A Social Geography of Canada

A Social Geography of Canada

Edited by Guy M. Robinson

Dundurn Press
Toronto & Oxford
1991

Design and Production: JAQ
Copy Editor: Margaret Hoogeveen
Printing and Binding: Gagné Printing Ltd., Louiseville, Quebec, Canada

Dundurn Press wishes to acknowledge the generous assistance and ongoing support of **The Canada Council, The Book Publishing Industry Development Program of the Department of Communications** and **The Ontario Arts Council.**
    Care has been taken to trace the ownership of copyright material used in the text, including the illustrations. The author and publisher welcome any information enabling them to rectify any reference or credit in subsequent editions.
        — J. Kirk Howard, Publisher

Canadian Cataloguing in Publication Data

Main entry under title:

A social geography of Canada

Rev. ed.
Essays originally published in honour of J. Wreford Watson.
ISBN 1-55002-092-7

1. Canada – Social conditions.   2. Anthropo-geography –
Canada.   I. Robinson, G.M. (Guy M.).   II. Watson,
J. Wreford (James Wreford), 1915–1990.

GF511.S63 1991   971   C91–094669–8

Dundurn Press Limited
2181 Queen Street East
Suite 301
Toronto, Canada
M4E 1E5

Dundurn Distribution
73 Lime Walk
Headington
Oxford, England
OX3 7AD

Contents

Part One: The Canadian Dimension

Part Two: The Urban Dynamic: Social Geographies of Urban Canada

Part Three: Beyond Main Street

Part Four: Planning, Society, and Environment

List of Tables

List of Figures

Contributors

Jacques Bernier, professor, Departement de géographie, Université Laval.

Pierre Camu, vice-president, Lavalin Inc.; former professor of economic geography, Université Laval; president of the St. Lawrence Seaway Authority; president of the Canadian Association of Broadcasters; and chairman of the Canadian Radio-Television and Telecommunications Commission.

Isobel P. Carlyle, former doctoral research student, Department of Geography, University of Edinburgh.

William J. Carlyle, professor, Department of Geography, University of Winnipeg.

Lyndhurst Collins, senior lecturer, Department of Geography, University of Edinburgh.

Leonard J. Evenden, associate professor, Department of Geography, Simon Fraser University.

Alan G. Macpherson, professor, Department of Geography, Memorial University of Newfoundland.

Jonathan O'Riordan, assistant deputy minister, Environmental Management Department, B.C. Environment, British Columbia.

Guy M. Robinson, senior lecturer, Department of Geography, University of Edinburgh.

Eric Ross, professor, Department of Geography, Mount Allison University.

W.R. Derrick Sewell, late professor, Department of Geography, University of Victoria.

P.J. Smith, professor, Department of Geography, University of Alberta.

John K. Stager, professor, Department of Geography, University of British Columbia.

D.R. Fraser Taylor, professor, Department of Geography, Carleton University.

Bernard D. Thraves, assistant professor, Department of Geography, University of Regina.

Ernest P. Weeks, former chairman, Canadian Saltfish Corporation; executive director, Atlantic Development Board, Canada; and visiting lecturer, Centre of Canadian Studies, University of Edinburgh.

J. David Wood, professor, Department of Geography, Joseph E. Atkinson College, York University.

Acknowledgements

To First Edition

In the compilation of a collection such as this, the editor has to rely upon a number of advisors – and more so if the editor and most of the contributors are separated by thousands of miles. So I owe a great debt to those who have assisted me at the various stages in the preparation of this collection, and without whom it would not have been completed.

I was grateful for advice received in the early phases of planning from Sandy Crosbie and from Wreford Watson himself who provided names and addresses of his former graduate students and former colleagues who he felt would have an interesting contribution to make to any geographical study dealing with Canada. After initial discussions in Edinburgh, the idea for this collection was formally aired to potential contributors after consultation with Ross Barnett, Barry Johnston and Derrick Sewell during my term as visiting lecturer at the University of Canterbury in New Zealand. Further discussions and correspondence with Doug Billingsley, Rik Davidson, Lou Gentilcore, Ron Jones, John MacNeil, Eric Ross, and David Wood also proved to be useful. A series of BBC radio programs compiled by Margaret Horsfield were the inspiration for part of the introduction to the section of the book dealing with rural Canada.

I have drawn on the expertise of numerous people to assist in the evaluation of the manuscripts and to suggest ways in which the collection could be improved. Each of the following deserve an individual mention: Helen Burton, Lyn Collins, Terry Coppock, Sandy Crosbie, Len Evenden, Bob Hodgart, Stephen Hornsby, David McMaster, Ged Martin, Briony Penn, Adrian Seaborne, Susan Smith, Michael Stanley, and Bernard Thraves.

I am indebted to Michael Anderson, dean of the Faculty of Social Sciences at the University of Edinburgh, for providing money from the Dean's Fund to help facilitate the word-processing of the individual manuscripts. The sterling work of the word-processors, Barbara, Helen and George Morris, and Shona Finlayson, is greatly appreciated, as is the assistance, not to mention the patience, of the typesetter, Sheila Edgar, who has been patient despite interminable editorial changes and procrastination.

The finishing touches to this volume were completed while I was a visitor in the Department of Geography, University of Melbourne and visiting tutor at University College, Melbourne. I am grateful for the facilities extended by both the University and the College.

Before the book went to press Derrick Sewell passed on. He had done a great deal to assist me in the early planning stages of this collection. As his neighbour for a while in 1984, I enjoyed many conversations with him and learnt much from him concerning matters both geographical and sporting. As time went by, his trans-Atlantic telephone calls about his own essay, the general "state of play" of the book, or the latest Queens Park Rangers result, became almost a regular Sunday event. I will miss his energy, enthusiasm and, not least, his friendship.

Guy M. Robinson
Ellis C
University College
Melbourne
October 1987

To Revised Edition

I am most grateful to Kirk Howard for encouraging the publication of a revised edition, and to Jacqueline Hope Raynor for her assistance with production and design. Steve Dowers uncomplainingly offered his time to track down the computer files containing the original chapters and then magically transferred them onto disk to make editing a much easier process. Anona Lyons also assisted with this, operating the new wonder of the age: a device for scanning text onto computer disk. The laborious checking of the files on these disks was rendered less tedious by unfailing encouragement from my wife, Susan, who also put up with numerous queries about English grammar and punctuation. Errors in the original edition were carefully sifted out by Alan Macpherson in an extremely helpful and generous feat of proofreading.

The revisions of my own contributions to the book were carried out in Brisbane in the Department of Geographical Sciences at the University of Queensland during my tenure of a University of Queensland travel award. I am very grateful for the facilities placed at my disposal during my stay there and for the kindness of the head of department, David Wadley, and his colleagues. Other assistance and encouragement was provided by Ged Martin and the Centre of Canadian Studies at the University of Edinburgh and by the University's Department of Geography.

I am also most grateful to the book's contributors for their speedy replies to my requests for revisions to their original chapters. Their swift responses to a very tight deadline were further indications of their respect for Wreford Watson, the inspiration for this volume, who sadly passed away some months before its publication. His memory will be cherished and his inspiration will endure.

Guy M. Robinson
Vinefields
Pencaitland
East Lothian
March 1991

Preface

Reviews of festschrifts invariably criticize the eclectic nature of such collections, usually complaining about lack of focus or pointing out that "only one essay in the book interested me!" In compiling this set of essays in honour of Wreford Watson, I was keenly conscious of such views and of how difficult it is to avoid a marked difference of approach, focus and content, even in this collection, which has a clearly defined subject. However, although I do not presume to have produced a collection beyond the reach of the usual criticisms, I have made a conscious attempt to create a book filled with cohesive and complementary essays.

This collection is intended to be more than an indication of the esteem that the contributors feel for Wreford Watson. Not only does it focus upon a topic, albeit a broad one, that was dear to Watson's heart, but it also attempts to reconcile the irreconcilable; it meets the contributors' desire to write on their own special topics and provides an undergraduate, academic and general audience with something beyond "only one essay of interest." To meet these aims the book has been divided into four parts, each with an introduction by the editor, summarizing the major topics of the individual essays. The introductions are intended to provide guides for a general audience, particularly one not resident in Canada. The individual essays cover specialist topics within the general subject matter of each section.

Throughout the text there are frequent references to Wreford Watson's work, both on Canada and geography in general. The four parts of the book are intended to highlight some of his major concerns and, necessarily, serve to give a different character to social geography than is usually recognized within the discipline of geography today. This is not a book written to reflect the modern trends of concern for social theory, presentation of particular philosophies, or political dogma. Rather, it is about places and people and is broadly concerned with where people live. Several contributions have drawn their inspiration from a tradition of human ecology and a concern for hard data. Yet the authors do not forget that behind the maps of social distribution lie the lives of everyday people and the unseen forces shaping those lives.

Part One

The Canadian Dimension

1 Introduction: Wreford Watson's Social Geography and a Social Geography of Canada

Guy M. Robinson

1.1 The Sociological Aspects of Geography

One of the catch-phrases associated with Expo '67, held in Montreal, was "Now we are 20 million." In the one hundred years after Confederation the population of Canada had increased more than six-fold from around three million in 1867 when "Canada [was] half a continent that had not excited the European imagination and was still largely the territory of Indian[s] and fur trader[s]" (Harris and Warkentin 1974, 328). In 1986, for the return of Expo to a Canadian venue, that being Vancouver, the corresponding catch-phrase could well have been "Now we are 25 million." During two decades a further five million inhabitants had been added and several new waves of immigrants had followed those that had shaped the distinctive social and ethnic mix of Canadian society. This mixing of people from diverse backgrounds, representing virtually every creed, colour and class, has long attracted the attention of social scientists, who have found in both Canada and the United States a wealth of opportunities for studying the ways in which settlers combined to produce a new society in the New World. For the geographer, the ethnic plurality has prompted studies of segregation, assimilation, ghettoes, and melting pots in a multiplicity of works on both small-scale residential differentiation and regional diversity. For Wreford Watson, as one of the new immigrants himself in the forties, the fascination was with the way in which Canada retained a multiculturalism whereby cultures had not "been melted down to form one image: . . . the image of Canada lies in the preservation of many images" (Watson and Watson 1977, 9).

When Watson began his own doctoral research in the forties on the social geography of Hamilton, Ontario, he and his contemporaries were part of a geographic discipline in which human geography was dominated by the notion of region. Hence, "it is the human element, and in that, perhaps above all, the social constituent, that distinguishes one place from another, and gives character to a region" (Watson 1957, 466). Perhaps it was the distinctiveness of the regions of Hamilton, with their striking social contrasts, that focused Watson's attention on the residential differentiation of the city. In Hamilton the processes by which such differentiation came about were clearly etched in the fabric of the city. For example, the sequences of invasion and succession, invoked in the writings of the Chicago ecologists (Park, Burgess, and McKenzie 1926) were depicted in Hamilton's "zones of compression" (Watson 1957, 493).

This type of social geography, which takes the cultural landscape as its basis, from which can be discerned regional differences associated not only with social characteristics, but also with economic activity and historical development, lent itself to both the broad brush and the detailed examination. The general lineaments of regions on a large scale, for example the Prairies, Central Canada, and the Maritimes, could be considered as well as the characteristics of urban social areas such as Cabbagetown in Toronto, the Latin quarter of Quebec City, or St. Boniface in Winnipeg. In Watson's case these huge differences in spatial resolution were handled deftly in his regional texts (Watson 1963, 1968) and in his other major works on Canada (e.g., Watson 1950, 1954a, 1962, 1965a, 1965b, 1977). At a time when the growth of systematic branches of the discipline was starting to promote specialized study of its various facets, his seminal work on "the sociological aspects of geography" made a clear attempt to define social geography (Watson 1951). His definition embraced "population (density, mobility, age and sex composition, and ethnic structure), settlement (rural and urban), social groups (home, work, play, worship groups) and social institutions and their function" (Watson 1957, 484).

This broad conception of the subject matter of the social geographer partially overlapped with what, at the time, were portrayed by some geographers as separate entities: racial geography and cultural geography (e.g., Sauer 1947; Taylor 1957). Arguments over this sub-division of knowledge into discrete categories and the numerous re-definitions of social geography as its popularity grew (see Johnston 1986) are not pursued here. Suffice it to say that Watson's social geography is what he himself and many of his graduate students practised during the past five decades. This fairly catholic interpretation of the subject has been followed in this volume. Population, settlement, social groups and social institutions figure largely in the considerations of a range of topics that come under the umbrella of social geography.

The systematic study of social geography has undoubtedly developed in ways unforeseen in the 1950s, but certain aspects of the methodological foundations utilized by Watson and others at that time have not been entirely eclipsed by subsequent modifications and additions. Social geography has been one of the liveliest branches of geography in recent years with a variety of empirical research, theoretical debate and philosophical innovation changing the character of the subject from its state as defined earlier by Watson, Houston (1953), and others (e.g., Gilbert and Steel 1945). However, the theme of the spatial structure of social interaction has remained as a central component, continuing the study of ideas about urban sociology and human ecology formulated at the University of Chicago during the 1920s and 1930s.

The consideration of the relationship between social and physical distance by Park and Burgess (1921) was echoed in Watson's work in which maps of the distribution of social phenomena were used as an important descriptive tool (e.g., Watson 1955). Jackson and Smith (1984, 71–79) describe Park's approach as "pragmatism" or "a version of empiricism which seeks to interpret the meaning and justification of beliefs in terms of their practical effects or consequences." Watson's work on Hamilton certainly deals with the physical consequences of the combined operation of factors such as physical environment, industrial growth, city institutions and social differentiation. Therefore, several of the core ideas of the Chicago sociologists are well represented: the city as an ecological community, land values as a reflection of the natural order, cycles of invasion and succession, and social areas containing a heterogeneity of lifestyles based on shared meanings and territorial control (Mellor 1977).

Although Watson's "sociological aspects of geography" deal in some detail with the study of society by geographers, there is little explicit attention to philosophical matters other than the tacit assumptions of positivism as embodied in the earlier work of the human ecologists. However, rather than moving himself and his research students farther down the road of empiricism and what Peach (1981) terms "spatial sociology," Watson retained and developed a focus upon people and places that were all too often overlooked within the quantitative revolution that dominated the discipline in the 1960s.

Watson's work, not surprisingly for a man who was very much a poet as well as a geographer, had much more in common with the geosophical writings of J.K. Wright (1947). These writings stressed that it was the minds of people that offered fertile ground for investigation, with the concept of people's sense of place providing a focal point for research. This aspect of humanistic geography (Entrikin 1976) is encapsulated in the opening sentence of Watson's (1979, 1) *Social Geography of the United States*: "The geography of any country is what people see in it, want from it and do with it . . . A social geography of America has evolved, reflecting the structure of society, the ends people have, and the means at their disposal. Essentially, this geography has been made through solving problems, and exploiting prospects." The social geography that emerges from the ensuing discussion is one in which the idea that "people make places" is at the fore. Thus, "social geography is an analysis not only of how people make places, but of how they think they do so: it is concerned with the perceptions behind the patterns" (Watson 1979, ix). With this interpretation of the subject it is possible to compare Watson's views with those of Ley (1982), Relph (1976), and Meinig (1979) among others, and to observe that his concern with regional differentiation in the 1950s was in terms of its interpretation in the daily lives of ordinary citizens.

Many of Watson's own sentiments, expressed three decades earlier when working on his study of Hamilton, have re-appeared in the literature in a slightly different guise in the humanistic approaches of David Ley – again with much emphasis on the study of a Canadian city, that being Vancouver (Ley 1981, 1985, 1986). Yet, it is pertinent to note that Ley has not completely discarded statistical analysis in favour of the humanists' preferred qualitative methods such as participant observation. His work on gentrification in Vancouver demonstrates that different methods, even philosophies, can be encompassed within the geographical investigation of a particular problem. Watson's own emphasis upon people's experiences, their views of their own city, and the way these translated into actions which reshaped and redefined the urban environment, was accompanied by both the interweaving of literary source as powerful metaphors for the human experience, and analysis of census data and surveys to present the urban dynamism in cartographic form. His work made no reference to the ideology utilized by the exponents of the structuralist method, which became prominent in social geography in the mid-1970s (e.g., Harvey 1973, 1975, 1978; Peet 1975). However, the ideas of the citizenry as operating within a well-defined framework established by the capitalist economic system and the concept of people as "structured agents" are well to the fore in Watson's (1983) depiction of Kirkland Lake. Here the controlling framework of the economic system is the central edifice in a situation in which "some people live bowered in beauty, and others are umbraged in ugliness" (Watson 1983, 391). That Watson recognized Kirkland Lake as "a place of alienation, injustice, and inequality" is an indication of a social geography stretching well beyond the parameters of spatial patterns, regional boundaries, and narrow ideologies.

In practical terms Watson's social geography extends past simple consideration of spatial patterns to an examination of major social issues such as violence, inner city collapse, immigration, ethnic segregation, the question of native Indians' rights, class structure, the reaction against city life, the growth of communes, and the excessive exploitation of natural resources. His *Social Geography of the United States* addressed all these issues, using literary sources as well as official statistics to generate an analysis designed to tease out the American image. The broad scope of this social geography seems to rest easily within the large dimensions of its North American setting, and is equally appropriate when applied to Canada as it is when applied to the United States.

1.2   A Social Geography of Canada

With a range of critical social issues similar to those of the United States, but with its own particular problems and characteristics shaped by its distinctive political, geographical, and historical background, Canada offers tremendous potential as a subject of study for social geographers wishing to pursue any one of the many-faceted strands of enquiry begun by Watson and others. This book draws together some of this work as carried out by Watson's graduate students, friends, and former colleagues. The topics themselves cannot be said to be an exhaustive coverage of the social geography of Canada in that they do not set out to make a systematic treatment of every major social issue or to make a detailed investigation of social differentiation within every region of Canada. However, they do cover a wide range of the subjects on which Watson himself wrote and the areas of interest in which he stimulated the research of his students and prompted his friends and colleagues to see with fresh eyes.

This collection is also a reflection of the evolution of social geography during the past five decades, and its different emphases: spatial patterns of residential differentiation and ethnic segregation; the analysis of census data; the mapping of the distribution of social characteristics; the consideration of the stuctures and processes underlying the surface configurations of society; and the review of the contribution of individuals and decision-makers as well as the acts of government by which Canadians have reshaped their social environment. To define the scope of the subject while encompassing a range of different approaches in which the attempt has been made to adapt method to subject, we have focused on key aspects of Canada's social geography. These aspects reflect Watson's main interests in the geography of his adopted country.

In Part 1, we examine the particular character created by the special mix of cultures and ethnic groups in Canada. This mixture has produced a particularly divisive issue within Canadian society: the competition between the citizens of British origin and those of French origin as is manifest in the struggle over the control of government and access to political power and control. This competition strikes at the very heart of the existence of the Canadian state and cannot be ignored in any study of Canadian society and its social institutions. The ways in which distinctive French- and British-Canadian societies have developed are considered in three studies of the evolution of the conflict between the French and the British, which has given rise to clear distinctions between the provinces of Quebec and Ontario. For the former the external and internal conflicts are considered against the background of separatism versus the notion of "une province comme les autres." For Ontario the solid economic platform for the development of a stable and cohesive society is emphasized from a historical perspective: how was this society formed and what characteristics does it exhibit?

Watson himself devoted much of his writing on Canada to examining the way in which Canadian society became essentially an urban society in which social, cultural, and ethnic differentiation represented regions in the micro-scale (see Part 2). The attempt is made in this collection to portray both ends of this regional spectrum: the regionalism and factionalism in the nation as a whole, including the conflicts of British versus French and Central Canada versus East and West; and the multi-faceted urban panorama including everything from house improvements in the suburbs to the nature of political control over urban territory to spatial patterns of ethnicity within cities. It is the dynamic nature of Canadian urbanism that has attracted many geographers and hence the central section of this collection comprises essays dealing with different aspects of this dynamism. Urban change has attracted many different approaches by geographers as they have struggled to understand the dynamics behind the total transformation of cityscapes and urban morphologies in the post-war period. Some of these various approaches are represented in Part 2.

If the nature of urbanization in North America is central to much of Watson's work, it must not be forgotten that he also dealt very sympathetically with the ever increasing marginalization of the native peoples (e.g., Watson 1956). He was a master at portraying the character of the people and landscapes beyond the confines of the city. For example, in his *Canada: Problems and Prospects*, he refers to the influence of the Scottish immigrants in shaping the rural and fishing economies of the Maritimes: "The Scottish settlers have kept their historic clannishness. Many of them still live as groups of related families in the glens of Cape Breton Island; they cherish the Gaelic; hold annual Gaelic Mods (singing, oratorical, and poetry competitions); and sport their Highland Games" (Watson 1968, 108). The landscapes of wide-open spaces, the grain elevators, and the fields of wheat on the Prairies are described in his

"Canadian Regionalism in Life and Letters," by using Anne Marriott's poetry (Watson 1965a). This rural domain, with its particular social problems of depopulation (see Watson 1947), reliance upon fluctuating markets for agricultural produce, and the rigours of farming in harsh northerly climes, merits its own section in this collection (Part 3), which also refers to some of the problems of Canada's native peoples.

In Watson's early career as a geographer, his field had not developed such an emphasis on systematic specializations as was to be produced in the 1960s and 1970s. Although Watson himself concentrated most of his attention on what today would be clearly recognized as social or cultural geography, he did not relegate the wider physical environment to the unimportant position allocated it by many modern human geographers. He was interested in the man-land relationship and the interaction between people and their environment, whether that environment was essentially a man-made one: the city, or a natural one: the Canadian Shield. This inter-relationship appeared as a central element in his work on how people perceived their own localities (e.g., Watson 1965b, 1967, 1971) as well as in his more specific work on the nature of the inter-relationship (e.g., Watson 1956, 1972). In this collection the opportunity to investigate the link between people and environment is pursued in Part 4 in essays considering planning policies, society, and the environment. Thus we take social geography to include applied aspects of social planning and the regulation of the use of environment for both economic purposes and societal benefit. This approach, too, is very much in keeping with Watson's own interests (e.g., Watson 1954b), which extended beyond the academic sphere in his work within the Nature Conservancy of the United Kingdom.

Together the four parts of this collection are offered as a celebration of Wreford Watson's contribution to scholarship within the discipline of geography. Subjects covered in some form in his own extensive literature are re-examined as a means of portraying many of the characteristics of Canada's social and cultural geography. The attempt has been made to keep in mind his axiomatic assertion that "people generate prejudice and prejudice governs place" by adhering as closely as possible, within the limitations of a diverse range of topics, to the view that "geography must be concerned with the unique place, expressed through the perceptions and images of it, entrenched in human culture and enshrined in the arts" (Watson 1983, 385). To this must be added the caveat that the arts must include cartography and a perceptive treatment of numbers as well as literature.

1.3   The Canadian Dimension

The first part of this book focuses upon broad divisions within Canadian society, the problems associated with the presence of the two "founding peoples," and an indication of the way in which the elements of Canada's social geography have developed over time. A personal view of social divisions in Canada is presented by Pierre Camu (chapter 2) by way of a prologue for all four parts of the book. The aspects of social differentiation he outlines have formed the basis for investigation by social geographers throughout the twentieth century. Problems associated with immigration, the organization of society into various socio-economic groups, and the growth of major urban complexes with their attendant social problems, have all attracted academic interest, argument, and debate. The immigrant, the city-dweller, the rich, and the poor, whatever their national or international setting, all merit special attention from geographers. However, Camu's brief discussion highlights a fundamental concern of geographers in their studies of society: the nature of the particular setting. This concern encompasses the peculiar characteristics of immigration into a given region, the special features of the cultural geography of an area, a comparison of the nature of urban life in various regions, and the influence of different political, economic, and social systems in creating macro-, meso-, and micro-scale differences.

Although social differentiation in Canada can be recognized in a variety of ways and at a variety of scales, perhaps even as part of a global continuum of social variation, there is, as well, a particular Canadian dimension. The unifying characteristics of a common history, federal politics, and continuity of economic and cultural development have engendered recognizable Canadian characteristics, which impart a uniquely Canadian dimension to numerous elements within the country's social geography. In some respects, it could be argued that Canadian society is merely an indistinguishable component of North American society in general: the fundamentals of Toronto's social geography are very similar to those of New York or Chicago. Yet, a range of distinguishing features can be cited to dispute this bald statement and emphasize particular Canadian, Ontario, or Toronto-specific dimensions. Perhaps the best starting point for consideration of these dimensions is with the notion of confederation and the political reality of a nation *a mari usque ad mare*, within which there existed not one but two "founding peoples."

1.3.1 Duality

The British North America Act (BNA Act) of 1867, which brought about Confederation, was justified by its supporters in French-speaking Canada such as Cartier, Galt and Langevin, on the grounds that, under the act, French Canadians would maintain a provincial identity, with Quebec City as their capital. The presence of French Canadians in the Federal Cabinet would prevent anglophone domination and restore some measure of equality between the two major groups within Canada. For others, notably Dorion's Parti Rouge, the BNA Act seemed a straightforward imposition by force of arms. The insignificance of the French minority within the dominating edifice of the mighty British Empire reduced nationalist sentiments to a concern for the maintenance of the French language and culture and a striving for greater political influence within the established Canadian system (Eccles 1972; McConnell 1977; Simeon and Robinson 1990). The sense of isolation felt by the French Canadians and French-speaking Quebecers especially, is depicted superbly in Ringuet's (1940) novel, *Thirty Acres:* the typical French Canadian farmer embedded in the ancient folkways of Quebec is forced to take notice of an alien English-speaking North America, partly because it provides employment for one of his sons and, ironically, also for the farmer himself in old age when he is "transplanted into a strange world, among strange people whose language he neither speaks nor understands" (Le Grand 1970).

Periodically, the conflict between the British and French Canadians has re-surfaced in the form of disputes over language rights (e.g., Laponce 1984). A recent instance occurred in the Alberta Legislative Assembly when the Speaker informed a member that he had no legal right to ask a question in French. Of Alberta's 2.2 million population about 30,000 (less than 1.5 percent) speak French and the incident in the legislature highlights the often-expressed discontent of the English-speaking majority, living 3,000 kilometres from Quebec, that they have to cope with a second official language. Also recently, but closer to Quebec, anti-French feeling was demonstrated in New Brunswick when government officials trying to promote wider use of the French language received a hostile reception. Similar attempts in Manitoba were abandoned after a similar response. Recently antagonism towards the official policy of bilingualism has achieved a political outlet via the Reform Party of Canada, a right-wing Alberta-based group whose message of "less government" and "no favours for Quebec" has gained popular support in English-speaking Canada. There may be the prospect of reduced government support for bilingualism if the ruling Conservatives seek to combat the appeal of the Reform Party by advocating some adjustments to the 1969 law that made Canada officially bilingual.

Burghardt (1978, 10) argues that the isolation of the French Canadians persisted until "true independence" came for Canada with the demise of the Empire and an increasing role for Canada in world affairs. From being a very small and insignificant minority in a larger whole, the French Quebecers and, to a lesser extent, the Acadians began to realize their importance within the federal structure. Indeed, history seems to have been underplaying the degree of access the French had to the federal Government in Ottawa afforded by Quebec's near total support for the federal Liberal party, which held office for the majority of the 1920s, 1930s, and 1940s under Mackenzie King and for 32 of the years between 1945 and 1987. Complaints of internal colonialism operating against Quebec were magnified in the 1960s and 1970s because of the comparatively poor economic performance of Quebec when set against that of western Canada (see for example, Table 3.4). This disparity was manifest in the net loss of over 200,000 inter-provincial migrants from the province in the 1970s. Between 1966 and 1981 only Manitoba and Saskatchewan had lower rates of growth of population. Quebec also suffered without the higher levels of wages and lower rates of unemployment in the more buoyant economies of Ontario, British Columbia, and the Prairie provinces. To counter this, both Quebec and the Atlantic provinces have been major recipients of federal transfer payments, drawing heavily upon the federal exchequer. In the 1980s, though, a resurgent Quebec economy altered the picture once more and helped create new attitudes to the status of the province both within Quebec and in the rest of Canada.

In the 1970s the expression of the desire of the French minority to retain its cultural integrity, added to economic marginality, was voiced most vociferously by a new French-speaking class of professionals and intellectuals within Quebec (Cook 1989). Hence, the rise of Quebec separatism under the Parti Québécois (PQ), which seemed such a potent and powerful political force in the late 1970s, was partly an element of a desire by French-speaking Quebecers to oust provincial control from an anglophone minority (Behiels 1985; McRoberts 1979; McRoberts and Postgate 1980).

The return to a Liberal provincial government in Quebec in 1985 did not represent a diminution in the desire for some form of greater recognition of Quebec's distinctiveness within the nation, no matter how difficult it might be to express this recognition. Rather, it may have reflected a basic reaction to a simple economic fact of life: as unemployment rises, it increases most in the regions where it is already highest. In the post-war years the rate of unemployment in Quebec has been consistently second only to that in the Atlantic provinces. Failure of the provincial government to alter this situation between 1976 and 1985, at a time of rising unemployment, may have cost them re-election as it seemed that economic issues rather than separatist policies were the main election issues in the provincial campaign of 1985.

The defeat of the PQ in the election of December 1985 brought an end to nine years in office. The manner of their defeat, in which the Liberals won 99 out of 122 seats in the provincial legislature, and the replacement of René Lévesque as the leader of the PQ seemed, temporarily, to have ended a period in which the separatist movement had become a major issue in Canadian politics. Several political observers at the time referred to the Liberal landslide as the first repudiation by voters of the independence option, although the PQ had removed the issue of sovereignty from its manifesto earlier in 1985 and it was referred to during the election campaign only as a distant vision and goal. Almost immediately upon assuming office the Liberals announced they would not enforce Quebec's French-language charter, Bill 101 enacted under the PQ, through which it is illegal in the province to display publicly a non-French sign. Another early signal of the new-found spirit of federalism was the return of the Canadian flag to its former place next to the speaker's chair in the Legislative Assembly. In addition, the new premier, Robert Bourassa, encouraged moves to open negotiations with the Canadian government over Quebec's possible future adherence to the new Canadian Constitution introduced in 1982.

It was difficult to imagine, though, that nationalist, even separatist, feeling in Quebec had been entirely buried, especially as the status of Quebec as a small French-language island in a sea of over 250 million mainly English-speaking North Americans had become more apparent. For some Quebecers a renewed sense of isolation had returned. For example, the Conseil de la Langue Française, a government agency concerned with long-term language policies, warned that Quebec was regressing rather than readvancing as a bastion of the French language in North America. The continuing domination of many aspects of Quebec's industrial and business life by the one-fifth of the province's population who are English-speakers exacerbated this situation (Dufour 1990).

There remains the paradox of a need felt by many French Canadians to maintain a clearly recognizable and distinctive identity, separate from other Canadians and yet belonging to the wider Canadian community. The distinctiveness continues to revolve around the retention of French as the spoken language and the fact that Canada is officially a bilingual country despite so many of the French-speakers being concentrated in just one province. An example of this paradox and of the distinctiveness of Quebec, despite the often-stated view that it is a "province comme les autres," was demonstrated in its representation as a separate delegation at an international francophone conference in Paris in 1986, despite the presence of a full Canadian delegation. The Quebec premier spoke on matters relating to language, culture and communications, while the Canadian delegate dealt with broad international, political and economic issues. Quebec's stature was further enhanced when the conference was held in the province in 1988.

Legal decisions and statements by both national and provincial politicians continue to highlight the centrality of the language issue to all views about Quebec's position within the federation. Thus, at the end of 1986 the Quebec Court of Appeal ruled that the law requiring signs on shops and other businesses to be in French was illegal. The law was held to have contravened the right of freedom of expression all Canadians were guaranteed by the Constitution. The Court ruled that the province could still require that signs be displayed in French, but could not prohibit signs in other languages. Just one day after this verdict was delivered, extremist separatist feelings were shown to be still in existence by the revival of the Front de Libération du Québec (FLQ), which fire-bombed a department store in Montreal that was displaying signs in English. The pro-independence terrorist front had ceased its activities in the early 1970s after kidnapping and murdering a Quebec Liberal cabinet minister in 1970 and also holding to ransom a British trade commissioner in the same year in an attempt to free jailed members of the FLQ.

Clearly, despite the electorate's rejection of the PQ, strong feelings in favour of some form of separatism have remained, and certain issues are capable of bringing such feelings to the fore in Quebec. However, language rights in particular have been of special significance. From the 1960s Quebec responded to the new influences being brought into the province by immigrants and the English-speaking media, especially television, by introducing a number of language laws and regulations. For instance, the children of immigrants must attend French-speaking schools, and the provincial law of French-only public signs has been enforced vigorously (via Bill 178 in the Quebec Legislative Assembly) despite objections by the provincial and federal supreme courts.

One major issue separating Quebec from more harmonious relations with the other provinces has been its rejection of the new Canadian Constitution when it was proclaimed in 1982. This constitutional estrangement from the rest of Canada has placed a notable strain upon the Confederation. However, in early 1987 there were signs that this particular potential source of future conflict would be removed by specific recognition of Quebec as a disinct society within the Canadian Confederation. This would have met one of the key conditions laid down by Quebec in return for its adherance to the new Constitution. It was thought that the possibility of a veto for the provinces over certain future constitutional amendments might also persuade Quebec to end its isolation. Yet major worries in the province over reform of the Senate, fisheries, and property rights remained and have qualified what the Quebec premier had called, "a historic breakthrough for Quebec as a Canadian partner" (see Johnston 1990). Subsequently, in 1990, the proposal of the Meech Lake Accord, a constitutional accord designed to recognize Quebec as a distinct society, failed to obtain the necessary unanimous ratification from the other provinces and therefore was defeated (Cohen 1990).

Many Canadians had seen ratification of the accord as the key to preventing the dissolution of the country itself (Burgess 1988). However, outside Quebec there remains strong resentment at the accord's proposed recognition of Quebec as a distinct society. This was particularly so in Manitoba and Newfoundland and, although the premiers of these two provinces signed the accord, they insisted that their respective legislatures should ratify the agreement even though it did not supercede the Charter of Rights. Subsequently, amidst a great deal of controversy, this ratification was not obtained. In Manitoba the role of a native Indian, Elijah Harper, was crucial in the failure to ratify the accord, highlighting the feeling among the native peoples that, like Quebec, they too could claim to be a "special case" that deserved particular attention in any constitutional accord (see Part 3). In Newfoundland there was opposition to the accord on the basis that special recognition for Quebec would detract from the need for strong federal government. Other concerns were expressed about how the accord could affect the nature of the relationship between the provinces and the federal government, the lack of formal input from non-politicians to the deliberations about the accord, and the general handling of the matter by the Mulroney government.

In January 1991, Quebec's ruling Liberal Party made its most clearly defined statement about the province's future since this failure to ratify the Meech Lake Accord. The statement went well beyond the constitutional change that had been blocked in June 1990 and proposed a new division of powers that, essentially, would make Quebec a politically autonomous state while maintaining an economic union with the rest of Canada. In this case, which stops short of full independence, the Quebec government would exercise full sovereignty in 22 jurisdictions, including all social policy, cultural affairs, education, housing, natural resources, agriculture and communications. The federal government would retain responsibility for defence, customs, currency and national debt management, and there would be shared responsibility for native affairs, justice, fisheries, and the post office. These proposals will be submitted to the Quebec Liberal Party Convention in the spring of 1991.

At the time of writing (January 1991), the 37-member commission (the Belanger-Campeau Commission) established by Quebec's premier, Robert Bourassa, after the failure of the Meech Lake constitutional talks, appears to be favouring a form of independence for Quebec. Such a development has also been supported by two-thirds of Quebecers according to opinion poll surveys completed at the end of 1990. Several commission members and the opposition Parti Québécois have suggested outright political independence or a "looser" association than exists at present with the rest of Canada. This new type of association could take a form similar to that between the member states of the European Community, with Quebec, the rest of Canada, and perhaps the United States forming a North American "common market." To this arrangement Quebec would bring an economy roughly the size of Belgium's, but with high business confidence based on its wealth of energy resources (hydro-electric power) and an expanding manufacturing industry. Thus many Quebecers view the prospect of an independent Quebec as an opportunity to join the elite of the small number of prosperous and economically strong nations.

Underlying this view is the fact that since the majority in Quebec rejected the Parti Québécois' push for independence in May 1980, there have been several important changes in Quebec. Two may be decisive in producing some form of separation between Quebec and the rest of Canada. First, the province has become more successful economically, building on its rich mineral and energy resources to reach a position in which many Quebecers feel their economy could not only survive independence but thrive if still able to enjoy easy access to the markets of the rest of North America. Second, there has been a growing feeling both within and outside of Quebec that the polarization between Quebec and the rest of Canada has grown so much that differences are now irreconcilable. Therefore, independence for Quebec seems to some to be the only possible outcome.

The non-partisan Belanger-Campeau Commission is expected to recommend a drafting of a Quebec Constitution that would oversee the province in some new form of sovereignty association with the rest of Canada. This implies political independence but a continued economic union. Meanwhile, other commissions established by several of the other provinces and by the Indian Assembly of First Nations are adding to the momentum towards major constitutional reform. Recommendations will be made to the federal parliament by the federally appointed Citizens' Forum on Canada's Future. This has been given a mandate "to launch a dialogue among people across the country and to encourage the development of a new consensus about Canada and its future." Comprising twelve people from several different spheres of national life, the forum is travelling to all the provinces, eliciting views on the country's future. Furthermore, a special committee of the Senate and Commons is expected to suggest a method of amending the Constitution. So 1991 and 1992 are likely to see the critical steps towards a clearer resolution of both Quebec's status and the nature of the Canadian Constitution, especially the division of federal and provincial powers. It is possible that referenda both in Quebec and nationally may play a part in these developments, especially as the idea of a referendum in Quebec, to be held in summer 1992, has been supported by the province's premier. In such a referendum Quebecers would be asked either to endorse a new deal with the rest of Canada, to be negotiated in the meantime, or to authorize separation as a fully independent country.

Poignantly, the death in 1990 of the novelist Hugh MacLennan was a reminder of the continuing divide between English- and French-speaking Canada. The title of his classic 1945 book, *Two Solitudes*, was often cited as an expression of the seemingly unbridgeable differences between francophone and anglophone cultures. The irony of this usage of *Two Solitudes* lies in the fact that MacLennan had taken the title from a definition of love by German poet Rainer Maria Rilke: "Love that consists in this, that two solitudes protect and touch and greet each other." It was this mutual protection and interaction between the two founding peoples that represented MacLennan's hopes for Canada as symbolized in his book in its account of the progress of a French-English marriage.

The establishment of a new constitution under the 1982 Constitution Act was a complex set of arrangements, which, among other things, created a Canadian Charter of Rights and Freedoms and divested the British Parliament of its power to amend the Canadian Constitution – termed as the "patriation" of the Constitution. Central to the debate was the question of whether provincial consent was required before the necessary amendment could be obtained from Britain, which would affect provincial rights, privileges, and powers. After much negotiation, Quebec was the only province actually to reject the decision to proceed with patriation. This illustrates the growing schism between that province and the federal government. However, at one time a "gang of eight" provinces objected to certain aspects of the new Constitution. What better illustration in recent times of the two significant dimensions of socio-cultural pluralism in Canada: biculturalism and an entrenched regionalism that exists in many forms? The regionalism manifests itself in a range of cultural, social, economic, political and historical characteristics within which the uneasy relationship between the "two founding peoples" has given rise to tensions capable of destroying the state itself. The two essays of this collection by Bernier (chapters 3 and 4) examine different aspects of this pluralism and address the "country's fissiparous regionalism" (Ley 1984, 98) with respect to the much publicized issue of Quebec separatism.

Both Camu (chapter 2) and Bernier highlight the fact that within the essential duality of Canadian society there is also a plurality, which is expressed in many different ways. Numerous indicators can be presented to portray this plurality, the most potent ones being those connected with ethnicity and measures of wealth which, taken together, have produced some of the fundamental differentiations upon which regional divisions of Canada may be based.

1.3.2   Plurality
1.3.2.1   Ethnic Diversity

For the first 80 years after the BNA Act, Canada was dominated by the presence of inhabitants of British and French descent, but after 1945 this dominance has been reduced, and to the already present German, Ukrainian, and Scandinavian minorities have been added significant numbers of southern Europeans, Asians, and West Indians (see Table 2.1). The ethnic mix has changed quite dramatically in some of the larger cities, notably Toronto, adding a plurality and a multiculturalism to the longer established duality referred to above. This change, reflecting the continuation of large-scale emigration to Canada, has brought with it a range of social problems and issues, and added an ethnic dimension to considerations of the social patterning of Canadian cities (see Part 2). Indeed, much of the receipt of migrants after 1945 has been channelled to the major cities. For example, in 1986 over half the immigrant population was resident in Ontario where they represented over one-third of

Toronto's population. Over one-fifth of the populations of Calgary, Hamilton, St Catharines/Niagara, and Vancouver in 1986 were immigrants. In the early eighties nearly three-quarters of the immigrants lived in cities of over 100,000 inhabitants compared with just 48 percent of the non-immigrant population (Statistics Canada 1984).

Great Britain remained the leading supplier of immigrants, accounting for six out of ten in Canada's immigrant population in the 1970s and early 1980s. However, the changing character of the flow of migrants is indicated in the fact that the 1981 census recorded India as the third leading supplier followed by Portugal, the Philippines, Jamaica, Vietnam, Hong Kong, Italy, and Guyana. Many of the immigrants from southern Europe, Asia, and the Caribbean followed the pattern set by previous generations of immigrants and settled in inner city areas, especially in Toronto, Vancouver, and Montreal. This pattern has given rise to particular problems, some of which are considered in Part 2. For example, of the immigrants arriving in the 1970s, 16 percent lived in high-rise apartments and 41 percent in multiple-unit dwellings compared with 4 percent and 26 percent respectively for the non-immigrant population. Similarly, 17 percent of immigrants arriving after 1971 lived in crowded conditions (more than one person per room) compared with 5 percent of the non-immigrant population. Yet this association with poor housing and inner city areas must not be over-emphasized as various other statistics show that, over time, many immigrants who have settled in Canada achieve a standard of living that exceeds that of the Canadian-born population. The willingness to adapt to new surroundings and to make a success of life in a new country, coupled with new immigration policies tying admission to education and occupational qualifications, has blurred some of the differences between the immigrant and host populations.

The Immigration Act of 1976 specified three classes of immigrants: family class (close relatives of permanent residents of Canada); refugees (those seeking refuge from persecution in their former countries of residence, and who do not have to qualify for entry under a points system); and independent and other immigrants who have to meet certain criteria for entry. Recently these criteria have placed less emphasis upon education and more upon occupational experience and demand for particular types of workers (Proudfoot 1989). This and the open policy towards refugees has fostered migration from beyond the traditional source areas of Britain, northern Europe and the United States. However, it has recently produced controversy especially with regard to the influx of refugees from Asia.

Although Canada has been a major recipient of both immigrants and refugees post-1945, following an influx of refugees in 1986 new and tougher immigration rules have been introduced. In the last four months of that year nearly 7,000 people arrived in Canada hoping to be accepted as refugees. The main groups involved were Turks, Iranians, Sri Lankans, Chileans and Ghanaians, perhaps in their diversity these people were a testament to Canada's reputation as a country that treats refugees with tolerance and consideration. However, in 1986 an estimated 12,000 people arrived in Montreal alone, claiming the status of refugee. In terms of emergency assistance and welfare payments, this cost approximately $40 million, paid jointly by the provincial and federal governments. Attempts to slow the speed of the processing of applicants wishing to be granted official refugee status and more rigid interpretation of refugee status are likely to reduce the numbers able to remain in Canada after they have been scrutinized. Ironically, these proposed changes were put forward just two months after Canada was awarded the United Nations-sponsored Nansen Medal for its open-door policy towards refugees from throughout the world and for support of official and private aid programs. Between 1979 and 1984 Canada received 129,000 refugees, a flow representing 23 percent of all Canadian immigrants. This placed Canada second among the industrialized countries with respect to the number of refugees received after 1945 as a proportion of population. The growing popularity of Canada as a recipient of refugees is indicated by the figures for claims to refugee status filed within Canada: from 1,600 claims in 1980 to 18,000 in 1986 and 25,000 in 1987 (Statistics Canada, personal communication). A bill to promote a revised refugee-determination system has now brought a distinction between "genuine refugees in need of Canada's protection" and people claiming refugee status but really seeking to enter Canada purely for economic motives.

The growth in the number of immigrants from Asia was thrown into high relief by the crash of Air India flight 182 off the west coast of Ireland on 23 June 1985 while on its way from Montreal to London. The possibility that this crash was caused by a bomb placed by militant Sikhs, as part of their struggle for an independent Sikh state in the Punjab, focused attention on the small Sikh ethnic minority in Canada. This interest was further aroused 14 months later with the arrest of 15 Canadian Sikhs in Montreal, Hamilton, and Vancouver Island on charges of committing or conspiring to commit various acts of violence in the name of their independence movement. Immigrants from non-traditional sources of supply have increased the cultural richness of Canada's major cities, but they have also brought a number of problems, some of which the country has yet to appreciate fully. In particular, old assumptions about the ethnic and linguistic composition of the major cities must be revised to take account of the growing multiculturalism: the recognition of the cultural and racial diversity of Canada and of the equality of Canadians of all origins (Bibby 1990).

Since 1971 the federal government has given particular recognition to the growth of non-British and non-French immigrants and also to the fact that, even at the time of the Royal Commission on Bilingualism in the late 1960s, 25 percent of the population were of non-British and non-French origin. This recognition has taken the form of various commitments to multiculturalism within a bilingual framework (Avery and Ramirez 1990, 86). In the Trudeau government of the early 1970s a minister of state responsible for multiculturalism was established within the Department of Secretary of State. Then in 1976 the present Multicultural Directorate was created. The minister is advised by the Canadian Consultative Council on Multiculturalism, which consists of over 100 representatives of various ethnic groups.

Several of the provinces have followed the federal government's example and have proclaimed policies of multiculturalism, pioneers being Ontario and the four western provinces. These policies have emphasized financial support for a wide range of ethnocultural organizations and educational projects, such as Ontario's

"English as a Second Language Program." These policies have sometimes been referred to as "red boots multiculturalism" because of their emphasis upon folk lore and pride in cultural tradition. However, in July 1988 the Mulroney government introduced a broader set of multicultural policies through the passage of Bill C-93, the Multicultural Act. This should direct more funds towards the implementation of policies to promote greater opportunities for the ethnic minorities, and is seen by some as an attempt to pursue structural multiculturalism rather than the more symbolic gestures dating from the early 1970s. This concern with ethnic minorities must be viewed in conjunction with policies towards the small but significant numbers of indigenous peoples who, at a relatively early stage in European colonization, were outnumbered by the colonists and then increasingly marginalized. The native peoples are a vital element of Canada's plurality and, increasingly, are finding a political voice to highlight their special needs and aspirations. (These issues are dealt with in greater detail in Parts 3 and 4.)

1.3.2.2 Regionalism

To the pluralism associated with ethnic and cultural diversity can be added another aspect of plurality within Canadian society, namely regionalism. The sheer size of Canada seems to dictate that regions and regionalism play a major role in the nation's life. The presence of a federal governmental system has created one fundamental element of regionalism in the existence of provinces, but it is the clearly recognized existence of the Maritimes, the Prairies, and other groupings of provinces that denotes a more concrete form of regionalism associated closely with the physical characteristics of particular parts of Canada (Brym 1986). Watson (1963, 230), citing Nicholson's (1954) work on internal boundaries in Canada, refers to this as "sectionalism": "In Canada significant sectional interests, traditions, and needs have divided the country into an Atlantic group of provinces, the Central Provinces, the Prairie Provinces, and British Columbia and the Yukon. Northern Canada is beginning to develop a sense of distinctness, as an area with its own pioneer problems and aims." As an alternative, he suggested a regionalism based on nodal regions centred on Vancouver, Edmonton, Winnipeg, Toronto, and Montreal (Watson 1962). Despite the simplicity of both this and the grouping of provinces, they have been outdated by social and economic changes during the past three decades (McCann 1982; Robinson 1983).

The major economic basis of regional diversity is emphasized by the uneven pattern of recent economic performance: industrial growth is strong in Ontario and a new dynamism has emerged in Quebec, yet western provinces are experiencing problems associated with falls in the prices of oil, grain, and minerals, and the Maritimes continue to lag behind. An important feature of this unevenness in the 1980s has been associated with fluctuations in oil prices. Their dramatic fall in 1986 produced significant problems for the Albertan economy, which had been buoyant throughout the 1970s as well as retarding development of offshore oilfields in the Atlantic and Arctic Oceans, and onshore in the western tar sands (Chapman 1985a, 1985b, 1989).

Before the fall in the price of oil in recent years, one of the major causes of tension within the federal structure was the disparity created by the economic boom enjoyed by Alberta, based largely on its oil industry. Although the Alberta provincial government agreed that there had to be some national recycling of revenues from oil, there was much concern that the rest of Canada was not paying a fair market price for this finite resource. However, with oil revenue of $100 per second (Foster 1979), Alberta in the late 1970s and early 1980s enjoyed the country's lowest tax rate, highest budget surplus, highest investment program, and virtually no sales tax.

This increase in Alberta's wealth highlighted contrasts with other provinces where the economy was less buoyant and social problems more apparent, especially in the early 1980s with reduced economic growth for the national economy. The change in fortunes in the late 1970s and 1980s was dramatic with regard to rates of unemployment. From a national average of just 3.4 percent of the labour force unemployed in 1966, this proportion had risen to 8.4 percent in 1978 and 10.5 percent in 1985. Significant regional variations stayed, though, with Atlantic Canada and Quebec remaining above the national average. As discussed by Bernier in chapter 3, between 1977 and 1983 the unemployment rate in all the Maritime provinces and Quebec moved closer to the national average (Table 3.4). Only in British Columbia did the unemployment rate remain above the national level and rise more rapidly than throughout Canada as a whole. Unemployment, of course, is just one of many social indicators that can be used as a reflection of the state of the economy, but it is a good indicator of the direct effect economic performance has upon the lives of the citizenry, as a range of social problems often go hand in hand with high levels of unemployment.

Another indicator of economic performance and its relationship with social change is migration. Thus, differential economic growth has been reflected in migration patterns through the renewal of a trend towards westward migration, Alberta showing a net gain of 280,000 migrants from 1971 to 1981 compared with 186,000 for British Columbia and 57,000 for Ontario, but a loss of 64,000 from Quebec. Other net losers were the Maritimes (including Newfoundland), Manitoba and northern Canada, though the general trend was in favour of population growth in all the provinces. The migrations tended to pick out those parts of the country experiencing economic growth. In effect this meant a focus upon major urban areas where the growing service sector was dominant and those parts of the country producing raw materials for export or developing "high-tech" industry (e.g., Cannon 1980; Steed and DeGenova 1983). The weakness of the Canadian economy was that, although the tertiary sector continued to expand in the 1970s and early 1980s, Canada has been very susceptible to fluctuations on the world raw material markets because of its over-reliance on production and export of raw materials.

The big cities have tended to prosper and grow while areas with older, established heavy industries have declined, and there has been an element of "boom and bust" for some of the areas reliant on raw materials. Unfortunately, the various regional economies have not co-ordinated their efforts to produce a balanced growth in the national economy (Davis 1982). North-south links with the United States have often proved stronger than east-west links within Canada (Hornsby et al. 1990), producing further tensions among the different parts of the country. The tendency for separate economic development of the regions has favoured western Canada and its rich resource base during the past two decades, promoting arguments from westerners concerning the payment of taxes to support those living in structurally weaker regions in the east. For example, the Prairie provinces and British Columbia have expressed a need for the four western provinces to exert greater control over federal spending in the West. A permanent western premiers' council has been created, which will voice "western views" on economic development. In terms of the French-British cleavage, the close links between Toronto and the north-eastern United States had helped to boost the city's economy in the 1970s and early 1980s compared with a slower development of key tertiary sector elements in Montreal (Semple and Green 1983). However, increased returns from Quebec's resource-based industries and a broadening of the province's service and industrial sectors has brought an economic resurgence to Quebec.

1.3.3   Unity

Burghardt (1978), in examining the possible consequences of separatism, remarked that, if it occurred, such an event would destroy the great Canadian corridor of the St. Lawrence, without which there would be no such viable land called Canada. This argument raises fundamental questions as to what holds such a large and diverse country together. What are the centripetal forces that have maintained this nation, given its size, physical diversity, sparseness and unevenness of its distribution of population, the presence of two founding cultures, and proximity to the many acculturating influences of the United States? The answer from Canada's dominant political figure of the 1960s and 1970s, Pierre Trudeau, is that foundation and continuation of the nation is based on a "common social will" (Trudeau 1968; Williams 1980). This will of the majority has surfaced in national surveys of public opinion (e.g., Kornberg et al. 1980) and, some may argue, in the defeat of the PQ in the elections for the Quebec Legislative Assembly in 1985, and in that party's failure to obtain a majority vote in the provincial referendum of May 1980. To a non-Canadian, such intangibles as "common social will" and a general consensus to resist the potential cleavages of regionalism and factionalism must be based in some small part upon a prevailing feeling of "Canadianness." This feeling is nourished by elements of common history since Confederation in 1867, by nationwide organizations and institutions, and by instruments of government that penetrate the daily lives of Canadians.

In 1985 a federal royal commission under the chairmanship of former federal finance minister Donald Macdonald, reported on the nature of the economic union and development prospects for Canada in the 1990s and into the twenty-first century. The report touched on many aspects of Canada's social and political fabric but, controversially, suggested the negotiation of a free-trade agreement with the United States, with whom there already existed over $160 billion of trade per annum, with Canada enjoying an annual surplus of $20 billion. Initial reaction from trade unions and Ontario, the most industrialized province, was opposed to the suggestion on the grounds that Canada would be the junior partner in such an arrangement and its political independence would be jeopardized. Arguments in favour of free trade included the view that free trade would strengthen the Canadian economy by increasing the market for its goods, that it would counter the possibly damaging growth of protectionist sentiment in the United States while, at the same time, demonstrating Canada's maturity as a nation and national confidence in its ability to compete with its larger neighbour. A major factor in government thinking appeared to be that Canada is exposed by being one of the few leading industrialized countries or trade blocs without an internal market population of 100 million or more. In a trade war Canada could suffer because of its small domestic market. Set against this have been nationalistic fears concerning the effect of free trade on the country's independence and the possibility of its political absorption into the United States.

Trade with the United States accounts for three-quarters of all Canada's trade with other countries, so such an agreement would only strengthen the already close ties. Yet, comments from Ontario government officials in August 1985 suggested that up to 30 percent of the province's manufacturing jobs could be threatened by the effects of reducing protectionism. Subsequently, the governments of other provinces, and especially Quebec, expressed concerns that their industry should not be affected adversely by any bilateral deal and argued for the right to be fully represented in any negotiations.

The Free Trade Agreement between Canada and the United States was finally ratified in 1988 despite strong opposition in Canada from the opposition Liberal and New Democratic parties. The agreement provides for a progressive dismantling of remaining tariff barriers between the two countries over a ten-year period beginning on 1 January 1989. At the time when the agreement was signed by Prime Minister Mulroney and President Reagan, in early 1988, annual trade between the two countries was $185 billion. This represents the biggest bilateral commercial partnership in the world and includes one-quarter of all Canadian exports. The United States exports more than twice as many goods to Canada than it does to Japan, and places one-third of its foreign investment there. In supporting the agreement, Canada's Conservative government emphasized four main advantageous outcomes from its implementation (External Affairs Canada 1987):

a) Ensuring industrial growth from a secure Canadian base
b) Encouraging new investment in Canadian enterprises
c) Creating a more stable and certain framework for co-operative relations between Canada and the United States (especially by increasing Canada's market access ten-fold)
d) Setting a bilateral precedent for global action (see Drache 1987)

Both countries have tried to pursue this global action in the Uruguay round of the General Agreement on Tariffs and Trade (GATT), albeit unsuccessfully to date.

Opposition to the agreement stressed that Canada could lose its economic independence, the opposition leader referring to the deal as "the Sale of Canada Act."

Among other fears was that regional inequalities might increase because of American investment being concentrated in enterprises located in already prosperous areas, notably the five major cities and mineral or energy developments in Alberta and Quebec. Also feared has been the threat to sovereignty and the probable job losses in the manufacturing industry, which may suffer from competition from firms in the United States. Some have argued that the agreement threatens Canada's cultural identity and could lead to eventual political union between the two countries. Contrary views from some economists have predicted that the agreement could increase Canada's gross national product by 5 percent during the nineties and create as many as 250,000 new jobs (Watkins 1986). In the 1988 general election, with the agreement as a major issue, the Conservatives were re-elected and their victory was seen as a general, if qualified, approval for free trade with Canada's southern neighbour. It should be noted, though, that the majority of voters voted for parties who were opposed to the agreement.

Perhaps the best illustration of the cement that binds Canadian society together is the nature of the relationship between Canada and the United States. There have been many instances when divisions within Canadian society have been submerged beneath a concern for the need to support national interests, especially when these have been perceived as being threatened by those of Canada's economically powerful neighbour. Although closer trading links have now been negotiated between the two North American neighbours, the Canadian government has continued to assert forcefully Canadian interests and points of view on certain issues. Two in particular attracted attention in the mid–eighties: Canadian sovereignty in the Arctic and pollution in the United States that was causing acid rain to fall on southern Canada.

Concern over the effects of acid rain on the environment, and forests and lakes in particular, has been manifest in calls for the United States and Canada to work together to halve acid rain emission by the mid 1990s. Various authorities suggest that more than half of Canada's acid rain is carried by prevailing winds from coal-burning power stations, ore smelters, and vehicle exhausts in the American Mid-West (e.g., Schmandt and Roderick 1985). On the issue of Canada's sovereignty over the waters enclosed by its Arctic archipelago, and in particular the North West Passage, the Americans are again called on to take action – this time in the form of official recognition of this status in return for the Canadian government facilitating transit routes between the islands. To enforce Canadian sovereignty in the Arctic, consideration has been given to purchase of a fleet of nuclear-powered submarines. Such vessels would be able to carry out defence functions under the Arctic ice cap as well as in the North Atlantic and along Canada's Pacific coast. Over both issues there remains the feeling in some quarters that it is still a case of a David and Goliath or big brother versus small neighbour. Elsewhere, dialogue between the two countries is now being seen increasingly as taking place between equals, with more mutual respect and understanding than had characterized previous negotiations (Cuff and Granatstein 1978).

One illustration of the concern over national identity in the face of the influence of "Big Brother" is the recent proposal by the Canadian Broadcasting Corporation

(CBC) to increase the amount of its Canadian content in order to change viewers' orientation. Their aim is to remove American commercial programs from the CBC network except for certain "high quality programs." This would produce a situation in which 90 percent of the programs on the CBC's English- and French-language services would be Canadian, supplemented by a range of material from around the world. The government was also urged to encourage privately owned networks, who tend to rely on cheaply purchased American fare, to readjust their schedules towards a national target of more than 50 percent domestic programming by the early 1990s. These plans illustrate the degree of cultural penetration that American radio and television have obtained in Canada. Over 95 percent of all the drama available on Canadian television comes from the United States, much of it regarded by many Canadians to be of extremely poor quality. In addition, most Canadians have direct access to the major American networks by cable from trans-border outlets (Collins 1989). An interesting footnote to the CBC's suggestions is their proposal to mount a counter-attack by beaming Canadian programs free of charge to U.S. cable companies.

1.3.4   Evolution

The concept of an evolving society in which various social characteristics are changing at different speeds throughout time is implicit in the preceding discussion as well as in the chapters by Camu and Bernier. The question, "how did the present pattern come about?" can partially be answered by a consideration of events that occurred during the past few years or even the period since the Second World War. Certain critical episodes in Canadian history that took place before 1945 helped shape the current social geography. Their importance has been hinted at, specifically with respect to the 1867 BNA Act. However, this is only one element in a rich history during the course of which a remarkable variety of cultural groups moulded distinct geographical environments throughout Canada. The story of these groups and the complex inter-relationships between the native peoples, the European settlers, and the land itself have merited considerable attention from scholars of many disciplines. Among them have been historians and historical geographers who have sought to show how Canada became, in Watson's (1968) terms, "the different America," and how the existing human imprint on the land came to be.

When examining current social patterns and major issues affecting Canadian society, the historical perspective is difficult to avoid. Its primary role in affecting duality, unity and plurality is all too evident. Above all, its centrality is crystallized in the maintenance of the Canadian state in the face of increasing American influence. Watson (1968, 7) described this as representing the attempt by both British and French Canadians to maintain the basic ways that they had inherited from Europe: "This brought and kept them together in Canada, and it made them develop the country in terms of that common feeling. Through this profoundly important factor, history came to dominate geography . . . developing the slender natural links between the regions of Canada to such an extent that the east-west geographical features . . . now became the main axes of development, and helped bind the nation together."

The inheritance from the past can be seen in thousands of different ways on various scales: the locations of different ethnic groups, the influence of the location of the railroad on the internal structure of the major cities, the way in which political structures have fostered or retarded economic development, and the effect of systems of land division on the rural landscapes. The links between the present social geography and the past are implicit in most of the studies in this volume. However, one study has been included that focuses explicitly on the way in which social geography has changed over time. This is the contribution by Wood (chapter 5), which examines the evolution of the social geography of southern Ontario, an integral part of Canada's "heartland" or "Main Street."

In this study, Wood selects a set of characteristics whose development can be traced for nearly two centuries, namely, demographic variables. He argues that in the early nineteenth century certain characteristics were established relating to fundamental social and political realities that remained as prime influences on the social pattern of the second half of the twentieth century. In particular, he singles out the way in which colonization of southern Ontario was planned, and the subsequent addition of the "flesh" of immigrants to the "skeleton" of the settlements and routeways developed in what was then part of Upper Canada. Five main phases of immigration are distinguished and examined in terms of long-term population dynamics. Within these dynamics the importance of urbanization and, subsequently, metropolitanization and suburbanization are recognized. These three processes represent a collective set of forces whereby southern Ontario was turned from a frontier of European settlement into a metropolitan society, perhaps even, in modern parlance, with elements of the post-industrial. Wood charts some of the main population dynamics within the build-up of agglomerating forces that produced the so-called Golden Horseshoe, stretching around the western end of Lake Ontario from east of Toronto to beyond Hamilton, and where today more than one in every six Canadians live.

In the forties some of Wreford Watson's first work in Canada was to study the city of Hamilton, where he learned about the features associated with social segregation and examined the forces that produced the micro-scale regionalization of the city (e.g., Watson 1945). As an illustration of the evolution of social geography, Wood returns to this study and compares Hamilton at the time of Watson's work with the city one hundred years earlier and also in more recent times. This comparison highlights the way in which the distribution of social classes and the growth of particular social problems crystallize and solidify in conjunction with major upheavals in the structural and economic fabric.

In terms of the formative elements of social geography that permeate the pattern of evolution portrayed by Wood, urbanization and migration appear to be the chief keys to the changing population characteristics that are examined. But they have operated in such a fashion that certain persistent structures within southern Ontario have been reinforced. Thus the MacDonald–Cartier Freeway and east-west road transport links can be compared with Whebell's (1969) corridors connecting, initially, urban islands in a sea of agricultural development on the eighteenth century frontier. Here is an example of modern society that, when placed under the microscope, reveals an onion-skin series of layers each building on, and often nearly reproducing, a previous pattern.

When describing present day population characteristics, or the three characteristics of duality, plurality and unity considered above, this complex and multi-faceted historical foundation must be referred to constantly if sense is to be made of the myriad of elements in social geography. Some of Watson's own work clearly demonstrated this, perhaps most vividly in his work on "relict features" in Halifax, Nova Scotia. Thus, "most regions are dynamic entities – especially urbanized regions. They develop a considerable number of structures to support their functions. These structures are changing, or are resisting change, both in nature and form. Their geographical description should, therefore, be dynamic" (Watson 1959, 141).

It is this dynamism amidst the persistence of certain crucial structures, such as federalism, the provinces, and Canada's physical geography, that has produced the Canadian dimension that forms the chief back-drop for the first part of this book and is present in numerous and diverse ways in all four parts.

References

Avery, D., and B. Ramirez. 1990. "Immigration and Ethnic Studies." In A.F.J. Artibise, ed., *Interdisciplinary Approaches to Canadian Society: A Guide to the Literature*, 77–116. Montreal and Kingston: McGill-Queens University Press.

Behiels, M.D. 1985. *Prelude to Quebec's Quiet Revolution: Liberalism versus Neonationalism*, 1945–1960. Kingston: McGill-Queen's University Press.

Bibby, R.W. 1990. *Mosaic Madness: Pluralism Without a Cause*. Don Mills: Stoddart Publishing Co.

Brym, R., ed. 1986. *Regionalism in Canada*. Toronto: Irwin.

Burgess, M. 1988. "Meech Lake: Whirlpool of Uncertainty or Ripples on a Millpond?" *British Journal of Canadian Studies* 3:15–28.

Burghardt, A.F. 1978. "Canada and Secession: Some Consequences of Separatism." In R.M. Irving, ed., *Readings in Canadian Geography*, 10–17. Toronto: Holt, Rinehart and Winston of Canada Ltd.

Cannon, J. 1980. "The Impact of Investment Incentives on Manufacturing Change: The Georgian Bay Region of Ontario." *Canadian Geographer* 24:131–48.

Chapman, K. 1985a. "Control of Resources and the Recent Development of the Petrochemical Industry in Alberta." *Canadian Geographer* 29:310–26.

———. 1985b. "Raw Material Costs and the Development of the Petrochemical Industry in Alberta Since 1975." *Transactions of the Institute of British Geographers* (new series) 10:138–48.

———. 1989. "Public Policy and the Development of the Canadian Petrochemical Industry." *British Journal of Canadian Studies* 4:12–34.

Cohen, A. 1990. *A Deal Undone: The Making and Breaking of the Meech Lake Accord.* Vancouver: Douglas & McIntyre.

Collins, J. 1989. "Broadcasting and National Culture in Canada." *British Journal of Canadian Studies* 4:35–57.

Cook, R. 1989. "The Evolution of Nationalism in Quebec." *British Journal of Canadian Studies* 4:306–17.

Cuff, R.D., and J.L. Granatstein. 1978. *American Dollars – Canadian Prosperity: Canadian-American Economic Relations, 1945–1950.* Toronto: Samuel-Stevens.

Davis, J.T. 1982. "Government-directed Money Flows and the Discordance between Production and Consumption in Provincial Economies, 1961–1979." *Canadian Geographer* 26:1–20.

Drache, D. 1987. "The Strategy of Canadian Trade Liberalization." *British Journal of Canadian Studies* 2:195–212.

Dufour, C. 1990. *A Canadian Challenge.* Lantzville: Oolichan Books.

Eccles, W.J. 1972. *France in America.* New York: Harper & Row.

Entrikin, J.N. 1976. "Contemporary Humanism in Geography." *Annals of the Association of American* 66:615–32.

External Affairs Canada. 1987. *The Canada-U.S. Trade Agreement in Brief; Trade: Securing Canada's Future.* Ottawa: Minister of Supply and Services Canada.

Foster, P. 1979. *The Blue-eyed Sheiks: The Canadian Oil Establishment.* Toronto: Collins.

Gilbert, E.W., and R.W. Steel. 1945. "Social Geography and its Place in Colonial Studies." *Geographical Journal* 106:118–31.

Harris, R.C., and J. Warkentin. 1974. *Canada Before Confederation.* New York: Oxford University Press.

Harvey, D.W. 1973. *Social Justice and the City.* London: Edward Arnold.

———. 1975. "Class Structure in a Capitalist Society and the Theory of Residential Differentiation." In R. Peel et al., eds., *Processes in Physical and Human Geography: Bristol Essays,* 354–69. London: Heinemann.

———. 1978. "Labor, Capital and Class Struggle Around the Built Environment in Advanced Capitalist Societies." In K.R. Cox, ed., *Urbanization and Conflict in Market Societies* 9–37. London: Methuen.

Hornsby, S., V.A. Konrad, and J.J. Herlan, eds. 1990. *The Northeastern Borderlands: Four Centuries of Interaction.* Fredericton: Acadiensis Press.

Houston, J.M. 1953. *A Social Geography of Europe.* London: Gerald Duckworth & Co.

Jackson, P., and S.J. Smith. 1984. *Exploring Social Geography.* London: George Allen & Unwin.

Johnston, D., ed. 1990. *Pierre Trudeau Speaks Out on Meech Lake.* Don Mills: Stoddart Publishing Co.

Johnston, R.J. 1986. "North America." In J. Eyles, ed., *Social Geography in International Perspective, 30–59.* Beckenham, Kent: Croom Helm.

Kornberg, A., et al. 1980. "Public Support for Community and Regime in the Regions of Contemporary Canada." *American Review of Canadian Studies* 10:75–93.

Laponce, J.A. 1984. "The French Language in Canada: Tensions Between Geography and Politics." *Political Geography Quarterly* 3:57–70.

Le Grand, A. 1970. "Introduction to Thirty Acres." In Ringuet (P. Panneton), *Thirty Acres*, ix–xiv. New Canadian Library, no. 12. Toronto: McClelland and Stewart.

Ley, D.F. 1981. "Inner City Revitalization in Canada: A Vancouver Case Study." *Canadian Geographer* 25:124–48.

———. 1982. "Rediscovering Man's Place." *Transactions of the Institute of British Geographers* (new series) 7:248–53.

———. 1984. "Pluralism and the Canadian State." In C. Clarke, D.F. Ley, and G.C.K. Peach, eds., *Geography and Ethnic Pluralism*, 87–110. London: George Allen & Unwin .

———. 1985. *Gentrification in Canadian Cities: Patterns, Analysis, Impacts, Policy*. Ottawa: Canadian Mortgage and Housing Corporation.

———. 1986. "Alternative Explanations for Inner-city Gentrification: A Canadian Assessment." *Annals of the Association of American Geographers* 76:521–35.

McCann, L.D. 1982. "Heartland and Hinterland: A Framework for Regional Analysis." In L.D. McCann, ed., *A Geography of Canada: Heartland and Hinterland*, 3–35. Scarborough: Prentice-Hall.

McConnell, W.H. 1977. *Commentary on the British North America Act*. Toronto: Macmillan of Canada.

McRoberts, K., 1979. "Internal Colonialism: The Case of Quebec." *Ethnic and Racial Studies* 2:293–318.

McRoberts, K., and D. Postgate. 1980. *Quebec: Social Change and Political Crisis*. Rev. ed. Toronto: McClelland and Stewart.

Meinig, D., ed. 1979. *The Interpretation of Ordinary Landscapes*. New York: Oxford University Press.

Mellor, J.R. 1977. *Urban Sociology in an Urbanized Society*. London: Routledge and Kegan Paul.

Nicholson, N.L. 1954. "The Boundaries of Canada, Its Provinces and Territories." *Geographical Branch Memoirs*, no. 2. Ottawa.

Park, R.E., and E.W. Burgess. 1921. *Introduction to the Science of Sociology*. Chicago: University of Chicago Press.

Park, R.E., E.W. Burgess, and R.D. McKenzie. 1926. *The City*. Chicago: University of Chicago Press.

Peach, G.C.K. 1981. "Conflicting Interpretations of Segregation." In P. Jackson and S.J. Smith, eds., *Social Interaction and Ethnic Segregation*, 19–33. London: Academic Press.

Peet, J.R. 1975. "Inequality and Poverty: A Marxist-geographic Theory." *Annals of the Association of American Geographers* 65:564–71.

Proudfoot, B. 1989. "The Setting of Immigration Levels in Canada since the Immigration Act, 1976." *British Journal of Canadian Studies* 4:233–56.

Relph, E.C. 1976. *Place and Placelessness*. London: Pion.

Ringuet (P.Panneton). 1940. *Thirty Acres*. Toronto: Macmillan Co. of Canada.

Robinson, J.L. 1983. *Concepts and Theories in the Regional Geography of Canada*. Vancouver: Talonbooks.

Sauer, C.O. 1947. "Cultural Geography." In E.C. Hayes, ed., *Recent Development in the Social Sciences*. Philadelphia and London: J.B. Lippincott.

Schmandt, J., and H. Roderick, eds. 1985. *Acid Rain and Friendly Neighbours: The Policy Dispute between Canada and the United States*. Durham, N.C.: Duke University Press.

Semple, R.K., and M.B. Green. 1983. "Interurban Corporate Headquarters Relocation Canada." *Cahiers de Géographie du Québec* 27:389–406.

Simeon, R., and I. Robinson. 1990. *State, Society and the Development of Canadian Federalism*. Toronto: University of Toronto Press.

Statistics Canada. 1984. *Canada's Immigrants*. Catalogue no. 99–936. Ottawa: Ministry of Supply and Services.

Steed, G.P.F., and D. DeGenova. 1983. "Ottawa's Technology-oriented Complex." *Canadian Geographer* 27:263–78.

Taylor, G. 1957. "Racial Geography." In G. Taylor, ed., *Geography in the Twentieth Century*, 3d ed., 433–62. London: Methuen.

Trudeau, P.E. 1968. *Federalism and the French Canadians*. Toronto and New York: St. Martin's Press.

Watkins, M. 1986. "A Canada-United States Free Trade Agreement: For and Against." *British Journal of Canadian Studies* 1:185–204.

Watson, J.W. 1945. "Hamilton and its Environs." *Canadian Geographical Journal* 30:240–52.

———. 1947. "Rural Depopulation in Southwestern Ontario." *Annals of the Association of American Geographers* 37:145–54.

———. 1950. "Canada: The Setting – its Geography." In G.W. Brown, ed., *Canada*, 120–42. Toronto: University of Toronto Press.

———. 1951. "The Sociological Aspects of Geography." In G. Taylor, ed., *Geography in the Twentieth Century*, 1st ed., 463–99. London: Methuen.

———. 1954a. "The Pattern of Canada's Post-war Growth." *Geography* 39:163–75

———. 1954b. "Basic Problems of Regional Planning in Canada." *Community Planning Review* 488–92.

———. 1955 "Geography – a Discipline in Distance." *Scottish Geographical Magazine* 71: 1–13.

———. 1956. "The Land of Canada." *Canadian Geographical Journal* 52:136–66.

———. 1957. "The Sociological Aspects of Geography." In G. Taylor, ed., *Geography in the Twentieth Century*, 3d ed., 463–99. London: Methuen.

———. 1959. "Relict Geography in an Urban Community: Halifax, Nova Scotia." In R. Miller and J.W. Watson, eds., *Geographical Essays in Honour of A.G. Ogilvie*, 110–43. London: Thomas Nelson & Sons.

———. 1962. "Canada and its Regions." *Scottish Geographical Magazine* 78:17–49.

———. 1963. *North America, its Countries and Regions*. London: Longmans Green.

———. 1965a. "Canada Divided: Problems of Region and State." *University of Edinburgh Journal* Autumn:146–58.

———. 1965b. "Canadian Regionalism in Life and Letters." *Geographical Journal* 131: 21–33.

———. 1967. "Mental Images and Geographical Reality in the Settlement of North America." *Cast Foundation Lectures, Univ. of Nottingham*, no. 3.

———. 1968. *Canada, Problems and Prospects*. Toronto: Longmans.

———. 1971. "Geography and Image Regions." *Geographica Helvetica* 1:31–4.

———. 1972. "Canada and its Environment." *Geographical Journal* 138:228–31.

———. 1977. "Images of Canada." Presidential Address to the British Association for Canadian Studies. *Bulletin of Canadian Studies* 1:1–15.

———. 1979. *Social Geography of the United States.* London: Longman.

———. 1983. "The Soul of Geography." *Transactions of the Institute of British Geographers* (new series) 8:385–399.

Watson, J., and J.W. Watson. 1977. *The Canadians: How They Live and Work.* Newton Abbot: David & Charles.

Whebell, C.F.J. 1969. "Corridors: A Theory of Urban Growth." *Annals of the Association of American Geographers* 59:1–26.

Williams, C.H. 1980. "The Desire of Nations: Québécois Ethnic Separatism in Comparative Perspective." *Cahiers de Geographie du Quebec* 24:47–68.

Wright, J.K. 1947. "Terrae Incognitae: The Place of Imagination in Geography." *Annals of the Association of American Geographers* 37:1–15.

2   Aspects of Social Differentiation in Canada

Pierre Camu

Social differentiation may be recognized in many ways. This essay outlines some of the fundamental social differences that exist in the vast country that occupies the northern half of North America and it is essentially a personal selection. As such it focuses upon elements that have produced distinctive facets of Canada's social mix and which, essentially, form the basic subject matter of the essays within this collection. It is intended as a brief guide to the sorts of topics that geographers have taken as their raw material for constructing a better understanding of the geography of Canadian society.

2.1   Ethnic Groups

The immigrant is a key factor in the composition of Canadian society. For decades Canada's population was dominated by its two major origins, the French and the British, upon which have been added waves of European immigrants after 1900 and, more recently, since the Second World War, immigrants from almost every country of the world (Table 2.1). In broad terms, the pattern of immigration has created three fundamental divisions in Canadian society: those between natives and non-natives, British and French, and these two founding or "charter" groups and other immigrants and their descendants.

In many respects it can be argued that there are two distinct cultural groups, the French- and English-speaking Canadians, because most immigrants have decided to learn English and have been integrated gradually into the largest of the two founding groups. Yet, the image of Canada as an Anglo-Saxon country prevails in the eyes of visitors, travellers, and observers, an image they gather from the predominance of spoken English, architectural styles, the judicial system and the parliamentary institutions. Even so, the fact remains that today, if 40 percent of the total population is of British origin, 60 percent is not, though more than two-thirds of that same population is able to express itself in English.

The "French fact" is a fundamental distinguishing feature of Canadian society: some 6.5 million French-speaking citizens live in Quebec and the two neighbouring provinces of New Brunswick and Ontario. The European immigrant of stock other than British or French is another vital component of Canadian society, with the concentration in the Prairies and some parts of Ontario. Despite the image of an Anglo-Saxon country, there are major ethnic differentiations. Yet, despite the arrival of hundreds of thousands of immigrants since 1951, and for every succeeding census year, at least 85 percent of Canadian citizens were born in Canada. Alongside the fundamental British-French dualism there remain complex networks of ethnic groupings, which play an important part in economic, political, and social

Table   **Composition of the Canadian Population by Ethnic (1981)**
2.1   **and Language Groups (1986)**

ETHNIC GROUPS			LANGUAGE GROUPS		
Origin[1]	*Number*	*Percent*	*Language[2]*	*Number*	*Percent*
British	9,674,250	40.2	English	15,334,085	60.6
French	6,439,100	26.7	French	6,159,740	24.3
Germans	1,142,365	4.7	Italian	450,320	1.8
Italians	747,97()	3.1	German	438,675	1.7
Ukrainians	529,615	2.2	Chinese	266,560	1.1
Native Peoples[3]	413,380	1.7	Ukrainian	208,410	0.8
Dutch	408,240	1.7	Portuguese	153,990	0.6
Chinese	289,245	1.2	Dutch	123,665	0.5
Scandinavians	282,795	1.2	Polish	123,120	0.5
Jewish	264,025	1.1	Greek	110,350	0.4
Polish	254,485	1.1	Others	1,934,920	7.7
Portuguese	186,105	0.8			
Others	3,451,920	14.3			
Total	**24,083,495**	**100.0**	**Total**	**25,309,330**	**100.0**

1. Ethnic origin refers to the ethnic or cultural group to which an individual or an individual's ancestors belonged on first coming to North America.
2. Language refers to mother tongue, that is the first language learned in childhood and still understood.
3. Includes 313,655 Indians of whom 47,235 are non-status Indians; 76,520 Métis and 23,200 Inuit – for definitions of these different groups see Bernier, chapter 3.

Sources: Census of Canada, 1981, Catalogue 93-933, Language, ethnic origin, religion, place of birth, schooling; *Census of Canada, 1986*, Catalogue no. 93-102, Language, Part I Table 1; *Census of Canada, 1986*, Catalogue no. 93-109, Ethnicity, Immigrants, and Citizenship, Table 2

organization. An indication of the importance of this "ethnic factor" is given in the two following statistics highlighted in *The Canadian Encyclopedia*: in the 1981 Census, 29 percent of Ontario's population, 35 percent of the population of British Columbia and 47 percent of the population of the Prairie provinces were comprised of immigrants of other than British or French origin; of 8 million Canadians of both non-British and non-French origins over 3 million learned a language other than English or French in childhood. On the one hand there is the retention of ethno-cultural differences, but on the other an integration into Canadian society of cultures and traditions from diverse origins. As these origins continue to grow through the receipt of new ethnic groups, from the Caribbean and South-East Asia for example, so the term "multiculturalism" becomes more appropriate. It has become a Canadian characteristic because immigrants in Canada have not been pressed to believe in a Canadian credo and to lose their identity to become Canadians as fast as possible. They have been encouraged to preserve their heritage, their roots, their culture, their crafts, and their arts.

Almost daily, new groups submerge the numerical importance of one group that has not been vociferous in the past, but whose origins are North American. These are the aborigines: the Inuit and the Indians, the first occupants of the land. These totalled 413,800 in 1981 or just over 1.7 percent of the total population. In contrast to many of the other ethnic groups within Canadian society, the native peoples tend to live on the margins, their very identity and heritage having been affected so greatly by the predominance of a more pervasive, dominant culture. The struggle to overcome the problems associated with marginality is crucial to the future well-being of the Inuit and Indians.

In contrast, the contribution of the second and third generation "immigrants" to a new Canadian society has been primordial and essential. They are the cement bonding a new society and nation out of the different linguistic and cultural groups. They are the new loyalists whose influence within Canadian society is impressive and, depending on the set of criteria chosen to rank the importance of a group in the Canadian mosaic, it could be said that their contribution is increasing every day.

2.2   The Labour Force

A second major differentiation of society comprises the variety of occupations and employment. The primary activities are the pursuit of a declining group of people such as the fisherman, the farmer, the lumberjack, the miner and the trapper and their families. They can be considered as one group, living and working closely with nature: their jobs are related to the great natural resources of the country; they are affected more than anyone else by weather and climatic conditions; their perception of the environment is different from those Canadians working in the industrial, manufacturing and construction sectors, and their family life must be adapted to their environment.

Another group of Canadians, consisting of those working in secondary activities, is large and concentrated in cities, metropolitan areas, or small towns, and is closely tied to the urban way of life. These are the "blue-collar workers," the producers and manufacturers, who live in small houses or apartments. Their physical environment is more limited than those in the primary occupations, and so are their patterns of activity. They spend their lives in a seasonal cycle that could be summarized by a few weeks of holidays per year in the outdoors, and the rest of the year at work in a given setting.

The large third group consists of those people working for the vast and varied world of services used by other Canadians. Trade is included in this category as well as the public services such as education, hospitals, police forces, and the civil service. These people work for either the state or themselves, but their livelihood depends on the other economic activities. Some have referred to this group as being engaged in tertiary, and even quaternary, activities, for example finance, banking, insurance, and head office operations. The "white-collar workers," the bureaucrats, and the self-made entrepreneurs all belong to this third group. It may be unfair to group them all into a single, large category, but their way of life in an urban setting is difficult to differentiate: their neighbourhoods, the cars they drive, the way they dress, the time they spend on the cultural activities of the theatre, concerts, music, and dining or at a second residence in the country, are some of the signs that separate them from the rest of society. They are the core of the citizens of any town or city, probably the most anonymous group of Canadians, but its most important in terms of political, social and economic influence.

The ratios between the three groups have changed in the post-war period as shown in Table 2.2. The largest group works in the service sector; it has increased from 47 to 65.9 percent of the total work force between 1951 and 1987, trebling its absolute numbers, while the percentages in both the primary and secondary sectors have fallen. The numbers involved in primary activities have declined by nearly 15 percent, but for secondary activities there has been a rise of nearly 20 percent during that 36-year period. These are, in general, the characteristics of an advanced, industrial society, and the socio-economic divisions so produced give rise to a set of social problems widespread throughout the developed world.

Table 2.2   Composition of the Labour Force in Work in Canada, 1951–87

Occupation	1951		1961		1971		1981		1987	
	No.[1] 000s	%	No. 000s	%	No. 000s	%	No. 000s	%	No. 000s	%
A	1,042.6	19.8	826.0	12.8	642.5	7.5	859.1	7.2	632	5.2
B	1,654.7	31.4	1,871.5	29.0	2,200.1	25.6	2,045.0	17.3	2,273	19.0
C	2,515.1	47.6	3,594.9	55.6	4,987.6	57.9	7,986.3	67.2	7,874	65.9
D	64.2	1.2	165.7	2.6	778.5	9.0	985.0	8.3	1,176	9.9
Total	**5,276.6**		**6,458.1**		**8,608.7**		**11,877.4**		**11,955**	

A Primary: farmers, loggers, fishermen, trappers, miners.
B Secondary: blue-collar workers, basically manufacturing, construction, and labourers.
C Tertiary and quaternary: services (white-collar workers), recreation, transport, and communications.
D Not stated.

1. Persons 15 years of age and over.

Source: Canada Year Book, 1980–81, Table 7.7. Statistics Canada provided special compilation for 1987.

Among the many characteristics that accompany the social division of the labour force, one worthy of mention as a symbol of the way in which employment patterns evolve over time, is the increase in the numbers of women as part of the gainfully-employed population. This trend started during the Second World War when many women were attracted by the salaries and the opportunities offered in the war industries. They came from the country, flocking into the cities or nearby towns to work in the factories while men were at war, and they never returned to the farm. In the mid-1980s the family with two wage-earners became a natural phenomenon of society. This has forced the creation and organization of day-care centres, nurseries and kindergardens; places of residence are empty during the day; the business hours of the retail trade have altered; transportation flows and movements have changed; and the patterns of cultural life are now compressed to certain evenings of the week or week-ends only.

In 1987 there were 5.1 million women at work in Canada; they comprised 43.2 percent of the total work-force. It is not surprising to note also that 80 percent of all women were working in the tertiary and quaternary sectors, especially in socio-cultural employment, the retail trade and public administration activities. Women are paid less than men, so some campaign for equal pay, equal rights, and equal treatment; some positions and jobs are still closed to them, in practice, if not in theory – an example of an inequality in Canada's contemporary, industrialized society.

Inequalities and, especially, the gap between the deprived of society and the wealthy can be seen in several other ways – the variations in housing, access to schooling and medical facilities, the ability to influence decision-making at a variety of levels, and differences in standards of living. The latter can be seen simply by looking at the way in which Canadians of all walks of life own or possess the trappings of a modern developed society: of almost universal use in the Canadian home is the bath and shower (98.8 percent), the telephone (97.6 percent), and the colour television (82.9 percent); more than two-thirds of Canadians have an electric washing machine (64.8 percent) and a clothes-drier (63.9 percent); more than half have one automobile (53.6 percent); and another 26.3 percent have two automobiles. For recreation 25 percent of Canadian households own a pair of cross-country skis, 20 percent have a tent for camping purposes, 48 percent have one bicycle, and some 8 percent have a snowmobile at the door (Statistics Canada, Catalogue no. 64-202). These are the statistics of a consumer society within which are hidden disparities and divisions associated with variations in disposable income. Deprivation and reliance on welfare payments in one socio-economic group can be contrasted with high consumerism and affluence in others. The intra-urban and inter-regional variation in these particular patterns of differentiation form a fundamental element of the social geographer's concern. They also contribute significantly to regionalism in Canada as suggested below (section 2.4).

2.3   Urban versus Rural

The division of Canada into three major groups based on their economic activities leads directly to another major social differentiation, the one between the rural and urban inhabitants, with a growing intermediary group of people who work in cities but live in the country or within a recognizable rural-urban fringe area, travelling back and forth everyday between their place of work and their place of rest. For Canada as a whole more than 50 percent of its population became urban around 1931, and, as indicated in Table 2.3, in the 1960s the proportion of the population classified as "urban" reached over 75 percent. The provinces with the largest rural population as a percentage of their total population were the Maritimes and Saskatchewan. In 1971 all the provinces had more than 50 percent of their population classified as urban except for Prince Edward Island. Quebec, which has been tagged for so long as a rural province because of the "habitant," its rural way of life, and its pleasant villages with the church as a focal point, has had a larger percentage of its citizens classified as urban rather than rural since 1921.

Table 2.3 **Distribution of the Population in Urban and Rural Areas, 1951–81**

	1951		1961		1971		1981	
	No. 000s	%	No. 000s	%	No. 000s	%	No. 000s	%
A *Rural*	5,381	38.4	5,538	30.4	5,157	23.9	5,907	24.2
Non-farm	2,553	18.2	3,465	19.0	3,738	17.3	4,867	20.0
Farm	2,828	20.2	2,073	11.4	1,419	6.6	1,039	4.2
B Urban[1]	8,628	61.6	12,700	69.6	16,410	76.1	18,436	75.8
< 5,000	1,519	10.8	3,258	17.9	2,876	13.3	5,843	24.0
5–100,000	3,849	27.5	5,288	28.9	7,637	35.4	10,035	41.3
> 100,000	3,260	23.3	4,154	22.8	5,897	27.4	2,558	10.5
	14,009		18,238		21,568		23,343	

1. People living in cities, towns and organized villages of 1,000 inhabitants and more, and villages of less than 1,000 but with a density of 1,000 inhabitants per square mile.

Source: Statistics Canada provided special compilation

In some respects it is surprising that in such a vast territory people are not only living in cities, but are also concentrated into a few large metropolitan centres and, with the exception of the Inuit and most Indian and Métis, the majority of Canadians live within 300 kilometres of the border with the United States, from the Pacific to the Atlantic Ocean. In theory there is still much space left for many immigrants. Canada has an ever present feeling of open space, of vast horizons, of long distances, of abundant space within its boundaries. Canada could support between 75 and 100 million people perhaps. But being practical, the available land, the good soils, the growing season, and the proportions of sunshine, rain, and snow could not sustain a very large population; it is not, after all, the most hospitable climate in the world. However, there is room for many more inhabitants; in fact, more usable land was occupied in the thirties than today. There has been a concentration of people in cities since the Second World War and this movement has been irreversible. Even so, it has not been a process devoid of problems: of crowding, of crime, of violence, and of vandalism – the negative aspects of urban life. For the new immigrants, though, it is still easier to integrate themselves into Canadian society via the largest cities and, subsequently, given favourable economic and social conditions, there is the possibility that they can select the type of employment and region in which they wish to live.

2.4   The Canadian Identity

There are some common factors that all Canadians share, irrespective of creed, faith, language, or origin, and these distinguish Canadians from other groups of people. They are namely, the notion and feel of winter, the notion of space and distance, the sharing of some unique and distinctive landscapes, the presence of the federal government, and the proximity to the United States.

Canada is snow-covered during almost four months of every year, from December to March. There are some exceptions such as in the lower Fraser Valley, and the areas around Victoria in British Columbia and the Niagara Peninsula in Ontario, but on the whole, everyone knows what snow is and how to cope with it. To withstand the harsh conditions Canadians have developed special construction standards for housing, buildings, maintenance of roads and highways, airports and railways. They manufacture typical winter clothing and practise sports such as skiing and skating, curling, and ice hockey that make winter more enjoyable. A song written by Gilles Vignault has become almost a second national anthem to French-speaking Canadians: "Mon pays, ce n'est pas un pays, c'est l'hiver." More than any other season, winter has marked Canadians and has been a principal factor of unification whose influences on Canadian society, it can be argued, have still not been assessed fully. Two geographers have described the effects and influences of winter on the Canadian way of life better than anyone else has done. Louis Edmond Hamelin, through his teachings, articles, and books such as *Le Canada* and *Nordicité canadienne*, has never underestimated the forces of winter on the inhabitants of the country. Pierre Deffontaines, in *L'homme et l'hiver au Canada*, described the effects of winter on types of houses, on problems of heating, on clothing, on food distribution, on transportation problems due to ice and snow, and on ways of life (Deffontaines 1957; Hamelin 1975; 1969). In general, winter in Canada is long, uncertain, unstable, wet, and snowy. It brings ice-cold temperatures, dryness in the Prairies, and is difficult and unpredictable everywhere.

Five and a half time zones separate Canadians in Newfoundland from those on Vancouver Island, and flying time from Montreal to Resolute Bay in the Arctic Islands is over ten hours. If you live in rural Saskatchewan, Manitoba, or even Alberta, you cannot walk to see your neighbour. It is preferable to take a truck, a snowmobile, or an automobile. How many stories have been told of young men driving hours to see their girl friends or fiancées for a few hours or for an evening? The majority of Canadians will never see all the provinces of the country; the North is not easily accessible, although it is becoming more so, and many citizens have never even been out of their own province. Just a look at the width of the major rivers to cross, of the Rocky Mountains and the Cordilleran chain in the West, the Great Lakes in the south, of the thousands of kilometres of coastline in the Atlantic provinces, demonstrates that the notion of space is directly associated with a vast territory where wilderness is never too far away.

A series of maps showing the networks of waterways, railways, roads and highways, locations of airports and landing strips, and of pipelines superimposed on a population map of Canada demonstrate in no uncertain terms the distances that must be covered to mail a letter, to visit a friend or relative, to send a package, to carry tonnes of resources and products, or just visit and discover the regions of the country. All Canadians share this notion of space and distance.

What they also share are the varieties of landscapes, both physical and cultural, that Canada possesses. These go much beyond the major physiographic regions, the huge drainage basins, the provinces where people live, their ward, their parish, their city, or their small world. It is the notion of "property" that bonds Canadians together. An example that illustrates better than anything else this notion of property occurred at the height of the Quebec crisis in the 1970s, when many friends were torn between a separate Quebec and the fact that they would also lose their *appartenance*, their shares of the Rocky Mountains. A separate Quebec would retain many attractive landscapes and yet would lose many, many more. Many other beautiful landscapes could be added to build up a list of "sights," of historical buildings, of huge developments such as the Saint Lawrence Seaway, the James Bay Hydro-electric project, or just maybe, an historical plaque at Batoche or a cairn on Cornwallis Island; it is this *patrimonie de la terre* that stopped those friends from voting for a separate Quebec. But for how long?

Winter, distances, and space can also be factors of isolation between Canadians, but for over one hundred years there have been crucial unifying elements overcoming the isolation. The presence of the federal government since 1867 has been predominant. Its main objective, at first and almost always subsequently, was to unify the country by building waterways, highways, airports, and landing strips; by facilitating the development of highways, pipelines, broadcasting systems of radio and television; by providing the post office service, the customs and excise, the financial and national defence infrastructures; and by keeping the direct responsibilities for foreign trade, immigration, external affairs and, partially, justice. After the initial phase of establishing and developing its responsibilities, the second objective has been to consolidate its power, provide a good responsible government, and improve the economic and social conditions of its citizens. This has been accomplished not without some epic battles with the ten provincial governments who, by definition, are closer to the people due to their basic socio-economic responsibilities.

Despite these major domestic responsibilities a constant preoccupation of the federal government has extended beyond the borders of Canada itself in the form of concern over the proximity of the United States – not only the geographical proximity of this major economic power, but its pervasive influence on Canadian life. This country's proximity has profound consequences. For example, the numerous connecting border crossings favour the coming and going of nationals of both countries, and of goods and products to the extent that more than 70 percent of the total foreign trade of Canada is with the United States. The two countries have complementary economies, a situation that has periodically led to considerations of an economic union, but this has always been rejected for nationalist reasons of which the crucial argument has been that if Canada joins the United States on an economic basis it is very likely to be absorbed or integrated politically at a subsequent stage.

Why would this be so easy? The answer lies in the similarities of the two societies and the two cultures. There is a North American way of life that Canadians share with Americans; it could be summarized in the similar types of houses, the dominance of the automobile, the mode of dress, and patterns of entertainment, eating, and working. The institutions such as the judicial, educational, health, and welfare systems are different, however, and so is the political structure, although there are many similarities between the powers, jurisdictions, and problems of states and provinces within the two federal systems.

What is more serious is the pull that the culture of the United States exercises on Canadian society. It is not only its attraction as the principal destination for Canadian tourists, a feeling exists that the United States is more than a friend; a feeling that the two nations are relatives, however distant the relationship. American radio, television, cinema, and theatre offer familiar music, films, and plays. The United States penetrates Canadian society in innumerable ways. It is so close that for some it is too close! It is an influence that has continually prompted Canadians to seek out their Canadian identity and to develop notions of separateness and distinctiveness in the face of the pull of the powerful American culture.

2.5   Regionalism

Because of Canada's size, its population of various ethnic groups, its two official languages, scattered over millions of square kilometres, its provinces, and its proximity to the United States, there exists a tendency towards the growth of regionalism, of provincialism, of cultural, social, and political pockets, and of *les petites parties* (the small local nations).

The growth of regionalism in Canada is almost a necessity. Some may disagree; others will recite the litany of efforts by the federal government to centralize and accumulate powers to govern more efficiently in order to protect the concept of "Canada" against its division into several units, like the Scandinavian countries. Indeed, it must be remembered that before the Act of Union in 1840, there were Lower Canada (Quebec) and Upper Canada (Ontario), and the colonies of Nova Scotia, Newfoundland, and New Brunswick, and that these regions existed with their own history, tradition, development, and characteristics. Today, at least four major regions are commonly identified: the Atlantic provinces consisting of Newfoundland and the Maritime provinces, Quebec, and Ontario, also considered as Central

Canada, and the West. The West could be subdivided into the Prairies and British Columbia. To this breakdown must he added the Northwest Territories and the Yukon, as the last frontiers, the land of the future, the proposed eleventh and twelfth provinces. There are differences between them all, sometimes almost imperceptible, sometimes as evident as the differences on the licence plates of automobiles, the road and highway signs, and other subtle but clearly visible features.

Canada is so vast and its territory so immense that it is natural to think in terms of regions. Because of their inherent rights and historical development, the provinces are the regions Canadians refer to when they identify themselves with their roots, connections, family links, and sense of belonging. The largest and oldest cities of the country have developed a heritage and a set of values that many Canadians are proud of, and they do not hesitate to name their "hometowns."

It is difficult to pinpoint and characterize the differences between the social groups of the Maritimes, the West, Ontario, and Quebec. The French-speaking society may be the easiest to differentiate, because of the language; though subgroups can even be distinguished among French-speaking Canadians, such as the Acadians, the Franco-Ontarians, the Manitobans, and so forth. It is more difficult to identify the English-speaking subgroups, though ethnicity and socio-economic factors provide fertile grounds for differentiation as has been suggested already.

The problem of regionalism arises when one or two regions or provinces are either frustrated by the dealings they have with central government, when it appears to be easier to go it alone, that is, to separate, or are so well off, so ahead of the rest, that instead of supporting the others, they feel they could do more for their citizens by separating rather than remaining within the Confederation.

It is the old quarrel between the "haves" and the "have nots"; one that arises because of the discrepancies or inequalities between regions that have a perennial high rate of unemployment and others that have a lack of basic resources, capital, or people. This notion of wealth is vital to the understanding of a modern society such as the Canadian one. Indeed, a fundamental social differentiation can be seen between classes of people based on wealth. This is translated into spatial terms in Table 2.4, which utilizes data on per capita disposable income.

The results confirm what other groupings of economic indicators could have revealed: that in 1961 the lower per capita disposable incomes were found in three of the four Atlantic provinces, as well as in Saskatchewan, and the higher were concentrated in Ontario, British Columbia, and Alberta. These comments are also true for 1971. Only Ontario, Alberta, and British Columbia were above the Canadian average per capita income of $1,400 in 1961 and $2,754 in 1971. Some interesting changes had happened by 1971, when Saskatchewan surpassed Nova Scotia, and British Columbia lost its first rank to Ontario, Quebec maintained its fifth rank.

By 1981 Ontario had lost first position to Alberta, while British Columbia kept its second rank. Saskatchewan increased its position again, registering the greatest gains, from seventh rank in 1961 to fourth rank in 1981. Meanwhile, Quebec had slipped to sixth. Four provinces were above the national average: Ontario, Saskatchewan, Alberta, and British Columbia. In 1985, the Atlantic provinces occupied the last four places; Ontario had regained its first place, Alberta had slipped into second, and British Columbia into third position. The disposable income of Quebecers increased to place the province fourth. Outside this classification, northern Canada, which in 1961 had an average disposable income above the national mean, had fallen below in 1971 and then rose again above the national average by 1985. There has been a certain consistency and equilibrium over the past 25 years that justifies the saying that those who are rich are getting richer, and those who are poor remain poor. The wealth accumulated over centuries in old cities such as Halifax, Quebec City, and Montreal compensates and offsets the low ranks of their provinces, as does not occur in the newer cities of the West. Yet Ontario and the West are definitely more wealthy. Their inhabitants possess of a greater disposable per capita income than those living in Quebec and in the Atlantic provinces. Overall, Ontario's society is still well-off as can be seen in the cultural landscape of southern Ontario, and in the variety, quality, and richness of its cultural and social life.

Table 2.4   **Per Capita Disposable Personal Income by Province, 1961–85**

PROVINCES	1961		1971		1981		1985	
	$	Rank	$	Rank	$	Rank	$	Rank
Newfoundland	860	10	1,893	10	6,498	10	10,125	10
Prince Edward Island	930	9	1,920	9	6,813	9	10,332	9
Nova Scotia	1,130	6	2,160	7	7,564	7	11,875	7
New Brunswick	1,000	8	2,080	8	6,968	8	10,837	8
Quebec	1,230	5	2,470	5	8,694	6	12,840	4
Ontario	1,640	2	3,130	1	10,379	3	15,094	1
Manitoba	1,350	4	2,630	4	9,930	5	12,594	5
Saskatchewan	1,090	7	2,390	6	9,931	4	12,288	6
Alberta	1,460	3	2,780	3	10,487	1	14,998	2
British Columbia	1,650	1	3,010	2	10,425	2	13,776	3
Northern Canada	1,830		2,480		9,841		15,642	
Canada (average)	1,400		2,754		9,587		14,342	

Sources:
1961   P. Camu, E.P. Weeks, and Z.W. Sametz, *Economic Geography of Canada with an Introduction to a 68 Region System* (Toronto: Macmillan, 1964)
1971   Unpublished compilation by Camu, Weeks, and Sametz
1981   National Income and Expenditure Account, Statistics Canada
1985   *Census of Canada*, 1986, Catalogue no. 93-114, *Total Income, Individuals,* Table 3

There is also clear evidence in Table 2.4 of five regions, or five groupings of provinces. The "have nots" are in the east. These are the four peripheral Atlantic provinces, which have the lowest disposable incomes. Their outlook is towards the sea when most of the country, including the federal government, has a continental approach to almost everything. Most of Quebec could be included in this "have not" category as well, but the Montreal metropolitan area makes the difference by increasing the average disposable income. Being predominantly French, the concept and the feeling of nationalism is stronger here than anywhere else in the country. It is definitely the second major region. Ontario, formerly Upper Canada, is the third region, one which is very conscious of being the cornerstone of economic, cultural, and social life in English-speaking Canada. The fourth region is the West, including the Prairie provinces and British Columbia. West of the Great Lakes and west of the Canadian Shield, the West is very much a unique part of the country. Its people's ancestors arrived from Europe only two or three generations ago. It is less conformist, more friendly, and closer to the land and the environment. In effect, it is the other half of Canada, though in saying this, another dimension is introduced. It is almost another country whose farms, towns, and cities are an extension of the patterns, imprints of settlement, and way of life in the American Midwest. The differences between the people living north and south of the 49th parallel reside in history, in the political institutions, and in the sense of belonging to another country.

The fifth region is the North, consisting of the Yukon and the Northwest Territories. This is the largest, the highest, and the least inhabited region; it is still controlled by the federal government. The land of the future, the last frontier, this territory has many problems that do not yet have solutions: there is no program for development or master plan for a basic approach. Louis-Edmond Hamelin and William Wonders have done much to awaken the interests of southern Canadians for the North and to arouse the hopes of its inhabitants, the Inuit and the Indians, though without much success. There remains an indifference, perhaps because the territory is too vast and there is still much to do south of the 60th parallel where, over one hundred years after the British North America Act, much energy and attention is still being devoted to resisting the attraction and pull from the United States leaving little zest and zeal to do anything for this fifth region, this "fifth estate."

Within the five regions lies the foundation of a Canadian society. Perhaps it is not possible to say there is a single Canadian society as such, but there are at least five groups of Canadians living in five distinct regions whose differences are not only geographical but socio-economic as well. It is in strengthening the concept of the five basic regions and their societies that eventually a more cohesive Canadian society might emerge.

In summary, the major differences among Canadians are within their occupations and ways of life, where Canada follows the trend of other western nations with large numbers of people working in tertiary and quaternary economic activities and in living more of an urban than a rural way of life. What differentiates this society, more than any other factors are the ethnic and linguistic divisions of the people into two or three broad groups: the British, the French, and the others, subdivided into several subgroups. The relationships between the majority and minority groups, the right to live and work and be serviced in one's own language, and other problems directly related to being a bilingual country, though not necessarily a bilingual society, have all been examined by several royal commissions in the past. It is almost a perennial problem, which increases or decreases depending on the political, economic and social tensions and stresses of the moment. This time it is more serious than ever. Quebec is flirting with the idea of sovereignty and may propose a new association with the rest of the country under a new confederation. Will the rest of Canada agree? The days of Confederation type one (1867–1992) are coming to an end.[1]

Notes

1. Spry 1971. Graham Spry was one of the most pertinent observers of the political climate and one of its best writers. This article demonstrates his unique understanding of the Quebec crisis of the 1960s and the appearance of the idea of separatism.

References

Deffontaines, P. 1957. *L'homme et l'hiver au Canada*. Paris: Gallimard et Presses de l'Université Laval.

Hamelin, L.E. 1975. *Nordicité canadienne*. Montreal: Hurtubise HMH.

——— . 1969. *Le Canada*. Paris: Presses Universitaires de France.

Spry, G. 1971. "Canada: Notes on Two Ideas of Nation in Confrontation." *Journal of Contemporary History* 6 (1): 173–96.

Statistics Canada. Catalogue no. 64-202.

3   Pluralism and National Unity
Jacques Bernier

3.1   A Country Born of Diversity

Both in its present territorial version *a mari usque ad mare* and in its institutional framework, the history of Canada dates back to the British North America Act (BNA Act) of July 1867. At that time Canada consisted of only Ontario, Quebec, New Brunswick, and Nova Scotia, but for the "founding fathers" the whole west, all the way to the Pacific Ocean, was regarded as part of the country. Thus, the new-born dominion purchased the Northwest Territories (Rupert's Land and the North-Western Territory) from the Hudson's Bay Company and established Manitoba as a fifth province in 1870. Then British Columbia was won over in 1871, as was Prince Edward Island in 1873. Finally, in 1905, as soon as the evolution of the "provincial districts" covering the area allowed it, Alberta and Saskatchewan were created. So by 1871 Canada stretched out from sea to sea and its territorial version-to-be was largely defined. The addition of the British colony of Newfoundland in 1949 hardly altered the territorial and demographic configuration of the country.

The birth of modern Canada was the result of both external and internal factors. On the one hand, London could safeguard its influence and interests in North America by preventing possible secessions or annexations to the powerful southern neighbour.[1] On the other hand, in Canada there was a desire to create a new and broader political community that would guarantee the existence of a dominion full of promises, and maintain the interests of leading bankers and merchants. This group could no longer rely on the imperial trade preferences that had been so profitable to the British colonies of America since the Napoleonic Wars.

This *raison d'être* has evolved since that time, but it is still partly valid. At the time of its creation modern Canada was in fact a settlement colony of the powerful United Kingdom whose distant influence was nonetheless real in some important affairs. In that respect, the situation has changed greatly; in 1931 the Statute of Westminster revoked all legal restrictions to the legislative autonomy of the country, and this, in practice, made it sovereign and independent. On the other hand, despite scepticism and hesitation in the beginning and despite subsequent problems, the desire of Canadians to maintain their country distinct from the United States of America and to belong to it, remained and even grew firmer.

The discussions and debates that preceded the BNA Act reveal that, in general, the founding fathers would have preferred a country with a highly centralized authority. Some of them even conceived Confederation as a transitory step towards the establishment of a more centralized system (Voisine 1977). Several good reasons militated in favour of a strong central state and indeed a unitary system. The attraction of the southern neighbour was already being felt in some regions. In addition to being vast and split up by physical barriers, Canada was sparsely and unevenly occupied by communities of various origin. But it would have been difficult, even impossible, to convince these communities, deeply rooted in their regions and often isolated from each other as they were, to accept a highly centralized and unitary political system (Garon 1977). Already at that time diversity was well implanted. It consisted not only of two peoples of French and British descent, but also of several communities that had developed mainly in a regional context. Thus, the diverse origin of the inhabitants, the varying conditions of their establishment, and the isolation of the main loci of settlement had already given rise to the regionalization of the country-to-be. The dualism and regionalism, which were determinant in the choice of the institutional framework of modern Canada, are unquestionably still major elements of the social, economic, and political fabric of the country. However, Canada has changed a great deal since the last decades of the nineteenth century, and its pluralism is more profoundly rooted and complex than it was in the beginning.

From an ethno-cultural point of view, the population of Canada comprises the British and French communities, often referred to as "the two founding peoples," "the two nations," or, more prosaically, as the elements of the historical duality of the country; several linguistic groups whose origin is neither British nor French and who seek to keep a part of their cultural heritage in the name of the Canadian cultural pluralism; and finally the native peoples (Indians, Inuit, and Métis) whose ancestors occupied the land centuries before the arrival of the first European settlers (see Table 2.1). Canadians of every extraction may be found almost anywhere in the country, but they are often concentrated in certain areas according to their country or region of origin. For instance, the French populate Quebec, adjacent northern New Brunswick, and northern and eastern Ontario; Europeans other than French and English populate the West and Ontario; and the Métis populate the Prairie provinces (see Table 3.1).

This ethno-cultural diversity is accompanied and sometimes coupled with a regionalism encouraged by both history and geography. These regional communities, whose identity and particular interests are rooted in history and local character, will be considered later in this essay.

The crisis of Canadian unity has been discussed and analyzed abundantly during the last 15 years or so and, in particular, since the election in Quebec in November 1976 of the Parti Québécois whose program's first article was to achieve the political sovereignty of Quebec (Parti Québécois 1978, 7). Radio, television, symposia, newspapers, books, and publications of all sorts have given the opportunity to experts, interest groups, and several ordinary citizens to give their views on the causes of the crisis and the ways to solve it. The Task Force on Canadian Unity (TFCU), whose mandate was in part to obtain the views of Canadians regarding the state of their country, met a wide cross-section of them during its national tour from Vancouver to Yellowknife to St. John's. Offhandedly shelved, as soon as released, by influential politicians who were determined to impose their own solution, the TFCU report, although written from a pan-Canadian perspective, summarizes in a telling and perceptive way what has been said and written on the question of Canada's future. It offers a penetrating analysis of Canadian society and puts forward forceful recommendations. This document, which could surface again to inspire a fundamental revision of Canadian federalism, constitutes a very useful synthesis that will be referred to often in this essay.

3.1.1   The British-French Duality

In accordance with the TFCU, British-French duality may be recognized as a phenomenon whose shape and significance are greatly influenced by the social, economic, and political context within which it lies (TFCU 1979, vol. 3, 22–23). British and French Canadians have coexisted more than two centuries in the vast territory that became Canada in 1867, and as a result there is a range of situations which have varied and do vary from region to region according to the demographic balance, the economic weight, the concentration, and, finally, the political power and aspirations of the communities. It is often with reference to one or the other of these diverse situations that duality is represented. While admitting the multifaceted and changing character of the phenomenon, it must be realized that duality in Canada as a key political fact refers to, above all, an essentially French Quebec as a major piece of an essentially British Canada. It is indeed this geopolitical reality that lies at the heart of the problem of Canadian unity.

In New Brunswick the Acadians, a sizeable minority representing 32 percent of the population of the whole province and nearly 55 percent in its northern areas, form a community whose numbers, territoriality and cohesion have already prompted it to hope for a more self-determinant control of its future. However, this specific community of French origin remains a minority in a not very populous province and does not represent a demographic and political weight on a national level that could be compared with that of Quebec. Partly concentrated in the northern and eastern counties of the province, Franco-Ontarians form the most numerous French minority in British Canada. Victim, however, of a strong assimilation – only 50 percent use French as their first language (Statistics Canada, Oct. 1983, Table 6) – this loose community's future depends mainly on that of Quebec within Confederation (see Tables 3.1 and 3.2).

3.1.2   The Regional Communities

Even though some Canadians, and many Quebecers in particular, tend to have an essentially dualistic view of Canadian society and thus to see British Canada as a monolith, regionalism also constitutes a significant cleavage in Canadian society.

From the very beginning, history and geography have favoured the development of regions in the country. On a national scale it is possible to think of Newfoundland and the Maritimes, Quebec and Ontario, and the Prairies and the West Coast, which sometimes are grouped together to form eastern, central, and western Canada. Even though references to three, four, five, or six regions correspond to a geographical and historical reality that transcends the provincial level, recent history shows that views and interests of the provinces often differ and that the provinces tend to embody the substance of regionalism more and more. It is true that the provincial framework provides an instrument of expression, pressure, and action that is not found at higher levels, and it may be that following the repeated utilization of this efficient connection, regional and provincial interests have come to merge. It is also possible to suggest that through their demands regional communities have induced provincial governments to behave more and more as their protagonists. Therefore, though it is justifiable from several points of view to speak of central Canada, the Maritimes, the Prairies, and the West Coast, the country's dynamics have required that regional interests find expression through and within the provincial framework.

Diversity in British Canada has several sources. There is the sheer size of the territory and physical barriers, whose impact, one or two centuries ago, could not fail to contribute to the isolation of the scattered communities. Furthermore, Canada was initially a series of colonies clearly distinct from each other, and until 1867 entities such as Upper Canada, New Brunswick, Nova Scotia, and British Columbia kept closer links with Great Britain than with each other. In addition to geography and history, there is ethnicity. British Canada is not made up only of those of British descent – these represent scarcely half of its population – but also of people from many horizons who have put down roots, mainly after 1900, in certain areas of western Canada in particular: namely, Europeans other than the British and French, West Indians, and Southern and South-East Asians emigrating to Canada after the Second World War. These people contributed greatly to the ethnic plurality of the country (see Figure 3.1 and Table 3.1).

While largely adopting the language and political attitudes of the British majority, these newcomers have kept certain features of their culture of origin, and in so doing have marked the identity of some provinces in a special way, in particular that of Alberta, British Columbia, Manitoba, and Saskatchewan.

This new contribution to Canadian society has generally strengthened regionalism in British Canada and has given it a new dimension and depth that Ottawa, according to some Quebecers, has taken pleasure in encouraging during the last two decades to counterbalance Quebec's claims based on cultural specificity. In addition, as in political terms the linguistic demarcation has proven to be more real than the ethnic differences, French Canadians have become used to thinking in terms of English rather than British Canada *(Canada anglais)*. Of course, this overshadows the fact that among the Canadians of Anglo-Celtic origin there are Scots, Irish, and Welsh elements. In the Maritimes, for instance, there were many Scots and Irish, both Catholics and Protestants, not to mention the Welsh. As noted earlier, Confederation, in giving the provinces considerable powers, confirmed and strengthened an already existing regional consciousness. As underlined by the TFCU (1979, vol. 3, 31), this was the case in Quebec where the "provincial government . . . has become the main instrument of Québécois's aspirations," but other provinces have also used their powers "to support and encourage what amounts to little less than the development of provincial societies."

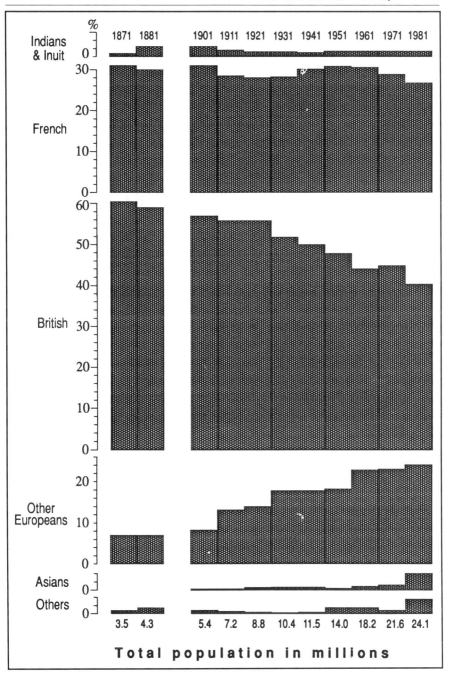

Figure   **Evolution in the Composition of the Canadian Population,**
3.1   **1871–1981**

> *Source*: Canada, Department of Indian Affairs and Northern Development,
> *Population indienne selon le sexe et la résidence le 31 décembre 1977*
> (1978), and *Atlas of Indian Reserves and Settlement of Canada* (1971)

Table 3.1   Composition and Distribution of Canadian Population, 1986 Census

Origin	N.W.T. Number	%*	Yukon Number	%*	B.C. Number	%*	Alberta Number	%*	Saskatchewan Number	%*	Manitoba Number	%*	Ontario Number	%*
British[1]	9,585	18.4	7,780	33.3	1,190,310	41.8	805,475	34.4	297,555	29.9	310,935	29.6	3,944,950	43.8
French	1,510	2.9	775	3.3	69,095	2.4	77,690	3.3	33,580	3.4	55,760	5.3	531,870	5.9
European[2]	2,800	5.4	2,650	11.3	481,750	16.9	507,210	21.7	267,925	26.9	278,165	26.5	1,696,835	18.9
Asian & African[3]	675	1.3	335	1.4	232,345	8.1	120,550	5.2	15,870	1.6	37,930	3.6	443,470	4.9
Indian[4]	7,590	14.6	3,165	13.6	56,955	1.9	34,490	1.5	43,385	4.4	40,960	3.9	51,165	0.6
Metis	2,205	4.2	80	0.3	3,930	0.1	16,880	0.7	12,220	1.2	14,270	1.4	3,715	—
Inuit	17,385	33.4	35	0.2	240	—	295	—	40	—	185	—	675	—
Other	800	1.5	445	1.9	44,550	1.6	40,575	1.7	9,655	1.0	29,975	2.9	311,840	3.5
Multiple Origin[5]	9,470	18.2	8,095	34.6	770,410	27.0	737,100	31.5	316,465	31.8	281,140	26.8	2,016,650	22.4
Total	52,020	100	23,360	100	2,849,585	100	2,340,265	100	996,695	100	1,049,320	100	9,001,170	100

	Quebec		New Brunswick		Nova Scotia		P.E.I.		Newfound-land		Canada	
	Number	%*	Number	%*	Number	%*	Number	%*	Number	%*	Number	%*
British[1]	380,265	5.9	329,310	46.9	542,190	62.7	86,410	69.0	501,775	89.0	8,406,540	33.6
French	5,019,055	77.7	233,850	33.3	53,415	6.2	11,140	8.9	11,320	2.0	6,099,060	24.4
European[2]	363,580	5.6	11,120	1.6	41,435	4.8	2,440	2.0	3,000	0.5	3,658,910	14.6
Asian & African[3]	111,445	1.7	3,050	0.4	6,835	0.8	685	0.5	1,095	0.3	975,095	3.8
Indian[4]	37,150	0.6	3,685	0.5	5,570	0.6	375	0.3	1,745	0.3	286,235	1.1
Metis	5,700	—	190	—	255	—	35	—	270	—	56,750	0.2
Inuit	6,470	—	10	—	135	—	—	—	1,810	0.3	27,280	0.1
Other	150,550	2.3	2,415	0.3	11,085	1.3	165	0.1	465	—	602,520	2.4
Multiple Origin[5]	380,275	5.9	118,230	16.8	203,230	23.5	23,840	19.1	41,710	7.4	4,906,615	19.6
Total	6,454,490	100	701,860	100	864,150	100	125,090	100	564,000	100	25,022,005	100

*   Percentage of total population.

1.   Includes the British single and the British only multiple categories.

2.   Other than British and French; mainly (85%) Germans, Italians, Ukrainians, Dutch, Poles, Portuguese, Scandinavians and Greek.

3.   Mainly (57%) Chinese and people from South Asia.

4.   Excluding the population on incompletely enumerated Indian reserves and settlements. For Canada there were 136 such reserves and settlements and the total population was estimated to be about 45,000.

5.   Predominantly (80.7%) of British and other origins.

Source: Statistique Canada, *Annuaire de Canada 1990* (Ottawa: Approvisionne-ments et Services Canada, 1989), A31–33.

Table   **The French Fact in Canada, 1986 Census**
3.2

| | Total | FRENCH MOTHER TONGUE | |
| | Population | Numbers | % of Total |
Region	(000)	(000)	Population
Canada	24,354	6,160	25.3
Quebec	6,291	5,317	84.5
New Brunswick	709	226	31.9
Northern New Brunswick[1]	398	213	53.5
Ontario	9,102	425	4.7
Northern and Eastern Ontario[2]	1,302	272	20.9

1. The six northern federal electoral districts of New Brunswick.
2. The 14 federal electoral districts of Northern and Eastern Ontario.

Source: Statistics Canada, *Profiles, Federal Electoral Districts – 1987 Representation Order: Part I* (Ottawa: Supply and Services Canada, May 1988), 1, 13, 14, 19, 55–98

It seems appropriate at this point to stress that the historical duality of the country and the increasing diversity of its population are not mutually exclusive. The cultural pluralism of the population lies within the scope of the basic Canadian dualism that preceded it and includes it. On the other hand, cultural pluralism is associated with regionalism to which it has given a new dimension if not a new life. Finally, dualism and regionalism are not two isolated phenomena but, on the contrary, are two inseparable aspects of Canadian diversity. In fact, the interweaving and the mutual influence of the two phenomena are such that it is impossible to understand one fully without referring to the other. It is evident, for instance, that dualism is a phenomenon that finds expression here and there in the country, but to understand its real significance its regional aspect must be realized. Although Quebec embodies one aspect of Canadian dualism, it also forms a distinct area of the country, and it is only in considering these two closely linked facts that its particular position in Canada may be understood. On the other hand, though regions in British Canada differ in many respects, they also share political attitudes and a vision of Canada that lies within the scope of the historical British-French duality.

3.1.3   The First Peoples

To give a picture of Canadian diversity in all its major aspects, in addition to the British-French duality and regional communities, the native peoples must be considered. The expression "native peoples," which is used in Canada to denote the first inhabitants, refers to Indians, Inuit, and Métis. In Canada there are actually some 300,000 status Indians, 22,000 Inuit, and 750,000 Métis and non-status Indians, who, altogether, represent about 5 percent of the total population of the country (TFCU 1979, vol. 3, 27) (see Table 3.3 and Figure 3.2).

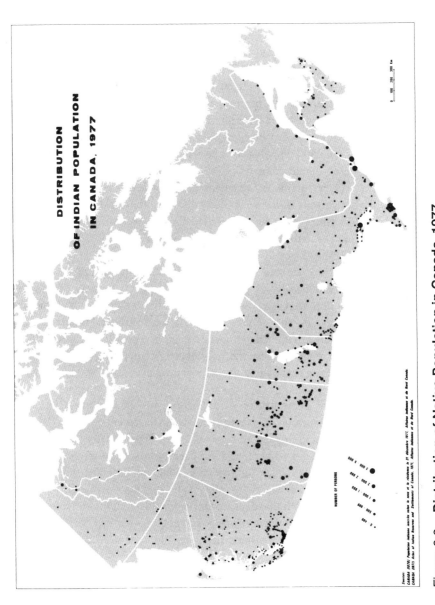

Figure 3.2   Distribution of Native Population in Canada, 1977

The term "Indian" broadly applies to anyone of Indian ancestry, including both status and non-status Indians. The expression "status Indian" designates persons registered, or entitled to be registered, under the Indian Act; it describes a legal status rather than an ethnic background, because it includes non-Indian wives of status Indian males. Non-status Indians are persons of native ancestry who, though calling themselves Indians, have either not been recognized as being eligible for registration under the Indian Act or have been enfranchised under the provisions of the act. Considerable controversy surrounds the processes whereby Indians have lost or been denied status. Métis are persons of mixed Indian and European ancestry who are neither registered nor entitled to be registered under the Indian Act. The terms "Métis" in French and "half-breed" in English were first applied to the offspring of unions between Indians and Europeans. In the nineteenth century these descendants became numerous enough, in what is now western Canada and the northern territories, to form an ethnic community separate from both the Indians and the Europeans. Descendants of those Canadians call themselves Métis today. Inuit (singular: Inuk) are persons of native ancestry speaking the Inuktitut language. At one time they were commonly referred to as Eskimos. According to an advisory opinion of the Supreme Court of Canada in 1939 the term "Indians" in the BNA Act includes Inuit (TFCU 1979, vol. 2, 4–5).

The specific identity and the particular situation of the native peoples are evident. Highly dispersed in small communities divided up by way of life and language but belonging to basically comparable civilizations at the time the Europeans arrived, they also share a presence in this land of several thousand years and the experience of the upsetting and traumatizing relations with Europeans. They were peoples of another age, too few and inadequately equipped to resist European settlers, who reduced them rapidly to a minority in their own land.

3.2   Diversity and Consensus

The interests, hopes, and dreams around which the country exists today may be found everywhere in European Canada, but they vary greatly in their tone according to region. From this point of view, the country may be divided up, first into Quebec and British Canada, which form the two wings of Canadian dualism, and secondly, into regions, which are at the root of the regionalism found in British Canada. Not surprisingly, both this dualism and regionalism, in their own way and extent, lie at the heart of the problem of Canadian unity. So far they have prevented the formation of a national consciousness strong enough to transcend basic cultural and regional centrifugal forces.

3.2.1   What Does Quebec feel?

Quebec represents the most significant French legacy in North America, and as such it considers itself as a particular and distinct entity vested with a special cultural and political purpose for Quebecers first, but also for French Canadians and Acadians scattered throughout Canada and even in the United States. This basic attitude is at the root of various aspirations, which seem to many Quebecers to be more and more difficult to satisfy within the framework of Confederation.

Regions	INDIANS[2]						INUIT[3]	
	Number of bands	Pop. living on reserves	Pop. living on establishments	Pop. living off reserves and estab.	Total number	Percentage of total population	Total number	Percentage of total population
Atlantic[4][5]	29	8,122	63	2,908	11,093	0.5	1,445	0.7
Quebec	39	19,209	5,518	5,448	30,175	0.5	4,775	0.1
Ontario	115	41,890	3,321	20,846	66,057	0.8	505	–
Manitoba	57	29,274	3,154	10,921	43,349	4.2	140	–
Saskatchewan	68	30,412	1,177	13,397	44,986	4.8	105	–
Alberta	41	25,355	2,117	7,690	35,162	1.9	315	–
British Columbia	194	33,888	796	19,634	54,318	2.2	290	–
District of Mackenzie[6]	16	8	7,261	272	7,541	–	15,495	34.1
Yukon	14	153	2,498	566	3,217	15.3	10	–
Canada	573	188,311	25,905	81,682	295,898	1.3	23,080	0.1

1. Status Indians registered under the Indian Act.
2. The Indian Act describes a reserve as "a tract of land, the legal title to which is vested in Her Majesty, that has been set apart by Her Majesty for the use and benefit of a band." "Establishment" designates Crown lands occupied by Indians or Inuit but not recognized officially as a reserve. As reserves were never provided officially by the government to Inuit, the Inuit were never granted specific land rights and their establishments are not officially recognized (CEITQ 1971, 4.1, 95–101, and 4.3, 203–8).
3. Year 1981.
4. 80% of the total number of Indians are in Nova Scotia and New Brunswick.
5. The Inuit are concentrated in Newfoundland where they add up to 0.2% of the total population.
6. Total number of Inuit refers to those in the Northwest Territories.

Note: These data and Figure 3.2 show clearly the highly scattered distribution of the native communities across Canada, the concentration of the Inuit in the Northwest Territories and Quebec, and, finally, the minority situation of these "First Canadians." They form a notable part of the population only in the Northwest Territories and the Yukon. More recent data containing the same level of detail as that for 1977 are not available, but the situation has not changed significantly.

Sources: Statistique Canada, 1978, 1; Statistique Canada, 1984, Table 1, 1.1–1.22

Abandoned by France in the middle of the eighteenth century, the "Canadiens," as they then called themselves, were sufficiently numerous and organized to persuade the new authority to come to some accommodations. These allowed the French to keep their religion, their language, their civil law, and, consequently, their collective distinctiveness. Suffice it to mention here the Quebec Act of 1774, hardly ten years after the conquest, the Official Languages Act two hundred years later, and, in the meantime, Confederation in 1867. The latter, it must be remembered, represented a compromise that made possible the political union of the British and French colonies in North America while preserving both of their identities.

For some people, the problem of Quebec is one of regionalism as met elsewhere in the country. To uphold such a view is to ignore both the difference in kind between the regional communities and the people of Quebec, and the scope and extent of their expressed grievances. The regional communities of British Canada share a basic attachment to Canada, and as critical as they may be of the actual regime, no disenchantment has effectively challenged the existence of the country. On the other hand, in Quebec is a distinctive community, highly conscious of its difference, which seriously questions its future within Canada. Both the nature and the importance of the Quebecers' grievances against Confederation confirm this. These grievances are political and socio-economic as well as cultural:

> The grave injustices and the national oppression to which the French-Canadian nation was subjected are part and parcel of the essence of the colonialist legislation that serves as a constitution for Canada.

> Ever since the industrialized era began in Quebec (and especially since World War II), all the governments elected by the people of Quebec have met with countless difficulties in trying to establish . . . within the confines of the confederative agreement, a coherent set of policies enabling the Quebec government to develop the life of our people in all its spheres of activity. (Montreal, TFCU 1979, vol. 2, 146)

Even though the Quebec Act of 1774 and, a century later, Confederation acknowledged the dualistic character of the colony, the two communities never agreed on a clear definition of the country's duality. Since the BNA Act came into effect, for instance, the decisive issue of division of powers between the federal and the provincial governments has been the subject of different and often contradictory interpretation. In British Canada the federal government was chiefly conceived of as a national institution responsible for the main affairs of the country and the national life, and the provincial government as a regional authority responsible for regional and local affairs. According to an opposite conception, French Canadians, and in particular Quebecers, insisted on seeing in Confederation a political system implying two orders rather than two levels of government sovereign in their respective fields of activities, a view conforming entirely with the idea of a pact between "two founding peoples" and with the Quebec will to endure as a distinct community. Supported by a

British Canadian majority, which had far fewer reasons to be afraid of a strong central government and even saw advantage in it, Canadian federalism has evolved towards a two-level system characterized by a predominantly central government that tends to intervene more often and more freely in provincial fields of activities as time goes by.

> The well-informed businessman can easily see that the Canadian Confederation has not allowed the French Quebecers as a majority to shape their economic future. Nor would a renewed federalism make this possible. (Montreal, *Conseil des hommes d'affaires québécois*, TFCU 1979, vol. 2, 144)

The Canadian federal system was not able to ensure an even and harmonious economic development of the country. As will be shown later, there exist in Canada regional economic disparities that threaten the cohesion of the country though they are not linked to the ethno-cultural duality. However, and this is certainly potentially more disruptive, the economic conditions of French Canadians have always been inferior to those of British Canadians across the land, not only in Quebec but also in New Brunswick, in Ontario, and in the western provinces. Today such disparities find expression particularly in lower incomes, a higher rate of unemployment, and a very weak participation in the economy at a high level. According to many, this long and painful experience of economic inferiority and submission represents a major element of the problem of Canadian unity. It has given French Canadians, and especially French Quebecers, the deep impression that Confederation has not allowed them to realize their economic development and has made them second-class citizens. As a consequence, Quebecers have gradually come to associate the objective of being master of their economy with the more global one of achieving a greater political autonomy.[2]

> I'll tell you how one turns to being a Quebecer after one has for a time thought of himself as a Canadian. At the time of the debate on the flag for Canadian unity, I went into a restaurant in Calgary, Alberta. There were some napkins on the table in front of my son. The napkins had small drawings on them. And they showed a beaver urinating on a frog. Underneath, one could read: "this is what the Canadian flag should look like." (Montreal, TCFU 1979, vol. 2, 142)

> In the richest city in Canada, which has gained the most from Confederation, we treat the French language as an alien language. The people who came from Quebec into our city last year – 1.7 million of them – were given no services, travel brochures, telephone books, nothing. How can these people feel that they are part of this country? (Toronto, TFCU 1979, vol. 2, 140)

We will never have a united Canada as long as Quebec is in Confederation. We will never have a united Canada until we have one language ... It is time that someone told Quebec to take us as we are or get out. (Toronto, TFCU 1979, vol. 2, 142)

In Quebec's French community there is a feeling of distinctiveness and a firm desire to assert it. But this sentiment is coupled with a fear of not being able to give free expression to the culture that embodies this distinctiveness and to make the whole country share this culture. This ambivalence, which is the origin of deep cultural grievances outside as well as inside Quebec, comes from another major dissention about the spirit of Confederation. From the very beginning and persistently ever since, Quebecers and French Canadians in general have seen Confederation as a pact that guaranteed both the cultural and linguistic rights of the "two founding peoples" not only in Quebec but also elsewhere in Canada. However, the federal government, the governments of the British provinces, and the English-speaking population in general have behaved as if the application of these reciprocal rights was limited to the case of Quebec and, in a mitigated way, to the federal institutions. Thus, although the rights of the British minority were recognized and respected in the province of Quebec, those of the French were denied outside Quebec in the key fields of education, judicial procedures, and public services, not to mention the language of work. It is important to note the passive, or indeed the negative, attitude of the federal government until recently in all its relations with French-speaking citizens and civil servants. In addition, there were a series of interdicts and suppressions concerning the status of the French language and the rights of French-speakers: the interdiction of French teaching in New Brunswick in 1870; the abolition of French in the schools of Prince Edward Island in 1877; the hanging of Louis Riel in 1884; the reduction to the minimum of the school rights of the French-speaking citizens in Alberta and Saskatchewan on their establishment as provinces; the exclusion of French as a teaching language in Ontario in 1912; and the interdiction to teach French in Saskatchewan in 1930. There were many measures, that slowed down, and in many cases bluntly discouraged, the development of a French way of life and culture outside Quebec, causing many French Canadians to begin considering Quebec as their homeland and Canada as a British country where their rights were simply denied.

These political, economic, and cultural grievances, which have evoked various disappointing experiences and situations, were at the origin of a growing dissatisfaction with Confederation among a great number of French Canadians. They explain Quebecers' ill feelings towards Confederation. A century of experience has convinced many of them that the BNA Act, as understood and put into practice by a majority British Canada, gives rise to unequal relations between the British and French communities, clearly to the detriment of the latter.

3.2.2   Newfoundlanders, Maritimers, Albertans, Westerners . . . or Canadians?

There can be no question that the strong sense of regionalism is a divisive force and a major obstacle to national unity. That is not to say, however, that strong regions are inconsistent with a more united Canada. They are merely inconsistent with a unified Canada. (Vancouver, TFCU 1979, vol. 2, 82)

Federal imperialism is the main problem of Confederation and the west and the east are the colonies. (Edmonton, TFCU 1979, vol. 2, 82)

It is sufficient to say that western alienation is primarily economic, geographic and psychological. It is economic because we feel that the policies of the Federal Government penalize the resource-based economies of the western provinces in order to assist the industrial and manufacturing economies of central Canada . . . Western discontent is geographic for obvious reasons – our distance from the nation's decision-making triangle and the physical and psychological barrier of three mountain ranges combine to make it difficult for us to understand – or even take an interest in – what is happening in the rest of Canada. Finally, our discontent is psychological – we do not feel that either the structure or the operation of some of our national institutions effectively converts western ideas into national policies, and hence we are inclined to withdraw from participation in those institutions. (Vancouver, TFCU 1979, vol. 2, 84)

. . . for the Maritimes have a regional identity which is seriously threatened by the existing pressures of the political framework which concentrated economic power, population, and general national attention on central Canada. (Halifax, TFCU 1979, vol. 2, 86)

We, in Newfoundland, both on the island and on mainland Labrador, feel very strongly that the federal machine is a machine which, unfortunately for us, shows little human concern for its most easterly province. We feel that it is a machine which can only regurgitate that which is fed into it, by those nearest to it, and that therefore it has but one answer to everything – the answer of central Canada. (Canadian Federation of University Women, St. John's, TFCU 1979, vol. 2, 86)

According to the TFCU, and rightly so, regionalism together with dualism constitutes a major element of the Canadian reality. It explains the way Canadians imagine themselves and the way they conceive and live out their citizenship and their institutions. As in the case of duality, regional communities existed before Confederation and were even a strong argument in favour of a federal system of government for the new country. The "Founding Fathers" had to imagine a set of

Table   **Incomes and Unemployment Rates by Province as a**
3.4   **Percentage of the Canadian Average, 1977 and 1987**

| | Canadian Average = 100 | | | | | |
| | Average Family Income | | Average Income after Tax | | Unemployment | |
Province	1987	1977	1987	1977	1987	1977
Newfoundland	75	68	81	70	209	196
Prince Edward Island	81	67	80	70	149	123
Nova Scotia	87	79	84	81	140	132
New Brunswick	80	75	84	77	148	165
Quebec	92	93	91	91	116	127
Ontario	112	109	112	110	69	86
Manitoba	91	93	93	97	83	73
Saskatchewan	91	92	92	94	82	56
Alberta	102	104	102	105	108	54
British Columbia	99	110	98	110	135	105
Canada	100	100	100	100	100	100

Sources: TFCU 1979, vol. 2, 197; Statistics Canada, *Household Survey Division, Family Incomes, Census Families – 1987* (Ottawa: Supply and Services Canada, 1989), Table 2, 16–17; Statistics Canada, *Household Survey Division, Income after Tax, Distribution by Size in Canada – 1987* (Ottawa: Supply and Services Canada, 1989), Table 2, 30–31; Statistique Canada, *Annuaire du Canada 1990* (Ottawa: Approvisionnements et Services Canada, 1989), Tableau 5.6, 5–25

institutions that would bring together in an effective whole the two communities and the regions and would at the same time respect their individual needs and allow them to develop harmoniously. But many Canadians believe that Confederation did not succeed in ensuring a proper economic and political balance between its main components. This is underlined as well as one could wish, first, by the growing number of provincial and regional claims and the arguments on which they are based, and second, by what was heard by the TFCU from one end of the country to the other during its national tour. The feeling of regional alienation has undoubtedly a political dimension in as much as the tensions it causes in the country are political. However, contrary to what happens in Quebec, the grievances this regional alienation gives rise to are basically economic in nature and essence. This emphasis on economy lies in the fact that British Canadians share a common political culture characterized, in particular, by a unanimous adherence to the idea of a united Canada *a mari usque ad mare* and to the essential aspects of Canadian federalism. These are the basic attitudes that both tone down the significance of the separatist remarks heard sometimes in the east and west, and partly invalidate the diagnosis of those who see regionalism in British Canada as an issue as crucial as that of Quebec. In fact, the claims of the provinces and/or regions of British Canada require a change of attitude in the approach of the federal government and an effective devolution of the federal administration, but they do not put into question the idea of a country united by a strong federal structure resembling that of today. Briefly, it is more a problem of attitudes and people than one of institutions.

Despite these arguments, it is no exaggeration to speak of alienation in some regions of British Canada, and it would be wrong to minimize the importance of the phenomenon.[3] For many easterners and westerners the historical and demographic weight of central Canada gives political influence in Ottawa to Ontario primarily, but also to Quebec, a political influence that is seen to be at the source of the regional disparities. Marked and deep-rooted, these disparities find expression in various fields such as employment, personal income, industrialization, cost of living, and education. Suffice it to refer to the socio-economic indicators that are most often used to stress these disparities: personal income and level of unemployment (see Table 3.4). The statistics in Table 3.4 show clearly that the Atlantic provinces experience the lowest rates of personal income and the highest rates of unemployment. They also indicate that the unemployment rate in Newfoundland has been between 50 percent of and double the Canadian average and treble the rate in Saskatchewan over the past decade. Apart from the worst moments of the Great Depression when the prairie crops were destroyed by drought, no region of Canada has at any time recorded as low a per capita income as the Atlantic region since comparable data were first collected on this topic in the 1920s. However, Quebec corresponds closely with the Atlantic provinces in having average incomes and unemployment rates respectively lower and higher than the Canadian average.

3.2.3   The First Canadians, A Moral Issue

The political venture that modern Canada embodies has only concerned Canadians of European descent and has completely left aside the native peoples. Today, in the name of liberty and multiculturalism, the native peoples can at last foresee the possibility of safeguarding their identity. This was not the case until recently because the federal government, which has exclusive jurisdiction over them,[4] has constantly favoured their assimilation without any real respect for their individual and collective rights.

> One of the greatest Canadian historical myths has been perpetuated during the current debate on national unity. I am speaking in particular of the myth suggesting that the French and English are the founding peoples of Canada. This statement is patently false. It is historically inaccurate and an insult to the Indian people of Canada. (National Indian Brotherhood, Ottawa, TFCU 1979, vol. 2, 30)

> We have not been recognized for what we as native people contributed, but only as savages running along with loincloths. (Fort Simpson, N.W.T., TFCU 1979, vol. 2, 30)

Our languages have no place in the parliaments or in the courts or in school today. Our culture has become a tourist aid to add colour to parades and festivals. (Wesley Band, Calgary, TFCU 1979, vol. 2, 30)

Certainly the most important priority in most Indian communities is not national unity . . . The basic day-to-day issues are housing, high unemployment, which is as high as 90 percent in many Indian communities . . . There is a sense of helplessness and hopelessness of a people who are on the bottom rung of decision-making powers. (Union of New Brunswick Indians, Moncton, TFCU 1979, vol. 2, 30)

The native peoples' past in Canada is rather dark, and this is exactly how they see it. Their grievances and claims attest to this basic perception. The native peoples are convinced that they have been exploited, rejected, and forgotten. They ask why so many standard histories of Canada begin only with the arrival of Europeans. They find it injurious and unjust for fellow Canadians to say that the French and British were the "two founding peoples," a statement that ignores the native peoples' historical contribution both before and after the arrival of the Europeans. They feel it is not possible to justify the series of laws and measures that, during the past century, have crushed the native communities, encouraged their massive acculturation, and provoked their marginalization to the extent of making them individually and collectively the most impoverished "Canadians" economically, socially, and politically.

As pointed out in the telling report of the Special Committee of the House of Commons on Indian Self-Government, "the extent of the social disintegration and deprivation arising from the history of relations between Canada and Indian Peoples" is bluntly recognized in a document published by the Department of Indian Affairs and Northern Development as recently as 1980. And it was confirmed in 1983 by officials of the Department of National Health and Welfare that conditions are not improving (House of Commons 1983, 14).

In spite of a strong feeling of humiliation and a deep bitterness, the native peoples still imagine their future to be within a Canadian context. However, this attitude comes with the proviso that certain basic claims or conditions be instituted. These are summarized under four headings by the TFCU: new constitutional arrangements should acknowledge the native peoples' right to "compensation" for the "historic disregard" of their treaty rights and for the numerous "hardships" that have been inflicted upon them; the right to contribute to the national decision-making process and to the daily conduct of the nation's business (left out of the discussions that led to Confederation, they should not be "overlooked again"); the right to be included in the constitution as "equal partners" with the French and the British should be acknowledged; the right for "self-determination" and the right to live according to their own belief and traditions should be recognized (TFCU 1979, vol. 2, 35).

3.3   Conclusion

This brief assessment of the diversity-consensus equation shows that Canada is much less cohesive, and much more divided, than may be thought at first sight. Two main factors are responsible for particular tensions: duality and regionalism, but only the former represents a decisive and immediate threat to Canada's integrity. This threat materialized dramatically with the election of the Parti Québécois on 15 November 1976. For the first time since it was created in 1867, the Canadian political union was seriously challenged. Never before had secession been sought with such a firmness of purpose. Fifteen years later, the Parti Québécois is no longer in power and has also lost its referendum on sovereignty-association. Nothing has really changed and Canada is still one country, but the problem remains to be solved, and it may be seriously suggested that it will persist to surface again and again as long as the existential Canadian challenge is not accepted: to live together while recognizing the fundamental duality of the country. The recent Meech Lake episode has confirmed this dramatically once more.

As Roy (1984) remarks pertinently, neither together nor separately do either Quebec or British Canada constitute homogeneous political communities endowed with a univocal political mission, and it is an error to reduce the country politically to the simplicity of the British-French duality. Such a view ignores the powerful movement of ethnic pluralism that has profoundly marked the personality of the country. On the other hand, Quebec and British Canada are strongly differentiated, and what distinguishes one from the other goes beyond the bounds of purely linguistic considerations. It is also an error to reduce the question of Quebec to one of regionalism and to refute dualism as one of the organizing principles in Canada.

Canada's duality is intrinsic, and as long as it is not clearly recognized and dealt with, the issue of Canadian unity will remain. As shown earlier, Quebec embodies Canada's duality and this basic fact makes this province a special entity in the country: *une province pas comme les autres*. Quebec's particular position explains its fundamental autonomist and nationalist attitudes. As Dion (1980, 44) points out, it is important that British Canada understands that the problem posed by Quebec is not that of a political party, but that of a society. It would be illusory to fight against the nationalism of the Parti Québécois with anti-nationalism. On the contrary, the answer is to put forward a conception of nationalism compatible with the idea of a united Canada. And this is not just a wild dream. An opinion poll taken at the request of the government of Quebec less than a year before the referendum on sovereignty-association confirms it clearly. So far, the most complete survey undertaken to understand the Quebecers' feelings for Confederation, this poll showed that among the people of Quebec there was a clear will for fundamental change as well as a marked desire to keep significant links with the rest of Canada.[5] Unfortunately, the patriation of the BNA Act and the proclamation of the Canada Bill fell short of Quebecers' requirements. As a result Canada is now a country whose fundamental law, its constitution, has been adopted by a factor of ten to one: accepted by all parties of all British majority parliaments and rejected by the two parties of the only French majority parliament. Thus, an exercise supposedly intended to make Quebec feel at home in the Canadian family once and for all resulted in its exclusion. Yet Canada is a country in which most Quebecers want to believe, and the Meech Lake endeavour has shown that there exists a constitutional answer which lies between full separatism and rigid symmetrical federalism: a solution that would reconcile both visions of Canada and prevent the country from breaking up.

Notes

1 The United States purchased Alaska from Russia in 1867, and they tried subsequently to collaborate with Louis Riel with the aim of annexing Rupert's Land, the Hudson's Bay Territory recently purchased by Canada (Morriset 1979).

2. A representative of the francophone sectors of the Quebec economy (TFCU 1979, vol. 3, 145).

3. In 1979 Frank Miller, then Ontario's treasurer, described the strong disagreement between Ontario and Alberta about the national policy on oil prices as the greatest threat ever to Canadian unity. The truth of this statement can be questioned, but nonetheless the fact remains that since the oil crisis, Ontario has been consistently and categorically opposed to a rapid increase in oil prices as this would be catastrophic for its industrial and commercial structure. It has argued that it has paid the price of Confederation when it had to, and that others must do the same now (*Le Soleil*, 26 September 1979, E1).

4. The federal government has exclusive jurisdiction over Indians and territories reserved for Indians under section 91, paragraph 24, of the BNA Act.

5. *Le Devoir*, 28 September 1979, and *Le Soleil*, 28 September 1979.

References

Commission d'étude sur l'intégrité du territoire du Québec (CEITQ). 1971. *Le Domaine Indien*. Vol. 1: *Rapport des commissaires; vol. 3: Études Juridiques*. Quebec: Éditeur Officiel.

Conseil Economique du Canada. 1977. *Vivre ensemble: Une étude des disparités régionales*. Ottawa: Approvisionnements et Services Canada.

Department of Indian Affairs and Northern Development. 1971. *Atlas of Indian Reserves and Settlements of Canada, 1971*. Ottawa: Supply and Services Canada.

———. 1980. *Indian Conditions: A Survey*. Ottawa: Supply and Services Canada.

Dion, L. 1980. *Le Québec et le Canada: Les voies de l'avenir*. Montreal: Québecor.

Garon, A. 1977. "La mise en tutelle (1830–1867)." In J. Hamelin, ed., *Histoire du Québec*, 345–74. Montreal: Éditions France-Amerique.

House of Commons. 1983. *Report of the Special Committee on Indian Self-government*. Ottawa: Supply and Services Canada.

Ministère des Affaires Indiennes et du Nord Canadien. 1978. *Population indienne inscrite selon le sexe et la résidence (bandes, districts, régions et Canada le 31 décembre 1977)*. Ottawa: Approvisionnements et Services Canada.

Morriset, J. 1979. "Louis Riel et le Mythe Canadien." *Le Devoir*, 23 April 1979, 4–5.

Parti Québécois. 1978. *Program officiel du Parti Québécois*. Montreal: Parti Québécois.

Roy, J.L. 1984. "Vivre ensemble differents." *Le Devoir*, 6 October 1984, 11.

Statistique Canada. 1973. *Recensement du Canada de 1971. Population: groupes ethniques*. Ottawa: Approvisionnements et Services Canada.

———. 1977. *La population active*. Ottawa: Approvisionnements et Services Canada.

———. 1978. *Comptes nationaux des revenus et dépenses, 1963–1977*. Ottawa: Approvisionnements et Services Canada.

———. 1984. *Recensement du Canada de 1981: Origine ethnique*. Ottawa: Approvisionnements et Services Canada.

Task Force on Canadian Unity (TFCU). 1979. *Report*. Vol. 1: *A Future Together;* vol. 2: *Coming to Terms;* vol. 3: *A Time to Speak*. Ottawa: Supply and Services Canada.

Voisine, N. 1977. "Province d'une confédération (1867–1892)." In J. Hamelin, ed., *Histoire du Québec*, 375–414. Montreal: Éditions France-Amerique.

4   Social Cohesion and Conflicts in Quebec

Jacques Bernier

Those aware of the evolution that Quebec has undergone over the past few decades generally agree that society in Quebec has experienced profound changes in its economic organization, social practices, and political attitudes. Although these changes have affected all aspects of society, undoubtedly they have had the most striking effect in the political sphere, at least from the viewpoint of outside observers such as Canadians from the other provinces. Among the most notable of these developments have been the emergence of political parties and movements, the ever increasing demands made by Quebec on the federal government and, finally, the calls for sovereignty and independence.

These sweeping changes have upset former balances and have given birth to differences and conflicts that have seriously affected the cohesion of society in Quebec. These conflicts have centred around the old French/English cleavage, as well as around new divisions that have manifested themselves among the French-speaking population. Given the multi-faceted nature of change, there is a problem of how to obtain a coherent picture of the social, economic, and political transformation. The intricacy of the various situations that make up the whole is very complex and any worthwhile analysis must take this complexity into account.

How then may the issue of social cohesion and conflicts in Quebec be approached? Without simplifying matters too much, it would seem that there is a choice of two different ways of addressing the issues: first, emphasis could be placed on cultural or national aspects and, second, social aspects of class and class relations could be given priority. In this instance, we choose the national approach. This is not meant to denigrate the importance of social class dynamics in Quebec and the role that they have played over the past two or three decades in the ferment experienced in Quebec society. Rather, it implies that this role is subsumed in the consideration of the broader issues in this study.

It is evident that the development and modernization of Quebec led leftist intellectuals and union leaders in Quebec to distinguish the interests of the working class and lower middle class, and to emphasize what separates them not only from the interests of the English-speaking minority, but also from those of the French-speaking middle classes. Yet this crucial observation did not diminish the pertinence to all classes of the issue of nationalisn. Although little inclined towards nationalism because of their ideology, those on the left of the political spectrum believe that the emancipation of workers in Quebec includes the national liberation of Quebecers, a national liberation that they hope to exploit to the good of the workers when the time comes. In short, in spite of the priority given to the question of social justice and even a certain distrust of nationalism, socialists in Quebec have set the interests of the working class within the framework of the political emancipation of Quebec. Quebec is seen as a dominated society both by the left and right and this explains why, over the last few years, the solidarity of French-speaking Quebecers has prevailed over any solidarity common to all Canadian working classes.[1]

4.1   Quebec: A Society That Has Undergone Profound Change

The problems of cohesion that society in Quebec has been experiencing are closely linked to the profound changes it has undergone during the past few decades. Since the mid-1940s Quebec's economy has experienced rapid development. Accelerated growth, which also affected the rest of Canada and the United States, had unique effects in Quebec. It shook the foundations of a society which, more than any other in North America, had resisted change, and lead this society to examine from a new perspective the crucial problem of its survival, that is, its relations with the rest of Canada and also with non-French-speaking Quebecers. The economic growth and social changes that followed in its wake also contributed to the birth of a class consciousness in the French-speaking community, which broke the ideological consensus that previously had united the various social classes.

Despite a tormented history, during the period following the conquest of 1760, French Canadians did not question their culture and the ideological universe that supported it until quite recently. Considering themselves the children of a beaten people, French Canadians felt culturally, economically, and politically dominated. They saw the conquest as an end to a glorious epic, an idyllic situation that they were to remember as a lost paradise. Longfellow's (1893) description of Acadia in *Evangeline* just prior to the deportation reflects this dramatic change. The history of this conquered people was then to become a long series of humiliations, frustrations, and fights for survival in terms of maintaining their basic rights and, in particular, their faith and their language in an Anglo-Saxon universe. Thus, in their collective vision, survival meant the rejection of any change in the economic order and, in particular, that of the creation of an industrial society. As Falardeau (1960, 30) stresses, this vision takes on specific traits in the speech of Mgr. L.A. Paquet (1915) given on 23 June 1902 and nicknamed the vade-mecum of the French Canadian patriot: "It was God's intention that the French Canadian have an agricultural vocation: he was to leave to others the worries of economic, industrial and materialistic life. His own inclination must tie him or make him return to the land. The instruments of his destiny are the cross and the plow."

Throughout the nineteenth century and the first decades of the twentieth century, their demography and economy were such that French Canadians continued to live in a rural and agricultural society. In spite of the industrialization of Montreal, the French-speaking population, which was less urbanized than the population of Quebec as a whole, was still 75 percent rural at the turn of the century. At that time, and even until the Second World War, the typical French Canadian described by Tocqueville (1957) in 1830 continued to live a traditional lifestyle: "Tenderly attached to the land which saw his birth, to his church tower, and to his family." Of course, the Quebec of the 1930s was different from that of 1830, but the spirit that reigned was much the same. Yet René Lévesque (1968) in his political manifesto, *Option-Québec*, published in 1968, described his fellow citizens in the following manner: "citydwellers, wage-earners, tenants. The standards of parish, village and farm have splintered" (McRoberts and Postgate 1983, 78). What had taken place in a few short decades?

When speaking about the profound changes that Quebec society has undergone, the expression "The Quiet Revolution" is generally associated with the brief period from 1960 to 1966. In reality the socio-economic and cultural changes that are associated with this period, and that explain the political agitation that Quebec was to experience from 1960 to 1966 and afterwards, had been in the making for a long time.

At the end of the 1950s Quebec was not very modern from a political standpoint. Government structures and activities as well as the public service were not well developed. The state made little attempt to intervene in the economic field, except to support financially the private sector, which served as the basis for primary services and the exploitation of resources. In the social arena this laissez-faire was even more evident, and the church was given complete freedom concerning both education and social services. Thus the economy was left to the private sector, while education, health, and welfare were left to the church.

Yet, the modernization and socio-economic development of Quebec were well underway during this period and required expansion in the sphere of governmental activity, with the support of an ever-growing and increasingly competent bureaucracy. Over the preceding decades society had slowly lost its rural character and the economy its agricultural basis. In spite of major efforts at agricultural land settlement, the exodus towards the towns and cities continued and accelerated because of the developing manufacturing sector. For example, between 1900 and 1920 this sector's contribution to the economy increased from 4 percent to 38 percent, and the exploitation of hydro-electricity and iron ore was begun. The agricultural sector also experienced important changes. Facing strong competition from western wheat producers, Quebec's farmers turned to dairy products and produce for the urban markets. The traditional farm disappeared, and rural Quebec became integrated into the urban economy (McRoberts and Postgate 1983). Society had been experiencing major changes graduated over half a century, changes that affected not only the elite, but the entire population. The two closely associated currents that had polarized the dominant values of French Canadian culture were having less and less of an effect on mentalities. The traditional social conception of the church had lost a great deal of its influence. Nationalism remained the decisive element of collective consciousness, but the link between faith and language was being replaced by the link between the economy and language.

In such a context, the Quiet Revolution, which served as the political catalyst of Quebec's renewal, was to give rise to a totally new Quebec in which the basic problem of survival, when considered in the light of this new context, would upset former balances.

It has often been said that the Quiet Revolution was an overstatement. This may be true if one believes that this movement resulted in few concrete changes in political processes or structures, and that it merely made Quebecers aware that, first, their society had undergone profound changes over the preceding half a century, and second, it was time to create an appropriate provincial administration. Yet, as is often argued, the expression is hardly an exaggeration if the profound and considerable ideological changes that this "revolution" produced were recognized. During this period ideas that had been dominant for more than a century were openly questioned and finally rejected by intellectuals and political leaders as a whole. This ideological turnabout meant a reconciliation with the economic and social modernization so feared in the past. It meant a departure from the idea that French Canadian society was mainly rural and agrarian.

Whether or not the expression "revolution" is justified, one thing is certain: during the 1960s Quebec became conscious of the profound cultural and socio-economic changes it had undergone, and Quebec took on a new ideology that was to completely change its views about its own nature and the means to ensure its survival.

Such changes and such a realization were to have disruptive effects on the Canadian political system and also on society in Quebec. Indeed, Quebec wished to redefine its position within Canada as a whole on the basis of these changes. In particular, ethnic and social divisions were intensified, and these divisions had major political implications.

4.2   The Old French/English Cleavage

As Painchaud (1984) points out, the concept of Quebec as a separate entity implies a homogeneous society. Although French-speaking Quebec may be "one of the most demographically homogeneous populations in the modern world" (Caldwell 1982, 62), all those who are familiar with Quebec know that the province as a whole is characterized by diversity. Moreover, this diversity is of a different type from that found in the United States or British Canada for example. In these two cases ethno-cultural differences express themselves within a common ideology in terms of a common general political vision and a common linguistic context. In Quebec's case, though, these differences seem much more pronounced because common integrating denominators such as basic political attitudes and a common language are absent. Quebec's various ethnic communities, in particular the English- and French-speaking communities, have lived alongside one another rather than becoming integrated. The reason for this state of affairs is that the two communities have been pursuing two different destinies. The cultural boundaries of the French-speaking majority never extended to different ethnic groups, and the French-English division or antagonism that appeared with the conquest has persisted.

After 1760 only the lesser seigneurs, a few merchants, and the "settlers" remained, and the victors became the new masters. Naturally, the colony was governed by the British administrators, first of all military and then civilian. But, moreover, British companies took over the fur trade and other commercial monopolies. British immigrants rapidly assumed the leading positions in the commercial sector.

Although Confederation gave Quebec, a province with a French-speaking majority, real powers in certain areas, and although the French-speaking population became involved increasingly in the economy, French-speaking Quebecers continued to consider themselves a minority and acted accordingly. To understand such behaviour, it must be realized that until recently the basic political framework was Canada as a whole, where the English-speaking population was in the majority and the French-speaking one in the minority. As Caldwell and Waddell (1982) explain in a very convincing manner, English-speaking Quebecers did not exist as a separate reality. Although within the province they were in the minority from a statistical standpoint, they acted as if they were in the majority; their leaders played an important role in the exercise of power, and the group as a whole saw itself as the expression in Quebec of Canada's British majority. Quebec's ethnic boundaries, which were poorly defined, had very little significance. One was either British Canadian or French Canadian and, in the minds of the former, these terms referred to two "nations" defined strictly in terms of language – one whose territory extended all across Canada and the other which was only tolerated in Quebec. It was only when French-speaking Quebecers relinquished the notion of French Canada in the 1960s and 1970s and adopted that of Quebec as the primary geopolitical point of reference for their collective identity, that the problem of identity for English-speaking Quebecers appeared.

This evolution, in fact, reflected a profound change of attitudes, which resulted both from a dream that failed to come true and from the demographic crisis of French-speaking Quebec.

Whether rightly or wrongly, Confederation led French Canadians to dream of a bi-national country whose French element could unfold not only in Quebec but from coast to coast. Forced to admit a century later that this was only a pipedream and that French-speaking Canadians outside Quebec were being assimilated, their reaction was to consolidate politically their positions in Quebec, the only place where they could ensure their survival as a community thanks to their majority position. French-speaking Quebecers thus ceased to see themselves first and foremost as a minority in Canada, but rather, to consider themselves a majority in Quebec, and a majority able to count on provincial mechanisms to exercise decisive power.

Thus, in the space of a few years the British Canadians of Quebec found themselves members of a minority – a minority of English-speakers living in Quebec. They were a minority that, until recently, had played the role of a majority, a minority that was in the majority elsewhere in the country and a minority to which the British North America Act (BNA Act) accorded certain rights and privileges. But, all the same, the status of the anglo minority was not to be so easily defended when the French-speaking community, intent on safeguarding its own interests, came to realize that the francophone identity could not be sustained by mere cultural and political affirmation but required legal action to limit the expansion of the minority. Indeed, in the late 1960s, French Quebec found itself threatened even on the demographic level. This threat came specifically from the English-speaking population which, thanks to the assimilation of immigrants, was increasing its relative strength in Quebec. The drop in the birth rate within the French-speaking community, the emigration of French-speakers out of Quebec, and their limited power of assimilation were responsible for this situation.

What could be done in view of such a problem except to stop the growth of the number of English speakers by preventing their schools from playing an assimilative role and by making French the everyday working language? These were necessary measures for the majority wishing to preserve its identity at all costs, but difficult to accept for the minority that, until recently, had been privileged by circumstances, thinking that it was protected by the BNA Act far more than it actually was, and whose demographic position was largely due to assimilation. Tetley (1982), in a telling personal account, echoes the English-speaking Quebecers' misunderstanding regarding the Constitution, Confederation, and linguistic rights. English-speaking Quebecers believed their language rights were enshrined in the BNA Act. In fact, the Constitution provided few language guarantees.

It took the English-speaking community several years to understand and accept the demographic crisis experienced by its French-speaking counterpart. For the first time, the English-speaking community began to ask questions about itself, something Quebec's French-speakers had been doing for two centuries, and something the English-speaking community had never done because of its previous position of strength. This reflection about themselves helped English-speaking Quebecers to realize that they were heterogeneous and not a cohesive community: an ethnically and culturally mixed population that shared a common language. The old image of a close-knit community concentrated in the Montreal region and made up of rich, unilingual Protestants of a British background was less true than ever, and in no way reflected the profound changes that the "English minority" had undergone over the years. As Caldwell and Waddell (1982) have clearly shown, the English community in Quebec is actually made up of a group of communities sharing a common language but having different cultures, classes, and geographical settings.

Even if in political terms the linguistic divisions are more significant than the cultural and political divisions, it is certain that in reality the heterogeneous nature of Quebec's English-speaking population limits the existence of a community cohesive enough to find the strength to survive. Yet the crisis has created a new ambiance. Most English-speaking Quebecers have grown sympathetic towards the use of French and this, of course, will encourage their political and social inclusion in the new Quebec. On the other hand, a growing number of French-speaking Quebecers acknowledge a rich British contribution to the history, culture, and identity of Quebec. These recent developments could give a new sense of identity to an English-speaking community based this time on the feeling of a common destiny.

4.3   Social Classes and National Consciousness among French-speaking Quebecers

At a time when the linguistic situation concerned a large number of the French-speaking Quebecers and set them against the English-speaking population, class divisions began to appear within the French-speaking community.

Aware of the major socio-economic gap that separated them, not only from the English-speaking population but also from the upper-class French-speaking community, members of the working class and the lower middle class began to ask themselves questions about their situation and soon realized that the Quiet Revolution had been more profitable to certain groups than to others. In particular, it had benefited the middle class who held positions in the bureaucracy. There was a general recognition that the fruits of the Quiet Revolution had been distributed rather unequally.

A document from the Confédération des Syndicats Nationaux (CSN), produced in 1971 and entitled "Ne comptons que sur nos propres moyens" (We can rely only on our own means), is a good illustration of this new awareness. It energetically condemned the errors of the Quiet Revolution, maintained that the Quebec state had remained in the service of British-Canadian and American capital, and explained that in the 1960s the rising French Canadian middle class and technocracy used the Quebec government to serve their own interests (McRoberts and Postgate 1983, 162).

The distrust felt by a group, or people, towards the religious, social, or political elite was not novel in Quebec, but this time it was taking place in a society that had been completely transformed socio-economically. What was questioned and what was at stake was no longer status or prestige in the traditional context, but wealth and power in a modern, capitalist context.

These conflicts, setting one part of the French-speaking population against another, might have seriously weakened the cultural and political solidarity among the French-speaking community and thus contributed to the consolidation of the Canadian political system. According to the literature on social classes, the class phenomenon, which goes hand in hand with economic development, generally leads to a decline in cultural and regional specificity and to a rise in social and political integration in multi-national countries. Although it may still be a little too early to reach a final verdict on this question, it can be argued that this has not been the case in Canada. There are two main reasons for this and they reinforce one another.

The first of these reasons, and undoubtedly of less importance, is what might be called the complicity between the middle class and the working and/or lower class – a complicity that is based on common interests. As Fournier (1977, 15) explains:

One of the main obstacles to the creation of a combined Canadian working class front lies in the advantage that the Quebec working class seems to obtain from the reforms put forward by the Quebec middle class (nationalist); indeed, the latter was only able to obtain certain reforms of the Quiet Revolution by making use of the support of elements of the labour movement and by paying the price for this support (easier access to education and health-care, creation of a better pension system, unionization of the civil service, modification of the Labour Code, increases in the minimum wages, etc.).[2]

The union establishment benefited greatly from this advantage, and for that reason the unions, without being really pro-sovereignty, came to support an ever-increasing autonomy for Quebec or a greater expansion of the Quebec state to the detriment of Ottawa. It should be remembered that the CSN and Centrale de l'enseignment du Québec (CEQ), two of the three most important union organizations in Quebec, recruit a large number of their members from the public sector and that the future of these employees is directly linked to the spending power and jurisdiction of Quebec. Yet the Fédération des Travailleurs du Québec (FTQ), few of whose members are from the public sector, has also always acted first and foremost as a Quebec union federation. This leads to the second and undoubtedly more important reason.

Even if no agreement as yet exists on the ideological common ground, the analyses made by the right and the left converge on one very important point: the emancipation of Quebecers involves the emancipation of Quebec. Thus, even for left-wing intellectuals, who are not very inclined to nationalism ideologically, the emancipation of workers requires the emancipation of Quebec. For both the left and the right, Quebec is basically a colony where the French-speaking population suffers the cultural and economic effects of colonialism. In addition to promoting cultural alienation, the colonial status is responsible for economic underdevelopment along with discrimination against French-speaking workers. Thus, the workers of Quebec have every incentive to liberate themselves from the control of the American and British-Canadian bourgeoisie and their tool: the federal government. In the words of the radical editors of Parti Pris (1965, 5):

> The Quebec nation lives in a country that does not belong to it, which has been taken away from it . . . The Quebec nation, because of Confederation, has neither control over its political nor over its economic life. This is a fact of utmost importance and it must be noted that Confederation is the framework for all the forms of domination under which Quebec suffers.[3]

There is no doubt that the election of the Parti Québécois (PQ) initially reinforced this view. The victory of the PQ in November 1976 was greeted with joy by trade unions, and during its first mandate René Lévesque's party never missed an occasion to boast convincingly of having the best interest of the workers at heart: "un prejuge favorable envers les travailleurs." The confrontations that took place between the government and the unions during the second PQ mandate rapidly dispelled this sentiment. Nevertheless, this way of seeing things never prevented the left from realizing that Quebec was not composed solely of workers and that the Quiet Revolution, by permitting the rise of a new French-speaking middle class, had reinforced the national middle class in Quebec.

Of course, such a perception of Quebec's social reality by left-wing intellectuals has bridled the left's nationalist fervour and has led it to place as much emphasis on social classes as on nationalism. Nevertheless, the changes advocated are confined within the framework of Quebec and remain completely compatible with, if not linked to, independence.

Several reasons can be cited to explain such a phenomenon. As has already been stated, it would be in the unions' interest to favour independence. The relative conservatism of British-Canadian unions and the specific interests of workers in Quebec as compared with British-Canadian workers are also important. These factors undoubtedly have a certain role to play, but it would seem that the fact of belonging to a distinct society is the deciding factor in this case. Quebec constitutes a distinct cultural and linguistic entity in Canada, and language and culture in a large way determine people's views and perceptions. In summary, although development and modernization have led a growing number of French-speaking persons to define themselves, whether consciously or unconsciously, in terms of social class and also to become aware of the differences of interest between the middle class and the lower class, this new awareness has not yet weakened the fundamental national solidarity of the French-speaking community.

4.4   Conclusion

In the words of McRoberts and Postgate (1983, 37), "by North American standards, the most striking fact about French Canadian society in Quebec is its continuity, its endurance over the centuries in an alien, sometimes hostile environment." There may be argument as to why Quebec survived as a distinct entity, but no one denies the fact of survival itself and its striking character.

Along with Gottmann and others, political geographers assume, rightly it seems, that the survival of a society depends, to a significant degree, on its ability to adjust to its external environment. Until recently, the French community in Quebec had adjusted to its North American environment by developing an ideology that made it impervious to outside influences and earned it an exceptionally high demographic growth rate, which made up for a strong emigration. The profound changes it has undergone over the past few decades has lead it to re-evaluate the problems of its survival. It is with this historical viewpoint, that one ought to confront the issues of social cohesion and conflicts in Quebec.

Notes

1. This essay is the result of many years of personal reflection during my time as a resident of Canada and of Quebec, as well as professional observation as a geographer. It would be difficult to give credit to all those who contributed to my contemplations. However, among several writings I read recently, which have provided stimulus for further thoughts and investigation, two were most useful: McRoberts and Postgate 1983 and Caldwell and Waddell 1982. These two books were particularly helpful for the sections dealing with the issue of social cohesion within the French-speaking community and the French/English cleavage.
2. Quoted in McRoberts and Postgate 1983, 171.
3. Ibid., 168.

References

Caldwell, G. 1982. "People and Society." In G. Caldwell and E. Waddell, eds., *The English of Quebec. From Majority to Minority Status,* 57–71. Quebec: Institut québécois de recherche sur la culture.

Caldwell, G., and E. Waddell, eds., 1982. *The English of Quebec. From Majority to Minority Status.* Quebec: Institut québécois de la recherche sur la culture.

Confederation des Syndicats Nationaux (CSN). 1971. "Ne Comptons que sur nos propres moyens." Document presented to the members of the Conseil confederal.

Falardeau, J.C. 1960. "Les Canadiens français et leur idéologie." In E. Wade, ed., *Canadian Dualism/La Dualite Canadienne,* 20–30. Quebec and Toronto: Les Presses de l'Université Laval and University of Toronto Press.

Fournier, M. 1977. "La question nationale: les énjeux." *Possibles* 1:7–17.

Levesque, R. 1968. *Option Québec.* Montreal: Éditions de l'homme.

Longfellow, H.W. 1893. "Evangeline. A Tale of Acadie." In *The Complete Poetical Works of Henry Wadsworth Longfellow,* 70–98. Boston and New York: Houghton Mifflin Company.

McRoberts, K., and D. Postgate. 1983. *Développement et modernisation du Québec.* Montreal: Boreal Express.

Painchaud, P. 1984. "L'archipel Québec comme objet de relations exterieures." *Le Devoir,* 3 December 1984, 7.

Paquet, L.A. 1915. "Sermon sur la vocation de la race française en Amerique." In *Discours et allocutions.* Quebec: Imprimerie Franciscaine Missionaire.

Parti Pris. 1965. "Manifeste 1965–1966." *Parti Pris* 3(1-2): 2–41.

Tetley, W. 1982. "The English and Language Legislation: A Personal History." In G. Caldwell and E. Waddell, eds. *The English of Quebec. From Majority to Minority Status,* 379–97. Quebec: Institut québécois de la recherche sur la culture.

Tocqueville, A. de. 1957. *Oeuvres Completes.* Vol. 5: *Voyages en Sicile et aux États-Unis.* Paris: Gallimard.

Waddell, E. 1982. "Place and People." In G. Caldwell and E. Waddell, eds., *The English of Quebec: From Majority to Minority Status,* 27–55. Quebec: Institut québécois de la recherche sur la culture.

5 The Population of Ontario: A Study of the Foundation of a Social Geography

J. David Wood

Two hundred and ten years ago southern Ontario was almost totally without human occupants. Today it is the most populous part of what is known as the heartland of Canada. It contains one-third of the total population of Canada, and it is currently attracting much more than its "fair share" of growth. Its metropolitan centre, Toronto, has become the most populous urban municipality in Canada.

The metamorphosis of Ontario from a wilderness to a heartland for half a continent still calls for attention from social geographers 40 years after Wreford Watson's pioneering contributions (Watson 1943, 1947, 1948, 1951). This essay reconstructs changes in distribution and composition of the population, from the earliest European settlement to the present, in an attempt to lay a foundation for social geographies of Ontario. There is an emphasis on the first century of the settlement when many persistent and fundamental social and political realities were established. The main themes taken up in this essay are, in order, the initiation of the European agricultural settlement, chronological variations in the size of the population, changes in its distributions and composition and, finally, some theoretical propositions bearing on the social geography.

5.1 Refugee Beginnings
5.1.1 American Upheaval

The bicentennial of the arrival of the first Euro-American agricultural settlers in Ontario was celebrated in 1984. The glorious accomplishments of these loyalists, and the modern re-creation and adornment of the early days, tend to disguise the fact that the loyalists were displaced persons escaping from a dilemma common throughout history. The Treaty of Paris which, in 1783, formally ended the American War of Independence, left no hope of recourse to the power of the mother country by those who had remained loyal. To avoid humiliation and worse, many of them chose to leave the new republic, abandoning the fruits of years and, in some cases, generations of endeavour.

The tens of thousands of refugees scattered in various directions: some to the Caribbean, some to the British Isles, a significant proportion to New Brunswick and Nova Scotia, and a few to the St. Lawrence valley east of the confluence with the Ottawa River. In the part of the Great Lakes basin that was to become Ontario, a minor proportion settled during the 1780s. These United Empire Loyalists numbered approximately 8,000 (apart from the 2,000 to 3,000 loyal Amerindians). The first few farming families actually settled on the Niagara frontier in 1780 (Gates 1968, 11;

Wilson 1981). This initial infusion of refugees was made up largely of the members of loyal militias, demobilized British troops, and their families. Because they had borne arms against the rebels, these military personnel were not welcome in the new republic. On coming into the new British territory, the loyalists closed the door, at least for a time, on their past. They began to build a new way of life that was consciously different in important respects from the directions being taken in the brash republic nearby (McCalla 1983).

5.1.2   The Trek to New Territory

Although it has not attained the same legendary dimensions, the trek of the loyalists was of similar scale to that of the *voortrekkers* in distance traversed, number of migrants, and dangers involved. Most of the loyalists who looked for refuge on the north side of the St. Lawrence basin had been residents of New York or Pennsylvania. Though today it may seem relatively close, it is unlikely that many refugees travelled less than 160 kilometres. The journey had to be made through largely uncleared forests, with their life's possessions commonly carried on a wagon drawn by oxen. No routes were suited to family travel: the trails were not well developed for cart traffic; wilderness streams required precarious fording; and the move might be forced at an inconvenient season.

Loyalists trekking from the vicinity of Albany, a common source area, would have journeyed at least 300 kilometres if they headed for the closest destination. Desirable areas would have required a trip of at least 400 kilometres. The earliest settlers around the Bay of Quinte, in 1784, completed their journey by boat up the St. Lawrence and into the east end of Lake Ontario. The gateways into what was to become Ontario were as distinct as those through a chain of mountains.[1] In practice, they were the three land bridges into peninsular Ontario, with entry by water being a little-used minor variation. Numerically, the most important gateway was the 210-kilometre stretch from the east end of Lake Ontario down the St. Lawrence River. A number of military units and loyal militias were offered land there on attractive terms, at demobilization, to form a protective buffer along the north shore of the river. The second ranking gateway was the Niagara frontier, to which groups primarily associated with New York militias made their way. The third gateway, less accessible and therefore less important, was at the far south-western corner opposite Fort Detroit. Here a well-established French community had sketched out long lots on both sides of the Detroit River. This gateway became especially important to that community in the 1790s when the fort and hinterland of Detroit were finally yielded to the United States, and settlers were forced to choose sides.

This tridentate influx meant that Ontario's earliest population occupied three pockets connected to each other only tenuously. In simple terms, the story of Ontario's population change was one of diffusion as people gradually settled further inland from the gateways. After about two decades, coalescence was beginning. By the 1850s the continuation of the process led to population concentrations almost the reverse of those of the 1780s.

5.1.3 Planning a Colony

The pattern of the population influx was influenced in the early years by a conscious and sophisticated plan for the colony. This plan was designed to yield a well-ordered, self-supporting, modestly progressive colony with most of the essential rights of the Mother Country.

The colonies gained their *raison d'être* from the postulates of mercantilism. Wherever it has been practised, mercantilism has embodied a degree of coercion because the colonies were unabashedly viewed as being tributaries to the economy of the Mother Country. Thus, protection of the system, usually in the form of a military presence, was characteristic. For this reason, and because of the obvious vulnerability of a boundary of 1,280 kilometres with the freshly independent United States, early Ontario invited military planning. At the formal establishment of a separate entity, in 1791, Ontario was endowed with a lieutenant-governor who was acutely aware of the need for a military plan, having himself tasted defeat in a late battle of the War of Independence. This lieutenant-governor was John Graves Simcoe. He is important to our considerations here because the plan he devised and the attempts he made to attract settlers laid the foundation for many of the perennial population characteristics of Ontario and some of the persistent weaknesses in the early scheme of settlement.

Within nine months of Simcoe's entry to the province, at the St. Lawrence gateway, he had traversed his domain from end to end, including long stretches on snowshoes. His military engineering background was applied to assessing the characteristics of the territory: the original description of southern Ontario as a *peninsula* appears in his correspondence.[2] Beginning in 1792 he began to substantiate the plan that was in his mind. The bases of the plan were:

a) a hierarchy of military strongpoints, including regional capitals, specialized posts (such as naval bases), and peripheral or frontier posts;
b) a network of military roads to link the various nuclei; and
c) a farming hinterland to supply each proto-urban centre.

But the military motive should not be allowed to overshadow Simcoe's other passion: to create an appropriate society for a loyal remnant of the Empire. This was to be brought about largely through the manipulation of the millions of acres of potentially valuable real estate in the province. Simcoe publicized his intention to attract well-to-do, influential individuals who would accept the responsibility for establishing self-contained settlements in return for large grants of land. This device for settlement of the colonies had a tenacious hold on the minds of imperial bureaucrats. It had been tried in the proprietary colonies such as Georgia early in the eighteenth century, and it was tried in the eastern Cape Colony, South Africa, in the 1820s (e.g., Christopher 1976, 63–67). All of these cases were at best only modestly successful; in Upper Canada in the 1790s it was almost a total failure because the agents failed to introduce the expected numbers of settlers.

Simcoe's plan of roads and defensive points, on the other hand, has provided a basic structure for population distribution that has been reinforced through subsequent developments. This structure includes the important east-west corridor from the Ottawa River to Windsor, an arm reaching around the west end of Lake Ontario and on to Niagara, and an opposite arm stretching north from Toronto to Lake Simcoe. The only important departures from the original plan, excluding the unforeseen, resource-based settlement in northern Ontario, are an extension up the Grand River valley to Waterloo, and the Ottawa exclave. The components of this all-important skeleton are displayed in Figure 5.1.

5.2   Variables Affecting Population Size

The population of a new agricultural territory is expected to grow, and although this does not inevitably prove to be the case, an ultimate increase certainly is the rule. There are two ways in which the population can increase: through immigration and through natural fertility. Both of these have had a major, though variable, role in population change in Ontario.

5.2.1   Immigration

The settlement of Ontario by agriculturalists of European stock was begun by the immigration of the loyalists in the 1780s. From that time, the flow of outsiders into the province has risen and fallen. There have been five periods in which immigration has been dominant. Its relative impact, however, has gradually decreased as the total population has grown, and there has been the countervailing influence of emigration. The main periods of immigration can be characterized as follows:

a) The Loyalist Period, ca. 1780–93, at the end of which the population amounted to about 21,000. This population was almost totally American-born, including the large, fluctuating French settlement in the vicinity of Detroit, the archetype loyalists near Niagara, at the east end of Lake Ontario, and down the St. Lawrence, as well as the roughly 3,000 Amerindians who chose to enter British territory. The retired British military settlers on the St. Lawrence were the only group not born in America.

b) The Post-Napoleonic Wars, ca. 1816–35. This was the first sizeable influx of settlers from the Old Country, and it set in motion a reshaping of Upper Canada, which by mid-century had given it a marked British flavour. Thousands of overseas immigrants began to arrive each year, and by the early 1830s over 50,000 were arriving in some years. Most of those entering by the Quebec route moved on to Upper Canada.

c) Potato Famine Aftermath, ca. 1847–55. Recent revised figures indicate that over 200,000 overseas immigrants entered Ontario during these years (Norris 1984). Even in the 1820s and 1830s the Irish were the most numerous in the immigration record. After 1846 their predominance was quite exceptional for a number of years. The passage to British North America offered a relatively cheap escape from the extreme destitution that gripped Ireland. At the end of the 1840s Ontario's population was growing by 10 percent each year.

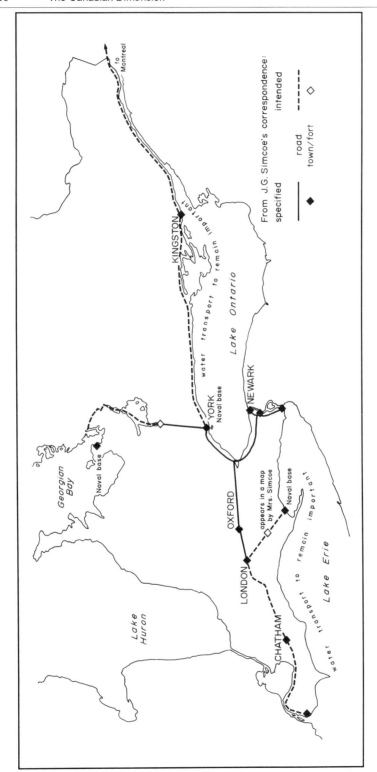

Figure 5.1 **Simcoe's Actual Settlement Plan for Upper Canada as Manifest in His Correspondence.**
Sources: Cruickshank (1923); Inglis (1963)

The rate of growth was moderated, however, through most of Ontario's history, by the opposing influence: emigration. It is suspected, for example, that many of the Irish who arrived on the shores of British North America moved on, without much delay, into the United States. But it was really with the 1850s that Ontario's "back door" was opened, so that both native-born and immigrants began drifting westward, first to the United States and then, after 1880, to western Canada as well. In simple figurative terms, Ontario became a huge migrant exchange, bringing overseas immigrants in from the east and shunting Ontarians and earlier immigrants out to the West. Large contingents of Ontarians settled in the western provinces, and this pattern of migration was not reversed until the end of the 1920s when the industrial and commercial influence of Ontario began to attract job seekers from both west and east (Taylor 1967). The reciprocation of the migration and the striking change in the balance are shown in Figure 5.2.

During the half century after 1855, when relatively cheap agricultural land had become scarce and industry had not yet become solidly established and diversified, Ontario ceased attracting large numbers of immigrants and suffered net losses to emigration. With the approach of the twentieth century, travel became easier and the distinction between immigration and emigration became blurred by people entering and leaving foreign countries more freely. So-called re-migration, in which erstwhile immigrants decided to return to their home countries, began to affect all parts of the New World. Argentina was hardest hit by re-migration, but even the United States experienced it at a level probably not much lower than that of Canada. (Thistlethwaite 1960, 38–42).

Immigration in the twentieth century displays two broad peaks:

d) Mass Overseas Influx, ca. 1905–13. Although immigration was much less important than high fertility as a component of population increase, Ontario did receive over 200,000 immigrants in each of the first three decades of the century. The most spectacular influx, when Canada suddenly became attractive again, coinciding with the improved technology of travel, occurred during the decade prior to the First World War. Although this is usually thought of as a mass movement to the prairie provinces, in fact Ontario was the principal destination throughout the period from 1900 to 1920, as can be seen in Table 5.1. However, the immigrants were much less important to Ontario than to the lightly-populated Prairies. By the end of the 1920s, this first peak of overseas immigration was being replaced by a strengthening internal flow of population to Ontario from most other parts of Canada, as shown in Figure 5.2b.

e) Post–Second World War Boom, ca. 1946–61. By the time the Second World War had ended, Ontario had become the main magnet both for immigrants and internal migrants. Toronto became the major immigrant destination of Canada. In 1961 42 percent of the city's population and one-third of those living in the metropolitan area had been born outside Canada, and in each case two-thirds had arrived between 1946 and 1961.[3] For the first time, British immigrants were outnumbered by other European immigrants, primarily from eastern and southern Europe. The census of 1981 reveals that 23.5 percent of Ontario's population was born outside Canada – the highest of any province. Kalbach and McVey (1979, 114–15) point out that immigration to Canada became important again at the end of the 1960s, and it will necessarily be important in the future because of the steady decline of the birth rate. It is well to point out, however, that as Canada's – and Ontario's – population has grown in the twentieth century, immigration has had less and less impact. Between 1961 and 1971, it

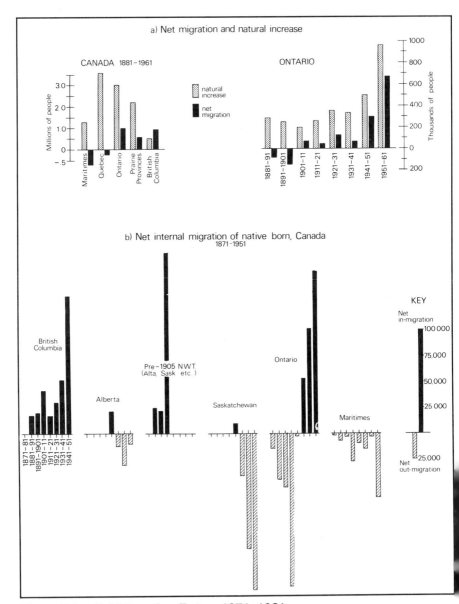

Figure 5.2   **Net Migration Rates, 1871–1961**

Source: Weir 1968, 139, 150

Table   **Distribution of Immigrants to Canada, Pre-1900 to 1921,**
5.1   **by Certain Provinces of Residence in 1921**

| | **% Distribution of Immigrants Arriving in Given Period** | | | | | | |
	Overall %	1919–1921	1915–1918	1911–1914	1900–1910	pre-1900	Immigrants Brit.	Foreign
Ontario	32.8	40.0	26.4	34.2	27.0	40.9	71.6	28.4
Manitoba	11.4	9.3	7.4	11.2	12.6	12.0	50.9	49.1
Sask.	15.3	10.6	16.8	15.8	18.9	9.5	33.5	66.5
Alberta	14.0	13.0	20.0	14.2	16.2	7.7	36.4	63.6
B.C.	13.3	12.7	12.2	12.6	13.8	14.5	61.7	38.3

Source: Census of Canada, 1921, Table 58

accounted for only about 15 percent of the growth, but Ontario stands out as a significant aberration from 1951 to 1956, when migration (primarily immigration from Europe) provided 47 percent of its dramatic increase (Macleod et al. 1972, 180).

Twentieth-century immigration has been characterized by the drawing power of cities, in contrast to the early immigration, which was overwhelmingly aimed at rural areas. Ontario society was dominated by agriculture until the end of the nineteenth century, but the movement toward urban places certainly had begun by the 1820s. Artisans with training in Britain or the United States began leaving their farms in order to serve the growing agricultural community. There had always been an overseas movement of people with capital, heading for new opportunities in the colonial urban centres. The classic rural-urban shift had begun in earnest in Ontario by the 1840s: a dozen totally rural townships reached their maximum population before 1851. It was the migration in the twentieth century, however, that was unequivocally bound for the urban centres in the older provinces of Canada. In fact, Ontario became predominantly urban before the beginning of the First World War, a decade earlier than Canada as a whole. Marshall and Smith (1978) demonstrate that the urbanization of Ontario's population was reflected in an impressive increase in new urban places (populations of 1,000 plus) in the 1860s and 1870s, which gave way to a greater and greater concentration in large cities in the twentieth century. At least one more phase has now been added: a relative decrease during the 1970s and 1980s, of the concentration in the large cities in favour of suburbanization and some small-city growth (see below).

5.2.2   Natural Increase

During periods when immigration was not providing large infusions, the population of Ontario continued to grow through fertility. At certain times, when high levels of fertility and immigration coincided, there was extraordinary growth. Cases in point would be the 1780s, the late 1840s, and, modern and less dramatic, the 1950s. At other times, when net migration was negative or at a very low level, natural

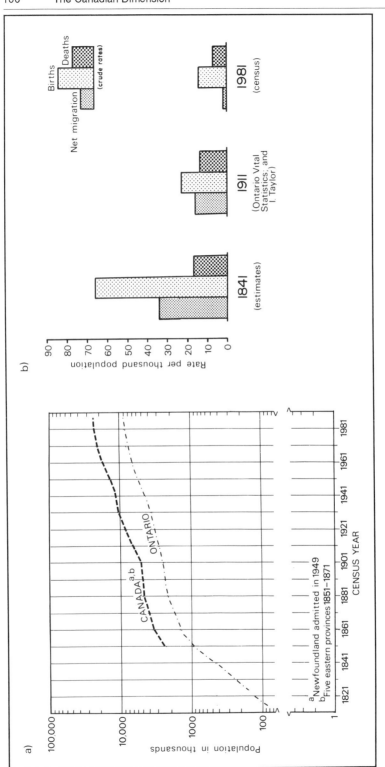

Figure 5.3a   **Population Growth, Ontario and Canada, 1811–1981**

Figure 5.3b   **Net Migration, Births, and Deaths, Ontario, 1841, 1911, and 1981**

Sources: Henripin 1972; Census of Canada 1921; and Census of Canada 1981.

Compilation from Statistics Canada and author's estimates (pre-1851)

increase has kept the population from decreasing. Therefore natural increase, though important throughout, really came into its own during periods when immigration was relatively low, notably from the late 1790s to 1815, the mid-1830s to the mid-1840s, the late 1850s to the beginning of the twentieth century, and from the years of the First World War until the end of the Second World War. The rate of natural increase in Ontario has at times ranked with the highest rates in human-population history, although over the two centuries there has been an overall, gradual decline.

Natural increase is the product of the relationship of two demographic components: births and deaths. Ontario in its pioneer era certainly lived up to Malthusian expectations for a new agricultural population surrounded by ample resources; that is, a doubling in 25 years by natural increase. Newly settled townships very quickly came to be dominated numerically by children, to the extent that over half the population would be under 16 years of age, usually to a proportion of 52 to 60 percent. The atmosphere of New World optimism led to a remarkable reproductive vigour. In the years around 1840 the birth rate as calculated by Henripin (1972) reached 66.9 per 1,000 yearly, which, although lower than rates set some years later during the opening of Manitoba and Saskatchewan, was higher than that achieved in Quebec even at the height of *la revanche des berceaux* (Henripin and Peron 1972). Postulating a concurrent death rate of about 17 per 1,000, it appears that natural increase by itself accounted for a growth of approximately 50 for every 1,000 in the population. From this point on, Ontario's birth rate went into a gradual decline: to 47.5 in the 1850s, 37.2 in the 1880s, and, after a dip around the turn of the century, a slight rise and fall again to 26.3 for the decade 1916–25. By 1937 it had slipped to 16.9; it rose again in the "baby boom" era to 26.8 in 1957, and then resumed its decline to 13.9 in 1983 (Henripin 1972, 366; Spelt 1968, 344; Statistics Canada 1984, 118). Apparently the baby boomers' babies caused it to rise again to 14.6 in 1988.

In the meantime, the death rate has followed a much less irregular trend. The adult population in the early decades, being relatively youthful, had a low death rate, except during periodic invasions by highly contagious diseases. Substantial infant mortality prior to the mid-nineteenth century raised the gross mortality rate. As the population has gradually aged over the past century and a quarter, the expected increase of the death rate has been more than offset by improvements in medical knowledge and provision. In the 1890s it ran about 12 per 1,000, rose to nearly 15 per 1,000 in the second decade of the twentieth century, and then decreased again in the 1930s to approximately 12. In 1961 it was 8.2, in 1983 7.2, and in 1988 7.5. The relative importance of the components of population change – net migration, births, and deaths – is displayed for three widely-spaced dates in Figure 5.3b. Despite variations in the components, overall growth has continued (Figure 5.3a).

5.2.3   Examples of Long-Term Population Dynamics

The variables in population change have created different patterns in different parts of Ontario. The six townships[4] analyzed in this section illustrate the range of data and dynamics found in what has been the overall growth of Ontario's population. The chosen townships have all been primarily rural throughout the

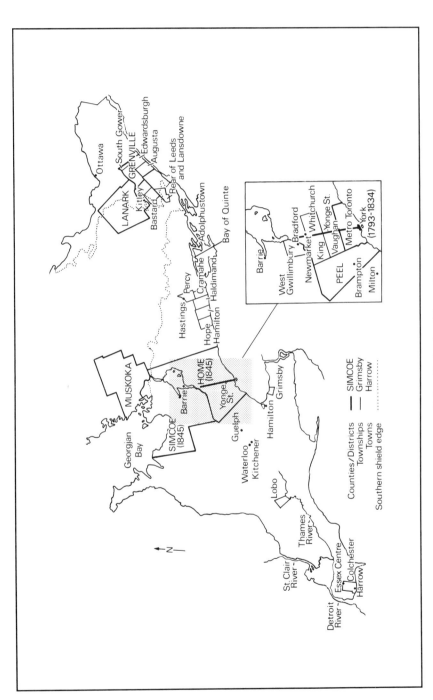

Figure 5.4   Ontario: Place-Names

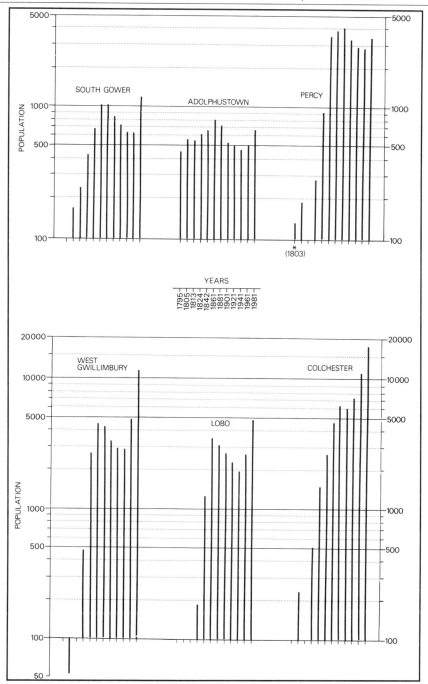

Figure 5.5   **Graphs of Long-Term Population Dynamics for Selected Parts of Ontario (logarithmic scale)**

Sources: Early municipal records; Censuses of Canada; *Smith's Canadian Gazeteer* (1846)

period; they have relied on the classic resource – land for agriculture – to maintain their population. They have also had constant boundaries. The prevalence of urbanized townships in Ontario is not denied by this choice; the discussion of urbanization is saved for later in the essay. These townships can be found on the location map (Figure 5.4), and thumbnail sketches of each, to complement the graphs in Figure 5.5, are provided in the next few paragraphs.

The survey begins with Adolphustown Township at the east end of Lake Ontario. It yields the oldest population series available for the province. A remarkable number of returns have been preserved because they were printed in 1899.[5] The originals have since disappeared. Adolphustown was part of the loyalist heartland of Ontario, the first settlers being refugees who reached the township in 1784. This township was cut into two small peninsulas by the arms of the Bay of Quinte, and its position has always been tangential to the main east-west thoroughfares. The township was almost entirely good potential farmland, the southern half being especially high-quality land. Original loyalist families have dominated the township throughout its history (Norris 1980). Their American heritage led to the early establishment of a town meeting and population record in Adolphustown (see the graph in Figure 5.5). Some of the earliest data for Adolphustown are included in the discussion of the characteristics of a frontier population (below).

The easternmost township was South Gower. It was 160 kilometres north-east of Adolphustown, and one tier back from the St. Lawrence River. Settlement began at the end of the 1790s. The land surface and soil quality were extremely variable, but most of the township was usable for agriculture. The search for farms and the location of the promising Rideau River system on the northern edge of the township resulted in the good land being quickly claimed. Neither South Gower nor Adolphustown had anything more urban than hamlets within their boundaries.

The data for Percy Township began a few years later than those for Adolphustown but at an earlier stage in the settlement. In fact, in the Percy figures the very first steps in the opening of a new township are revealed. All the townships in this long-term series, but especially Percy, are first viewed at a very early stage in their development.[6] The settlers who opened the township about 1798 formed one of the first offshoots from the early loyalist settlements. It was in the second tier of townships, like South Gower, about 19 kilometres back from the Lake Ontario shore, which had begun to be settled slightly earlier. A village called Hastings began to grow irregularly in Percy Township towards the end of the nineteenth century, and by 1981 it held just under 1,000 people.

West Gwillimbury was very much a fringe settlement in 1805. It probably owed its population primarily to being just off the north end of the main government road, Yonge Street. It lay on the west side of the southern extremity of Lake Simcoe, although access to the lake was difficult and not of much consequence until later in the century. Except at its south-eastern and north-western corners, which were excessively wet, the township was very attractive for agriculture. An agricultural service centre, Bradford, grew on the success of the market gardening developed in the south end of the township since the 1920s. This centre has been the main focus of the mushrooming growth in the township during the past 20 years.

Lobo Township lay at the great southerly bend of the Thames River, just west of London. It consisted almost entirely of superior agricultural land. Once settlement began, about 1820, rapid increase in population characterized the next 40 years. Since that time, Lobo has displayed the gradual decrease, followed by the post–Second World War increase, that was common to a great many southern Ontario farming townships.

Colchester Township was near the old French Canadian settlement on the Detroit River. Being in a coastal location, less than 16 kilometres from this outpost of French colonization, it was eligible for overspill at an early date. It is thought that the first agricultural settler arrived in 1784, at the same time that Loyalists were moving into the eastern extremity of the province. Colchester was to become a noted agricultural area, although the north half of the township was hampered by poor drainage. Two urban centres eventually developed: Essex Centre, which grew in the last quarter of the nineteenth century at the north-east corner of the township to a population of 1,400 by the turn of the century; and Harrow, which was closer to the lake in the south and only rose above 1,000 by 1941.

Almost all these farming townships mirror the pattern of growth of the Canadian-born component in the provincial population as a whole (see Figure 5.2b). There was rapid increase until the middle of the nineteenth century, followed by substantial loss in the last four decades of that century and until the 1920s, but once again reversed after 1930. In the past few decades, these townships have been caught up in the pervasive urbanization of southern Ontario.

5.3   Changing Population Distributions
5.3.1   Contrasting Two Centuries

The major contrast between the 1780s and the 1980s, apart from the absolute numbers involved, lay in where the people lived. The initial distribution, as mentioned above, was tied to the three gateways into the province from east and south. In fact, even in 1794 there were sizeable contingents that had still not crossed from the east side of the Niagara River and the west side of the Detroit River (as indicated on Figure 5.6). At the same time, dissemination had begun from the gateways: an exclave was taking shape on the north side of Lake Ontario around the site of the new capital, York (Toronto), a tentacle of settlement was reaching along the Lake Ontario shore from the east; and a vigorous incursion was advancing from the south-west up the valley of the Thames River. This opening scene also displayed a conglomerate population barely touched by the homogenization typical of New World settlement. The far eastern end of the province was dominated by Gaelic speakers, most of whom were families of Highlanders who had served with the British military forces during the American rebellion. At the other extremity of the province, along the Detroit River and the lower Thames, numerical superiority was with the French-speaking population, which had occupied that area for nearly half a century. The other major ethnic group, although made up of distinct components, was

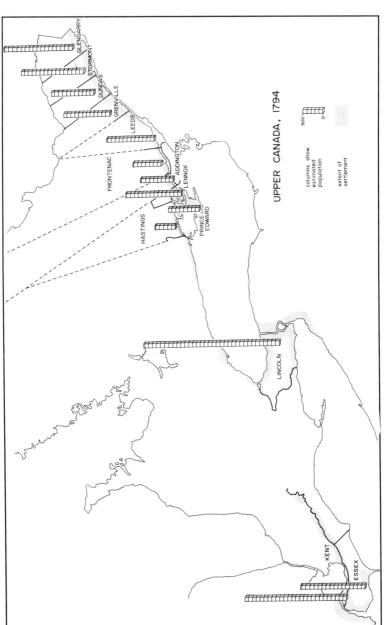

Figure 5.6   **Distribution of Population, Upper Canada, 1794 (excluding Amerindians and Imperial troops)**

Source: Cruickshank 1924, vol. 2, 293

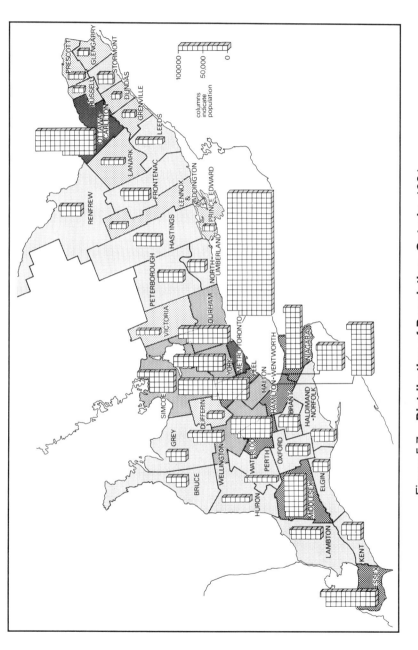

Figure 5.7   **Distribution of Population, Ontario, 1981**
Source: Census of Canada, 1981

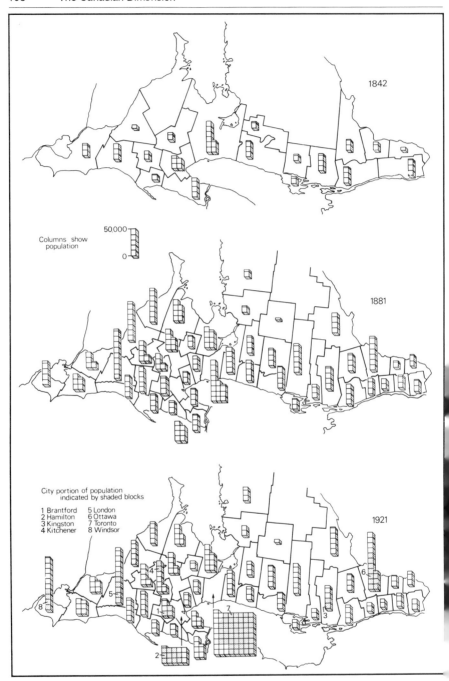

Figure 5.8   **Distribution of Population by Counties, Ontario, 1842, 1881, and 1921**

Sources: *Census of Canada, 1871*, vol. 4; *Census of Canada, 1931*, vol. 1, Table 1a.

the native Amerindian. Concentrations of them lived along the Detroit River and around Lake St. Clair, in the Grand River Valley, at the north-west corner of Lake Ontario, and on the north side of the Bay of Quinte.

By 1981 the focus of population in southern Ontario had clearly shifted from the edges to the centre. The primacy of Metropolitan Toronto stands out starkly in diagrammatic form on Figure 5.7. Other areas not represented on the 1794 map, but of great importance today, are London, Hamilton, and Ottawa. Although certain parts of the province, including sections of some cities, are associated with a particular ethnic group, the process of homogenization has diluted or obliterated the separateness in most cases. The past 60 years have been primarily an era of acculturation in which large numbers of immigrants have been assimilated with little more than a ripple – in marked contrast to the early decades, when immigrant waves carved indelible features on the demographic face of Ontario.

5.3.2   Intervening Distributions

A shift of the centre of gravity of population towards the Head-of-the-Lake (the west end of Lake Ontario) and Toronto and its hinterland had occurred by 1842, the year that marked the first attempt at a comprehensive census (see Figure 5.8). There was also vigorous growth in the vicinity of London and along the north shore of Lake Ontario. Although settlement had begun confronting the limits along the edge of the Shield in the eastern and central parts of the province, there was still the extensive, untapped and unsurveyed, north-western sector of the peninsula, "The Queen's Bush," to be occupied. It was opened to settlement less than ten years later, with the penetration by colonization roads (Norris 1984). Colonization roads were also used slightly later to entice homesteaders onto the southern portion of the Shield between Georgian Bay and the Ottawa Valley.

Population continued to fill up the fringes and spread into new territory, although by the middle of the nineteenth century many long-settled agricultural townships were reaching their maximum numbers. The initiation of a railway network in the 1850s led first to a renewed extension of settlement, but by the 1860s it was encouraging a profound reorganization, expressed especially in the crystallization of an urban hierarchy and a readjustment of economic relationships down to the level of the myriad of villages (Spelt 1983). The map for 1881 (Figure 5.8) reveals that the outward extensions of 1842 had continued and strengthened. These included a notable reinforcement of the concentration around London, and a push beyond to the shores of Lake Huron, a spectacular infilling of what had been the empty Queen's Bush in 1842, an increase in the townships around Georgian Bay and even into the Shield lands of Muskoka. The cities were launched into rapid growth, and Toronto was approaching its status as a primate city, being two and a half times the size of Hamilton.

A further 40 years takes us just beyond the First World War, when Ontario's population had become more than half urban. The map of the distribution in 1921 (Figure 5.8) shows how the urban centres were asserting their influence. The most striking example, Toronto, had reached more than half a million in a total provincial population of less than three million. The population had begun to consolidate around

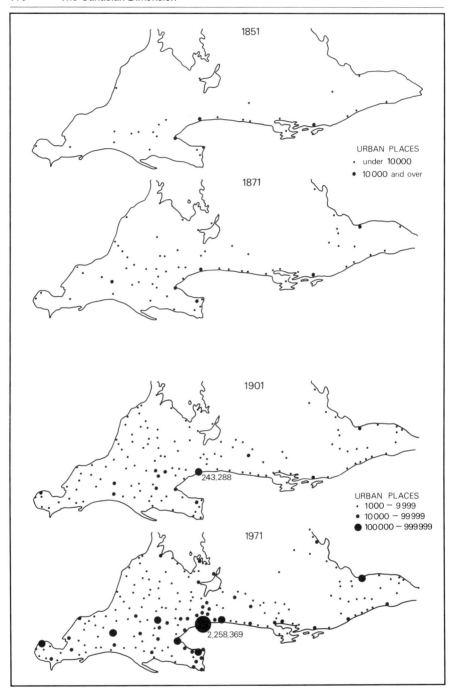

Figure 5.9   **The Developing Urban System in Southern Ontario, 1851–1971**

Source: Marshall and Smith 1978, 25–26

other cities as well. Hamilton accounted for 114,000 of Wentworth County's 153,000, which, with Toronto, made the western end of Lake Ontario the pre-eminent focus for the province's population. The provincial highway system, which was to link major urban centres especially along the Lake Ontario shore, was being developed and would lead in three or four decades to the modern highway-based distribution. There was some reiteration of the old gateway concentrations through urban growth around Windsor in the south-west and the Welland Canal in Niagara. Ottawa and London had increased to three or four times their 1881 sizes, but other cities, such as Kingston, had had very modest growth (Osborne 1975). Most parts of Kingston's rural hinterland had actually decreased in population. Losses were occurring in many agricultural counties, including Lanark and Grenville on the east side of the Shield edge, and also at the other extremity approaching Lake Huron. Marked growth had taken place in many parts of northern Ontario since the penetration of that area by the transcontinental railway in the 1880s but, ultimately, the catalysts most influential in changing Ontario's population were at work in the urban centres in the south.

5.3.3 The Emergence of Urbanization

The beginnings of the European settlement in Ontario were non-urban, except for some clustering around military strongpoints. But, in Europe at this time, urbanization was in full flood, most dramatically in association with industrialization. Over half a century would pass before industrialization would become an important stimulant to urban growth in Ontario, but in the meantime nuclei began to form around government administration on the one hand, and around the workshops and services required by the dominant agricultural community on the other.

The rural-urban shift got under way at an early date. Upper Canada was characterized by a large surplus of men in the population in keeping with all agricultural frontiers, but women gained numerical dominance in the towns. In Kingston, for instance, it occurred at least as early as 1835: 1,257 females to 1,165 males, age 16 years and over; and in Toronto by 1836: 4,861 to 4,793, all ages (Martin 1967, 184; 1967, 189). A reasonable explanation for this contrast is that women, especially in the young, working age group, were moving in substantial numbers from country to town in pursuit of employment. This characteristic became more pronounced as time passed. In the second half of the nineteenth century Ontario moved towards an urban majority. In 1851, 17 percent of the population was in urban places of 1,000 or more; by 1881, the proportion was approaching 29 percent; and, as mentioned earlier, half the population was urban by the beginning of the First World War. By 1951, when most of the immigrants to Canada were heading for Ontario, and when most of the Ontario immigrants were heading for cities (Yeates 1982, 114–15), the urban proportion was 65 percent.

An analysis of the distribution of the urban population prompts a re-examination of the effect of Simcoe's plan and the headstart it implanted in certain parts of the province.. In 1949 D.W. Kirk argued that the structure provided by Simcoe's military roads and the planned military and administrative centres became the skeleton on which the flesh of the 1850 – and even the 1950 – urban hierarchy built up. And, although Kirk's interpretation of Simcoe's ideas was even more ambitious than appears to have been intended by their ambitious originator (see Figure 5.1), the argument holds up rather well. The shadow of Simcoe's plan can be seen to take shape in the series of maps from Marshall and Smith's (1978) analysis of the urban system of southern Ontario (see Figure 5.9). The string of main towns up the St. Lawrence, along the north shore of Lake Ontario, and extending west to the Detroit River lies on Simcoe's military road; the importance of the Niagara frontier survives from the 1790s. This urban system was traced out from the St. Lawrence River entry to Windsor, almost step by step, by the visitation of cholera in 1832 and 1834, following the routes of ingress, but tending to break out first in the larger centres (Pyle 1969).

By 1971 Simcoe's plan still stands out distinctly. The road north from Toronto, to tap the upper lakes, is studded with an urban constellation. The largest towns and cities (10,000 people or more) are almost all found in proximity to the structure of 1794, except for Ottawa, Kitchener-Waterloo, and the latter's immediate neighbours. What is even more impressive is the discovery by Marshall and Smith (1978, 31) that of the 22 places they call "persistent gainers," all but four or five clearly owe their success to Simcoe's plan (see also Whebell 1969). Ottawa was one of the persistent gainers beyond the Simcoe influence. It gained some notoriety in the nineteenth century, through its connections with the construction of the Rideau Canal, the timber activity in the watershed of the Ottawa River, and its selection as capital of the new Dominion. But Ottawa is primarily a twentieth-century creation that has risen since the 1920s to its present status as the second-largest conglomeration of population in Ontario. With Hull on the Quebec side of the river, Ottawa is now designated the "National Capital," and as with Brazilia and Canberra, it carries on a life that transcends or ignores its local milieu. Large infusions of money by the federal government, especially since the Second World War, have transformed it into a world-class administrative city.

Urbanization has become the major influence on the distribution of Ontario's population. The high concentrations within formal urban boundaries, along with relatively high tributary populations, together form a greatly extended linear distribution with intersecting arms from which there is a rapid gradation to rural density (see Figure 5.1a). Less pronounced lines of development stretch from Windsor along the Detroit and St. Clair rivers, north from the Lake Ontario shore to Peterborough, and up the Ottawa Valley. The long band of settlement from Windsor to the Ottawa River is the larger part of what Yeates (1977) has coined the "Main Street" of Canada, although the section along the St. Lawrence River is a corridor more of passage than of development. The way he has chosen to represent the population in southern Ontario can provide an appropriate summation of the process we have followed from the 1780s. He has classified census subdivisions according to mean population density (using measures modified from Russwurm 1970), as follows: (a) 0–10 persons per square kilometre (sparsely populated), (b) 10–25 persons per square kilometre (rural), (c) 25–60 persons per square kilometre (semi-urban), and (d) more than 60 persons per square kilometre (urban) (Yeates 1985, 43–47). The resulting pattern for 1981 is displayed in Figure 5.10.

5.3.4   Metropolitanization and Suburbanization

In less than 200 years Ontario has passed through the grand transition from rough-and-tumble frontier to a metropolitan society. Toronto has emerged as a metropolis since the Second World War and was granted a metropolitan government in 1953. The city attracted an inordinate proportion of the migrants entering the country during the 1950s. Whereas Toronto and its immediate neighbours had a population of about 925,000 in 1941, by 1961 the same municipalities, as Metropolitan Toronto, had doubled to nearly 1.9 million (Nader 1975, 230). It was the key-stone to an agglomeration euphemistically labelled the Golden Horseshoe, which enclosed the whole west end of Lake Ontario, from east of Toronto to beyond Hamilton, accounting for approximately 2.8 million people. By 1981, Metro Toronto Census Metropolitan Area (CMA) alone contained a fraction under three million people, and southern Ontario could boast another ten cities of 100,000 or more. This city domination is illustrated effectively by the "isodemographic" map, in which the size of each entity is a representation not of land area but of population (see Figure 5.11).

Ontario is not at the end of a demographic process, although the metropolis is sometimes thought to be so. There has been a move beyond the metropolitan condition – not to a true post-industrial society, though there are many signs of impending, profound change, but at least to an alternative to the continual funnelling of population into one huge conurbation. The metropolis continued to grow vigorously until the early 1970s, but that decade brought an abrupt halt to some prevailing trends. Most significant was a redirection of job-seekers toward developments in the western provinces, especially Alberta and British Columbia. This meant that the greatest growth rates between 1976 and 1981 occurred in western cities rather than in Ontario. The Toronto CMA, for instance, recorded a net loss (-0.7 percent) in internal migration, though thanks to continued immigration and natural increase it had an overall growth of 7 percent, which is slightly above the 6.1 percent mean for CMAs (Simmons and Bourne 1984, 32).

The other notable demographic feature of the 1970s was a widespread slowdown of growth in metropolitan areas in favour of less focused growth. The latter took the form of suburbanization, scattered beyond the formal boundaries of CMAs, and of rapid increase in some medium-sized cities. Oshawa, the automobile-industry city 40 kilometres east of Toronto, grew by 14.1 percent to 154,000 between 1976 and 1981, and took a further jump to 203,500 by 1986. Suburbanization has been going on, of course, for decades; indeed, one might even identify its beginnings in the late nineteenth century when Toronto began annexing adjacent municipalities. It is obvious that part of Oshawa's growth is suburbanization, because it is within the modern commuter range of Metro Toronto. This also accounts for major components of the growth of other small cities from 1976 to 1981; for example, Barrie (11.7 percent to 38,423, and to 48,287 by 1986), Newmarket (20 percent to 29,753, and to 34,923 by 1986), and, closer to the doorstep of Metro Toronto, Brampton (44 percent

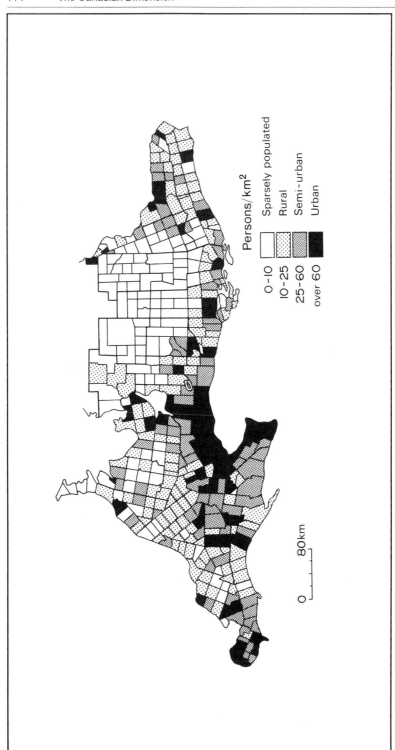

Persons/km²

0-10   Sparsely populated

10-25   Rural

25-60   Semi-urban

over 60   Urban

0   80km

Figure 5.10 **The Distribution of Population in Southern Ontario by Density Classes, 1981**

Source: Yeates 1982

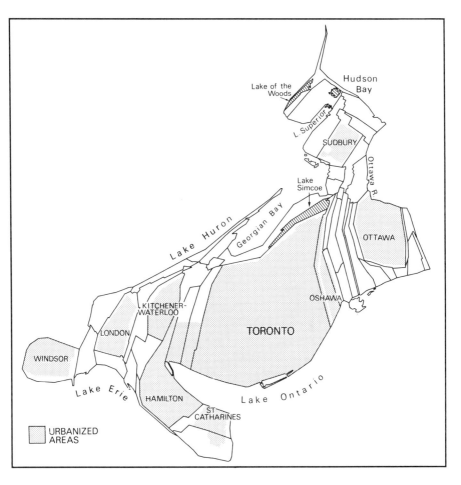

Figure 5.11 **An "Isodemographic" Map of Ontario, Based on the 1961 Census**

Source: Skoda and Robertson 1972

to 149,030, and to 188,498 by 1986), and Milton (35.2 percent to 28,067, and to 32,037 by 1986).[7] In most of these cases annexation has added considerably to the numbers.

The 1980s have brought yet another important transition. The lure of the West has notably declined, and the industrial heartland appears to be reasserting its attractiveness. After the setback in Alberta's petroleum-based economy in 1982, the internal migration in the year 1982–83 led to some surprising statistics. The "winners" of the 1970s – primarily Alberta and British Columbia – had been cut back drastically and, indeed, Alberta registered a net loss of population for the first time in twelve years. Ontario and the other eastern provinces, except Quebec, had net gains (Statistics Canada 1984, 50). The Toronto Census Metropolitan Area returned to vigorous growth, with a 14 percent increase between 1981 and 1986, to 3,427,200. Conditions in the foreseeable future are expected to dampen the fluctuations in migration and population change generally. It seems likely that greater stability, including some consolidation of the metropolitan primacy, will characterize this decade's population distribution.

5.4   Changing Population Composition

The consideration of the size and distribution of a population tends to be panoramic, whereas composition delves into structure and material. There have been unusual demographic features as well as striking changes in Ontario's population history. This section views a range of compositions, from rude frontier to established agricultural district to small industrial city.

5.4.1   Characteristics of a Frontier Population

The loyalists who came in the 1780s did not establish a typical frontier society. Many of them were people who would not willingly have chosen the hardships and hazards of an unopened wilderness. The large, American-born component generally had been established landowners. They came into the new territory with families, tools, animals, and probably a little capital. Because of this head start, the loyalist townships were not what one would designate as true frontier communities, not "stage one" of a new settlement. But it took only about a decade for offspring of the loyalists to begin moving afield and, with other land seekers, to carve out a true frontier. Data are available for the first few years of some of the frontier townships, allowing reconstruction of that rudimentary demography.

The earliest evidence is from the simplest form of census: the annual report from the township clerk naming heads of households and indicating the number of their dependants. The earliest clerk's reports that have survived, dating from the 1790s, are for townships in eastern Ontario, in every case settled by the relatively well-established loyalists. But there is also a good selection of records from "second generation" townships, dating from the early years of the nineteenth century, some of which provide a usable succession of data. The most basic information from the returns is the simple population total, which is displayed in Figure 5.12. Two loyalist townships, Edwardsburgh on the St. Lawrence and tiny Adolphustown on the Bay of

Quinte, neither of which was modified by significant urban growth, are included for comparison. The loyalist township of Augusta, which eventually spawned the town of Prescott, is also used for some early comparisons. This mixture of new with partially settled townships provides data that can be used to assess some widely held assumptions about frontier and peri-frontier populations. The expectation of continuous growth from the entry of the first settlers is not supported by these data. Eight of the ten townships suffered setbacks in population growth in the early years, and in some cases – especially with South Gower and Percy, which were one tier of townships back from the water routes – irregularity of growth was chronic, at least in the first two decades.

The main dynamic underlying this irregularity was the transiency of the people. It has been shown that at a much later stage in the process of agricultural settlement in Ontario, when census data were available, the degree of transiency was remarkably high. Even in a well-endowed township the turnover of population between one decennial census and the next could easily approach 60 percent (e.g., Gagan and Mays 1973). The fragmentary records from the years around 1800 suggest that in the earliest settlements the amount of movement was just as high. It was not unusual for over half the householders to leave the township in a ten-year period.[8]

A striking feature of the early settlements was the numerical predominance of adult males over adult females. After ten years of settlement in the loyalist township of Adolphustown, in 1794, there was an adult male-female ratio of 145:100. It seems that Augusta had a similar ratio at the end of the 1790s. The newest townships, however, had a relatively low ratio of around 120:100. The evidence indicates that the newly opened townships, such as Bastard, Percy, and South Gower, at least in the first decade of settlement, were being populated more by young families than by single men – recalling the "daughter colonies" that had characterized the early dispersion of the New England settlements. In general in eastern Upper Canada, however, single men living by themselves were common. This caused a lowering of the size of average household and family. Even in the well-established Adolphustown in 1794, the average household was only 4.96 persons. As Norris (1980) documents in his multi-faceted study of the township's demography, that average gradually increased over the next 15 years to more than seven. The truly frontier townships actually had a slightly higher early average, in the range of 5 to 5.5, but the mode (approximately four persons) was the moderate-sized young family.

A heavy predominance of men, and especially the surplus of single men, certainly helped to stimulate the transiency that was ubiquitous on the frontier, although even having a family and owning property did little to moderate the rate of movement (e.g., Curti 1959, 65). The number of spare men had a powerful effect on the institution of marriage. In fact, a single woman of marriageable age was rare. The rush to family formation was reflected in the early average age of mothers at the birth of their first child. Data from two townships in the first decade of the nineteenth century indicate that about half the women had their first child before they reached twenty years of age.[9] The most common spacing between the ages of the half dozen

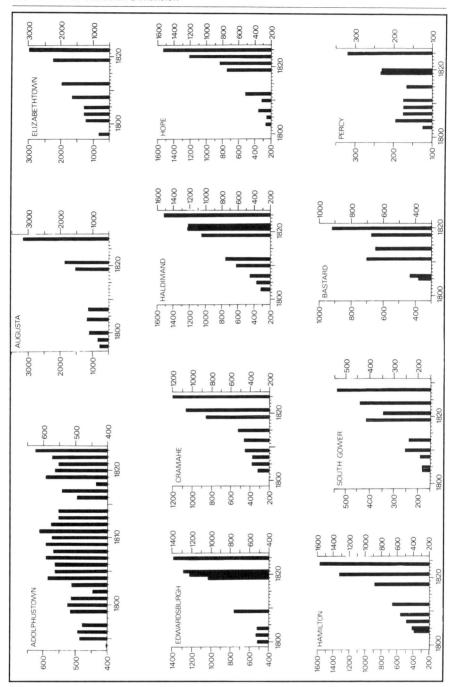

Figure 5.12 **Early Population Totals for Frontier Townships, Eastern Ontario, ca. 1800**

Source: Township clerk's reports in Municipal Records, RG 21, Archives of Ontario

or more children in a family was just under two years. It was not unusual for a township to double its population in 10 to 15 years, much of it through natural increase. It should not be surprising, therefore, to find that the population pyramids for the selected early townships are close to that of a classic young population. They are dominated by an extremely wide base (see Figure 5.13). In the townships of the sample, children (under 16 years of age) accounted for between 52 and 61 percent of the population in the decade centred on the year 1800. (For a complementary discussion see Wood 1988.)

5.4.2   The Home District, 1840s

The Home District was not one of the gateways to Upper Canada, nor was it settled in the first decade of the loyalist influx. But, as its name suggests, it was intended to play a significant role in the development of the province. In the great arch of southern Ontario the Home District, both in location and in function, was to be the keystone. After Simcoe decided in 1793 to make Toronto the provincial capital, people began to trickle in; but even by 1799 the district was said to have contained only 224 souls (presumably not counting migratory Amerindians) (Martin 1967, 189).

The physiography of the Home District modified the distribution and indirectly the composition of the population. The district, which was divested of the Simcoe portion in 1845, was a sector stretching from the Lake Ontario shore up an agriculturally rich incline to a huge morainic ridge across King and Whitchurch townships, then sloping from the ridge northward to the basin of Lake Simcoe and across a complex of deep glacial deposits and troughs to the shore of Georgian Bay. The whole area had been covered heavily by forest, which gradually disappeared as settlement pushed north on Yonge Street and other north-south and intersecting roads. There was little settlement to speak of as far north as Lake Simcoe until the late 1840s, and even in the mid-1840s there was a great deal of unoccupied land in the three northern and western tiers of townships.

By the 1840s the Home District was aspiring to its expected status, having become the most populous district by 1832, with a total European stock of 40,650 (nearly double that of 1827). Despite a rebellion that agitated the province in 1837–38, the Home District recovered quickly and launched into a period of development in concert with its spectacularly growing city. By 1842 the district had a population of about 57,000, while Toronto had an additional 15,336.[10] According to the census of 1848 the district's population had skyrocketed to 84,312, and Toronto's to 23,503. It is apparent simply from these gross population figures that this central sector of the province was a focus of massive change. It was an arena of the main dynamics of New World settlement. A partial census dating from 1842 and an almost complete census from 1851–52 provide a statistical frame for the 1840s.[11]

It is notable that the ratio of male to female adults in the Home District of the 1840s was, at least on average, rather close to that of the truly frontier townships at the beginning of the century. In 1842 most of the townships beyond those along the lakeshore or Yonge Street had a ratio greater than 120 adult males to 100 adult females (adulthood beginning at 14 years for this census only; otherwise at 16 years).

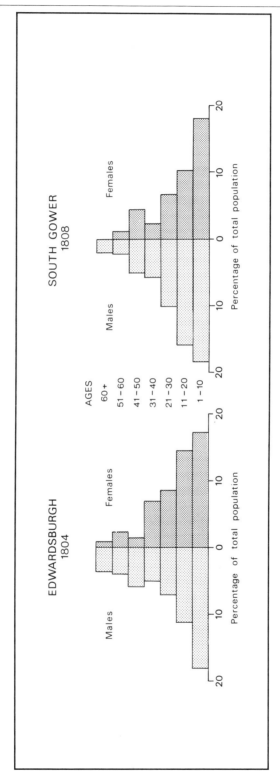

Figure 5.13 **Population Pyramids: Edwardsburgh Township, 1804, and South Gower Township, 1808**

Source: RG 21, Archives of Ontario (calculated P. Orr)

This seems to have been maintained through the 1840s, at least outside Toronto, judging by a partial census of 1848. By 1851, however, only a third of the townships, scattered across the district, had a ratio over 120:100. The numbers of men and women had begun to even out, most noticeably in eight townships beyond the moraine ridge, which had all registered over 140:100 in 1842 but in 1851 were all below that figure, four of them even below 120:100. There was a contrast in conditions between "front" and "back" townships; that is, between those in the well-developed areas along the lakeshore and fronting on Yonge Street and those on or north of the great moraine barrier. The back townships underwent slower improvement because of location and variable land quality, and also experienced a renewed *Irish* frontier in the late 1840s (discussed later in this section).

Around 1840 Upper Canada was registering a remarkably high birth rate, according to Henripin's (1972, 366) calculations. It appears that in the 1830s the surplus of births over deaths was accounting for about 60 percent of the increase in Upper Canada. Therefore, the youthful portion of the population was relatively large, as it had been in the frontier townships. The Home District was partaking fully of this "population explosion." In Vaughan Township in 1842, children under 16 years of age accounted for 52 percent of the population, which was in the range of the settlements of 40 years before. For the whole Home District that year, including the city of Toronto, the proportion was slightly over 50 percent. It seems that the rural populations, in general, were almost as bottom heavy as the populations of the frontier townships had been: the southern half, later to become York County, averaged 51.7 percent children in 1841, while the northern half, called Simcoe, averaged 53 percent.[12] The average size of a Home District household, which could embrace farm labourers, domestics, young relatives, or boarders in addition to the nuclear family, was 5.9 persons in 1842.

Throughout Upper Canada the population prior to the War of 1812 had been predominantly American. The Home District, however, had a strong infusion of British-born settlers because of its role as the administrative hub. The district went through its most significant growth in the late 1820s to about 1835, and again in the 1840s. The growth was a product of natural increase and British immigration, so that by the 1840s the adult population was heavily British, and in some townships predominantly so. In 1842 persons of British birth accounted for 38 percent, and in 1851 42 percent, of the total population. But a closer look at the data reveals important distinctions within the British population. The Irish, with no separation between northern and southern, were the largest component under the British label (in 1842 40.7 percent, and in 1851 51.6 percent of the British-born), and there were townships where Irish-born settlers must have accounted for the majority of adults. These were usually the less accessible areas, into which the Irish flooded particularly in the late 1840s. By 1851 they represented the majority of British in a solid band of townships from immediately west of Toronto north to Georgian Bay (Wood 1975). The English and the Scots were more evenly distributed across the region, though the English, almost everywhere, were more numerous than the Scots. The main change between 1842 and 1851 was the dramatic increase in the Irish after 1846.

The very large proportion of British-born settlers in the population draws attention to the massive migration that brought it about. The Home District of the 1840s was a creation of the immigration, just as in the 1850s and 1860s it gradually became a re-creation of the railways. The migration was a profoundly complex process made up of a multitude of individual motives, needs, routes, and stages. The moves were not always westward, although that was the prevailing orientation. Quite often migrants travelled to and fro, sometimes retracing earlier paths. This was not always to higher status jobs, nor necessarily from rural to urban locations. The convoluted patterns of many migration paths in early Ontario may have had something to do with its peninsular nature, but it also raises the suspicion that, during the nineteenth century, migration in the New World was more complex than the simple westward flow that is commonly imagined.

5.4.3   The People of Hamilton – 1851 and 1950

In step with many other parts of the world, Ontario has been urbanizing rapidly. This process has involved the expansion of the influence of the cities and urban culture as well as the growth of the cities themselves. Since shortly after its founding in 1813, Hamilton has been one of the largest and most dynamic urban nuclei in Ontario. Its success, unlike most cities in the province, has been based on heavy industry. In the middle of the nineteenth century it was just beginning to fashion its industrial foundations, and in most ways it was like many competing, scrambling, lively Victorian cities: an "ambitious little city," as it called itself (Katz 1975, 1; Osborne 1975). Hamilton also was typical in having no clear grip on its future, despite the protestations of its boosters. Change and unpredictability were the order of the day at the inauguration of the railway era. Hamilton may be examined, however, to see how its population composition compares with that of the general Ontario milieu and, in brief, how its social geography survived a century of profound challenge and evolution.

There is a striking indication of the population flux in the male-female ratios around the middle of the century. For example, the figures for 1848 show Hamilton with a total of 5,360 males to 4,529 females (118:100), which was closely comparable with most rural districts in the province, while the older cities like Toronto and Kingston had the expected female predominance (95:100 and 92:100 respectively). Three years later, however, Hamilton exhibited equal numbers of males and females (7,059 and 7,053; but the *adult* ratio was 104:100), while Toronto was at 97:100, Kingston at 100:100, and the rapidly developing London maintained the same ratio as in 1848 (ca. 100, 100). If these figures can be believed, therefore, Hamilton's population swung from a composition in 1848 that was much like the early frontier townships, to one like the contemporary urban centres of 1851. Unlike in the frontier townships, it was unusual for a person in the city to live alone, boarding with a family being the common alternative (Katz 1975, 36).[13]

It is quite remarkable that, despite the exceptional fluidity of population in the New World during the nineteenth century, a number of demographic regularities appear. Hamilton was extraordinary, even for a young Canadian city, in the proportion of its population that came from overseas. In the pioneering analysis carried out by Katz and his research team, the proportions are highlighted: 29 percent were born in England and Wales, 18 percent in Scotland, 32 percent in Ireland, and 8 percent in the United States. Only 9 percent had been born in the province (p. 23). Ethnic differences certainly were noted in mid-century Hamilton, and a tendency for Scots to locate their residence away from Irish can be shown. A more persuasive observation is that the city was residentially mixed "despite some clustering and a modest tendency for the wealthy to live near the center of the city" (p. 23 and Appendix 1).

Related to the immigrant character of the city was a surprising amount of transiency, a characteristic deeply embedded in pioneering long before the 1850s. One expression of this is that about three-quarters of the living accommodations were rented (p. 25), which was certainly not what the mobile population in the frontier townships had been aiming for. Land *ownership* had been the goal of the rural settlers. In Hamilton, ownership of real estate was restricted to only a quarter of the population, and Katz found that about 88 percent of the wealth in property was held by 10 percent of the population, hardly frontier equality (p. 25). At the same time, it is somewhat surprising to find that between the censuses of 1851–52 and 1861 roughly 35 percent of the population remained in the city – a figure very close to that indicated above for rural townships in the Home District and other parts of the province at about that time (e.g., Gagan 1981, ch. 5).

Some other comparable features arise from the demography of the family. Hamilton was much closer to equality between the numbers of men and women in 1851, and the proportion of children, at 42 percent, was much smaller than it had been in the frontier townships. The average size of household (5.8 persons) was quite similar to that of an agricultural township into its second generation. The larger households in the city were usually those of the more affluent, although they were large because of employees and boarders rather than larger numbers of children (p. 34). Just as the well-to-do and poor were intermixed in Hamilton's residential blocks, so were the different sizes of household. Families, which averaged about 4.4 members, also varied throughout the city, with differences related more to occupational type and ethnic background than to location. Katz found that many characteristics of household and family were strikingly similar to those of contemporaneous populations in England and even an eclectic selection of earlier populations. Almost 80 percent of households were composed of a simple nuclear family (pp. 34–41, 219–25).

Hamilton in the early 1850s was a paradox on a number of counts. It was still essentially a pedestrian city, although it had an emerging central business district. Also, it had wealthy residents close to the core, as well as some of its poorest, just as it had wealthy and poor on its fringes. Hamilton presented, to the frustration of scholars, "an imperfect fit between the arrangement of people in geographical and social space" (p. 342). It is probably appropriate to think of Hamilton at this time as having been *geographically in transition*, particularly transition to the railway era. It was common for towns in Ontario to begin a metamorphosis in central land use in

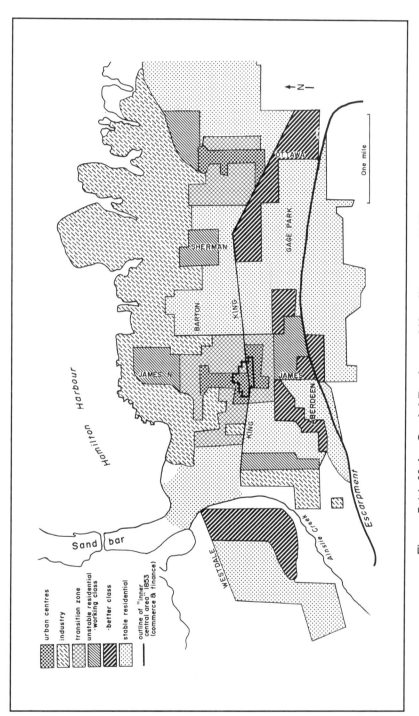

Figure 5.14 **Major Social Regions of Hamilton, ca. 1950**
Sources: Watson 1951; Davey and Doucet in Katz 1975, Appendix 1

anticipation of the coming of a railway line. In more general terms, the city was a paradox in Katz's judgment because it embraced at one and the same time "the rigidity of its social, economic, and demographic structures with . . . immense transiency . . . and . . . fluid experience of its . . . people" (pp. 14–15). On its unique small stage were played out the two great themes of nineteenth-century urban history: transiency and inequality (p. 17).

In 1950, Hamilton had solidified many of its functions and land uses, and thereby its social geography. It was now by no means a pedestrian city. It had produced, according to Watson's (1951) analysis, two important business districts, one of which had been identifiable in the 1850s.[14] It had grown to 175,000 people, and had carved out a large hinterland to the west and south. It had become the most highly industrialized city in Canada. Its well-to-do no longer resided around the central business district but on the topographically attractive fringes. But, more important to the social geographer, the social distance between the industrial owners/ managers and the workers was exaggerated by the relative deficiency of middle-class business and professional groups. In terms of the fabric of the city, instability was displayed by large transition zones and "shatter belts" of changing real estate under compression by expanding industry and other businesses (see Figure 5.14).

Watson observed that although the bulk of the population lived north and east of the city centre, the social facilities to serve that population were seriously deficient. Reminiscent of the 1850s is the claim that a large proportion of the population crowding into Hamilton in the 1950s was "foreign born, poor, and with a limited education" (p. 493). The reception areas were close to the city centre and the lower-paid industrial jobs that such immigrants were forced to take. For most of them, Hamilton was still perforce a pedestrian city. By studying the case loads of a variety of social agencies, Watson discovered a marked discontinuity between the number of cases and the provision of facilities that would be expected to ameliorate problems. The institutions vacated the shatter belts and the unstable working-class residential areas, where Watson found "a remarkable concentration of unemployment, neglect, desertion, and delinquency . . . " (p. 495). Any institutions that remained within reach of the unstable residential areas, such as the fine old churches, the central library, and the Conservatory of Music, were "further away from [the nearby residents] socially than from the remotest suburbanites" (p. 492).

In 100 years Hamilton had been transformed into a major industrial city. Within the flux of the post–Second World War scene, certain population features had crystallized. Transiency was still going on apace, but residential intermixture was no longer accepted as normal. The centre of the city, too, was no longer residentially desirable, and some of the gracious structures of the 1850s were incongruities or downright problems in the 1950s. The population had gradually shifted outward by the familiar process of decay and leapfrogging, but ironically – as with Toronto, Detroit, and Chicago – not towards the waterfront, which was usurped by heavy industry representing a more formidable barrier even than the escarpment to the south. Like the largest of Ontario's cities, Hamilton had again become a mecca for migrants as it had been in the middle of the nineteenth century, thus reinstituting the demographic potpourri of an immigrant city. In 1986 Hamilton, with a population of 557,000 in its Census Metropolitan Area, was still an immigrant city, and it had not yet managed to reclaim much of its waterfront from heavy industry.

5.4.4   A Twentieth-Century Urbanized Population

From the time that Ontario became predominantly urban, it has continued to have the largest urban proportion of any of the provincial populations. The only provinces which approach Ontario in this respect are Quebec, Alberta, and British Columbia, with respectively 77.6, 77.2, and 78 percent of their population being urban in 1981, while Ontario had 81.7 percent. Ontario's urbanization proceeded rapidly, especially after the Second World War. In 1931 the percentage was 61.1, at a time when Canada as a whole was only 53.7 percent urban. By 1955 Ontario's population was three-quarters urban.

Ontario has followed a demographic course that has diverged in various ways from that of most other parts of Canada. Its urbanization has been one reflection of this. In overall growth the Ontario population has increased at times when Canada's in general has not. There have also been times when Ontario fell behind the national rate of growth, as Table 5.2a illustrates. Until the 1970s the cumulative total had been heavily in Ontario's favour. Between 1971 and 1981, however, although the total population of Canada increased by 12.9 percent, Ontario only added 12 percent. This retardation in Ontario was concurrent with the shift of large population increases to the western provinces. The Toronto CMA, as noted earlier, joined Ontario in being a net loser in terms of internal migration during this decade. The 1980s, however, showed a reversal of that loss, with Ontario and British Columbia being the only provinces to gain significantly from interprovincial migration.

Ontario has also stood out from most of the other provinces in the calculation of median age. A population with a median age below 30 years is considered to be young, and presumably growing rapidly through natural increase. Although Ontario is not young, neither is it the only part of Canada with a relatively old population. It has consistently stayed well above the median age figure for the rest of the country (as shown in Table 5.2b), and yet is still growing vigorously. The reasons for the higher median are a lower birth rate and a greater immigration, the latter having drawn primarily from the young and middle working ages (Kogler 1969, 5). Ontario's population has grown not from the bottom up but from the middle up.

Because Ontario contains 36.6 percent of the Canadian population (1990), its population pyramid is quite similar to that of the country as a whole. Yet, hidden by the similarity is another important contrast in composition. This is the foreign-born proportion which, as alluded to in the discussion of variables affecting population size, has been quite influential in certain periods. In the nineteenth century Ontario had by far the largest foreign-born population in Canada, and even in 1901, 46.3 percent of Canada's foreign-born were in Ontario. With the opening of the western interior this proportion was reduced, but after the Second World War it rose rapidly, until by 1971 it was up to 51.8 percent. This hundred-year high has been increased through immigrant influxes during the past two decades. Ontario has attained a

Table **Annual Increase in Population in Ontario and Canada, Selected**
5.2a **Years, 1942–68**

| | Average Annual Increase (%) | |
	Ontario	Canada
1942	2.5	0.7
1943	0.8	1.4
1946	2.3	1.6
1947	2.0	2.1
1948	2.4	2.1
1949	2.4	2.0
1950	2.1	1.9
1951	2.8	1.8
1952	4.1	2.8
1953	3.2	2.4
1954	3.5	2.7
1955	3.0	2.6
1960	2.4	2.1
1961	2.0	2.1
1962	1.8	1.9
1963	2.0	1.8
1964	2.3	1.7
1968	2.1	1.4

Source: Kogler 1969, 17

Table **Median Age of Population for Ontario and Canada, 1901–81**
5.2b

| | MEDIAN AGE (Years) | |
	Ontario	*Canada (excl. Ontario)*
1901	24.1	21.9
1911	25.8	22.8
1921	26.8	22.5
1931	27.8	23.5
1941	29.9	25.7
1951	30.1	26.5
1961	28.4	25.2
1976	28.6	c.26.9
1981	30.0	29.0

Sources: Kogler 1969, 5; *Census of Canada, 1976*; data for 1981
from sample survey by Institute for Social Research, York University

primacy reminiscent of its status in the middle of the nineteenth century, but in a much larger arena. The foreign-born, however, have not formed as large a part of Ontario's population in relative terms as of other less populous provinces, especially those in the West. In 1931, foreign-born residents made up 23.4 percent of Ontario's population of 3.4 million, whereas they made up nearly 24 percent of 8.6 million in 1981. In the past four decades Ontario has attracted the largest numbers of immigrants; for example, in 1981 Ontario was the intended destination of 43 percent (54,890) of new immigrants, more than twice as many as any other province (see Figure 5.15), while in 1989 more than half the 192,000 immigrants were heading for Ontario.

In the past century Canada has gradually changed from having a majority of males to a majority of females. Ontario has moved even further in this direction. It provides a striking reversal of the demography of the early generations when, for instance, in the 1840s there were approximately 114 males for each 100 females. By 1981 that ratio had become 97.8:100, which a century ago would have been characteristic only of Ontario's largest urban centres. Immigration is reinforcing this transition because in recent years a majority of immigrants have been female (Statistics Canada 1984, 116).

Ontario's urbanized population has moved a long way in its occupational structure from its totally agricultural predecessor of the early nineteenth century. There has been a plummetting of employment in all primary activities except mining but, on the other hand, a spectacular rise in employment in the service sector and, especially since the 1950s, of women in the workforce. By far the largest single occupational category in 1981 was "clerical." The main sectors, of 23 ranked according to "employment by industry," are "Service" (communities, business, and personal) at 27.9 percent, "Trade" (16.3 percent), "Public Administration" (6.9 percent), and "Finance, Insurance, Real Estate" (5.9 percent). In the decade 1971 to 1981, these were the only sectors to register significant growth (Ontario Task Force 1985).

5.5   Population as a Key to the Social Geography of Ontario

The argument that population is the fundamental grist for the geographer's mill is an old one. Certainly the presentation and manipulation of the population characteristics of Ontario provide most of the basic ingredients for a social geography. This final section will sketch a possible framework for a social geography of Ontario.

5.5.1   Shifting Densities

In the 1780s Ontario was at the end of the most remote branch of the imperial system in central North America. The settlers in what was then western Quebec were only tenuously linked with the outside world. The main areas of settlement straddled the central line of the St. Lawrence River system, because people were uncertain about where the international boundary line would eventually be drawn, and uncertain to which stretch of new territory they should attach themselves. There was only a tentative lapping of settlement onto the northern flanks of the basin,

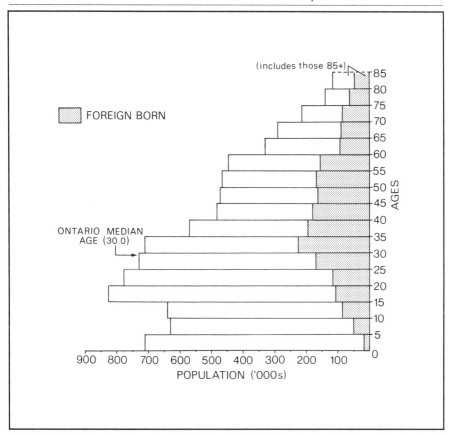

Figure 5.15 **Foreign-born Population and Total Population in Ontario by Age Groups, 1981**

Sources: *Census of Canada, 1981* and (for data on foreign-born) sample run by Institute for Social Research, York University, from Statistics Canada computer tapes

through the three portals. What has happened in the intervening two centuries has been a gradual occupation of peninsular Ontario, proceeding generally from east to west, at least until the Lake Huron shore was reached about 1850. The heaviest concentrations of population have migrated from around the initial entry points to locations more closely related to Simcoe's system of roads and administrative centres, leaving a pattern almost the reverse of that of 1785.

Another fundamental development was Ontario's move from the end of the road in the Empire to being an important crossroads for an evolving Canada in the mid-nineteenth century, to serve, indeed, as its "field headquarters." In current terminology, southern Ontario has shifted from periphery to core. From being prized out of wild Indian Territory in the 1780s, it metamorphosed into the most vital part of

Canada's Heartland, and the most heavily populated.

5.5.2   Some Components and Trends

Certain characteristics need to be noted in summation. The celebrated numerical predominance of males over females, especially among adults, which seems to have been characteristic of a new country, has now gone; Ontario in the 1990s has a slight overall predominance of females. Demographically Ontario is becoming an old country.

This raises the subject of the ageing of the Ontario population. From the early situation, where over half the population were children, there has been a gradual, though not continuous, lessening of this proportion, so that currently children less than 16 years of age account for just under 25 percent of the population. At the same time there has been an increase in the proportion of people over 65 years of age, so that policy discussions are now held concerning the ageing of the population and its implications.

The most spectacular trend in Ontario's population history has been the relentless urbanization. From being a totally rural society in 1790, with nothing more urban than three or four villages clustered around defensive sites, Ontario has steadily become more and more urban. Today over 80 percent of the province's population is reckoned to be urban, with just under 35 percent embraced by the Toronto CMA alone. It is this highly urban character that makes Yeates's term, "Main Street," so appropriate. Hardly any corner of southern Ontario is far off Main Street, and thus hardly any corner escapes the urban culture and pressures that can now be communicated almost instantaneously through the telephone network, television satellite dishes, powerful radio transmissions, and other modern media.

The variable flows of migration have formed a major undercurrent in the story of Ontario's population. Initially, Ontario was the terminus for large numbers of migrants, but from the 1840s it has also served as a way-station for opportunity seekers who have moved on to the United States or Western Canada or elsewhere. With changes in conditions in Ontario, the number of migrants coming and the number staying has fluctuated. Along with the other expressions of transiency, this has been profoundly important in population change and, except for the last 45 years of the nineteenth century, the ups and downs of net migration have tended to go hand in hand with the modulations in the overall rate of growth. A significant modification in the composition of the immigration has occurred in the past 30 years, with first a major increase in immigrants from southern Europe and, more recently, a notable increase in immigrants from Asia. This has accompanied a relative decrease in the traditionally overwhelming proportion from the British Isles.

The celebrated demographic transition of the industrialized world is usually presumed to have occurred in Canada. But a serious student finds it rather difficult to track. Taking Ontario as an example, it is apparent that the transition did not start with the classic initial condition. It was a society prematurely interrupted by the American Revolution and, whether or not it had been at some point in the demographic transition, the new beginnings in the wilderness of Upper Canada were a potpourri of stages. Upper Canada did not start with high birth and death rates, although once the loyalists got established, high birth rates reflected their optimism. Also, Ontario had a kind of second round of very high birth rates, accompanying the large overseas immigrations from the 1820s to the 1840s, although the death rates probably did not approach those of a truly pre-industrial peasant society. At what point did Ontario slide into the demographic transition? The truth of the matter is that the concept is too inflexible and its terminology too inadequate to account for the gamut of population origins and dynamics found on New World frontiers. It is often conceded that Ontario went through a different kind of demographic transition than did the Old World. Transition it was, certainly, but that is a natural process in all populations. What will help us distinguish common and unique characteristics are detailed studies like the one initiated in this essay.

5.5.3   Persistent Structures
5.5.3.1 A View of Main Street
There are certain patterns in the population geography of Ontario which, while different from the original tentative incursions, have been in place long enough to be termed persistent. The most readily apparent is the one named "Main Street." It has been developing for more than 180 years, but it has been given new emphasis in the past couple of decades by the construction of a major artery that links it from end to end; the Macdonald-Cartier Freeway. This artery has simply expedited the form of circulation that has played the most consequential role, namely the motor vehicle. There is now multifaceted reinforcement, of course, by electronic media and other less visible systems that have effectively undermined the traditional distinction between urban and rural. A good social geography of Ontario would reveal the many ramifications of Main Street. One illustration of its influence, on population density, can be seen in Figure 5.10.

5.5.3.2 Whebell's Corridors
An elaboration and precursor of the Main Street model is found in Whebell's (1969) description of corridors as the most effective form of urban-based development in new agricultural territories. Whebell advanced the argument that an influential plan like that of Simcoe would be reiterated and strengthened through the usual progression of settlement innovations: "the pattern of New World settlement was essentially set . . . before the major innovations in transportation . . . [The] location and spacing of major urban centers . . . derived from earlier periods" (Whebell 1969, 3).

Whebell takes southern Ontario as the case study of New World settlement to illustrate his theory. He displays five stages which, while progressing, intermingle through time. Moving from subsistence, the following stages are characterized in turn by powerful participants in settlement change: commercial agriculture, and its need for markets; railways; motor roads, which add flexibility but tend to reinforce the hierarchy built by the railways; and divided super-highways, which complete the domination by the largest cities. In Ontario these embraced the period from the early nineteenth century to the middle of the twentieth century.

The significance of Whebell's theory for our purposes lies in its focus on an initial, choice site – a point or zone of "contagion" from the Old World – with good accessibility to an interior territory, and on the persistence of the centres and facilities that had a head-start or "pre-emption" (Freeman 1985). The corridors that Whebell believes have been entrenched in the social landscape, as well as on the ground, are illustrated in Figure 5.16. These corridors are composed of transportation facilities linking major towns and cities. The social importance comes from the corridors serving as routes of innovation, thus leading to contrasts from place to place with "a degree of regularity termed 'culture gradient,' which extends downwards along the corridor from the senior town most accessible, historically, to Europe. Secondary diffusion takes place laterally from the corridor into areas between or away from corridors" (Whebell 1969, 4). Some of the corridors in Ontario, such as the Air Line, Sagamo, and Grenville, were established by railways, but in all cases they are paralleled by important roads. The Conestogo and Dundas are now almost indistinguishable because a super-highway is routed between them. Some, like the Egremont and the Upper Ottawa Valley, are secondary appendages. All these corridors, it should be noted, reveal their presence fairly distinctly in the population densities of Main Street (see Figure 5.10).

5.5.3.3 **A House Divided**

The first four decades of agricultural settlement in Ontario were encouraged for the purpose of establishing a non-republican going concern. The antipathy towards the neighbour to the south was kept fresh through a variety of antagonistic manoeuvres and altercations. During the 1780s and 1790s British influence was confronted and gradually pushed north across the St. Lawrence basin, and the forts on the south side were given up in 1796. The War of 1812 reopened many old wounds and inspired the British to considerably strengthen their fortifications, including the monumental Rideau Canal construction to provide a defensible route north of the St. Lawrence. The building of the Welland Canal, at the end of the 1820s, was an attempt to neutralize the economic aggression that had been greatly stimulated by the building of the Erie Canal through New York state. These efforts, among others, have become part of the Ontario experience and have provided a settlement structure that might not have been predicted given the physiography of the basin.

The St. Lawrence basin, in effect, has been bifurcated. There is one St. Lawrence for Ontario and another for the United States. It has not fostered the heavy population concentration that one might expect of such a great routeway, notwithstanding the important transportation lines traversing the north side. The centres of economic power have been peripheral to it. Only recently has the river, as the St. Lawrence Seaway, become the major water link from the interior to the Atlantic Ocean, superseding the Erie Canal. The valley of the upper St. Lawrence, which Watson (1963, ch. 8) described as a "zone of divergence," in this sense, though it was at odds with the natural system of the river basin, has had an impact on the social geography. It is largely because there was no unified development of the basin that there is an

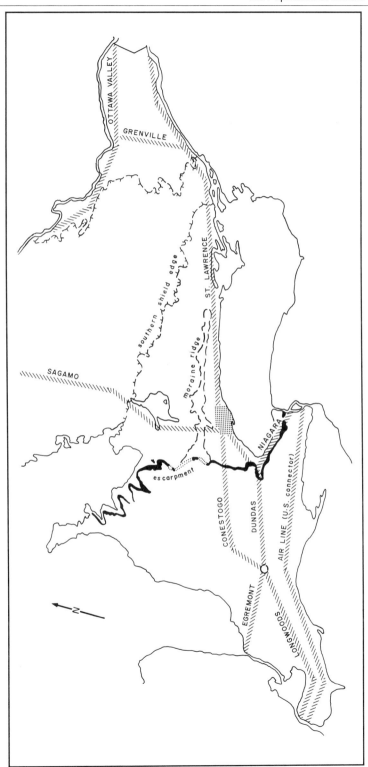

Figure 5.16 **The Corridors of Settlement in Southern Ontario**
Source: Whebell 1969, Figure 6

independent structure on the Ontario side which forms Main Street. The divergence was reinforced by the railway network, after the era of the Rideau Canal, and later by major highways.

5.6   Conclusion

Population is not the whole of social geography. Watson's (1951, 482–84) conceptualization of social geography also included the examination of rural and urban settlement forms, social groups, and social institutions and their functions, the analysis of all of which was dedicated to the differentiation of the earth's regions. But, in social geography probably more than any other branch of geography, Hooson's (1960, 16–17) insistence on population as foundation has had a sympathetic reception: "The distribution of population is the key to the whole geographical personality of a region [because] *ideas about place* come closer to the heart of our subject matter than place itself, and find their cumulative reflection in the distribution of population."

The story of Ontario has been that of the much-vaunted palimpsest; it was transformed from a wilderness tramped by a few hundred transient Amerindians into a heavily populated scene of industry and commerce 200 years later. The contagion that brought this to pass consisted of relatively small infusions of people, first from within North America and later via a trans-Atlantic routeway, reinforced by an impressive reproductive vigour that lasted for over a century. This population filed into the rural and urban settlements, cultivated and enhanced living conditions through a great variety of social groups, and regularized its society and environment by establishing social institutions. The population was not the whole story, but it was certainly the foundation.

Acknowledgements

I am grateful to the Institute for Behavioural (now Social) Research at York University, and its Director, Dr. Gordon Darroch, for a research fellowship in 1984 under which much of the groundwork for this essay was done. I have also benefited from perceptive reading of the work by Eric Winter and Brian Osborne, and from discussions with John Warkentin. The cartography was ably executed by Janet Allin.

Notes

1. The name first given, when Quebec was subdivided in 1791, was Upper Canada; in 1840 the name became Canada West, then Ontario in 1867.
2. Simcoe to Sir Joseph Banks, Pres. Royal Society, 8 January 1791. In Cruikshank 1923, vol. 1, 18.

3. From the *Report of the Royal Commission on Bilingualism and Biculturalism* in Palmer 1975, 13.

4. In its usage in Ontario, a township is a block of land much smaller than a county, divided into rows of rectangular farm lots usually of 40.5 or 81 hectares each. This does not apply to a purely urban development, in which case the term "town" is used.

5. Ontario Department of Agriculture, *Appendix to the Report of the Ontario Bureau of Industries, 1897* (Toronto: Government of Ontario, 1899), particularly 27–50. These figures, along with all the early figures, especially prior to the 1861 census, must only be accepted with caution.

6. The 1803 data for Percy are gathered from the Municipal Records (RG 21) at the Archives of Ontario. All the data for 1805 in this essay come from the National Archives of Canada, RG 5 B 26, vol. 1.

7. Based on figures in *The Canadian Almanac and Directory, 1984*, and *The Canadian World Almanac . . . 1991*.

8. For example, Assessment records for Grimsby Township, in RG 21, Archives of Ontario, reveal a 40 percent loss from 1799 to 1806.

9. These calculations were executed in a course essay by my graduate student Ms Patricia Orr.

10. The available sources are equivocal; consider Smith 1846, 81; and *Census of Canada, 1871*, vol. 4, 135.

11. Careful analysis of returns from these censuses reveals inconsistencies and other deficiencies, especially for that of 1842, but the scarcity of alternative documentation legitimizes cautious use. There are no returns for the City of Toronto for 1851–52.

12. These calculations are based on tables in the *Census of Canada, 1871*, vol. 4.

13. Most of the following depiction of Hamilton in the mid-nineteenth century is based on Katz (1975), and reference to it is by page numbers in parentheses.

14. The page references which follow in parentheses are from Watson 1951.

References

Christopher, A.J. 1976. *Southern Africa*. Folkstone: Dawson.

Cruikshank, E.A., ed. 1923–31. *The Correspondence of Lieut. Governor John Graves Simcoe*. 5 vols. Toronto: Ontario Historical Society.

Curti, M. 1959, *The Making of an American Community: A Case Study of Democracy in a Frontier County*. Stanford: Stanford University Press.

Freeman, D.B. 1985. "The Importance of Being First: Preemption by Early Adopters of Farming Innovations in Kenya." *Annals of the Association of American Geographers* 75, 17–28.

Gagan, D. 1981. *Hopeful Travellers. Families, Land and Social Change in Mid-Victorian Peel County, Canada West*. Toronto: University of Toronto Press.

Gagan, D., and H. Mays. 1973. "Historical Demography and Canadian Social History: Families and Land in Peel County, Ontario." *Canadian Historical Review* 54: 27–47.

Gates, L. 1968. *Land Policies of Upper Canada*. Toronto: University of Toronto Press.

Henripin, J. 1972. *Trends and Factors of Fertility in Canada, A 1961 Census Monograph.* Ottawa: Dominion Bureau of Statistics.

Henripin, J., and Y. Peron. 1972. "The Demographic Transition of the Province of Quebec." In D.V. Glass and R. Revelle, eds. *Population and Social Change,* 213–32. London: Edward Arnold.

Hooson, D.J.M. 1960. "The Distribution of Population as the Essential Geographical Expression." *Canadian Geographer*, no. 17:10–19.

Innis, M.Q., ed. 1965. *The Diary of Mrs. Simcoe*. Toronto: Macmillan.

Kalbach, W., and W. McVey. 1979. *The Demographic Bases of Canadian Society.* 2d ed. Toronto: McGraw-Hill Ryerson.

Katz, M. 1975. *The People of Hamilton, Canada West. Family and Class in a Mid-nineteenth Century City.* Cambridge: Harvard University Press.

Kirk, D.W. 1949. "Southwestern Ontario. The Areal Pattern of Urban Settlements in 1850." Unpublished Ph.D thesis, Northwestern University.

Kogler, R. 1969. "An Analysis of Population Growth Trends in Ontario." *Ontario Economic Review* 7:4–17.

McCalla, D. 1983. "The 'Loyalist' Economy of Upper Canada, 1784–1806." *Histoire Sociale/ Social History* 14:279–304.

Macleod, B., C. Ivison, and N. Bidani. 1972. *Patterns and Trends in Ontario Population.* Toronto: Ontario Institute for Studies in Education.

Marshall, J.U., and W. R. Smith. 1978. "The Dynamics of Growth in a Regional Urban System: Southern Ontario, 1851–1971." *Canadian Geographer* 22:22–40.

Martin, R.M. 1967. *History of the Colonies of the British Empire ... From the Official Records of the Colonial Office.* 1843. Reprint. London: Dawsons of Pall.

Nader, G.A. 1975. *Cities of Canada.* Vol. 1, *Theoretical, Historical and Planning Perspectives*. Toronto: Macmillan.

Norris, D. 1980. "Household and Transiency in a Loyalist Township: The People of Adolphustown, 1784–1822." *Histoire Sociale/Social History* 13 (2): 399–415.

———. 1984. "Migration, Pioneer Settlement, and the Life Course: The First Families of an Ontario Township." In D. H. Akenson, ed., *Canadian Papers in Rural History,* vol. 4, 130–52.

Ontario Task Force on Employment and New Technology. 1985. *Occupational Employment Trends in Ontario, 1971–1981*. Toronto: Ontario Government.

Osborne, B.S. 1975. "Kingston in the Nineteenth Century: A Study in Urban Decline." In J.D. Wood, ed., *Perspectives on Landscape and Settlement in Nineteenth Century Ontario,* Carleton Library no. 91, 151–89. Toronto: McClelland and Stewart.

Palmer, H., ed. 1975. *Immigration and the Rise of Multiculturalism*. Toronto: Copp Clark.

Pyle, G.F. 1969. "The Diffusion of Cholera in the United States in the Nineteenth Century." *Geographical Analysis* 1:59–75.

Rodgers, J.D. 1911. *A Historical Geography of the British Colonies.* Vol. 5: *Canada.* Oxford: Clarendon Press.

Russwurm, L.H. 1970. *The Development of an Urban Corridor System: Toronto to Stratford Area,* 1941–1966. Toronto: Queen's Printer.

Simmons, J., and L.S. Bourne. 1984. "Recent Trends and Patterns in Canadian Settlement, 1976–1981." *Major Report, Centre for Urban and Community Studies, University of Toronto,* no. 23.

Skoda, L., and J. C. Robertson. 1972. "Isodemographic Map of Canada." Geographical Papers, Lands Directorate, Environment Canada, no. 50.

Smith, W.H. 1846. *Smith's Canadian Gazetteer.* Toronto: Rowsell.

Spelt, J. 1968. "Southern Ontario." In J. Warkentin, ed., *Canada. A Geographical Interpretation,* 334–95. Toronto: Methuen.

———. 1983. *Urban Development in Southcentral Ontario.* Carleton Library no. 57. Ottawa: Carleton University Press.

Statistics Canada. 1984. *Current Demographic Analysis.* Catalogue no. 91-209E. Ottawa: Statistics Canada.

Taylor, I.C. 1967. "Population Migration to and from Ontario." *Ontario Economic Review* 5 (7–8): 3–15.

Thistlethwaite, F. 1960. "Migration from Europe Overseas in the 19th and 20th Centuries." *Rapports, XIe Congress Internationale des Sciences Historiques* 5:32–60.

Watson, J.W. 1943. "Urban Development in the Niagara Peninsula." *Canadian Journal of Economics and Political Science* 9:463–86.

———. 1947. "Rural Depopulation in South-Western Ontario." *Annals of the Association of American Geographers* 37:145–54.

———. 1948. "The Influence of the Frontier on Niagara Settlement." *Geographical Review* 38:113–19.

———. 1951. "The Sociological Aspects of Geography." In G. Taylor, ed., *Geography in the Twentieth Century,* 463–99. London: Methuen.

———. 1963. *North America. Its Countries and Regions.* London: Longman Green.

Weir, T. 1968. "The People." In J. Warkentin, ed., *Canada: A Geographical Interpretation,* 137–76. Toronto: Methuen.

Whebell, C.F.J. 1969. "Corridors: A Theory of Urban Growth." *Annals of the Association of American Geographers* 59:1–26.

Wilson, B. 1981. *As She Began: An Illustrated Introduction to Loyalist Ontario.* Toronto: Dundurn.

Wood, J.D. 1975. "The Settlers and the Land: Pioneer Experience in the Home District." *Families* 14:108–25.

———. 1988. "The Population of an Agricultural Frontier: Upper Canada, 1796–1841." In R. Hall, W. Westfall, and L. MacDowell, eds., *Patterns of the Past: Interpreting Ontario's History.* Toronto: Dundurn.

Yeates, M.H. 1977. *Main Street: Windsor to Quebec City.* Toronto: Macmillan.

———. 1982. "The Industrial Heartland in Transition: Problems and Prospects of an Urbanized Region." In L.D. McCann, ed., *Heartland and Hinterland. A Geography of Canada,* 100–31. Scarborough: Prentice-Hall.

———. 1985. "Land in Canada's Urban Heart-land. "*Land Use in Canada.* Series no. 27. Ottawa: Lands Directorate, Environment Canada.

Part Two

The Urban Dynamic:
Social Geographies of Urban Canada

Introduction:
Urbanization and the Urban Dynamic

Guy M. Robinson

6.1　The Urban Image

One of Wreford Watson's main areas of interest was the image or character of urban North America. What were the features within the urban landscape that gave it a particular distinctiveness? What spatial arrangements of individual functions and land uses could be distinguished? How had these arrangements come into being? And how did the character of the city shape the lives of its inhabitants? Watson's early work concentrates upon those social processes that were socially organized or internal to the city, and deals with socio-cultural life in terms of the development of social groups, social customs, and cultural, religious, and ideological processes.

The micro-scale regionalization of the city was a key consideration in this type of urban study, with the internal structure of cities being outlined with respect to areal differentiation on the basis of socio-economic status and function. In his descriptions of the various "social areas" Watson portrays adverse societal features such as crime, poverty, and bad housing that were to become a focus of study for both geographers and sociologists: positivists, humanists, and Marxists alike. In terms of Dunleavy's (1982, 14) description of the development of urban studies, Watson's work can be categorized as forming part of the "central tradition" of the Chicago school, with the addition of both the geographer's interest in land use and spatial definitions and a socio-cultural interest reminiscent of some sociologists' community studies.

Another facet of Watson's interest in the urban geography of North America was the evolution of the urban system as a whole and, in particular, the role of the city in its regional context. Within the regional framework he adopted (e.g., Watson 1963, 1968a, 1968b), he was able to demonstrate the way in which Canada's urban system differs markedly from that of other countries. The most crucial factors contributing to this difference are the presence of the national boundary, the functional specialization of the regional economies, the vast distances between regions, the importance of both the natural resource base and recent public initiatives, and the lack of an endogenous, cumulative settlement pattern (Simmons and Bourne 1984, 49).

In the 1970s and 1980s these distinctive characteristics received considerable attention from both geographers and scholars in other disciplines, drawing attention to particular issues and problems facing this heavily urbanized country (e.g., Bourne et al. 1974; Gertler and Crowley 1977; Nader 1975; Simmons 1974, 1981; Stelter and Artibise 1986; Yeates 1985). In terms of the general structure of urban development in Canada, overviews have tended to emphasize the distinction between those urban centres within the core of "Main Street" consisting of southern Ontario/south-western Quebec, and the periphery comprising the rest of Canada (McCann 1982). Another crucial distinction was made between those centres at the top of the urban hierarchy, especially Montreal and Toronto, and those at a lower level (e.g., Simmons 1978). Of these two distinctions the former gives prominence to a lack of manufacturing in the periphery with the exception of primary processing. This in turn emphasizes the reliance of the peripheral urban centres upon world markets for their primary specialization, especially those producing iron ore, oil, pulp and paper, or wheat. In addition, the greater wealth generated within the core by the greater range of economic activities has produced a differentiation not completely offset by western Canada's oil revenues. When examining the urban hierarchy, critical distinctions arise relating to the benefits and diseconomies associated with extreme size. On the one hand there are the economies of scale: the flourishing tertiary and quaternary sectors, good access for the majority of the population to a wide range of services and utilities, and a diversity of employment opportunities, social contacts, and facilities for recreation. But set against this are the problems created by congestion: pollution, overcrowding, disparities between rich and poor, and a range and magnitude of social problems generally not experienced in smaller communities.

These distinctions mean that the image of the city held by both its residents and outsiders can be many-sided (e.g., Boissevain 1970; Klodawsky and Spector 1985; Watson 1977). The high degree of social variation, especially pronounced in the larger cities, is likely to colour the reaction of certain groups to the city and to urban living. One aspect of this image is examined by Collins (chapter 7), who presents the changing face of Canadian cities in terms of their dynamism and distinctiveness from their American counterparts (Goldberg and Mercer 1980; Mercer 1979; Mercer and Goldberg 1986). He points out that although many non-Canadians still think of the country in terms of wide open spaces, forests, prairies, and pioneering enterprise, for the majority of Canadians the realities of urban living shape their lives and the lineaments of their social geography. The dynamism of the cities and the increasing concentration of population in cities at the top of the urban hierarchy is attributed to the influx of people from rural areas and small towns, the receipt of immigrants from sources other than the traditional suppliers, and the higher birth rates associated with those immigrants.

Some of the main changes in the "cityscape" are considered by Collins together with the effects of redevelopment and changes in provision of urban transport. The chief impression conveyed is of the emergence of cityscapes closely resembling the Manhattan profile, with high-rise reflective glass towers dominating central business districts (CBDs). Banks, insurance companies, and major business groups have often competed with one another to erect bigger or more eye-catching buildings, a process that has been most apparent in the larger cities, but which has also taken place in smaller centres. This change has reflected the growth of the tertiary sector within the Canadian economy and the nature of competition within and between different elements of this sector. Some competition between cities has also contributed to the construction of new buildings with original designs, often built in the "grand manner," the fully enclosed sports stadia, large shopping malls, and the redevelopment of waterfrontages in Halifax, Montreal, Quebec City, Toronto, and Vancover (Holdsworth 1986).

Major retail complexes have also been a feature of this trend towards large-scale development. Many have been built as part of the growth of the suburbs, in the form of suburban or out-of-town shopping centres. However, one of the most well-known is the Eaton Centre in the heart of downtown Toronto, functioning as what Ilbery and Healey (1990, 260) describe as a "super-regional centre" with over 100,000 square metres of covered shopping space, over 100 individual units, and a range of facilities/ services in addition to retailing. Currently the world's largest such complex is the West Edmonton Mall, 9.5 kilometres west of Edmonton, described by Johnson (1987) as a "mega-regional centre." This has 480,000 square metres of gross leasable space, providing room for over 800 stores and over 100 restaurants. It covers 110 acres and is enclosed by a $950 million roof (Hopkins 1990). In addition, it has 19 theatres or cinemas, a hotel, a "fantasy land" amusement park, an ice rink, and a water park.

The dynamism reflected in the surge of new building since the early 1960s, has been accompanied by a changing concern for the way in which Canadian cities should appear. Alongside the influences of economic forces, there have been inputs from city fathers and the "urban gatekeepers" such as banks and building societies, which Collins illustrates with respect to the installation of public transport systems. The changing attitude of local government towards expressways in Toronto has had a significant effect upon the evolving urban morphology and, similarly, the particular option chosen with respect to public transport systems has influenced morphology in other major cities.

Onto the changing image of the built environment can be grafted the image left by inhabitants of that environment. In Canada, for much of the last one hundred years, those inhabitants have been primarily of either British or French descent. So, for example, the image of Toronto was largely of a rather staid city dominated by ex-British stock: something of a bridge between British and American urbanism. In the 1980s, though, Toronto is very much a multicultural North American city. A variety of ethnic groups are represented in the city, and in many cases they have created distinctive areas associated with ethnic churches, ethnic shops, and the clustering of households of ethnic groups in particular areas. Black, brown, yellow, and a variety of shades in between, have been added to the white of the Anglo-Saxon Protestant stock. Cultural and ethnic diversity has radically altered the social geography of Toronto, making it more akin to the type of social patterning associated with large cities in the United States. On a smaller scale the same sort of diversity is described by Isobel Carlyle (chapter 9) in connection with Winnipeg, and can be compared with the duality in Ottawa-Hull referred to by Taylor (chapter 8). Thus Part 2 of this book looks more closely at certain urban issues, taking up several of the themes pursued in Watson's own work: the changing image presented by the city, the development of distinctive "social areas," the growth of the suburbs, the territorial expansion of those cities at the top of the urban hierarchy, and the future of the city.

6.2   Urban Social Areas

Taylor (chapter 8) concentrates upon the spatial distribution of the two principal ethnic groups in Ottawa-Hull in terms of three socio-economic characteristics: language, education, and income. Utilizing computer cartography, he demonstrates both the high degree of spatial differentiation between British and French Canadians in Ottawa-Hull, and the changing nature of the distributions since 1951. The French Canadians remain concentrated in Hull and Vanier, but bilingualism has spread because this ability is so important in a city dominated in terms of employment by the demands of government service. Hence, the number of people speaking only French has dropped and, as this characteristic places people at an economic disadvantage, it tends to be associated with lower-income groups. Increasingly, these groups have become concentrated in those parts of Hull that do not supply workers to the high-rise federal government office complexes built since 1970 in downtown Hull. A similar correlation between education and income has been drawn, with a hint of the influence of increased ethnic diversity. Since the early 1960s, distinctive Italian and Chinese communities have developed and, more recently, a small cluster of Vietnamese immigrants has formed in an area of low-income housing in Hull. The Italian community became sufficiently well established by the early 1980s for some of them to move out of the initial reception area in which they had congregated.

The pattern followed by the Italian immigrants in Hull has been repeated by several of the groups living in Winnipeg, where there are several long-established ethnic communities as well as more recent immigrants. As Carlyle (chapter 9) describes, ethnic variety in the city is manifest in a wide array of religious establishments and retail outlets; and even banks and credit unions often have a specific ethnic connection. Indeed, the diversity in Winnipeg compares with that of Toronto where it has developed more recently. In Winnipeg the immigrants of the last two decades have been added to four major existing groups: the British, Ukrainian, German, and French, each with their own characteristic spatial distribution (see Artibise 1975; 1977).

Whereas Taylor uses computer cartography to portray distributions and to illustrate socio-economic differentiation, Carlyle uses indices of segregation, a measure first popularized by geographers and sociologists in the 1950s (e.g., Duncan and Duncan, 1955). The high index for the French Canadians in Winnipeg, clustered in St. Vital and St. Boniface, contrasts with the low index for those of British origin, who are distributed much more evenly throughout the city. The index for the Ukrainians, the second largest group after the British, suggests a certain degree of clustering, though not to the same extent as the French. The third largest group, the Germans, have tended to follow the classic pattern of dispersing into the general community after initial settlement in the poorer reception areas of central Winnipeg and the north end. Similar dispersion, associated with suburbanization and the acquisition of jobs commanding higher incomes, has been characteristic of the Scandinavians and Dutch. More recently arrived immigrants, such as the Italians, the Chinese, and other Asian groups, tend either to live in or near their original reception area or to retain close social links with other members of their own ethnic group (Davis and Krauter 1971; Kobayashi 1988).

This ethnic and cultural mosaic is examined by Carlyle in terms of the distinctive social areas of Winnipeg, recalling the type of regional differentiation portrayed by Watson for the Hamilton of the 1940s. The existence of Winnipeg's ethnic sectors testify to the continued operation of processes creating ethnic segregation, assisting or retarding assimilation and generally shaping the character of each distinctive part of the city (Driedger 1978; Rotoff et al. 1990). The ethnic dimension is an addition to the social distance that separates groups in less ethnically diverse Canadian cities, and it has given both Winnipeg and Toronto characteristics typical of many American cities, and yet with different ingredients: for example, French, Germans and Ukrainians instead of Hispanics and blacks (e.g., Breton et al.1990).

6.3   Suburbanization

Although the transformation of the downtown and inner suburbs has attracted much attention in the 1980s, most major Canadian cities have experienced the continuing growth of urban sprawl involving large-scale development of new residential properties and the quest for political control by big cities over adjacent small townships. Two aspects of this urban growth are considered in this essay: the improvement of residential accommodation by means of expanding domestic living space, and the territorial conflict between growing urban centres and the surrounding administrative units.

6.3.1   Enclosing and Improving

The two most dominant aspects of urban growth after 1945 have been the continued outward expansion of the urban area, and the more recent counter-developments of the improvement of inner-city areas as a means of offering an alternative to living in outer-suburban areas and commuting long distances to work. On the one hand, there is the operation of centrifugal forces pulling people away from the inner city and, on the other, there are centripetal forces bringing people back to the inner city, or at least making it easier for people to stay relatively close to the downtown through the provision of improved accommodation. This is not to say that the two sets of forces are in balance, because the continued loss of agricultural land to urban sprawl indicates that during the 1970s and 1980s physical expansion of the city has continued. People who have moved from inner suburbs to more spacious accommodation in the outer suburbs have often subsequently moved farther out to more desirable locations even more distant from the inner city, and increasingly to settlements beyond the confines of the principal urban area (e.g., Brunet 1980).

Alongside this process of suburbanization and the operation of centrifugal forces, Evenden (chapter 10) describes a process representing centripetal forces, namely domestic residential improvement and non-migration. The improvement he highlights is the expansion of domestic space by the building of some form of extension onto single-family, detached dwellings (see also Phipps 1983). Although this phenomenon of life in residential suburbs may be taken for granted, Evenden reveals that in his study area on Vancouver's north shore, the amount of extra living space created by such extensions added space equivalent to 20 percent of all space created in newly completed single-family dwellings in the early 1980s.

Evenden's study of this phenomenon examines the reasons behind the building of such home extensions, the characteristics of those involved, and the extent to which "staying and building" represents a direct alternative to moving to a larger property. In particular, he relates the construction of additional living space to the household life-cycle involving families with one or more children of school age. Other important factors revealed are the government programs offering favourable loans as a form of mortgage subsidy and subsidies on the costs of insulating houses. But such programs are transitory, and there appear to be more fundamental reasons for families to commit themselves to residing in a particular location. If the improvement is not performed to realize a profit by selling the property, then it usually results from a commitment to a particular school, and forms part of a consolidating process within the suburbs that Evenden refers to as "the landscape of residential enclosure."

Accompanying the growth of this landscape has been the emergence of what might be termed the "landscape of improvement." Indeed, to the other various social changes affecting Canadian cities in the 1980s, this one has received more attention from geographers. Usually referred to as the process of gentrification (London 1980), this phenomenon has been found throughout the developed world. Several distinctive features have characterized its appearance in Canadian cities, such as the "deconversion" of rooming houses in both Montreal and Toronto into single household dwellings, the development of instant Victoriana as in Bulwerk Village, Toronto, and the frequent association of gentrification with political conflict, though less so than in the United States where an ethnic factor has also been of great importance. In recent years three areas in Canadian cities have proved to be most susceptible to gentrification. These are the inner residential areas in close proximity to the downtown, especially those near the presence of an existing elite social group, such as the presence of the Inglewood condominiums in Hamilton; areas in close proximity to neighborhoods associated with a counter-culture or groups often set apart from the rest of society, such as homosexuals and political activists; and areas in close proximity to certain amenities, having ease of access to downtown retailing and services and a generally attractive environment, such as neighbourhoods with views of Vancouver Harbour or parks in Ottawa and Toronto.

Numerous factors have contributed to the emergence of this type of development as an important phenomenon in cities throughout North America, Western Europe, and Australasia. Different interpretations have been presented from a variety of perspectives (e.g., Jackson 1985; Ley 1986; Rose 1983; Smith, N., 1982; Smith, P.J., 1981), and attention has been focused especially upon community action, the role of institutions, and the extent of displacement involved. Ley (1984, 1986) cites four significant factors: demographic changes, the role of the housing market, the attractions of the inner city, and the nature of economic restructuring, primarily in service-oriented, white-collar regional centres. The key demographic change has been the movement of the "baby boom" generation into the housing market since the late 1960s. This generation has had smaller families and so, generally, has been more willing to take accommodation in the type of smaller dwelling found in the inner suburbs. Such areas have also been seen as an alternative to living in outer suburbs where inflated house prices have effectively excluded most first-time buyers. So, the inner suburbs can be seen as areas of second choice, supplying a demand for those unable to afford to purchase property elsewhere.

The inner city may also present many opportunities for renting properties, so that while some districts may become dominated by young, middle-class home-owners, others will be occupied by less wealthy groups renting their accommodations, such as students, artists, single-parent families, and young office-workers. This rented sector of housing has often been transformed in the 1970s and 1980s by developers taking advantage of low land values by buying up land and properties, and under-taking renovation and restoration, or wholesale rebuilding (Fincher 1984a), such as the Market Square development in Toronto. Economic restructuring has raised the demand for such accommodation near the CBD simply by increasing the number of workers in this part of the city. For example, in the 1960s and 1970s the amount of office space in downtown Toronto and downtown Vancouver tripled (Code 1983).

One key variable in the social differentiation of the suburbs is housing tenure. Both Evenden's study and much work on gentrification focus upon the owner-occupier side of the housing market. The work of Harris (1984) and Pratt (1986), the latter using a Vancouver case study, shows that home ownership offers access to capital gains and accumulation of wealth, with important connections existing between housing tenure, social class, and political attitudes. For example, the renters tended to be less conservative in their voting practices, and to be more supportive of strikes, protests, and social welfare provisions. From Pratt's study it appeared that associations between political attitudes and housing tenure occurred primarily among the skilled non-manual and lower-level managerial positions. The explanation for this may lie in different levels of union membership and hence variation in political awareness among classes. To this must be added the emergence of major housing problems, especially in the larger cities. For example, for Vancouver, Ley (1984) shows that as redevelopment has occurred in inner-city areas such as Kitsilano, working-class tenants have been displaced. Subsequently, despite city planning initiatives, many of these people have experienced the growing problem of being unable to afford new accommodation because of shortages of low-rent housing and their replacement with new property developments aimed at middle-class buyers. The result is the re-emergence of higher-class areas close to the CBD and more clearly defined high- and low-status sectors within the inner city (e.g., Harris 1986; Wolfe et al. 1980).

6.3.2   Urban Expansion and Local Government

The aspect of urban expansion investigated by Smith (chapter 11) is that of the development of urban morphology with respect to political control of territory by a developing metropolitan area. He focuses on two of the most rapidly growing major urban areas in Canada in the 1970s and 1980s: Calgary and Edmonton. In both cases rapid suburban development has not only brought about the growth of the built-up area but has also affected more outlying communities, which have become dormitory settlements while experiencing very rapid rates of population growth. Calgary and Edmonton have exercised their territorial claims within the same legal and administrative framework. But though both have pursued vigorous courses of territorial expansion, they have met with very different rates of success. Calgary has achieved a much more consolidated form than Edmonton, around which suburban municipalities have pursued their own territorial aspirations aimed at preserving local self-government. Smith examines these contrasting situations, dealing with their patterns of growth over time and the different effects of such factors as the growth of the oil industry, the emergence of new industrial nodes, the creation of new residential settlements beyond the confines of the metropolitan area, and the influence of a special royal commission on the development of the two cities. His conclusions are that, at the time when rapid suburbanization developed in the early 1960s, there were already several satellite communities around Edmonton, including the presence of the Strathcona industrial corridor, which actively resisted incorporation into the larger metropolis. With more rapid organic growth around Calgary, incorporation of suburban expansion was rendered easier, though various decisions by provincial authorities assisted this process. The resulting contrast between the two cities is shown by the figures for 1981 that 18 percent of the population within a 40-kilometre radius of central Edmonton lived outside the city's jurisdiction compared with just 2.6 percent for Calgary.

In terms of the development of communities the significant aspect of these different types of territorial development is in the control exerted over the type of growth allowed in particular localities. Around Edmonton, suburban communities have been able to organize themselves effectively, exhibiting a sense of belonging to a small municipality rather than a large metropolis. There seems to have been a case of communities expressing a wish to be "of the city but not in it," at least in jurisdictional terms.

Smith's study shows that municipalities are essentially "creatures of the provinces." They are subject to a variety of legislative, judicial, and administrative controls and are heavily dependent upon provincial and federal financial assistance. So it is important to recognize this political reality when considering conflict between different authorities. In terms of promoting land development, though, most city councils have more power and freedom of action, and this has been seen after 1945 in the encouragement of urban renewal schemes by municipal politicians who so often have had close ties to local business interests. In the 1970s this led to direct conflict between local governments on the one hand and urban citizens' movements on the other. Pressure for development encouraged the building of new expressways, demolition and renewal of old neighbourhoods and the creation of high-rise buildings in downtown areas. Although disputes were often taken to arbitrators such as the Alberta Local Authorities Board and the Ontario Municipal Board, the urban reforms of the 1970s swept away many old neighbourhoods and produced drastic changes in land use (Cullingworth 1984; Weaver 1976, 1977). However, the influence of community groups has been seen to have brought about a recent trend towards restoration rather than demolition and the challenging of developers' and planners' desires to focus upon the prominence of the automobile in their schemes (Artibise and Stelter 1979, 1982; Fincher 1984b; Simmons 1986; Villeneuve 1982).

6.4   Urban Futures

The continuation of urban expansion, as manifest in suburbanization and the spread of the commuter belt, is one of several themes taken up by Thraves (chapter 12), who summarizes several of the aspects of urban change considered in this part of the book. His summary takes the form of a view of urban Canada at the beginning of the next millenium. Geographers have not been noted for prospective studies, perhaps accepting that the myriad of influential variables impinging social and economic change cannot be analysed systematically, as is required for making accurate predictions. However, in this case the concern is with likely changes during just one decade, the 1990s, and with further elaboration of the trends in urban development covered in the other essays in this section. Three themes in particular are considered: the prospects for further urbanization and urban growth, the changing physical structure of Canada's cities, and the changing social structure.

In the first of these three themes the dominant post-war process of metropolitanization has been replaced by the relatively slow growth of the largest Census Metropolitan Areas (CMAs), and the more rapid expansion of smaller CMAs and non-metropolitan communities (see also Soroka 1987). This trend is likely to continue given the presence of certain diseconomies associated with the large CMAs, such as congestion, pollution, and the high costs of land, labour, and housing. To overcome these diseconomies "greenfield" sites for new industries have been adopted and metropolitan influence has been extended, facilitating longer range commuting and the growth of small- and medium-sized towns within the general vicinity of the metropolis. However, Thraves recognizes that these are regional differences in this process, especially apparent in the economic downturn in western Canada in the 1980s. Urban growth in this region has been particularly dependent upon the international markets because of the natural resource industries, and this is likely to continue for several years, raising doubts over prospects for sustained urban and economic growth. Similar doubts exist for the Maritimes, with their greater reliance upon government-related employment, and the influence of both federal and provincial programs to stimulate economic growth.

While, as Collins points out, a strong image of the Canadian city after 1945 has been its dynamism and growth, urban diseconomies are promoting new trends in urban growth similar to those found both in western Europe and the United States. The tendency for pronounced migration away from the central areas of the major cities has become apparent, with the receipt of immigrants balancing such an outflow only in certain cases. At a time of only slow population growth through an excess of births over deaths, this has highlighted the existence of many social and environmental problems in inner-city areas, and has been associated with major changes in the physical structures of cities: suburban sprawl, the suburbanization of retailing and industry, a question-mark over the future of downtown areas, and the pronounced separation of rich and poor. Despite the slow growth phase currently being experienced, Thraves believes that these trends will continue and so will exert continued pressure upon the small supplies of the most productive agricultural land. But trends towards redevelopment and gentrification of inner suburbs and the downtown may also be accentuated given sufficient capital to support urban renewal (e.g., Bourne 1978).

In terms of the changing social dimensions of the city, Thraves gives special attention to two particular groups: the elderly and new immigrants. Both are occupying a larger proportion of the Canadian population and both are associated with special problems requiring careful attention from federal and provincial governments. The rate of growth of the proportion of population 65 years of age and over has been reduced in Canada by the influx of new, young immigrants, but the concentration of the elderly in particular CMAs and parts of CMAs presents particular strains for the social services and public transportation, and for the declining proportion of working population having to provide the supporting tax-base. Again, the implication is that, given the uneven distribution of the elderly, such problems will tend to be focused upon particular areas, especially as there is a close relationship between the distribution of the elderly and low-income households. The division between prosperous outer suburbs, dominated by young, upwardly mobile families, and the more congested inner suburbs with high proportions of elderly or recently arrived immigrants, is likely to be reinforced. Of course, the simplicity of this pattern is destroyed by the return to the inner city of "high class" areas associated with redevelopment and gentrification.

The continuation of immigration from the Caribbean, Asia, and Latin America is likely to promote further diversification of the Canadian population. Especially in the largest cities, these immigrants are likely to contribute to more growth of distinctive ethnic "quarters" and to the development of multiculturalism. Thraves notes that such a process will further differentiate between the three main magnets for immigrants, Montreal, Toronto, and Vancouver, and other urban centres. Problems associated with high levels of segregation for certain new immigrant groups, and the low incomes associated with much of the employment they obtain, are likely to conflict with the ideals accorded multiculturalism and with concepts of social and economic equality for all immigrant groups (Calif 1978).

The trends highlighted by Thraves and the other contributors to Part 2 of this book suggest that, despite pervasive influences from the United States, Canadian urbanization and the character of Canadian cities are likely to retain a distinctiveness that reflects critical differences in the forces shaping the cities on either side of the border. Though it is difficult to make hard and fast distinctions between the influence of different value systems, in Canada greater collectivism, the prominence of public enterprise, provincial rather than federal interventions in urban planning, and perhaps greater acceptance of multiculturalism and of interpersonal differences are all promoting more positive attitudes to the city while not eliminating the forces that produce suburbanization and even de-urbanization.

References

Artibise, A.F.J. 1975. *Winnipeg: A Social History of Urban Growth.* Montreal: McGill-Queen's University Press.

——. 1977. *Winnipeg: An Illustrated History.* Toronto: James Lorimer & Co.

Artibise, A.F.J., and G.J. Stelter, eds. 1979. *The Usable Urban Past: Planning and Politics in the Modern Canadian City.* Toronto: Macmillan.

——, eds. 1982. *Shaping the Urban Landscape: Aspects of the Canadian City-Building Process.* Ottawa: Carleton University.

Boissevain, J. 1970. *The Italians of Montreal: Social Adjustment in a Plural Society.* Ottawa: Queen's Printer.

Bourne, L.S. 1978. "Perspectives on the Inner City: Its Changing Character, Reasons for Decline and Revival." Research Papers, Centre for Urban and Community Studies, University of Toronto, no. 94.

Bourne, L.S., et al. 1974. *Urban Futures for Central Canada: Perspectives on Forecasting Urban Growth and Form.* Toronto: University of Toronto Press.

Breton, R., W.W. Isajiw, W.E. Kalbach, and J.G. Reitz. 1990. *Ethnic Identity and Equality: Varieties of Experience in a Canadian City.* Toronto: University of Toronto.

Brunet, Y. 1980. "L'exode urbain, essai de classification de la population exurbain des cantons de l'est." *Canadian Geographer* 24:385–405.

Calif, N. 1978. *Multiculturalism and the Government of Canada.* Ottawa: Minister of Supply and Services.

Code, W.R. 1983. "The Strength of the Centre: Downtown Offices and Metropolitan Decentralisation Policy in Toronto." *Environment and Planning A* 15:1361–80.

Cullingworth, B. 1984. "Land Use Policy Issues in Canada." *Land Use Policy* 1:343–56.

Davis, M., and J.K. Krauter. 1971. *The Other Canadians.* Toronto: Methuen.

Driedger, L. 1978. *The Canadian Ethnic Mosaic.* Toronto: McClelland and Stewart.

Duncan, O.D., and B. Duncan. 1955. "Residential Distribution and Occupational Stratification." *American Journal of Sociology* 60:493–503.

Dunleavy, P. 1982. "Perspectives on Urban Studies." In A. Blowers, C. Brook, P. Dunleavy, and L. McDowell, eds., *Urban Change and Conflict: An Interdisciplinary Reader,* 1–16. London: Open University Press/Harper and Row.

Fincher, R. 1984a. "Identifying Class Struggle outside Commodity Production." *Environment and Planning D: Society and Space* 2:309–28.

——. 1984b. "The State Apparatus and the Commodification of Quebec's Housing Cooperatives." *Political Geography Quarterly* 3:127–43.

Gertler, L., and R. Crowley. 1977. *Changing Canadian Cities: The Next 25 Years.* Toronto: McClelland and Stewart.

Goldberg, M.A., and J. Mercer. 1980. "Canadian and United States Cities: Basic Difference, Possible Explanation and Their Meaning for Public Policy." *Papers, Regional Science Association* 45:159–83.

Harns, R. 1986. "Home Ownership and Class in Modern Canada." *International Journal of Urban and Regional Research* 10:67–86.

Harris, R. 1984. "Class and Housing Tenure in Modern Canada." Research Papers, Centre for Urban and Community Studies, University of Toronto, no. 153.

Healey, M.J., and B.W. Ilbery. 1990. *Location and Change: Perspectives on Economic Geography*. Oxford: Oxford University Press..

Holdsworth, D.W. 1986. "Architectural Expressions of the Canadian National State." *Canadian Geographer* 30:167–71.

Hopkins, J.S.P. 1990. "West Edmonton Mall: Landscape of Myths and Elsewhereness." *Canadian Geographer* 34:2–17.

Jackson, P. 1985. "Neighborhood Change in New York: The Loft Conversion Process." *Tijdschrift voor Economische en Sociale Geografie* 76:202–15.

Johnson, D.B. 1987. "The West Edmonton Mall – From Super-regional to Mega-regional Shopping Centre." *International Journal of Retailing* 2:53-69.

Klodawsky, F., and A. Spector. 1985. "Mother-Led Families and the Built Environment in Canada." *Women and Environments* 7:12–17.

Kobayashi, A., ed. 1988. "Asian Migration to Canada." *Canadian Geographer* 32:351–62.

Ley, D.F. 1984. "Inner City Revitalization in Canada: A Vancouver Case Study." In J.J. Palen and B. London, eds., *Gentrification, Displacement and Neighbourhood Revitalization*, 186–204. Albany: State University of New York Press.

———. 1986. "Alternative Explanations for Inner-City Gentrification: A Canadian Assessment." *Annals of the Association of American Geographers* 76:521–35 .

London, B. 1980. "Gentrification as Urban Reinvasion: Some Preliminary Definitional and Theoretical Considerations." In S.B. Leska and D. Spain, eds., *Back to the City*. New York: Pergamon Press.

McCann, L.D., ed. 1982. *Heartland and Hinterland, a Geography of Canada*. Scarborough: Prentice-Hall.

Mercer, J. 1979. "On Continentalism, Distinctiveness and Comparative Urban Geography: Canadian and American Cities." *Canadian Geographer* 23:119–39.

Mercer, J., and M.A. Goldberg. 1986. "Value Differences and Their Meaning for Urban Development in Canada and the United States." In G. J. Stelter and A.J.A. Artibise, eds., *Power and Place: Canadian Urban Development in the North American Context*, 343–94. Vancouver: University of British Columbia Press.

Nader, G.A. 1975. *Cities of Canada*. 2 vols. Toronto: Macmillan.

Phipps, A.G. 1983. "Housing Renovation by Recent Movers into the Core Neighbourhoods of Saskatoon." *Canadian Geographer* 27:240–62.

Pratt, G. 1986. "Housing Tenure and Social Cleavages in Urban Canada." *Annals of the Association of American Geographers* 76:366–80.

Rose, D. 1983. "Reconceptualizing Gentrification: Beyond the Uneven Development of Marxist Urban Theory." *Environment and Planning D – Society and Space* 2:47–74.

Rotoff, B., R. Yereniuk, and S. Hryniuk. 1990. *Monuments to Faith: Ukrainian Churches in Manitoba*. Winnipeg: University of Manitoba Press.

Simmons, J.W. 1974. "The Growth of the Canadian Urban System." Research Papers, Centre for Urban and Community Studies, University of Toronto, no. 65.

————. 1978. "The Organisation of the Canadian Urban System." In L.S. Bourne and J.W. Simmons, eds., *Systems of Cities: Readings on Structure, Growth and Policy*, 61–69. New York: Oxford University Press.

————. 1981. "The Impact of Government on the Canadian Urban System." Research Papers, Centre for Urban and Communities Studies, University of Toronto, no. 126.

————. 1986. "The Impact of the Public Sector on the Canadian Urban System." In G.J. Stelter, and A.F.J. Artibise, eds., *Power and Place: Canadian Urban Development in the North American Context*, 21–50. Vancouver: University of British Columbia Press.

Simmons, J.W., and L.S. Bourne. 1984. "The Canadian Urban System." In L.S. Bourne, R. Sinclair, and K. Dziewonski, eds., *Urbanization and Settlement Systems: International Perspectives*, 49–70. Oxford: Oxford University Press.

Smith, N. 1982. "Gentrification and Uneven Development." *Economic Geography* 58:139–55.

Smith, P.J. 1981. "Residential Land Use Change in Inner Edmonton." *Annals of the Association of American Geographers* 71:536–51.

Soroka, L.A. 1987. "Male/Female Income Distributions, City Size and Urban Characteristics: Canada, 1970–1980." *Urban Studies* 24:417–26.

Stelter, G.A., and A.J.F. Artibise, eds. 1986. *Power and Place: Canadian Urban Development in the North American Context*. Vancouver: University of British Columbia Press.

Villeneuve, P. 1982. "Changement social et pouvoir municipal à Québec." *Cahiers de géographie du Québec* 26:223–33.

Watson, J.W. 1963. *North America, Its Countries and Regions*. London: Longmans Green.

————. 1968a. *North America, Its Countries and Regions*. London: Longmans Green, 2nd edition.

————. 1968b. *Canada, Problems and Prospects*. Toronto: Longmans Canada.

————. 1977. "Images of Canada." *Bulletin of Canadian Studies* 1:1–15.

Weaver, J.C. 1976. "Approaches to the History of Urban Reform: Introduction." *Urban History Review*, no. 2 (1976): 3–11.

————. 1977. *Shaping the Canadian City*. Toronto: Institute of Public Administration of Canada.

Wolfe, J.M., G. Drover, and J. Skelton. 1980. "Inner-City Real Estate Activity in Montreal: Institutional Characteristics of Decline." *Canadian Geographer* 24:349–67.

Yeates, M.H. 1985. "Land in Canada's Urban Heartland." Land Use in Canada Series, Lands Directorate, Environment Canada, no. 27.

7   Canadian Cities: Recent Developments and the Changing Image

Lyndhurst Collins

Wreford Watson's concern with imagery in general (Watson 1967, 1970, 1971, 1977) and with Canada in particular (Watson 1950, 1956, 1962, 1968, 1972) has provided a broad research framework in connection with his promotion of Canadian studies both in the United Kingdom and in Canada. One of his main contributions in this respect has been the stimulation of a genuine interest in Canada in a wide-ranging audience. His success has been achieved, in part, by adopting an external viewpoint (e.g., Watson and Watson 1977) and by making international comparisons of spatial processes (Watson 1983). Within this context the aim of this chapter is to consider some of the recent developments that have taken place in many of the major Canadian cities, in order to explain the changing image of urban Canada. The reason for doing so is that a substantial body of literature has focused attention on the North American city (Yeates and Garner 1976) as a concept that exists both in the United States and Canada. Canadian cities have been described and analysed in detail (Nader 1975) as separate entities, but over the last ten years or so increasing attention has been devoted to identifying the distinctiveness of Canadian cities as compared to their American counterparts (Goldberg and Mercer 1980, 1986; Higbee 1976; Hodge 1971; Mercer 1979; Ray and Murdie 1972). It is suggested in this essay, that recent developments in Canadian cities have contributed quite significantly to creating this distinct image.

Today, Canadian cities are new, rapidly expanding, clean, and in some cases they have some of the most dramatic profiles that can be viewed anywhere. This is especially true of Toronto, which is dominated by the CN Communications Tower, claimed by Torontonians to be the world's tallest free-standing structure. Canadian cities exude dynamism, and this is partially a reflection of the rapidly changing ethnic composition of the cities, which have been greatly influenced since 1945 by major influxes of Italians, Greeks, Poles, Hungarians, West Indians, and, more recently, Asians. Canadian cities are now exciting places in which to live and, though not big by international standards, many of them provide sophisticated cultural and recreational facilities that would be the envy of many large cities in Europe.

For many Europeans, the dominant image of Canada is still one of a country involved in the production of primary goods such as lumber, grain, minerals, and, to a lesser extent, oil. The European image of the Canadian landscape is dominated by extensive prairie, limitless forests, barren rocky mountains, snow-covered wastelands, and innumerable lakes large and small, all of which provide the scene for rough outdoor living, isolation, and pioneering enterprise (Simmons and Simmons

1974). These are, of course, all part of Canada, and the search for the Canadian identity within Canada usually includes all these elements (Harris 1979). But most Canadians, over 80 percent of them, are concentrated in a relatively small number of cities located in a narrow strip, a few hundred kilometres wide, located along certain portions of the Canada-U.S. border. Despite its vast area and enormous natural resources, Canada is more urbanized today than many West European countries.

The rapid expansion of Canadian cities since 1945 contrasts sharply with the experience of most European cities, especially those in the United Kingdom. Although it is difficult to make accurate comparisons through time because of the changes in the definition of metropolitan boundaries, especially in Canada where the boundaries have been substantially extended to incorporate suburban and ex-urban developments, the trends are quite clear.

Canadian cities have experienced significant growth rates. The three largest cities more than doubled their populations between 1951 and 1981. Toronto almost trebled its size during this period and by 1976 replaced Montreal as Canada's largest metropolitan centre. Even the core cities of all the metropoli increased their populations between 1951 and 1971, which was also a period of massive suburban development. Other Canadian cities have undergone the same process, especially Calgary and Edmonton, both of which had the greatest increase in their populations between 1976 and 1981 at 26 percent and 17 percent respectively. The trend in the growth pattern has been the same for all Canadian cities (except Windsor in Ontario, which experienced a population decline); only the rate of change has varied over the country, the national average increase in population from 1976 to 1981 for the 70 largest urban centres being 5.6 percent.

These important and, in some cases, dramatic changes in the urbanization of Canada can be attributed to three main causes. First, the movement of population from small, rural settlements to bigger towns and cities has been substantial and fairly constant throughout the post-war period. Second, the largest Canadian cities in particular have been the destination of a very large flow of immigrants arriving from Europe, the Caribbean, and South-East Asia, who have tended to settle in well-defined ethnic areas in each of the different cities. Concentrations of immigrants in certain areas have been particularly noticeable among the Italians, Greeks, Portuguese and Chinese, though less obvious among the northern Europeans. Third, these immigrants, most of them young married couples, have generated a much higher birth rate than the average recorded for Canada as a whole.

7.1   Changes in the Urban Landscape

The urban growth that has been stimulated by these changes has had a fascinating and profound result on the landscape, which reflects the interplay of technological, economic, political, and social forces. Canadian cities stand as bold monuments not only to the enormous wealth of resources in Canada but also to the enterprise of its inhabitants. Against this background of general urban growth in Canada, the aim is now to look at the changes that have taken place and that continue to take place within some of the individual Canadian cities.

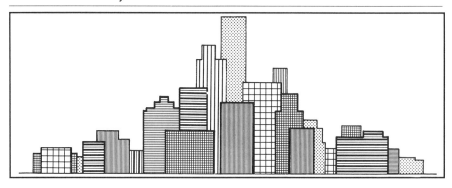

Figure 7.1   **Canadianville 1985**

In terms of physical appearance there is now a striking similarity in the central cores among all major Canadian cities; indeed, the appearance is common to most cities in North America (Goldberg and Mercer 1980). This similarity is most closely represented by their profiles, which have assumed the inverted cone or pyramidic shape. The apex is located at the heart of the downtown area or central business district (CBD), which tends to be the site of the tallest building or skyscraper. With increasing distance away from this point, buildings decrease in height. This classic profile, illustrated in Figure 7.1, can be explained in terms of land values and bid rents. In other words, the process of economic competition has created those buildings that now dominate Canadian cities. This is in sharp contrast to the cultural (religious) and institutional forces that initially created the dominant buildings in European cities, buildings that, in most cases, have remained dominant despite the appearance over the past two decades of high-rise office and apartment blocks. Spires, steeples, cathedrals, and castles still capture the eye from any vantage point overlooking many European cities. It is not possible with many European cities, to point from a distance outside the city, with any guiding principle, to that part of the city that contains the peak land value. In Canadian cities this. can be done with relative ease. The Manhattan profile of New York is now repeated on a lesser scale in Montreal, Ottawa, Toronto, Winnipeg, Edmonton, Calgary, and Vancouver.

The pyramid profiles of Toronto, Montreal, and Vancouver, begun during the 1960s, were the first to be established. Calgary's rapid vertical growth occurred in the early 1970s as a direct result of the Albertan oil developments. Edmonton, Saskatoon, Regina, Winnipeg, and Ottawa also experienced growth during this decade. Since 1980 Saint John, in New Brunswick, has been striving to change its old image, created by a skyline hitherto dominated by port facilities; its skyline is now dominated by modern, though modest, high-rise buildings. Farther east, Halifax is experiencing one of the most rapid developments, proportionately speaking, of all Canadian cities. Offshore oil developments, though now stalled, have changed Halifax in recent years just as Albertan oil changed Calgary 15 years ago. For the first time, Halifax is experiencing a period of significant growth without the aid of military conflict. The new, reflective-glass towers, containing banks, insurance companies, and related offices, have transformed the otherwise staid appearance of a garrison town, and have given Halifax the physical stamp of being the primary city of the Atlantic provinces.

One exception to these general trends is St. John's in Newfoundland. Despite the recent addition of Atlantic Place, a multi-storey building/mall with 20 shops and offices located at the centre of Water Street, the magnificent harbour setting of St. John's is still overshadowed by the Basilica of St. John the Baptist on the hill; the urban skyline remains low and uninterrupted by high-rise towers. St. John's, then, reputed to be the oldest city in North America, continues to be dominated by cultural rather than by commercial buildings.

What can often distinguish the profiles of the major Canadian cities from those of most of their southern neighbours, however, is their newness. This pristine quality is matched in some U.S. cities such as Houston, Dallas, and Denver, but many of the cities in the United States, though now dominated by the modern, tinted-glass skyscrapers, still contain many of the heavy slab structures inset with relatively small window spaces. The Empire State Building in New York is perhaps the best-known example. In Canada this type of structure can also be found at a much smaller scale, especially in the "chateauesque" Canadian Pacific hotels topped by their distinctive copper roofs now greened by the weathering process. One of the best Canadian examples of the early style of skyscraper is the old Imperial Bank of Commerce Building in Toronto, which, until the 1960s, was the tallest building in the Commonwealth. Today, this building is almost hidden among the new giant structures.

The reflective-glass office towers of Montreal, Toronto, and Vancouver are less than 20 years old, while those in Calgary, Ottawa, Winnipeg, and other Canadian cities of similar size are the products of the last ten years; those in Halifax are even more recent. These new, finger-like structures have replaced the old railway hotels as the dominant structures in those Canadian cities that owed their first real spurts of growth to the railways along which these luxurious hotels were built. Most of these hotels assumed a style epitomized by the Nova Scotian in Halifax, or the Royal York in Toronto. Only in Quebec City does the major hotel, Chateau Frontenac, remain the dominant feature of the urban landscape, especially when viewed across the St. Lawrence from Lévis. However, the developing skyline of Saint John is dominated by the new Hilton Hotel. Saint John, therefore, can be seen to be at a very early stage of downtown development. There is no doubt that the new profiles of Canadian cities are the direct result of economic forces (Bourne 1967; Kerr 1968; Spelt 1973), but they are forces that have been influenced to a considerable extent by prestige, a factor which cannot be measured accurately in economic terms.

This quest for prestige reflects the fierce struggle between competing firms *within* the individual urban centres. Generally, these competitors have been banks, insurance companies, and related financial enterprises. In Toronto, for example, the pre-eminence of the Bank of Commerce was first challenged in the early 1960s by the Toronto-Dominion Bank, which pushed up the first "tall glasshouse" in the city. It became a landmark and its prestige was secured. In order to build this high, however, the Toronto-Dominion had to win the support and approval of the planners by providing adequate open space around the centre and also by providing underground malls linking the surrounding streets in the downtown area. Throughout the 1960s the Bank of Commerce negotiated frantically to secure more land in order to supplant the Toronto-Dominion as the tallest and most prestigious building in the city. This was not purely rational economic behaviour; the concern was with prestige, though it could be argued that indirect economic benefits would accrue to the winner of the game. When the Bank of Montreal decided to move its head office to Toronto from Montreal in the early 1970s, at the height of the Quebec separatist movement, it was determined to build higher than either the Toronto-Dominion or the Bank of Commerce. Here, again, concessions had to be made and a new elaborate concourse containing shopping facilities had to be provided at ground level to appease the planners. The game was ended when the Royal Bank of Canada, who were now forced to build anew, decided not to compete in the tall towers race but, instead, pushed up a spectacular twin triangular block with gold tinted glass in front of the downtown area. Height was replaced by opulence. Here it must be emphasized that this was a general process that was repeated throughout the Canadian urban system; the game was the same, only the players were different.

In most cities the institutional framework, represented by the planners, has favoured high-rise development. In Ottawa until the mid-1970s, however, there were strong pressures to prevent high-rise development close to the Parliament buildings. Such height-restricting policies are common in many European cities; in Edinburgh, for example, regulations prevent any building from rising above the level of the castle. In Ottawa, the taller the building, the farther it had to be from Parliament. If continued, this process would have created a conical rather than a pyramidic profile. But, by the 1980s, general economic pressures were such that the familiar configuration of "Canadianville" had been assumed: Ottawa began to look like just another Canadian city. During this decade limits to further vertical growth have been imposed in most Canadian cities, though developers still seek and find ways of building higher than the general principles permit. A good example is the Sun Alliance development on the western edge of downtown Toronto at the south-east corner of King Street at Simcoe. By agreeing to preserve St. Andrew's Church, the developers have been allowed to "transfer" the height of the building that otherwise could have been built on the site of the church, to the height of a new building on an adjacent site. This "transfer of density" procedure allowed for a much higher tower than would be permitted under more stringent planning regulations.

The profiles of Canadian cities have been affected not only by the competition among enterprises *within* the individual cities, but also by competition *between* cities. A large part of this has been stimulated by the quest by both Toronto and Montreal to become Canada's leading city. Both cities have been engaged in developing grandiose schemes, but the CN Communications Tower has given Toronto a distinctive landmark that endorses its pre-eminence in size gained over the last decade. Much earlier, however, in the early 1960s Toronto had already taken steps to assume the image of a modern city by promoting international competition for the design of its new city hall. The winning design undoubtedly gave the core of Toronto a futuristic appearance. Similarly, following the lead taken by Vancouver and followed by Calgary with its "Saddledome," other Canadian cities are planning to build enclosed air-conditioned stadia that will guarantee year-round sport at the highest level. The most recent move in this direction has been made in Toronto where the world's largest retractable-roofed stadium has been built, covering an area of 3.25 hectares and tall enough to enclose a 25-storey apartment block. Completed in 1989, the "Skydome" further enhances Toronto's new-found image as an international city capable of providing top-class sporting facilities regardless of weather conditions. These structures are the newest additions to the city profiles, and though not part of the downtown proper, except in Vancouver and Toronto, they are being built within easy access. The process of redevelopment in the three largest Canadian cities involves major changes of land use around the CBDs; the area involved in all cases is quite significant. Traditionally, these areas were occupied by heavy industrial activity linked to the rail and port facilities.

7.2   Redevelopment and the New Image

The process of waterfront redevelopment was started initially in Montreal during the 1960s in preparation for the Montreal World's Fair (Expo '67). This event was secured for Montreal by an aggressive policy under Mayor Drapeau, which subsequently attracted the Olympics in 1976 as part of the quest to gain increased prestige for the city. Both events were economic disasters, but Expo '67 was used as a medium for changing the whole nature of the St. Lawrence River with the building of islands made of material dug to make the tunnels for Montreal's new subway system. Many of the Expo buildings still remain today as centres for recreational activity. Similarly, Vancouver has used Expo '86 to provide it with the same sort of facilities and waterfront activity secured by Montreal 20 years earlier. Stanley Park, on the north-western tip of the peninsula, has always provided downtown Vancouver with easy access to green space; in much the same way Montreal has been served by the open space of Mount Royal, and Toronto by Toronto Island and High Park. But in Vancouver a spectacular waterfront redevelopment of False Creek, to the south of the CBD, for Expo '86, together with the construction of a substantial number of town houses and marinas, has transformed a large tract of hitherto unsightly industrial/port land into one of North America's urban showcases. Added to this is the continuing transformation of some of the old harbour facilities along the southern shore of Burrard Inlet with the Pan-Pacific development. All these changes are giving a new image to the traditional zone of transition or blight around Vancouver's CBD. This image reflects the dynamic changes at the national level, involving the tendency to move away from a primary/secondary based economy to one more dominated by services and recreational pursuits (Ley 1981, 127–28).

The speed, scale, and dynamism of these changes are more evident in Toronto than in any other city in Canada. Toronto's CBD has long been prevented from expanding southwards towards Lake Ontario by the large physical obstacles presented by the rail and port facilities. By the mid-1960s, however, most of the old industrial areas to the east and west of the downtown area along the lakeshore had been cleared. Their sites were levelled and hastily set up as temporary car parks. Similarly, during the 1970s, many of the old, unsightly port facilities were closed down or moved farther east. The scene was now set for extensive improvements and modifications, and the change over the last ten years has been dramatic. Most of Toronto's waterfront is now occupied by marinas, shops, restaurants, exhibition halls, hotels, condominiums, and a conference centre. Nearby is the CN Observation Tower, with its rotating restaurant from which it is possible to gain a 360-degree perspective of the whole metropolitan area and, on a clear day, a view of the spray rising from Niagara Falls 67 kilometres away. Access to the CN Tower from the CBD is provided through a glass-enclosed walkway over an extensive layout of railway tracks. This is the first step in an attempt to enclose this physical barrier and, when the enclosure is complete, the CBD will be able to spread unhindered to the waterfront.

Undoubtedly, this will be a major achievement, but what is more important than all these commercial and recreational developments is the construction of high-rise apartments and condominiums along the very edge of the water (Skaburskis 1984). Some are entirely new constructions whereas others are imaginative conversions of old port buildings and warehouses; the ground floor of one such building has been refurbished with boutiques while the reinforced roof has been used to support a stack of condominiums. Condominium living has become increasingly popular in Toronto, where O'Reilly (1985) estimated that the average condominium cost $172,000 in 1985. Residential accommodation along the waterfront itself is for those in the highest-income brackets, but to the east of the CBD and on land recently occupied by heavy industrial activity, co-operative housing schemes for lower-income groups have been constructed, such as the St. Lawrence complex. The tree-lined avenues and luxurious grassy banks in sight of the CBD tower blocks disguise the fact that much of this land was previously occupied by unsightly dilapidated housing. Part of the emphasis in this redevelopment process, therefore, is on moving people back into the heart of the city (Brown and Burke 1979), which itself is becoming a more attractive place in which to live.

Whereas the emphasis of the 1960s and 1970s was on vertical growth and pure commercial development, the emphasis of the 1980s is on improving the quality of the environment (Ley 1981, 1986). The latter is particularly evident in the smaller cities of Quebec City, Saint John, and Halifax-Dartmouth where waterfront developments have taken the cities back to the water's edge. There is a difference, however, between the developments in these smaller eastern cities and those taking place in Vancouver, Montreal, and Toronto. In the big cities the emphasis is on construction to provide new facilities and amenities. In the smaller eastern cities the emphasis is on the restoration of historic buildings and on the conservation of a cultural heritage. In Quebec City, L'escalier Petit-Champlain, formerly called the "break-neck stairs," leads down to the Lower Town where boutiques and restaurants now abound amid the rows of gentrified houses along Rue Petit-Champlain, itself a street lined with traditional eighteenth-century wrought-iron lampstands with attractive hand-made glass bowls. At the centre of Lower Town, Place Royale, the cradle of French civilization in North America, has been completely restored to its former glory by the provincial government. Many of the surrounding houses have been restored to the style of the late eighteenth century while others, being beyond repair, have been replaced with modern replicas. Approaching Quebec across the St. Lawrence on the ferry from Lévis, Lower Town now presents a view that cannot be very different from the same view in the eighteenth century. Within the town the restaurants and boutiques perform the same functions as their eighteenth-century counterparts. The success of this redevelopment has been acknowledged by UNESCO, which lists Quebec City as a World Heritage Site.

In Halifax the traditional wooden buildings, as opposed to the more substantial stone buildings in Quebec City, have been preserved, but in many cases their functions have been changed. During the 1960s and early 1970s the advent of container shipping, the construction of the new A. Murray McKay Bridge across the Narrows, and the spread of the new suburban shopping malls began to threaten the viability of the CBDs in Halifax and Dartmouth. To revitalise these areas the Nova Scotia Department of Development and the Federal Department of Regional Economic Expansion, on a 20:80 percent cost share basis, set up the Waterfront Development Corporation in 1976. Its catch phrase of "bringing back the waterfront" has captured the imagination and pride of Haligonians.

The resulting newly constructed museums, the harbour walk, the preserved historic properties containing converted warehouses for shops, boutiques and restaurants, along with the award-winning newly built Sheraton Hotel constructed according to traditional lines with copper roofs, provide Halifax with an attractive waterfront. But it is also a working waterfront, and the two functions operate side by side in clean, quiet harmony.

The same approach to waterfront development has been adopted by Saint John, where Market Square functions as a focal point. This area, overlooking Market Slip where the loyalists from the United States landed in 1783, is a mixture of old and new brick buildings encompassing the new Trade and Convention Centre linked to the high-rise Hilton International Hotel. The adjacent mall, joined to the CBD by underground walkways, stands on the water's edge. Inside this complex every effort has been made to emulate the heavy-timbered internal structure of the Old City Market, which is located in the heart of the CBD and which is the oldest common-law or farmers' market in Canada. The present brick building was erected in 1876, and its roof is supported by hand-hewn timbers reminiscent of an inverted galley hull. There is a clear emphasis, therefore, in these three eastern cities, on preservation and conservation in their push to redevelop their respective waterfronts.

7.3   Transport and New Attitudes

The new concern about how Canadian cities should appear and function is also reflected in terms of changing attitudes towards expressways and public transport systems. The expressway building era started early in Toronto during the 1950s and early 1960s. By then Toronto had been encompassed by the east-west Queen Elizabeth Way and Gardiner Expressway to the south along the lakeshore, by the north-south Highway 427 to the west, by the north-south Don Valley Parkway to the east, and to the north by the east-west Highway 401, which was designed to by-pass the northern fringe of the built-up area. So rapid has been the suburban expansion of residential and industrial activity that today the 12-lane Highway 401, one of the busiest stretches of road in the world, simply bisects the urban area. The boom years of the 1960s stimulated ever-increasing growth in all Canadian cities, and mayors were elected to office on the basis of their aggression and promises to build bigger and wider expressways, which in turn fostered increasing use of the motor car and subsequent outward expansion. In the same way that commercial and financial institutions can be identified as being responsible for the early vertical growth at the centres of Canadian cities, so too can residential and industrial activities be identified as the major contributors to their lateral or areal expansion. Here a contrast can be made with many cities in the United Kingdom, where much of the initial vertical growth was attributed to residential tower blocks; Glasgow is a good example of this phenomenon.

By the early 1970s the attitude towards the construction of new expressways through Canadian cities had changed quite abruptly. Following the example set by Vancouver in 1968–69, the people became concerned with the "inequality of life," and right across Canada city mayors were being elected who were not only opposed to building new expressways but were also prepared to prevent the completion of those under construction. One exception was the mayor of North York. Elsewhere in Toronto powerful citizen protest groups joined forces and, through successful lobbying, halted the construction of the Spadina Expressway, which was designed to bisect the "Toronto Box System" with a north-south route from Highway 401 in North York to the heart of the downtown area. Similar action in Montreal halted the Ville de Marie (east-west) autoroute. In Toronto the expressway had already been partially completed before the project was halted, and the land for the rest of the expressway had already been purchased and cleared. The empty lands are commonly referred to as the "Spadina Trench" or "Davis's Ditch" because Bill Davis was the premier of the provincial cabinet that made the final decision to halt construction. Viewed from the air it is puzzling to see such a wide road leading, literally, to nowhere. However, the proposed route of the expressway is now occupied, for the most part, by the Spadina Subway.

A parallel concern with the provision of rapid transit systems has enabled Toronto and Montreal to develop two of the world's finest subway systems. The Montreal system, hastily started and partly completed for Expo '67, is magnificent; the tile mosaics that adorn the stations would not be misplaced in many public and civic buildings. Both systems are clean and efficient. The Montreal system is perhaps best known for its rubber wheels, introduced to provide increased efficiency in the braking system necessary for the very short journeys through and around Montreal's underground city. In Toronto the subway system is fully integrated with a very efficient bus network that is now acting as a model for new systems in Europe where, until recently, public transport systems in general have been more available than in North America. Arguably, the world's best integrated public transport system is found in Toronto. As the Toronto system has been extended and halted at intervals, complexes of apartment blocks have mushroomed around the temporary terminals and remain today as permanent reminders of the construction cycles. Other Canadian cities, especially Calgary and Edmonton, have built Light Rail Transit (LRT) systems on the surface through the downtown areas, while Vancouver has built the first elevated and fully automated (driverless) Skytrain.

7.4   Residential Patterns and the New Social Composition

Most of the suburban residential expansion around Canadian cities takes the form of a mix of detached and semi-detached homes, row or terrace housing, and blocks of high-rise apartments. The general aim has been to cater to a wide variety of household types and income levels. The high-rise apartments are often concentrated at the intersections of the arterial roads, thus placing high-density development adjacent to public transportation. Generally speaking, the farther one moves from an arterial intersection, the lower is the residential density. Overall, the suburbs present an appearance that is far from being uniform and monotonous. What is perhaps more important, their social composition is also notably diverse.

To most North Americans, residential space is an important concept, and houses in Canada are advertised on a square footage basis; in the United Kingdom, in contrast, houses are advertised according to the number of rooms and few home-owners know the area of their house. In the Canadian suburbs one goal is to own 223 square metres or more. Also, again in contrast to most cities in the United Kingdom where suburbs are often dominated by local authority housing estates, Canadian suburbs are essentially middle class and far removed from the older, less desirable properties closer to the city centres, which tend to be occupied by the more recent immigrant groups. The ambition of these immigrants is to save money as quickly as possible so that they too can move to the relative tranquility of the suburbs. For many, owning a home in the suburbs is a major indication of personal success.

Canadian suburbs can be contrasted to those around British cities not only by the character of the residential neighbourhoods but also by the facilities they contain. Apart from the neighbourhood shopping plazas, which are comparable in size and function with the largest found in the United Kingdom, Canadian suburbs contain giant complexes located at key intersections on the highway system. These have become regional shopping centres and in some cities they pose a real threat to the very existence and survival of downtown retailing. The biggest and most recent example of such a complex is the West Edmonton Mall in Alberta, which opened in 1983 and which is currently the largest in the world, with about 483,000 square metres or the equivalent of 108 football fields all under cover. As well as the main tenants, comprising Eaton's, the Hudson's Bay Company, Sears, Safeway, and Zellers, the West Edmonton Mall contains under one roof 828 other stores. These include 110 restaurants that are open every day until midnight (collectively advertised as "North America's largest Gourmet World"), 19 cinemas, an automobile showroom, an amusement fairground that spreads over several acres, and an ice palace skating rink. The walkways are marble-lined, air-conditioned, spacious, and luxuriously adorned with spectacular fountains, geysers, and ornamental trees. The total ease of access both to the site itself and from the car parks to the stores, combined with complete protection from the bitter cold of winter and the stifling heat of summer, make the centre highly attractive. Indeed, it is difficult to see how downtown Edmonton can compete successfully against what is, in effect, a highly accessible shopping centre under one roof.

This type of competition has been met effectively in both Toronto and Montreal and to a lesser extent in Vancouver. In these cities, the basement levels of the major downtown office buildings and hotels contain a diverse array of specialized shops and restaurants. These clusters of retail facilities are interconnected by extensive networks of underground passageways, which also provide access to the rapid transit systems in Toronto and Montreal. This form of underground development is most extensive and best exemplified in Montreal, which has been described as "the first city of the 21st century." In Toronto, moreover, the new Eaton Centre adds further protection from the weather by turning the retail district of the CBD inside-out. Built in the form of a cavernous, glass-domed corridor, reminiscent of the Crystal Palace, the Eaton Centre has taken much of the pedestrian traffic off neighbouring Yonge Street and brought it indoors. It is as if a suburban shopping mall of the latest design had been deposited in the very centre of the city.

All in all, the physical appearance of Canadian cities has undergone a radical transformation since the early 1960s. The rapid growth of all the major cities, both vertically and laterally, bespeaks an economic dynamism that in turn reflects the country's wealth of natural resources. But another type of change has also taken place: Canadian cities have become more cosmopolitan. This development, without a doubt, reflects the contributions of recent immigrants to the diversity of Canada's urban population.

Successive waves of immigrants have carried to Canada, and to the cities in particular, a wide variety of cultures. Well-known examples of urban ethnic distinctiveness include the concentration of Irish in St. John's, of Germans in Kitchener (the town was called Berlin until the First World War), and of Ukrainians in the cities of the Prairies. Undoubtedly, the most important is the juxtaposition of French and English in Montreal – a combination, in the traditional francophone view, of *entrepreneurs anglais et bucherons canadiens.* From the point of view of ethnic *diversity,* however, most observers agree that Canada's most interesting city is now Toronto (e.g., Kamoue 1975). In little more than 30 years, Toronto has evolved from being a bland and rather puritanical community, composed largely of persons of British stock, into being a multi-cultural metropolis in which persons of the traditionally dominant white, Anglo-Saxon, Protestant variety (the WASPs) are now definitely in a minority. No longer can Toronto be described succinctly as "a British town on American soil" (Firth 1966, 87). The soil may be American, at least in a continental sense, but the dominant British character of the population is declining.

The largest single non-British ethnic group in Toronto is the Italian community, which numbered approximately 400,000 in 1981 according to the Census of Canada. This makes Toronto the twelfth-largest Italian city in the world, and the second-largest outside Italy (behind New York). In addition to the British and the Italians, Toronto contains significant numbers of Ukrainians, Poles, Hungarians, Germans, Portuguese, Greeks, Jews, Iranians, and West Indians. One final group deserving mention is the "Orientals," this being, in reality, a heterogeneous group that encompasses substantial numbers from such widely different sources as Hong Kong, Singapore, Taiwan, Malaysia, Vietnam, China, and the Philippines. The resulting multi-cultural character of the city's population finds visible expression in numerous ways, including elements of domestic architecture (arches and wrought iron may identify an Italian household; a statue of the Madonna by a porch reveals a Portuguese), a plethora of ethnic newspapers, various cultural events (among which the annual West Indian festival, Caribana, is the largest), and a seemingly endless variety of distinctive restaurants and shops.

The typical pattern followed by each major group of immigrants has been for an initial concentration to develop in a "reception area" often close to the CBD. Normally, these reception areas are run-down residential districts where large houses, formerly occupied by middle-class and even upper-class residents, have been subdivided into flats in order to accommodate lower-income households at high densities. In Toronto, the principal reception area is Parkdale, a zone of once-elegant Victorian housing that runs westwards from the CBD towards High Park and the valley of the Humber River. Virtually every major group of immigrants that has come to Toronto since the end of the Second World War settled initially in some part of this relatively small section of the urban area.

As each immigrant group becomes more affluent and acculturated, it tends to move outwards towards suburban areas, some, in time, vacating the reception area completely. But there are wide differences in the extent to which the various ethnic groups remain spatially segregated. Some groups, even as they increase in numbers and diffuse outwards, remain tightly clustered in new areas, ultimately forming well-defined sectors. The outstanding examples of such sectors are the Jewish community, closely associated with the location of synagogues, and the Italian community of Toronto. Other groups, in contrast, become more widely dispersed throughout the city, though in these cases a definite nucleus may be left behind in or near the original reception area. In Toronto, for example, Greeks and Poles (excluding Polish Jews) are now scattered widely throughout the metropolitan area, and no continuous sectors tracing the expansion of these groups can be found. Yet the Greek core area along Danforth Avenue is a highly distinctive feature of the social geography of the East End; and in Parkdale there are still shops along Roncesvalles Avenue where Polish is understood more readily than English.

The Orientals constitute a special case. Appreciable numbers of Orientals are present in all large Canadian cities, and in every case this ethnic group is dominated numerically by what may be termed the "True Chinese," that is, persons who were born, or whose parents or grandparents were born, in Hong Kong, Taiwan, or the People's Republic of China. The True Chinese, however, fall into two quite distinct categories, which have different social origins and, most interestingly, different patterns of geographical distribution within Canadian cities. First, there are what may be called the "Old Chinese." The Old Chinese, with few exceptions, are descendants of indentured labourers who travelled from China to Canada (and, in even greater numbers, to the United States) during the late nineteenth century to work on the construction of the transcontinental railroads. After the railroads were completed, the labourers gravitated to the cities, and within every city, adjacent to the CBD, they created a distinctive Chinatown. The early inhabitants of these Chinatowns were poor; for reasons that are not entirely clear, many of their decendants have remained in this lower-income group. The Chinatowns are still in place, and their general standard of living is well below the urban average.

Recently, however, a second category, which may be termed the "New Chinese," has appeared. The New Chinese are persons who have arrived in Canada mainly from Hong Kong since about 1975. It is generally acknowledged that these immigrants are persons who wished to remain within the British Commonwealth, and who feared that, if they did not leave Hong Kong, their economic freedom might be curtailed by China when the British lease expires in 1997. The New Chinese display several interesting features. First, they are numerous – certainly in the thousands, and possibly in the tens of thousands. Second, they are affluent; their general standard of living is clearly well above the Canadian urban average, and a remarkable number of them are outright millionaires. Third, and no doubt reflecting their wealth, they have not settled in Canada's Chinatowns. Instead, they have moved directly to the suburbs, showing a preference for the high-class areas and frequently buying a substantial house through an intermediary, cash on the nail, even before they set foot in Canada. In Toronto, for example, the New Chinese have shown a marked preference for the north-eastern suburbs, particularly Agincourt, where the elegant, new shops in the small but well-appointed Chinese mall, known as the Dragon Centre (actually a converted roller-skating rink), bear witness both to their numbers and to their economic strength.

In general, during the post-war period Canadian cities have absorbed a diverse array of immigrants without falling prey to the uglier forms of inter-racial and inter-ethnic strife. To be sure, there have been some nasty incidents. Many of these, however, have been manifestations of "imported" disagreements with roots in the participants' countries of origin – as with the long-standing antipathies between Armenians and Turks, or between Sikhs and Hindus. Resentment of newcomers by members of the "host society" does not appear to be a significant problem.

7.5   Conclusion

This overall view, impression, or image of Canadian cities lends support to the earlier observation of Watson and Watson (1977) that the urban revolution is currently the most notable trend in Canadian geography and that it is dividing Canada more and more into urban-based regions. The Watsons also suggested that the future of Canada lies with its great cities. This overview has shown that, in the last ten years, significant changes have continued to take place in the largest cities. Undoubtedly, Canadian cities have assumed new images, some of which have given them an international dimension. The revitalization of Canadian cities, and especially the attempt by many of them to redevelop their waterfronts for both economic and cultural reasons, have turned large tracts of hitherto unsightly industrial land into attractive areas with suitable amenities that complement the commercial opulence of the modern CBDs. These in turn have emerged as "Contemporary Cathedrals" (Collier 1977), and their form is a result, in part, of keen competition among firms within the respective cities and also of the keen rivalry among the cities for prestige.

Canada was founded on the basis of two dominant cultures, the British and the French. During the post-war period, however, this dominance has been severely eroded by mass immigration from other countries, so that today Canada is not only a bilingual country but also a truly multi-cultural society. The new cultures, which are concentrated in ethnic areas within the larger cities, have not yet been "melted down" to form one image. These separate cultures coexist in juxtaposition and in relative harmony within the confines of the larger cities. To some extent, therefore, the "image of Canada still lies in the preservation of many images" (Watson and Watson 1977, 9).

Acknowledgements

I wish to acknowledge the generous assistance provided by the Canadian High Commission through their Faculty Enrichment Scheme, which financed extensive travel across Canada in 1985. During the visit I was given valuable assistance and information by Professor John Mannion (Memorial University, Newfoundland), Mrs. Joan Marshall (Concordia University, Montreal), and by Professor Larry Bourne (University of Toronto). I would like to give special acknowledgement to Professor John U. Marshall (York University, Toronto) for his substantial comments, many of which are included, on the new social composition of Canadian cities.

References

Bourne, L.S. 1967. "Private Redevelopment of the Central City." Research Papers, Department of Geography, University of Chicago, no. 112.

Brown, P., and P. Burke. 1979. *The Canadian Inner City 1971–76: A Statistical Handbook.* Ottawa: Central Mortgage and Housing Corporation.

Collier, R.W. 1977. *Contemporary Cathedrals: Large Scale Developments in Canadian Cities.* Montreal: Harvest House.

Firth, E.G., ed. 1966. "The Town of York, 1815–1834: A Further Collection of Documents on Early Toronto." Publications of the Champlain Society, no. 8.

Goldberg, M.A., and J. Mercer. 1980. "Canadian and U.S. Cities: Basic Differences, Possible Explanations and Their Meaning for Public Policy." *Papers and Proceedings of the Regional Science Association* 45:159–83.

———. 1986. *The Myth of the North American City*. Vancouver: University of British Columbia Press.

Harris, C. 1979. "Within the Fantastic Frontier: A Geographer's Thoughts on Canadian Unity." *Canadian Geographer* 23:197–200.

Higbee, F. 1976. "Centre Cities in Canada and the United States." In J.W. Watson and T. O'Riordan, eds., *The American Environment: Perceptions and Policies*, 145–60. New York: John Wiley & Sons.

Hodge, G. 1971. "Comparisons of Urban Structure in Canada, the U.S. and Great Britain." *Geographical Analysis* 3:83–90.

Kerr, D.P. 1968. "Metropolitan Dominance in Canada." In J. Warkentin, ed., *Canada: A Geographical Interpretation*, 531–55. Toronto: Methuen.

Kamoue, L. 1975. *The Social Structure of Metropolitan Toronto*. Toronto: Metro Toronto Planning Department.

Ley, D.F. 1981. "Inner City Revitalization in Canada. A Vancouver Case Study." *Canadian Geographer* 25:124–48.

———. 1986. "Alternative Explanations for Inner City Gentrification: A Canadian Assessment." *Annals of the Association of American Geographers* 76:521–35.

Mercer, J. 1979. "On Continentalism, Distinctiveness, and Comparative Urban Geography: Canadian and American Cities." *Canadian Geographer* 23:119–39.

Nader, G.A. 1975. *Cities of Canada*. 2 vols. Toronto: Macmillan of Canada.

O'Reilly, D. 1985. "Condominium Living Is Becoming More Popular in Toronto." *Real Estate News,* 18 October, C3.

Ray. D., and R.A. Murdie. 1972. "Canadian and American Urban Dimensions. In B.J.L. Berry, ed., *City Classification Handbook,* 181–210. New York: John Wiley & Sons.

Simmons, J., and R. Simmons. 1974. *Urban Canada*. Toronto: Copp Clark.

Skaburskis, A. 1984. "Condominium Demand: How the Market Evolved and Changed." *Habitat* 27 (4): 41–5.

Spelt, J. 1973. *Toronto*. Toronto: Collier-Macmillan.

Watson, J.W. 1950. "Canada: The Setting, Its Geography." In G.W. Brown, ed., *Canada,* 120–42. Toronto: University of Toronto Press.

———. 1956. "The Land of Canada." *Canadian Geographical Journal* 52:136–66.

———. 1962. "Canada and Its Regions." *Scottish Geographical Magazine* 78:137–49.

———. 1967. "Mental Images and Geographical Reality in the Settlement of North America." Cast Foundation Lectures, University of Nottingham, no. 4.

———. 1968. *Canada, Problems and Prospects*. Toronto: Longmans Canada.

———. 1970. "Image Geography: The Myth of America in the American scene." *Advancement of Science* 27:1–9.

———. 1971. "Geography and Image Regions." *Geographica Helvetica* 26:31–4.

———. 1972. "Canada and Environmental Analysis and Control." *Geographical Journal* 138:77–91.

————. 1977. "Images of Canada." *Bulletin of Canadian Studies* 1:1–15.

————. 1983. "Centre and Periphery: The Transfer of Urban Ideas from Britain to Canada." In J.H.C. Patten, ed., *The Expanding City: Essays in Honour of Professor Jean Gottmann*, 381–411. London: Academic Press.

Watson, J., and J.W. Watson. 1977. *The Canadians: How They Live and Work.* Toronto and Newton Abbot: David and Charles.

Yeates, M.H., and B.J. Garner. 1976. *The North American City.* New York: Harper & Row.

8   Mapping the Socio-economic Landscape of Ottawa-Hull

D.R. Fraser Taylor

8.1   Watson's "Social Himalayas" and Computer Cartography

Wreford Watson in his chapter entitled "The Sociological Aspects of Geography" published in 1951 in Griffith Taylor's book, *Geography in the Twentieth Century*, made a strong case for the field of what he called social geography. Watson was a pioneer in this field, which he defines as "the identification of different regions of the earth's surface according to association of social phenomena related to the total environment" (Watson 1957, 482). In his discussion of the concept Watson argued that social factors are every bit as important as physical factors in understanding the geography of a region. He recognized that regions can be differentiated "as much by their social content as by their physical character" (Watson 1957, 463).

Watson (1957, 468) argued that "the cultural landscape is the concrete representation of man's adaptation of his environment," and that this landscape has concrete forms such as fields, mines, houses, and factories. He took this argument further, however, by posing a simple but provocative question: "But why stop at the concrete representation?" (Watson 1957, 468). His argument is that "it is the immaterial force that is the really significant thing in the geography of a region" (Watson 1957, 468), and that both the immaterial and material aspects of Man's activities must be considered in portraying the geographic base of society.

He demonstrated this by presenting the social geography of the city of Hamilton, Ontario, stressing the dynamism of change over time. In discussing Hamilton he argued that, "Its character as a region depends not on the influence of natural material force, in the environment, but on social forces which re-adapt and reorganize the areas and give it a unique character" (Watson 1957, 496). He looked at the geography of recreational institutions, which he saw as largely the social geography of the group they serve. He introduced the concept of social distance, which could keep some institutions remote from those who live quite close to their location, and at the same time, make the same institutions socially close to those who are geographically remote from them. His conclusion is that "unless the geographer takes account of these *social Himalayas* he cannot give an adequate, far less a complete picture of the geography of a region; but when he tries to consider them then certain patterns become obvious, that would otherwise be obscure, while the connections between patterns, and the explanation of their distributions, will be more evident" (Watson 1957, 497–98). Since the publication of Watson's pioneering work outlining the characteristics of this systematic branch of the discipline, social geography has developed as a major field of geographical thinking and analysis, utilizing many of Watson's ideas as its basic building blocks.

One of these "building blocks" that finds particular expression today in conjunction with cartographic representation is the imaginative phrase "social Himalayas." Indeed, developments in computer-assisted cartography now make it possible to portray what were previously considered to be immaterial or invisible elements of the cultural landscape in a concrete form. Cartographers can now depict the socio-economic landscape of a city as effectively as the concrete cultural landscape of that city or the physiography of the landscape on which the city is built. The social Himalayas have become reality on the graph plotters and visual display units of a new generation of cartographers.

Cartographers, using data from the population census and other data bases, have developed increasingly sophisticated mapping and analytical techniques to illustrate socio-economic variables. From the early use of distribution maps of single variables, the field has moved to the use of increasingly sophisticated multi-component maps and maps derived from factorial analysis and trend surface analysis. Here the influence of the computer has become increasingly evident. Indeed, one of the earliest uses of computer-assisted cartography was in the field of the mapping of census variables, as illustrated by the early use of programs such as SYMAP for this purpose. Computer-generated atlases using census variables began to appear in the late 1960s (Taylor and Douglas 1970) and are now commonplace. Interactive electronic atlases are now being developed (Siekierska and Taylor 1991).

As mapping techniques improved in sophistication, new illustrative techniques that used multiple colour component mapping were developed, such as those produced by the U.S. Bureau of the Census (Broome and Witiuk 1980). Modern computer-assisted cartography allows considerable manipulation and analysis of socio-economic data, and when a third dimension is added to the illustrative techniques, Watson's social Himalayas appear as real peaks on a modern computer map. Computer-assisted cartography can easily portray the socio-economic landscape of a city in the same form as a three-dimensional model of the physical landscape. Watson's imaginative ideas can now be given new visual expression.

The purpose of this chapter is to demonstrate how elements of the socio-economic landscape can be mapped using computer techniques and, in the process, lead to an increased understanding of the dynamics of Ottawa-Hull in the National Capital Region, the area used for exemplification. Computer-assisted cartography is not the only analytic tool available to the social geographer, but it can gives insights into spatial patterns and processes in a way that other techniques cannot. It can also portray, in a unique way, the social Himalayas of which Watson wrote.

8.2   A New Cartography for Mapping Social Variables

The use of the computer in cartography is now commonplace and widely accepted (Rhind et al. 1984; Carter 1984), and it may be argued that the technological transition" (Monmonier 1985) that has taken place in cartography has been so widespread that we are now witnessing the emergence of a "New Cartography" (Taylor 1985) to respond to the challenge of the information age. Within a decade there is unlikely to be any commercial cartographic production that is not influenced to a substantial degree by computer techniques. Even at the level of the individual cartographer producing one-of-a-kind maps, the personal computer is likely to play an increasing role.

In the initial stages the field of computer-assisted cartography was dominated primarily by technical concerns but, although technical concerns are still of importance, the emphasis is moving away from producing maps and graphics utilizing a computer to a different set of demands. Concerns over hardware and software are being replaced by the much more significant question of brainware. Bouille (1984) has argued that computer technology started with hardware for which software was developed and only then – and only as a last step – were the uses considered to which this technology was to be put. In extreme cases this became a technological solution searching for problems to solve. He argued that this process must be completely reversed.

Computer-assisted cartography needs to be much more responsive to the uses to which new techniques can be put, with technical developments responding to the needs determined by "brainware." There is considerable scope for more imaginative cartographic responses utilizing the strengths of both new computer techniques and new procedures for transmission of information (Slocum and Egbert 1991). The development of the new field of computer visualization is especially promising in this respect (Taylor 1991). The computer has revolutionized cartography in technical terms, but because cartographers, in the main, did not control or initiate these technological changes, their full cartographic potential has yet to be realized. The field has changed so rapidly that the hard-copy map is now only one of a number of modern cartographic products, and by the year 2000 it may not even be the most common one. A recent description of cartography is as follows: an information transfer process that is centred about a spatial data base that can be considered, in itself, a multifaceted model of geographic reality. Such a spatial data base then serves as a central core of an entire sequence of cartographic processes, receiving various data inputs and dispersing various types of information products" (Guptill and Starr 1984, 1–2).

Spatial data bases contain a wealth of information including much data of direct relevance to social geography. Utilizing this data, various analyses of socio-economic variables can be made. It will be argued that the portrayal of these variables cartographically as socio-economic surfaces in three dimensions is an especially useful approach.

8.3   The "Social Himalayas" of Ottawa-Hull

The twin cities of Ottawa-Hull stand in the valley of the Ottawa River close to the edge of the Canadian Shield, which rises to the north in the form of the Gatineau Hills. In terms of the concrete cultural landscape there have been dramatic visible changes since the establishment of both Ottawa and Hull in the nineteenth century. In recent decades many visible changes, such as high-rise office towers, multi-level highways, and gigantic shopping centres, with their attendant hectares of concrete parking lots, have transformed the concrete cultural landscape, but at the same time the socio-economic landscape has been changing just as dramatically, but less visibly.

The basic source of data used to construct elements of the socio-economic landscape of Ottawa-Hull was the Census of Canada. Language, education, and income levels were chosen as three key variables for illustrative purposes. Of course, these are not the only variables representing social differentiation in Ottawa-Hull, but they are particularly significant because they reflect some of the wide differences that exist, and there are interesting inter-relationships among them. It can be argued that economic status is correlated with both educational level and language ability, and that the peaks and valleys of the various surfaces bear some similarity to each other.

Language ability in Canada's national capital has always been a key variable. The ability to speak and write English well has been a key factor in social differentiation, and this did not begin to change significantly to include the same abilities in French until after 1967. Those unable to function in either English or French are always at a disadvantage in a city where the federal government employs a very high percentage of the work force. There is a strong spatial differentiation in the language surfaces and these surfaces illustrate well some of the social Himalayas to which Watson refers The same applies to educational levels, which are a key to vertical mobility in Canadian society, and nowhere are the social Himalayas more strikingly illustrated than in terms of income levels. The three variables chosen are also ones on which there is reasonably consistent comparative data available for the last four full censuses, allowing the portrayal of change over time in the socio-economic landscape of the region.

Data were extracted for census tracts for the years 1951, 1961, 1971, and 1981. For language, percentages were calculated by census tract for four categories of official language spoken – French only, English only, both English and French, and neither French nor English. For education, percentages were calculated for the highest levels of education (greater than grade 13) and the lowest educational levels (less than grade 9). For income, the median family income for Ottawa-Hull for each time period was calculated and expressed as 100 percent. Values for each census tract were then calculated relative to this median and expressed in percentage terms.

There were two major problems with the data: the changes in the boundaries of the census tracts, and the fact that for 1981 a 20 percent sample was used for some variables rather than a complete sample as in earlier censuses. The latter problem is insoluble but, as the sample was carefully selected, data for each census period were considered comparable. The boundaries of the census tracts for 1981 were used to digitize the base map (Figure 8.1). Over the 30-year period the number of census tracts increased from 42 to 92 but, as this was achieved by subdividing large census tracts into smaller ones, spatial comparisons over time could be achieved. As the data were plotted by centroid, values for the earlier, larger census tracts could be attached to the smaller 1981 tracts without significant loss. In some instances, though, this meant that the same value was attached to as many as ten 1981 tracts now found within the original larger 1951 tract (see Table 8.1).

Table   **Median Family Income by Census Tract, Ottawa-Hull, 1951–81**
8.1

				Census of Canada Mean Family Income				
Tract	1981	1971	1961	1951	Tract	1981	1971	1961	1951
1.01	53.02	93.79	126.13	96.61	38	49.93	77.05	79.30	93.59
1.02	124.27	93.79	126.13	96.61	39	65.58	64.68	79.20	95.53
2.01	145.97	158.00	126.13	96.61	40	65.92	69.41	81.36	94.92
2.02	134.96	158.00	126.13	96.61	41	56.79	61.81	78.10	92.87
2.03	120.92	158.00	126.13	96.61	42	41.60	62.01	73.09	88.08
3	131.11	131.02	106.05	101.81	43	79.13	78.59	90.26	105.47
4	88.69	98.60	106.05	101.81	44	124.40	114.98	126.79	154.71
5	107.25	135.43	134.13	101.81	45	97.79	94.87	104.56	106.92
6	142.98	167.71	138.18	101.81	46	64.61	67.38	77.60	84.50
7.01	144.96	146.35	138.18	101.81	47	53.78	53.78	69.96	82.36
7.02	97.06	146.35	138.18	101.81	48	132.95	74.16	83.18	90.37
7.03	148.91	146.35	138.18	101.81	49	62.48	82.65	91.30	103.58
8	110.49	122.49	138.18	101.81	50	73.60	82.28	95.69	108.97
9	120.70	137.09	138.18	101.81	51	112.87	105.09	107.75	125.44
10	92.18	113.16	138.18	101.81	52	53.00	60.78	80.97	96.53
11.01	100.52	113.42	119.27	93.92	53	44.25	58.28	74.45	83.05
11.02	95.76	113.42	119.27	93.92	54	67.83	73.05	82.91	91.90
12	74.51	85.87	91.57	93.92	55	57.12	61.32	77.26	85.50
13	75.58	89.29	99.74	93.92	56	86.55	69.55	86.50	97.14
14	55.63	76.04	83.86	111.23	57	124.10	115.06	110.54	124.34
15	98.45	88.12	93.17	104.26	58	92.95	103.57	97.71	94.60
16	125.05	115.47	130.93	145.08	59	96.40	98.75	109.30	149.15
17	121.60	92.88	109.30	123.67	60	76.49	98.45	109.30	149.15
18	103.92	77.91	94.23	108.97	61	104.92	103.57	97.71	94.60
19	124.37	117.86	128.34	145.97	62.01	94.45	103.57	97.71	94.60
20.01	103.69	112.17	123.09	102.57	62.02	59.42	81.43	94.23	96.01
20.02	104.97	112.17	123.09	102.57	100	75.94	89.62	92.98	96.01
21	77.47	91.12	99.62	102.57	101	63.45	79.10	90.07	96.01
22	64.63	83.37	123.75	102.57	102	73.05	86.94	85.91	96.01
23	116.47	128.91	123.75	102.57	103	56.27	74.06	84.63	96.01
24	116.29	135.70	123.75	102.57	104	284.98	183.67	189.02	222.86
25	128.29	150.00	139.96	126.20	110	62.18	68.19	75.56	91.82
26	113.20	110.61	111.60	102.93	120	51.10	68.93	93.30	88.64
27	85.19	98.89	111.60	102.93	501	53.22	70.44	73.88	88.28
28	92.20	112.89	115.84	102.93	502	64.70	74.50	89.77	91.34
29	71.54	71.93	92.39	102.93	503	109.17	88.39	81.45	94.68
30	90.96	87.95	92.39	102.93	504	72.11	79.72	89.55	94.48
31	103.69	112.21	108.71	126.20	505	82.56	85.92	72.50	85.42
32.01	106.97	138.33	142.31	126.20	507	56.87	68.96	79.42	79.42
32.02	139.21	138.33	142.31	126.20	508	62.80	84.01	79.42	79.42
33.01	96.75	99.41	107.24	113.88	509	82.78	93.20	79.42	79.42
33.02	91.62	99.41	107.24	113.88	510.01	108.51	116.67	108.15	108.15
34	138.35	137.43	158.09	197.86	510.02	107.24	116.67	108.15	108.15
35	70.13	77.47	83.42	88.76	511.01	89.93	98.11	108.15	108.15
36	135.68	108.23	114.63	137.56	511.02	103.99	98.11	108.15	108.15
37	77.95	90.81	104.11	116.98					
Region	$28,006	$10,889	$5,877	$2,484	Region	$28,006	$10,889	$5,877	$2,484

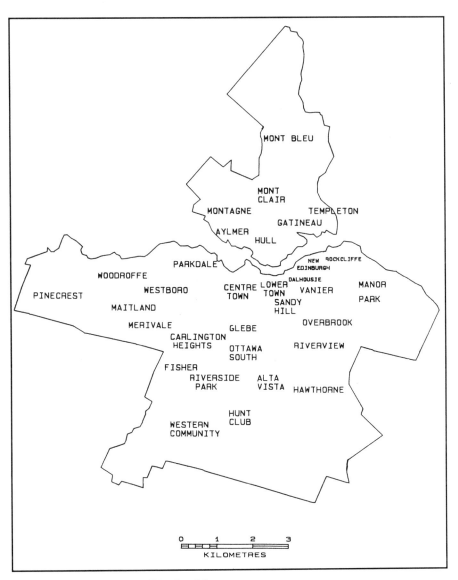

Figure 8.1   **Ottawa-Hull Index Map**

Source: Census of Canada, 1981

Produced by MIGS Cartographic Research Unit, Carleton University

Three computer mapping programs were used in portraying the data: SYMAP, PREVU, and MIGS. SYMAP is one of the earlier computer mapping programs, developed by the Laboratory for Computer Graphics and Spatial Analysis at Harvard University in the 1960s (Carter 1984). Since plotters became commonplace as computer peripherals, the line printer output from SYMAP is used less frequently for cartographic production, although it is still used for analysis, especially by urban and regional planners. In this instance the production of maps using SYMAP was an intermediate step required to produce the input for PREVU. For the purposes of the presentation of socio-economic surfaces in three dimensions, the data were first turned into maps of continuous surfaces using the excellent general interpolation algorithm, which is an integral part of the SYMAP program (Monmonier 1982). These maps provided the data for PREVU, a program developed at Carleton University. The viewpoint used for all PREVU illustrations is from the south-west (Figures 8.2, 8.4, 8.6, 8.8, 8.10, 8.12, and 8.14). MIGS is a choropleth mapping program developed in the Cartographic Research Unit at Carleton University by Stephen Prashker (Prashker and Taylor 1983). Figures 8.3, 8.5, 8.7, 8.9, 8.11, 8.13, and 8.15 show the same data as Figures 8.2, 8.4, 8.6, 8.8, 8.10, 8.12, and 8.14, but in these instances the data have been presented as discrete percentages within the boundaries of each census tract. The data are also available in tabular form, but only one table (Table 8.1) is reproduced here for comparative purposes showing the percentage above or below the median family income (expressed as 100 percent) by census tract for each time period. The table clearly shows the impact of census subdivision between 1951 and 1981.

8.3.1 Language Surfaces

Language is a key variable in understanding the socio-economic realities in Ottawa-Hull. Canada has two official languages – English and French – and between 1971 and 1981 the government of Canada implemented its official language program to encourage employees in the public service to develop a facility to work in both of them. The influence of the public service in the National Capital Region, of which Ottawa-Hull is the core, is pervasive and extremely significant. The cities are essentially dominated, in employment terms, by the demands of government service. Prior to 1971 English was the language of all but the lower echelons of the civil service, and this shows up clearly in the surfaces. Between 1971 and 1981 there was a dramatic change (Figures 8.3 and 8.7). Bilingualism (defined as the ability to work in both English and French) became necessary for advancement in the public service. In addition, local boards of education introduced French-immersion programs in what were previously unilingual English schools. Between 1971 and 1981 the officially bilingual population of Ottawa-Hull increased from 32.65 percent to 40.15 percent, whereas those speaking only English dropped from 53.48 percent to 48.67 percent, and those speaking only French from 13.07 percent to 10.41 percent.

In the case of people speaking English only (Figures 8.2 and 8.3) the shape of the language surfaces did not alter much, with the surface for 1971 being virtually the same as that for 1981 (Figure 8.2). However, there was an overall decline in the percentage of people in this category and, whereas in earlier census periods there were many parts of Ottawa where 80 percent or more of the inhabitants spoke only English, by 1981 only one such tract remained (Figure 8.3). The dominance of English in Ottawa persisted and the sharp difference between Ottawa and Hull in linguistic terms also continued.

Those speaking only French are concentrated in Hull and, to a lesser extent, in Vanier, but as figures 8.4 and 8.5 show, there has been a significant change in the shape of the surface, especially in Hull. The number of people speaking French only in areas such as Mont Bleu, Montagne, and Aylmer has dropped significantly. These are areas of newer middle- and high-income housing developments where growing numbers of bilingual civil servants of predominantly French Canadian origin have chosen to live. In economic terms, to speak French only in Ottawa-Hull is a disadvantage. As a result, people speaking only French tend to be found in lower-income areas of Hull such as Gatineau and Templeton. There is also a relationship between the concrete and socio-economic landscapes of Hull, as a significant number of new high-rise federal government office complexes have been built in downtown Hull.

The highest percentages of the officially bilingual population (Figures 8.6 and 8.7) are concentrated in Hull and Vanier and, as mentioned above, there has been a marked increase in the western and northern parts of Hull. There has also been an expansion from Vanier eastwards.

Figures 8.8 and 8.9 show the distribution of people speaking neither French nor English. In 1951 there were only 0.20 percent of the entire population in this category, but by 1961 this had increased to 0.98 percent. The concentration of the Italian and Chinese communities is clearly visible in centretown from 1961 onwards. It is interesting to note that although some movement has taken place when some of the upwardly mobile members of the Italian community moved out of "Little Italy," the ethnic concentrations have persisted over time. More recent immigrants, especially those of Vietnamese origin, have settled in lower-town Hull where low-income housing is more prevalent. This language "sub-surface" is rarely given the attention it deserves, but is a very real element in the socio-economic landscape.

8.3.2   Education Surfaces

Figures 8.10 and 8.11 show the percentage of people with education levels less than grade nine, the lowest levels of educational achievement. Figures 8.12 and 8.13 show the opposite end of the educational spectrum, those with educational levels greater than grade 13 which, in essence, shows those with some college or university education. The mean level of education has increased dramatically, especially since 1971. The graphic picture is distorted to some extent by lack of consistency in statistical definitions. For the three earlier census periods the figures relate to the population of five years of age and over, while the figures for 1981 relate to the population of 15 years of age and over. This does not affect Figures 8.12 and 8.13, but does impact significantly on Figures 8.10 and 8.11. Despite this distortion the general trend in educational surfaces reflects a "social revolution" in Ottawa-Hull beginning in the late 1960s. The population was infinitely better educated by 1981.

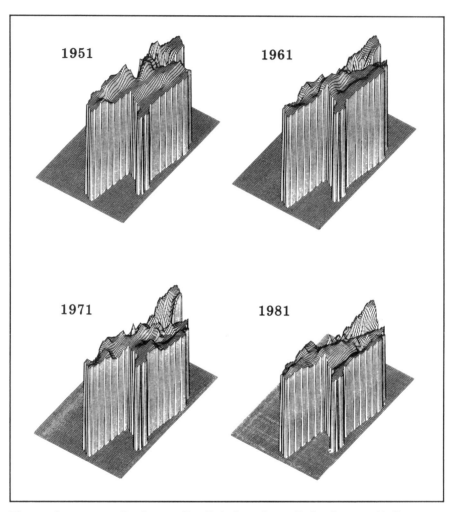

Figure   **Language Surfaces: English-Speakers Only, Ottawa-Hull,**
8.2   **1951, 1961, 1971, 1981**

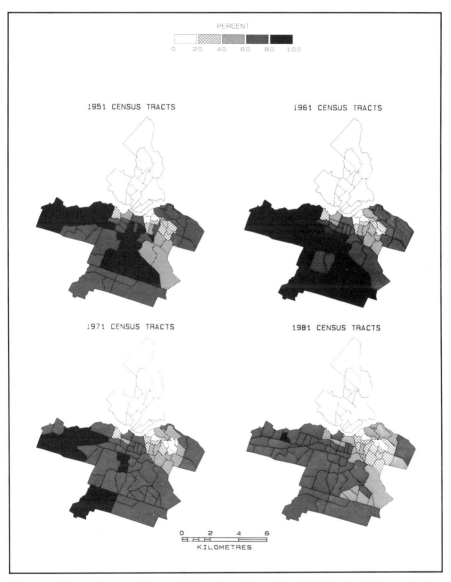

Figure **Percentage of Population Speaking English Only, Ottawa-Hull,**
8.3   **1951, 1961, 1971, 1981**
Produced by MIGS Cartographic Research Unit, Carleton University

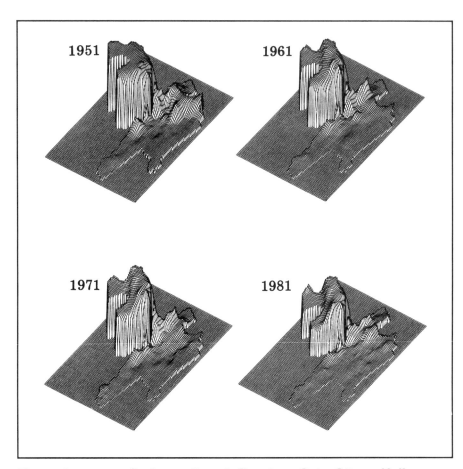

Figure   **Language Surfaces: French-Speakers Only, Ottawa-Hull,**
8.4   **1951, 1961, 1971, 1981**

Figure **Percentage of Population Speaking French Only, Ottawa-Hull,**
8.5   **1951, 1961, 1971, 1981**
Produced by MIGS Cartographic Research Unit, Carleton University

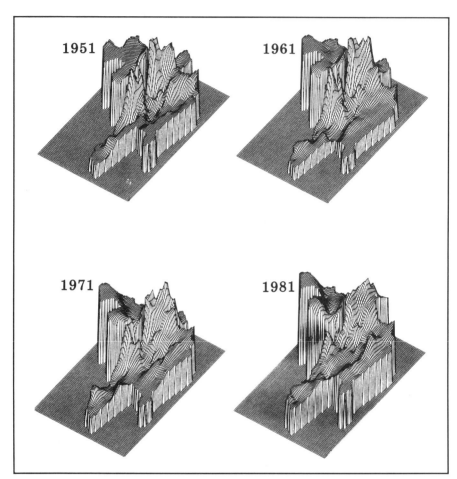

Figure   **Language Surfaces: English- and French-Speakers,**
8.6   **Ottawa-Hull, 1951, 1961, 1971, 1981**

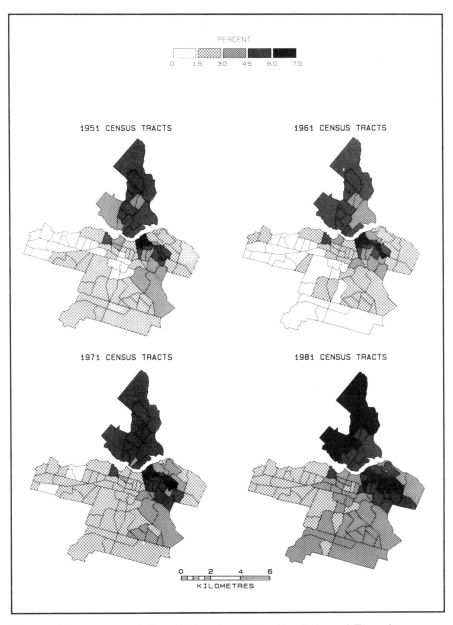

Figure
8.7
Percentage of Population Speaking English and French, Ottawa-Hull, 1951, 1961, 1971, 1981

Produced by MIGS Cartographic Research Unit, Carleton University

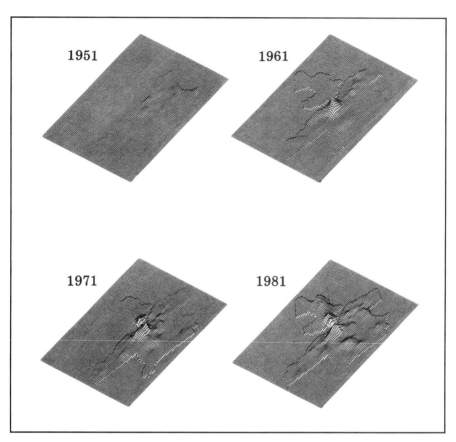

Figure   **Language Surfaces: Non-English-Speakers and**
8.8   **Non-French-Speakers, Ottawa-Hull, 1951, 1961, 1971, 1981**

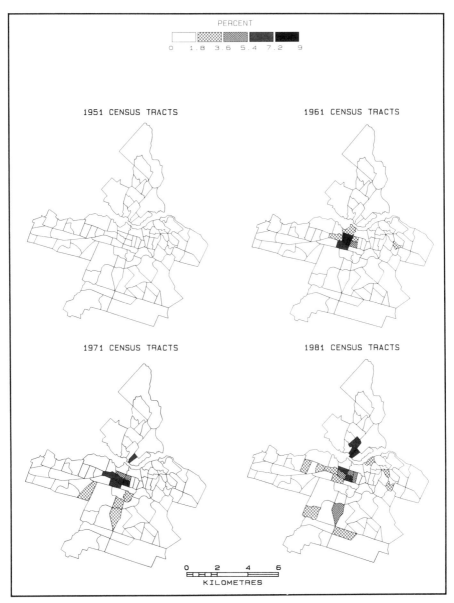

Figure **Percentage of Population Speaking Neither English nor**
8.9 **French, Ottawa-Hull, 1951, 1961, 1971, 1981**
Produced by MIGS Cartographic Research Unit, Carleton University

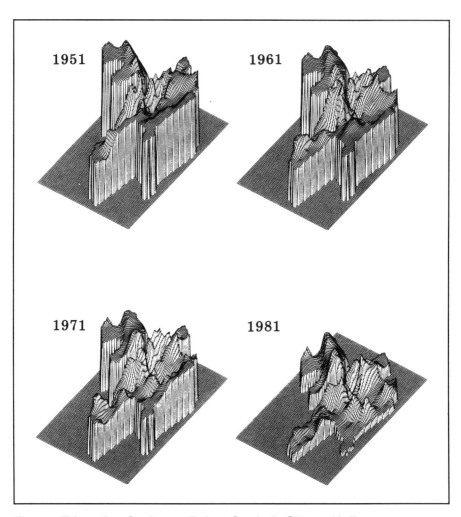

Figure   **Education Surfaces: Below Grade 9, Ottawa-Hull,**
8.10   **1951, 1961, 1971, 1981**

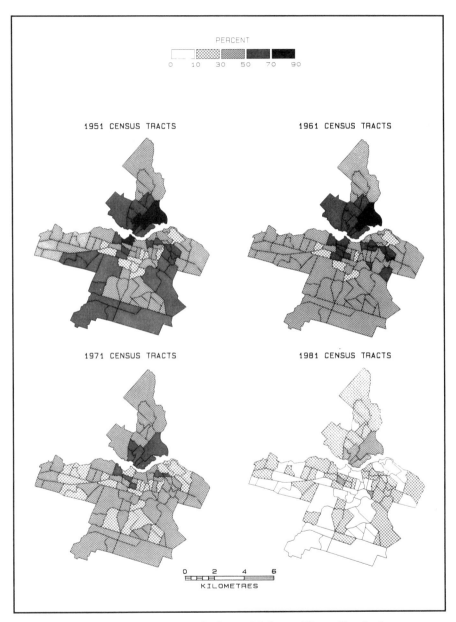

Figure   **Percentage of the Population with Less Than Grade 9**
8.11   **Education, Ottawa-Hull, 1951, 1961, 1971, 1981**
Produced by MIGS Cartographic Research Unit, Carleton University

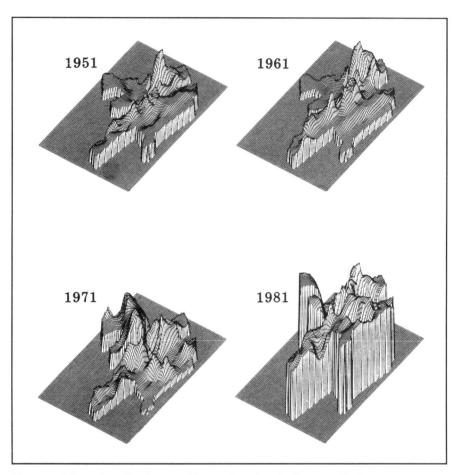

Figure   **Education Surfaces: Above Grade 13, Ottawa-Hull,**
8.12   **1951, 1961, 1971, 1981**

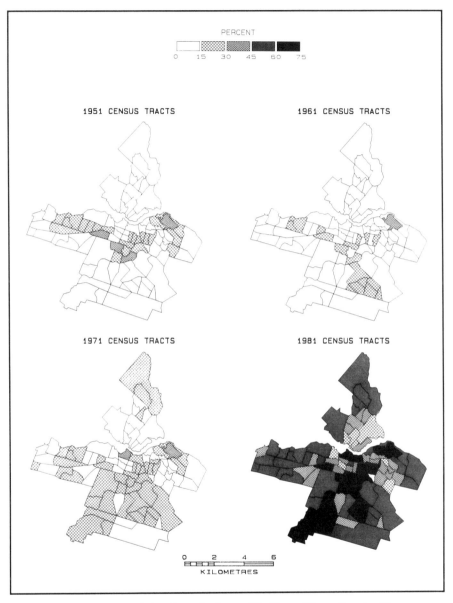

Figure   **Percentage of the Population with More Than Grade 13**
8.13   **Education, Ottawa-Hull, 1951, 1961, 1971, 1981**
           Produced by MIGS Cartographic Research Unit, Carleton University

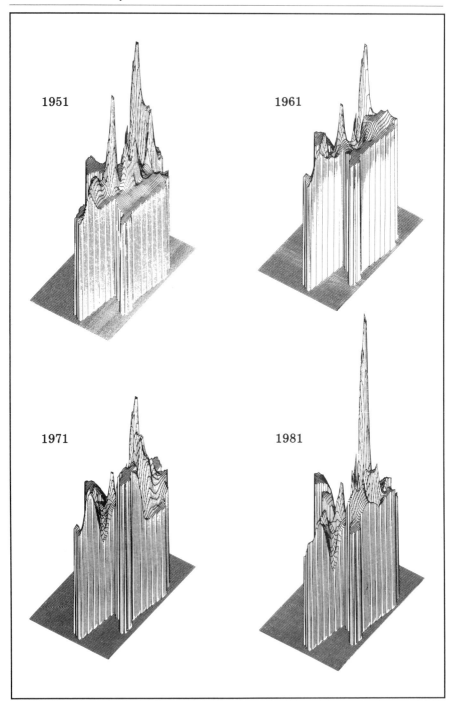

Figure   **Income Surfaces: Median Family Income, Ottawa-Hull,**
8.14   **1951, 1961, 1971, 1981**

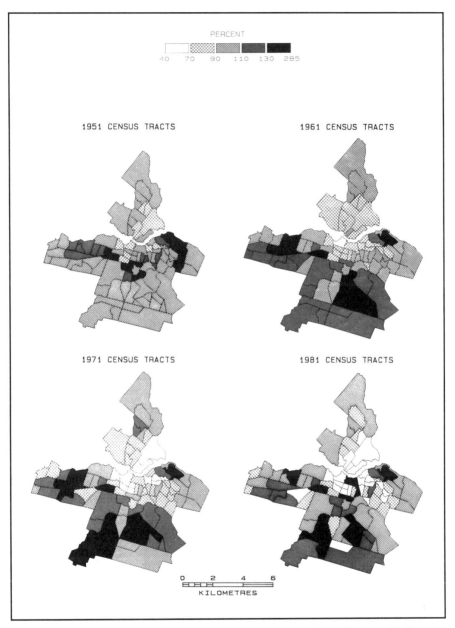

Figure **Family Income as a Percentage of the Median, Ottawa-Hull,**
8.15 **1951, 1961, 1971, 1981**
Produced by MIGS Cartographic Research Unit, Carleton University

The educational surfaces show interesting spatial relationships. Those areas where there is a higher proportion of people speaking neither English nor French have the highest proportions of people with the lowest levels of education, followed by those areas with the highest proportion of people speaking French only. Although these relationships were strongest in the earlier censuses, they still persisted, but much less strongly, in 1981.

Although all areas of Ottawa-Hull have benefited from increased education, some have benefited more than others. The changes in the surface in Hull show the influx of more highly educated, bilingual civil servants especially between 1971 and 1981.

8.3.3   Income Surfaces

Figures 8.14 and 8.15 show the final element chosen to illustrate the socio-economic surface of Ottawa-Hull, namely that of family income. As shown in Table 8.1, the median family income in the region rose from $2,484 in 1951 to $28,006 in 1981. Figures 8.14 and 8.15 have been constructed not to show absolute increases in income, but the percentage above or below the median, which would appear as 100 percent in Figure 8.15. The physically small area of Rockcliffe Park dominates Figure 8.14, and this dominance persists over all census periods, with the difference being at its greatest in 1981. In income terms, Rockcliffe Park is the Mount Everest of Ottawa-Hull, and it stands in sharp contrast to adjacent areas of the city.

Family income levels are related to both education and language. Families with the lowest income levels are found in those census tracts with the highest proportion of people speaking neither French nor English who also have the lowest educational levels. Although levels of education and language also give a good general explanation for the existence of higher-income areas, they are by no means the only explanatory factors in operation.

8.4   Conclusion

This chapter has illustrated the use of computer-assisted cartography for creation of visible socio-economic surfaces. The approach used has been selective rather than comprehensive. Many more variables, resulting in many more illustrations, could have been chosen, but limitations of space made this impractical. In the information era, computer-assisted cartography has a special role to play in creating new forms of cartographic representation and new ways of communicating information. None of these diagrams could have been easily or quickly produced by conventional means, and the diagrams help to bring alive the social Himalayas and other features of the cultural landscape of which Watson wrote many years ago.

The nature of this volume demands that the cartography used be in the form of hard copy. Had this limitation not been present then the nature of the socio-economic surface of Ottawa-Hull could have been much more fully explored in an interactive fashion on a terminal. The three-dimensional diagrams could have been rotated to give different views of the same surface. Surfaces can be viewed from any point in the region and some idea of the perceptions of the inhabitants of these areas might be achieved as a result. The view of a socio-economic surface from the top of a peak is very different from that at the bottom of a valley! (Taylor 1977). The nature and form of the variables chosen and the inter-relationships explored could also have been in the hands of the user, rather than those of the author. Sophisticated interactive cartographic information systems have now been developed with hundreds of variables. A system being developed by the municipality of Burnaby in British Columbia has over 3,000 variables on the municipality available on an interactive basis (Juhl 1986). New communications technologies such as videotex and videodisc are increasing the availability of data bases to users, and we are not far away from the time when ordinary citizens will have the same access to information as the planners. The electronic atlas of Canada, which will provide many of these capabilities, is currently being developed (Siekierska and Taylor 1991).

Computer-assisted cartography offers new ways both of understanding and illustrating social geography and of making its findings more easily available and understandable. What is in essence a "New Cartography" is emerging to respond to the demands of the information era. Cartographic analysis and presentation has its drawbacks, but it has two major advantages for the social geographer: it uses space as the key variable, and it communicates spatial patterns and relationships graphically. Modern cartography provides an interesting way to further the imaginative social geography of which Wreford Watson was a pioneer.

Acknowledgements

The author would like to acknowledge the research assistance of Elise Refuse, David Saab, Stephen Prashker, and Christine Earl in the preparation of this chapter.

References

Bouillé, F. 1984. "Educational Geomatics for New Look Cartographers." *Technical Papers of the 12th Conference of the International Cartographic Association* 1:820–29.

Broome, F.R., and S.W. Witiuk. 1980. "Census Mapping by Computer." In D.R.F. Taylor, ed., *The Computer in Contemporary Cartography,* 191–217. Chichester: John Wiley and Sons.

Carter, J.R. 1984. *Computer Mapping: Progress in the 80's.* State College, Pennsylvania: Resource Publications, Association of American Geographers.

Guptill, S.C., and L.E. Starr. 1984. "The Future of Cartography in the Information Age." In L.E. Starr, ed., *Computer-assisted Cartography Research and Development Report,* 1–15. Washington D.C.: International Cartographic Association.

Juhl, J.M. 1986. "Automated Mapping." *The DEC Professional* 5 (4): 1–9.

Monmonier, M. 1982. *Computer-assisted Cartography: Principles and Prospects.* Englewood Cliffs: Prentice-Hall.

———. 1985. *Technological Transition in Cartography.* Madison: University of Wisconsin Press.

Prashker, S., and D.R.F. Taylor. 1983. "MIGS: A Microcomputer Mapping System for Cartography in Developing Nations." In B. Wellar, ed., *Automated Cartography: International Achievements and Challenges,* vol. 1, 480–87. Ottawa: Proceedings of the Sixth International Symposium on Automated Cartography.

Rhind, D., N. Green, H. Mounsey, and J. Wiggins. 1984. "The Integration of Geographical Data." In *Technical Papers of the Austra Carto One Seminar,* 237–55. Perth: 12th ICA Conference Committee.

Siekierska, E., and D.R.F. Taylor. 1991. "Electronic Mapping and Electronic Atlases: New Catographic Products for the Information Era – The Electronic Atlas of Canada." *CISM Journal* 45 (1): 11–21 (Spring 1991).

Slocum, T.A., and S.L. Egbert. 1991. "Cartographic Data Display." In D.R.F. Taylor, ed., *Geographic Information Systems: The Microcomputer and Modern Cartography.* Oxford: Pergamon Press.

Taylor, D.R.F., and D.H. Douglas. 1970. *A Computer Atlas of Ottawa-Hull.* Ottawa: Carleton University.

Taylor, D.R.F. 1977. "Graphic Perception of Language in Ottawa-Hull." *Canadian Cartographer* 14: 21–34.

———. 1985. "The Educational Challenges of a New Cartography." In D.R.F. Taylor, ed., *Education and Training in Contemporary Cartography,* 3–25. Chichester: John Wiley and Sons.

———. 1991. "Geographic Information Systems: The Microcomputer and Modern Cartography." In D.R.F. Taylor, ed., *Geographic Information Systems: The Microcomputer and Modern Cartography.* Oxford: Pergamon Press.

Watson, J.W. 1957. "The Sociological Aspects of Geography." In G. Taylor, ed., *Geography in the Twentieth Century: A Study of Growth, Fields, Techniques, Aims and Trends,* 3d ed., 463–99. London: Methuen & Co.

9   Ethnicity and Social Areas within Winnipeg

Isobel P. Carlyle

As the longest established of the five major cities of the Canadian Prairies, Winnipeg exhibits characteristics in its social geography that stem from the four or five generations that have inhabited it. Yet, at the same time, Winnipeg demonstrates many of the recent social changes common to North American cities. Both the unique features of the city's physical geography and the sequential migration into the city of different ethnic groups during succeeding decades have contributed to the rich diversity of the city's social geography.

If one approaches Winnipeg, the provincial capital of Manitoba, from the level land of the surrounding Red River Valley, the city presents the typical profile of most cities in North America. One- and two-storey suburban houses spread out over the plains, up to 13 kilometres from the centre in some directions: evidence of unremitting suburbanization. The skyscrapers of the city's business nucleus, most no more than 15 years old, appear as a grey cluster culminating in their apex at the intersection of Portage Avenue and Main Street, the longstanding centre of the city (Bellan 1978, 255) (see Figure 9.1). This intersection is itself little more than a kilometre north and west of "The Forks," the confluence of the two principal rivers of the eastern part of the Prairies, the Red River and the Assiniboine River.

Much of this physical appearance – and the confluence site – is little different from many another Canadian city. Yet, Winnipeg belies the normality of its appearance in the distinctiveness of its social, and particularly ethnic, geography. A closer look at the city's landscape reveals an almost incredible variety of churches and religious meeting places, which run the gamut from Scottish Presbyterian churches to a Ukrainian Catholic cathedral with its four spectacular bulbous towers. The city's retail establishments show another aspect of ethnic variety: there are Korean corner stores, German delicatessens and a shop selling traditional German dress, Jewish butchers serving kosher fare, an old-style British grocery store, and restaurants of almost every imaginable national type. Even banks and credit unions sometimes have ethnic connections. The ethnic balance of the city's population is substantially different from that of Canada as a whole. In this regard Winnipeg bears similarities to cities in the United States, although the specific ethnic groups found in Winnipeg, and their proportions, are not typical of any American city.

In studies of Canada's urban areas, Hill (1976) considered Winnipeg to be the nation's most ethnically diverse city. Of other major Canadian cities, Toronto now approaches Winnipeg in the diversity of its ethnic mosaic, but this is a recent phenomenon begun little more than a decade ago, whereas ethnic diversity in Winnipeg has been established for many years. It is the purpose of this essay, first, to show the cosmopolitan nature of the city's people and the cultural landscapes that have arisen from this; second, to show how distinct social regions have developed along ethnic lines; and, third, to demonstrate trends among ethnic groups that can be expected to continue in the future.

9.1   Ethnic Groups

In 1981, 564,473 people lived within the metropolitan confines of Winnipeg, an increase of 0.64 percent on the total for 1976. The population of the Census Metropolitan Area (CMA), which includes suburban overspill and the rural-urban fringe, as well as residents within the city limits, rose from 578,217 to 584,842 (1.15 percent) within this five-year period. By 1986 this total had risen to 625,305, a 6.9 percent increase since 1981.

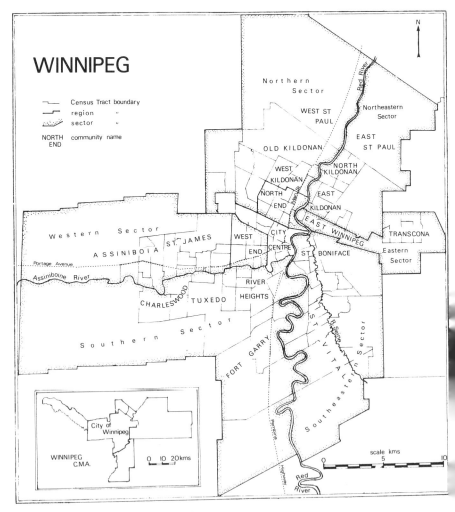

Figure   **Winnipeg: Location Map**
9.1

Table **Recent Changes in Population in the Major Cities of the**
9.1 **Prairie Provinces**

	Population 000s				
	1971	**1976**	**1981**	**1986**	**% 1971–86**
Calgary CMA	403	471	593	671	+67
Edmonton CMA	496	556	657	698	+41
Regina City	141	150	163	187[1]	+32
Saskatoon City	126	134	154	20[1]	+60
Winnipeg CMA	550	578	585	625	+14

1. CMA.

Sources: Census of Canada, 1981, "Selected Characteristics: Winnipeg," Catalogue
no. 95-940 (vol. 3, series A), and Catalogue no. 99-942; *Census of Canada,
1986*

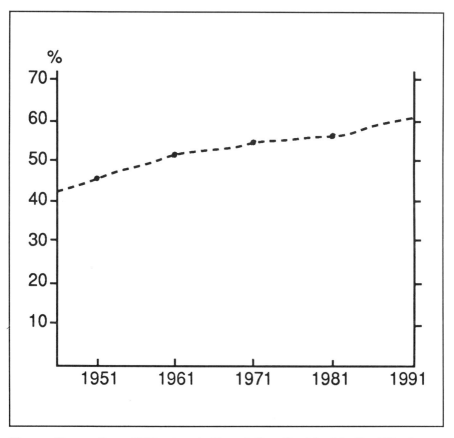

Figure **Proportion of Winnipeg's Population Resident in the Winnipeg**
9.2 **CMA, 1951–81**

For several decades such a sedate rate of growth has contrasted with the mushrooming of the populations of the cities in Alberta and has deprived Winnipeg of its long-held pre-eminent status as the most populous Prairie city (see Table 9.1). However, within Manitoba, Winnipeg continues to increase its proportion of the total provincial population. From 46 percent in 1951, Winnipeg now holds 59 percent (1986) of the province's population (Figure 9.2). Against a backdrop of comparatively slow growth, the social geography of Winnipeg has changed relatively rapidly.

In Winnipeg there are 32 ethnic groups of more than one thousand people mentioned in the population census of 1981, and some of these, such as the British (Scottish, English, Welsh, and Irish), the Scandinavian (Icelanders, Norwegians, Swedes, and Danes), and the Germans (Germans and Mennonites) can be subdivided further, increasing the number of ethnic groups. Additionally, the census does not collect figures for certain ethnic groups, such as Americans or Métis. Other ethnic groups, including Jews, appear in the statistics for religious groups.[1]

Since there are only small disparities between urban and rural birth and death rates in Manitoba, the continued growth in the proportion of the province's population that lives in its provincial capital is largely a result of in-migration. This movement of population from rural Manitoba, and also the rest of Canada, the United States, and from other countries, has been a major factor in the development of the city's special ethnic characteristics. The influx from rural areas has been important in establishing the British, Ukrainian, Mennonite, and French groups. Additionally, native Indians have provided one of the most recent in-migrations to enlarge the city's population at the expense of the rest of the province.

In the early growth of Winnipeg's population, migration from other regions of Canada was especially important, as groups already well settled in eastern Canada, principally Scots and English from Ontario, and a few French Canadians, relocated westwards. But, as well as internal migration, there have been sequential waves of migration directly to Winnipeg from both town and country in the British Isles, northwest Europe, Slavic Europe, and, more recently, Mediterranean Europe. Asian sources – China, Korea, and, recently, India, Vietnam, and the Philippines – have also added an increasing flow of people. In 1971, 7,305 people were listed as being of Asian ethnic origin: 1.3 percent of the total population; by 1981, 19,690, representing 3.4 percent of the total population, were enumerated as having an Asian birthplace.[2] Although these figures are not directly comparable, as the latter also includes some non-Asians, these percentages indicate a substantial increase. A small Chinese community has been prominent since the late nineteenth century, and has increased from about 500 people prior to the First World War to 6,195 in 1981. Also, since many recent arrivals are Asian or from the islands of the Pacific Ocean (15,670 Filipinos were recorded in the 1986 census), the racial composition of the population has altered. The overall effect is small, but because newcomers are concentrated in the inner areas of the city, in a "Zone of Transition," changes in racial composition are important at the local level in these areas.

One consequence of these recent changes in immigration has been a shift in the proportion of the population attending different Christian denominations. Long-established ethnic groups in Winnipeg attend Anglican, United Church, Ukrainian Catholic, Mennonite, and Roman Catholic churches as their principal places of worship, while Jews attend synagogues. Newer ethnic groups, including the Vietnamese and Filipinos, are often Roman Catholic, or profess an oriental religion. Roman Catholics and Ukrainian Catholics increased from 171,800 to 199,225 (16 percent) in the decade 1971–81. On the other hand, the main Protestant denominations, the United Church of Canada (the former Methodist, Presbyterian, and Congregational churches), and the Anglican Church have respectively declined from 129,100 to 122,360 people (–5.2 percent), and from 69,590 to 60,435 people (–13.2 percent). This has occurred despite population increases among the varied groups that attend Protestant denominations, including those that are not the traditional groups adhering to these two churches. The combined total of believers in Eastern religions has now reached 6,615 people.[3]

The proportions of each ethnic group to the rest have also been changing, as can be demonstrated for the four major groups: the British, Ukrainian, German, and French. In 1981 the British were most numerous, as would be expected in any city of English-speaking Canada. Yet, they have not formed a majority of the city's population since 1951, and their overall proportion continues to fall (39 percent in 1981 compared with 43 percent in 1971). In the 1986 census, of the 392,480 people in the Winnipeg CMA recording a single ethnic origin (as opposed to a multiple one) 32.3 percent were British. Even so, this does not diminish their position as the most numerous ethnic group in the city, nearly three times as numerous as the second-ranking Ukrainian group (Figure 9.3), which represented 12.2 percent of those claiming single ethnic origin in 1986.

The distribution of the British throughout Winnipeg is in keeping with their plurality: they are found in all census tracts, including areas where other ethnic groups are dominant. To a large extent, their distribution reflects that of the city's population as a whole. As Winnipeg has expanded, so has the British ethnic group. Their index of residential segregation is very low, this being a measure of their dispersion throughout the general population (Figure 9.4).[4] Yet a pattern of preferred residence for this group is not entirely lacking. Changes since the Second World War have tended consistently towards ever more extensive suburbanization. The traditional British area of St. James and West End Winnipeg (Figure 9.1) has extended farther and farther into Assiniboia and the commuter village of Headingley. At the same time, this group has expanded into all other suburbs.

Although detailed information on the English, Irish, Scots, and Welsh was available in early censuses, very little is published at present. The Irish are not listed as a separate group despite the independence of the Republic of Ireland. Unpublished data is not readily available except on a provincial basis, which breaks down the British group in Manitoba for 1981 as follows: English, 58 percent; Irish, 12 percent; Scottish, 19 percent; Welsh, 1 percent; and mixed British origins (and unclassified), 10 percent.

Numerically, Ukrainians form the second-largest ethnic group in Winnipeg, with nearly 59,000 people, or 11 percent of the total in the CMA in 1981. As with the

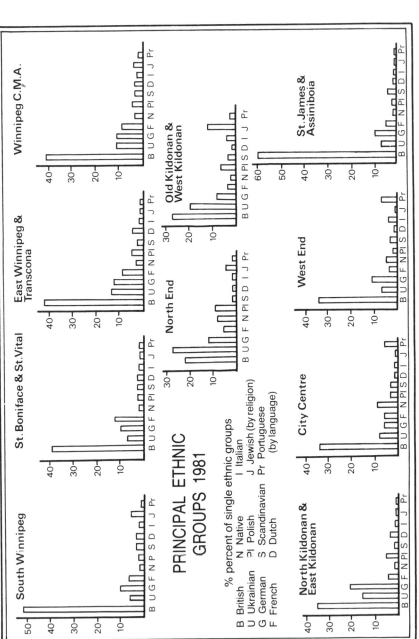

Figure 9.3   **Principal Ethnic Groups in Winnipeg, 1981**

British, this percentage is lower than at the previous decennial census. In both instances part of the decline is apparent rather than real, a result of census enumeration allowing multiple ethnic origins to be tabulated.[5] Although the Ukrainian group is scattered throughout the urban area, and shows the strong propensity to suburban expansion of most other groups, nevertheless it still favours certain locations. For example, there remains a high ratio of Ukrainians who live in the North End and adjacent suburbs north of the Canadian Pacific shunting yards, the area hitherto preferred by this group. But, compared with a decade or more ago, fewer Ukrainians live in the inner North End, since many young families have moved to the newer suburbs of West and Old Kildonan to the west of the Red River, or to Elmwood, East and North Kildonan on the east bank. Ukrainians are sparsely represented in the wealthier suburbs south of the Assiniboine River, though less sparsely than previously.

The German ethnic group comprises German Canadians of long standing, Mennonites, and more recent immigrants from Germany. There were 45,880 single-origin Germans recorded in the 1986 census (11.7 percent of all single origins). The Mennonites, in particular, are distinct, because they are a separate religious sect, some of whose number (19,105 in Winnipeg by religion in 1981) are found in census totals for Dutch and Russian, as well as German, ethnic groups (Fromson 1965, 77). With 55,000 people, the German subgroups combine to form the third most numerous ethnic group, and comprise 11 percent of the city's population.[6] Soon after the Second World War, the distributions of the German groups were not too dissimilar to the main Slavic groups (Ukrainian and Polish), with many Germans living in the poorer central areas of Winnipeg, and the North End. The special Mennonite settlement in North Kildonan was still small, and few Germans lived in any of the city's suburbs or in the wealthy areas of south Winnipeg. Today, the pattern of residence has changed completely; few Germans now live in the inner North End, having moved out to more comfortable suburbs. There remains a distinct German population in the West End, but their overall distribution in 1981 was similar to that of the British and the general population. The principal exception to this generalization is the high density of Germans of Mennonite origin in North Kildonan.

The foregoing three ethnic groups, British, Ukrainian, and German, account for over half the city's population. This, in itself, displays the contrast between Winnipeg's ethnic mosaic and that of English-speaking Canada, or even Canada as a whole, in either of which a combination of French and British groups comprises well over half the people. Although early French development in Winnipeg attempted a "two nations" concept, striving for equal importance with the British, this never happened, primarily due to a lack of immigration from either Quebec or France. The French ethnic group is the fourth most numerous in the city.[7] Over 38,000 people, or 7.5 percent of the population of the Winnipeg CMA, are of French ethnic origin (35,085 of single French ethnic origin in 1986). They are concentrated on the east bank of the Red River around the nucleus of the Cathedral of St. Boniface. This cluster of French Canadians in St. Boniface and St. Vital constitutes the largest such group in Canada west of Ontario.

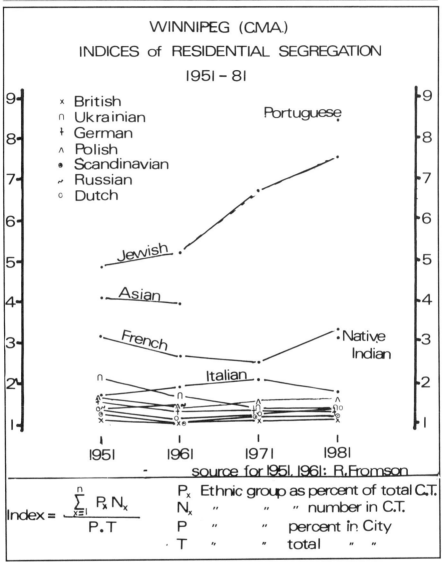

Figure 9.4   **Winnipeg CMA: Indices of Residential Segregation**

The proportions of French and British in Winnipeg reflect those in Manitoba as a whole, in part, at least, because the city contains such a large part of the province's population. However, the ratios differ substantially from those of the rest of Canada: for 1981 the British are slightly less well represented (39 percent compared with a national figure of 40 percent), and the French are much less well represented (7.5 percent versus 27 percent). Of the remaining major ethnic groups, the principal ones are Polish (3.7 percent), Jewish (3.0 percent), native Canadian (2.5 percent), Dutch (2.4 percent), Scandinavian (2.1 percent), and Italian (1.7 percent).

The Polish group has similarities with the Ukrainian in general distribution, although they have remained closer to the North End. Native Canadians, almost entirely Indians rather than Inuit, are probably undercounted in the census. In Winnipeg, most Scandinavians are Icelanders; they are found throughout the city, with no particular clustering in any one area. The Dutch include both Mennonites, who have moved into the city from rural southern Manitoba over the decades, and immigrants arriving directly from the Netherlands. Italians are usually recent immigrants, and there are clusters in the West End and in Fort Rouge, but they also follow the trend towards suburban residence. Even more recently arrived, generally, the Portuguese are concentrated in the West End, and have not yet dispersed to the outer fringes of the metropolitan zone.

Jewish groups show a binodal distribution: one cluster in West Kildonan beyond the North End, the other in River Heights and Tuxedo (Figures 9.4 and 9.5). The original Jewish area was the North End, where they settled along with the first wave of continental European immigrants to reach the city. This area has expanded outwards, becoming a little more suburban, although in this regard both the Jews and the Chinese resist the strong suburbanization of the other established groups. Their movements and relative growth patterns since 1951 have been from the poorer inner zones of the North End to the adjacent inner suburbs or to the wealthy inner suburbs south of the Assiniboine. Unlike the other longstanding cultural groups, Jews have avoided the newly settled outermost suburbs and the rural-urban fringe. As with the Chinese, this may be ascribed largely to their desire to retain a distinct identity. As Fromson (1965, 91–99) has shown, the move to River Heights and Tuxedo has occurred mainly since the war, as this group has become more prosperous. In 1971 most of the Jewish group lived north of the Canadian Pacific Railway (CPR) tracks, with a minority living south of the Assiniboine. By 1981, the two clusters were nearly equal in number.

Recent developments in immigration directly from foreign countries have added to the already considerable cultural diversity. Since the Second World War, a steady stream of refugees fleeing war and revolution has included Latvians, Lithuanians, Estonians, and Finns from the Baltic; Armenians, Albanians, Greeks, Czechs, Slovaks, Rumanians, and Russians from Asia Minor and eastern Europe; and Belgians, Spanish, and Swiss from western Europe. In this list are merely a few of the polyglot groups that have rarely gained individual attention in Winnipeg, and yet collectively account for over 15,000 people. Sikhs, Vietnamese, Greeks, Portuguese and Chileans are among the arrivals of the last decade; they have often been refugees from political turmoil.

This brief outline of the principal ethnic groups in Winnipeg shows that some of them, notably the British, Icelandic, Dutch, and German, live throughout the city, displaying weak tendencies to reside in particular zones, and thus displaying considerable assimilation. One can look in vain for specifically Dutch or Icelandic churches, banks, or stores. Similarly, the Canadian-born children of immigrants from Germany do not always use the stores that cater to their parents. These groups have indices of residential segregation that are little above unity.[8] Others, like the newly

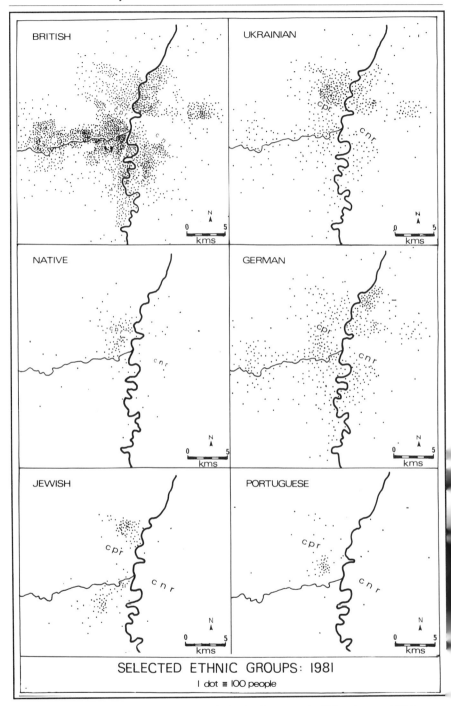

Figure 9.5   **Location of Selected Ethnic Groups in Winnipeg, 1981**

arrived Portuguese and, as urban residents, native Indians, or the long-settled French and Jews, are concentrated in particular neighbourhoods. These groups have indices of residential segregation that are well above unity. Consequently, different parts of the city have developed unique cultural balances, some of which have altered slowly over the generations (Figure 9.4).

Indices of residential segregation, calculated for the city's census tracts, show that over time there has been increasing assimilation of the principal ethnic groups into the suburbs. The British are scattered throughout the city in a fashion not too different from the population as a whole: even in regions of distinct culture, such as French St. Boniface, they are often the second ethnic group. In West Kildonan, one of the two Jewish nuclei in the city, although Jews are the largest single group, the British are actually more numerous in three of four census tracts. A breakdown into even smaller areal units would be necessary to pinpoint the real concentration of the Jewish community. Other prominent cultural groups are also dispersed: Ukrainians, Germans, Dutch, and Icelanders all have indices of 1.1 to 1.4, which characterize almost random distribution. Newly arrived groups have high indices of segregation as a consequence of "huddling" together in low-income, low-rent areas, which are not extensive in Winnipeg. Jews have a high index, which has actually increased over time as a result of further clustering associated with their unique religious and social position.

While it is obvious that ethnic groups such as the Germans and Icelanders have been assimilated into the predominantly Protestant Anglo-Saxon society of the city, the low indices of some groups mask a certain lack of assimilation. In this respect, the index does not sufficiently emphasize levels of assimilation that are only moderate. This can be seen in the case of the Ukrainians. Although this group is found throughout the city, more are still in North Winnipeg than south of the tracks (Figure 9.5).

9.2   Ethnic Sectors: The Social Areas of Winnipeg

The recognition of distinctive internal city regions was a feature of the pioneering work of human ecologists in Chicago, building on the ideas of Park, Burgess, and McKenzie (1925). Their identification of zones and sectors in social terms has been taken up in a multitude of studies that have made use of their concepts about population, namely that populations are segregated residentially by social class, and so "observable patterns of residential segregation in spatial terms can be discerned within the city" (Carter 1981, 251). Geographical studies of the "social areas" of cities have progressed from testing of the ecologists' hypotheses to multivariate taxonomies to more complex models and considerations drawing attention well away from the conventional basis of pattern analysis (Jackson and Smith, 1984). However, within the early post-war literature, one of the best examples of a description of distinctive social areas that uses some of the ideas of the ecologists, was Watson's (1957, 484–98) work on Hamilton, Ontario. This described the social regions of the city using the ecologists' terms – "transition zone," "segregation," and "social distance." A portrayal such as this, based on an interweaving of themes relating to distributions, social structures, functions, and processes, is no longer central to many studies by geographers of the social characteristics of residential areas. However, Winnipeg's distinctive ethnic geography lends itself to such a portrait which, in itself, recalls the regional differentiation stressed in Watson's views on social geography.

In Winnipeg the physical growth of the urban area has created concentric rings of housing of different types and ages. Land use, on the other hand, shows considerable multi-nodal aspects, with such foci as the Central Business District, the Brooklands-Airport-Inkster wholesale and industrial zone, and the University of Manitoba. However, considering the regionalization of ethnicity, there is strong sectorial development.

In the establishment of this sectorial pattern the city's basic physical geography has been a factor. Winnipeg owes much of its shape to the Assiniboine and Red rivers, with the three reaches of the rivers creating sectors, and the smaller River Seine enhancing the development of sectors east of the Red River. The boundaries of the rural river lots, which early settlers based on the major watercourses, are parallel with the principal determining lines of the modern street system. The historical Portage Trail along the westward-reaching tributary, the Assiniboine River, and the Pembina Trail parallel with the reaches of the Red River north and south of the confluence, are the precursors of the three backbones upon which the modern street system has evolved (Weir 1978, 4). The city has rarely been circular at any stage of its expansion, because new additions have tended to follow the northern, southern, and western extensions along the rivers (Carlyle 1974, 28–30). To the north, suburban development was discouraged because of the prior existence of linear settlement and market gardening leading to Selkirk, once a commercial rival to Winnipeg. This has encouraged development in the downstream direction of the Red River. On either bank of the rivers there is little urban spread farther than four kilometres away from the bank. Rather than one, single, all-embracing grid pattern, as is common in most modern North American cities, Winnipeg has a series of three intermeshing gridirons, which further demonstrate the characteristics of sectorial growth.

To some extent, these "ethnic sectors" in Winnipeg correspond with the rural areas in which the same ethnic groups dominate. Thus, the British are found in southwestern Manitoba and also the western suburbs of St. James and Assiniboia; the Slavs live in the Interlake north of the city and in the city's North End; and the French live in the south-eastern suburbs of St. Boniface and St. Vital and in south-eastern Manitoba. These connections between the rural areas and the nearest urban sector suggest the maintenance of social contacts between town and country.

The open swathe cut through northern Winnipeg by the airport, the Canadian Pacific shunting and switching yards, the Symington yards and Transcona shops of the Canadian National Railway, the Winnipeg aqueduct with its railway, and all the associated activity, has created further sectors. One sector (the northern) can be seen between the Red River and the Canadian Pacific Railway yards; a second (the western) between these latter and the Assiniboine River; a third (the southern) south of the Assiniboine (which could be divided into two); a fourth (the south-eastern) between the Red River and the Seine River with the nearby Canadian National

Railway yards; a fifth (the eastern); and a sixth (the north-eastern) between the railway yards and the Red River (Figure 9.1).

Within each sector the familiar change from older, inner suburbs to newer, more dispersed, and often wealthier, outer suburbs normally exists. In defining the regions used in the following sections, these sectors have sometimes been divided further. Census tract boundaries, which frequently define the real boundaries of the regions, have been used in delineating the exact boundaries in order that the ethnic character of each region can be more accurately ascertained. No attempt has been made to divide Winnipeg into an exhaustive list of small regions. The regions chosen are broad urban zones, and it will be noticed that several smaller community areas are often named as being within particular sectorial regions (Peach 1975).

9.2.1   The City Centre[9]

This region includes the Central Business District and a large part of the zone of transition, which lies to the north and north-west, between the business area and the railway yards. This is the area of the city that provides the most employment.

As its focus this region has the chief financial district, concentrated around the intersection of Portage Avenue and Main Street. This district is the direct successor to the original commercial core of a century ago. Westwards, this uninhabited zone continues along the central retailing corridor of Portage Avenue and its side streets. On the southern side of the retail area is found a zone extending from the provincial legislature and law courts in the west, to the railway station, just short of the river, in the east. Public buildings, provincial government offices, medical clinics and ancillary activities, hotels, car parks, and apartments are characteristic of land use. Although the residential component of land use is sporadic, the population increases southwards towards the banks of the Assiniboine River. Armstrong Point is an enclave of high-class housing within a meander of the Assiniboine River.

North of the business and retail districts lies much of Winnipeg's zone of transition, where delapidated residential streets intermingle with waste areas, scattered improvement districts, and small-scale manufacturing such as the "pin trade." The city's "pin trade," comprising the manufacturing of clothing, especially gloves, fashionable ladies' wear, work clothes, and winterwear and furs suitable for Winnipeg's climate, markets its products across Canada. It provides employment to new immigrants, because most of the work can be done without an understanding of either English or French. Clothing firms make use of the older buildings in this area. The zone of transition is something of a no-man's land, as is commonly found in larger cities between the central business district and the residentially undesirable railway yards.

In its ethnic balance this city region is obviously quite different from suburban areas. Although it has some similarity with the North End or the Inner West End, it has its own unique features. Essentially, residential housing in this neighbourhood consists of apartment blocks, both new multi-storey structures and older three- and four-storey brick structures, and rented private housing, often of very substandard quality. Simultaneously, the luxury penthouse is side by side with skid row (Rowley 1978; Barber and Brook 1980).

New immigrants to Canada from Asia and Portugal, among others, make use of the inexpensive houses to be found in the poorer fringes of the central area. The small Chinatown has been a feature here for decades, but it has fallen into decay. It is now being rebuilt as an even more distinctive set of buildings. Chinese style architecture is being juxtaposed with western styles in a new complex, comprising apartments, and facilitates for commerce and cultural activities. For different reasons, the poor among the well-established ethnic groups, the British, French, Métis, Ukrainian and Icelandic, also live on the fringes of downtown.

In common with the North End, the central-fringe zone of transition is also home for many native Indians, whose migration into Winnipeg from reserves in both northern and southern Manitoba has been fraught with innumerable problems. Alcoholism, crime, poverty, unemployment, and complete maladjustment to urban living are just a few of the difficult, and sometimes disastrous, problems that they confront. It is probable that the census figure of 13,260 native Indians in Winnipeg is a substantial under-enumeration of people with mainly native Indian ancestry. The number would swell considerably if the census were to include the French-speaking Métis and English-speaking Métis (once known as "Half-Breed" or occasionally "country-born"), respectively of part-Indian, part-French Canadian ancestry, and part-Indian, part-British Canadian ancestry. The mixed-race Métis groups, however, usually regard themselves as a unique entity separate from French, British, and native Indians alike. Prior to the 1981 census, most French Métis, being French speakers, would include themselves in the French group for census purposes in the absence of their own specific group; likewise, most English-speaking Métis would list themselves under the British group. For example, most of the Scottish Orcadian fur-traders in the Selkirk Settlement married Indian women, and most of their descendants have disappeared entirely into the British group, only a small minority continuing to regard themselves as Métis of Scottish-Indian ancestry. Many of the other fur traders who retired to the Selkirk Settlement were already Métis of Indian and either French or Scottish origin (Mailhot and Sprague 1985). There is some evidence of a subtle nuance in the different attitudes of the French and British to the Métis. Descendants of the French and Indian settlers appear to have more awareness of their background as Métis. Despite this, they have been obliged to list themselves as French until the 1981 Census, in which "French and other" ethnic origin is included, although this is still not a Métis classification *per se*. In recent years, as in the past, non-Indian women of many different origins – Icelandic, for example – have married Indians and become treaty Indians themselves. Their descendants are mixed-blood treaty Indians. There are also mixed-race people from rural Manitoba, Ontario, and elsewhere. Thus, the mixed-race groups merge racially with the French, British, Indians, and others.

Even assuming that Métis are excluded, under-enumeration of native Indians appears to be present, partly because many of them have a transient lifestyle. treaty

Indians from a particular band and reserve generally cannot retain their rights and privileges, which may be substantial, if they live permanently off the reservation. Consequently, many visit, rather than reside in, the city, even though their visits may be of several months' duration every year. The large number of such temporary residents increases the Indian population.

The total native population has been estimated to be as high as 50,000 people, but this undoubtedly includes Métis – and probably more than would regard themselves as Métis. Somewhere between 13,260 and 50,000 lies the true figure. Relative to the total population of 560,874 in the city, this seems to be one of the largest proportions of native Indians to be found in any Canadian or American city of over half-a-million people; within Canada, Regina and Saskatoon are the only sizeable cities with similar ratios.

Inevitably, there are immense social problems associated with the influx of so many Indians from reserves (Baxter 1968; Driedger 1978; Driedger and Church 1974; Clark and Gleave 1973). Traditional native skills, valuable in remote areas only a generation or two in the past, have never been marketable in the city. Hence, unemployment is rife and income is low, even where an occupation is found. Many younger Indians drift aimlessly in and out of crime and unemployment. Up to two-thirds of the unattached individuals of this central area are officially classified as having a low income ($7,152 or below in 1981); over one-third of families are regarded as having a low income.[10] The effect upon the cultural landscape is obvious. For example, along this section of Main Street, pawn shops, derelict premises, run-down department stores, and second-hand clothing stores succeed bars and dilapidated hotels.

The unemployment rates among adults over 25 years of age in this region are the highest in the city: 20.6 percent in census tract 24 and 21.2 percent in census tract 25, compared with only 3.4 percent over the whole city.[11] Much of this unemployment is concentrated among Indians.

Other social problems arise. Natives who move into the city are by no means a homogeneous group. Different bands do not always speak the same language or dialect. While English can usually be used as a common language, this is not an invariable solution. Older natives do not always speak English, and even younger people from remote reserves may not understand it. In one senior citizens' home, native women from different bands are unable to speak to one another.

9.2.2   The Northern Sector[12]

The northernmost sector of the city comprises the North End, the newer suburbs of West Kildonan and Old Kildonan, and some more indefinite suburbs west of Old Kildonan. The North End itself has always had a very distinct social geography, which has made the area well-known throughout Canada. Its origin lies in the immigration of the early years of the twentieth century. Between 1900 and 1914 the population of Winnipeg increased very rapidly from 50,000 to 275,000. Since 1896 the vigorous immigration policies of the eastern Canadian establishment had encouraged continental Europeans to emigrate to the Prairies. Prominent among the great influxes were those of the east and central Europeans: Austrians, Bohemians, Bukovinians, Czechs, Galicians, Hungarians, Ruthenians, Serbs, Slovaks, Catholic Ukrainians from the western Ukraine, and others, all from the hegemonic Austro-Hungarian Empire. Added to these were Poles, Russians, Russian and German Jews, and Germans. After their long journey by train and steamer, they boarded the train again in eastern Canada for the last leg to Winnipeg. As they came off the railway trains, without work and unable to speak English, they were temporarily housed in immigration sheds. From there, many found their way to the "ethnic quarter": the North End – right beside the railway that had brought them. Here they became trades-men, industrial workers, and skilled workers in a crowded, polyglot, and cosmopolitan area.

Frequently, the new immigrants displaced railway workers of English or Scottish origin, so that the phenomenon of ethnic succession was already at work in the burgeoning city at the turn of the century. The growth of this city region was also aided immensely by the construction of bridges and an underpass to allow access southwards across the CPR yards to the rest of Winnipeg and its more varied employ-ment opportunities.

East European immigrants, Jewish, Polish, and Ukrainian especially, have formed a substantial portion of the population in the North End. In addition, there has remained some British, though the once numerous Germans have moved, for the most part, to the suburbs. These groups formed the social core of the region, but subsequently most of the European groups have tended to move northwards into neighbouring suburbs, followed by some southward movement dispersing into wealthy suburbs. However, almost half the Ukrainians in Winnipeg and over two-fifths of the Poles still lived in the North End in 1951. By 1961 these had declined to somewhat over a third and, by 1971, to no more than a quarter. In 1981, only 17 per-cent of Ukrainians and 18 percent of Poles lived in the traditional North End.

The outward movement has not yet been sufficient to totally alter the character of the region. Main Street, the principal commercial zone of these neighbourhoods, forms a unique traffic artery through the region, with a succession of retail stores, offices, banks, and small workshops. Polish delicatessens, Ukrainian credit unions, many tiny corner grocery stores, Ukrainian Catholic churches with their spectacular bulbous towers, and small single-family industries colour the cultural landscape of this area.

As the people belonging to the original ethnic groups that populated the North End have moved or died, the population has declined dramatically, registering a decrease of 12.9 percent during the five years before 1981 alone, compared with an overall increase of 0.8 percent for the city of Winnipeg. Even so, ethnic succession is still evident in the influx of new ethnic groups that have partly taken their place; this is especially so in the inner southern streets. Native Indians are one of the main groups of recent arrivals, and they generally occupy inexpensive accommodation in small, old houses and decaying apartment blocks.

Main Street continues north-eastwards from the North End into the progres-sively newer suburbs of West Kildonan and Old Kildonan (Figure 9.1). Likewise, much of the ethnic character of the North End continues into West Kildonan. Of the 52 percent of Winnipeg's Jewish community who live north of the CPR tracks, four-fifths now live in this region, mostly in West Kildonan. The Polish community is less concentrated, but can still be found throughout this sector. Of the major ethnic groups of the city, the British are evenly represented, the Ukrainians are more numerous and the Germans less numerous than expected, while the French are hardly represented at all.

9.2.3   The Western Sector[13]

The West End is a zone of mixed land use and primarily aging buildings. Only along the arterial highway of Portage Avenue is there a substantial number of new and renovated buildings. Behind this commercial facade the streets consist of detached houses, built very close together, ranging up to 95 years of age in the section closest to the city centre (Artibise 1975). Newer houses, either infilling or occasionally rebuilding, line some streets, but most houses are old, and many are maintained indifferently. Some older apartment blocks, rooming houses, and subdivided houses add to the possibilities for a high population density. The inner half of this region has the highest population density in the city: 5,545 people per square kilometre.[14] Although this is by no means astronomical as urban densities go, it contrasts significantly with the density for the entire city: 988 people per square kilometre. [15]

As a result of the cheapness and availability of lodgings, new immigrants from beyond the province are attracted, or compelled, to live here. Because these lodgings are often better than those left behind in their native countries, the element of compulsion is often small. As in the North End, a sequence of occupance by different ethnic groups may be discerned. In 1951 the original residents, middle-class British, were by far the most numerous. However, by then they were either moving out or aging. The British element has continued its steady decline, although it is paradoxical to note that here, as in many ethnically distinct and apparently non-British areas of the city, people of British origin remain in substantial number.

By 1961 the West End had many immigrants direct from Germany (Table 9.2). But the number of Germans had already started to fall by 1971, and by 1981 had almost declined to the level attained in 1951, as recently arrived Germans became more established, learnt English well, assimilated, and dispersed throughout Winnipeg.

The West End has never had many French Canadians, Jews, Dutch, Mennonites, or Poles. Ukrainians, however, have always been present in moderate numbers, the West End being an alternative to their early preferred location in the North End. Recent ethnic changes have probably been greater than in any other city region. The new immigrants include Filipinos, Vietnamese and other South-East Asians, East Indians, and Pakistanis among the Asian groups. Among smaller groups represented there are Chileans, Sikhs from India, and blacks from the Caribbean, Guyana, and Britain. The varied elements of the ethnic succession are reflected in the urban landscape. There are still German butchers here, but a Korean grocery store, a

Table   **The German Ethnic Group, Winnipeg West End**
9.2

Census	Population
1951	3,013
1961	8,761
1971	6,975
1981	3,870

Sources: Fromson 1965, 82; *Census of Canada*

Portuguese community hall and church, and Indian restaurants are more appa- rent. Conspicuous by their absence are the spacious layouts of suburban shopping centres.

In the most run-down neighbourhoods, native Canadians from rural Manitoba are crowded into small, old, often-rented accommodations. The differences in race and appearance between this city region and the rest of the city have thus become clear-cut; whether the long-term prospects for assimilation are good is debatable. In over a century of constant immigration by a totally heterogeneous European popu- lation, assimilation has generally been calm and peaceable; very few hostile eruptions have occurred, and there have been comparatively few ugly incidents. But newer immigrants are often racially different from those of the past, a change that has prompted concern for the possible emergence of problems that have afflicted both American and British cities.

This region obviously has special social characteristics. The people of the established ethnic groups, British and German, tend to be elderly and live more to the western outer edge of the area. The inner zone has very distinctive social charac- teristics, which are slowly extending throughout the region. Little more than half the people have English as a mother tongue, compared with almost three-quarters in the city as a whole, and as much as a third have less than the nine years of schooling mandatory in Canada, or in many of the countries from which Canada has received immigrants in the past. Although some students from the nearby University of Winnipeg room here, the percentage of people with post-secondary education is among the lowest in the city. People with professional skills are almost totally absent.

Lack of education combines here with poverty and several social problems. Single-parent families are frequent. Households with one person, often with little or no income, are common and there is a constant turnover in occupancy.[16] Most houses have low market value (less than $40,000 in 1981, compared with over $50,000 in most of the suburbs); rents are correspondingly low. Similarly, family income is small; on average, it is little more than half that of the wealthy southern, western, and outer suburbs.

Winnipeg has expanded westwards along the Assiniboine River and Portage Avenue to a greater extent than it has to the north or south along the Red River. North of the Assiniboine, St. James and Assiniboia, with 67,624 people in 1981, form one of the city's most populous suburbs. This region has expanded steadily since the

Second World War from its nucleus in the former City of St. James, itself the successor to the Parish of St. James. At the start of this century, St. James formed an urban area substantially separate from Winnipeg, and much of the inner part of the region retains its individuality with a civic centre, large library, community offices, and its own school division and police department.

St. James and Assiniboia form the most predominantly British – mainly English and Scottish – sector of Winnipeg, with the British forming 60 percent of the population.[17] In addition to outgrowth from the core of St. James, it also owes much to the westward movement from the West End, which was almost entirely Scottish and English half a century ago. There has been some immigration from the United Kingdom to St. James but, nevertheless, only 5 percent of the population were born in Britain. By far the major group are long-established British Canadians of English or Scottish ancestry (Figure 9.3). Compared with Britain, where English outnumber Scots by 9:1, English and Scots are much more evenly represented in St. James. A precise statistic is difficult to determine – intermarriage is one of many complications, but a survey of surnames would suggest 2:1 or even 1:1 as a ratio. Of the 40 percent who are not British by descent, most are members of the other major ethnic groups: German (9.8 percent), Ukrainian (7.2 percent), French (5.1 percent), Icelandic (3.5 percent), and Dutch (2.3 percent).

St. James shows the typically strong trend towards suburbanization found in the city as a whole. From 1976 to 1981 only the westernmost fringes of the suburbs showed an increase in population. Inner suburbs, which were themselves outer suburbs 20 years ago, have been static or declining. Much of the demographic increase has been further westwards beyond the city boundaries in Headingley or St. Francois Xavier. In spite of the severity of the winter, which might be expected to encourage people to live closer to employment and services, the desire for new and more spacious accommodation appears to have no end.

As people have moved, one-storey shopping centres with vast car parks have been established to cater to the new, affluent residents. Large supermarkets, one- and two-storey department stores, small clothing shops, and stores providing services such as shoe-mending or hairdressing spread themselves along shopping malls. "Polo Park" and "Unicity," at the inner and outer ends, are just the largest of such centres in this sector, and are the two largest shopping centres of upwards of a dozen throughout the city. Portage Avenue is itself a ribbon of considerable commercial development. The urban landscape of this ribbon indicates features of the Canadian norm – the main banks, credit unions, stores such as "Eaton's" (T. Eaton Co.) and "The Bay" (Hudson's Bay Co.), restaurant chains, and churches.

9.2.4   The Southern and South-Eastern Sectors[18]

For most of its existence, this southern sector has been the most wealthy, and this wealth continues to be a prime characteristic. Especially near "The Forks," small pockets of poorer streets do exist, but households in most of the sector have considerably higher incomes than do those in any other part of the city: in 1980, average household income was $29,032, in contrast to $23,208 for the city as a whole, with five of its 25 census tracts recording an average of over $35,000.[19]

Despite the major flood control measures that the city has adopted since the early 1960s, of paramount consideration in the three-quarters of a century of residential growth in the southern sector has been its generally well-drained nature. Another advantage is the accessibility of the Central Business District, just across the Assiniboine River. Paradoxically, the rivers also act as physical and social barriers, separating these neighbourhoods from poorer areas.

Construction of houses and streets suitable for a wealthy area began at the turn of the century with elegant, tree-lined avenues, planned elm boulevards, and the large houses and ample lots of Wellington Crescent and Crescentwood, along the southern bank of the Assiniboine (Artibise and Dahl 1975). Later, building continued in River Heights and Tuxedo, while the suburbs of Fort Garry have grown up in the vicinity of the University of Manitoba, which occupies a spacious site on the banks of the meandering Red River.

Almost all ethnic groups are represented here. The principal exceptions are new immigrants, such as the Portuguese, and native Indians. All the long-established cultural, national, racial, and religious groups are represented. However, the British are in the majority, and Germans form the second most numerous group: Ukrainians, French, and Dutch are somewhat under-represented. Some members of newer immigrant groups, such as Italians and East Indians, having made a swift economic success of life in Canada, have moved into the exclusive sections of this sector. The well-established Chinese are also a feature of the ethnic balance. The proportion of the Jewish community that lives in the wealthiest streets of Tuxedo and River Heights has also risen steadily, from 11 percent in 1951 to 39 percent in 1971, and now nearly half (45 percent) of the city's Jews report a residence south of the Assiniboine in 1981.

Across the Red River from downtown Winnipeg and facing the confluence with the Assiniboine, St. Boniface grew up as a separate city. The most culturally distinct of all the different foci, St. Boniface, with its cathedral, was in existence just as early as Winnipeg's embryonic nucleus of Portage Road, Garry (Main) Street, and Fort Garry (Weir 1978, 4–5).

French Canadians form the main ethnic group in this sector, particularly in the inner nucleus of St. Boniface, in the streets near the cathedral and its accompanying administrative buildings. Here, French form over half of the population, with the second ethnic group accounting for little more than a quarter.

The magnificent Roman Catholic cathedral was accidently razed, but it has been partially rebuilt in a modern idiom. The ecclesiatical zone, with the archbishop's residence, several nunneries, and St. Boniface College – an affiliate of the University of Manitoba – is a central area around which other activities have evolved. St. Boniface Hospital, a well-known teaching hospital, is nearby. Street names are French, as are many of the commercial establishments, and there is a French library. In the urban landscape there are many reminders of past French leaders. In particular, Louis Riel is honoured, the hero of the French Métis who led the rebellion of 1869 against forces from eastern Canada. Here is evidence of the connection that the French community has with Métis and native Indians.

As the population and houses in the streets behind the cathedral have aged, new generations have moved south-eastwards and southwards into St. Vital, where the sector between the Red River and the small River Seine remains at least partly French. French Canadians show some of the strongest sectorial development of any ethnic group in Winnipeg. They tend to be absent from other sectors; conversely, too, many other ethnic groups, especially newer immigrants, such as Italians, Portuguese, and Asians, are absent from this zone (Matwijiw 1979, 56; Nicholson and Yeates 1969). Hence, this region is quite ethnically distinctive, although it is worth pointing out that even here the other major ethnic groups are moderately represented.

9.2.5   The Eastern and North-eastern Sectors[20]

The eastern sector is primarily an industrial zone along the northern side of the Canadian National Railway (CNR) tracks leading to the CNR yards and workshops of Transcona. As a sector it is less distinct ethnically than it is distinct in terms of this type of industrial land-use. All groups are found here with those of British-descent being in the majority only in Transcona. However, although the British are very numerous here, the presence of almost all other ethnic groups mutes the region's cultural distinctiveness.

North Kildonan, stretching from the east bank of the Red River over the prairie, has its own cultural character. In 1921, Mennonites, who had previously eschewed the "evils" of city life in favour of a traditional and conservative lifestyle in the remote rural areas of Manitoba, decided to build a settlement very near Winnipeg. Presumably, the intention was to enjoy the economic and social benefits of a large city, while at the same time retaining many of their traditional values. The impact on the cultural landscape is to be seen in the presence of the Mennonite Bible College and Mennonite churches that feature services in German as well as English.

Although Mennonites have since spread throughout all areas of the city, the settlement has gone on flourishing and North Kildonan still has a high proportion of Mennonites. Even here, though, with city expansion into the area, British are the most numerous group, but Dutch and German (mainly Mennonite) together make up a quarter of the population. Ukrainians are the other main group to favour this region.

As the outer suburbs are approached, so the social characteristics of the population change. In this respect each sector is a functional region in which the generations move outwards. From older couples living in family houses in the inner suburbs, whose children have left, whose houses are up to 90 years old, and whose mortgages are paid, there is a continuum of social change as outer and newer rings of suburbs are encountered. The outermost suburbs are still gaining population, with numerous children and young couples living in new houses. Unpaid mortgages and double-income couples go hand-in-hand. The ethnic mix that is found here is consistent with the rest of the sector in which they are located, juxtaposed with the overwhelming presence of older, established ethnic groups. Thus, British, Ukrainian, German, Icelandic, French, and people who are a mix of these ethnic groups tend to predominate. Many would regard themselves now as Canadians and not as members of other ethnic groups.

On the other hand, several of the more culturally different inner zones of Winnipeg are characterized by the absence of some, rather than the presence of other, ethnic groups. The long-established groups have moved out of these streets as they have decayed. New immigrants to the city, whether from outlying Manitoba, as are native Indians, or from foreign countries, as are Greeks, Portuguese, and Italians, rarely have the resources or inclination to make an immediate move to the new outer suburbs, where the bulk of Winnipeg's population lives. If they are poor, cannot speak English well, and lack education, they remain in places such as the West End. The more literate, who have modest means and are able to acquire better jobs rapidly, often rent accommodation in one of the many apartment blocks, staying there even if they become quite prosperous. Even those who achieve rapid business success tend to move to the inner suburbs of River Heights and Tuxedo, instead of moving to the outer suburbs.

In the future, the varied cultural and ethnic circumstances of the different sectors of Winnipeg will undoubtedly continue. However, the suburbs show less segregation than the inner city areas, and a slow decline in the ethnic differences between sectors may be expected. With language barriers and ingrained cultural attitudes being less prevalent than they were in the past, at least for long-established urban groups, intermarriage between groups is considerable. People of different ethnic groups are now showing an interest in each other's ethnic traditions, as is shown by the popularity of the annual "Folklorama," a unique and vital festival of ethnic culture and customs. For the first time, in 1981, the census recorded multiple ethnic origins, and these form a significant 11 percent of the city's population, no doubt a portent of the future. There are over 8,000 people of mixed British and French origin, and nearly 30,000 people who are a mixture of British and a non-French group. Yet, even so, the retention of a considerable degree of cultural identity for each sector is assured for the immediate future, certainly as far ahead as the beginning of the twenty-first century.

Notes

1. The term "ethnic" is used here as an all-inclusive term to describe any significant group of a particular national origin, race, language group, religion or sect, culture, or any other attribute that distinguishes it. The group usually shares a common genealogy and particular location of origin in the Old World.

   The census of Canada regards the term "ethnic group" as a reference to the "roots" of the population; it should not to be confused with citizenship or nationality. Paternal ancestry and language "on first coming to this continent" were the main determinants until the 1981 census, when multiple origins were first included. For the city as a whole the populations of 38 ethnic groups were published in 1981. Unpublished data on nine major ethnic groups (British, Dutch, French, German, Italian, native, Polish, Scandinavian, and Ukrainian) were obtained for each census tract; information on language and birthplace (for the Portuguese) and religion (Jews) increased this to 11 groups for each census tract.

Americans and Canadians could arguably be regarded as an ethnic group, but the census does not collect such statistics. Neither are census statistics collected for Métis, who, in the past, were often included in the French or British groups, but are, in reality, a distinct and sizeable group. In 1981 they would mostly be included in the totals for French and British of multiple ethnic origins.

2. *Census of Canada, 1971*, "Population and Housing Characteristics by Census Tracts," Catalogue no. 95-753, series B; and *Census of Canada, 1981*, "Population by Ethnic Origin," Catalogue no. CTC81B13, microfiche.

3. *Census of Canada, 1971*, "Population and Housing Characteristics by Census Tracts," Catalogue no. 95-753 (CT-23B), series B; and *Census of Canada, 1981*, "Selected Social and Economic Characteristics," Catalogue no. 95-981 (vol. 3, series B).

4. A recurring theme of American sociological literature has been to refine the measurement of levels of segregation that may be observed in urban areas. Various indices have been employed to measure segregation (see Lee 1977, 171–73), two of the commonest being those used first in the 1950s by Duncan and Duncan (1955) and Taueber and Taueber (1965) in testing theories of the Chicago ecologists. The Duncans' Index of Dissimilarity *(ID)* represents the proportion of a population of sub-group *y* that would have to relocate among a set of *n* sub-areas to have a distribution equal to that of another sub-group *x*.

1. $$ID = \sum_{i=1}^{n} \frac{(x_i / \Sigma x_i) - (y_i / \Sigma y_i)}{2} \quad x \quad 100$$

where,

x_i = proportion of group *x* occurring in sub-area *i*,

y_i = proportion of group *y* occurring in the same sub-area *i*.

If the total population *t* were to be used, then a correction factor may be applied to eliminate what would be *y*'s presence within *t*. This gives the Index of Segregation, *IS* used in this essay.

2. $$IS = \frac{ID}{1 - \frac{\Sigma y_i}{t}}$$

A value of *IS* near one indicates dispersion of a group throughout the city whereas values tending away from one suggest a tendency towards segregation.

The value of the index is affected by the number of sub-areas, *n*, and their size. The number of areas used for purposes of calculation influences the absolute level of the index, so that a ranking of degrees of segregation may vary with the scale with which the indices are calculated. Hence, the indices can only be used as general indicators of the degree of segregation, and great care is required in their interpretation (see Woods 1976).

5. *Census of Canada, 1981*, "Selected Social and Economic Characteristics," Catalogue no. 95-981 (vol. 3, series B).

6. *Census of Canada, 1981*, "Population by Ethnic Origin," Catalogue no. CTC81B13, microfiche.

7. *Ibid.*

8. That is, the native Indian group is not combined with the Métis, the statistics for this last group being uncertain.

9. Census Tracts 013-5, 022-7, 032-3, and 542.

10. *Census of Canada, 1981*, "Metropolitan Atlas Series: Winnipeg," Catalogue no. 99-922, 63–5.

11. *Census of Canada, 1981*, "Selected Social and Economic Characteristics: Winnipeg," Catalogue no. 95-981.

12. Census Tracts 034-6 and 041-9 (North End); 050.01–.02, 051.01–.02, 052, 550-3, 560.01–.03 (Old Kildonan and West Kildonan).

13. Census Tracts 016-21, 028-31 (West End), and Census Tracts 530–541 (St. James and Assiniboia).

14. Census Tracts 016-8, 020-1, 028-30.

15. *Op. cit.*, Footnote 11.

16. *Census of Canada, 1981*, "Metropolitan Atlas Series: Winnipeg," 7–65.

17. *Census of Canada, 1981*, "Population by Ethnic Origin," Catalogue no. CTC81B13.

18. Census Tracts 001–012, 500.01–.03, 501.01–.02, 510, 520, 521, 522.01–.02 (River Heights, Tuxedo, Charleswood and Fort Garry); Census Tracts 100.01–.02, 101.01–.02, 102.01–.04, 103–5, 110.01–117 (St. Boniface and St. Vital).

19. *Census of Canada, 1981*, "Selected Social and Economic Characteristics: Winnipeg," Catalogue no. 95-981.

20. Census Tracts 037–040, 120.01–.03, 121–3 (Transcona and East Winnipeg); Census Tracts 130.01–.02, 131–4, 140, 141.01–.02, 142.01–.02, 150 (inner part) (North Kildonan and East Kildonan).

References

Artibise, A.F.J. 1975. *Winnipeg: A Social History of Urban Growth.* Montreal: McGill and Queen's University Press.

Artibise, A.F.J., and E.H. Dahl. 1975. *Winnipeg in Maps, Winnipeg par les Cartes: 1816–1972.* Ottawa: Public Archives of Canada.

Barber, S., and C. Brook. 1980. "The Historic Winnipeg Restoration Area: A Brief History." *Prairie Forum* 5:219–36.

Baxter, R.S. 1968. "The Statistical Analysis of the Structure and Form of Urban Areas, With Particular Reference to Winnipeg." Paper presented at Canadian Association of Geographers' Conference, Calgary.

Bellan, R. 1978. *Winnipeg First Century: An Economic History.*Winnipeg: Queenston House Publishing.

Carlyle, W.J. 1974. "Growth, Ethnic Groups and Socio-economic Areas of Winnipeg." In T.J. Kuz, ed., *Winnipeg 1874–1974*, 27–41. Winnipeg: Manitoba Department of Industry and Commerce.

Carter, H. 1981. *The Study of Urban Geography*. London: Edward Arnold.

Clark, B.D., and M.B. Gleave, eds., 1973. "Social Patterns in Cities." *Special Publications, Institute of British Geographers*, no. 5.

Driedger, L. 1978. "Ethnic Boundaries: A Comparison of Two Ethnic Neighbourhoods." *Sociology and Social Research* 62:193–211.

Dreidger, L., and G. Church. 1974. "Residential Segregation and Institutional Completeness: A Comparison of Ethnic Minorities." *Canadian Review of Sociology and Anthropology* 11:30–52.

Duncan, O.D., and B. Duncan. 1955. "A Methodological Analysis of Segregation Indexes." *American Sociological Review* 20:210–17.

Fromson, R. 1965. "Acculturation or Assimilation: A Geographic Analysis of Residential Segregation of Selected Ethnic Groups: Metropolitan Winnipeg, 1951–1961." Master's thesis, University of Manitoba.

Hill, F.I. 1976. "Ethnicity and the Cultural Mosaic." In D.M. Ray, ed., *Canadian Urban Trends*, vol. 1, 229–84.

Lee, T.R. 1977. *Race and Residence: The Concentration and Dispersal of Immigrants in London*. Oxford: Clarendon Press.

Mailhot, P.R., and D.N. Sprague. 1985. "Persistent Settlers: The Dispersal and Resettlement of the Red River Métis, 1870–85." *Canadian Ethnic Studies* 17:1–30.

Matwijiw, P. 1979. "Ethnicity and Urban Residence: Winnipeg, 1941–1971." *Canadian Geographer* 23:45–61.

Nicholson, T.G., and M.H. Yeates. 1969. "The Ecological and Spatial Structure of the Socio-economic Characteristics of Winnipeg, 1961." *Canadian Revue of Sociology and Anthropology* 6:162–78.

Park, R.E., E.W. Burgess, and R.D. McKenzie. 1925. *The City*. Chicago: Chicago University Press.

Peach, G.C.K. 1975. *Urban Social Segregation*. London: Longman.

Rowley, G. 1978. " 'Plus ca change ...' A Canadian Skid Row." *Canadian Geographer* 22:211–24.

Taueber, K.E., and A.F. Taueber. 1965. *Negroes in Cities*. Chicago: Aldine Publishing.

Watson, J.W. 1957. "The Sociological Aspects of Geography." In G. Taylor, ed., *Geography in the Twentieth Century*, 463–99. 3rd ed. London: Methuen.

Weir, T.R. 1978. *Atlas of Winnipeg*. Toronto: University of Toronto Press.

Woods, R.I. 1976. "Aspects of the Scale Problem in the Calculation of Segregation Indices: London and Birmingham 1961 and 1971." *Tijdschrift voor Economische en Social Geografie* 67:169–74.

10   The Expansion of Domestic Space on Vancouver's North Shore

Leonard J. Evenden

10.1   General Considerations
10.1.1   Introduction

To see two or three workmen labouring together on a house in order to add a bedroom, extend a kitchen, or expand some other aspect of dwelling space seems so common in greater Vancouver as to be hardly worth notice. Yet it is precisely because this is such a common sight that geographical attention is merited: amid all the public discussion concerning the availability and affordability of housing, the relationship of the construction industry to the health of the economy, the social implications of housing policies, and the questions of aesthetics in building design, there is a persistent though unheralded activity of adding new space to dwellings already in existence. It is curious that this particular point has been addressed so little in the geographical or housing literature because, although individual projects are often very small, certain of them are of major proportions, and in aggregate they are so numerous as to make an important contribution to the level of construction activity. Some idea of the importance of this activity can be seen in the finding that, for the time period of this study, the amount of extra living space created by constructing additions to pre-existing houses in the study area was equivalent to about 20 percent of all space created in newly completed single-family dwellings over the same time span in the same area.

This expansion space is important for other reasons, too. If at any given time a substantial number of households is engaged in its construction, it follows that the existing housing stock is inadequate in its provision of space, that households find this to be a worthwhile investment of their funds, time, and labour, or that other motives, such as the creative release of energy, may be at work. Indeed, it appears that all of these factors give impetus to the building of new household space. To enquire into the continuous creation of this living space thus requires an examination of the extent of these additions and of the circumstances surrounding their devising. This is at once a geographical problem of identifying the magnitude and distribution of expansion space and a behavioural problem concerning the motives for the creation of such space by individual households. Thus, the creation, form, and extent of expansion space is the subject here, and the first purpose is to delineate the extent of its occurrence in one particular study area, namely the north shore of greater Vancouver, and to outline the intended uses of such space. The second purpose is to explore some of the characteristics of the population engaged in building additions to their houses, emphasizing the stage of household development in its relation to this activity.

Much attention regarding the changing of the spatial arrangements of household living has focused on the decision to move, and thus on intra-urban mobility (Brown and Moore 1970; Short 1978; Simmons 1968). Such a perspective highlights the social sorting of the population as families and individuals place themselves in the landscape in order to bring together their shelters with the locations of their daily obligations of work and social relations. During recent decades people have been much on the move, migrating over long distances from country to city and between cities, and over short distances within cities and neighbourhoods. This has also been a time of rising expectations, and the quality of housing has generally improved.

But there is another population, in fact the larger one, which moves only infrequently and has comparatively stable work and social relations. A relationship may be drawn between this settled population and the existing housing stock. Because housing is durable, the accumulated stock satisfies at any moment most of the demand for shelter (Hamilton 1978). New structures satisfy only a relatively small proportion of this demand. If housing standards or the demand for housing should increase, it follows that the current standing stock would have to be modified to meet the higher standards or greater demand. The replacement of buildings is one way in which this can be accomplished, but what is much more common is the renovation and enlargement of existing dwellings. This effort, cumulative in the landscape, is largely that of the settled population. And in this study the population of those expanding their houses was found to be remarkably stable, inhabiting their dwellings for over a decade before expanding them, and remaining for a number of years afterwards. Thus, there is not a quick profit motive as expressed in property improvement and rapid resale. Rather, there is a more rooted population making provision incrementally for new space, and revising the arrangements of existing space to suit personal needs and desires.

The most frequent approach to studies of change in the built environment is probably the ecological, with its vocabulary of invasion and succession and derivative concepts (Bourne 1981). In this approach land uses change in response to a variety of socio-economic pressures emanating from the downtown core, the force of which has the capacity to require the modification of buildings. So the transition zone, ringing the central business district, is perhaps the most dynamic, with filtering processes both up and down the social scale being associated with dwelling conversions. It might be tempting to think that additions to pre-existing dwellings form part of this conversion process, but it is not clear from the present study exactly what the position of this activity would be in relation to the filtering processes. Studies of the transition zone emphasize the conversion and subdivision of houses for the purpose of intensifying land use and, generally, a zone characterized by rapid change and land-use complexity may be observed. In his seminal study of the nature of social geography, Watson (1957) noted that, at least for Hamilton, "transition zone" may be too weak a term to describe the geographical effect of such a clash of pressures, and suggested that "shatter belt" would be better. But in the present study there is no distributional pattern of occurrence that would correspond to a land-use zonation model, and newer houses seem as likely to be expanded as older ones. The principal locational attribute of this activity is diffuseness throughout the districts of single-family dwellings. Thus, the traditional ecological approach must be set aside in favour of a focus on the process and the landscape, one that is subject, perhaps, to much less external pressure than the landscapes of other areas in the city. The pressures exerted for building modification seem to come from the inhabitants of the dwellings themselves. For the moment, it is preferable to view the process of expanding dwellings as a development in society's ability to provide and consume heated space (Laaksonen 1981).

10.1.2 Definitions and Context

"Expansion space" refers to enclosed space that has been added to a pre-existing house; space that is roofed and otherwise sealed against the weather, and that is functionally incorporated into the dwelling. Because it is normally heated, this additional space might also be thought of as "winter space," a term that serves to distinguish expansion or additional space from the built forms of other purely seasonal extensions to household living space, such as patios, balconies, and swimming pools.

The "dwelling" is taken to mean the detached single-family house, inhabited by a single household. If the occupier is also the owner, it may be assumed that the social unit of the household is the decision-making authority. The decision to expand the house, and the consequent actions, together constitute the moment of space creation in the cycle of existence of both the household and the physical dwelling. This is the moment of change in the built environment, during which the links between human agency and material consequences are exposed for observation.

Official sources of data published by governments include this activity and its spatial consequences within reporting categories that are too wide in their scope to permit the consistent identification of additional space.[1] Such terms as "conversions," "additions and alterations," and "renovations" mask the necessary detail, and reporting practices, even at the municipal level, do not allow for the clear separation between projects that add new space to dwellings and those that merely alter the forms of existing space (McCann 1975; Phipps 1983). Thus, for the purposes of this study, the focus of which is single-family dwellings, it was necessary to create the data from more detailed sources as will be discussed below.

A further contextual issue concerns the role of governments in promoting change in the residential built environment. In an attempt to forestall the decay of inner-city areas, government programs throughout the 1970s promoted the concept and subsidized the activity of renovating existing houses within designated areas (Mercer and Phillips 1981). Even though privately owned houses were involved, an element of social housing was present in that participants qualified for assistance partly on the basis of income. But renovations sponsored by these programs were mainly intended to improve the existing housing stock by renewing utility services and repairing structural faults. Additional space was not considered to be an important outcome. So the modification of dwellings as sponsored by such programs is not of direct concern here. Further, such housing renovation, coupled with a concern for area revitalization, which has also received official support, has served to draw attention not only to housing conditions but also to urban renewal and redevelopment (Ley 1981; Wong 1978). This has also meant drawing attention to the inner city rather than to the whole residential environment. While these major trends have been to the fore in public awareness, perhaps dating from the 1969 Federal Task Force on Housing and Urban Development, the unsubsidized practice of adding new enclosed space to existing houses has proceeded without fanfare throughout the entire urbanized greater Vancouver area.

Indeed, this activity has not only been widespread throughout the city but has also characterized the whole historical period. The material result – enclosed living space – is an integral part of the dwelling, and thus, in the townscape as a whole, it represents the collective intentions of households towards "the central reference point of human existence" (Relph 1976, 20). One of the objectives of this paper is to direct attention to this pervasive element in the built environment which, perhaps because of its common occurrence, small unit scale, geographical dispersion, and obscurity in the usual records, is normally overlooked.

The procedure that must be followed in an expansion project is that plans, once drawn, must be submitted for approval by the municipal building inspector. When approval has been granted, and permits bought, work on the project may proceed. Permits may be obtained by the householder, the designer, or the contractor. Thus, the sequence of steps can vary. Contracts may be agreed contingently prior to the purchase of permits, or construction firms may be approached afterwards. Often a householder serves as his or her own contractor and project manager, and sometimes will personally do all the construction work. Whatever the case, at designated points in the construction process inspections are required before work may continue. With activity thus punctuated by inspections, the project goes to completion when a final inspection is made. In this way the dwelling is enlarged and the consumption of indoor space by the household increases. This extra space will be passed on eventually, upon the sale of the property, and it might provide the necessary room to allow for the subdivision of the dwelling in some future phase of land-use intensification. Therefore the use-value of the dwelling is enhanced simultaneously with a potential increase in exchange value. In the single-family residential environment as a whole the quantity of enclosed, heated living space is constantly increasing.

In the same way that intra-urban migration has been regarded as a response by households to perceived needs to alter the circumstances of dwelling in the city, the assumption is made that the widespread practice of adding space to single-family dwellings is not incidental. Rather, it is a patterned response to the changing conditions of urban living by adapting built structures. This response is activated individually by households to satisfy their perceived wants and needs, and operates within certain constraints including building regulations, limitations of cost and design, and the self-imposed dictates about the appropriate level of change necessary to satisfy the desire for more space. The actions of households, in constructing additional domestic space, work to satisfy the perceived needs. But whereas the result of satisfying the same needs by relocation constitutes a redefinition of social space in the city, the result of satisfying these needs by creating additional space includes specific modifications to the built environment, modifications that cumulate into the future.

10.1.3 The Study Area: Vancouver's North Shore

Metropolitan Vancouver comprises a core of four municipalities, namely the three cities of Vancouver, New Westminster, and North Vancouver, and the District Municipality of Burnaby. These are surrounded in turn by a complex of over a dozen suburban municipalities, Indian reserves, and "unorganized areas." The north shore is physically separated from the rest of the urbanized area by Burrard Inlet and English Bay (Figure 10.1). Its connection to Vancouver by bridges and a ferry, its historic participation in the life and work of the harbour and port, and its intimate involvement in regional government serve to tie this area firmly into the general metropolitan fabric. Yet it is essentially suburban and there exists a distinct north shore identity. Community identity is also apparent in the formation of the three municipalities that make up the area, namely the city of North Vancouver and the two district municipalities of North Vancouver and West Vancouver. The latter two are sprawling residential communities, the first surrounding the city of the same name. Together they extend some 40 kilometres from east to west, while rising away from the foreshore up the flanks of the north shore mountains to a maximum permitted building elevation of some 1,200 feet (366 m) in West Vancouver, and a little less at 1,050 feet (320 m) in North Vancouver.[2]

West Vancouver was created as a separate municipality in 1912, out of North Vancouver district territory, following the division in 1907 of the north shore into the district and city of North Vancouver. Urban and community developments have been patterned, ever since, by the somewhat divergent personalities of these three municipalities. In this paper municipal differences serve as comparative reference points throughout the discussion. Thus, it is useful to characterize, briefly, settlement in the study area with reference to municipal development and to interaction with the city of Vancouver.

The city of North Vancouver had its origins in the sawmilling village of Moodyville, founded in the 1860s. To this day it remains the industrial heart of the north shore. In recent years, however, the waterfront area has been transformed from one which was wholly industrial to one which now includes major office buildings and numerous retail outlets. The pressure for redevelopment implied by the waterfront changes has resulted in the replacement of neighbourhoods of small, single-family dwellings by low-rise apartment blocks and commercial buildings in a pattern clearly expressive of succession theory. "Zone of transition" or "shatter belt" would be appropriate concepts for describing this limited area. The district of North Vancouver, in contrast, comprises several distinct valley and coastal communities and, in parts, is dominated by a forested, if no longer rural, landscape. Its housing tracts are very extensive, however, and its population, in excess of 65,000, is almost twice that of each of the other two municipalities (Table 10.1). It serves as a dormitory suburb for downtown Vancouver.

Table   **Populations, Households, and Dwellings, 1981**
10.1

	North Shore	City of North Vancouver	North Vancouver District	West Vancouver District
A. Source: *Census of Canada, 1981*				
Population	135,047	33,952	65,367	35,728
Population in private households	133,225	33,445	64,775	35,005
Mean number of persons/household	2.6	2.1	3.0	2.6
Mean number of persons/family	3.0	2.7	3.2	3.0
Mean number of children at home	1.1	0.8	1.3	1.1
Occupied private dwellings (a)	51,580	16,120	21,945	13,515
Occupied single detached dwellings (b)	30,930	4,810	16,810	9,310
(b)/(a) x 100 *	60	30	77	69
B. Source: Author's survey				
Mean number of persons/household	3.9	3.9	4.2	3.6
Mean number of adults/household	2.4	2.1	2.5	2.3
Mean number of children/household	1.6	1.8	1.7	1.5
Children by age (as % of total)				
0 – 5 yrs	30	17	34	29
6 – 12 yrs	45	61	38	51
13 – 18 yrs	24	22	26	20
Mean ages of adults:				
(years) M	44	44	43	46
F	42	42	42	45

* This represents the dividend of "Family persons in private households" and "Families in private households."

Source: *Census of Canada, 1981*, Catalogue no. 95-903 (vol. 3, profile series A), Table 1

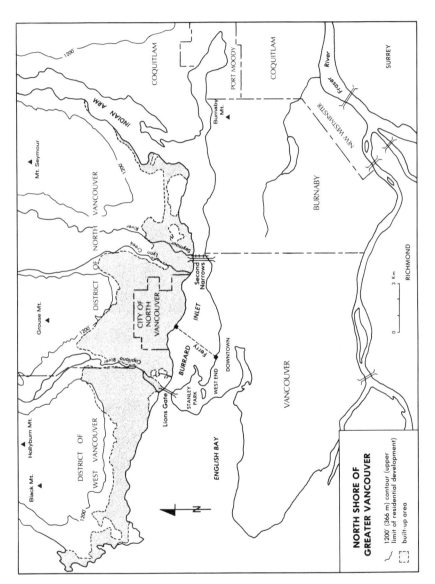

Figure 10.1 The North Shore of Greater Vancouver

West Vancouver, in its early years, comprised little more than a string of small coastal settlements along the alternately sandy and rocky shoreline that forms the northern strand of English Bay. It has always had the character of an amenity community, lying as it does on the open-sea side of the first narrows at Stanley Park, with its beaches, promontories, and slopes enjoying a southern exposure. Indeed, the summer cabin was an important early form of building there, and numbers of these remain as winterized and much elaborated homes in the streets accessible to the beaches. Isolated examples may also be found farther up on the wooded hillsides.

During the 1930s the Lions Gate suspension bridge was built by the Guinness interests in order to serve the further development of their extensive holdings on the upper slopes of West Vancouver. In fact, this bridge came to have enormous significance, because it became the principal gateway to the whole north shore, especially the western half (Evenden 1978). Even before the Lions Gate bridge was opened, however, the railway bridge at the Second Narrows carried automobiles on a lane beside the track.[3] The main impetus for the development of suburbs in the eastern part of the north shore came with the completion in 1959 of the Second Narrows road bridge. Having lost its ferry service to downtown Vancouver the previous year, and lying equidistant from both bridges, the city of North Vancouver was now by-passed and comparatively isolated. Thus, in relative spatial terms, the rapid growth on the north shore during the 1960s emphasized residential areas accessible to the bridges and away from the central area. The districts of North and West Vancouver were the twin foci of this expansion. The landscape brought into existence in this way consists overwhelmingly of single-family detached dwellings (Table 10.2).

With the inauguration in the mid-1970s of a new foot-passenger ferry, the Sea-Bus, connecting the central waterfront of the city of North Vancouver to downtown Vancouver, a new era in the development of the north shore was initiated, one which echoes the earliest settlement by focusing geographically at the point of original attachment. The ferry has breathed new life into the central city of North Vancouver, doubtless adding to the pressure to redevelop some of the surrounding areas, as noted above. But the residential geography of the north shore remains dominated by the single-family dwelling and, despite the variety and contrasts across this large suburban region, the practice of expanding houses is common throughout.

In Vancouver, and indeed throughout the west, housing has had a short dynamic history. There have been periods of considerable pressure on housing, and the time of the urban area's growth has been so short that the response to the housing need has included an emphasis on standard plans, units, and forms, and on pre-manufactured components. But while standardization of components is characteristic of much modern construction anywhere, its combination in British Columbia with the historical practice of building houses almost entirely of wood, and with the tradition that ordinary people commonly take part in the construction and renovation of their own homes, creates the circumstances in which it is relatively easy for householders to consider major alterations to their dwellings in order to solve their living space problems (Holdsworth 1979, 1986). Certainly, for the "up-market" house the contribution of the talented architect has always been important. But the vast bulk of the residential landscape comprises a variety of modest house forms. Individual dwellings are commonly set in standard lots of some 65 feet (19.8 m) by 120 feet (36.6 m). Although there is much variation in these dimensions, the important point is that there exists a spatial-legal constraint on permitted expansions, because by-laws regarding set-backs from property boundaries, and height, impose upper limits on the possibilities for expansion.

Despite the existence of these regulations the amount of space enclosed in the original structures of many suburban houses could effectively be doubled before reaching the limits of the building envelope as set in the by-laws, and many dwellings could be expanded by more. For much of the area this implies a low density of single-family dwellings: an underbuilt residental landscape. Historically, there has been little concern that there would not be sufficient room to expand a house because the permissible limits are broad, and householders have had considerable freedom to experiment with various expansion forms. This is changing in some neighbourhoods under the pressures of modern development, as builders seek to maximize the scale of new houses in order to take full advantage of properties they are developing or redeveloping. But until the mid-1960s, low density suburbs were virtually universal in the metropolitan area, and they still predominate in the 1980s. It is in this context that the north shore serves as a case study of the wider metropolitan Vancouver area.

Table 10.2	Residential Land Use, 1982, and Dwelling Completions, 1975–80			
	North Shore	City of North Vancouver	North Vancouver District	West Vancouver District
Total land area (ha)	26,893	1,232	16,560	9,101
Total residential area (ha) (a)	3,358	406	1,595	1,357
Total area of single-family dwellings (ha) (b)	3,088	310	1,485	1,295
(b)/(a) x 100	92.0	76.4	93.0	95.4
Completions of new dwellings (c)	7,681	2,699	3,406	1,576
Completions of new single-family dwellings (d)	2,633	273	1,766	594
(d)/(c) x 100	34.3	10.1	51.9	37.7
Mean annual completions of single-family dwellings	439	46	294	99

Sources: Canada Mortgage and Housing Corporation and Greater Vancouver Regional District

10.2   Expansion Space: Magnitude, Distribution, and Characteristics
10.2.1   Approach and Method

Empirical data were collected from records kept by the three north shore municipalities. All building permits issued during the six-year period, 1975–80, were inspected, and those referring specifically to the construction of enclosed heated expansions to single-family dwellings were extracted. This yielded a "basic list" of 2,457 cases from which a 10 percent sample was drawn at random. This procedure was necessary in order to isolate expansions from other forms of work reported in the same category in the records – everything from the erection of car ports to the construction of patios. It should be stressed that the sample does not represent all dwellings but only those that were expanded during the study period, and for which permits were bought.

Permits themselves were used only for sample selection. Information recorded on them is often sketchy, referring to intentions as cross-referenced to building plans. Thus, it was the plans themselves that were the principal source of data. The most important forms of space expansion, to be discussed in the following section, refer to floor areas of additions and to rooms added and extended.

Within each municipality there is a consistent approach to the application of by-laws and in the methods of keeping records, although there are differences between jurisdictions. The municipal units were preserved as the geographical basis for the compilation of data, and they provide the framework for comparative perspectives across the north shore. This also reflects the varying municipal personalities as developed historically. In the case of aggregate additions it is possible to show cartographically a more detailed distribution.

10.2.2   The Expansion of Dwellings
10.2.2.1 Aggregate Space

Across the north shore as a whole some 114,500 square feet (10,635 m^2) of space were added to the houses in the sample during the six years of the study period (Table 10.3). Keeping in mind that this quantity represents a 10 percent sample of all places that were expanded, the total amount of space enclosure may be seen, by extrapolation, to be considerable. As would be expected by virtue of its large size, the greatest share, fully 50 percent (57,382 square feet; 5,330 m^2), is found in North Vancouver district. West Vancouver, with over a third of the total (41,020 square feet; 3,810 m^2), occupies the middle position in a ranking by municipality, while North Vancouver city with 14 percent (16,132 square feet; 1,498 m^2) ranks lowest. The mean size of expansion is 464 square feet (43 m^2), or a square of just over 21 feet (6.5 m), and the values for each municipality are close to the figure for the north shore. The typical expansion is smaller, however, as expressed in the median values, and there are greater differences among the municipalities by this measure. West Vancouver's median is higher by 28 square feet (2.6 m^2) than that for North Vancouver city, and the value for the district of North Vancouver rises by a further 29 square feet (2.7 m^2) to 309 square feet (28.7 m^2). The differences, at about 10 percent

Table   **Aggregate Space**
10.3

	North Shore	City of North Vancouver	North Vancouver District	West Vancouver District
Pre-Expansion Areas (square feet)				
Total	452,109	57,136	227,713	167,260
Mean	1,868	1,731	1,836	1,968
Median	1,833	1,665	1,813	1,922
Range	520–5,844	663–2,862	520–3,805	686–5,844
N	242	33	124	85
Areas of Additions (square feet)				
Total	114,534	16,132	57,382	41,020
Mean	464	489	463	456
Median	300	252	309	280
Range	16–2,213	40–2,213	26–1,658	16–2,152
N	247	33	124	90
Post-Expansion Areas (square feet)				
Total	566,643	73,268	285,095	208,280
Mean	2,342	2,220	2,299	2,450
Median	2,212	2,147	2,228	2,228
Range	690–7,294	690–4,048	900–3,805	814–7,294
N	242	33	124	85

Note: In five cases in West Vancouver the records are incomplete as to pre-existing structures.

increase between municipalities, are marked, but they are also in keeping with the comparative demographic characteristics. North Vancouver district has the highest number of children living at home, while the city has the lowest (Table 10.1). Thus, the pressures for expansion, as related to stage in the life cycle, correspond to the actual evidence of expansion. This is considered later.

The results of two calculations demonstrate how extensive is the practice of expanding dwellings, and they also show the overall relationship of house expansion to the existing housing stock. In 1981 there were 30,930 "occupied single detached private dwellings" on the north shore (Table 10.1). If all such dwellings are assumed to be involved in expansion activity, and the total additional space by extrapolation from the sample is 1,145,340 square feet (106,379 m^2) (Table 10.3), then it can be seen that this activity would add about 37 square feet (3.4 m^2) to each and every house, or a space measuring approximately six feet by six feet (1.8 m).

Perhaps an even more dramatic illustration of the magnitude of activity would be to express additional space in terms of house equivalents. If the total additional area of enclosed space is taken in terms of the mean pre-expansion size of house (1,868 square feet; 173 m^2), then the number of mean house equivalents would be 613. Over the six-year study period this would represent the addition of just over 100 house equivalents annually to the total housing stock. If the same calculation is made on the basis of post-expansion sizes of dwelling, then the number of house equivalents would be 489 or 81 per year. Given that the total number of new houses actually completed on the north shore during the six years was 2,633,[4] for a mean annual total of 439, it can be seen that the proportionate amount of expansion space that was added annually to the already built environment was considerable. On the basis of these data it appears that between 18 and 23 percent more space was created in the environment of single-family dwellings than can be accounted for by reports of new single-family house completions alone.

Although municipal comparisons provide insights into how these data, in broadly aggregated forms, reflect the character of well-understood places of municipal jurisdiction, cartographic analysis permits a spatial description of the patterns of housing expansion across the whole area, emphasizing neighbourhoods and localities (Figure 10.2). Areas with corresponding high values, as between pre-expansion sizes and areas of additions, may be traced, as may areas having low values of pre-existing sizes but large expansions. The latter are apparent in the main areas of North Vancouver city and directly to the north about three kilometres, in the valley communities lying just north and east of the Second Narrows, and in some isolated fragments in the far western part of West Vancouver. The former relationship is most clearly found in the "British Properties," the exclusive suburb founded by the Guiness interests, which lie some three kilometres north of the First Narrows, and in the neighbourhoods of the lower Capilano valley. Well to the west, the pattern is dominated by small additions being attached to comparatively large houses. The patterns found in the eastern and western extremities of the north shore are fragmented and complex on an area basis, for the settled localities are small and complicated by a difficult rocky and wooded terrain. Thus, the principal patterns are to be observed in the central regions where there is easy access to the bridges.

The distribution of proportionate increases makes explicit the area relationships between the two variables of pre-exisiting sizes of dwelling and expansions. High ratios occur in a broad and sinuous east-west zone extending from the valley communities just north of the Second Narrows to about five kilometres west of the First Narrows. An intersecting extension occurs to the north from the city of North Vancouver, and a second may be found stretching to the north along the slopes on the west side of the Capilano valley. Together these form a concentric pattern around the neighbourhoods of the lower Capilano.

10.2.2.2 Partitioned Space

Dwellings comprise not only simple space as measured by some standard measure, such as square feet or square metres, but also space as allocated to different purposes and divided by partitions or walls into enclosures. To divide space in this way is to provide for functional specialization by area. Such definition may be

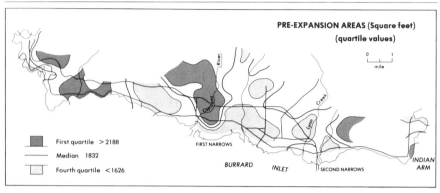

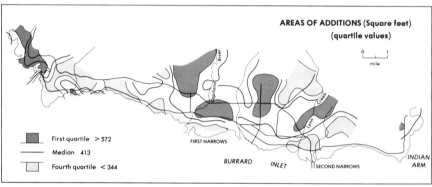

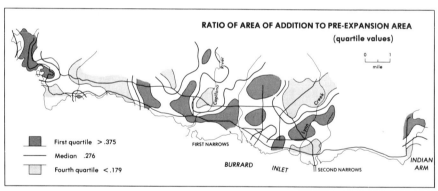

Figure   **Relationship between Pre-expansion Areas and Areas of**
10.2   **Additions to Single-Family Detached Dwellings**

accomplished without walls, but the existence of these firm, and perhaps sound-proof, partitions imparts a rigidity to the spatial arrangement of the house that reduces functional flexibility and may constrain desirable changes in the uses to which the spaces are put. Realizing this as one of their problems, the householder and designer must strike an appropriate balance between a pattern dominated by enclosed spaces and one that is markedly open within the dwelling. The first has the disadvantage of loss of flexibility but has the merit of providing for privacy. In contrast, open areas

Table   **Partitioned Space**
10.4

	North Shore	City of North Vancouver	North Vancouver District	West Vancouver District
Rooms added				
Total	502	80	251	171
Projects adding rooms:				
Number	195	26	106	63
Percentage	79	79	86	70
Mean number of				
rooms per project	2.6	3.1	2.4	2.7
Rooms extended				
Total	133	13	57	63
Projects extending rooms:				
Number	83	9	37	37
Percentage	34	27	30	41
Mean number per project	1.6	1.4	1.5	1.7
Projects adding and extending rooms				
Total: Number	35	3	21	11
Percentage	14	9	17	12

have the advantage of flexibility in the use of space but the disadvantage of loss of privacy. Thus, there is a tension in the organization of space within the modern dwelling, the recognition of which is central to the household's resolution of the problem of creating a spatial framework suitable to its needs and desires.

The idea of expanding the house to create more space stands in contrast to the idea of subdividing space to control it in certain desired ways. Yet the two are not completely separate in the expansion project, for the addition of a room accomplishes both while an extension to an existing room only adds to existing space. This is a practical expression of the tension involved in designing changes to meet the needs for both privacy and additional space. Therefore, the forms of additions are distinguished here as between new rooms and extensions to existing rooms (Table 10.4). New rooms represent space that can be closed off from the rest of the dwelling by doors, whereas extensions represent enlargements of existing rooms. For the north shore as a whole, 502 separate rooms were added to the sample of houses studied during the six-year period. More than three-quarters (79 percent) of projects involved additions of rooms. It is common for two or three rooms to be added in a given project but the extension of existing rooms is less than half as common. West Vancouver stands out, however, with just over 40 percent of projects involving extensions. At 1.7 it also has the highest mean number of rooms extended per project.

Some ambiguity in assessing such figures is inevitable because structural considerations often require the opening up and alteration of the existing house in order not only to attach an expansion but also to integrate it into the spatial order of rooms and functions. Thus, a third category was created, comprising places in which both additions and extensions were worked together in the design. This is a less important category, but it is interesting that the city of North Vancouver has the lowest proportion of this type, whereas the district of North Vancouver has the highest. In any given project all three forms of addition may be represented.

There is no doubt that the cost of extending rooms is proportionately higher than it is for adding them, and the municipal distribution of construction in this category conforms with the comparative average incomes among the municipalities. As noted, West Vancouver has the largest number of rooms extended per project, and the largest proportion of projects involving extensions. Thus, houses there appear to be expanded less for the necessity of extra partitioned space or privacy, and more for convenience and pleasure. In contrast, with the highest number of rooms added per project, houses in the city of North Vancouver seem to be under pressure for more partitioned space. The district of North Vancouver generally occupies an inter-mediate position in these relationships. It stands out, however, in the "rooms added" category in that between 80 and 90 percent of its expansion projects involve such additions while just under one-third include extensions. This may be credited, to a certain extent, to the municipality's position as the principal child-raising munici-pality on the north shore (Table 10.1). The evidence of this study supports this claim because of the district's greater proportionate emphasis on adding bedrooms and general purpose family rooms. Some 18 percent of all the projects in this district were for such rooms, in contrast to 12 percent each for the city and West Vancouver.

10.2.2.3 Functional Space

The purposes for which expansion spaces are intended reveal the spatial needs of evolving households. Table 10.5 indicates these purposes and their relative importance by frequencies and proportionate emphases for both municipalities and functions. The list of functions itself was derived from entries made on plans accompanying applications for permits, each category representing a number of terms. For example, the category of "hallways/entrances" represents the following terms: hall, entrance, entrance hall, entrance lobby, foyer, mud room, enclosed entry, entrance and closet, hall and nook, lanai, and atrium. In all, some 60 terms were reduced to the eight categories given in the table.

Bedrooms, general purpose family rooms, bathrooms, and public rooms together comprised 70 percent of all additions. Additions of bedrooms were overwhelmingly the most numerous, with North Vancouver district and West Vancouver having 43 and 39 percent respectively of the north shore total. Bedrooms and bathrooms are commonly considered together in the modern house, as "master bedrooms" usually have "en suite" bathrooms, while a second bathroom serves the other bedrooms. Thus, the construction of new bathrooms and the remodelling of existing ones commonly accompany the addition of new bedrooms. For the north shore as a whole, one new bathroom was built, or an existing one was expanded, for the addition of every two to two-and-one-half bedrooms.

Family and public rooms were the other two most numerous types of addition, with a marked contrast between the two north Vancouvers. The district accounted for the greatest proportion of family rooms on the north shore. This functional type was represented more strongly there than in either the city or West Vancouver, and more strongly than in any other category than the bedroom. These proportions are higher than they are for public rooms (living and dining rooms) but the opposite is true for the city. Family rooms are described in the data sources as dens, recreation rooms and by a variety of similar terms, whereas public rooms refer only to living and dining rooms. So the emphasis is quite different between the municipalities, and it points out the district's role as a place for growing families. Of the four most important categories the bathroom represents the most inflexible space by virtue of its specialized plumbing installations and the necessity for privacy. The utility and kitchen categories are also important as measured by their frequency of construction, but about one-half of the additional utility spaces were for storage and therefore required little specialized installation, except perhaps for shelves and hooks. Kitchens (and kitchen equipment, which is becoming increasingly sophisticated and demanding of space) require periodic renewal, and they have changed in the last generation from being comparatively small rooms to being open and spacious, easily accommodating a table for family meals and often serving as a place for informally entertaining friends. Thus, the kitchen has come to serve as the dining room to some degree and the latter has commonly been reduced to a "dining area" in an expanded open living room. Nevertheless, it appears that the desire to dine away from the kitchen remains, for the dining room accounted for the majority of expansions in the category of public rooms. It would seem that there is considerable ambiguity in the modern house surrounding the dining function: in standard plans, even for large and expensive houses, the dining room is often no more than an area in an open plan living room; sometimes the kitchen serves or usurps the dining area's purpose, especially in informal entertaining, but an effort is often made to enlarge it if it is already present, or to create a new one if it is not.

The remaining categories are less frequently represented and refer both to the private spaces of specialized interests within the household, for example the office, dark room, or music room, and to the public spaces surrounding entrances and passageways, spaces which are often underbuilt in first construction. But it is evident from the pattern of intended uses that there was a concentration of effort to create space to serve the basic and common needs of the household rather than to create specialized spaces to serve more esoteric interests.

10.3   Stayers and Builders

To move to another dwelling may be a more costly way to obtain extra space than to add to a current residence. But there is no doubt that many expansion projects involve much more labour and effort than would a move. There is also the possibility that the actual costs of construction will exceed the estimates, especially in older

Table   **Expansion Rooms and Spaces by Activity: A Functional**
10.5   **Classification**

	North Shore	City of North Vancouver	North Vancouver District	West Vancouver District
Bedrooms	195	36 (19)	84 (43)	75 (39)
	[30]	[33]	[28]	[32]
Family rooms:	94	13 (14)	53 (56)	28 (30)
general activity	[15]	[12]	[18]	[12]
Bathrooms	83	12 (15)	42 (51)	29 (35)
	[13]	[11]	[14]	[13]
Public rooms	80	17 (21)	36 (45)	27 (34)
	[12]	[16]	[12]	[12]
Utility rooms	56	11 (20)	21 (38)	24 (43)
	[9]	[10]	[7]	[10]
Kitchens	52	9 (17)	23 (44)	20 (39)
	[8]	[8]	[8]	[9]
Hallways/entrances	46	5 (11)	24 (52)	17 (37)
	[7]	[5]	[8]	[7]
Family rooms:	34	3 (9)	18 (53)	13 (38)
specialized activity	[5]	[3]	[6]	[6]
Unfinished/unknown	5	3 (60)	2 (40)	0 (0)
	[1]	[3]	[1]	[0]
Total	645	109	303	233

(-) Percentage of category total (row)
[-] Percentage of municipal total (column)

houses in which unforeseen problems are commonly encountered. Further, once started on an expansion, householders frequently see possibilities they had not previously considered and decide to enlarge the scope of their project. This combination of risk and effort implies that a considerable commitment to the existing dwelling must be made in order to initiate and carry out an expansion project. Plans must be conceptualized, drawn, and procedures must be followed. A major disruption to family life may also occur, especially during larger and more ambitious projects. Some families remain in their houses during work, but others move out altogether. Many feel considerable strain and tension. The project often takes longer to complete than anticipated, thereby increasing the tension but also demonstrating the commitment. The mean number of months for project completion on the north shore, as reported by households, was 13, varying from 7 in North Vancouver city to 15 in West Vancouver, while in North Vancouver district the mean coincided with the area-wide average. In a general way this variation in completion time reflects the complexity of the projects being undertaken. In some cases it indicates a lengthy "wind-down" time during which householders complete the finishing tasks themselves. But lengthy completion times also testify to the dedication of householders to the projects and the houses.

In Canada capital gains tax is not applied to proceeds realized in the sale of a principal residence, so the assumption is sometimes made that to improve a dwelling is a behaviour largely motivated by a desire to protect household equity and to realize profits in a generally rising real estate market. While this is certainly an important consideration, it would appear that this is not the complete explanation because, in this study, over 200 of the 247 households in the sample were still living in the same houses that they had expanded, three years after the date chosen for the conclusion of the study. For those who expanded their houses in 1975, this meant an eight-year interval following expansion. Further, it was discovered that the mean length of residence before expansion was 12 years. These figures show that this is a comparatively stable population, emphasizing a long-term commitment to maintain the fabric of the dwelling and to adapt it by expansion if necessary.

In such circumstances the life cycle of the household must be taken into account to help explain varying housing needs, which develop over time. The ways in which households come to understand their own needs might not be identified easily, but the fact that they conclude that additional space is required, coupled with other data about the stage of development of their households, provides a basis for identifying the relationship between household needs and an expanding residential landscape.

In order to inquire into the relationship between expansion activity and the course of the household life cycle, a mailed survey of all available households in the sample was conducted. Availability for postal contact was determined by whether the households that had expanded their houses were still living in them at the time of the survey. Thus, 203 questionnaire forms were sent to householders still residing, in the spring of 1983, in the houses they had expanded during the six-year study period. Of these there were 98 usable replies, a response rate of 48 percent.

Households were asked to indicate how the decision to expand their dwelling was related to stage of household development. Because this is a perceptual issue, as stated, yielding only a summary impression of whatever deliberations took place to arrive at the decision to expand, more factual information regarding stage of household development was sought as well. In this the life-cycle stages suggested by Duvall (1967), and applied in Australia by McLeod and Ellis (1982), formed the basis of classification. This classification is useful here because it held that the needs of the family are closely tied to the maturation stage of the oldest child: the space needs of the oldest child set the pattern for allocating household space to children, with the need for future space for younger siblings being projected from this experience. Because they include the overwhelming number of cases here, only stages three, four, and five out of the eight suggested by Duvall are included.

Table   **Stage of Household Life Cycle at the Time of House Expansion**
10.6

Stage	North Shore	City of North Vancouver	North Vancouver District	West Vancouver District
	%	%	%	%
3	21	17	24	17
4	40	58	37	37
5	21	8	24	20
Total	**82**	**83**	**85**	**74**

Stages: 3 – Couple, age of eldest child less than 6 years (pre-school)
4 – Couple, age of eldest child between 6 and 12 years (elementary school)
5 – Couple, age of eldest child between 13 and 17 years (secondary school)

10.3.1 The Household Life Cycle and Dwelling Expansion

Over 80 percent of expansion dwellings on the north shore are inhabited by households in the third, fourth, or fifth stages of life-cycle development (Table 10.6). Stage four, characterized by having the oldest child in elementary school, is the stage when most renovations take place. This is especially evident in the city of North Vancouver where the pressure for additional space drops markedly upon the household's entry into the fifth stage. The patterns for the two district municipalities are symmetrical across the stages.

There are difficulties in interpreting life-cycle patterns with cross-sectional information. What might be called the flow-through or vintage effect of more than one child passing through their various stages of development at the same time within the same household cannot be accounted for directly (McLeod and Ellis 1982, 178). Yet the pressure to expand dwelling space relates to this wider perspective, which involves the household's experience of meeting the space needs of all household members at all times. Recognizing this, the following can be suggested. Experience in the uses and adequacy of dwelling space will form the basis from which parents will project and plan for future space needs. If there is a pre-schooler following an older sibling, and if space is already at a premium, then the appraisal of future needs might lead to the opinion that more space will be required. This in turn might lead to a decision to expand the premises. Similarly, if the household has reached stage five, when the oldest child is in secondary school, it will be apparent that the space needs of the oldest normally will exceed those of individual younger siblings, and will virtually coincide with those of an adult. Thus, to project the future needs from that point, to contemplate the space demands of a period when two or more children will be of secondary school age, might also lead to a decision to expand.

The impact of life-cycle developments upon space requirements will vary among households, depending on the number of children present and the available

Table   **The Sharing of Bedrooms by Children**
10.7

	North Shore	City of North Vancouver	North Vancouver District	West Vancouver District
Separate bedrooms at time of survey				
Yes (%)	89	100	86	92
No (%)	11	0	14	8
Have children ever shared bedrooms in present house?				
Yes (%)	43	33	52	31
No (%)	57	67	48	69

space. But given that, on average, surveyed families had only 1.6 children living at home at the time of house expansion and a mean family size of 3.9, it seems appropriate in general to think of the flow-through effect in terms of families with no more than two children (Table 10.1). As a rule, the north shore family appears to expect to provide a private bedroom for each child by the later years of elementary school, and certainly for the secondary school years. This can be inferred from the knowledge that virtually no modern houses have fewer than two bedrooms, and so to construct a third or fourth in a two-child household is to provide for a private room for each child. This is borne out further by information concerning the sharing of bedrooms by siblings (Table 10.7). At the time of the survey fully 89 percent of the children in the sample of households had separate bedrooms, but 43 percent had shared their bedrooms in the expansion dwelling at some time in the past. It is from this experience of sharing, and from the expectations of privacy, taken together in relation to the household life cycle, that the pressure to expand arises. This is especially marked for the district of North Vancouver, already cited as the chief child-rearing municipality on the north shore, where about one-half of the children have shared bedrooms in contrast to the approximately one-third for the other municipalities. In a few isolated cases across the north shore, households felt the pressures related to the obligations of caring for elderly family members, but these were of marginal importance.

10.3.2 Staying and Building

This essay began by observing how common is the practice of building additions to single-family detached houses in greater Vancouver. The extent and some of the characteristics of the residential landscape produced by this activity are shown for the north shore for the period 1975 through 1980. The life cycle of the household is seen to have features that correspond to the moment of expansion, the inclusive event that includes all the decisions, actions, and results of adding new space to pre-existing dwellings. The hundreds of additions built each year to the standing stock of houses are cumulative. The effect is to make the single-family dwelling progressively larger, a point that can be expressed for the north shore as the increase from a mean pre-expansion floor area of 1,868 square feet (173 m^2) to a mean post-expansion area of 2,342 square feet (217.5 m^2), or in terms of the median values, from 1,833 to 2,212 (170 to 205).

In particular, the pressures felt by households to increase their living space relate principally to the need to provide space for growing children. This is evident because of an emphasis on the construction of bedrooms and family rooms. Paradoxically, the number of persons per household on the north shore has declined over the years, as it has in general, the relationship between the rate of change of numbers per household and increased amounts of heated space being neither direct nor simple. If gauged by the ability of householders to build and maintain such space, however, not only is a higher standard of housing demonstrated, but also an increased standard of living is shown.

Other factors that might contribute to the motivation to expand can be acknowledged, but their importance is difficult to gauge. Those related to the time period of the study include the "energy crisis" of the 1970s, because of its associated volatile but generally high rates of interest for mortgages. In 1981, in an attempt to slow the rate of defaulting and to encourage the purchase of new dwellings, the provincial government offered favourable loans as a form of mortgage subsidy. With careful planning it might have been possible for a householder to take advantage of this as a factor in expansion work. Loans were to be repaid by 1986. Although this program was not implemented until just after the study period, the conditions that gave rise to it were apparent during that time. Further, beginning in 1977, a federally sponsored program to subsidize the cost of insulating existing houses may have prompted some householders to seize the opportunity to renovate extensively, including expanding the premises, at the same time as insulating. This program terminated in 1986. Many households made use of both these government programs. A more diffuse but no less real matter was the frenzied atmosphere of the real estate market and the uncertainty of the value of investments. From this there emerged the opinion that to put personal resources into the household's principal residence was a wise financial strategy. Such factors as these have their role in explaining the degree of expansion activity, but to disentangle them from one another would be a task for further research.

Furthermore, these factors are ephemeral. On the one hand, they point to influences that at any time might involve individual households in the processes contributing to the form of the building cycle. On the other hand, the length of tenure of stayers and builders, coupled with the considerable amount of effort required to expand a house, suggests that there are more fundamental reasons for engaging in this activity than merely taking advantage of a favourable but time-limited loan. Indeed, the way of life in the community itself is involved – for example, the matter-of-fact manner in which householders approach sometimes daunting tasks requiring skills in carpentry, plumbing, electrical work, painting, and more; the availability and reasonable cost of tools; and the standardization of component materials. Together, these and other factors form a complex set of relationships underlying the observable building activity of any moment or time period. Not only is it a common sight to see work in progress on expansion projects, but the evidence of such work undertaken over the years is apparent everywhere.

Households must rationalize their activity in personal terms. To embark on an expansion project is a traumatic experience for some, and there are those who would never contemplate such an effort. But for others the urge to create additional living space seems so strong that they build additions not only well beyond what would be necessary for their personal use but also beyond what would reasonably augment the value of the property. In this way the residential landscape of enclosure is constantly being enlarged, a development clearly related to both the progression of family life and a general rise in the standard of living.

Since this study was completed there have been numerous developments in the formation of residential landscapes in the Vancouver area. Certain general points may be made. A severe economic recession occurred during the early years of the 1980s, and the provincial and local economies were slow to recover. By the end of the decade a certain measure of prosperity was evident, paralleling the experience of the 1970s. But many homeowners, having overextended their indebtedness during the 1970s, were severely tested financially during the early 1980s. As a result a mood of fiscal caution developed, and personal debt clearance became a matter of priority for many. This mood continued through the second half of the decade and into the 1990s. A central fact conditioning such an outlook was the deliberate national policy of maintaining high rates of interest as a technique for controlling inflation.

Because the activity of building additions (and, in general, renovating houses) varies with the rate of interest, and in view of the mood of caution that had developed, the rate of construction of additions during the 1980s, as defined in this study, was probably lower than it might otherwise have been. This inference can neither be confirmed nor denied by reference to the accompanying table (Table 10.8), which shows raw totals of building permits issued during the second half of the decade. The figures are not directly comparable between muncipalities. However, inspection suggests a decreasing significance of the single-family dwelling in the central city of North Vancouver, a city increasingly being redeveloped with multiple dwelling units. Further, the possibly greater stability of income in the wealthier West Vancouver, as compared with the district of North Vancouver, may be inferred. West Vancouver has little more than half the population of North Vancouver district, but it issued approximately three-quarters as many permits for broadly equivalent types of building projects. In addition, the scope of the projects was greater, as can be seen by a comparison of average values.

Table   **Permits Issued for Additions and Alterations to Single-Family**
10.8   **Dwellings, 1985–89 (annual totals)**

	City of North Vancouver[1]		District of North Vancouver[2]		District of West Vancouver[3]	
	No.	$'000s	No.	$'000s	No.	$'000s
1985	115	949	406	5,421	256	5,994
1986	100	1,039	362	3,735	264	6,950
1987	108	951	294	4,989	251	7,393
1988	99	840	351	5,418	276	8,553
1989	88	816	361	6,415	302	12,655
Total	510	4,595	1,774	25,978	1,379	41,545
Mean Value of Permits	$9,010		$14,644		$30,797	

1. Data for North Vancouver city refer to both single-family and two-family dwellings, but not to multiple-family dwellings.
2. Data for North Vancouver district refer to a "Miscellaneous" category of permits, which includes additions and alterations. Whether the items included refer only to single-family dwellings cannot be known without reference to each project individually, as was the case in the original study. But most permits would refer to single-family dwelling projects as those dwellings form the overwhelming majority in the District.
3. Data for West Vancouver refer to single-family dwellings only.
Source: Municipal reports

Acknowledgements
I should like to acknowledge the support of the Canada Mortgage and Housing Corporation, the cordial reception and help from the authorities in all three north shore municipalities, and the assistance of Neil Kellock and Kathy Emmott. R.R. Squirrell and M. Wheat produced the maps.

Notes

1 For example, Statistics Canada uses the following categories for building permits: single-family dwellings, cottages, double dwellings, row housing, apartments, and conversions *(Building Permits Annual Summary)*.

2. All dimensions of building and property are given here first in imperial units, as appropriate to the historical development of the built environment. Even now, with dimensional lumber being produced and marketed to metric standards, the imperial system dominates the parlance of the building industry. Lumber manufactured to metric specifications was only beginning to be available at the end of the study period.

3. I am grateful to Mrs. Joan Rheumer for alerting me to this point.

4. Canada Morgage and Housing Corporation.

References

Bourne, L.S. 1981. *The Geography of Housing*. London: Edward Arnold.

Brown, L.A., and E.G. Moore. 1970. "The Intra-urban Migration Process: An Actor-oriented Approach." *Geografiska Annaler* 52B:1–13.

Duvall, E.M. 1967. *Family Development*. 3d ed. Philadelphia: J.B. Lippincott.

Evenden, L.J. 1978. "Shaping the Vancouver Suburbs." In L.J. Evenden, ed., "Vancouver: Western Metropolis," *Western Geographical Series*, vol. 16. Victoria: University of Victoria.

Hamilton, S.W. 1978. "The Land Market in Metropolitan Vancouver." In L.J. Evenden, ed., "Vancouver: Western Metropolis," *Western Geographical Series*, vol. 16. Victoria: University of Victoria.

Holdsworth, D. 1979. "House and Home in Vancouver: Images of West Coast Urbanism, 1886–1929." In G.A. Stelter and A.F.J. Artibise, eds., *The Canadian City: Essays in Urban History,* Carlton Library, no. 109. Ottawa: Macmillan.

———. 1986 "Cottages and Castles for Vancouver Home-seekers." *BC Studies* 69–70:11–32.

Laaksonen, K. 1981. "Factors Affecting the Floor Area in the Town of Riihimaki, Southern Finland (in 1980)." *Fennia* 159:379–480.

Ley, D.F. 1981. "Inner City Revitalization in Canada: A Vancouver Case Study." *Canadian Geographer* 25:124–48.

McCann, L.D. 1975. "Neighbourhoods in Transition: Processes of Land Use and Physical Change in Edmonton's Residential Areas." *University of Alberta Studies in Geography*. Edmonton: University of Alberta.

McLeod, P.B., and J.R. Ellis. 1982. "Housing Consumption over the Family Life-cycle: An Empirical Analysis." *Urban Studies* 19:177–85.

Mercer, J., and D.A. Phillips. 1981. "Attitudes of Homeowners and the Decision to Rehabilitate Property." *Urban Geography* 2:216–36.

Phipps, A.G. 1983. "Housing Renovation by Recent Movers into the Core Neighbourhoods of Saskatoon." *Canadian Geographer* 27:240–62.

Relph, E. 1976. *Place and Placelessness.* London: Pion.

Short, J.R. 1978. "Residential Mobility." *Progress in Human Geography* 2:419–47.

Simmons, J.W. 1968. "Changing Residence in the City: A Review of Intra-urban Mobility." *Geographical Review* 58:622–51.

Watson, J.W. 1957. "The Sociological Aspects of Geography." In G. Taylor, ed., *Geography in the Twentieth Century,* 463–99. 3d ed. London: Methuen.

Wong, S.T. 1978. "Urban Redevelopment and Rehabilitation in the Strathcona Area: A Case Study of an East Vancouver Community." In L.J. Evenden, ed., "Vancouver: Western Metropolis," *Western Geographical Series*, vol. 16. Victoria: University of Victoria.

11 Community Aspirations, Territorial Justice, and the Metropolitan Form of Edmonton and Calgary

P.J. Smith

Edmonton and Calgary are alike in so many respects that they might almost be regarded as twins, or at least as jealous siblings. The very intensity of their rivalry, which permeates virtually all aspects of life, bespeaks the strength of their similarities (Seifried 1990). Yet they display some critical differences as well, of which one of the most striking to geographers is the forms of their respective metropolitan areas. The purpose of this essay is to offer an explanation for this difference in form, with particular emphasis on what political geographers know as the political organization of space; that is, the organization of metropolitan territories into local government jurisdictions, and the implications for the spatial pattern of urban development. Of central importance here is the notion that territorial jurisdiction is determined primarily by the needs and desires of the various communities that occupy the metropolitan space, and by the political will with which they pursue their separate interests (Soja 1971, 32–52; Williams 1971, 36–49). Territory is inseparable from community. It has meaning only to the extent that it fosters community identity, by nurturing the unique sense of place that any spatially bound community must have. It also follows that territory, the objective reality, is subjectively determined, an expression of human values and beliefs, hopes and fears. As Wreford Watson (1976, 15) has explained: "The geographer must be concerned with the standards of living men *demand*, with the things they *want*, and with the *ideas* at their command. It is these immaterial things which, as they make a material impact on the landscape, make the geography of a country" – or, as we might add, a city.

11.1 The Frames of Reference for Territorial Determination in Alberta

Territory, according to Gottmann (1973, ix), is the unit in the political organization of space by which relations between a community and its neighbours are defined. Gottmann wrote this with national territories in mind, but his axiom is no less apt for metropolitan space. The powers and privileges of local governments are so intimately bound up in their territories, and the demands on their territorial bases are so great, that intra-metropolitan relations are likely to be riddled by territorial considerations. Particularly during times of rapid growth and change, such as those that Edmonton and Calgary have experienced over the last 40 years, the logic of initial jurisdictional arrangements is quickly outgrown. Yet the pace of adjustment seems always to lag behind, no matter how vigorously the various local governments may press for change (Honey 1976, 461). The root of their problem is simple: there is no new territory to be distributed. To change an existing jurisdictional pattern requires the *redistribution* of territory, a condition that holds great potential for political conflict, as competing municipalities attempt to satisfy their individual aspirations.

In general, there are only two means by which metropolitan territory can be redistributed. The first is for a superordinate authority to impose its own solution by ordering that the structure of local government be reorganized. In Canada, under the constitutional division of powers, there is no question that provincial governments have this prerogative, and most have exercised it from time to time (Makuch 1983, 28–51). Some have even imposed sweeping reorganizations on their largest metropolitan centres (Brownstone and Plunkett 1983; Kaplan 1982; Rose 1972), but no Albertan government has yet been willing to take that step. Although Toronto and Winnipeg have sometimes been put forward as models of reform, especially for the Edmonton area, the official view in Alberta is that territorial problems are best resolved through the machinery of local determination, which is the second general approach to redistribution (Masson 1985, 52–81). Most commonly, if a municipal government believes there is a need for redistribution, it must make its case before a neutral arbitrator (National League of Cities 1966; Sengstock 1960). In Alberta, this is an administrative tribunal known as the Local Authorities Board.[1]

Those who arbitrate territorial disputes are concerned fundamentally with the equity of existing distributions and possible redistributions. They must therefore be guided by some conception of territorial justice, although there is no agreement on the criteria of a just distribution (Harvey 1973, 101–18). In practice, questions of functional needs and administrative efficiency tend to become entangled with questions of democratic rights and freedoms (Sharpe 1970), and the value of territory as a material resource has to be weighed against its symbolic value as a manifestation of community (Batey and Smith 1981, 199–202). The arbitrators must also deal with the ethical dilemma of the reformer's paradox, as described by Rescher (1966, 121): "Given an imperfect existing initial distribution, any redistribution in the interests of arriving, from the standpoint of justice, at a superior distribution runs headlong into the pattern of existing claims that cannot – in the interests of the very justice that provides the rationale for the entire enterprise – be pushed aside as an irrelevant obstacle."

Of course, bids for territorial redistribution do not always conflict with a "pattern of existing claims." A common situation in Alberta has been for an urban municipality to seek to expand into an adjacent rural one, by applying to the Local Authorities Board for permission to annex raw land for which a clear development need can be established. If the rural municipality has no aspirations of its own towards that land, the application may not even be contested. When competing aspirations enter the picture, however, the decision becomes profoundly more complicated. As rural municipalities are urbanized through the process of metropolitan expansion, they become increasingly dependent on their built-up areas for tax revenues. Industrial development is desired particularly, and is an especially acute source of conflict among metropolitan local governments. Some rural municipalities may promote large-scale residential development as well, in the belief that an established population of confirmed suburbanites offers the best buffer against a central city's territorial expansion. A good example is the emergence of the cities of Nepean and Gloucester on Ottawa's boundaries (Coleman 1969; Fullerton 1974; Wesche and Kugler-Gagnon 1978).

The growth of metropolitan areas is further accompanied by a proliferation of urban jurisdictions, which are also likely to have to react, sooner or later, to the threat of absorption by the central city. The normal expectation is that they will resist with all the force they can muster, although this does not hold true in all situations. Because metropolitan communities vary widely in their circumstances of origin and development, metropolitan political relations are shaped largely by the local patterns of these differing circumstances (Zikmund II 1975). At one extreme, following Williams's lifestyle hypothesis, it is possible to conceive of communities that are strongly united around a distinctive lifestyle that they have the wherewithal to sustain and that they have deliberately set out to protect through municipal incorporation (Williams 1967). For such communities, any threat to territory is an attack on autonomy and lifestyle values, and so must be opposed. Equally, however, at the other extreme, it is possible to conceive of suburban municipalities with so few advantages, material, social, or environmental, and so little prospect for self-improvement, that independence becomes an intolerable burden.

The conclusion to which this leads, as a framework for comparative analysis, is that prospects for territorial redistribution through local determination are conditioned by the unique circumstances of place and time. To understand why metropolitan areas differ in their spatial adaptations to the pressures of growth and change, it is necessary (among other things) to understand the local contexts of territorial determination, that is, the contexts that apply at those times when crucial decisions are taken. There are two considerations here. The first, which sets the political-geographical context, is the varied circumstances of origin and development among the local communities, and the attitudes towards territory to which they give rise. The second, which derives from the juridical context, concerns the balance that is struck, in the decision process, between the justice of redistribution and the justice of existing claims (Cox and Johnston 1982, 7). In practice, the two considerations are inseparable, because existing claims and the desire for redistribution are themselves a function of community circumstances.

11.2   Bases for a Comparative Study of Edmonton and Calgary

Edmonton and Calgary offer an unusual opportunity for a comparative case study of the way in which the outcomes of attempts at territorial redistribution, and hence metropolitan form, are shaped by the local context. The two cities fall under the same provincial jurisdiction, and so have exercised their territorial claims within the same legal and administrative framework. They are also of comparable size and have grown at much the same rate throughout their histories. Finally, both cities have consistently regarded the consolidation of their metropolitan territories under their own jurisdiction as the only reasonable model of urban polity, and both have pursued vigorous courses of territorial expansion. But whereas Calgary achieved a consolidated form in 1964, and is still essentially consolidated today, the Edmonton metropolitan area has become increasingly fragmented. A pattern of political conflict has become entrenched as well, as suburban municipalities in the Edmonton area have pursued their own territorial aspirations, which run counter to those of Edmonton.

Given that the cities of Edmonton and Calgary have sought an identical aim through the same adjudicative procedures, how can the different spatial outcomes be explained? One obvious possibility, which has long been seized upon by municipal politicians from Edmonton, is that the two cities have been treated differently by the Local Authorities Board, perhaps with the collusion of the Alberta government. This interpretation is typified by the following outburst, to which a former alderman gave vent after a particularly sharp setback to Edmonton's hopes in 1964:

> The City of Calgary was permitted to expand its boundaries to include industrial areas. Why is the government through its autocratic Board discriminating against this city? Why have we not heard a word of protest from the Members of the Legislative Assembly who were elected to represent this city, three of whom are in the Cabinet? . . . Let the Provincial Government come out from behind the Local Authorities Board, from whose decisions there is no appeal, and assume its responsibility to the citizens of this city.[2]

Similar charges have been levelled on other occasions, but an exhaustive examination of the board's decisions from 1946 to 1974 revealed them to be groundless (Diemer 1975). The apparatus of territorial determination has been applied consistently and, by its own criteria, fairly, to both metropolitan areas, and cannot be called upon to explain their present differences in spatial organization.

Another possible explanation, raised by Masson (1985, 70–76) in his book on local government in Alberta, is that metropolitan relations have been conducted more fractiously and self-interestedly in Edmonton than in Calgary – or anywhere else in Canada, if Sancton's (1983, 301) interpretation of territorial competition is accepted: "Although Canadian suburbanites have generally tried to resist either annexation to the central city or metropolitan government, they have done so without the passion or commitment of their American counterparts. The main reason for this difference is the absence in Canada of the racial dimension to metropolitan political conflict." As Masson points out, Edmonton's experience gives the lie to this generalization, and it does so without the confounding factor of racial prejudice. A more important question is still being begged, however. Given that political relations in the Edmonton metropolitan area are peculiarly fractious, from what does the fractiousness derive and why has it not been characteristic of the Calgary area as well? The answer to be presented here is that the explanation is basically geographical. The differences in political behaviour are themselves rooted in differences in spatial form between the two metropolitan areas. Those differences in form have been reinforced, in turn, as outcomes of the differences in political behaviour, but they derived initially from different patterns in the circumstances of community origin and development.

Table 11.1   **Population and Municipal Status of Urban Places within 40 Kilometres of the Centres of Calgary and Edmonton in 1946 and 1986**

	1946		1986	
	Population	Status	Population	Status
Calgary	100,044	city	636,104	city
Bowness	none recorded	unincorporated	—	amalgamated with Calgary
Forest Lawn	646	village	—	amalgamated with Calgary
Montgomery	none recorded	unincorporated	—	amalgamated with Calgary
Airdrie	198	village	10,390	city
Cochrane	405	village	4,190	town
Okotoks	694	town	5,214	town
Edmonton	113,116	city	573,982	city
Beverly	1,171	town	—	amalgamated with Edmonton
Jasper Place	none recorded	unincorporated	—	amalgamated with Edmonton
Beaumont	none recorded	unincorporated	3,944	town
Bon Accord	none recorded	unincorporated	1,355	town
Calmar	none recorded	unincorporated	1,087	town
Devon	—	—	3,691	town
Fort Saskatchewan	921	town	11,983	city
Gibbons	none recorded	unincorporated	2,335	town
Leduc	920	town	13,126	city
Morinville	735	town	5,364	town
New Sarepta	none recorded	unincorporated	314	village
Sherwood Park	—	—	30,400	unincorporated
Spruce Grove	none recorded	unincorporated	11,918	city
St. Albert	804	town	36,710	city
Stony Plain	720	town	5,802	town

Sources: Census of the Prairie Provinces, 1946; Census of Canada, 1986

11.3   Circumstances of Community Development in the Edmonton and Calgary Metropolitan Areas

Edmonton and Calgary entered the post-war period with pronounced physical similarities. Their populations were relatively small (Table 11.1); they had large tracts of undeveloped land; and they were burdened with an excess of poorly serviced, partially built-up subdivisions. Environmental improvement was the immediate, pressing need, not territorial expansion, although this soon changed after subsequent events. At the census of 1961, Edmonton's population had increased to 280,000 and Calgary's to 250,000. Both cities had made some territorial gains, but population growth had spilled beyond their boundaries into low-status dormitory suburbs where a further 70,000 people were then living.

A trend to fringe development began early in both cities, on land that had been subdivided into building lots during the western real estate boom of 1908–12. The smallest and most scattered of these developments were absorbed by the cities, piece by piece, over many years, but the five largest were to prove more problematic. These were the communities of Jasper Place and Beverly near Edmonton, and Bowness, Montgomery, and Forest Lawn near Calgary, all of which experienced a surge of growth after 1946. Their initial attractions were cheap land and low taxes, but the houses were generally small and poorly built, services of all kinds were deficient and sometimes unsafe, and environmental amenities were virtually non-existent. Then, under the influence of the new boom conditions, the residents began to demand a higher level of services. Building and development controls were implemented, in an attempt to break away from the "shack-town" image, and the communities gave voice to their emerging sense of collective responsibility by obtaining incorporation as towns.[3] However, these rising aspirations were to become a source of severe frustration. To varying degrees, all five communities were tax-poor, and they faced the common dilemma of trying to upgrade themselves with inadequate resources.[4]

Meanwhile, even as this similarity of metropolitan form was gaining substance, large and ultimately more significant differences were taking shape. They were a function of three factors: the spatial pattern of initial settlement; the scale and location of industrial development; and the emergence of high-status residential suburbs in close proximity to Edmonton. The present-day implications are summarized in Figure 11.1, from which it can be seen that there are 13 separate urban places within a radius of 40 kilometres from the centre of Edmonton, including 11 that are now firmly established as satellites. Two of these satellites – Sherwood Park and Devon – are "new communities" on greenfield sites, but the remainder date from the period of agricultural colonization that began late in the nineteenth century. All had small populations in 1946 (Table 11.1), although five were incorporated as towns, indicating a long-established foundation of organized community life. In the Calgary area, by contrast, there are only three urban places within 40 kilometres of the city centre. As well, they were very small in 1946, and only one was incorporated as a town at that time.

It is evident, then, that the Edmonton area entered the post-war period with a denser pattern of established urban centres than the Calgary area. This meant that

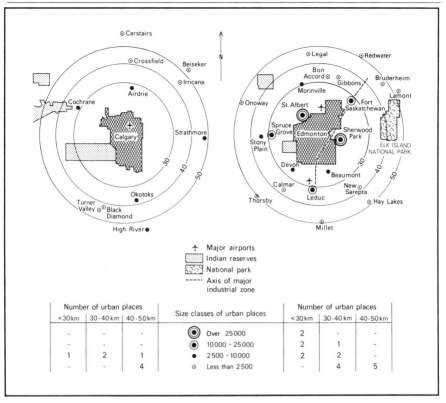

Number of urban places			Size classes of urban places		Number of urban places		
<30km	30-40km	40-50km			<30km	30-40km	40-50km
-	-	-	◉	Over 25 000	2	-	-
-	-	-	◉	10 000 - 25 000	2	1	-
1	2	1	●	2 500 - 10 000	2	2	-
-	-	4	⊙	Less than 2 500	-	4	5

Figure   **Urban Places in the Environs of Calgary and Edmonton,**
11.1   **Classified by 1981 Population and Distance from City Centres**

there were more potential development nodes in the vicinity of Edmonton, a point that was not lost on either the planners for the Edmonton region or their elected officials. All but one of the towns were represented on the regional planning authority that was created in 1950, and they made their growth aspirations clear from the beginning.[5] The planners therefore proposed that the Edmonton metropolitan region should be organized on the model of the British new towns, with a compact central city enclosed by a green belt and a circle of satellite towns that would be permitted to grow in a controlled fashion. The key elements of that concept have long since proved to be unenforceable, but the principle of dispersed development has at least persisted, despite repeated objections from the city of Edmonton.

In the Calgary area, regional planning took a different orientation from the outset. At first, Cochrane and Airdrie were the only outlying centres under the planning authority's jurisdiction, but neither was then thought to be an attractive growth point. Nor were towns that were added shortly after, such as Okotoks, High River, and Strathmore. Eventually, as highway connections improved and Calgary itself became greatly enlarged, all of these places took on some dormitory function, but in the 1950s and 1960s the Edmonton model of large-scale dispersal was deliberately rejected. With no competitive communities within close proximity, regional planning policy has been focused upon the containment of urban development within the boundaries of the city of Calgary. The corollary, of course, is that the boundaries must always expand in advance of development needs.

The contrast in development policy between the two metropolitan areas gained further impetus from the spatial effects of Alberta's burgeoning oil industry. In Calgary the immediate impact was concentrated *within* the city, most notably in the demand for office accommodation in the central business district (Saarinen 1963); in Edmonton, where industrial development was the major consequence, the most significant effects were felt *outside* the city boundaries. The explanation is rooted in the oil industry's origins before the First World War, when attention was focused on the Turner Valley area, south-west of Calgary. Edmonton had little part in this early activity, and at no time since has it competed with Calgary's historic role as the centre for investment, exploration, and administration (Zieber 1971). Yet when the first oil strikes were made in 1947 and 1948, they were close to Edmonton, which then emerged as the logical centre for the new transport and processing systems and for the new businesses that provided supplies and services to the oilfields. There were three direct consequences of long-term importance:

a) Several small towns in the Edmonton area were transformed from agricultural service centres into industrial growth points. Leduc and Redwater, for instance, became oilfield service centres, and Fort Saskatchewan, by virtue of its location on the North Saskatchewan River, with a ready supply of natural gas close at hand, was quick to attract major petrochemical and metal-smelting plants (Smith 1962). Fort Saskatchewan still stands as the most successful industrial satellite in the Edmonton metropolitan area, and it set a model that other towns have tried to emulate.

b) In the late 1940s the town of Devon was created as a planned service centre for the Leduc-Woodbend oilfield. Since this function has been unable to generate sustained growth, steps have recently been taken to convert Devon into a detached suburb of Edmonton.

c) Much of the industrial development spawned directly by the oil industry has been located in the rural municipalities abutting on Edmonton. This pattern became established early, as the first oil pipelines skirted the city to reach the hub of the transcontinental distribution network, in the County of Strathcona immediately east of Edmonton. A variety of industries, such as refineries, petrochemical factories, and pipe fabricating plants, were drawn to this area as well, forming the nucleus of a major industrial complex known locally as the Strathcona industrial corridor. Today, it is part of an extended industrial zone that stretches from Leduc to well beyond Fort Saskatchewan (Figure 11.1). Strathcona's success also encouraged other rural municipalities to seek industrial development, a desire that the regional planning authority, in all justice, has been unable to deny.

Another consequence of Strathcona's industrialization was the creation of the dormitory suburb of Sherwood Park (Gahr 1979).[6] In 1951 the Edmonton District

Planning Commission received notice that a real estate developer wished to build a new community just east of the Strathcona industrial corridor. The need for workers' housing was cited in justification, although the site's easy access from Edmonton ensured that it would be just as attractive to commuters. To the planning authority the proposal was a travesty of satellite town theory, but this opinion carried no weight with the Strathcona Council, which was shrewd enough to see political advantage in the project. It was only a matter of time before the city of Edmonton would covet Strathcona's industrial land, and the best defence was thought to lie in being able to demonstrate that the tax revenues from industry were being applied to the needs of a large resident population. For this reason, Sherwood Park has never sought incorporation (Alberta Municipal Affairs 1977), although it ranks with St. Albert as the largest of Edmonton's satellite communities.

Sherwood Park and St. Albert are of comparable status. They are well-designed communities, offering a high level of environmental and social amenities to middle-income families. Yet their origins were very different. St. Albert was founded in 1861 as a Catholic mission and became one of the leading centres of French settlement west of Winnipeg. It has always had a special cultural cachet, which has enhanced the authority it has been able to command in local affairs. When the first metropolitan plan was being drafted, its planners worried that St. Albert was too close to Edmonton to be anything more than a dormitory suburb. The force of this concern has been demonstrated over the past 35 years, yet there was never any question that St. Albert had as much right to grow as more distant towns, such as Fort Saskatchewan and Leduc. Indeed, its growth aspirations were given powerful sanction in 1957 when it was designated a "new town" and so became eligible for special assistance from the provincial government, to help it cope with the initial problems of rapid suburbanization.[7]

In summary, the post-war metropolitan areas of Edmonton and Calgary were both alike and different in the geographical bases on which the individual municipal governments had to seek territorial determination. Among the similarities the most critical were related to the need to adapt to the pressures of rapid growth while, at the same time, coping with the desire to improve servicing standards and environmental quality. These matters were to dominate intra-metropolitan relations until the 1960s, when the future of the low-status suburbs was finally decided. They also gave rise to a perception that Edmonton and Calgary were facing common problems for which an identical solution was appropriate. In part that was correct, but only in part. Edmonton entered the post-war period with a settlement pattern that was already more complex than Calgary's, and the complexity was enhanced by subsequent trends. This, in turn, gave rise to conflicts over territory and development that never existed in the Calgary area.

11.4   The Reformer's Paradox and the Low-Status Suburbs

By the mid-1950s it had become apparent in both Edmonton and Calgary that the cities' territorial bases were inadequate for sustained growth. Calgary's pressures were more acute, however, partly because a greater proportion of its

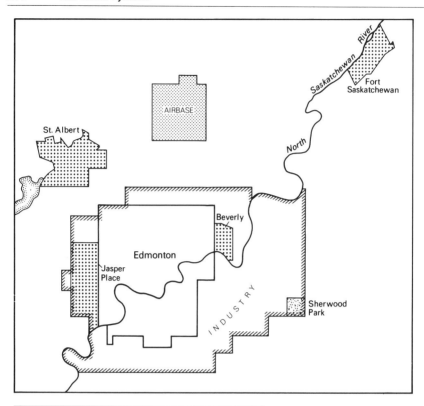

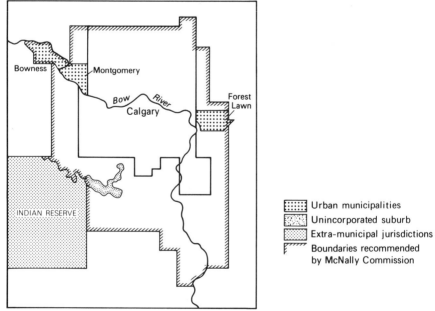

Urban municipalities

Unincorporated suburb

Extra-municipal jurisdictions

Boundaries recommended
by McNally Commission

Figure   **Political Organization of the Metropolitan Space of Edmonton**
11.2   **and Calgary in January 1956 (drawn to the same scale)**

Edmonton

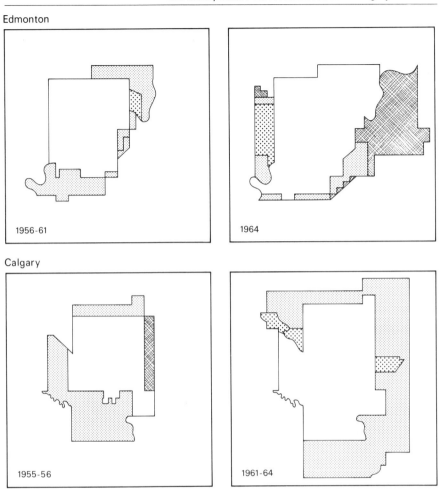

Calgary

Amalgamation approved	Annexation approved	Annexation refused

Figure   **Territorial Expansion of Edmonton, 1956–64, and Calgary,**
11.3   **1955–64 (drawn to the same scale)**

territory was considered unsuitable for development at that time, and partly because there had been less spillover into suburban municipalities. To some extent, Jasper Place and Strathcona acted as safety valves for Edmonton, and as long as a highly constrained, compact form of development was envisaged, concern about the city's long-term land needs could be deferred. Even so, it was clear that Jasper Place and Strathcona were erecting barriers against Edmonton's eventual expansion – barriers of a scale and kind that Calgary did not have to face (Figure 11.2).

Given these differences in territorial circumstances, it was only to be expected that Calgary would be more aggressive than Edmonton in its pursuit of annexation through the 1950s (Figure 11.3) (Bettison et al. 1975; Diemer 1975). Edmonton was also inhibited, as Calgary was not, by recommendations put forward in 1956 in the *Report of the Royal Commission on the Metropolitan Development of Calgary and Edmonton*, the so-called McNally Commission. This was established primarily to advise the government on ways of overcoming the fiscal problems of raising service delivery to a uniform standard throughout the two metropolitan areas, but it was also given a broad mandate to "recommend the boundaries and the form of local government which will most adequately and equitably provide for the orderly development of school and municipal services." As it turned out, this became the commission's major contribution.

Although the McNally Commission devoted a great deal of attention to the equity of existing territorial arrangements, at no point did it address the concept of equity as a fundamental intellectual problem. Rather, it made its own ideological assumptions, from which a particular view of equity emerged almost inevitably. Of central importance, the commission adopted the functional values that were then entrenched in the metropolitan reform movement, and so seized on the idea that consolidation of each of the two metropolitan areas would be the only acceptable approach (Figure 11.2). This allowed three closely related ends to be satisfied. First, said the commissioners, laying down their most basic principle, metropolitan areas are social and economic units which can be most "efficiently and effectively governed by one central municipal authority."[8] Second, cities must have ample "growing space" under their jurisdiction, if an "orderly" pattern of urban development is to be achieved. Finally, as long as municipal governments were heavily dependent on property taxes for their revenues, it was "unjust and inequitable" that jurisdictions within the same metropolitan entity should vary greatly in their property tax bases, and hence in their ability to meet their servicing needs. Equity was tied to functional requirements, and consolidation was thought to be the best way of ensuring that all members of a metropolitan community would have "equitable" (that is, equal) access to existing tax resources. It naturally followed that alternative conceptions of metropolitan form, based on contrary values, such as local autonomy or the pro-tection of established lifestyles, received absolutely no consideration.[9] By definition, they could lead only to inefficiency and injustice.

In retrospect, the McNally Commission's most important service was to force the various local governments in the two metropolitan areas to articulate their concerns and aspirations for the first time. For their part, the suburban towns expressed a strong desire for autonomy and self-improvement, although these were admitted to be impossible dreams for municipalities that could not afford to meet the costs of improvement. The only feasible alternative was amalgamation with Edmonton or Calgary, which the McNally Commission regarded as the logical course anyway. In one of its most carefully reasoned arguments, the commission concluded that the central cities were to blame for the "tax poverty" of the suburbs, because they effectively prevented the suburbs from gaining any substantial investment in non-residential property. Thus, continued the commission, it was only just that the cities should assume responsibility for the cost of upgrading the towns. Amalgamation was the obvious mechanism.

The cities, needless to say, offered a different view. Justice, to them, lay with the established claims of their own hard-pressed ratepayers, who should not be expected to take on extra costs for the benefit of suburban residents. Amalgamation could be tolerated only if it was part of a comprehensive consolidation that extended well beyond the developed metropolitan areas. What the cities wanted for themselves was to have absolute control over all future urban development so that fragmentation of authority could never again disrupt the metropolitan order. Only at this large scale could the cost of absorbing the suburban towns be seen as an acceptable trade-off.

For as long as the question of amalgamation remained unresolved, which meant until the early 1960s, the suburban towns did what they could to secure industrial assessment. However, in the presentations to the McNally Commission, only Forest Lawn expressed serious hopes for an independent future, based on its claim to a large part of the industrial land reserve for the Calgary area – a claim advanced in direct competition with the city of Calgary.[10] That particular contest was resolved in 1961, when the Local Authorities Board approved the transfer of a large block of rural territory to Calgary (Figure 11.3). Since Forest Lawn's vision of industrialization was then in ruins, the amalgamation of the two communities was ordered at the same time. Montgomery and Bowness followed in 1963 and 1964, completing the trade-off that Calgary had declared itself willing to accept. Not only had it gained jurisdiction over a large land base, it had opened the way to untrammelled expansion in the future by clearing its boundaries of embarrassing obstructions. Thus, in Calgary's case, the universe unfolded as the McNally Commission had decreed it should.

The same was not true of Edmonton for two reasons, both reflecting misjudgements on the part of the McNally Commission. In the first place, although the commission understood that Edmonton's metropolitan form differed in several respects from Calgary's, it considered the differences to be of degree rather than of kind. The future of Sherwood Park and the Strathcona industrial corridor were the most serious points at issue. The former was described as "a metropolitan tragedy," an offence to the commission's sense of orderly development; the latter was viewed as a grave injustice, because its tax wealth was inaccessible to the communities in greatest need. On the other side, the County of Strathcona argued that its tax advantage was by no means as great as was commonly supposed, particularly when its own long-term development plans and service needs were taken into account. If anything, the available evidence supported the county's position, but the commission gave that no credence. Instead, to paraphrase Rescher (1966), it regarded Strathcona's established claims as an irrelevant obstacle to its vision of an enlarged and unified Edmonton, and so pushed them aside.

In the second place, the McNally Commission completely misjudged the will of the government of Alberta, and the strength of its attachment to the ideals of local autonomy and responsible self-government. The commission's broad mandate to the contrary, the government had no intention of imposing wholesale changes on patterns of territorial jurisdiction that had evolved largely out of community wishes. Any action had to come on the communities' own initiative, through the machinery of local determination. Moreover, the minister of municipal affairs openly supported the construction of satellite towns, including Sherwood Park, so the commission's recommendations ran directly counter to his personal convictions. What he had expected, it seems, was advice on fiscal reforms and tax equalization measures that would allow all governments in both metropolitan areas to share the benefits of growth and improvements to services, without necessarily giving up their independence or surrendering large blocks of territory (Batey and Smith 1981, 210–11).

Unfortunately, it was several years before the significance of these attitudes became apparent, because there was no official response to the McNally Commission's report. For Calgary, the uncertainty did not matter. There, the suburban towns were not really a threat to the city's expansion plans, and it had little to lose by pressing ahead with normal annexation procedures. Indeed, with the authority of the McNally Commission behind it, Calgary could cast itself in a selfless light in its relations with the towns. Edmonton's position was altogether more clouded, especially with respect to Strathcona. Like Calgary, Edmonton believed that it had to secure control over a long-term supply of industrial land to make the amalgamation trade-off feasible. That pointed to eastward expansion into the Strathcona industrial corridor, but it was obvious that any move in that direction would be fiercely contested. Worse still, as events were to confirm, Edmonton's image in such a contest would be that of a bully-boy, carrying out a "tax-grab" that would impoverish the county. The McNally Commission's report therefore gave Edmonton a clear incentive to wait for the provincial government to act.

Over the next decade Edmonton regularly called on the government to order the consolidation of the metropolitan area, in accordance with the McNally recommendations. In the meantime, however, the city was running out of developable land, and had no option but to begin a series of annexations. As in Calgary, the first moves were cautious ones, securing rural territory that was desired for residential use. Amalgamation with Beverly was accepted at this stage as well (Figure 11.3), in part to try to enhance the city's standing before the Local Authorities Board in the real contest to come – the bid for the Strathcona industrial corridor. Edmonton also believed that if it was to have any chance of success against Strathcona it would have to show its willingness to amalgamate with Jasper Place. The bid was therefore presented in the form of a trade-off package: Jasper Place for the industrial corridor, with Sherwood Park thrown in on grounds that it would be too large a responsibility for the County of Strathcona to maintain once it had lost its industrial tax base (Bettison et al. 1975, 265–72; Smith and Diemer 1978).

In the outcome, to its great dismay, Edmonton was hoist with its own petard. The Local Authorities Board refused to accept a package deal, arguing that it had to judge the cases against the separate municipalities on their individual merits. In effect, the board delivered two decisions. In the first, the amalgamation of Edmonton and Jasper Place was ordered. As with the other suburban towns, the board came to the conclusion that the cost of improvement was too great for the ratepayers of Jasper Place to bear, whereas the same cost would be miniscule when spread amongst Edmonton's much larger body of ratepayers. In the second decision, the annexation from Strathcona was largely refused, following the same kind of logic. In this instance, the board concluded that the cost to Strathcona of losing the most valuable part of its territory would far outweigh the financial benefit to Edmonton. In economists' terms, Edmonton had fallen victim to the "tyranny of the small," meaning that in any assessment of relative costs and benefits between two parties of greatly unequal size, the smaller must always have the advantage over the larger.

The board's decision forced Edmonton to accept that the immediate metropolitan area would be only partially consolidated, an outcome rendered all the more galling by the knowledge that Calgary had completed its consolidation in the same year. The fact that the McNally Commission had recommended consolidation for both cities was further salt in Edmonton's wound. But whereas the commission's conception of equity was framed solely around functional values, the board had adopted the view that it must give equal consideration to the democratic or participatory values that the commission had explicitly discounted. Where functional needs could be judged to be more important, as in the case of the low-status suburbs, territorial redistribution was an equitable solution. However, Strathcona posed a different ethical problem for the board, which concluded that it would not be right to reduce a responsible self-governing community to an impoverished rump, to allow Edmonton to gain a relatively small fiscal benefit. Thus, the Strathcona contest gave clear notice that the reformer's paradox was critically important to the Edmonton metropolitan area. Unlike Calgary, where the juridical balance slipped easily and quickly to the side of redistribution, the justice of existing claims had become a decisive feature of Edmonton's local context.

11.5   Implications for the Evolution of Metropolitan Form

With the blessing of hindsight, it can be seen that the evolution of metropolitan form in Edmonton and Calgary was critically affected by the events of the 1950s and early 1960s. This was a period in which fundamental decisions were made about patterns of jurisdiction and urban development, and in which attitudes towards territorial relations formed and hardened. By 1964 the two cities were settled into intrinsically different growth patterns.

The nature of the difference can best be appreciated by reference to a developmental theory, such as Zikmund's four-stage model of metropolitan form (Zikmund II 1975, 47–50). In the late 1950s, when Edmonton and Calgary were still comparatively small and uncomplicated, their metropolitan areas fitted Zikmund's description of the second or "emerging" stage of metropolitan development. This has two main characteristics: the central city is clearly dominant over its suburbs, and its boundaries are largely open. Eventually, however, if suburbanization continues, as it threatened to do in Edmonton's case, the central city will be completely enclosed. This is Zikmund's third stage, and it is characterized by viable and well-organized suburban communities that are able to resist the central city's expansion. The focus of development then shifts to the suburbs and satellite towns, beyond the jurisdiction of the city government. This was a prospect that Edmonton and Calgary were equally anxious to avoid, in effect by truncating Zikmund's evolutionary sequence. But whereas Calgary succeeded so completely that it regressed to stage one in the model

– a stage of no suburban development – Edmonton was merely able to retard its suburbanization for a time. The theoretical explanation is that Calgary ca. 1960 represented a very early phase of stage two development whereas Edmonton was already in transition to stage three, a process marked by the emergence of communities of the Strathcona type. The more advanced the trend to suburbanization, and the more nearly a metropolitan area approaches a stage three condition, the more difficult it is to reverse the sequence through the machinery of local determination.

City officials in Edmonton came to essentially the same conclusion in 1964. The failure of their attempt to annex the Strathcona industrial corridor left them convinced that the Local Authorities Board was not an appropriate body to pass judgement on the justice of a complex redistribution where the interests of several municipalities had to be balanced in a single decision. As long as the board insisted on treating territorial claims as a direct contest between legal equals, the tyranny of the small would be an insuperable obstacle to Edmonton's aspirations. Hence that passionate plea: "Let the provincial government come out from behind the Local Authorities Board" – because only the provincial government had the authority to order that territory from several municipalities be consolidated at one sweep.

Over the next 15 years Edmonton made several approaches to the government, but all were rebuffed. The period was also marked by an expanding scale of metropolitan development, as the growth of the suburbs and satellite towns

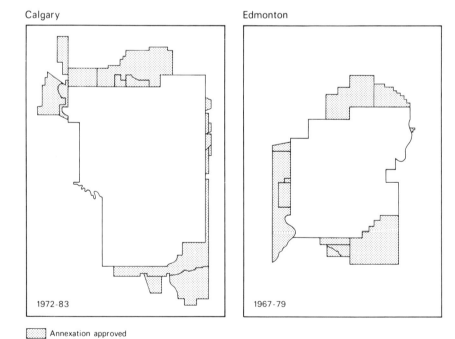

Calgary   Edmonton

1972-83   1967-79

▒ Annexation approved

Figure   **Territorial Expansion of Calgary, 1972–83, and Edmonton,**
11.4   **1967–79 (drawn to the same scale)**

quickened. In 1961 the urban population of the area within 40 kilometres of the centre of Edmonton was about 340,000, of which 95 percent lived in the central city (including Beverly and Jasper Place). By 1986 the total had increased to 700,000, with close to 130,000 (18 percent) outside Edmonton (Table 11.1). By North American standards this was still not a particularly high level of dispersal, but it was in striking contrast to Calgary where only 20,000 people out of a total of 655,000 lived in towns over a comparable area. An early stage of satellite development had become evident, most notably in Airdrie, which has grown rapidly since 1976, but this trend poses no threat yet to Calgary's own expansion. In Zikmund's terms, Calgary is still in the first stage of metropolitan development and is likely to remain so for the foreseeable future.

For Edmonton, by contrast, the expanding scale of metropolitan development can be interpreted as a renewal of Zikmund's evolutionary sequence after the absorption of the low-status suburbs. It was also accompanied by increasingly independent behaviour on the part of the metropolitan municipalities, as the setting for territorial competition was enlarged. Edmonton made some important gains in the 1970s (Figure 11.4), but so too did the other urban communities, all of which annexed territory from their rural neighbours. Four of the largest (St. Albert, Fort Saskatchewan, Leduc, and Spruce Grove) also obtained city charters, a largely symbolic gesture but one that gives them the same municipal status as Edmonton. Moreover, all of the municipalities, rural as well as urban, have taken steps to assume more direct control over their local planning systems, underscoring Williams's (1967) suggestion that the power to regulate land use is one of the most potent means of protecting lifestyle values. In fact, the issue of planning jurisdiction erupted into open conflict in 1982–84, when the current version of the metropolitan plan was under review. The strategy favoured by the regional planners was to concentrate development in Edmonton and the largest satellites, but this was rejected by the regional municipalities, which wished to be free to set their own growth policies (Bayne 1986).

These behaviours manifest a growing challenge to Edmonton's dominance in its metropolitan region, which is a key characteristic of the transition from stage two to stage three in Zikmund's model. At the same time, Edmonton was escalating its own response to its growth pressures, the effects of which were compounded by a building sense of frustration over the provincial government's failure to intervene (Smith 1982). The first step occurred in 1968, when an eminent political economist advised that Edmonton's territory should be roughly twice as large as the McNally Commission had proposed only 12 years before (Hanson 1968). St. Albert was included within the new boundary as well, and so was drawn into territorial conflict with Edmonton for the first time. Then, in 1978, after having been told once again that all claims for territorial redistribution had to be directed to the Local Authorities Board, Edmonton submitted an application of staggering but logical boldness – logical, that is, if the problem of the tyranny of the small was to be overcome. The application called for Edmonton to annex Strathcona County in its entirety, along with St. Albert and large portions of two adjoining rural municipalities (Figure 11.5).

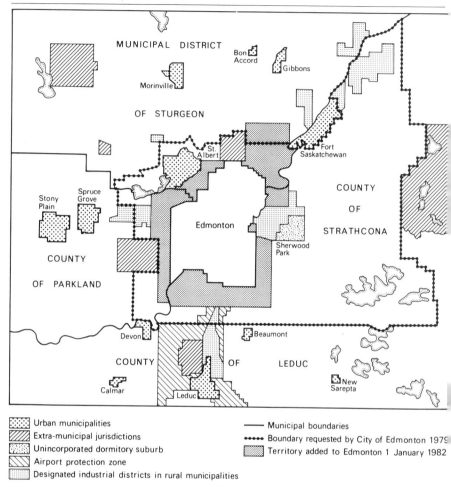

Figure   **Edmonton's Annexation Bid of 1979 and Its Effect upon the**
11.5   **Political Organization of Edmonton's Metropolitan Space, 1985**

The aim was to consolidate the whole of the inner-metropolitan area under Edmonton's jurisdiction. Edmonton also found cause for optimism in an important procedural change that had just been enacted.[11] This empowered the provincial cabinet to vary any decision of the Local Authorities Board in any way it saw fit, which meant that Edmonton's case was really being addressed to the cabinet, at least indirectly.

The decision that was finally announced in 1981 was a masterpiece of compromise (Plunkett and Lightbody 1982).[12] On one side, cabinet recognized Edmonton's right to unobstructed growth, and so granted extensions along all sections of the city's open boundary, even including land that Edmonton had not requested. The city's territory was doubled thereby, giving a land base that should be adequate for development until well into the twenty-first century. On the other side, cabinet affirmed, in the strongest language, its desire to protect the autonomy of St. Albert and Strathcona. The county lost heavily from Edmonton's expansion, and for this it was compensated with special grants, but Sherwood Park and the original core of the industrial corridor were untouched. Cabinet also hoped to ensure the long-term viability of Sherwood Park and St. Albert by raising their population targets from 30,000 to 70,000. This marked the influence of the only truly unequivocal evidence produced by the long, bitter, and exceedingly costly hearing process – the evidence, supported by scientifically conducted attitude surveys, that the residents of Sherwood Park and St. Albert were almost unanimously opposed to the loss of their communities (Burton 1979).[13] They were living verification of Williams's lifestyle hypothesis.

In one sense, cabinet's decision gave Edmonton what it had wanted ever since the McNally Commission, in that the provincial government had finally been forced to make a judgement on Edmonton's territorial ambitions. In its substance, however, the decision differed only in scale from that delivered in 1964 by the Local Authorities Board. Cabinet had had to confront the reformer's paradox exactly as the board had done, and it arrived at essentially the same balance between the justice of redistribution and the justice of existing claims. It has also deferred the need for a further round of territorial competition into a remote future, although that decision in itself may have guaranteed that the metropolitan area will complete the transition to Zikmund's stage three before Edmonton has another chance to extend its boundaries. The city already marches with St. Albert and touches upon Fort Saskatchewan; Devon and Beaumont are barely beyond the southern boundary; and other major obstructions (an Indian reserve, airport control zones, and suburban industrial development) leave little room for manoeuvring even now. The real decision on the political organization of Edmonton's metropolitan space may simply have been delayed for 40 or 50 years.

Notes

1. The authority to rule on applications for annexation or amalgamation was vested in the Board of Public Utilities Commissioners, which became the Public Utilities Board in 1960.
2. *Edmonton Journal*, 4 June 1964.
3. Bowness was incorporated as a village in 1948 and raised to a town in 1951; Forest Lawn became a town in 1953; Montgomery was incorporated as a town in 1958; and Jasper Place first became a village and then a town in 1950. Only Beverly, a coal-mining settlement, which was incorporated as a town in 1914, remained unchanged.
4. The fullest description of conditions in the five suburbs is in *Report of the Royal Commission on the Metropolitan Development of Calgary and Edmonton* (Edmonton: Queen's Printer, 1956), chaps. 3 and 4.

5. Based on the annual reports of the Edmonton District Planning Commission.

6. See also *Report of the Royal Commission on the Metropolitan Development of Calgary and Edmonton* (Edmonton: Queen's Printer, 1956), chap. 5, 30–33.

7. The *New Towns Act, 1956* was designed primarily to assist in the development of new resource towns, such as Devon and Drayton Valley, but it was also available to established communities facing the prospect of unmanageable growth. See H.N. Lash, "New Towns and Provincial Assistance" (Paper presented at the annual meeting of the Town Planning Institute of Canada, Banff, September 1956).

8. Ironically, the economic and social unit was not defined to include St. Albert, which was completely excluded from the McNally Commission's consideration despite its proximity to Edmonton (Figure 11.2). The omission has never been explained.

9. In one of the commission's most revealing asides, local autonomy was described as "a legal, constitutional myth which ought to be exploded," since local governments in Canada have no rights other than have been expressly conveyed to them by a provincial government. *Report of the Royal Commission on the Metropolitan Development of Calgary and Edmonton* (Edmonton: Queen's Printer), chap. 6, 88.

10. "Brief Submitted to the Royal Commission on the Metropolitan Development of Calgary and Edmonton on Behalf of the Council of the Town of Forest Lawn" (December 1954). Of the five towns, Forest Lawn was the only one to be consistently opposed to amalgamation throughout the period from 1946 to the early 1960s. The others sought amalgamation on various occasions, although Jasper Place, in a rare burst of confidence, reversed itself in a late submission to the McNally Commission, *Edmonton Journal*, 18 May 1956.

11. First, in an amending statute in 1975, cabinet was empowered to "approve or disapprove" a board order. To this was added in 1978 the power to "vary" an order.

12. See "Report and Decision Concerning the Edmonton Annexation Application" (Released by the Minister of Municipal Affairs, Alberta, June 1981).

13. See also *St. Albert Community Attitude Survey* (Edmonton: Earl Berger Ltd., 1980).

References

Alberta Municipal Affairs. 1977. *The Hamlet of Sherwood Park: A Review of Alternate Forms of Government*. Edmonton: Alberta Municipal Affairs.

Batey, W.L., and P.J. Smith. 1981. "The Role of Territory in Political Conflict in Metropolitan Fringe Areas." In K.B Beesley and L.H. Russwurm, eds., "The Rural-urban Fringe: Canadian Perspectives," Geographical Monographs, Atkinson College, York University, no. 10, 199–217.

Bayne, P. 1986. "Regional Planning and Local Autonomy in the Edmonton Metropolitan Region, 1981–1984." Master's thesis, University of Alberta.

Bettison, D.G., J.K. Kenward, and L. Taylor. 1975. *Urban Affairs in Alberta*. Edmonton: University of Alberta Press.

Brownstone, M., and T.J. Plunkett. 1983. *Metropolitan Winnipeg: Politics and Reform of Local Government*. Berkeley: University of California Press.

Burton, T.L. 1979. *A Strathcona County Residents Survey*. Edmonton: Makale and Kyllo Planning Associates Ltd.

Coleman, A. 1969. "The Planning Challenge of the Ottawa Area." Geographical Papers, Department of Energy, Mines and Resources, Ottawa, no. 42.

Cox, K.R., and R.J. Johnston. 1982. *Conflict, Politics and the Urban Scene*. London: Longman.

Diemer, H.L. 1975. "Annexation and Amalgamation in the Territorial Expansion of Edmonton and Calgary." Master's thesis, University of Alberta.

Fullerton, D.H. 1974. *The Capital of Canada: How Should It Be Governed?* Ottawa: Information Canada.

Gahr, G.A. 1979. "Sherwood Park: Residents' Attitudes Toward a Dormitory Satellite of Edmonton." Master's thesis, University of Alberta.

Gottmann, J. 1973. *The Significance of Territory*. Charlottesville: University Press of Virginia.

Hanson, E.J. 1968. *The Potential Unification of the Edmonton Metropolitan Area: A Fiscal Study of Annexation and Amalgamation*. Edmonton: University of Alberta.

Harvey, D.W. 1973. *Social Justice and the City*. London: Edward Arnold.

Honey, R.D. 1976. "Metropolitan Governance." In J.S. Adams, ed., *Urban Policymaking and Metropolitan Dynamics: A Comparative Geographical Analysis*, 425–62. Cambridge: Ballinger Publishing Co.

Kaplan, H. 1982. *Reform, Planning and City Politics: Montreal, Winnipeg, Toronto*. Toronto: University of Toronto Press.

Makuch, S.M. 1983. *Canadian Municipal and Planning Law*. Toronto: Carswell Co. Ltd.

Masson, J. 1985. *Alberta's Local Governments and Their Politics*. Edmonton: Pica Pica Press.

National League of Cities, Dept. of Urban Studies. 1966. *Adjusting Municipal Boundaries: Law and Practice*. Washington, D.C.: National League of Cities.

Plunkett, T.J., and J. Lightbody. 1982. "Tribunals, Politics, and the Public Interest: The Edmonton Annexation Case." *Canadian Public Policy* 8:207–21.

Rescher, N. 1966. *Distributive Justice: A Constructive Critique of the Utilitarian Theory of Distribution*. Indianapolis: Bobbs-Merrill Co.

Rose, A. 1972. *Governing Metropolitan Toronto: A Social and Political Analysis 1953–1971*. Berkeley: University of California Press.

Saarinen, T.F. 1963. "The Changing Office Functions in Calgary's Central Business District." Master's thesis, University of Chicago.

Sancton, A. 1983. "Conclusion: Canadian City Politics in Comparative Perspective." In W. Magnusson and A. Sancton, eds., *City Politics in Canada*, 291–317. Toronto: University of Toronto Press.

Seifried, N.R. 1990. "Edmonton and Calgary: Perception and Reality of Rival Cities." In P.J. Smith and E.L. Jackson, eds., *A World of Real Places: Essays in Honour of William C. Wonders*, 163–73. Studies in Geography, University of Alberta.

Sengstock, F.S. 1960. *Annexation: A Solution of the Metropolitan Area Problem*. Ann Arbor: Michigan Legal Publications.

Sharpe, L.J. 1970. "Theories and Values of Local Government. *Political Studies* 18:153–74.

Smith, P.J. 1962. "Fort Saskatchewan: An Industrial Satellite of Edmonton." *Plan Canada* 3:4–16.

———. 1982. "Municipal Conflicts Over Territory and the Effectiveness of the Regional Planning System in the Edmonton Metropolitan Area." In *Kulturgeographische Prozessforschung in Kanada*, 207–23. Heft 4: Bamberger Geographische Schriften.

Smith, P.J., and H.L. Diemer. 1978. "Equity and the Annexation Process: Edmonton's Bid for the Strathcona Industrial Corridor." In P.J. Smith, ed., "Edmonton: The Emerging Metropolitan Pattern." Western Geographical Series, University of Victoria, no. 15, 263–89.

Soja, E.N. 1971. "The Political Organization of Space." Resource Papers, Association of American Geographers, Commission on College Geography, no. 8. Washington, D.C.

Watson, J.W. 1976. "Image Regions." In J.W. Watson and T. O'Riordan, eds., *The American Environment: Perceptions and Policies,* 15–28. London: John Wiley and Sons.

Wesche, R., and M. Kugler-Gagnon, eds. 1978. *Ottawa-Hull: Spatial Perspectives and Planning.* Ottawa: University of Ottawa Press.

Williams, O.P. 1967. "Lifestyle Values and Political Decentralization in Metropolitan Areas." *Southwestern Social Science Quarterly* 48:299–310.

———. 1971. *Metropolitan Political Analysis: A Social Access Approach.* New York: The Free Press.

Zieber, G.H. 1971. "Inter- and Intra-city Location Patterns of Oil Offices for Calgary and Edmonton, 1950–1970." Ph.D. thesis, University of Alberta.

Zikmund II, J. 1975. "A Theoretical Structure for the Study of Suburban Politics." *Annals of the American Academy of Political and Social Science* 422:46–60.

12   Urban Canada 2001

Bernard D. Thraves

The purpose of this essay is to provide a brief assessment of prospective change in Canada's urban system to the year 2001. In recent years the nature and intensity of this change has been influenced by a succession of exceptional political and economic events. Examples include the flight of business from Quebec following the election of the Parti Québécois government in 1976, and the decline in investment and exploration in Alberta's oilfields following the enactment of the National Energy Policy in 1980. Such events have strongly influenced the intensity and direction of inter-provincial migration and related urban growth rates (Robinson 1981, 21; Statistics Canada 1984a). Because similar events may override the "normal" processes of change in the period to 2001, precise forecasts of urban change based on the manipulation of demographic and economic data sets are of doubtful value. Consequently, the forecasts presented here are concerned with general themes in urban development and are deliberately conservative in their argument. The first theme outlines the current dimensions of Canada's urban system and examines the prospects for further urbanization and urban growth. The second theme describes the physical structure of Canada's cities and concentrates on the liabilities posed by urban deconcentration. The third theme examines the social dimensions of Canada's cities and draws attention to the increasing significance of their elderly and new immigrant populations.

12.1   Canada's Urban System

In Canada the designation "urban" denotes all communities with populations in excess of 1,000 inhabitants. On this basis, 76 percent of Canada's population were classified as urban in 1981, and 56 percent lived within census metropolitan areas (CMAs).[1] At the same time, urban communities occupied less than 1 percent of national territory and were situated predominantly in southern Canada. The basic dimensions of this system were determined before 1920 with the closure of the land frontier in western Canada.[2] Since then the predominant form of urban development has been in the vicinity of existing urban communities, or in small, highly specialized, and relatively isolated settlements in the provincial north, Yukon, and Northwest Territories.

The economic development of Canada's cities has varied considerably. This variation reflects the contrasting wealth of their hinterlands, their degree of centrality within the North American market, and their ability to retain experienced labour and attract new investment (Walker 1980, 78–86). Since Confederation these factors have tended to favour cities in central and western Canada. For most of this period the traditional staple industries of eastern Canada have been less competitive in international markets, and have generated less domestic industry through linkage economies than the newer staples of central and western Canada (Gertler and Crowley 1977, 105–12; Marr and Paterson 1980, 425–38). In addition, national economic policy and foreign investment have tended to favour the concentration of secondary manufacturing and tertiary activity in central Canada (Pomfret 1981, 189–99).

During the twentieth century the most distinctive aspect of Canadian urbanization has been the emergence of a nationwide system of large metropolitan centres (Nader 1975, 210–14). Until the mid-1960s these centres accounted for an ever increasing share of the urban population, and the dominance of the three largest centres, Montreal, Toronto, and Vancouver, was viewed with particular alarm (Lithwick 1970). Since then, however, the combined growth rate of all the CMAs has approximated that of the entire urban system, while the growth rates for individual CMAs have become increasingly varied (Statistics Canada 1984b). For example, the growth rates of Montreal, Hamilton, and Winnipeg have slowed appreciably, and absolute losses of population have been recorded in Sudbury and Windsor. In contrast, quite vigorous growth has been experienced in Calgary, Edmonton, Ottawa-Hull, and St. Catharines-Niagara. In addition, the proportion of Canada's population classified as urban has stabilized at around 76 percent. To a considerable extent the phenomenon of counter-urbanization reflected in these data represents a movement of people to medium-sized towns and exurban environments around the large cities. Explanations for these movements are found in "pull" factors such as increased privacy, security, and choice of lifestyle, and in "push" factors such as the high cost of urban housing and disenchantment with suburbia (Bryant et al. 1982, 72–76). Also, post-war developments in transportation and electronic communication have helped extend the benefits of urban lifestyles to exurban environments.

What are the prospects for further urbanization and urban growth in this system? To answer this question some indication of Canada's expected population growth is required. Recent forecasts suggest that low fertility and immigration rates will contribute to declining rates of population growth in the next few decades (Statistics Canada 1985a). On this basis, Canada's population should total between 27.8 and 30.3 million by the year 2001, with forecasts at the lower end of this range being favoured by most analysts (e.g., Barney et al. 1981, 66–68; Yeates 1985, 73). Within this environment of slow growth the level of urbanization may still increase, but differences in the growth rates of individual urban areas are expected to become much more pronounced (Robinson 1981, 78). Important factors in the growth rates of individual communities are likely to include their current size and centrality within the urban system, and their endowment in physical and human resources. At the same time, the continued extension of urban-oriented lifestyles within exurban environments will further reduce the significance of urban status as traditionally defined (Russwurm 1980, 292). On this basis several arguments seem persuasive.

First, the relatively slow growth of Canada's largest CMAs is likely to remain slow unless means are found to combat their urbanization diseconomies. These diseconomies include the highest costs of land development, labour, and housing, and the costs to industrial production and individual health caused by increased congestion and pollution. Because of these drawbacks, new and expanding industrial developments in central Canada may be located in medium-sized CMAs or in non-metropolitan communities. In this context, the recent siting of new car plants in Quebec at Bromont (by Hyundai), and in Ontario at Alliston (by Honda) and Cambridge (by Toyota), seems instructive. For this reason, relatively promising growth prospects are expected for small- and medium-sized communities within the commutersheds of the large metropolitan areas. In central Canada at least, these communities are expected to form industrial and residential nodes within an emerging system of highly dispersed regional cities (Russwurm 1980; Bryant et al. 1982, 219–22). However, there is the risk that this growth may simply transfer some of the problems of the large cities to the smaller communities. For example, rapid growth may lead to poor development design, the overtaxing of local infrastructure and social services, conflict between long-term residents and newcomers, and the impairment of the environmental advantages sought in smaller communities (Robinson 1981, 93–98).

Second, somewhat uncertain growth prospects face many of the urban centres in western Canada. In recent decades, communities such as Calgary, Edmonton, and Vancouver have experienced mounting prosperity based on the development of forest, hydrocarbon, and other mineral resources in their hinterlands. Expanding economies in these communities have attracted an increasing proportion of Canada's new immigrants and inter-provincial migrants, and have helped shift the centre of gravity of Canada's population away from the industrial heartland of central Canada. Currently, however, the downturn in the world oil market, low grain prices, and the prolonged recession in the British Columbian economy have emphasized the problems associated with the lack of industrial diversification in much of western Canada (Rhéaume 1986, 43). In addition, the region is still handicapped by its distance from the major national and international markets. In short, the prosperity and continued growth of many centres in western Canada will depend on improved markets for natural resource industries, or on their ability to develop more diversified industrial bases. The immediate prospects for either of these developments is not encouraging (Gusen 1984, 10).

Third, growth prospects in eastern Canada will remain tied to direct employment opportunities in the public sector and to government-sponsored development initiatives. Historically, the region's poor resource base and weak manufacturing sector have been reflected in considerable economic hardship. Remedies for this situation have been sought in the regional economic development programs of the federal and provincial governments. The prime example of this has been the work of the Department of Regional Economic Expansion (ECC 1977, 145–72). In addition, direct employment in public administration and defence industries has provided a major component of the economic base in such cities as Halifax (18.4 percent of 1981 labour force) and St. John's (12.7 percent), and in smaller communities including Charlottetown (14.4 percent), Gander (19.9 percent), and Fredericton (18.2 percent). The precise impact of government programs and direct employment on the economic well-being of eastern Canada is difficult to measure. However, it is generally conceded that long-term improvements in the economy must, in part, be attributable to government intervention (Sitwell and Seifried 1984, 164). These improvements are indicated by a significant slowing of the traditional net migration losses from three of the four provinces, and by some closure in the gap between regional and national per capita income and employment levels (Sitwell and Siefried 1984, 132–33). Similarly, it is unlikely that the economic well-being of eastern Canadian cities can be sustained unless future governments remain committed to regional development initiatives. This point is dramatized by the recent setbacks in economic growth, which can be attributed in part to reduced job creation in the public sector (Rhéaume 1986, 42). Ironically, eastern Canada's familiarity with economic stagnation and slow growth, of population may prove psychologically advantageous in the slow growth environment of the next few decades.

Fourth, relatively weak development prospects are anticipated for Canada's single-resource towns. Most of these towns are located in the provincial north, Yukon, and Northwest Territories, and are engaged in mining, forestry, or other resource-based activities. Typically their economic viability is dependent on markets and investment decisions taken in distant metropolitan centres or outside Canada. This combination of factors is considered to be the root cause of socio-economic and psychological hardships among residents, and their consequent sense of "settlement" rather than "community" (Gertler and Crowley 1977, 250–60). In the past decade the viability of many resource towns has been adversely affected by generally poor markets for most industrial raw materials and by volatile changes in resource industry investment (EMR 1985, 1.1–1.3; Statistics Canada 1986a). This situation has been especially critical for mining towns and has contributed to economic retrenchment, population losses, and a general slowdown in the pace of northern development (Statistics Canada 1984a). In certain instances, for example at Schefferville, this has meant the total collapse of the local urban economy (Bradbury and St-Martin 1983). It seems certain that the prospects for these communities will remain tied to distant market factors. Consequently, their competitive position will depend on the restoration of global markets for industrial raw materials, the favourable investment priorities of multinational corporations, and technological advances in the development of new resources and products (EMR 1985, 1.3–1.4). Even with improvement in these factors, northern resource development is unlikely to encourage the establishment of new resource towns. Instead, the high capital costs of new townsite development may be diverted into existing communities, as is already the case for most new developments in the forest industry (McCann 1980, 219–26). This strategy would be consistent with regionally based attempts to improve economic stability and community services in resource towns (Gertler and Crowley 1977, 263–64).

Finally, the increasing likelihood of population decline in large urban areas may generate a sense of pessimism in which inaction or unimaginative planning may lead to more substantial decline (Robinson 1981, 86). To date, Canadians have been accustomed to a philosophy of urban development that stresses economic growth and physical expansion, or quantitative rather than qualitative aspects of development (Russwurm 1980, 292–94; Lorimer 1981). The social and economic costs of such development are expressed in the aforementioned urbanization diseconomies, the neglect of minority group interests, and a general disregard for environmental issues. European experience demonstrates that this form of development occurs when the harmonious relationship between man and environment ("cultural rationality") is subordinated to the demands of the marketplace ("economic rationality") (Hall 1977, 105–10). Fortunately, the expected lower growth rates of post-industrial Canada may help to establish greater balance between these components of urbanism. For example, a slower growth rate in Calgary might help the city to avoid the kind of social service and physical planning problems posed by rapid urban development, as it experienced in the 1970s (Robinson 1981, 78–79).

12.2   The Physical Structure of the City

Perhaps the most immediate physical characteristic of Canadian cities is their low density and extensive development pattern. This structure has become accentuated since the 1950s and reflects the massive suburbanization of residential development, industry, and commerce. Suburban residential development has been encouraged by rising personal incomes, high rates of automobile ownership, substantial growth in the rate of new household formation, and a desire for more privacy and space (Nader 1975, 71). Because of these factors, the population of the suburbs in every CMA now exceeds that of its corresponding central city (Mitchell and Bond, 1980). The suburbanization of retailing to serve the suburban population has been accomplished in the development of large shopping malls. These malls, which have been promoted by major property developers, first appeared in the mature suburbs during the 1950s. Since then they have appeared at an increasing scale with each new phase of suburban development (Nader 1975, 79–82). The suburbanization of industry has reflected a shortage of industrial sites in the inner cities, changes in the type and technology of industrial production, increasing use of inter-modal transportation systems, and municipal involvement in the planning and promotion of industrial parks (Walker 1980, 228–42; Bryant et al. 1982, 118–19).

Arguably, the suburbanization of Canada's cities has provided an improved living environment and lifestyle for suburbanites. Nevertheless, suburbanization has also resulted in major social and economic costs to certain citizens' groups and to society at large. For example, costs to the elderly, the poor, and small business interests have included the decline of retailing in the central business district. Costs to the municipality, and hence the public at large, have included the mounting financial burdens of providing public transit, road maintenance, and garbage and snow removal. However, perhaps the greatest cost of suburbanization has been the permanent loss of prime agricultural land. For example, between 1966 and 1976 urban growth in cities with populations of 25,000 or more consumed approximately 150,000 hectares of rural land (Warren and Rump 1981).[3] Of this total, 62 percent were classified as improved agricultural land. During the same period, urban growth in the vicinity of Toronto consumed over 17,000 hectares of which 82 percent were improved. Some of this loss has been inevitable insofar as most urbanized areas are located in areas with moderate to high agricultural potential. Most critically, however, the loss has included irreplaceable speciality crop areas (Kreuger 1978), and has occurred at a rate greater than the rate of growth in population (Bryant et al. 1982, 98–101; Yeates 1985, 5–6). Yet, to date, effective controls on suburban land development are restricted to a few jurisdictions such as Vancouver and Victoria.

What are the prospects for change in the physical structure of Canadian cities? In answering this question several arguments seem relevant. First, massive change in the physical environments of Canada's cities has normally been restricted to speculative phases during their early development or to periods of expansion during resource-led booms. Examples include the rapid growth of urban settlements in the Prairies prior to the First World War and the more recent oil-based booms in Calgary and Edmonton (Artibise 1981, 15–21; Nader 1976, 337–38). This type of development is not anticipated in the slow-growth environment of the next few decades. Nevertheless, continued deconcentration of the large metropolitan centres could result in unprecedented rates of urbanization in small towns and exurban environ-ments (Robinson 1981, 93–98; Bryant et al. 1982, 219–22). Moreover, the emerging pattern of regional city systems is expected to perpetuate existing high rates of rural land consumption. One estimate for the Windsor-Quebec axis indicates that 94,000 hectares of rural land[4] may be consumed in direct losses to urban development between 1981 and 2001 (Yeates 1985, 73–84). The same study suggests that a further 574,000 hectares may be consumed in indirect losses to urban-orientated services, and to land withdrawn from agricultural production in anticipation of urban development. Even if this forecast is overly pessimistic,[5] the implication is still clear: Canada's most productive agricultural resource will remain under sustained develop-ment pressure throughout the forecast period. Further, if agricultural output is to be maintained, or even increased, the losses of productive land must either be replaced, or the productivity of the remaining resource must be increased. The Canadian experience has shown that such circumstances are likely to increase dependence on energy- and technology-intensive agricultural systems (Manning 1978).

Second, the suburbs and the inner cores are likely to remain the most active areas of change within the major urban centres. However, unlike the experience of the last few decades, the level of activity in the cores may increase relative to that in the suburbs. This view is based on anticipated changes in the characteristics of Canadian households. By the mid-1990s most of the post-war baby-boom population will have passed through the household-formation life-cycle stage. Because of this, the pres-sure for residential and retailing developments in the suburbs should ease somewhat. In addition, growth in the proportion of single-person households, including those of the elderly, may increase demand for non-family housing in inner-city neighbour-hoods. Indeed, this trend is already evident in the gentrification of old neighbour-hoods (such as Toronto's Cabbagetown and Vancouver's Kitsilano district), and in the redevelopment of derelict urban core properties (such as Toronto's Harbourfront and Winnipeg's Portage Avenue project) (Ley 1981; Frampton 1985). Many of these projects represent joint financial commitments on the part of the public and private sectors, and add to longstanding programs in urban renewal. However, a major drawback of such inner-city revitalization is its tendency to displace low-income households (Bourne 1981; Phipps 1982). Consequently, the provision of an adequate supply of moderately priced housing in inner-city neighbourhoods could become a significant issue in Canada's post-industrial cities, and especially if white-collar professional employment remains concentrated in the central business district (Ley 1981).

Third, the operation of zoning by-laws should ensure that most land uses in the major urban centres remain relatively fixed, and that new developments are compatible with existing land uses. Prevailing rates of conversion and obsolescence mean that only a small fraction of the urban environment is likely to change through redevelopment (Russwurm 1980, 273). Similarly, the market economy will continue to determine individual access to housing. For this reason, the urban poor will still live in the aging housing stock of the inner city. In contrast, the middle-class will remain more comfortably accommodated in suburbia, and increasingly in exurbia or the gentrified parts of the inner city. For these reasons, the physical appearance of Canada's cities in 2001 will substantially resemble that of the mid-1980s. The forces of change simply act too slowly to expect otherwise.

12.3   The Social Dimensions of the City

In socio-demographic terms the residents of Canada's cities form a series of minority groups, membership of which is determined by such factors as income, age, family status, and ethnic status. For the majority of urban residents their minority group membership allows a satisfactory, and perhaps comfortable, lifestyle. For the members of some groups, however, urban residence is fraught with constant hardships, which stem from their lowly position within the market economy, or from their adverse relationships with other minority groups. Two minority groups, the elderly[6] and new immigrants, are selected for discussion.

Between 1951 and 1981, Canada's elderly increased from 7.8 percent to 9.7 percent of the total population (Statistics Canada 1984c). This increase maintains a trend established in the 1920s, and mirrors the aging process observed in most industrialized countries. In the Canadian case, however, periodic waves of high net immigration have slowed the process. The distribution of the elderly reflects the impact of past immigration, but more especially the locational preferences of internal migrants. Currently, the elderly are relatively overconcentrated in certain CMAs, for example Victoria (17.0 percent of its 1981 population) and Vancouver (11.5 percent), but tend to be underconcentrated in rapidly growing cities such as Calgary (6.1 percent), and in frontier cities such as Chicoutimi-Jonquière (6.0 percent). At the intra-urban scale the elderly are usually overconcentrated in core areas or older suburban locations. For example, 9.2 percent of Regina's total population is elderly, and yet over 20 percent of the core area population consist of elderly persons compared with less than 1 percent in some new suburban locations (Statistics Canada 1984d).

The economic status of Canada's elderly tends to be lower than that of most Canadians. In 1983, low-income households accounted for 25.3 percent of the elderly, but only 17.1 percent of all Canadians (Statistics Canada 1985b). Moreover, low incomes were particularly prevalent among unattached elderly women. Corresponding data for urban areas are not readily available. Nevertheless, most cities exhibit a strong association between the distributions of elderly persons and low-income households.[7] Explanations for the low-income status of the elderly are found in the weak indexing and transferability provisions of many private pension schemes, the unavailability or inadequacy of pensions for work traditionally performed by women, and the immaturity of the Canada and Quebec Pension Plans (Powell and Martin 1980).

What change in the status and needs of the elderly can be expected in the period to 2001? Several arguments seem relevant. First, the increasing life expectancy of Canadians and the continuation of recent declines in fertility and immigration should produce a more-rapid aging of Canada's population. Because of this, it is expected that the elderly will form between 12.8 percent and 14.0 percent of the population by 2001 (Statistics Canada 1985a). At the same time, the locational preferences of the elderly are expected to reinforce inter-urban differences in their distribution (Shulman 1980, 32). Second, the financial status of the elderly should improve during the forecast period. This improvement will be related to the maturation of more equitable pension schemes, and to the higher social status of new retirees (Statistics Canada 1984c). Of course, this improvement will do little to enhance the status of those already retired. Third, relative and absolute increases in the number of elderly persons will have important implications for the provision of health care, housing, transportation, and social services (Stone and Fletcher 1982). This point is worth considering in more detail.

Understandably, Canada's elderly have a much higher rate of utilization of hospitals than the general population. Consequently, significant increases in costs of health care can be expected as more of Canada's elderly survive into old age (over 75 years). Also, the rate of household formation among the elderly is expected to increase more rapidly than the elderly population itself. This extra demand for housing will be heightened by the need to provide improved housing designs and housing services for the elderly. Conversely, the use of private automobiles by the elderly is likely to decline. This decline will place additional responsibilities on public transportation services. If services are designed to meet the special needs of the elderly, the costs to public transit systems could rise significantly.

In administrative terms the responsibilities for these services are shared by all levels of government. In practice, however, the physical demand for services and many of their immediate costs are expected to have the most affect on the large urban centres (Shulman 1980). Also, the demand for services for the elderly is expected to increase throughout the forecast period, and to intensify in the early decades of the next century. Demand at that time will be enhanced by the retirement of the baby-boom population. Consequently, both the quality and cost of these services may be influenced by the type of initiatives undertaken in the period to 2001.

Canadian history reveals that immigration has almost always played a key role in national economic development (Gertler and Crowley 1977, 51–61; Marr and Paterson 1980, 172–78). Moreover, in every decade since 1867 immigrants to

Canada have formed a larger segment of the population than their counterparts in the United States (Mercer 1979). In 1981 this segment accounted for 16 percent of the population. Of this total, 89 percent lived in urban areas compared with 73 percent of the non-immigrant population (Statistics Canada 1984e). More striking still, 74 percent of immigrants lived in CMAs compared with only 47 percent of the non-immigrant population. However, these data disguise the very unequal regional distribution of immigrants. Cities in eastern Canada have been relatively unsuccessful in attracting immigrants. In contrast, successive waves of immigration, most notably in the two decades prior to the First World War and in several periods since the Second World War, have stimulated rapid growth in the cities of central and western Canada (Mercer 1979). Furthermore, the cosmopolitan nature of these cities has increased significantly since the enactment of revised immigration legislation in 1967 (Richmond and Kalbach 1980, 183–200). This legislation was designed to eliminate "discrimination on the basis of race or nationality . . . for all classes of immigrants" (Manpower and Immigration Canada 1974, 33). Since this pronouncement, considerable changes have occurred in the sources and diversity of Canada's immigrants. The most profound change has involved an absolute and proportionate increase in the number of immigrants from Asia, the Caribbean, and Central and South America (Statistics Canada 1984a, 1984f).

What role can immigration and new immigrant communities be expected to play in the future development of Canada's cities? Again, several arguments seem persuasive. First, current population forecasts indicate that as fertility declines, population growth will become increasingly dependent on immigration (Statistics Canada 1985a, 43–46). Second, it seems unlikely that Canada will neglect its traditional role of providing sanctuary to refugees, and equally unlikely that the world community will fail to provide an abundant supply of the same. As in the past two decades, most of these refugees are likely to be drawn from Third World countries. For this reason, their cultural origins are unlikely to match those of Canada's non-immigrant and older immigrant communities. Third, and somewhat less likely, Canada may experience a substantial increase in immigration in response to national population objectives or demands from the industrial sector (Statistics Canada 1984g, 94–96). In this case immigrants are most likely to originate from areas with skilled labour surpluses in traditional countries of origin.

It is unlikely that the impact of immigration will be experienced evenly across the country. As in the past, urban areas in receipt of large numbers of immigrants will tend to grow faster than non-recipient areas. If current trends continue, the major demands for housing, employment, and social services related to immigration will be experienced in the cosmopolitan centres of Montreal, Toronto, and Vancouver, and to a lesser extent in the other major centres of central and western Canada. Consequently, Canadian cities may become increasingly divided into those that duplicate in microcosm Canada's official multicultural status, and those that typify the more traditional dualism of English and French Canada. This situation might be moderated if the federal government becomes more active in steering immigrants to certain targeted communities or sectors of the economy. Such action is unlikely, however, for it would almost certainly unleash widespread criticism at a time when the government is already sensitive to its part in previous "relocations" of minority immigrant groups.

The concentration of new immigrants within a few of the larger cities may reinforce undesirable aspects of ethnic segregation. Among Canada's oldest ethnic communities the persistence of ethnic neighbourhoods has been attributed to factors of social choice rather than to social status or occupational differences (Ley 1984, 103–6). However, the same explanation may not hold true for Canada's new immigrant communities. For example, data for Winnipeg indicate that high levels of segregation among East Indian, Filipino, and Vietnamese immigrants are associated with exceptionally low median incomes and massive concentration in blue-collar occupations (Statistics Canada 1986b). Undoubtedly, the low socio-economic status of these groups may be explained, partly, because their arrival in Canada is so recent, and their English-language skills are poor.[8] The period to 2001 should indicate whether this status is purely temporary, or if it reflects the inability of Canadian society to translate multicultural ideals into social and economic equality for all immigrant groups.

12.4   Conclusion

The preceding discussion has focused on prospective growth in Canada's urban system, and on change in the physical structure and social dimensions of individual urban communities. The position is taken that the incidence of exceptional events prohibits the presentation of statistically precise development forecasts. Currently, the decline in world oil prices has slowed development forces in parts of western Canada, and has further postponed the return of a "Golden Age" to eastern Canada. Also, while low oil prices are expected to stimulate growth in the urban-industrial core of central Canada, the pursuit of liberalized trade with the United States provides an uncertain development outlook for this region. Beyond these events, however, the growth of Canada's urban system is reasonably predictable. The fundamental strengths and weaknesses of Canada's geography should continue to favour the urban communities in central and western Canada. At the same time, differences in the growth rates of individual cities will become increasingly pronounced, and will pose different types of development problems. Thus, the continued decentralization of population and industry from larger cities will require planning strategies that stress the social and economic opportunities of "decline." Conversely, rapid growth in smaller urban centres and exurban environments must guard against the transfer of urbanization diseconomies to these locations. In most respects the physical appearance of urban centres in 2001 will closely resemble that of the mid-1980s. This absence of change over much of the urbanized area can be predicted on the basis of existing land-use controls and prevailing rates of obsolescence, and by the fairly rigid socio-spatial divisions into which cities are divided. In socio-demographic terms, however, the prospects for change are somewhat greater. The general ageing of Canada's population will be experienced in all urban centres, but especially in those with existing large concentrations of elderly.

The need for improvements in a wide range of social services for the elderly will challenge the fiscal and humanitarian resources of these communities, especially as more of the elderly survive into old age. Similarly, future patterns of immigration are likely to favour Canada's most cosmopolitan cities. Here the challenge will be to provide a level of financial security and social opportunity consistent with the ideals of multiculturalism.

Notes

1. A Census Metropolitan Area (CMA) is the main labour-market area of an urbanized core having a population of 100,000 or more.
2. In this essay western Canada refers to the Prairie provinces and British Columbia, central Canada refers to Ontario and Quebec, and eastern Canada refers to the four Atlantic provinces.
3. This amount is equivalent to adding two Montreals to Canada's urbanized area.
4. This is the equivalent of adding another Toronto or five Hamiltons to the axis.
5. Actual losses will depend on the interaction between many uncertain factors including rates of population growth, energy costs, and the locational preferences of individual households and industrial entrepreneurs.
6. The elderly are defined as persons of 65 years and over.
7. Victoria is exceptional in this context insofar as its elderly population has an income that is higher than the average (Nader 1976, 425).
8. The same data base shows that English-speaking West Indian immigrants have income and occupational profiles similar to those of the numerically dominant British group.

References

Artibise, A.F.J. 1981. *Prairie Urban Development, 1870–1930*. Booklet 34. Ottawa: Canadian Historical Association.

Barney, G.O., P.H. Freeman, and C.A. Ulinski. 1981. *Global 2000: Implications for Canada*. Toronto: Pergamon Press.

Bradbury, J.H., and I. St-Martin. 1983. "Winding Down in a Quebec Mining Town: A Case Study of Schefferville." *Canadian Geographer* 27:128–44.

Bourne, L.S. 1981. *The Geography of Housing*. London: Edward Arnold.

Bryant, C.R., L.H. Russwum, and A.G. McLellan. 1982. *The City's Countryside: Land and Its Management in the Rural-urban Fringe*. London: Longman.

Economic Council of Canada (ECC). 1977. *A Study of Regional Disparities*. Ottawa: ECC.

Energy, Mines and Resources (EMR). 1985. *Canadian Minerals Yearbook, 1983–1984: Review and Outlook*. Ottawa: Mineral Report, Energy, Mines and Resources: no. 33.

Frampton, A. 1985. "Toronto's Harbourfront: An Exciting Blueprint for Urban Revival." *Canadian Geographic* 104 (6):62–69.

Gertler, L.O., and R.W. Crowley. 1977. *Changing Canadian Cities: The Next 25 Years*. Toronto: McClelland and Stewart.

Gusen, P. 1984. "Mounting Pressure on Western Resource Industries." *Canadian Business Review* 11 (3):6–10.

Hall, P. 1977. *Europe 2000*. London: Duckworth.

Krueger, R.R. 1978. "Urbanization of the Niagara Fruit Belt." *Canadian Geographer* 12:179–94.

Ley, D.F. 1981. "Inner-city Revitalization in Canada: A Vancouver Case Study." *Canadian Geographer* 25:124–48.

———. 1984. "Pluralism and the Canadian State." In C. Clarke, D.F. Ley and G.C.K. Peach, eds., *Geography and Ethnic Pluralism*, 87–110. London: George Allen

Lithwick, H. 1970. *Urban Canada: Problems and Prospects*. Ottawa: Central Housing and Mortgage Corporation.

Lorimer, J. 1981. "The Post-Developer Era for Canada's Cities Begins." *City Magazine Annual 1981* 1 (1):6–11.

McCann, L.D. 1980. "Canadian Resource Towns: A Heartland Hinterland Perspective." In R.E. Preston and L.H. Russwurm, eds., "Essays on Canadian Urban Process and Form II." Publication Series, Department of Geography, University of Waterloo, Waterloo, no. 15, 213–72.

Manning, T.W. 1978. "The Agricultural Potentials of Canada's Resources and Technology." In R.M. Irving, ed., *Readings in Canadian Geography*, 141–48. 3rd ed. Toronto: Holt, Rinehart and Winston.

Manpower and Immigration Canada. 1974. *The Immigration Program, Part 2: A Report of the Canadian Immigration and Population Study*. Ottawa: Manpower and Immigration Canada.

Marr, T.W., and D.G. Paterson. 1980. *Canada: An Economic History*. Toronto: Gage Publishing.

Mercer, J. 1979. "On Continentalism, Distinctiveness and Comparable Urban Geography: Canadian and American Cities." *Canadian Geographer* 23:119–39.

Mitchell, B., and W. Bond. 1980. "Urban Profiles." In H.J. Adler and D.A. Brusegard, eds., *Perspectives Canada*. Vol. 3, 185–239. Ottawa: Statistics Canada.

Nader, G.A. 1975. *Cities of Canada*. Vol. 1: *Theoretical, Historical and Planning Perspectives*. Toronto: Macmillan.

———. 1976. *Cities of Canada*. Vol. 2: *Profiles of Fifteen Metropolitan Centres*. Toronto: Macmillan.

Phipps, A.G. 1982. "A Utility Modelling Approach for Measuring the Costs of Displacement: An Application to the Core Area of Saskatoon." *Urban Geography* 3:328–54.

Pomfret, R. 1981. *The Economic Development of Canada*. Toronto: Methuen.

Powell, B.J., and J.K. Martin. 1980. "Economic Implications of Canada's Aging Society." In V.W. Marshall, ed., *Aging in Canada: Social Perspectives*, 204–14. Don Mills: Fitzhenry and Whiteside.

Rhéaume, G. 1986. "The Challenge of Creating Jobs." *Canadian Business Review* 13 (2) 41–43.

Richmond, A.H., and W.E. Kalbach. 1980. *Factors in the Adjustment of Immigrants and their Descendants*. Ottawa: Ministry of Supply and Services: Statistics Canada Catalogue 99-761E.

Robinson, I. 1981. *Canadian Urban Growth Trends: Implications for a National Settlement Policy*. Vancouver: University of British Columbia Press.

Russwurm, L.H. 1980. "The Developing Spatial Form of Canadian Cities." In R.E. Preston and L.H. Russwurm, eds., "Essays on Canadian Urban Process and Form II." Publication Series, Department of Geography, University of Waterloo, Waterloo, no. 15, 273–366.

Shulman, N. 1980. "The Aging of Urban Canada." In V.W. Marshall, ed., *Aging in Canada: Social Perspectives*, 27–34. Don Mills: Fitzhenry and Whiteside.

Sitwell, O.F.G., and N.R.M. Seifried. 1984. *The Regional Structure of the Canadian Economy*. Toronto: Methuen.

Statistics Canada. 1984a. *Current Demographic Analysis: Report on the Demographic Situation in Canada 1983*. Ottawa: Ministry of Supply and Services. Catalogue no. 91-209E.

———. 1984b. *Urban Growth in Canada*. Ottawa: Ministry of Supply and Services. Catalogue no. 99-942.

———. 1984c. *The Elderly in Canada*. Ottawa: Ministry of Supply and Services. Catalogue no. 99-932.

———. 1984d. *Regina: Metropolitan Atlas Series*. Ottawa: Ministry of Supply and Services. Catalogue no. 99-929.

———. 1984e. *Population: Place of Birth, Citizenship, Period of Immigration*. Ottawa: Minstry of Supply and Services. Catalogue no. 92-913.

———. 1984f. *Canada's Immigrants*. Ottawa: Ministry of Supply and Services. Catalogue no. 99-936.

———. 1984g. *Current Demographic Analysis: Fertility in Canada – From Baby-boom to Baby-bust*. Ottawa: Ministry of Supply and Services. Catalogue no. 91-524E.

———. 1985a. *Population Projections for Canada, Provinces and Territories*. Ottawa: Ministry of Supply and Services. Catalogue no. 91-520.

———. 1985b. *Income Distributions by Size in Canada*. Ottawa: Ministry of Supply and Services. Catalogue no. 13-207.

———. 1986a. *Capital Expenditures of Domestic and Foreign Controlled Establishments in Manufacturing, Mining and Forestry*. Ottawa: Ministry of Supply and Services. Catalogue no. 61-215.

———. 1986b. *Tabulations 6001-PO2584T1 to 6001-PO2584T6 in Customized Census Tabulations for Winnipeg CMA, 1981*. Ottawa: Census Operations Customer Services.

Stone, L.O., and S. Fletcher. 1982. *A Profile of Canada's Older Population*. Montreal: The Institute for Research on Public Policy.

Walker, D.F. 1980. Canada's Industrial Space-economy. Toronto: Wiley and Sons.

Warren, C.L., and P.C. Rump. 1981, "The Urbanization of Rural Land in Canada: 1966–1971 and 1971–1976." Land Use in Canada Series, Lands Directorate, Environment Canada, Ottawa, no. 20.

Yeates, M.H. 1985. "Land in Canada's Urban Heartland." Land Use in Canada Series, Lands Directorate, Environment Canada, Ottawa, no. 27.

Part Three

Beyond Main Street

13 Introduction: Rural Canada — Urbanization, Depopulation, and the North

Guy M. Robinson

13.1 The Heart of the Nation?

In 1986, 5.75 million members of the Canadian population, representing 23 percent of the total, were classified as living in rural areas. This may be considered to be an artificial estimate because it is based on an arbitrary measure of what constitutes an urban settlement: a minimum of 1,000 inhabitants. Nevertheless, it is still a strong indication that a significant proportion of Canadian society lives outside the major metropolitan centres. This rural society has been eroding steadily during the twentieth century as the balance of the population distribution has shifted in favour of the cities, and the larger metropolitan centres in particular. Rural depopulation has affected many parts of the countryside outside commuting range of the big cities. The rapidity with which this has reduced the numbers in rural areas can be gauged from the fact that the farm population fell by over 60 percent, from around 3 million in 1951 (about 21 percent of the population) to just over 1 million in 1981 (about 4 percent) and to 890,490 (3.5 percent) in 1986. This represents a fall of 72.4 percent between 1931 and 1986. But despite its small numbers, the farm population, and Canadians reliant upon primary activities as their main economic support, dominate vast parts of the country, especially if those involved in hunting, fishing, logging, and mining in northern Canada are included. It can be argued that the division between urban and rural, however defined, is as important in social terms as the traditional divisions of Canada into regions.

Not surprisingly for a geographer brought up in the "regional tradition," much of Watson's own writing emphasizes regional diversity. Watson portrayed this diversity in many ways, perhaps most vividly in an article entitled "Canadian Regionalism in Life and Letters," in which he draws upon various novels and poems depicting life in Canada (Watson 1965). Yet this literature, chosen to depict the strong character of Canadian regionalism, also demonstrates the way in which differences in the rural economy and primary activity dominated this regionalism. From fishing in Newfoundland in Pratt's (1944) *The Cachalot,* to Hemon's (1921) habitants of Quebec in *Maria Chapdelaine*, to the rapidly changing Ontario countryside of Creighton's (1939) *Spring Burning*, to the vastness of the Prairies in Grove's (1922) *Over Prairie Trails*, and to the different types of "wildscape" in British Columbia and the north in Mackay's (1948) *Nunc scio, quid sit amor* and Smith's (1943) *The Lonely Land*, the heart of Canada is shown to be firmly rural. At the same time, the division between this diverse rural realm and the rapidly changing, developing cities is also drawn.

Watson's literary perspective on regionalism stresses the way in which Canadian writers who wrote before 1950 often exhibited their close ties to a particular region as well as to the land in general. Increasingly, from this time, much Canadian literature has reflected aspects of Canadian nationalism, be it the Quebec nationalism of the Quiet Revolution or the search for a distinct identity, a Canadianness, within the rest of Canada. Given Watson's (1983) stated views on the importance of literature as a source material for geographers, it is appropriate at this point to consider how Canadian authors in the 1970s and 1980s have established a recognizable Canadian identity, and how it is tied closely to the land, to rural and small-town Canada. In some ways it marks the end of a search for identity that has brought Canadian writers to what Sutherland (1982, 484) calls a "brand-new beginning, perhaps the first genuine Canadian beginning."

The apparent fragility of the "Canadian identity" is well illustrated in the search for "the great Canadian novel." In the 1950s and 1960s there seemed to be a great need within Canadian literature to assert Canadianness as part of a search for identity. The search was gradually replaced in the 1970s and 1980s by a more confident and prolific output containing sharper images of Canada and Canadians. From only 30 novels published in English in Canada in 1960, the number had risen to 400 by 1984, and Canadian authors were portraying a wide range of Canadian lifestyles and societal problems, some peculiar to Canada and others of a more general nature. Watson's own summary, in the 1950s, of regionalism in Canada as expressed in poetry and literature could be extended today to a much wider range of material, which could embrace authors whose reputations have taken on an international standing. Authors such as Alice Munro, Margaret Laurence, and Margaret Atwood have developed their own "nationalism" in which the myths and legends of Canada have been established as a firm "spiritual" foundation competing with the more dominant forces emanating from the United States and Europe. The impact of the colonial heritage is clear in Laurence's (1974) *The Diviners*, in which Morag Gunn's Scottish background is emphasized. Many of the characters in Atwood's (1969, 1976) *The Edible Woman* and *Lady Oracle* confront basic concerns of identity and survival that could well apply to Americans as well as Canadians. However, there are very recognizable Canadian characters in these books as well as in the novels of respected Canadian authors such as Robertson Davies and Timothy Findley, even though they have not always given their books a specific Canadian setting. For example, Findley's (1984) *Not Wanted on the Voyage* uses Noah's Ark as its point of departure, but has a landscape drawn directly from southern Ontario, and Mrs. Noyes appears as an Ontario farm wife of the early twentieth century. Similarly, Dunstan Ramsey, in Davies's (1971) *Fifth Business*, lives on the edge of fantastic events and fantastic people as he makes his spiritual quest, but remains a familiarly Canadian character.

Neither Davies nor Findley conform to a stereotype, in that they don't create romantic portrayals of Canada. Instead of dealing with the wilderness, perhaps what many non-Canadians would expect in a Canadian novel, they write of things mythic and strange, though still fixed firmly in their own landscapes and people. Davies's (1971, 1972, 1975) Deptford trilogy and the work of W.O. Mitchell, Bill Valgardson, and Alice Munro among others, also convey a tremendous sense of place, giving a special meaning to rural and small-town Canada. For example, the transition from life in small, essentially agricultural, communities to the big city and an urban society is vividly created in Munro's (1978) *Who Do You Think You Are?* This presents several portrayals of the Canadian countryside, of the land itself, to which many Canadians remain closely attached and, beyond that, to the author's own ethnic origins across the Atlantic. Authors like Valgardson have followed the example of W.O. Mitchell (1947) whose classic *Who Has Seen the Wind?* vividly portrays the landscape and people of a small settlement on the Saskatchewan prairies as told through the boyhood of Brian O'Connel. The evocation of place, the situation, and the feelings of the people in rural Saskatchewan can be compared with Valgardson's accounts of Icelandic communities in Manitoba and Munro's accounts of rural southern Ontario. Yet while Mitchell's communities seem to be unaffected by the outside world, Valgardson (1980) presents the opposite. For example, in *Gentle Sinners* he shows how fishermen on Lake Winnipeg are exploited by processing companies dominated by the mafia from Chicago. The fishermen are in bondage to the fishing companies who own their homes and their possessions. This man-made oppression competes with the natural harshness of an environment that produces both temperatures of -40C and devastating blizzards, to create a difficult existence. Valgardson, as a fourth generation Canadian himself, also associates this harshness with that of his Icelandic roots, reflecting the original settlers' apparent willingness to exchange one harsh environment for another.

Rural Manitoba is also the setting for several of Margaret Laurence's novels. In *A Jest of God* (1966), for example, the fictional town of Manawaka is based upon Neepawa, 190 kilometres west of Winnipeg. This was where her grandparents had settled, in a community that was half Scots-Irish and half Ukrainian. Both groups were close-knit, but the divide between the two was a gulf not easily bridged. Although there may no longer be such a clear ethnic division in Neepawa or many other small rural communities, important distinctions remain. For example, different religious groups often play major roles in influencing the life of rural societies and in developing a coherent community divided along religious lines. Such divisions, lurking below the surface and often closely associated with ethnic or religious background, are brilliantly and humourously portrayed for rural Minnesota in Garrison Keiller's (1985) *Lake Wobegon Days*. Equally perceptive accounts can be found from a Canadian context in Davies's Deptford trilogy in which a population of 800 in rural Ontario is catered to by five churches: Roman Catholic, Baptist, Methodist, Presbyterian, and Anglican. The last catered primarily to the poorer citizens and tended to be looked down upon as were people from even smaller communities who were "rustic beyond redemption."

The plot in Davies's trilogy centres around three men seeking to escape from their small-town home, but carrying with them its legacies of puritanism, Calvinism, opportunism, and narrowness. The message seems to be that escape is really impossible; the inheritance of small-town rural life and of generations of tradition is never entirely submerged even by years of travel or life in new, but alien, surroundings. This same message permeates several of Alice Munro's works. She writes about the south-western Ontario she left behind before moving to British Columbia, in her books such as *Friend of My Youth* (Munro 1990). Her countryside is one inhabited by a people whose ancestors had been European peasants until the last generation: people who had come to a new land, carved out a life for themselves closely resembling the one they had left behind, and who were essentially unchanging and unwilling to relinquish their hold upon the land that had only been won and tamed with tremendous personal sacrifice. Yet, Munro also writes of the changing rural communities immediately before and after the Second World War when a new generation was tempted away from the stability of the countryside by the seemingly wonderful life of big cities and the world beyond the farm. Her writing contains many restless characters yearning to break free from their rural confines and who have a keen awareness of the differences between rural and urban.

Both the set of authors considered by Watson and the more recent group of "international" Canadian authors referred to above give portrayals of a rural Canada that is able to permeate the lives of Canadians even when they are divorced from the land by many years lived in big cities. As Margaret Laurence remarked, "whatever I am was shaped and formed in that sort of place (Manawaka) and my way of seeing, however much it may have changed over the years, remains in some enduring way that of a small-town prairie person" (Sutherland 1987, 2). This hints at a commonly held view that farm and small-town life is superior to life in the city (e.g., Robinson 1990, 13) – a Canadian rural ideal that many urban dwellers have invoked as part of their search for a better environment in which to live. This search has helped to foster the so-called population turnaround in the last 20 years in which urban residents have migrated beyond the outer suburbs of major urban centres to swell the numbers in small outlying townships. In many cases the migrants continue to lead "urban lives" and live in housing indistinguishable from that of the outer suburbs, but the attraction of the rural environment, with its promise of a higher quality of life, has exerted a powerful pull. This pull may extend to individuals whose only link with rural Canada was through grandparents or great-grandparents who worked on the land.

13.2   Urbanization

The notion of small-town and rural Canada, which exists in southern Ontario and southern Quebec (Yeates's [1975] "Main Street Canada"), as well as in the Maritimes and the Prairies, has been altered since the 1960s by the growing spread of metropolitan influence over the countryside. The flow of population from the country to the towns has been replaced by a counter-current decanting people from the cities, and their inner areas in particular, to the outlying suburbs and beyond to small communities now considered to be part of the extended city. This process of "population turnaround" (Joseph et al. 1988) can be seen throughout Canada, but has been most influential in conjunction with the growth of the largest cities, and hence its significance within "Main Street." Formerly sleepy small towns and farming communities have been caught up in the urbanization process with the arrival of commuters, second-home owners, hobby farmers, branch plants and retired former city dwellers. The nature of the communities have been altered because the new-comers have so often outnumbered their rural hosts. It is this process of the extension of the metropolitan tentacles, in so many diverse ways, that is considered by Robinson (chapter 14) who refers to the emergence of the "city beyond the city" (Bryant et al. 1982; Coppack et al. 1988). The implication is that while Main Street may once have been regarded as a series of urban nodes with close connections one to another, those connections have now become more and more diffuse, urban hinterlands have spread and the rural interstices between the nodes have been altered dramatically (Coffee and Polese 1988). More than ever before, the countryside is being placed under urban pressure: on the one hand from urban sprawl and, on the other, from the continued loss of population from the more remote rural communities to urban centres.

Robinson considers the first aspect of this pressure, urban sprawl, with respect to both changes in the physical appearance of the rural-urban fringe, and the social composition of communities in this area. In recent years, one of the chief concerns about the physical character of the fringe has been the loss of prime agricultural land (Furuseth and Pierce 1982; Crewson and Reeds 1982; Bryant et al. 1982). Given the scarcity of such land within Canada, it is not surprising that the country possesses a sophisticated land-use monitoring program which permits analyses of changing land uses. Using data from this program, Robinson notes an acceleration of loss of land to urban sprawl in the late 1970s. The highest relative increases in urban land use occurred in association with small towns, but the greatest absolute increases were apparent around the major metropolitan centres, primarily Edmonton, Ottawa-Hull, Toronto, and Vancouver. Disturbingly, prime agricultural land accounted for half of the total land converted to urban use.

Two areas where particular efforts have been made to curtail urban sprawl from covering high-quality farmland have been the Niagara Fruit Belt and the Okanagan Fruit Lands, both major areas of intensive agricultural activity. Robinson briefly reviews the special policies introduced in these areas to preserve agricultural land. While not completely preventing loss of farmland, stricter designations of the type of land available for urban expansion, adherence to clearly stated control policies, and the influence of local pressure groups have all helped to reduce sprawl in both areas.

The statistics on the increase of land devoted to urban uses shows the highest absolute gains for areas close to the major metropolitan areas. This tends to reflect the character of outmigration from the central and inner suburban districts of the largest cities to communities lying beyond the continuously built-up area. Thus, this population turnaround has become a potent force in changing the character of small towns and former farming communities in the metropolitan hinterlands. The social character of the out-migration is considered by Robinson with respect to Toronto where the most rapid growth of population in the 1970s and 1980s has occurred in the outer suburban areas and some of the small communities lying between the city and

Georgian Bay to the north. Effectively, farmers and ex-urbanites now live in the same locale, and the social character of former rural communities has been altered dramatically.

The out-migrants have tended to be young professionals, supplemented by blue-collar workers (who have largely shed working-class patterns of social interaction), people moving out of the city to retire, and perhaps also second home owners and hobby farmers. So there are often several types of exurbanite settling in the rural-urban fringe area (e.g., Dahms 1986; Sinclair and Westhues 1974; Walker 1977, 1987). The majority of the newcomers retain a variety of close links with the city, either by commuting regularly to work or by retaining links with friends and family closer to the city centre. The city can also remain the focus for recreation and entertainment, though in some cases this attraction may be supplanted by the type of outdoor pursuits offered by a more rural setting. Often it is the newcomers who take over local organizations, associations, and even politics, sometimes coming into conflict with long-established residents or creating different groups among the newcomers. In short, a new set of "national" and essentially urban values are brought into the countryside, overshadowing the "local" rural values. Newcomers swarm into close-knit communities and often destroy the very characteristics of those communities that they found so attractive in the first place. It is a destruction of the rural way of life every bit as effective as paving over a green field for a new out-of-town shopping mall.

13.3   Depopulation

Carlyle (chapter 15) examines another aspect of population change in rural areas: depopulation. In his study of the Prairies he notes that while the major cities there have grown very rapidly during the past three decades, a significant amount of this growth has been supplied by out-migration from rural communities and the small service centres that developed on the Prairies during the first few decades of European settlement. Given that pioneering agricultural occupation only occurred after 1870 and was still under way on a large scale in certain areas in the 1920s, in the Peace River district for example, the movement from a simple agricultural society to one caught up in the metropolitanization process has been extremely rapid. This speed of change, coupled with the type of farming characteristic of the Prairies, has produced a very distinctive social and economic response. The predominantly large-scale family-operated farms remain, but they have become even larger and more reliant upon the substitution of machinery for labour. The sparsely settled nature of the Prairies has been accentuated, and the loss of hamlets and small villages has placed severe strains upon the maintenance of services and utilities for the farmers that remain. Although this is a familiar story in many rural areas remote from metropolitan centres, in the Prairies the element of large distances between farms and service centres adds an extra dimension to the picture. To accentuate the problem, there has been relatively little migration from the major cities back into the surrounding rural areas (Davies 1990).

The problem of declining services in rural areas is well illustrated by the measures adopted in 1990 by the national railway network, Via Rail, which more than halved its number of routes following a reduction in its annual subsidy received from the government from $600 million to $350 million. The rail mileage was also halved, and the labour force cut by 38 percent. Subsequently Via Rail has revealed to the Royal Commission on National Passenger Transportation that many of its remaining "remote services" are uneconomical because they attract few customers. Eight routes in particular have been highlighted as significant loss makers: Montreal–Jonquiere, Montreal–Senneterre, Senneterre–Cochrane, Sudbury–White River (currently part of Via Rail's transcontinental service), Winnipeg–Churchill, Pas–Lynn Lake, Jasper–Prince Rupert and Wabowden–Churchill. It remains to be seen whether these routes will join the numbers already closed throughout rural Canada.

Losses of one vital rural service, the post office, are likely to be increased as Canada Post accelerates the conversion of its entire network of 5,221 rural post offices to private operations by 1996. Many of the current postmasters are likely to quit after conversion because of the unsatisfactory differential between their current pay rates as employees of Canada Post and the wage rates for staff of private rural outlets. For Canada Post the attraction of the new arrangements will be a potential saving of up to one billion dollars.

Carlyle's analysis of rural depopulation on the Prairies considers the basic demographic changes involved, the evolving economic basis of the rural Prairies and changes to key social and economic institutions. These institutions include the once dense rail distribution network, rural schooling, and the distinctive ethnic mosaic that began with the occupation of the Prairies by a range of different groups of people. The changes he analyses refer primarily to the quickening of the process of depopulation since the 1930s when the rural population was at its peak. Subsequently, the farm population has fallen by three-fifths, so that only 12 percent of Prairie population lived on farms in 1981. Less than one-third of the total population was in rural town-ships while over half were in Calgary, Edmonton, Regina, Saskatoon, and Winnipeg.

This transformation has been marked by an uneven pattern of depopulation, closely associated with the changing basis of the farm economy. Urban sprawl and agricultural intensification related to production for the expanding urban market have brought some increases in population in "rural" areas, especially in the Edmonton–Calgary corridor, but in areas dominated by extensive agriculture there have been losses of over half the population post-1930. Such losses have been most pronounced in areas reliant upon extensive wheat production, and hence the highest rates of depopulation have been in southern Saskatchewan (e.g., Dale 1988; Seaborne 1988). Pockets of irrigated agriculture have enabled some areas to retain higher population densities and to diversify production. Depopulation has brought a consolidation of rural services and a number of farm mergers, more than doubling the average farm size over a period of just 45 years. However, the emergence of a minority of very large holdings exists in conjunction with the survival of a majority composed of smaller holdings, so that the modal size of holding is still less than 325 hectares. (In Canada as a whole the average size of holding in 1986 was 231 hectares – two-and-a-half times larger than in 1931.) Those farms that remain, though, have been part of a process in which, to survive, farmers have had to become more efficient and more business-like to combat the forces exerted by the high costs of supplies on the one hand and competitive retailers and wholesalers on the other. Agribusiness and rising efficiency have accompanied depopulation on the Prairies as have increased indebtedness and reliance upon outside support. The agribusiness developments have involved movements away from the norm of single-family operation of farms through the growth of corporate structures and co-operatives. Outside support has often taken the form of subsidized shipment of grain. If smaller holdings have been retained it has often been through the growth of part-time farming on a seasonal basis, further eroding the traditional pattern of rural communities (Todd 1980, 1981).

Carlyle's description of the rationalization of the rail network for shipping grain and livestock to market, and of problems involved in sustaining a viable system of schooling in dwindling communities, is essentially a "broad-brush" picture for a very large region. He also describes particular features for one specific ethnic group out of many on the Prairies: the Hutterites (see also Evans 1985). This broad sweep, plus selective case study, can be compared with the more intimate, single-community approach adopted by Ross (chapter 16) in which he similarly considers the overriding phenomenon of depopulation. He focuses on the example of Pictou Island, Nova Scotia, giving a vivid portrayal of the small community at its height during the operation of lobster fishing in the first half of the twentieth century. This picture of an isolated, tightly knit, community, reflecting its Scottish origins and only gradually coming to terms with twentieth-century technology, is one that could be drawn for many others in the Maritimes, albeit with different origins and different cultural traits. In effect, Ross makes an eloquent statement on behalf of a "golden age" of rural life in the Maritimes, picking out details that represent crucial aspects of community life: the seasonal round of farm chores, Saturday-night gatherings, tales of the "old country," the arrival of new workers each summer, the long, harsh winter, and a prevailing self-sufficiency. This is a vivid reminder that social geography deals with the lives of individuals and their communities, and a good example to demonstrate how large-scale processes such as rural depopulation affect many single communities, not just regions at an aggregate level.

For Pictou Island, depopulation was heralded by the almost imperceptible increase in contact with and dependence upon the mainland. The consolidation of schools in Nova Scotia meant that children had to leave the island to attend high school. Often whole families left the island rather than sending their children over to the mainland to board. Eventually, in 1971, the island school was closed, and the few remaining parents with young children followed the others to the mainland. Before this, though, the community life of the island had already been undermined in a variety of ways: the influence of radio and television, the demise of the lobster fishery, the establishment of unemployment benefits reducing the need to combine fishing with farming, the undercutting of Pictou Island's potato production by growers on Prince Edward Island, and children born on Pictou Island but educated on the mainland failing to return. From a maximum population of 230 in 1921, Pictou Island had only 20 inhabitants by 1971. Meanwhile, many other rural communities in the Maritimes suffered large outflows of population and, with little receipt of immigrants or growth of major urban centres, the Maritimes' share of the Canadian population fell to less than 10 percent.

Ross's portrait of Pictou Island is of a community slipping into terminal decline, whereas Carlyle's of the Hutterites on the Prairies is of several communities retaining population numbers and a distinctive way of life by retaining their religious beliefs and maintaining a high degree of isolation from the rest of society to keep at bay elements thought to be disruptive. In chapter 17 Macpherson shows how these disruptive elements have caused much damage to the Indian and Inuit communities.

Macpherson conceptualizes demographic, social, and economic changes in Newfoundland in terms of two *longues durées*. The first of these, the *grande longe durée*, represents the occupation and dominance of native groups dating back some 9,000 years. The second, the *petite longue durée*, refers to the coming of European settlement from the seventeenth century. In seeing economic and social development in these terms, he places in context the co-existence of Indians and Europeans over the past 500 years and introduces a dimension of present-day society not considered in any detail in the previous chapters: the presence of the native peoples and their role in society. His portrait of the transition from the sole occupation of Newfoundland by native groups to permanent occupation and dominance by Europeans, points to the conflicts that developed, to attitudes generated towards the native peoples by the Europeans, and to the lives of native peoples today.

The contact with whalers, traders, and the early permanent settlers effectively brought about the demise of the Beothuck, the native group that had inhabited Newfoundland. They were replaced by the Micmac Indians, who survived and even flourished in proximity to European society (Pastore 1978) until the decline of the caribou herds brought an end to their traditional way of life on Newfoundland, the island. However, Inuit continue to occupy parts of Labrador and have laid claim to special rights to protect their culture and traditional way of life (Stix 1982). Yet the very existence of such a claim illustrates the extent to which Inuit and Indians occupy a socially dependent and marginalized position with respect to the majority European society. Hence, the *petite longue durée* in all ten provinces has tended to obliterate the achievements of the native groups. They have become a small minority, and a problem minority at that, in the land they once occupied, unchallenged by external threat.

The picture Macpherson paints of the *petite longue durée* in Newfoundland is of a society that began by relying heavily upon the fisheries. The society remained overly dependent upon this industry for a long period. Despite a four-fold increase in population since 1869, the degree of urbanization has been significantly less than in Canada as a whole. There is very little population in dispersed communities inland, and the legacy of the fishing industry's dominance of the economic and social fabric is very evident. The British ethnic group, which established the first prolonged European occupation of Newfoundland, has retained a greater dominance than in any other province.

Various indicators can be used to illustrate the way in which the economy of the Maritimes has lagged behind the growth of the economics of western and central

Canada. This hold-up can also be translated into social terms, as Macpherson does for Newfoundland in terms of education: relative to the rest of Canada the province has a significantly small proportion of its population educated above grade 9, and this proportion is lowest away from the major metropolitan centre, St. John's, and other urban centres. This is cited as an indicator of Newfoundland's peripherality vis-à-vis the rest of Canada, not just in geographical terms but with respect to economic and social development. Other disparities cited show high unemployment rates (double the national average), low average earnings (20 percent below the national average), and high levels of out-migration of population between the ages 15 and 24 years. It remains to be seen whether current and future exploitation of offshore oil reserves has any pronounced effect on these disparities, and on the economy of the Maritimes as a whole. The Hibernia field is estimated to have recoverable oil reserves of between 525 and 650 million barrels, or an economic life of about 15 to 20 years. Peak production of 110,000 barrels of light oil per day is predicted for 1998.

Macpherson also highlights the problems experienced by the east coast fisheries in recent years. Lower catch quotas have been introduced to preserve fish stocks, but a consequence has been a growing reliance upon aid packages for the fishing communities. Of the federal program, the largest has been a $500 million package announced in 1990 for the purpose of funding retraining programs and local employment projects. Three-fifths of this money is expected to go to communities in Newfoundland, which also received $130 million allocated to the Federal Community Futures Program, which is modelled on similar ventures introduced in Newfoundland to aid rural communities after the cross-province railway was abandoned in 1988.

13.4   Native Peoples: The Other Canadians

There is another rural realm lying beyond both the areas of direct metropolitan influence and the more extensive districts dominated by a steadily diminishing farm population. This is the largest part of Canada; this largely untamed wilderness, much of it in northern Canada, is snow-covered for a substantial part of the year. It also supports a thinly scattered human population, and is the one area where, at least in terms of numbers, the native peoples are dominant (see Usher 1982; Brody 1981). Just how thinly populated the northern part of Canada is, can be seen from the following statistics for the largest political subdivision in this region (and in Canada itself), the Northwest Territories: it occupies 3.4 million square kilometres or 34.1 percent of the national area, yet it has just 52,000 inhabitants; of its population, just under half (46.3 percent) are concentrated in small urban centres, primarily Yellowknife and Inuvik; and it has just 64 communities in all. This difference and separateness is further emphasized by the distinctive ethnic pattern of the Northwest Territories, with native peoples representing 59 percent of its population. Almost all the non-native residents are concentrated in the Mackenzie Valley, mainly in the larger settlements such as Inuvik, Hay River, and Fort Simpson.

A multiplicity of native peoples are present in northern Canada, including both Indian groups and Inuit,[1] though the latter constitute the majority in the Arctic regions. The distinctive problems of all the native peoples have come increasingly to the attention of the rest of Canada during the 1970s and 1980s, partly because of the "drift southwards" to the cities by certain native groups, and also because of the greater efforts directed towards exploitation of the natural resources of the Canadian north (Berger 1977; Brody 1975). The latter has renewed conflicts over access to land and destruction of traditional ways of life. Meanwhile, the migration of native peoples to the cities of southern Canada has significantly altered their population distribution, so that in 1986, out of a total of 711,720 (2.8 percent of Canada's population), the greatest number (167,375) lived in Ontario and about 35 percent of the Indian, Métis, and non-status Indians lived in urban or semi-urban areas.[2]

There is a variety of different groups of native peoples in Canada, each with distinctive cultural, social, and economic patterns (e.g., Getty and Lussier 1983). But following the European settlement and dominance of the white society, many of the problems faced by the native peoples became common ones, and there has been a tendency towards the marginalization of all native groups in economic, social, and political terms. The reduction in numbers following the introduction of diseases such as smallpox and influenza contributed to this marginalization, with some groups such as the Mackenzie Inuit and the Sadlermiut decimated. The most numerous of the native groups are the Indians, 286,230 single-ethnic-origin Indians being recorded in the 1986 census, plus 262,730 multiple-ethnic-origin Indians, 59,745 single-ethnic-origin Métis, and 91,865 multiple-ethnic-origin Métis. However, problems of obtaining satisfactory enumeration in remote areas, and the absence of acceptable and consistent definitions of Métis and non-status Indians, reduce the accuracy of the census. Other surveys (e.g., DIAND 1980) suggest there may be as many as one million Métis and non-status Indians. The Inuit population of just 27,290 single-ethnic-origin and 9,175 multiple-ethnic-origin is small in comparison.

13.4.1 The Indians

The social geography of the Indians is dominated by the continued concentration of this group on reserves. Although the proportion living on reserves is gradually falling, in the early 1980s just over two-thirds were still on reserves scattered throughout Canada. There are 2,242 reserves in total, covering 25,954 square kilometres, but the majority of these are in remote or rural farm districts. Strong pro-rural traditions remain in Indian society, and rural reserves are supported by a wide range of community services paid for by the federal government. However, the communities on the reserves have been affected by the penetration of new ideas and market forces so that, increasingly, traditional ways of life have come to be regarded as inferior to the more materialistic way of life offered in urban Canada. This attitude has been most prevalent among the young who are also given a "push" factor for leaving the reserves in the form of depletion of the environmental resources required for sustaining traditional hunting, fishing, and fur trapping. Although 11 percent of the population of registered Indian bands are urban because the bands are located in or adjacent to urban areas, there has also been out-migration from rural reserves to cities, especially in Ontario and British Columbia. This out-migration has also characterized smaller Indian bands, reserves where there has been a longer tradition of working outside the reserve, bands with higher education levels, areas with more racially integrated schools, and bands with poorly developed local organization.

Much publicity has been given to the social problems encountered by Indians who have migrated to cities, but there appears to be great regional variation in the severity and extent of these problems. For example, Indians living in the small towns of the northern Prairies and northern Ontario have tended to suffer from very limited economic opportunity, lack of well-developed, urban Indian ethnic institutions, and the simple organization of the Indian bands themselves. Anti-Indian feeling has often been high in such communities. In contrast, the greater maturity of urban Indian ethnic institutions in the large cities of Quebec, southern Ontario, southern Alberta, and British Columbia has reduced problems by facilitating greater ease of assimilation (e.g., Price 1979). Yet social problems are pronounced for Indians both on and off reserves and for Inuit. For example, the native representation in penitentiaries is seven times greater than the non-native figure (per head of population); native death, illness, and accident rates are two to four times the national average; one in every three Indian families lives in crowded conditions; only half the Indian homes have running water; participation in higher education is much lower than for the rest of the population, despite the creation of special programs such as that at the Indian Federated College in the University of Regina; and employment rates for natives are the lowest of any ethnic group in Canada (see Brody 1971).

The problems of young Indians have been highlighted repeatedly by such incidents as the deaths of six Indians aged between 16 and 34 years in the community of Peerless Lake, northern Alberta, in 1985 because they drank photocopying fluid. Although this area has been the scene of work by oil companies, there have been few employment opportunities for Indians, mainly because of their poor qualifications (Bone and Green 1986). For many younger Indians, Moose Milk, Brewpot, or Moonshine have provided temporary respites to the situation in which they find themselves: caught between two cultures. The dubious attractions of alcohol have only served to produce a rate of alcoholism among Indians that is 13 times the national average, and an incidence of violent death five times as high. Stories of Indians being deprived of their traditional hunting and fishing are common, and their aimless existence of relying upon government welfare has spawned growing social problems.

Since Confederation these problems have been viewed by federal and provincial governments within the context of a series of statutes referring to native peoples. The first "Indian Act" was passed in 1876, but it has been amended and altered significantly. Despite substantial modification the current act still gives a large amount of discretionary control over Indian affairs to non-Indian institutions, especially with regard to the regulation of Indian reserves (Bartlett 1980; Weaver 1980). Until the 1940s, government policy towards native peoples largely ignored the Inuit, and denied the need for special responsibility for Métis and non-status Indians. Since the 1940s, though, federal policies have moved increasingly towards encouraging greater autonomy for all the native cultures, by recognizing and funding native political organizations, by encouraging self-determination and responsibility for their own affairs, and by increasing financial inputs to special programs for native peoples.[3] From 1966 these programs have been primarily under the jurisdiction of the Department of Indian Affairs and Northern Development (DIAND), which is responsible for the administration of the resources and affairs of the Northwest Territories and the Yukon Territory as well as dealing with Indian affairs. The department's budget exceeded $2 billion per annum in the mid-1980s, but funding for native peoples by federal government has consistently been less than 2 percent of its annual budget (Comeau and Santin 1990; Hawkes 1989).

There has been much criticism of federal government expenditure on native affairs. One charge is that the allocation of funds has been insufficient to deal with worsening socio-economic conditions in Indian communities. Another has been that in the late 1970s and early 1980s the Indian and Inuit Affairs Program (IIAP) received a growth in its budget below the rate of growth in expenditures for the social programs of other Canadians. There has also been continued criticism of the way in which funds to the IIAP have been allocated to particular categories of expenditure. For example, less than 10 percent of funds has been directed to initiatives aimed at job creation and economic development. Education has taken between one-third and 40 percent of the funds and most of the remainder has been allocated to welfare dependency programs. Federal policy has continued to place more onus upon the provinces and Indian band authorities to develop their own assistance programs and stimulation of economic development. This has also been the case for the Inuit (Clark 1990).

13.4.2 The Inuit

The Inuit, those of single ethnic origin numbering just over 27,000 at the 1986 census, have never been subject to the Indian Act and have tended to remain outside federal programs until the 1950s. Subsequently, several aspects of federal assistance to the Inuit have been geared towards self-help and communal co-operation to provide a basis for economic and social development. Although some aspects of the traditional way of life remain, acculturation over the past three centuries has significantly altered Inuit society. Replacement of a nomadic and semi-nomadic existence by fixed settlement has been one major change. Language and several aspects of culture have also been altered: for instance, the Inuit have embraced Christianity, and their language, Inuktitut, has taken in many English words and anglicizations. Government activity has established schools, nursing stations, airports, and other communications as well as new housing. However, some important aspects of culture and way of life have been retained, such as traditional child-rearing practices, concerns about the environment, respect for individual autonomy, and maintenance of arts and language. Thus, from the early 1970s, the Inuit Tapirisat of Canada has attempted to protect and foster Inuit cultural and individual rights, establishing an Inuit Language Commission and a Land Claims Office.

Stager (chapter 18) considers certain aspects of recent development in the Canadian north and, specifically, the role of co-operatives as agents of change. The focus upon co-operatives is a useful one in terms of highlighting the way in which the federal government has sought to assist local self-help and self-determination without necessarily relying upon large injections of capital. The Inuit co-operatives, initiated in 1959, were an attempt to introduce the Inuit of the eastern Arctic to a money economy. Their aim was to produce goods for local consumption or export, but they soon expanded into consumer co-operatives, importing goods from southern Canada for retailing. Other functions soon developed such as municipal services and the provision of tourist accommodation.

Stager notes that because traditional Inuit society was based upon small-group living in which individual activity was geared towards general group welfare, the formal co-operative structure was quickly and easily adopted. This form of organization spread rapidly, with the co-operative competing with the Hudson's Bay Company for customers in 29 settlements by the mid-1980s. The co-operatives have become a major part of northern life within a short space of time, having an impact on the small communities in various ways. For example, they have played a leading role in encouraging local arts and crafts, while also acting as a major economic force. In settlements that have co-operatives, roughly one-sixth of the families benefit directly from wages drawn from the co-operative and, except for the government, the co-operatives are the largest employers in the north. Yet Stager argues that the most important role of the co-operatives is not the economic one, but the way in which they give the Inuit experience of working within an imposed framework. The co-operatives have frequently provided valuable business and administrative experience to Inuit who have moved subsequently into leading roles in the community. However, problems remain over obtaining people with sufficient skills at managerial levels, and key personnel have often been introduced from the south.

Although each co-operative acts as an independent community association, they serve a wider role throughout northern Canada by virtue of the existence of two federations of co-operatives, one for the Northwest Territories and one for northern Quebec. These provide important centralized facilities, such as accounting, auditing and educational departments, the one for northern Quebec functioning particularly effectively. This type of integration is important as the co-operatives increasingly become an integral part of the northern economy and society.

Out-migration of Inuit from their northern homeland has been relatively small. This has meant that, with more Inuit living in fixed settlements, greater pressure is being placed upon local economies to provide employment as well as social conditions that are available elsewhere in Canada. Lack of opportunities for economic advancement is accompanied by numerous signs of the continued problems of adjusting to a new way of life, and assimilation into the majority culture. For the co-operatives a major problem is the threat to their stability posed by funding for other forms of business activity and development. If development programs do not take account of the important role of the co-operatives, three decades of steady progress could be lost without providing the Inuit with any greater prospect of economic advancement. A new factor that may affect the change in the viability of the co-operatives is the sale of the Hudson's Bay Company in March 1987. The sale of 178 frontier posts and stores, at a time when they were carrying a $2.5 billion debt, will create a different economic climate in the north and may change the nature of the competition facing the co-operatives.

The 1990s are likely to be a critical decade during which the problems of northern development will either multiply rapidly with the threat of severe social problems, or the northern native peoples will be brought closer to national norms and will be able to take advantage of a wider range of opportunities. The administrative context within which development will occur has been altered because, following a plebiscite in May 1987, the future administration of the Northwest Territories will be based upon a division between an eastern territory called Nunavut, inhabited mainly by Inuit (Merritt et al. 1989), and a western territory, Denendeh, occupied by Indians and mixed Indian groups, plus around 17,000 non-native peoples and 2,500 Inuit. The estimated population of Inuit in Nunavut is 17,000. Under this arrangement they will have the homeland they have long sought and one in which they represent 85 percent of the population. However, the 11,000 Indians, Métis, and non-status Indians in the western territory will be in the minority in an area that will also include Inuit groups in the western Arctic. A further change in the future could be the transfer of responsibility for native peoples from the DIAND to more specialized federal departments.

13.4.3 The Growing Politicization of the Native Peoples

Some of the native peoples' long-held resentment about their place within Canadian society was symbolized in the 54-day "stand-off" between a group of Mohawk Indians and the Canadian Army at Oka Hill in the Mohawk territory of Kanesatake, Quebec, in the summer of 1990. Although the dispute began after Mohawks moved to block the extension of a golf course onto land they claimed as their own, the dispute soon became symbolic of their grievances. The expression of these grievances revealed a number of factions to be present within the Mohawks themselves, reflecting the fact that the Indians as a whole comprise a number of different groups whose differences have not been entirely submerged by either a number of tribal agreements or the 1876 Indian Act. In the case of the Mohawks, they were one of six feuding "nations" united under the Iroquois Confederacy prior to the arrival of the European colonists. The dispute at Oka Hill became a vehicle for one group of Mohawks to assert that they were a "separate nation" requiring greater recognition by both Indians and other Canadians. Attention was also focused on the original goal of the Indian Act, which had encouraged assimilation of native peoples into Canadian society, imposed an elected council system and native dependence on government funding.

That such a dispute should have arisen so recently may seem surprising if one considers that, following the establishment of the Charter of Rights and Freedoms in the 1982 Constitution, an amendment to the Indian Act was introduced in 1985 (Bill C-31), designed to eliminate certain "anomalies" in the status of Indians. Most notably these referred to enfranchisement, whereby Indians could only escape their status as "wards of Ottawa" by officially giving up their Indian status. This bill also eliminated the loss of Indian status that Indian women experienced when marrying a non-Indian. However, many native peoples have undoubtedly retained a strong distrust of "white" government and especially the federal government, which has been perceived to have used stalling tactics over the settling of land claims and to have "capped" post-secondary education funds for native peoples.

To the Mohawks' dispute can be added the role of Elijah Harper, a Dene chief from Manitoba, in the debate over the Meech Lake Accord. Harper refused to support the constitutional agreement in the Manitoba Legislative Assembly because native peoples had been left out of the process of reaching the Accord. He demanded that native peoples should be afforded the same "distinct society" status that the accord proposed for Quebec. Thus, his stand was seen by many as further indication of the native peoples' growing frustration with their position in Canadian society (see Krotz 1990). This frustration has not been eased by victories in the courts over certain land claims, and it is likely that further protests will occur over land disputes, the potential conflicts over hydro-electric projects in northern Quebec being probable flashpoints. Of the land claims already settled, the largest in Canadian history was that in 1990 in the eastern Arctic, giving 17,000 Inuit ownership of an area the size of Alberta. The federal government has now announced an intention to examine all land claims by native peoples by the end of the century. To this end $15 million per annum has been allocated to deal with over 500 specific claims. However, both the amount of money and the procedures for settling claims have been strongly criticized by the native peoples' organizations.

The theme of continued conflict between increasingly politically aware groups of native peoples and federal/provincial governments over traditional claims to land (and its mineral rights) is taken up in Part 4 of this book where reference is made to three of the most celebrated conflicts: the James Bay hydro scheme, the Mackenzie Valley pipeline, and South Moresby in the Queen Charlotte Islands.

Notes

1. *Indians*: People legally defined as Indians are known as status Indians. Among status Indians there are two groups: treaty Indians and registered Indians outside treaty areas. "Treaty" refers to an agreement between the Crown and a specific group of Indians who are regarded as having surrendered their land rights for specified benefits. Registered Indians are Indians in areas where treaties were not made or Indians in treaty areas who, for various reasons, are not covered by the treaty (see Bartlett 1980).

   Non-status Indians: People of Indian ancestry who have either inter-married with non-Indians or who have abandoned their status rights so that they have lost their legal status, although they still retain a recognizable Indian identity.

Métis: Given several historically variable terms, such as *"michif," "bois brule," "chicot," "half-breed," "country-born,"* and *"mixed blood."* The term is applied generally to people of dual Indian-white ancestry but, more specifically, it defines a particular socio-cultural heritage and is used as a means of ethnic self-identification (see Lussier and Sealey 1978; Peterson and Brown 1984).

Inuit: Translates as "people." Originally termed "Eskimos" or "eaters-of-raw-meat" by Indian groups. They are one of the original peoples to inhabit northern Canada and speak a common language: Inuktitut or Inuttituut.

2. In the 1986 census, people were able to specify either single or multiple ethnic origins. Thus, people of both Indian and British descent could record this multiple ethnic origin and be counted in the total of multiple origins as both Indian and British. In this chapter data referring to the native peoples have been taken from Statistics Canada (1989, 1990).

In the 1981 census, with a different set of definitions employed, 293,000 status Indians were recorded, plus 75,000 non-status Indians, 98,000 Métis, and 25,000 Inuit.

3. *Indian Self-government in Canada: Report of the Special Committee*, Catalogue no. XC2-321/ 9. 1983.

References

Atwood, M.E. 1969. *The Edible Woman*. Toronto: McClelland and Stewart.

——. 1976. *Lady Oracle*. Toronto: McClelland and Stewart.

Bartlett, R. 1980. *The Indian Act of Canada*. Saskatoon: Native Law Centre, University of Saskatchewan.

Berger, T.R. 1977. *Northern Frontier, Northern Homeland*. Ottawa: Minister of Supply and Services Canada.

Bone, R.M., and M.B. Green. 1986. "Accessibility and Development of Métis Communities in Northern Saskatchewan." *Canadian Geographer* 30:66–71.

Brody, H. 1971. *Indians on Skid Row*. Ottawa: Northern Science Research Group, Department of Indian Affairs and Northern Development.

——. 1975. *The People's Land: Eskimos and Whites in the Eastern Arctic*. Harmondsworth: Penguin.

——. 1981. *Maps and Dreams*. Vancouver: Douglas and McIntyre.

Bryant, C.R., L. H. Russwurm, and A.G. McLellan. 1982. *The City's Countryside: Land and its Management in the Rural-urban Fringe*. London and New York: Longman.

Clark, B. 1990. *Native Liberty, Crown Sovereignty: The Existing Aboriginal Right of Self-government in Canada*. Montreal and Kingston: McGill–Queen's University Press.

Coffee, W.J., and M. Polese. 1988. "Locational Shifts in Canadian Employment, 1971–1981: Decentralization Versus Decongestion." *Canadian Geographer* 32:248–55.

Comeau, P., and A. Santin. 1990. *The First Canadians: A Profile of Canada's People Today*. Toronto: James Lorimer & Co.

Coppack, P.M., L. H. Russwurm, and C. R. Bryant, eds. 1988. *Essays on Canadian Urban Process and Form.* Vol. 3: *The Urban Field.* Waterloo: Department of Geography, University of Waterloo.

Creighton, A. 1939. *Cross-country.* Toronto: Macmillan.

Crewson, D.M., and L.G. Reeds. 1982. "Loss of Farmland in South-Central Ontario from 1951–1971." *Canadian Geographer* 26:355–60.

Dahms, F.H. 1986. "Diversity, Complexity and Change: Characteristics of Some Ontario Towns and Villages." *Canadian Geographer* 30:66–71.

Dale, E.H., ed. 1988. "The Future Saskatchewan Small Town." Western Geographical Series, Department of Geography, University of Victoria, no. 24.

Davies, R.W. 1971. *Fifth Business.* New York: Signet.

———. 1972. *The Manticore.* New York: Signet.

———. 1975. *World of Wonders.* New York: Signet.

Davies, W.K.D. 1990. "What Population Turnaround?: Some Canadian Prairie Settlement Perspectives, 1971–1986." *Geoforum* 21:303–20.

Department of Indian Affairs and Northern Development (DIAND). 1980. *Indian Conditions: A Survey.* Ottawa: DIAND.

Evans, S.M. 1985. "Some Developments in the Diffusion Patterns of Hutterite Colonies." *Canadian Geographer* 29:327–39.

Findley, T. 1984. *Not Wanted on the Voyage.* New York: Delacorte Press.

Furuseth, G.J., and C.G. Pierce. 1982. "A Comparative Analysis of Farmland Preservation Programs in North America." *Canadian Geographer* 26:171–206.

Getty, A.L., and A.S. Lussier, eds. 1983. *As Long as the Sunshines and Water Flows: A Reader in Canadian Native Studies.* Vancouver: University of British Columbia Press.

Grove, F.P. 1922. *Over Prairie Trails.* Toronto: McClelland and Stewart.

Hawkes, D.C., ed. 1989. *Aboriginal Peoples and Government Responsibility.* Ottawa: Carleton University Press.

Hemon, L. 1921, *Maria Chapdelaine.* Toronto: Macmillan.

Joseph, A.E., P.D. Keddie, and B. Smit. 1988. "Unravelling the Population Turnaround in Rural Canada." *Canadian Geographer* 32:17–30.

Keiller, G. 1985. *Lake Wobegon Days.* New York: Penguin.

Krotz, L. 1990. *Indian Country: Inside Another Canada.* Toronto: McClelland and Stewart.

Lawrence, M. 1966. *A Jest of God.* Toronto: McClelland and Stewart.

———. 1974. *The Diviners.* Toronto: McClelland and Stewart.

Lussier, A.S., and D.B. Sealey, eds. 1978. *The Other Natives: The Métis.* Winnipeg: Métis Federation Press.

Mackay, L. A. 1948. *The Ill-tempered Lover and Other Poems.* Toronto: Macmillan.

Merritt, J., T. Fenge, R. Ames, and P. Jull. 1989. *Nunavut: Political Choices and Manifest Destiny.* Ottawa: Canadian Arctic Resources Committee.

Mitchell, W.O. 1947. *Who Has Seen the Wind?* Toronto: Macmillan.

Munro, A. 1978. *Who Do You Think You Are?* Toronto: Macmillan.

———. 1990. *Friend of My Youth.* London: Chatto.

Pastore, R. 1978. "The Beothucks." *Museum Notes*, no. 1. St. John's: Newfoundland Museum.

Peterson, J., and J.S.H. Brown, eds. 1984. *New Peoples: Being and Becoming Métis in North America.* Lincoln: University of Nebraska Press.

Pratt, E.J. 1944. *Collected Poems.* Toronto: Macmillan.

Price, J.A. 1979. *Indians of Canada: Cultural Dynamics.* Scarborough: Prentice-Hall.

Robinson, G.M. 1990. *Conflict and Change in the Countryside: Rural Society, Economy and Planning in the Developed World.* London and New York: Belhaven Press.

Seaborne, A.A. 1988. "The Problem of Economic Viability in Saskatchewan's Small Towns." In E.H. Dale, ed., "The Future Saskatchewan Small Town." Western Geographical Series, Department of Geography, University of Victoria, no. 24, 99–116.

Sinclair, P.R., and K. Westhues. 1974. *Village in Crisis.* Toronto: Holt, Rinehart and Winston.

Smith, A.J.M. 1943. *News of the Phoenix and Other Poems.* Toronto: Ryerson Press.

Statistics Canada. 1989. *Canada's Population – From Ocean to Ocean.* Catalogue no. 98-120. Ottawa: Supply and Services Canada.

———. 1990. *Canada's North — A Profile.* Catalogue no. 98-122. Ottawa: Supply and Services Canada.

Stix, J. 1982. "National Parks and Inuit Rights in Northern Labrador." *Canadian Geographer* 26:349–54.

Sutherland, F. 1987. "Margaret Laurence, 1926–1987." *Canadian Plains Bulletin* 15(1):1–2

Sutherland, R. 1982. "A Literary Perspective: The Development of a National Consciousness." In W. Metcalfe, ed., *Understanding Canada: A Multi-disciplinary Introduction to Canadian Studies,* 401–84. New York and London: New York University Press.

Todd, D. 1980. "Rural Out-migration and Economic Standing in a Prairie Setting." *Transactions of the Institute of British Geographers* (new series) 5:446–65 .

———. 1981. "Rural Out-migration in Southern Manitoba: A Simple Path Analysis of Push Factors." *Canadian Geographer* 25:252–66.

Usher, P.J. 1982. "The North: Metropolitan Frontier, Native Homeland?" In L.D. McCann, ed., *Heartland and Hinterland,* 411–56. Scarborough: Prentice-Hall.

Valgardson, W.D. 1980. *Gentle Sinners.* Ottawa: Oberon Press.

Walker, G. 1977. "Social Networks and Territory in a Commuter Village, Bond Head, Ontario." *Canadian Geographer* 21:329–50.

Walker, G.E. 1987. "An Invaded Countryside: Structures of Life on the Toronto Fringe." Geographical Monographs, Atkinson College, York University, no. 17.

Watson, J.W. 1965. "Canadian Regionalism in Life and Letters." *Geographical Journal* 131:21–33.

———. 1983. "The Soul of Geography." *Transactions of the Institute of British Geographers* (new series) 8:385–99.

Weaver, S.M. 1980. *Making Canadian Indian Policy: The Hidden Agenda, 1968–1970.* Toronto: University of Toronto Press.

Yeates, M.H. 1975. *Main Street.* Toronto: Macmillan.

14   The City Beyond the City

Guy M. Robinson

Maurice Yeates's book, *Main Street*, examines the development of the area stretching some 1,170 kilometres from Windsor in the south-west to Quebec City in the north-east (Yeates 1975). This area, referred to by others as the "Heartland" (e.g., Ray 1971) or "Central Canada" (e.g., Bourne and Mackinnon 1972), covers nearly 179,200 square kilometres and contains the greater part of the population of Canada. It is clear in Yeates's study that although Main Street consists primarily of major cities such as Toronto, Montreal, and Hamilton plus numerous smaller towns, it also includes numerous urban-area fringes "where families supported by urban [employment] and those supported by non-urban employment are intermingled" (Yeates 1975, 7). Furthermore, the area contains pockets of productive farmland to which the term "rural" might be more correctly applied than even "semi-rural" or "semi-urban." Yeates does not claim strictly defined limits to Main Street, yet it is clear that even this area, with its close associations with large-scale urbanization and industrial development, has interstices and urban hinterlands that comprise what are, essentially, its rural dimensions. It is on these areas – the rural-urban fringes and the "city's countryside" (e.g., Bryant et al. 1982) – that this chapter focuses, giving special attention to the rural-urban fringe in Ontario, to the changing nature of communities inhabiting the fringe, and to associated land-use conflicts.

14.1   The Dynamics of the Rural-Urban Fringe in Canada

The centrifugal forces within the process of urbanization in Canada have received much attention from geographers and from scholars in related disciplines. The forces have been examined principally in terms of the changing patterns of land use, the changing structures of land management, and the characteristics of and problems affecting those communities in the areas concerned. To gain a better understanding of the emerging socio-cultural characteristics in the city's countryside, it is necessary first to examine these centrifugal forces and their effects upon land use and land management, drawing upon the extensive literature covering these topics.

The process of urbanization in Canada has created what Bryant et al. (1982, 3) term "the regional city," which covers not only the built-up core of the urban area but also an area around this core which, in the case of the largest cities, may have a radius of up to 120 kilometres. This growth of a concentrated urban area surrounded by a more dispersed urban form has been a significant element within the transformation of Canadian society from being largely rural to predominantly urban. However, the dispersed nature of the urban form has only really become of major significance since 1945, when the increased ownership of cars by private individuals permitted the extended separation of workplace and residence. The enlargement of the maximum commuting zone between household and workplace has brought with it the growth of suburbs attached to the urban core as well as the growth of both existing and new settlements in the area beyond these suburbs. Within this simplistic division of core, suburbs, and outlying settlements, Russwurm (1975, 1977), among others, has recognized a more complex mixture of different land uses characterizing the area beyond the suburbs. This mixture includes ribbon development, uses requiring large amounts of space (e.g., stockyards), and various types of development of residential property belonging to commuters or retired urban workers. Other more subtle forms of urban influence on land use also occur by way of increased non-farm ownership of land and modifications to agricultural land use. Second-home ownership and development of property for short "holiday lets" may also become features of the city's countryside.

In the 1960s there was a clear "rural renaissance" in which many non-metro-politan areas started to grow at nearly double the rate of their metropolitan counter-parts (Berry 1976, 1980). This phenomenon has continued into the 1970s and 1980s as migration from cities to the surrounding countryside has frequently replaced the formerly dominant pattern of migration in the opposite direction. Particularly in Main Street, non-metropolitan and mid-size Census Metropolitan Areas (CMAs) have grown at a faster rate than the larger CMAs as decentralization and migration from larger to smaller centres has formed the basis of a shift in the focus of population growth (Coffee and Polese 1988; Preston and Russwurm 1977, 18–24). This pattern of decentralization reflects a complex web of decision-making relating especially to the growth of service industries and the diseconomies of location in large cities. These have produced a desire to seek homes beyond the urban core and suburbs. Changes in transport, communications, personal mobility, and the needs of industry have also enabled the establishment of a more diffuse urban form, placing increased pressure on agricultural land and changing the composition of communities in areas affected (Bourne 1978; Preston and Russwurm 1977; Smit and Conklin 1981).

Forces at work behind this urbanization of the countryside include the increased mobility of the population, economic factors associated with the costs of transpor-tation, land, housing, and local taxes, and the changing life-styles and desires of indi-viduals. In particular, changing demographic and environmental contexts, housing availability, employment opportunities, and public policy have been the key deter-minants of dispersal (Herington 1984).

The various processes that shaped the more diffuse urban form have been studied in a variety of ways, with certain aspects attracting special attention. For the geographers the key issues have been land-use competition, especially the loss of prime agricultural land; the changing nature of communities, including a focus on the groups in society that are involved in migrations associated with the dispersal of population; and the planning of the changes occurring in the city's countryside, especially the regulation of land-use competition through legislation affecting the land and housing markets. This range of topics reflects the recognition that various forces have not only significantly modified the visible landscape of the rural-urban fringe, but have also altered the composition of the communities inhabiting the area, reshaping the economic infrastructure of the fringe (Robinson 1990, 25–58). Both the social and landscape changes in the city's countryside are considered in this chapter, referring especially to the northward sprawl of Toronto – the prime Canadian example of the ever increasing spread of metropolitan influence over a wide hinterland.

14.2   The Northward Expansion of Toronto

A brief comparison between the Toronto Metropolitan Area (MA), its suburbs and its rural-urban fringe reveals the different characteristics of the fringe (Figure 14.1). The population of the fringe is growing rapidly, and it is the domain of young families – with a higher size of household and fewer non-family households than the other two areas (Simmons 1984, 26). Figure 14.1b shows the pattern of population gain and loss for 1981–86 in the hinterland of Toronto. It is a pattern that is repeated throughout much of the Developed World: a decline in parts of the inner city and inner suburbs, while the outer suburbs and adjacent smaller urban areas grow quite rapidly. In Toronto's case it is the communities of the adjacent regional municipalities that have grown the fastest (York, 39.1 percent; Peel, 20.7 percent; Durham, 15.0 percent; and Halton, 6.9 percent, compared with 2.6 percent for the Toronto MA itself). But, within the regional municipalities the greatest proportional increases have been in those parts that form a part of the fringes of the Toronto CMA, such as Vaughan (119.2 percent), Markham (48.8 percent), Ajax (43.5 percent), Pickering (29.7 percent), and Brampton (26.5 percent). This is the new commuter belt, receiving the latest wave of migrants to leave the city's suburbs. Formerly separate urban centres, such as Pickering, Whitby, and Oshawa to the east, and Mississauga, Oakville, and Brampton to the west, have become part of the general urban sprawl along Lake Ontario. To the north the receipt of out-migrants has been pronounced in former small towns such as Markham, Newmarket, and Vaughan, again all within about 50 kilometres of downtown Toronto. Indeed, within this area of the outer parts of the Toronto CMA are nine of the 20 fastest-growing urban municipalities in the country – with Vaughan (first), Markham (third), Ajax (fourth), Pickering (sixth), Brampton (seventh), Whitby (eighth), and Richmond Hill (tenth) all in the top ten.

North of the CMA, for example in the vicinity of Holland Marsh, there exists an increasingly intensive agricultural production belt, with sod farms and vegetable-growing. Beyond this belt, the pattern of growth is more irregular. Growth has tended to be concentrated more in certain small towns, such as Bradford (19.7 percent) and Beeton (8.3 percent), and in townships with good communication links to Toronto rather than in smaller farming communities (e.g., Essa: -3.2 percent). The influence of Highway 400, from York to Barrie and Orillia, is apparent in its contribution to growth as far as the north-western shores of Lake Simcoe. Farther north, holiday developments and retirement homes have swelled numbers in some communities near Georgian Bay, such as Elmvale (24.3 percent) and Coldwater (12.4 percent). Thus, out-migration from the city has involved both young families and those in older age groups.

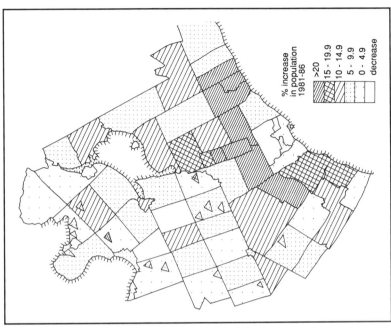

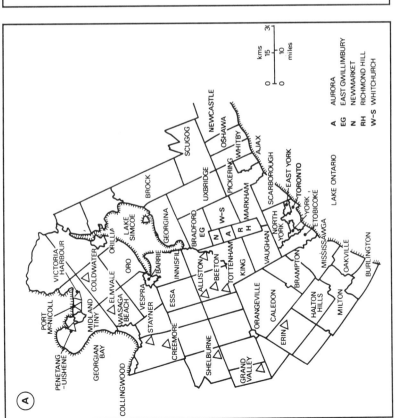

Figure   Toronto and Its Hinterland: a) Administrative Districts;
14.1   b) Changes in Population, 1976–81

The wave of population growth extending beyond the Toronto CMA has been an uneven one, favouring certain localities at the expense of others. Several townships and small towns have tended to remain beyond the orbit of the Toronto commuter belt, especially beyond the 90-kilometre mark. These include Collingwood, Midland, and Port McNicoll. Beyond this distance from Toronto, though, are a number of resort areas now attracting second-home owners and tourist developments. For example there are ski-fields near Algonquin Provincial Park and also closer to the city in the Georgian Lakelands region (where advertisements highlight the fact that the ski-fields are within 90 minutes drive from the city). Blue Mountain and The Peaks, 13 kilometres west of Collingwood, are the most popular ski resorts. Here "mountain" condominiums are now being built.

Of the satellite towns immediately north of Toronto, Markham provides a good illustration of the processes behind the rapid growth. Markham nearly trebled its population from 56,000 in 1976 to over 150,000 in 1990, and it is displacing Scarborough as an attractive location for recent immigrants. Scarborough has approximately one-third of Toronto's Chinese community, but Chinese and other newcomers from Hong Kong and Taiwan are being attracted to Markham by employment opportunities there in small businesses and a number of high-tech companies. In 1990 *The Emigrant* magazine listed over 330 computer-related companies employing over 14,000 workers out of a total 50,000 jobs in Markham. In particular, the intersection of Highways 401 and 404 has become the site of Canada's greatest concentration of high-tech businesses. Companies such as American Express, Apple Canada, IBM Canada, Mitsubishi, Samsung, and others dealing in computer software, information services, and financial services have located here, often making this their corporation headquarters. There are a total of 21 industrial parks in the town, mainly east of Highway 404.

Markham provides just one of several possible illustrations of how a range of business interests, but especially the rapidly expanding service industries in banking, insurance, and information technology, are migrating to the fringes of the metropolitan area. Another good example is that of North York between the end of the subway line and Highway 401. In this area, between 1976 and 1990, 892,800 square metres of new office space were established, nearly 40 percent of which were built in the last five years of the 1980s. A further 1.172 million square metres are planned for the early 1990s. In contrast, there has been almost no new office construction since 1977 in the City of York and the Borough of East York because they are in a no-man's-land between major transit routes. The lack of a coherent regional strategy in the northern fringes of the city has contributed both to increased urban sprawl and to spiralling land costs in those locations best served by good transport links to the central city. In some cases land can cost as much as one-third of the total development costs, which is twice the current average for American cities.

Recent in-migration has been a major factor in the population growth occurring in both the satellite towns and smaller outlying communities. This is indicated in Table 14.1, which gives some details of population increase in those municipalities of 5,000 inhabitants and over in 1986. Of the 46 places tabulated, half experienced more rapid growth between 1981 and 1986 than in the previous five-year period. However, both the spatial pattern and the role of in-migration remained very similar. The importance of in-migraton is suggested in column A of Table 14.1, which shows that in most of the more rapidly growing communities around one-third of the inhabitants aged five years and over had in-migrated from other administrative areas within the period 1981–86. Of the 12 fastest-growing places, nine of them had proportions of in-migrants in excess of 30 percent. In contrast, several of those with slow growth or a decline in population had proportions of under 20 percent – notably within the Toronto MA, such as East York (14.6 percent), York (14.8 percent), and North York (16.5 percent).

An examination of the influx of population to the attractive wooded hills of the Oak Ridges Moraine in the municipalities of King, Vaughan, Caledon, Beesley, and Walker (1990) found that three-quarters of the newcomers to the area had urban backgrounds, the majority being young families moving north from Toronto. However, farther away from the metropolis, migrants may have a less urban background. For example, in a study in the Guelph-Stratford region less than half the non-farm residents in three urban fields had come from a town of over 10,000 and only 30 percent had been raised in a city (Joseph et al. 1988; Dorin and van Rietbergen 1990).

It was the Toronto CMA that was the main target for migrants from other provinces (column B), with the city of Toronto having nearly a quarter of its recent in-migrants from Canadian provinces other than Ontario. Immigrants, too, were attracted to the Toronto CMA, but especially to the traditional areas of immigrant receipt (column C), such as the city of Toronto, North York, East York, Scarborough, Etobicoke, and Mississauga – places still providing a range of employment opportunities for newly-arrived immigrants. As column C shows, immigrants comprised one-quarter to one-third of the in-migrants to these places.

Beyond the Toronto CMA the slowest rates of growth, and some population losses, occurred in the more rural townships where farming has remained the dominant activity. This includes a number of townships north of Lake Simcoe (e.g., Rama and Matchedash) as well as some closer to Georgian Bay (e.g., Flos and Nottawasaga). In the last two townships, the selectivity of the wave of population growth is well illustrated: Stayner Town and Elmvale Village have grown, partly through tourist-related development, while the population numbers in the surrounding hamlets and farms has remained almost unchanged.

While a more detailed breakdown of the population changes, in terms of age and sex structures, ethnic groups, and occupational groups, would give better definition to the types of development being experienced beyond the city and its adjoining suburbs, this brief survey does illustrate certain key points in the evolution of the city's countryside. It is clear that there have been some very rapid increases of population in a semi-circular belt around Toronto. This has pushed the continuous built-up area even farther beyond the downtown and generated a looser structure for the urban form. However, the growth of population has gone well beyond this suburban belt to reach small towns, villages, and hamlets that were previously dominated by farming and other rural activities. These have now been brought very

Table   **Population Growth in Toronto and Vicinity, 1981–86**
14.1   **(for places of >5000 population)**

	1981–86	1976–81	A	B	C
		% Population Increase			
Vaughan	119.2	64.1	34.7	5.1	9.2
Markham	48.8	37.1	34.2	12.7	11.8
Ajax	43.5	24.2	39.0	9.5	4.8
Pickering	29.7	42.2	33.0	9.3	5.4
Aurora	28.5	14.2	37.7	7.1	5.1
Brampton	26.5	38.0	27.9	15.1	9.7
Whitby	24.9	24.7	35.7	10.7	5.1
Richmond Hill	23.8	8.8	28.9	9.7	6.1
Bradford	19.7	45.1	36.2	6.7	5.1
Mississauga	18.7	15.0	26.1	17.9	14.7
Newmarket	17.4	20.0	30.9	11.6	5.2
East Gwillimbury	16.5	18.1	32.1	5.1	4.8
Oakville	15.0	9.9	28.2	22.7	11.1
Milton	14.1	35.2	27.9	15.0	5.6
Scugog	12.8	13.7	27.0	10.8	3.2
Georgina	11.8	8.5	29.8	9.9	2.1
Whitchurch-Stouffer	11.6	5.2	27.4	7.4	3.6
Caledon	11.3	18.8	28.0	7.2	6.8
Barrie	11.1	11.7	26.3	13.7	4.6
Innisfil	9.5	15.7	30.3	8.7	2.5
Scarborough	9.3	14.5	16.8	16.1	29.2
Wasaga Beach	8.9	-5.6	33.1	9.1	1.6
Oro	8.8	11.3	25.1	6.8	6.5
Tiny	8.8	7.3	25.0	5.0	0.8
Brock	8.0	5.0	27.0	5.6	2.7
Vespra	7.8	14.6	24.7	4.9	3.7
Tecumseth	6.8	11.5	25.3	5.5	5.5
Uxbridge	6.1	2.1	25.9	5.2	3.9
Newcastle	5.7	0.9	20.4	7.6	4.2
Oshawa	5.2	9.8	19.8	17.7	6.3
Orangeville	5.1	12.8	26.8	8.8	3.6
King	5.0	8.3	28.1	5.3	6.6
Penetanguishene	4.9	-2.7	24.9	7.4	4.1
Orillia Town	3.9	7.9	22.4	8.1	1.6
Tay	3.4	-0.9	22.0	10.3	4.9
Toronto City	2.2	-5.4	20.0	23.3	32.3
Burlington	1.6	10.1	20.7	16.7	8.4
Etobicoke	1.4	0.5	15.1	16.5	24.8
Halton Hills	1.1	2.1	20.5	12.5	7.2

	A	B	C		
Collingwood	0.9	8.5	22.1	6.6	2.7
York	0.6	-4.8	14.8	18.8	32.6
Orillia City	0.5	-1.9	19.6	12.1	4.2
Midland	-0.3	4.2	21.5	3.8	7.8
North York	-0.6	0.2	16.5	17.9	37.0
East York	-0.9	-4.7	14.6	17.3	29.4
Essa	-3.2	-4.1	48.5	43.4	6.4

A   In-migrants 1981–86 as a proportion of the population aged >5 years old in 1986 (based on 20 percent sample survey).

B   Proportion of migrants 1981–86 from another Canadian province (based on 20 percent sample survey).

C   Proportion of immigrants among the migrants 1981–86 (based on 20 percent sample survey).

Source: *Census of Canada 1986*, Catalogue no. 94-111, *Population and Dwelling Characteristics, Ontario*, Parts 1 and 2

definitely within the urban sphere of influence, with traditional rural residents often becoming a small minority in the midst of newcomers who work in the city and have other ties with Toronto, which means that their focus is on the city rather than on the locality of their new domicile. However, this growth beyond the suburban belt has been selective spatially, associating most closely with good communication links with Toronto or the attraction of amenities for retirement migration and second-home ownership. Small towns have not always proved attractive locations for the out-migrants, though some, Alliston, Beeton, and Bradford for instance, have been associated with rapid growth through the development of local employment opportunities, such as assembly-line plants.

14.3   Changes in the Social Geography of the Rural-Urban Fringe

The population changes associated with the growth of the city beyond the city have produced a new pattern of social and economic life in those communities affected by the influx of newcomers from the city. The in-migrants have frequently located in townships previously dominated by farming households, which were at the centre of life in small, rural communities. Thus, while the direct conversion of agricultural land to urban use is the most obvious physical expression of the urbanization of the countryside, Bryant (1986, 168) notes two other sets of demands that may produce a response from farming and the agricultural community. These are a demand for labour, resulting from expansion in opportunities for non-farm employment, and a demand for agricultural produce and services associated with the changing nature of the urban market. In addition to the sale of farmland, these other demands produce effects associated with alterations in the patterns of farm investment, rentals, and labour input. Of these changes within farming activity itself, geographers have focused attention upon the development of part-time farms and hobby farms in the rural-urban fringe (e.g., Layton 1978, 1979, 1981), the nature of change in agricultural land use associated with urban expansion (e.g., Bryant 1974, 1984; Sinclair 1967), and the underlying structures producing the changing landscape of the city's countryside – for example, the rural land market (Bryant 1982; Rodd 1976). In all of these studies the focus of attention has tended to shift away from the resource of the land itself to that of societal response to urbanization and to the nature of the communities within the rural-urban fringe.

Studies of social changes in the rural-urban fringe have concentrated on the pattern of migration that has produced changes in population and the evolution of the communities themselves in terms of their composition and social relationships (Gilg 1985, 67; Robinson 1990, 25–58). The expansion of these communities as they increasingly take on the role of the "commuter village" has brought changes in both the composition of and the functional relationships within the communities. A wealth of literature on the types of changes occurring in other parts of the developed world indicates a recognizable urbanization of people in the rural-urban fringe, with communities moving away from the characteristics attributed to the rural communities at the one extreme of the so-called rural-urban continuum (e.g., Pacione 1984, 152–56). This change was summarized for the United States by Anderson's (1963, 8) comment that "the American ideal of home, community and work was clearly rural and puritanic. Industrialism and urbanism combined in various ways to shock established norms." In simple terms, the change has meant that farmers and exurbanites now live in the same locale. Yet it is clear that within the evolving communities there are important differences of outlook and attitude, in part conditioned by the fact that farmers still use the land for its production function and former urban residents use it for its "place and play function" (Bryant et al. 1982, 46).

Gertler and Crowley (1982, 282) recognize five different groups of people who now inhabit the fringes of major Canadian cities. In addition to the advancing tide of exurbanites who still work in the city and retain their social ties with the city, there are part-time dwellers such as owners of cottages, second homes, and hobby farms; part-time farmers who live on a farm, operate it, but have a job in the city; full-time farmers or those continuing in other forms of full-time primary activity in the urban fringe; and other ruralites who are the remnants of traditional rural society, such as farm labourers and those involved in the provision of services in a network of hamlets and villages.

Layton's (1978, 1979, 1981) work on farmers in the rural-urban fringe of London, Ontario, gives further definition to these last three groups as he also identifies clearly recognizable groups of farmers: those completely reliant upon farming for their income and those who were either part-time or hobby farmers with non-farm employment to supplement their income. The hobby farmers had a more urban background and purchased farms as a place of residence and for personal recreation. Yet, even 44 percent of this group of farmers farmed on a strongly commercial basis rather than maintaining an interest in just farming for pleasure. The hobby farmers had tended to purchase land in the aesthetically more attractive areas. Their willingness to pay large amounts of money inflated land prices. This was preventing the amalgamation of commercial farm units with the result that the family farmer was gradually disappearing in favour of either very large agribusinesses or small part-time and hobby farmers.

For southern Ontario, one of the best examples of the nature of social changes in commuter villages is provided in Gerald Walker's (1976, 1977) studies of Bond Head, a community of 683 people (in 1971), located 64 kilometres north of Toronto. Like many small settlements in the area, Bond Head comprises two kinds of communities: the old village with its close ties with communities in the surrounding countryside; and a new housing estate, constructed in 1968, containing 110 houses occupied mainly by people from the professional-managerial group, Toronto-born, and commuting to Toronto to work. By 1977 this new suburban population out-numbered the rural villagers by approximately 2 to 1. However, even in the old village there had been penetration by former urban residents in the form of retired people from Toronto or urban workers who had purchased houses within the nucleus of the old village.

Walker's analysis of the social networks of the inhabitants of Bond Head focused on the two distinguishable communities there: a rurally oriented group, consisting largely of retired people, and a group of "suburbanites" living in the new housing estate (see also Smit and Flaherty 1981). Yet, in effect, the latter consisted of several different social sub-groups with minimal inter-group cohesion. "The suburb had a small group, short distance, friendship and middle-class orientation more characteristic of an urban community" (Walker 1977, 347). Hence, the overall pattern of community and territory on the housing estate closely resembled that found by Clark (1968) for suburban Toronto. Among the suburbanites, half the households derived their incomes from blue-collar labour, although they had largely shed working-class patterns of interaction. So they were part of a private and familistic lifestyle in which social ties often mirrored the link with Toronto, retained by virtue of commuting to work there. In contrast, the villagers had relatives and friends living locally and had reinforced their sense of a local community "by creating an institutionally complete world" of church, school, and a few shops. Change within Bond Head was continuing in the form of the gradual disappearance of the old village.

Walker's (1974, 1975) further studies of three townships in south Simcoe County, 80 kilometres north of Toronto, suggest that the farming community and the former urban residents are pursuing different objectives. The urban-centred focus of the exurbanites even extends to the political sphere as it is the farmers who still control local politics in the three townships. This may be a case where conflicts between the established population and newcomers have not occurred, but there is much potential for such problems to arise. For example, the presence of an influx of young families putting pressure on existing educational provision can raise local tax rates as can the need to provide other services and utilities for the newcomers (Joseph and Smit 1981; Joseph et al. 1989).

In their study of Elora, a village of 1,500 people located on the fringes of Guelph and Waterloo, Sinclair and Westhues (1975) illustrated the type of conflict that can occur. In Elora, conflicts arose between the newcomers, who opposed a new apartment development, and the established population who generally looked favourably upon the scheme. It seems the newcomers were seeking what Pahl (1965) terms "the village in the mind." that is, a particular type of desirable residential environment in a rural area. While that particular environment may have been altered significantly by their very presence, they still wanted to protect it from any further alteration and hence the opposition to the development scheme.

Similar work by Dahms (1977, 1980) has shown that for Wellington County, on the western periphery of Toronto's urban field, part of the spatial organization of small communities still exists quite independently of the core city. Several of the small settlements had not only gained population since 1960, but they had also acquired new functions in the form of specialized retailing and services plus employment. Access to such functions proved as convenient as access to work or shopping for residents of several such communities, and hence these smaller centres tended to subsume some of the roles of the higher-order centres. In particular, he noted the establishment of a range of new businesses, often of a specialized nature or associated with regional and national franchises. The employment opportunities afforded by such establishments means that small towns of about 1,000 people can often provide close to 300 jobs and encourage daily in-commuting to work (Hodge and Qadeer 1983, 91–92).

These various changes in the city's countryside cannot be divorced from either local or regional planning initiatives. The impress of local, regional, provincial, and federal government has grown in the post-war decades influencing even micro-scale features of social and spatial organization. Thus, planning has had a major influence upon population distribution and the changing character of rural communities. The Toronto area again provides good examples of this.

Following the rapid growth in the 1950s and 1960s of rural townships adjacent to expanding urban areas, several cities annexed rural townships. This often provoked conflict between the urban and rural parts of the new administrative unit, especially if such moves were perceived by the rural inhabitants as being a licence for urban sprawl. However, for Toronto, a form of regional government has been developed in which existing counties have been amalgamated in a system that combines cities, towns, and villages under one regional municipality. Again there is the prospect of conflicts between urban and rural interests, but also the opportunity for co-operation to generate strict zoning of land use and stringent planning controls to channel urban growth to specific locations.

In particular, such planning has had to regulate the real estate market. The nature of this market plays a major role in determining the nature and pattern of urban expansion. Contrast, for example, development through the development industry as opposed to rural residential development on an individual basis. The variability of the real estate market around Kitchener and Waterloo has been demonstrated by Bryant (1982), highlighting spatial variability associated especially with the relative importance of farmer-to-farmer transactions, the role of intermediate actors and their involvement in multiple chains, property size of land in the market, and value per unit area. The latter has risen sharply as, for long periods in the last three or four decades, the land market around Canada's urban areas has been buoyant, reflecting the demand for land for building development. This buoyancy has been translated into substantial losses of land for urban uses and the introduction of a number of new planning controls to regulate land-use competition and to protect valuable farmland from urban sprawl.

14.4 Land-use Conflicts

If social changes in the city's countryside have been widespread during the past two or three decades, then the changes to the physical appearance of that countryside have been equally dramatic. These alterations in the landscape have been an integral part of geographical investigation into the various economic and social forces involved in the expansion of urban areas. Indeed, in the monitoring of land-use changes around the major cities, Canada has developed information systems that are among the most advanced in the world. This detailed monitoring provides a most useful complement to the social and demographic changes described above.

14.4.1 The Canada Land Use Monitoring Program (CLUMP)

The continued loss of agricultural land, especially to urban sprawl, has been of major concern throughout the Developed World. In the Canada Land Use Monitoring Program (CLUMP), Canada can claim one of the best information systems for charting this and other changes in the pattern of land use. CLUMP was established in 1978 to provide an information system on changing land use, for use by researchers from various disciplines, planners, land resource managers, and policy-makers (Rump and Hillary 1987; Rump 1983). It was intended to complement the land capability surveys of the Canada Land Inventory. In so doing it was designed to monitor land use and change in land use both spatially and sequentially. Hence, CLUMP is intended to provide an information system capable of answering questions relating to the location of changes in land use and the rate of change, as well as examining whether high-quality land is allocated to its most productive use. The role of government policies can also be monitored as can the way in which various land-use policies are sustaining the land resource base.

Four different types of area have been selected for special attention as part of CLUMP. These are urban-centred regions (UCRs),[1] prime resource lands, rural areas, and wildlands. The first three of these may all contain land within the realm of the rural-urban fringe, though only the first named specifically covers the fringe when it deals with the "city's countryside" for urban centres with populations of over 25,000. For such areas the data produced by CLUMP permit a description of the pattern, type, and rate of change of land use, analysis of loss of high-capability agricultural and other resource lands to urbanization,[2] and the correlation of changing land use with growth of population. The basic mode of operation of CLUMP is indicated in Figure 14.2.

CLUMP has produced special fact sheets for a number of individual urban-centred regions plus information on the rates of loss of land to urban uses. In addition, as part of the Land Use in Canada series, there has been a detailed study by Warren

THE CANADA LAND USE MONITORING PROGRAM (CLUMP)

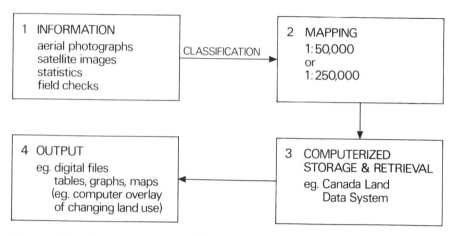

Figure   **The Canada Land Use Monitoring Program (CLUMP)**
14.2

and Rump (1981) on the urbanization of rural land between 1966 and 1976 (see also Gierman 1977) and a study by Yeates (1985) of land use in the Windsor–Quebec City axis. The pattern revealed by Warren and Rump (1981) for 1966–71 and 1971–76 may be compared with the findings of the Lands Directorate (1985a; Warren et al. 1989) for 1976–86. Together these studies provide an excellent overview of the extent of change in land use in the rural-urban fringe and of the components of that change.

14.4.2   Changing Rates of Loss of Rural Land, 1966–86

Between 1966 and 1986 just over 744,000 acres (301,400 hectares) of rural land were converted to urban uses in UCRs, the most rapid rate of conversion occurring between 1976 and 1981. This rate represented an increase of 59 percent compared with the amount of conversion between 1971 and 1976, but only a 14 percent increase on the rate of conversion between 1966 and 1971. However, the amount converted between 1981 and 1986 was only 56 percent of that from 1976 to 1981. The largest losses of land to urban use were associated with the expansion of the major cities, especially Toronto, Edmonton, Calgary, and Montreal where a 1 percent growth in the urban population produced a 1.5 percent increase in land under urban use (Yeates, 1985, 6–7).

In British Columbia the rate of loss for 1976–81 was almost three times that for 1966–71 and 1971–76, but the rate was substantially reduced for 1981–86 and in all provinces the amount of loss of prime agricultural land fell in the 1980s. This reflects tighter controls on urban encroachment onto such land and also the diffusion of the effects of urban sprawl to areas with less prime land. This diffusion has also carried the tendency towards urban sprawl down the urban hierarchy.

Table 14.2 Total Rural Land (TRL) and Prime Agricultural Land (PAL)* Converted in the Canadian UCRs for Four Monitoring Periods, 1966–86

Province (No. of UCRs)	1966–71			1971–76			1976–81			1981–86			1966–86		
	TRL ha	PAL ha	PAL as % of TRL	TRL ha	PAL ha	PAL as % of TRL	TRL ha	PAL ha	PAL as % of TRL	TRL ha	PAL ha	PAL as % of TRL	TRL ha	PAL ha	PAL as % of TRL
B.C. (7)	7,515	1,154	15	7,665	1,690	22	23,372	5,272	23	6,778	1,244	18	45,330	9,360	21
Alta. (5)	14,698	8,911	61	12,279	8,936	73	11,077	6,821	62	13,637	6,761	50	51,691	31,429	61
Sask. (4)	1,487	951	64	2,410	2,090	87	4,507	2,509	56	2,209	1,368	62	10,613	6,018	65
Man. (2)	5,199	4,733	91	1,441	1,356	94	3,975	3,433	86	2,431	1,925	79	13,046	11,447	88
Ont. (26)	36,952	29,125	79	21,260	16,558	78	27,070	20,276	75	20,670	17,081	83	105,952	83,040	78
Que. (19)	15,632	8,409	54	11,082	5,486	50	17,609	7,346	42	6,264	3,671	59	50,587	24,912	49
N.B. (3)	1,803	292	16	2,798	868	31	4,830	892	18	1,917	373	26	10,848	2,425	22
N.S. (2)	1,810	663	37	1,143	582	51	3,928	1,481	38	1,162	321	28	8,043	3,047	38
P.E.I. (1)	307	309	99	414	414	100	1,523	1,463	96	34	13	38	2,280	2,197	96
Nfld. (1)	685	–	0	672	4	<1	1,085	10	>1	608	1	>1	3,050	15	>1
70 UCRs	86,090	54,545	63	61,164	37,984	62	98,976	49,503	50	55,210	32,758	59	301,440	174,790	58

* Prime Agricultural Land (PAL) is defined as land within Agricultural Capability Classes 1, 2, and 3 (see Lands Directorate 1976).

Source: Warren et al. 1989

Table   **Increase in Area, Population Growth, and Rate of Conversion**
14.3   **of Rural Land for UCRs, by Population Class, 1966–86**

Population Class (No. of UCRs)	Area Increase		Population Increase		Rate of Land Conversion ha/1000 Change in Population	
	% 66–86	% 81–86	% 66–86	% 81–86	66–86	81–86
25,000–50,000 (26)	16.4	3.3	6.2	1.5	196	242
50,001–100,000 (18)	12.5	4.0	5.3	2.9	175	141
100,001–250,000 (13)	13.4	4.9	9.9	3.6	101	104
250,001–500,000 (4)	14.8	3.2	14.2	5.2	78	50
>500,000 (9)	42.9	6.6	64.4	6.3	50	53
70 UCRs	41.0	5.4	33.0	5.4	74	64

Source: Warren et al. 1989, 11

In absolute terms it is still the major cities that are dominating the conversion of rural land, the larger UCRs having the smallest relative but largest absolute expansions in their urban land uses. The nine UCRs with a population in excess of 500,000 had the highest population densities and accounted for 78 percent of the population increase in the UCRs between 1981 and 1986, and for 66 percent of the total rural land converted, while only increasing their urban area by 7 percent. The smaller centres have greater relative increases and are urbanizing more land per capita (Table 14.3) (Cournoyer 1987). This difference between small and large UCRs is demonstrated clearly in Alberta where the two cities dominating the urban hierarchy, Calgary and Edmonton, increased their urban population by 26 percent and 17 percent respectively between 1976 and 1981. Yet, their urban areas expanded at a rate well below the national average of 11 percent. This contrasted with the experience of smaller towns in the same province, such as Lethbridge and Red Deer, which had smaller proportional increases in population, but experienced greater relative growth of their urban areas. Table 14.3 also shows that, for all UCRs, the rates of increase in both urban area and population size were substantially lower for 1981–86 than the average rates over the 20-year period between 1966 and 1986.

The differential changes in the amount of land converted to urban uses may be related to variations in population growth by measuring the number of hectares of rural land converted per 1,000 increase in urban population (Table 14.4). Between 1976 and 1981, rural-to-urban land conversion in the Maritimes was associated with relatively small increases in population, suggesting low-density urban sprawl. Elsewhere, and especially in Alberta and Ontario, much higher-density use of land was associated with the conversion. In the early 1980s, though, the national rate of conversions was almost one-half that between 1976 and 1981. Only New Brunswick maintained a very high rate of rural land conversion per 1,000 population increase,

Table 14.4 **Rates of Land Conversion; Percentage Increase in Area and Population of UCRs, by Province, 1976–86**

	Rate of Land Conversion ha/1000 Change in Population		Area Increase %		Population Increase %	
	81–86	**76–81**	**81–86**	**76–81**	**81–86**	**76–81**
B.C.	51	84	6.0	16.6	7.2	9.2
Alta.	132	46	9.8	8.5	6.9	21.4
Sask.	51	96	8.0	19.3	10.2	10.7
Man.	66	791	5.2	9.4	5.3	0.8
Ont.	46	80	5.8	8.1	6.7	5.4
Que.	82	334	3.2	10.3	1.8	1.3
N.B.	979	1,657	4.1	15.9	0.8	1.2
N.S.	81	1,193	2.7	9.7	3.9	1.0
P.E.I.	13	1,580	0.6	26.0	7.0	3.0
Nfld.	86	109	5.0	9.6	4.8	6.5

Sources: Lands Directorate 1985a; Warren et al. 1989

and there had been substantial reductions in Manitoba, Quebec, Nova Scotia, and Prince Edward Island. In part this reflected tighter controls on urban sprawl, especially attempts to protect the limited amounts of top-quality agricultural land.

Between 1981 and 1986 prime agricultural land accounted for 59 percent of the land converted in Canada as a whole, illustrating the conflict between urban growth and the retention of the best agricultural land (Williams and Pohl 1987). More than 55 percent of prime agricultural land lies within a 160-kilometre radius of major metropolitan areas (Neimanis 1979). The concentrated nature of the pressure on this good-quality land is further illustrated by the UCRs around Toronto. The region bounded by Toronto, Barrie, and Windsor converted 14,500 hectares of agricultural land to urban uses between 1981 and 1986, of which nearly 94 percent were prime agricultural lands, with 65 percent in Agricultural Capability Class One. The Toronto UCR absorbed 10,047 hectares of prime land during this period, compared with 4,036 hectares around Edmonton, 2,665 around Montreal, and 498 around Vancouver. This continued loss of good land around Toronto also reflects the considerable amount of population growth within Toronto's urban field, as discussed earlier: 30 percent of the population of Main Street, or one in every six Canadians, now lives within 65 kilometres of the city's CN Tower (Yeates 1985, 51). Meanwhile, between 1976 and 1986 Montreal's share of the population of Main Street fell as office and financial activities moved away to Toronto, which continued to develop a more dynamic manufacturing sector (Code 1983; Semple and Green 1983; Szplett 1983, 1984). More recently, though, this contrast between Canada's two biggest cities has decreased somewhat because Montreal has seen a renewed confidence in its service and industrial sectors.

One other notable change in land use in the rural-urban fringe is in the diversity of uses to which the land is put. This has increased in conjunction with growth in the forms of ownership. These changes were illustrated in Punter's (1976) study of four townships within 64 kilometres of Toronto during the period 1954–71. Active agricultural use dropped substantially (by 35 percent) at the same time as a major reduction in owner-occupation of farmland. Recreational land use increased seven-fold and residential land use more than doubled. Two categories of ownership increased greatly: corporate ownership, especially in the investment-developer category, and absentee ownership by individuals who purchased a second home (Punter 1974, 50–53). Corporate ownership of land marked the growth of land development by large public companies organized to operate, design, construct, manage, and market major residential or business projects (e.g., Martin 1975, 1984). This trend, in part, accounted for a sharp upward trend in land prices pushing farming activity off the land and promoting speculative purchasing in the real estate market. For example, in terms of land converted to urban use in the UCRs in Canada between 1981 and 1986, 11 percent was classified as "abandoned agricultural land," 23 percent as "land with no perceived activity," and 32 percent as "land in transition." These categories largely represent land held speculatively, often in transition from former agricultural use. The UCRs in Alberta and Ontario absorbed 70 percent of the land in transition between 1981 and 1986, while 41 percent of the total land converted in Quebec was abandoned agricultural land.

14.4.3 The Loss of Agricultural Land in Sensitive Areas: The Niagara Fruit Belt and the Okanagan Fruit Lands

Perhaps the area that has received the most attention with regard to the direct loss of agricultural land to urban sprawl has been the Niagara fruit belt, the centre of Canadian wine and soft-fruit production (Figure 14.3). The Niagara Peninsula, forming the western end of the so-called Golden Horseshoe, has a population of some 370,000. The fruit belt, to the north of the Niagara Escarpment, is one of only three small areas in Canada capable of growing tender fruits such as cherries, grapes, peaches, pears, and strawberries (Kreuger 1965). One of the critical problems has been that much of the urbanization in the peninsula has occurred in the areas of the most intensive fruit-growing and on land of the best quality (Kreuger 1984; Seguin 1987). Agricultural land use is threatened by the growth of internal centres such as St. Catharines and Niagara Falls, external pressures from Hamilton and Toronto, the routing of a main trunk road (the Queen Elizabeth Way) through land of high agricultural capability, and the development of recreation and mineral extraction (Krueger 1977, 1978). The amount of land devoted to fruit and vines in the fruit belt in 1951 was 21,450 hectares. Thirty years later less than half the acreage of tree crops remained, and the total agricultural acreage had fallen by 20 percent. Although the vineyard area had increased (29 percent) through new plantings along the Niagara Escarpment, the competition for prime fruit-growing land was great.

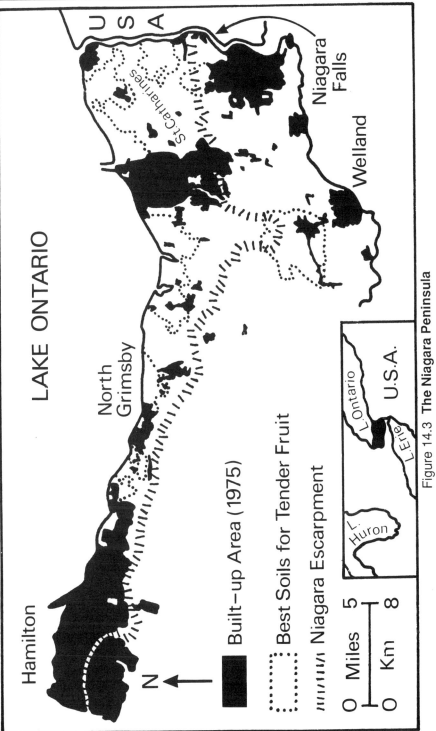

Figure 14.3 **The Niagara Peninsula**

The high rate of loss of farmland in the 1960s was one of the factors that brought about the establishment of regional government in 1970 in the form of the Regional Municipality of Niagara (Jackson 1985, 1986). Its policy plan of 1973 stated one basic objective: "to protect the agricultural industry and its resources." After ten years of public hearings and enquiries, boundaries of permitted urban development were established that were in broad agreement with the wishes of the citizens' conservation group, the Preservation of Agricultural Land Society (PALS). This ten-year period represented a time of major political activity related to the demarcation of the boundaries of urban areas. Many felt that the policy plan proposed urban boundaries far in excess of future requirements (Gayler 1982a, 1982b): "The urban area boundaries had obviously been drawn so liberally to accommodate the expansion desires of all the local municipalities. While the policy objectives espoused the preservation of the fruit lands, the urban area boundaries maps appeared designed to encourage the destruction of the unique agricultural resources" (Kreuger 1984, 294).

In general, municipal and regional politicians were unwilling to reduce the area designated for urban development. They paid lip service to the goal of protecting agricultural land, but the need for cheap housing and industrial land to help solve the economic problems of the region put pressure on them to release land for development. After 1978, however, boundary disputes were brought before the Ontario Municipal Board (OMB), with PALS using a Green Paper on *Food Land Guidelines*, produced by the Ontario Ministry of Agriculture and Food (1978), to argue for reduced urban area boundaries. These guidelines provided specific criteria to assist local governments in designating agricultural land within their official plans (Furuseth and Pierce 1982, 58–60). As a result of the hearings, over 2,025 hectares of land, primarily in the northern part of the peninsula, were removed from urban designation, and the OMB advocated strict control policies outside the urban boundaries, based on soil capability rather than on existing levels of production (Jackson 1982). These policies meant highly restrictive measures on development outside the urban area boundaries, which meant that the rural areas of the fruit belt could only be developed for agricultural purposes (Gayler 1990; Regional Municipality of Niagara 1988).

Work by Krushelnicki and Bell (1989), who used Ontario Registry Office records on land transactions to monitor loss of agricultural land during the period of sustained pressure from urban development between 1967 and 1981, revealed that significant amounts of land outside the urban area boundaries were being sold at prices beyond the price land for agricultural use would normally command. They termed this the "urban price shadow," as it represented land that had moved into the urban land market – land purchased by people anticipating non-agricultural use. Such purchases were especially prevalent in the mid-1970s, but after the OMB hearings there was some contraction of the urban shadow, especially around Grimsby and St. Catharines. Some evidence of the too generous urban area boundaries was provided by the fact that, within the boundaries, one-quarter of land sales remained within the agricultural price range. However, only 5 percent of such purchases were made by farmers, and, outside the boundaries, transactions involving non-agricultural purchasers were as numerous as those involving farmers. Some of these non-agricultural purchases involved speculators and developers who often bought the small parcels produced by the increased fragmentation of agricultural land. Other purchases included transactions for recreational development or for the establishment of hobby farming.

Controls on urban development have also been suggested by the Niagara Escarpment Commission, created in 1973 by the provincial government. The commissioner has a mandate to balance the needs of existent economic activities against the need to protect the Escarpment, which constitutes a valuable natural and scenic resource. In April 1986 the Niagara Escarpment Plan was established to preserve and develop an area around the Escarpment covering 1,900 square kilometres. Under the plan, 90 percent of the plan area will be brought under one of three protected categories: Escarpment Natural Areas, Escarpment Protection Areas, and Escarpment Rural Areas. These will be under the jurisdiction of a parks system that will acquire land throughout the designated area. In this way it is intended to preserve resources while also offering educational and recreational opportunities. The implication is that further control over urban sprawl has been established, though its potential effective-ness has already been questioned (e.g., Johnston and Smit 1985).

Similar problems of conflict between urban and prime agricultural land occur in British Columbia where the few pockets of land suitable for food production are situated in close proximity to concentrations of population. Prime agricultural land is very limited in the province: the Fraser Valley and the Okanagan, the two most important areas of fruit production, having only 109,459 hectares of prime land (Capability Classes 1 to 4) (B.C. Select Standing Committee on Agriculture 1978) (Figure 14.4). The pressure of urban expansion upon this land has been great, with one estimate suggesting that in the 1960s and early 1970s over 6,000 hectares of prime agricultural land were being lost annually to this competing use (Lands Directorate 1980, 19). The scale of this conflict and the severe shortage of agricultural land prompted an early response from the provincial government, which pioneered legislation to establish a comprehensive agricultural land protection policy.

In 1973 a land-zoning program was introduced to protect farmland; the program paid special attention to the need to maintain and develop family farming (Bray 1980; Stupich 1975). Zoning and regulatory controls over agricultural resources and Agricultural Land Reserves (ALR) were placed in the hands of a Provincial Land Commission. The ALR, covering 4.9 percent of the province, acts as an area zoned exclusively for farming so that its designation supercedes all other land planning and zoning decisions (Wilson and Pierce 1984). To remove land from the ALR, local authorities have to make special petitions to the commission or the provincial government. Various surveys in the late 1970s suggested that the integrity of the ALR was being preserved and that there was widespread support for the farmland protection policy (Malzahn 1979; Manning and Eddy 1978; Raynor 1980). Indeed, Pierce's (1981) survey of the rates of conversion of farmland in the province showed that land transfers out of the ALR were much slower than before the act. Support for the policy from farming interests reflected an additional element associated with the

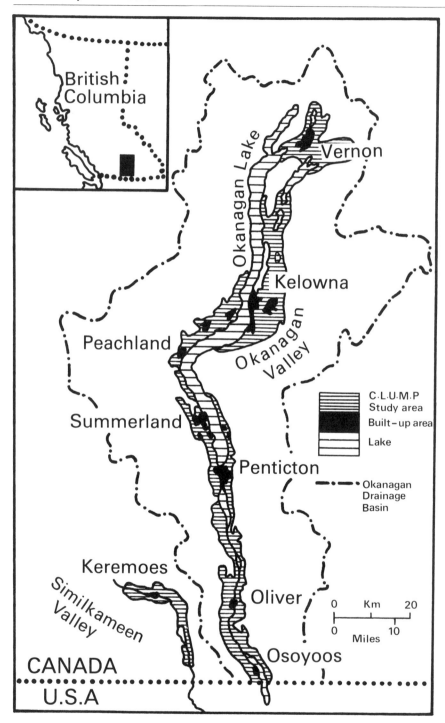

Figure I4.4 **The Okanagan Valley**

ALRs, namely the Farm Income Assurance Act, which provided financial assistance to farmers. This created a trade-off for farmers: while they lost potential land value though the "freeze" on development, they gained income protection.

Despite these encouraging findings, high rates of loss of agricultural land were apparent for several of the smaller towns in British Columbia in the late 1970s. This may indicate some localized relaxation of the strict enforcement of the ALRs, but also reflects increases in low-density housing in rural-urban fringe locations. For example, the Victoria Metropolitan Area experienced a growth in its urban population of only 6 percent between 1976 and 1981, while its rural counterpart experienced a 32 percent increase (Lands Directorate 1985b). This was associated primarily with conglomerations of low-density housing. Some of this development involved infilling on existing subdivided land, but good-quality farmland was also affected, and it is clear that communities needed to develop further plans to guide and control urban and suburban growth more effectively. Subsequent trends suggest that such planning has indeed occurred and is restricting losses of agricultural land.

Although only two examples of measures to preserve farmland have been considered here, several others could have been given to reflect the widespread concern with such policies in both Canada and the United States (Hiemstra and Bushwick 1989). For example, parallel to British Columbia's approach is that of Quebec, where a stringent zoning system was introduced in 1978 under the Loi sur la Protection du Territoire Agricole. Thus, British Columbia and Quebec represent the adoption of strong central controls on farmland preservation in contrast to Ontario's more decentralized plans (Glenn 1985). Neither central controls nor decentralization have been entirely satisfactory, though, simply because of the powerful pressures that urban development can apply. For example, Bunce (1991) notes that on the northern fringes of the Toronto CMA, where it has been the policies of the local municipalities that have been most important in determining rates of loss of farmland, urban sprawl has not been greatly restricted by agricultural designations. Using the example of Markham, he notes that agricultural designations have tended to be used as holding categories for future development. In this case the planners' boundaries between urban and rural simply acted as devices for slowing urban sprawl instead of creating firm protection for agricultural land. Future tests of the effectiveness of existing controls on prime farmland throughout Canada will undoubtedly be posed by continuing low-density urban sprawl and by arguments that rising farm output to land ratios reduce the need to protect all high-quality farmland.

The overriding impression of the hinterland of both large and small Canadian cities in the 1970s and 1980s is of cities extending their influence farther and farther from the urban core. The nature of the influence can be seen in an obvious fashion in terms of new buildings, heralding the arrival of out-migrants in previously small, "undisturbed" communities, and the loss of agricultural land. But it can be seen in many other, and often very subtle, ways: the change in agricultural land use as farmers respond to changing market conditions associated with urban influence, the rise in land values as the land market responds, the emergence of new organizations in small communities to oppose certain types of change, and new opportunities and challenges for areas that for decades were just part of small-town or rural Canada. The city beyond the city continues to reshape the countryside, especially in Canada's heartland, but also throughout the nation.

Acknowledgements

I am indebted to the Carnegie Trust for the Universities of Scotland and to the Travel and Research Funds of the University of Edinburgh and the Department of Geography, University of Edinburgh, for financing research in Canada. During this research I was especially grateful for the assistance provided by Jean Seguin of the Lands Directorate, Environment Canada, and for the hospitality of Professor David Wood and his family. I am also grateful to the following institutions for assistance during the collection of material for this essay: Ryerson Polytechnical Institute, the University of Toronto, McMaster University, York University, Brock University, and Carleton University. The maps and diagrams were skilfully drawn by Elizabeth Clark and Anona Lyons.

Notes

1. Urban-centred regions (UCRs) comprise all land in a Canadian Metropolitan Area (CMA), Census Agglomeration (CA), or other urban centre with a population of 25,000 or greater using 1981 Census of Canada statistics. Minor boundary modifications were made to exclude areas where topographic features prohibit potential settlement (Lands Directorate 1985a, 7). CMAs are defined by Statistics Canada as the main labour market area of an urbanized core or continuous built-up area having 100,000 or more people. CAs are geostatistical areas created by Statistics Canada and comprise at least two adjacent municipalities that are at least partly urban. The urbanized core of CAs must have between 2,000 and 100,000 people, and a population density of at least 386 per square kilometre.
2. The conversion statistics from rural to urban land use are derived from the UCRs component of CLUMP (see Lands Directorate 1985a, 7)

References

Anderson, N.L. 1963. "Aspects of Rural and Urban." *Sociologia Ruralis* 3:8–22.

Beesley, K.B., and G.E. Walker. 1990, "Residence Paths and Community Perception: A Case Study from the Toronto Urban Field." *Canadian Geographer* 34:318–30.

Berry, B.J.L. 1976. "The Counter-urbanization Process: Urban America Since 1970." In B.J.L. Berry, ed., *Urbanization and Counter-urbanization.* Beverly Hills: Sage Publications.

———. 1980. "The Urban Problem." In A.M. Woodruff, ed., *The Farm and the City: Rivals or Allies?*, 37–59. Englewood Cliffs: Prentice-Hall:.

Bourne, L.S. 1978. "Some Myths of Canadian Urbanization: Reflections on the 1976 Census and Beyond." In R.M. Irving, ed., *Readings in Canadian Geography,* 124–39. 3rd ed. Toronto: Holt, Rinehart and Winston.

Bourne, L.S., and R.D. Mackinnon, eds. 1972, "Urban Systems Development in Central Canada." Research Papers, Department of Geography, University of Toronto, no. 9.

Bourne, L.S., and J.H. Simmons. 1979. "Canadian Settlement Trends: An Examination of the Spatial Pattern of Growth 1971–76." Centre for Urban and Community Studies, University of Toronto, Major Reports, no. 15.

Bray, C.E. 1980. "Agricultural Land Regulation in Several Canadian Provinces." *Canadian Public Policy* 6:591–604.

British Columbia Select Standing Committee on Agriculture. 1978. *Inventory of Agricultural Land Reserves in British Columbia, Phase I.* Victoria, B.C.: Legislative Assembly.

Brown, D.L., and J.M. Wardwell, eds. 1980. *New Directions in Urban-Rural Migration: The Population Turnaround in Rural America.* New York: Academic Press.

Bryant, C.R. 1974. "The Anticipation of Urban Expansion: Some Implications for Agricultural Land Use Practices and Land Use Zoning." *Geographica Polonica* 28:93–115.

———. 1982. "The Rural Real Estate Market: Geographic Patterns of Structure and Change in an Urban Fringe Environment." Publications Series, Department of Geography, University of Waterloo, no. 18.

———. 1984. "The Recent Evolution of Farming Landscapes in Urban-Centred Regions." *Landscape Planning* 11: 307–26.

———. 1986. "Agriculture and Urban Development." In M. Pacione, ed., *Progress in Agricultural Geography,* 167–94. Beckenham, Kent: Croom Helm.

Bryant, C.R., L.H. Russwurm, and A.G. McLellan. 1982. *The City's Countryside: Land and Its Management in the Rural-Urban Fringe.* London and New York: Longman.

Bunce, M.F. 1991. "Local Planning and the Role of Rural Land in Metropolitan Regions: The Example of the Toronto Area." In G.M.R.A. van Oort, L.M. van den Berg, J.G. Groenendijk, and A.H.H.M. Kempers, eds. *Limits to Rural Land Use: Proceedings of an International Conference Organized by the "Commission on Changing Rural Systems" of the International Geographical Union (IGU), Amsterdam, Netherlands, 21–25 August 1989,* 113–22. Wageningen: Pudoc.

Clark, S.D. 1968. *The Suburban Society.* Toronto: University of Toronto Press.

Code, W.R. 1983. "The Strength of the Centre: Downtown Offices and Metropolitan Decentralisation Policy in Toronto." *Environment and Planning A* 15:1361–80.

Coffee, W.J., and M. Polese. 1988. "Locational Shifts in Canadian Employment, 1971–1981: Decentralization v Congestion." *Canadian Geographer* 32:248–56.

Cournoyer, R. 1987. "The Use of the Assessment Roll to Determine Urban Land-Use Change in the Province of Quebec." In P.C. Rump and N.M. Hillary, eds., *Monitoring for Change: Workshop Proceedings,* 79–84. Land Use in Canada Series, Lands Directorate, Environment Canada, no. 28.

Dahms, F.A. 1977. "How Ontario's Guelph District Developed." *Canadian Geographical Journal* 94:48–55.

———. 1980. "The Evolving Spatial Organization of Small Settlements in the Countryside – an Ontario Example." *Tijdschrift voor economische en social Geografie* 71:295–306.

Dorin, P.K., and A. van Rietbergen. 1990. "Lifetime Mobility: Interrelationships of Labour Mobility, Residential Mobility and Household Cycle." *Canadian Geographer* 34:33–48.

Furuseth, O.J., and J.T. Pierce. 1982. *Agricultural Land in an Urban Society.* Resource Publications in Geography, Association of American Geographers, Washington, D.C.

Gayler, H.J. 1982a. "The Problems of Adjusting to Slow Growth in the Niagara Region of Ontario." *Canadian Geographer* 26:191–206.

———. 1982b. "Conservation and Development in Urban Growth: The Preservation of Agricultural Land Use in the Rural-Urban Fringe of Ontario." *Town Planning Review* 53:321–41.

———. 1990. "Changing Aspects of Urban Containment in Canada: The Niagara Case in the 1980s and Beyond." *Urban Geography* 11:373–93.

Gertler, L.O., and R. Crowley. 1982. *Changing Canadian Cities: The Next 25 Years.* 2d ed. Toronto: McClelland and Stewart.

Gierman, D.M. 1977. "Rural to Urban Land Conversion." Lands Directorate, Environment Canada, Occasional Papers, no. 16.

Gilg, A.W. 1985. *An Introduction to Rural Geography.* London: Edward Arnold.

Glenn, J.M. 1985. "Approaches to the Protection of Agricultural Land in Quebec and Ontario: Highways and Byways." *Canadian Public Policy – Analyse de Politiques* 11:665–76.

Herington, J. 1984. *The Outer City.* London: Harper and Row.

Hiemstra, H., and N. Bushwick, eds. 1989. *Plowing the Urban Fringe: An Assessment of Alternative Approaches to Farmland Preservation.* Fort Lauderdale: Florida Atlantic University/Florida International University Joint Center for Environmental and Urban Problems.

Hodge, G., and M.A. Qadeer. 1983. *Towns and Villages in Canada: The Importance of Being Unimportant.* Toronto: Butterworths.

Jackson, J.N. 1982. "The Niagara Fruit Belt: The Ontario Municipal Board Decision of 1981." *Canadian Geographer* 26:172–76.

———. 1985. "Management of Rural Resources: The Niagara Peninsula." Paper presented to Management of Rural Resources Conference, University of Guelph, Ontario.

Jackson, J.N., ed. 1986. "The Niagara Region: Trends and Propects – The Challenge of Change." Occasional Publications, Department of Geography, Brock University, no. 4.

Johnston, T., and B.E. Smit. 1985 "An Evaluation of the Rationale for Farmland Preservation Policy in Ontario." *Land Use Policy* 2:225–37.

Joseph, A.E., P.D. Keddie, and B. Smit. 1988. "Unravelling the Population Turnaround in Rural Canada." *Canadian Geographer* 32:17–30.

Joseph, A.E., and B.E. Smit. 1981. "Implications of Exurban Residential Development – A Review." *Canadian Journal of Regional Science* 4:207–24.

Joseph, A.E., B. Smit, and G.P. McIlravey, 1989. "Consumer Preferences for Rural Residences: A Conjoint Analysis in Ontario, Canada." *Environment and Planning A* 21:47–64.

Kreuger, R.R. 1965. "The Geography of the Orchard Industry of Canada." *Geographical Bulletin* 7:27–71.

———. 1977. "The Destruction of a Unique Renewable Resource: The Case of the Niagara Fruit Belt." In R.R. Krueger and B. Mitchell, eds., *Managing Canada's Renewable Resources*, 132–48. London: Methuen.

———. 1978. "Urbanization of the Niagara Fruit Belt." *Canadian Geographer* 22:179–94.

———. 1984. "The Struggle to Preserve Speciality Crop Production in the Rural-Urban Fringe of the Niagara Peninsula of Ontario." In M.F. Bunce and M.F. Troughton, ed., *The Pressures of Change in Rural Canada*, 292–313. Toronto: Department of Geography, York University.

Krushelnicki, B.W., and S.J. Bell. 1989. "Monitoring the Loss of Agricultural Land: Identifying the Urban Price Shadow in the Niagara Region, Canada." *Land Use Policy* 6:141–50.

Lands Directorate. 1976. "Land Capability for Agriculture: A Preliminary Report." *Canada Land Inventory Report*, no. 10. Ottawa: Environment Canada.

———. 1980 "C.L.U.M.P." Discussion Papers, Land Use Monitoring Division. Ottawa: Environment Canada.

———. 1985a. "Urbanization of Rural Land in Canada." *Land Use Change in Canada, Fact Sheets*, no. 85–84. Ottawa: Environment Canada.

———. 1985b. "Victoria Urban-Centred Region 1976–1980." *Land Use Change in Canada, Fact Sheets*, no. 85–86. Ottawa: Environment Canada.

———. 1986. *Urbanization of Rural Land in Canada: Supplementary Tables for Fact Sheet 85–84*. Ottawa: Environment Canada.

Layton, R.L. 1978. "The Operational Structure of the Hobby Farm." *Area* 10:242–46.

———. 1979. "Hobby Farming." *Geography* 65:220–23.

———. 1981. "Attitudes of Hobby and Commercial Farmers in the Rural-Urban Fringe of London, Ontario." *Cambria* 8:33–44.

Malzahn, M. 1979. "B.C.'s Green Acres: A Look at the Future of Farmland in B.C." *Urban Reader* 7:14–19.

Manning, E.W., and S.S. Eddy. 1978. "The Agricultural Land Reserves of British Columbia: An Impact Analysis." Land Use in Canada Series, Lands Directorate, Environment Canada, no. 13.

Martin, L.R.G. 1975. *Land Use Dynamics on the Toronto Urban Fringe*. Ottawa: Environment Canada.

———. 1984. "Urban Diversion and Land Market Dynamics on the Rural-Urban Fringe." In M.F. Bunce and M.J. Troughton, eds., "The Pressures of Change in Rural Canada." Geographical Monographs, York University, no. 14, 181–201.

Neimanis, V.P. 1979. "Canada's Cities and Their Surrounding Land Resources." *Canada Land Inventory Reports*, no. 15. Ottawa: Lands Directorate, Environment Canada.

Ontario Ministry of Agriculture and Food. 1978. *Food Land Guidelines.* Toronto: Queen's Printer.

Pacione, M. 1984. *Rural Geography.* London: Harper and Row.

Pahl, R.E. 1965. "Urbs in Rure: The Metropolitan Fringe in Hertfordshire:" Geographical Papers, London School of Economics, no 2.

Pierce, J.T. 1981. "Conversion of Rural Land to Urban: A Canadian Profile." *Professional Geographer* 33:163–73.

Preston, R.E., and L.H. Russwurm. 1977. "The Developing Canadian Urban Pattern: An Analysis of Population Change, 1971–1976." In R.E. Preston and L.H. Russwurm, eds., *Essays on Canadian Urbanization,* 1–30. Department of Geography, University of Waterloo.

Punter, J.V. 1976. *The Impact of Exurban Development on Land and Landscape in the Toronto-Centred Region, 1954–1971.* Ottawa: Central Mortgage and Housing Corporation.

Ray, D.M. 1971. "Dimensions of Canadian Regionalism." Geographical Papers, Department of Energy, Mines and Resources, Ottawa, no. 49.

Raynor, I. 1980. *Canadian Public Priorities, the Canadian Mortgage and Housing Corporation Survey.* Ottawa: Supply and Services Canada.

Regional Muncipality of Niagara. 1988. *Regional Niagara Policy Plan: Office Consolidation.* Thorold, Ont.: Regional Municipality of Niagara.

Robinson, G.M. 1990. *Conflict and Change in the Countryside: Rural Society, Economy and Planning in the Developed World.* London and New York: Belhaven Press.

Rodd, R.S. 1976. "The Crisis of Agricultural Land in the Ontario Countryside." *Plan Canada* 16:160–70.

Rump, P.C. 1983. "Land Inventories in Canada." In R.L. Gentilcore, ed., *China in Canada: A Dialogue on Resources and Development.* Hamilton: McMaster University.

Rump. P.C., and N.M. Hillary, eds. 1987. "Monitoring for Change: Workshop Proceedings." Land Use in Canada Series, Lands Directorate, Environment Canada, no. 28.

Russwurm, L.H. 1975. "Urban Fringe and Urban Shadow." In R.C. Bryfogle and R.R. Krueger, eds., *Urban Problems,* 148–64. Rev. ed. Toronto: Holt, Rinehart and Winston.

———. 1977. *The Surroundings of Our Cities.* Ottawa: Community Planning Press.

Seguin, J. 1987. "The Use of Air Photography for Monitoring Land-Use Change in Canada's Fruitlands." In P.C. Rump and N.M. Hillary, eds. "Monitoring for Change: Workshop Proceedings." Land Use in Canada Series, Lands Directorate, Environment Canada, no. 28, 69–74

Semple, R.K., and M.B. Green. 1983. "Interurban Corporate Head-quarters Relocation in Canada." *Cahiers de géographie du Québec* 27:389–406.

Simmons, J.W. 1984. "Key Processes in Canadian Settlement Trends." In L.S. Bourne and J.W. Simmons, eds., *Proceedings of an Invitational Seminar on Urbanization: Canadian Perspectives on Urban Growth and Decline,* 21–27. Vancouver: Centre for Human Settlements, University of British Columbia.

Sinclair, P.R., and K. Westhues. 1975. *Village in Crisis.* Toronto: Holt, Rinehart and Winston.

Sinclair, R. 1967. "Von Thunen and Urban Sprawl." *Annals of the Association of American Geographers* 57:72–87.

Smit, B.E., and C. Conklin. 1981. "Future Urban Growth and Agricultural Land: Alternatives for Ontario." *Ontario Geographer* 18:47–55.

Smit, B.E., and M.F. Flaherty. 1981. "Resident Attitudes toward Exurban Development in a Rural Ontario Township." *Professional Geographer* 33:103–12.

Stupich, D.D. 1975. "British Columbia Passes Vital Land Legislation." In R.C. Bryfogle and R.R. Krueger, eds., *Urban Problems Revised,* 328–30. Toronto: Holt, Rinehart and Winston.

Szplett, E.S. 1983. "The Current State of Office Location and Office Functions in Canada: 1. Managerial Aspects of the Firm." *The Operational Geographer* 1 (2): 35–39.

———. 1984. "The Current State of Office Location and Office Functions in Canada: 2. Office Location and Linkage." *The Operational Geographer* 1 (3): 27–31.

Walker, G. 1974. "Social Interactions in the Holland Marsh." *Ontario Geography* 8:52–63.

———. 1975. "Social Networks in Rural Space: A Comparison of Two Southern Ontario Localities." *East Lakes Geographer* 10:68–78.

———. 1976. "Social Perspectives on the Countryside." *Ontario Geographer* 10:54–63.

———. 1977. "Social Networks and Territory in a Commuter Village, Bond Head, Ontario." *Canadian Geographer* 21:329–50.

Walker, G.E. 1987. "An Invaded Countryside: Structures of Life on the Toronto Fringe." Geographical Monographs, Atkinson College, York University, no. 17.

Warren, C.L., A. Kerr, and A.M. Turner. 1989. "Urbanization of Rural Land in Canada, 1981–86." *State of the Environment Fact Sheet*, no. 89–81. Ottawa: Environment Canada.

Warren, C.L., and P.C. Rump. 1981. "The Urbanization of Rural Land in Canada: 1966–1971 and 1971–1976." Land Use in Canada Series, Lands Directorate, Environment Canada, no. 20.

Williams, D., and A. Pohl. 1987. "'Let them eat houses!' The Implications of Urban Expansion onto Good Farmland." In C. Cocklin, B. Smit, and T. Johnston, eds., *Demands on Rural Lands: Planning for Resource Use,* 85–96. Boulder and London: Westview Press.

Wilson, J.W., and J.T. Pierce. 1984. "The Agricultural Land Commission of British Columbia." In M.F. Bunce and M.J. Troughton, eds., "The Pressures of Change in Rural Canada." Geographical Monographs, Department of Geography, Atkinson College, York University, no. 14, 272–91.

Yeates, M.H. 1975. *Main Street.* Toronto: Macmillan.

———. 1985 "Land in Canada's Urban Heartland." Land Use in Canada Series, Lands Directorate, Environment Canada, no. 27.

15 Rural Change in the Prairies

William J. Carlyle

15.1 Introduction

Many changes have taken place in the rural parts of the Prairies during the past 50 years. To a large degree human and animal labour have been replaced by machines. Mechanization of agriculture has led to fewer and larger farms while, at the same time, the total amount of farmland, and especially improved land, has increased. Automobiles, trucks, and better roads have shortened travel time, and the focus of rural life has shifted away from the local setting to a wider, more urban-oriented, one. Rural people have come to expect, and many have achieved, a standard of living equal to that of urban inhabitants. Indeed, in almost all aspects of cultural life, there has been a lessening of the distinction between rural and urban over the past one or two generations.

Changes similar to these have taken place in much of the industrialized world, but there are significant geographical differences in the extent, pace, and background of these changes in Canada. On the Canadian Prairies agricultural settlement did not begin in earnest until the 1870s, and the transition from pioneer settlement to the development of a relatively simple agricultural society and, more recently, to a complex, industrialized, urbanized, and increasingly metropolitan-dominated way of life has taken place over the short time span of 50 to 100 years. This sequence of change occurred over hundreds and even thousands of years in longer-settled regions of the now industrialized world. Thus, upheaval, dislocation, adjustment, and new beginnings rather than stability and gradual change have been characteristic of life on the Canadian Prairies from the onset of agricultural settlement.

The climate, soils, and generally flat to undulating topography of the Prairies all have lent themselves to the development of large-scale mechanized agriculture based on extensive cash grain and grain-fed livestock production for markets distant from this relatively sparsely populated region. In the process, Prairie farms, which were always very large, by world standards, for family-operated farms and well above the norms for most industrialized regions, have become even larger, and progressively fewer farmers are needed to till even more land overall than a generation or two ago. Unlike many industrialized and urbanized regions, except near the few large cities, there has not been an influx of rural non-farm people to counterbalance the flight from farms and the decline of small, rural service centres.

Ever since the days of the fur trade, the development of transportation has been vital to Canadians, as befits a nation so thinly spread over such a vast area. Nowhere in Canada is this more true than the Prairies, where the railway and initial settlement were symbiotic. The railways carried the exports of agricultural produce and the imports of manufactured goods that allowed commercial development of the region.

Until recently, most long distance movements of people and goods, both within and to and from the region, were carried by rail. Because of this and the fact that the railway provided the only direct link between the Prairies and the rest of Canada, railways have become a symbol of the region. Grain elevators dotted along the railways have also become stereotypes of Prairie life. The necessity of access to service centres, with their railways and grain elevators, made the development and condition of roads of the utmost importance to the early settlers on the Prairies, and this concern is no less strong today. Indeed, the Prairies undoubtedly have as great a mileage of developed roads per rural dweller as any agricultural region on earth, if not greater.

Roads have been vastly improved on the Prairies over the past 50 years and this, together with motorized transport, has expanded the economic and social horizons of the rural inhabitants. Partly as a consequence of these changes, the railway and grain elevator network has been thinned out, and there has been a widespread decline of unincorporated hamlets and small villages. This shift from the local and agricultural to the regional and urban has also affected the systems of schooling, which were developed at an earlier time for quite different conditions than those prevailing today in rural parts of the Prairies.

Another characteristic of the Prairies that stems from the beginning of agricultural settlement has been the ethnic and religious mosaic. Peoples from many countries and regions of North America and Europe began life anew on the Prairies, often in ethnically homogeneous blocks. Especially the more disadvantaged or religious of them viewed the Prairies as a "Promised Land" or a "New Jerusalem" (Rees 1988; Smillie 1983). The difficulties of prairie homesteading, the commercialism of life in North America, and time itself have wrought many changes on the way of life and the cohesiveness of these groups.

The purpose of this essay is to examine the ways and degrees to which these characteristics of prairie rural society have changed over the past half century, and to suggest trends for the foreseeable future. The essay will be confined to a discussion of the main settlement zone of the Prairie provinces. Areas north of this zone and Indian reserves, national parks, and military camps within it will not be considered. Changes in the distribution and types of rural population within the main settlement zone will be examined first, because they are both the cause and consequence of many other rural trends.

15.2   Population Change

The settlement frontier, here defined as a population of 72 in a typical 93-square-kilometre township or an average of 0.75 people per square kilometre expanded relatively slowly on the Prairies from 1870 to 1900. Thereafter, it spread rapidly, filling in the remaining parts of the parkland and moving into the arc of mixed-grass prairie stretching from south-eastern Saskatchewan to the Rockies (Figure 15.1). Pioneer settlers did not move into the drier core south of this arc until the second and third decades of the twentieth century. By 1931 most of the suitable agricultural land, except for parts of the Peace River district in north-western Alberta, had at least been thinly populated (Kerr and Holdsworth 1990).

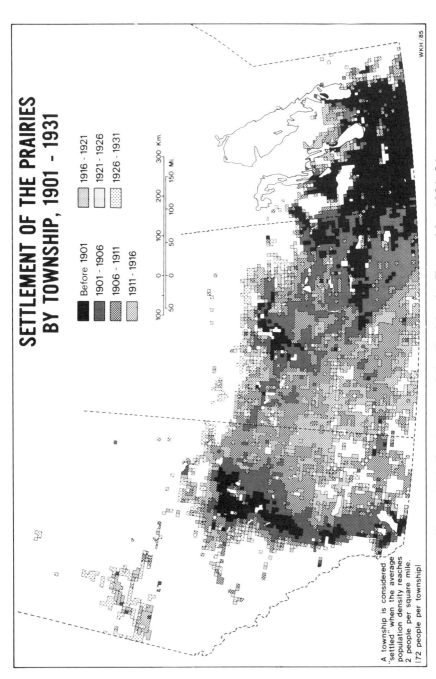

SETTLEMENT OF THE PRAIRIES BY TOWNSHIP, 1901 - 1931

Before 1901
1901 - 1906
1906 - 1911
1911 - 1916
1916 - 1921
1921 - 1926
1926 - 1931

100   50   0   50   100   150   200   300 Km.

0   50   100   150 Mi.

WKH/.85

A township is considered "settled" when the average population density reaches 2 people per square mile. (72 people per township)

Figure 15.1 Settlement of the Prairies by Township, 1901–31

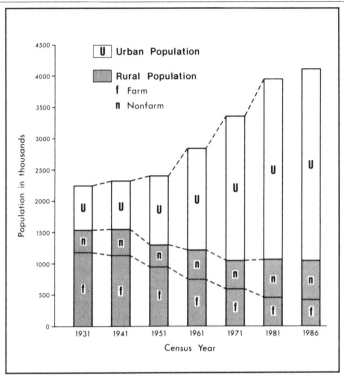

Figure 15.2   **Rural Farm, Non-farm, and Urban Population on the Prairies, 1931–81 (data are for the main settlement zone, and exclude Indian reserves, national parks, and military camps within it)**

Throughout this period most settlement was rural, and rural attitudes and institutions were hallmarks of the Prairie region. Moreover, rural life was largely synonymous with farm life, and the characterization of the Prairies as an agricultural region, both in terms of livelihood and outlook, was apt until at least the 1930s.

The rural population of the Prairies peaked in the 1930s. Since then, the farm population has declined by almost two-thirds, and by 1986 people living on farms comprised only 10 percent of the total population in the main zone of settlement (Figure 15.2). However, the rural non-farm population, defined for census purposes as "people living in incorporated or unincorporated nucleated centres of less than 1,000 people or in dispersed rural non-farm dwellings," has increased by some 90 percent since 1931.[1] Overall, the rural population has declined by almost one-third between 1931 and 1986, and now comprises only one-quarter of the total population of the Prairie region. During the same period, and especially since the 1950s, the urban population has risen dramatically in absolute terms and as a proportion of the total population of the Prairies (Smith 1984). The largest centres have accounted for most of this growth, and by 1986 slightly more than half of all Prairie people lived in the metropolitan centres of Winnipeg, Edmonton, Calgary, Regina, and Saskatoon.

Growth and decline in the rural population since the 1930s have been distributed unequally both spatially and temporally within the Prairies (Figure 15.3). Since the 1960s, the rural non-farm population located in close proximity to the larger urban centres, and many of the smaller ones, has increased progressively as more and more people who work in cities and large towns seek a rural residence. Where these increases in the rural non-farm population have exceeded losses in the population on farms, such as around Winnipeg and in the Edmonton to Calgary corridor, the overall rural population has risen. In addition, the farm population near the large urban centres has tended to decline less than in the rest of the region, and in a few districts even to increase, because off-farm incomes derived from jobs in the cities help maintain many farms as economic units. Also, there exists here an opportunity for smaller more intensive farms to develop because of the close proximity to urban markets (Carlyle 1989). Increases in population occurred from 1936 to 1976 on the northern and western fringes of settlement, including the Peace River district, but within this overall growth there was a slight decrease from the peak rural populations recorded earlier in the period (Vanderhill 1982). Elsewhere, increases have been largely confined to parts of southeastern Alberta, where irrigated agriculture has been developed or expanded in recent years (Figure 15.3).

Zones of moderate decrease in the context of the Prairies, up to 49 percent, surround the areas of increase at either end of the region (Figure 15.3). In these zones, the same urban influences, although weaker, have mitigated rural losses.

The vast central core of the region, however, has felt the full force of agricultural change with no offsetting urban influences. In most districts within this central region, the rural population, here largely synonymous with farm population, has declined by 50 percent or more since the 1930s (Figure 15.3).

Mechanization of agriculture has led to fewer but larger farms and a reduction of hired labourers on farms. The number of people per farm household has decreased considerably since the 1930s, mainly because of the decline in average size of families. In farming districts where there has been no influx of rural non-farm people, a decline of one-quarter in the rural population can be attributed to this change alone. In addition, more so than in the past, grain farms are operated by people who reside most of the year in sizeable urban centres, and hence form part of the urban rather than rural population. Another reason for the decline is that farmers today expect a higher standard of living than they did in the 1930s. The agricultural resources that once could support several families now maintain only one farm family at a higher level of material well-being.

These changes in the aspirations and numbers of the farm population, together with railway abandonment, the closure of grain elevators, and the shortening of travel time brought about by motorized transport and better roads, have all combined to cause the bypassing and decline of many of the smaller service centres on the Prairies. Although in recent years there has been an overall rise in the rural non-farm population, increases have been largely confined to zones near the larger towns and cities. Rural non-farm losses associated with the decline of hamlets and small villages are much more typical.

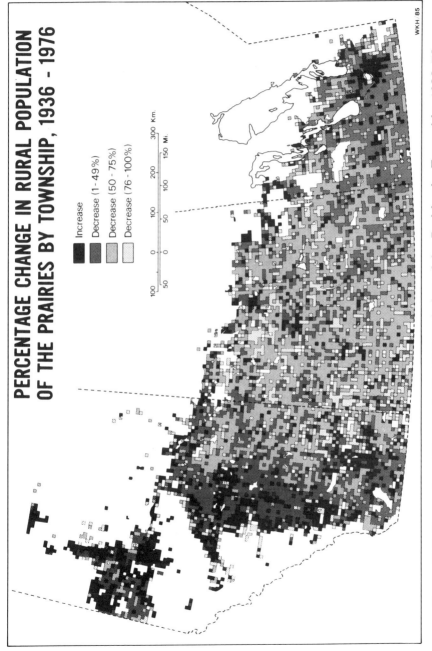

PERCENTAGE CHANGE IN RURAL POPULATION
OF THE PRAIRIES BY TOWNSHIP, 1936 - 1976

Increase
Decrease (1 - 49%)
Decrease (50 - 75%)
Decrease (76 - 100%)

Figure 15.3 Percentage Change in Rural Population of the Prairies by Township, 1936–76

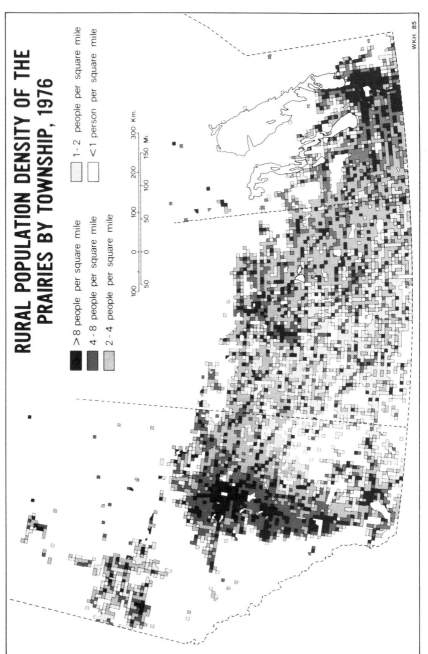

Figure 15.4 Rural Population Density of the Prairies by Township, 1976

Hence, over most of the Prairie region, what were already low population densities in 1936 have been reduced to even lower levels at the present time (Figure 15.4). Indeed, a large part of the region would not be considered settled or even occupied, by standards used in many parts of the world (e.g., Hart 1975, 62–63). These changes in population can be attributed mainly to technological and economic forces, although social considerations, too, have contributed. The causes of these changes and their effect on the prairie landscape will now be considered.

15.3   Land and Livelihood

Regulations set by the Dominion government assured that most Prairie farms during the pioneer period were of about the same size, if not of equal productivity. Farms initially comprised a quarter-section of about 65 hectares arranged in a square, 0.8 kilometres to a side. To this could be added another quarter-section by pre-emption or purchase of railway, school, or Hudson's Bay Company land (Martin 1973). Common problems facing the pioneers promoted mutual aid and encouraged a feeling of closeness and equality. Elizabeth B. Mitchell, who visited the Prairies just before the First World War, graphically summed up Prairie society in an English-speaking settlement as follows:

> Entertaining is not "a social duty," but a simple pleasure. You entertain not "the best people" but either people you like or the wayfarers who have to be put up for the night because there is nowhere else for them to go. Perfect democratic equality is hardly to be found on earth, but one is very near it here, where every man is a farmer or the son of a farmer or going to be a farmer, and the hired-man may play bezique very pleasantly with the master of evenings after working shoulder to shoulder with him all day. (Mitchell 1981, 145–46)

There is ample evidence, however, to show that many English-speaking settlers were less than socially democratic in their view and treatment of settlers of other backgrounds, notably peasant groups from central and Eastern European (e.g., Lehr and Moodie 1980). Notwithstanding this, there was undoubtedly far less social and economic stratification in the Prairies than would be found in most parts of the world in the early 1900s.

Inevitably, as time went on, some farmers were able to expand the size of their farms more than others, but in 1936 quarter- and half-section farms still predominated on the Prairies. Mechanization of agriculture, which had begun on the Prairies almost from the beginning of settlement, gathered force after the Second World War, and has led to progressive increases in the size of farms. Indeed, for the Prairies as a whole, the average size of farm increased from 152 to 370 hectares between 1936 and 1986.[2]

These hectarages do not tell the entire story. Farms of two quarter-sections (130 hectares) or less comprise about three-tenths of all Prairie farms, and almost six-tenths are less than five quarter-sections (324 hectares). However, the overall average size is increased by the presence of a minority of large and very large holdings. An

Table   **Size of Farm by Gross Farm Sales: Prairie Provinces,**
15.1   **1966 to 1981**

Size of Farm by Gross Farm Sales (constant 1975 $)	Percentage of Census Farms			Percentage of Total Gross Farm Output		
	1966	**1971**	**1981**	**1966**	**1971**	**1981**
< 10,000	42	36	30	10	7	3
10,000–24,999	36	35	26	31	23	11
25,000–49,999	17	19	24	30	27	23
50,000–74,999	3	5	10	10	12	16
75,000–99,999	1	2	4	5	6	10
>100,000	1	3	6	14	25	37
Farms (000s)	195	175	155			
Gross Sales (millions of constant 1975 $)				3721	4322	5845

Source: Statistics Canada, unpublished data

analysis of the size of farm by value of output is even more revealing. Of particular note is the increasingly large proportion of the total output of Prairie farms that is accounted for by a small number of highly productive farms, notably those with sales of $100,000 or more (see Table 15.1). Many of these farms have large hectarages, but some, especially those in Manitoba and Alberta, are medium to small farms devoted to intensive production of livestock, poultry, or crops.

It is clear therefore that mechanization and specialization, together with differences in management skills and natural conditions, have led to an increasing disparity in the economic well-being and geographical size of Prairie farms, and that capital and output on farms have become more and more concentrated into fewer and fewer hands. Whether this trend has created a rigid social hierarchy among farmers is debatable. The author's experience, which has been largely confined to farms in Manitoba, would suggest that the social differences are not as much as might be expected.

For example, when visiting one of the largest farms in south-west Manitoba, a grain and cattle operation comprising about 5,460 hectares or 55 square kilometres with a market value of some seven million dollars, the author was surprised that the two brothers who together owned the farm lived with their families in modest bungalows and lacked any obvious social or economic pretensions, other than that expressed in their farm machinery. Two hired hands worked with the brothers on an apparently informal social basis, much as described by Elizabeth B. Mitchell. Another instance is that of an acquaintance of the author who lives in Winnipeg and who the author knew as a "part-time" farmer for several years before discovering that, in addition to a job in Winnipeg, he ran a grain farm of about 6,475 hectares, or the equivalent of 100 quarter-section pioneer homesteads.

In the Prairies, there is little ostentatious show of wealth or social stratification accompanying the enlargement of farms and the disparities in the size of farms. Many Prairie people, however, are concerned and even alarmed by the suddenness and scale of farm closures and the change in attitude towards agriculture and agricultural land.

Between 1936 and 1986, the number of Prairie farms decreased by slightly more than one half, from 300,000 to 149,000. In most farm districts there has been no compensatory increase in rural non-farm dwellings, so the remaining farmsteads are increasingly far apart, except where clustering has developed along main roads through the physical relocation of existing farmsteads and the building of new ones. Thus, although even at the height of farm settlement 50 or so years ago there was a very bare human landscape, it has now become even more lacking in signs of human occupancy. Over large tracts only unfenced fields and transportation routes, with perhaps oil pumps moving up and down like perpetually pecking birds, attest to man's presence. While it is true that farmers today can travel over rural roads at up to 80 to 90 kilometres in an hour in most weathers, thereby expanding their social and economic space, the fact remains that the prairie landscape is becoming increasingly devoid of that most basic element of human occupance, the farmhouse.

This process has been most extreme in parts of the short-grass prairie of south-western Saskatchewan and south-western Alberta, where farms and ranches are more easily measured in square kilometres than hectares and, in addition to the disappearance of three-quarters or more of the farmsteads, some entire hamlets and small villages have become virtual "ghost towns." One writer, speaking of this area, commented:

Everywhere sagging silhouettes of farms and ranches are reminders that homesteads were just a short phase in the early accumulation of prairie resources, a phase initiated and foreclosed by banks and railroads. With populations clustered at ever-widening coordinates, the prairie itself becomes the space in between, a surface to be harvested, drilled and navigated by ever more efficient machines. Small towns ungraced by asphalt simply got in the way of the fields. (Johnson 1984, 120)

Yet, it is overly simplistic to attribute the disappearance of farms and decline of small service centres to any single cause or a limited number of causes, such as "banks and railroads," because these are but manifestations of wider economic and social forces affecting Prairie society.

From a strictly economic point of view, the decline in the number of Prairie farms is understandable, even predictable. What has happened on the Prairies is not unique; it is part of a much wider trend in all free-market industrialized countries towards fewer and larger farms brought about by mechanization, specialization, and commercialization of agriculture. In the process capital has increasingly replaced labour and land in farm production, and farmers themselves have had to increase their management and business skills. A rising proportion of farm costs is being devoted to off-farm purchases of commodities such as seeds, fertilizers, herbicides, pesticides, and machinery and equipment, as well as chartered accountants, tax lawyers, and other professional services. Farmers who, for one reason or another, have not been able to adapt to these changes have had to give up farming, and their land and other assets have gone to those who have successfully adjusted to economic conditions. Similarly, banks, railway and grain elevator companies, and others who are part of the agricultural production process have had to keep their books in order, as expressed in higher interest rates and rationalization of services.

Most Prairie farmers appear to accept this economic order, and there can be no denying that output from Prairie farms, except in years of extremely poor weather or infestations of grasshoppers, is higher than ever before, and that many, and perhaps most, of the farmers enjoy a higher standard of living than in the past. At the same time, many farmers and others concerned with prairie rural life feel betrayed, confused, or powerless in the face of these impersonal economic forces. Prairie farmers are particularly upset by the fact that they have to accept world market prices for their grain and, more specifically, because grain prices have not been increasing at a rate commensurate with farm costs. In addition, because so much of Prairie grain is exported, sudden and wide swings in the market are commonplace, which adds a high degree of uncertainty to what, because of natural hazards, is already a risky venture. Rising interest rates add to this problem because most farmers have accumulated considerable debt in trying to expand and adapt their holdings to accommodate the prevailing economic conditions.

These economic problems have been offset to a degree by financial support from outside the farming community. The shipment of grain on the railway has long been subsidized, mainly by the railway companies. More recently, through a series of *ad hoc* programs, the federal government has paid substantial amounts to Prairie farmers in years of extreme financial hardship, and permanent price support schemes are under consideration. This government support can be viewed as a response to the heavy subsidization of agriculture in the European Community, which competes for markets with Prairie farmers. Even with financial support, however, many Prairie farms are in a precarious financial state and, increasingly, farmers and their families resort to off-farm work to supplement income from agriculture.

Government settlement policy in pioneer days guaranteed that single-family farms predominated on the Prairies. Despite much publicity to the contrary, the vast majority of Prairie farms, indeed more than 95 percent, are still family farms. However, there has been a trend in recent years towards new types of family farm. To an increasing degree, there has been the establishment of nuclear and extended family partnerships and corporations (Table 15.2). Partnership and multiple-family corporate farms allow resources to be pooled, discounts to be obtained by bulk purchases, greater efficiency in the use of large machinery, collective planning of farm and financial decisions, and some tax advantages. In addition, a considerable proportion of farmers operating what the census lists as "individual or family farms" share purchases, farmwork, machinery, and equipment with their neighbours, usually family members, in an attempt to reduce overall costs (Carlyle 1983a). Another way

Table **Types of Farm Organization on the Prairies, 1971 and 1986**
15.2

Type	Percentage 1971	Distribution by Type 1986
Individual or Family[1]	91.8	84.3
Partnership	5.9	10.8
Legally Constituted Company		
(Corporation): Family	1.7	4.0
Other	0.2	0.3
Other Types[2]	0.4	0.6
Number of Farms	**174,653**	**148,544**

1. Defined as "privately operated by an individual" in 1971 and as "individual or family" in 1981, the change in 1981 being made to take into account the contribution of spouses and children to the running of a farm where there is, nevertheless, only one principal operator.
2. Hutterite colonies, institutional farms, and community pastures owned by the local, provincial, or federal government are included with this type.

Source: Censuses of Canada

to reduce costs involves attempts to arrange the parcels of farm units in a spatially efficient manner (see Carlyle 1983b). This has become of greater concern in recent years, as necessity has led most Prairie farmers to acquire land across roads or completely separated from their farmstead piece.

The quest for ever increasing efficiency has sometimes produced results that have alarmed people, including many farmers who are interested in the natural environment. One focus of concern stems from the fact that rising costs and large-scale machinery have led many Prairie farmers to expand their improved hectarage to the long-term detriment of the environment. Woodlots have been cleared on agriculturally marginal land, and field shelterbelts that were planted to reduce soil erosion by wind have been removed. Poorly drained depressions have been infilled to the detriment of wildlife and local ground water supplies. These modifications have sometimes been made more to avoid the necessity of slowing down and making turns to avoid these obstacles than to acquire additional farmland. The Canadian Wheat Board has contributed to the environmentally inadvisable improvement of land through its policy of not allowing farmers to claim unimproved land on their allotment of hectarage for grain delivery. This policy entices farmers to improve and cultivate marginal land, so that their allotment can be increased (Sawatzky 1979). Taxation of unimproved land also contributes to the problem. Farmers attempt improvement of poor land to get some income from it instead of paying taxes on unimproved land, from which there is no financial return. However, this tendency towards a more cost efficient but open and less varied landscape has been offset to a degree by the activities of some public and private agencies, such as the Prairie Farm Rehabilitation Administration and Ducks Unlimited, who have assisted farmers in planting field shelterbelts, maintaining or creating wetlands, and sowing erosion-susceptible soils with forage rather than grain crops.

Changes over the last 50 years have also affected the institutions or institutional framework of Prairie rural society. Some of the most important of these institutions will now be examined.

15.4   Social and Economic Institutions
15.4.1   Railways and Grain Elevators

Each phase in the economy and mode of living of Prairie people during the historic period has been identified by a few aptly chosen symbols. Indian cultures in the eighteenth and nineteenth centuries were portrayed by and for people of European origin through description, sketches, and paintings of the Indians themselves, their horses and skin tents, and the bison herds on which so much of their livelihood and culture depended. At the same time, canoes, boats, boatmen, oxcarts, furs, traders, and trading posts encapsulated the European presence in the region. The period of agricultural settlement that followed was represented by ox- or horse-drawn ploughs, virgin land being cleared and broken, lonely homesteads of sod or logs, and immigration sheds packed with people of a variety of dress and culture. In more recent years, the main images of prairie life have been of wheat fields ripening or being harvested under a vast blue canopy punctuated by cotton-ball clouds, railways or section roads stretching to a distant vanishing point on an uninterrupted horizon, and grain elevators pointing skywards, like cathedrals, breaking an otherwise horizontal geometry. Scenes similar to other regions of North America, such as delapidated houses in city centres and modern homes sprawling across suburbia and beyond, dairy and vegetable farms, lake and riverside cottages, and airports are seldom portrayed. Yet, with the rapid urbanization of recent years, most Prairie people now spend the greater part of their lives amid these undepicted landscapes, and an increasing number seldom see at first hand the rural scenes by which the Prairies are presented to outsiders.

Even within the rural areas, a large proportion of people live on the fringes of urban centres, and have little to do with open spaces, grain elevators, or wheat fields. More likely, they are preoccupied with ponies for their children, the condition of roads, water and sewerage facilities, and the cost of commuting daily to nearby cities for work and recreation.

Vast areas of the Prairies, though, are still almost wholly populated by farming people and, in these areas, many of the established symbols of prairie life still have an aptness and a validity. To an increasing degree, however, even these areas are undergoing change to such an extent that a new or revised set of images will have to be developed. Farmsteads are still dispersed and physically isolated, but social contact outside the home is probably greater than ever before because farm people can travel as much as 100 kilometres in an hour and generally have more leisure time for social activities than formerly. For many, farming is only a part-time occupation, supplemented by work in an urban centre and, in many cases, the farm is operated seasonally from a permanent residence in the urban centre itself. Thus, even in what appears to be a traditional farming district, there is often a strong urban influence both on the economy and the manner of living.

Two well-known symbols of prairie life, railways and grain elevators, are also undergoing change. These two features were essential to early agricultural settlement on the Prairies. A network of railways brought in people and goods, and hauled grain and livestock produced in the region to distant markets and ports. Small service centres, each in turn with one or more elevators for storing and trans-shipping grain, were established at intervals of 8 to 16 kilometres along the railways, within easy access by horse-drawn wagon of the farms in the vicinity. Once established, the network remained virtually unchanged for many years. Recently, however, there has been a large-scale reorganization of the system in response to changing economic and social conditions, albeit against the wishes of much of the rural community.

By the 1930s about 2,000 railside grain delivery points, comprising some 5,500 grain elevators in all, served farmers in the Prairie region. These numbers changed little until the early 1950s. Since then, at first slowly, and then more rapidly, the numbers have declined. Overall, between 1953 and 1983, the number of grain elevators and grain delivery points declined from 5,368 to 2,784 and from 2,078 to 1,175 respectively (Figures 15.5 to 15.7) (Canadian International Grains Institute 1982, 150–51; Canadian Grain Commission 1983, xi). A small proportion of these losses has occurred on short spur lines or sidings, where one or two elevators sat isolated beside a farmer's field. Most commonly, however, the elevators have been removed from service centres. In most cases, redundant elevators have been demolished in situ or purchased by farmers for storage of grain.

Loss of one or more elevators from a service centre that has others is not viewed too seriously, because the surrounding farming community continues to use the remaining elevators, which are usually enlarged in storage capacity as the others are closed. But farmers and townspeople alike become considerably concerned when a delivery point comprising only one or more elevators is completely removed from a community, and even more so if an entire railway branch line and all its delivery points become redundant (Figures 15.5 to 15.7). Loss of a delivery point forces farmers to go farther afield to deliver grain, thereby adding to their expenses, and townspeople, particularly in very small centres, anticipate a loss in trade because farmers will no longer be visiting the centre to deliver their grain.

Viewed in a wider context, however, there is considerable justification for these changes. Farmers now haul grain by truck, not horse-drawn wagon, making a haul of 30 or 50 kilometres not unreasonable. Also, grain handling has become concentrated in a few large companies instead of many small ones. This has facilitated the closure of small, inefficient elevators and the expansion of others. In a similar manner, the railway companies can justify the abandonment of uneconomic branch lines.

Strong resistance by the farming community to these closures and abandonments is understandable, but probably is not based primarily on the economic considerations put forward. Farmers themselves have contributed to the decline of

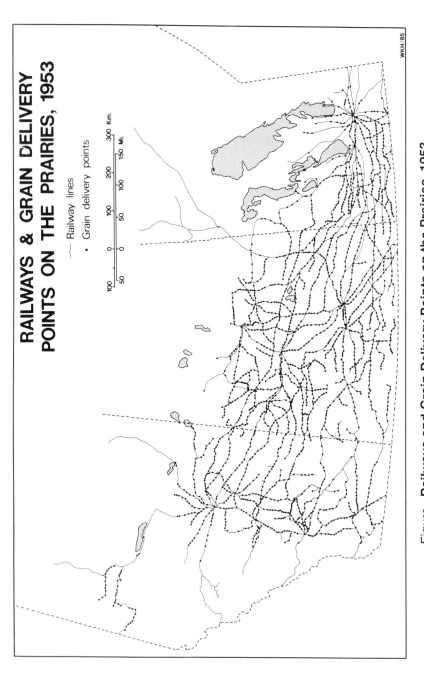

Figure   Railways and Grain Delivery Points on the Prairies, 1953
15.5

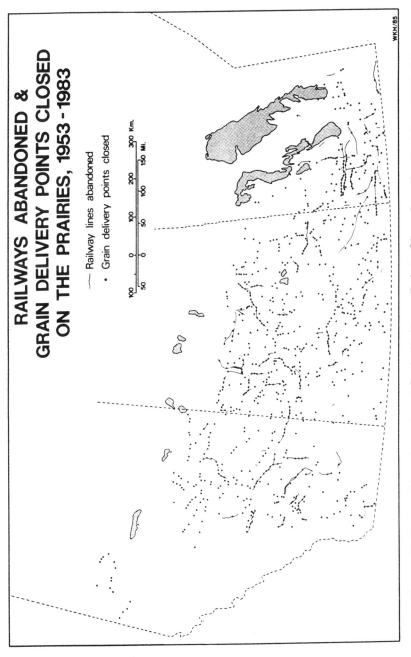

Figure   Railways Abandoned and Grain Delivery Points Closed on the Prairies, 1953–83
15.6

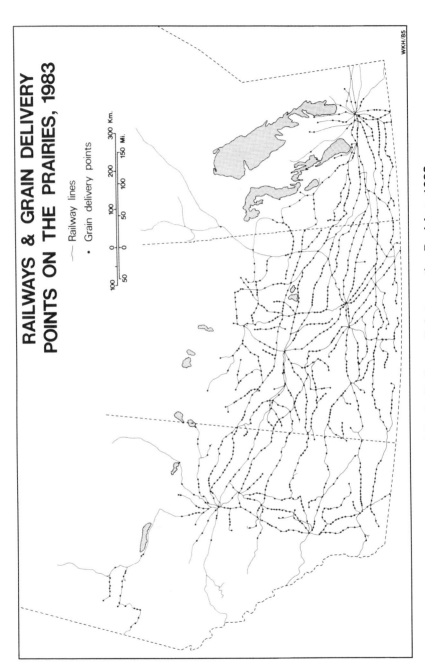

RAILWAYS & GRAIN DELIVERY POINTS ON THE PRAIRIES, 1983

— Railway lines
• Grain delivery points

WKH/85

Figure Railways and Grain Delivery Points on the Prairies, 1983
15.7

small service centres by bypassing them to shop, worship, educate their children, and conduct leisure activities at distant, larger urban centres. Not infrequently, these activities also involve grain delivery at the larger centres (Wilson 1981, 126–44; Zasada 1969, 19). Moreover, farms on the Prairies increasingly comprise separated pieces of land several miles apart, and grain from the different pieces is often hauled to different delivery points. Thus, the closure of a specific delivery point is less economically disadvantageous than it would have been in earlier times when farms were compact and only a single delivery point was used. All of the above trends began long before the widespread closure of delivery points and abandonments of railway lines, so even where it can be demonstrated that a service centre has declined since closure of a delivery point or rail line, it is difficult to determine cause and effect. It is noteworthy, in this regard, that the very hamlets, small villages and towns that farmers were bypassing previously, are those from which most delivery points and rail lines have been removed in recent years. For example, of the 189 places in Saskatchewan that lost their delivery points between the crop years 1970–71 and 1975–76, only seven had more than 100 people in 1971 and only 13 had more than 50 people.

It may well be, then, that the very strong opposition to these closures is to be found elsewhere, in the minds and perceptions of rural people rather than primarily in their pocket books. The main reason may well be that rural people resent having so little control over these changes. While it is true that public hearings are held concerning proposed rail-line abandonments, the ultimate decision lies with the railway companies and the federal government. Similarly, the grain handling companies themselves decide which elevators should be consolidated. Another possibility is that rural people view these closures as just a beginning of a process that will greatly accelerate if not opposed from the start. In particular, they may fear that a system of very large inland terminal elevators, similar to that recently built at Weyburn, Saskatchewan (whose capacity is 10 to 15 times that of many Prairie elevators), will become established across the Prairies, leading to the disappearance of most of the remaining grain elevators and delivery points and much of the branch-line railway network, as well as the decline of many service centres (Kulshreshtha 1982). At a deeper level, it may be that because agricultural settlement and the establishment of small service centres on the Prairies were, in a sense, creations of the railway and grain elevator system, the loss of them is viewed as the death of a way of life, which indeed it is.

15.4.2 Schools

The system of public schools established in rural areas of the Prairies during the period of pioneer settlement was based on those of the longer-settled regions of Ontario and the United States, from which many of the early settlers came (Dawson and Younge 1940, 159–82; Masson 1985, 86–87).[3] The chief characteristic of this system was small local schools that were controlled and financed by the surrounding community.

In agricultural districts, schools were dispersed across the landscape in much the same manner as the farms. These schools were established at intervals of about six or seven kilometres to allow ready, if not easy, access to children travelling on foot or by horse. A school district with a locally elected board of trustees was established for the attendance area of each school, or about 30 to 40 square kilometres. Rural schools generally provided instruction only to grade 8, and all grades were taught by a single teacher in one room. By the mid-1930s, about 9,000 such one-roomed elementary schools and school districts were in operation in rural parts of the Prairies (Wilson 1967, 344).[4]

These schools met the needs of rural society during the early period of settlement, when the prevailing view was that there should be local control over schools and that a grade 8 education was sufficient, or more than sufficient, for farmers' sons and daughters. By the early 1900s, however, a demand had arisen among some farmers for secondary education for their children. This was met in several ways, including the addition of some high-school grades to the elementary school, correspondence courses, and the consolidation of several school districts for the establishment of a high school, while leaving the elementary schools and districts separate as before. Otherwise, farm children had to be sent to schools in villages, towns, or cities, access to which was only permitted if classroom space was available after meeting the needs of urban children (Dawson and Younge 1940, 174–75; Wilson 1967, 341–42).[5] In most cases farm children had to be boarded in the urban centre, away from their families. Under such circumstances it is not surprising that only a small proportion of farm children completed high school, even among families who favoured further education. In summary, an elementary education at a local school was all that the majority of farm families wanted or could arrange until the end of the main period of settlement.

During the past 50 years the system of rural schooling has undergone revolutionary change. The one-roomed, public elementary school has virtually disappeared from the prairie landscape. In its stead have arisen elementary and high schools, or composites of both, divided into separate classrooms for each grade and staffed by teachers who are specialized according to subject. These schools are located in towns, villages, and, infrequently, hamlets, and children in the surrounding rural areas are bussed to and from them daily.

The process by which this change took place is a complex one, only summarized briefly here. Horse-drawn and motorized school vans for transporting children in rural districts to centralized schools were in limited use on the Prairies by the 1920s. At first they were considered appropriate only for transporting children to high schools. They were not favoured or much used for conveying children to elementary schools because of the travel time, hazards associated with weather and poor roads, and the necessary separation from family. In time, however, and particularly during the post-war period, improvements in roads and vehicles reduced both travel time and much of the uncertainty surrounding travel over rural roads. These developments, coupled with farm depopulation and a growing realization among the farming community that a better standard of education was required for their children and that this could only be achieved through centralization of schools in urban centres, all contributed to the decline of the dispersed one-roomed elementary school. Changes in school administration, particularly the formation of school divisions and transfer of much of the decision-making about schools to the divisional from the district level, furthered the process. Rural school divisions, each comprising about 60 to 80 school districts, were formed in Alberta in the decade after 1936. Divisions of a similar size were formed in Saskatchewan between 1944 and the mid-1960s, and in Manitoba between 1959 and the early 1970s (Carlyle 1987).

The closure of schools and removal of decision-making from the rural districts themselves was not done easily or without strong opposition. Some rural people clung to the view that an elementary education provided by a local school under their watchful eyes was sufficient. Others, although favouring centralization and more advanced and better standards of education in principle, feared that their children would abandon rural life for the towns in the process of becoming educated. Almost all farmers and other dispersed rural dwellers were united in viewing the closure of the local school as affecting far more than just the educational life of the community because many social functions were held in the school house (Mitchell 1981, 70; Funk 1971, 106).

This opposition slowed down the removal of schools from farming districts but did not prevent it, and today the "new" system has been in effect long enough for most farming families to view it as being the normal or accepted system. Among the older people, however, there is much nostalgia for the local one-roomed school, the teachers they came to know so well and, above all, the wider significance of the school house to the social life of the community. While examining a list of recent publications on the local history of Prairie rural communities, one can find among the titles the names of local schools and school districts, such as Minnehaha, Picnic Lake, Broomhill, Beaver Crossing, Cherry Grove, Dry Gully, Windcrest, Piety Hill, Thistledown, Badger, or Bluff. After seeing these, it would be a hard-hearted person indeed, who did not share in the sense of loss that rural people feel for their schools now that they are gone.[6]

While the once ubiquitous local public school has disappeared from farming districts, there are still a few private one-roomed schools located along rural roads amid a dispersed farming population. Most are operated by conservative Christian groups such as Seventh Day Adventists or Mennonites. A small number of public schools serving only farm children are still in operation, but they are found in Mennonite farm villages or on Hutterite colonies, and not amid dispersed farmsteads.[7]

5.4.3 Ethnic Groups

People of British and French origin comprised the vast majority of Canadians when the Dominion of Canada was formed in 1867. Ontario was mainly British, Quebec largely French, and the Maritimes had a sizeable Acadian French minority among the British majority. Other ethnic groups, such as Mennonites in Ontario and Germans in Nova Scotia, were relatively insignificant. Overall, the two main groups tended to keep apart from each other geographically, socially, and economically, both in their cultural strongholds and in the areas where they were in the minority, such as the British in the eastern townships of Quebec and Acadians in the Maritimes. This formed what Hugh MacLennan (1945) described as "two solitudes."

This duality persisted in eastern Canada until recently, when the arrival of large numbers of immigrants, notably from southern Europe, Asia, Guyana and other parts of the Caribbean, produced a more varied cultural mix. However, most of these recent arrivals have gone to the urban centres, especially the very large ones. The truly rural areas of eastern Canada are still populated very largely by people of British and French origin, albeit with more geographical and social intermingling than a century ago.

The addition of the province of Manitoba to the Dominion in 1870 did not alter the pattern established in eastern Canada, as the inhabitants of the Red River Settlement, which comprised most of Manitoba's population at that time, were mainly of British or French heritage, although most also had native Indian ancestry. However, this early duality was short-lived on the Prairies, and by the early 1900s the region was populated by people of many national and ethnic origins. Thus, multiculturism, not biculturism, has long been the reality on the Prairies.

The main groups in this mosaic each occupied well-defined geographical tracts of the Prairies by the early 1900s, even before the end of the main period of rural settlement. Since then, some groups have expanded from their core areas, and others have lost ground, but in general the geographical map of ethnicity established early in the twentieth century has persisted to the present day. Thus, people of Ukrainian origin still predominate in the moist and quite heavily wooded areas (parkland) where their ancestors settled at the turn of the century; Mennonites still form a large proportion of the total population on land reserved for settlement by them in Manitoba and Saskatchewan in the late nineteenth century; the Mormon presence is still strong in their area of settlement in southern Alberta; and clusters of people of French and German origin approximate their centres of initial settlement, all against a backcloth of the most widespread and numerous group, the British. Among the British, too, there are concentrations according to initial settlement by place of origin, be it Ontario, the United States, or the United Kingdom, and also by sub-groups such as Scottish, Irish, or English.

The geographical patterns of earlier years have been preserved to a large extent, but the cultural landscapes of each group have not. Only a few Mennonite farmers continue to live in street villages, or strassendorfs, and the custom of dividing their open fields into strips, was abandoned by 1930, and leaves little trace on the landscape. The distinctive Ukrainian farm buildings, of whitewashed plaster over logs with a thatched roof, are today found only as museum pieces. Other styles of farmstead brought by them to the Prairies persist only in a small number of older structures that are fast disappearing. Homes and barns constructed of field or quarried stone are still fairly numerous in areas of Ontario-British settlement, but few, if any, are of recent origin. Churches and church architecture have perhaps lasted best among the elements of the built environment brought to the Prairies by the cultural groups (Sawatzky 1970; Warkentin 1959; Friesen 1977; Lehr 1980, 195; Schlichtmann 1976, 71). Indeed, so complete has been the disappearance of distinctive ethnic landscapes on the Prairies that cultural groups and government agencies have recently begun to establish heritage sites, where key elements of surviving earlier settlement are gathered together, reconstructed, and often placed alongside contemporary replicas (Artibise and Friesen 1990).

While the cultural landscape has become more uniform and North American on the Prairies, there is considerable debate concerning the degree to which the cultural integrity of each group has been preserved, as manifested by social customs, language, religion, perceptions, and attitudes. It is beyond the scope of this essay to examine this aspect of Prairie cultural groups, but it can be said that the distinctiveness of every group is still readily apparent in their main areas of settlement. For example, most Mennonites in rural areas, and especially on farms, still speak low German as a first or second language, and attend church several times a week. Similarly, Ukrainian is commonly spoken at home by members of that group, and in rural areas where Ukrainians predominate it is sometimes used before English in conversation outside the home.

Among the main ethnic groups on the Prairies, the Hutterites stand out clearly as the one that has most resisted cultural integration with Canadian and North American society, so this group will be examined in more detail.

15.4.3.1 The Hutterites

The Hutterian Brethren, or Hutterites, are the most recent of the main groups to settle on the Prairies, but this does not explain the preservation of their culture. It is, rather, their particular form of Christianity, a variant of the wider Anabaptist movement, which gives them a distinct identity. The underpinning of Hutterite life is a belief in spiritual oneness: the brotherhood of all believers, which is expressed in worldly terms by communal ownership of material goods. They believe that their spiritual and communal life can best be maintained by living together in small family groups, engaging in agriculture, and observing strict standards of worship, dress, work, and play. Officially and, to a large degree, in practice, they do not use birth control.

These aspects of Hutterite life have set them apart, socially and geographically, from the mainstream of Prairie life. Groups of 10 to 15 families live together in nucleated farm settlements, or colonies, amid the prevailing single-family households and dispersed farmsteads of the Prairie region. All assets of the colony – buildings, machinery, and land – are communally owned by the colony members, in contrast to the private and generally individual ownership of other Prairie farms. Each established Hutterite colony has its own tiny, one-roomed public school, in a time when almost all other farm children are bussed to hamlet, village, or town schools. Hutterite children are generally educated only to grade 8, although a few colony schools do have instruction to the grade 9 or 10 level. Hutterites see no benefit in formal education to more advanced levels, except for a limited amount of training for specific jobs. Indeed, they fear that higher education would be detrimental, because it would be necessary for children to leave the colony and would expose them to worldly ideas and temptations, both in and out of school. This attitude is but part of a general tendency for Hutterites to isolate themselves from the rest of society. This aspect of Hutterite life has been criticized by many rural people, some of whom claim that the social and economic life of service centres near Hutterite colonies has suffered adversely in consequence. However, rural people are even more concerned, some to the point of hostility, over the rate of growth of the Hutterite population, which has until recently been one of the highest of any group in the world, and its corollary, the acquisition by Hutterites of an ever-increasing proportion of Prairie farmland.

The rate of expansion of the Hutterites on the Prairies has been truly remarkable. Seventeen colonies relocated from South Dakota to Alberta and Manitoba in 1918 and 1919 (Figure 15.8). By 1950 the founding colonies and their offshoots, plus a few others that relocated from the United States, totalled 60 colonies, excluding two renegade colonies not officially recognized at inception by the Hutterian Church. By 1984 established colonies, that is, colonies sufficiently developed to be financially independent of the others, numbered 218, and 22 more were in the process of being established.[8] Two colonies were excommunicated between 1951 and 1984, raising the number of renegade colonies to four.

No data on the number of Hutterites on the Prairies have been available until recently, but a rough estimate of their number can be made by assuming that each colony has about 80 to 90 people. Data obtained from Statistics Canada, although not as precise as might be desired, show that the Hutterite population on the Prairies rose from about 6,200 in 1951 to 16,200 in 1981. During this same period, the Hutterite proportion of the total farm population rose from 0.7 percent to 3.3 percent. There has been a corresponding increase in the amount of land farmed by the Hutterites. By 1984, colony land, the vast majority of which is owned, rather than rented or leased, by the Hutterites, totalled about three-quarters of a million hectares. This amount, however, represents only some 1.5 percent of all Prairie farmland.

For a considerable time after they settled on the Prairies, little attention was paid to the Hutterites. As their numbers grew rapidly and many new colonies were formed, however, farmers in or near their areas of concentration in Alberta and Manitoba grew increasingly anxious. By the 1940s and 1950s this led to limits being established in both provinces; maximum area for individual colonies was set as well as a minimum distance between existent and new colonies. In Manitoba, the number of colonies in a single rural municipality was also controlled (Ryan 1977, 33–34; Hoestetler 1974, 133–35). The restrictions in Alberta were passed by the provincial legislature; in Manitoba they took the form of an agreement the Hutterites signed with the Union of Manitoba Municipalities to avoid legislated controls. These restrictions are no longer in effect, but many rural people across the Prairies remain strongly opposed to the continuing expansion of the Hutterites.

Whether the rate of growth of the Hutterite population and landholdings will continue to follow past trends, and whether this will lead to a reintroduction of

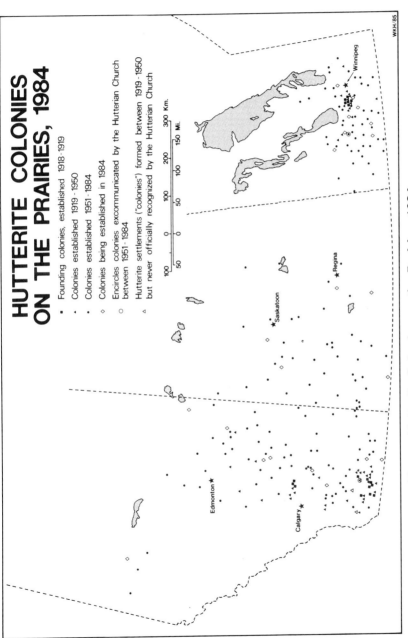

Figure Hutterite Colonies on the Prairies, 1984
15.8

controls, is debatable. Until 1950 the Hutterites had an average growth rate of population of more than 4 percent per annum (Eaton and Mayer 1954, 44). In recent years, however, this rate has declined considerably. The Schmiedeleut Hutterites in Manitoba, who comprise more than one-third of all Hutterites on the Canadian Prairies, had an annual growth rate of population of only about 2.25 percent from 1970 to 1981, and the Hutterites in North America as a whole increased at an average annual rate of only 2.4 percent from 1977 to 1980 (Boldt 1983, 235–37; Peter 1980, 109). That women are getting married at a later age partially accounts for this decrease. Another important contributing factor appears to be a recent increase in the number of Hutterite women who have been allowed to terminate their reproductive capacity on the grounds that additional pregnancies would endanger their health (Peter 1980, 105; Peter and Whitaker 1982, 269–71). This relaxation of the official Hutterite policy on birth control is but one sign that women are gaining more influence than formerly in what is still a patriarchal society. But for whatever reason it has occurred, the decline in the rate of growth of the Hutterite population should lead to corresponding decreases in the rates of expansion of colonies and acquisition of land, and if the downward trend in growth of population is sufficient, tensions with neighbouring farming communities could be much reduced or disappear entirely.

Other changes are also occurring which may reduce conflicts. The Hutterites favour and promote continued mechanization of farmwork and other activities in the colonies. This may lead to surplus labour in the Hutterite colonies. Such a development, together with the low returns and financial uncertainties characteristic to agriculture, may make commercial manufacturing an attractive alternative or supplement to farming. Moreover, there is nothing in the beliefs and traditions of the Hutterites to prevent this from occurring. Agriculture first became the exclusive economic activity of the Hutterites only in the eighteenth and nineteenth centuries in southern Russia. Before this, during the golden age of Hutterite culture in Moravia during the late sixteenth and early seventeenth centuries, manufacturing was an important part of the Hutterite economy, and some Hutterites even worked regularly off the colonies (Hoestler 1974, 27–61). A few colonies on the Prairies have already begun to make and sell such items as roof trusses, heat exchangers, stainless steel table-tops, and hog-barn equipment.[9] If such diversification were to become wide-spread it should reduce the need for land by the Hutterites, and thereby relieve tensions with the other farming communities, even without a continued decline in the rate of growth of population. On the other hand, new conflicts may arise. A harbinger of things to come has appeared in Manitoba, where most colonies engaged in commercial manufacturing are located. Some Manitoban businessmen have begun to complain that the Hutterites have an unfair economic advantage in that they do not pay colony members directly for specific jobs, thereby allegedly undercutting the legislated minimum wage, and they do not pay workers' compensation premiums because there is no employer-employee relationship.

Whether these and other changes presage a breakdown in the established way of life of the Hutterites on the Prairies is open to question. Although it is true that each of the Hutterite sects, Schmiedeleut, Dariusleut, and Lehrerleut, has excommunicated or refused to officially recognize at least one entire colony, there have only been four such occurrences in 66 years, and only one since 1962.[10] It is noteworthy in this regard that Hutterite colonies are held together by both their faith and a requirement that adult members must sign a declaration to forgo all claims to colony assets if they should decide to abandon communal life. This declaration, which has been upheld in Canadian courts of law, makes the partial break-up of a community extremely unlikely.

Although social forces are important, the geographical distribution of Hutterite colonies on the Prairies should not be overlooked entirely in assessing the long-term viability of the group. The fact that most colonies are located in the dry belt of the prairies could lead to widespread economic problems and many bankruptcies of colonies if another prolonged drought should occur in the area.

Yet, the strength and resilience of the Hutterite faith and the society to which it has given rise should not be underestimated, as the history of the group has clearly demonstrated. Change will undoubtedly occur in the Hutterite way of life on the prairies, but rather than being quick and highly disruptive, it is likely to be slow, cautious, and controlled.

15.5   Prospect

Rural areas of the Prairies have undergone many far-reaching changes during the past half-century. It is difficult to ascertain whether these changes will continue to take place at the same pace and in the same direction as they have in the past, but some trends appear evident. The number of farms and farm population will probably continue to decline, but at a slower rate than they have in the last three decades. Many of the smaller, uneconomic farms have already been eliminated, and the era of relatively inexpensive oil and gas, required in large amounts to fuel the farm machinery necessary to handle increasingly large hectarages per farmer, appears to be nearing an end. Further enlargement of farms may well involve mainly pooling of assets through the formation of partnerships and several-family corporations, rather than continued consolidation into larger units of single-operator farms. Artificial fertilizers and pesticides, being partly derivatives of the petrochemical industry, are expected to increase in price as the oil industry declines, and this may lead to decreasing yields on farms unable to afford them in the amounts used today.

A majority of the present plans to further reduce the network of railway branch lines on the Prairies will be implemented, and there will undoubtedly be continuing economic rationalization of the network of grain elevators. However, it is doubtful that large inland terminal elevators will entirely or even significantly replace country elevators in the foreseeable future. Nevertheless, many hamlets and small villages will continue to decline. Some villages will be forced reluctantly to disincorporate, and their separate identities will slowly be lost through merger with surrounding rural districts. There will be some additional centralization of rural schools, and this will mainly involve the closing of schools in hamlets and small villages. Hutterite colonies will continue to expand, but at a slower rate than formerly, and a considerable number of colonies will probably turn to manufacturing to supplement their farm enterprises.

It is uncertain whether the rate of increase of the rural non-farm population near large urban centres will be maintained. The desire for rural living by people tied closely to the city for their livelihood continues to be strong, and this desire is frequently within reach, especially if both spouses are wage earners and they have a small family. On the other hand, rising costs of travel, and increases in taxes to provide the modern services so much in demand by the residents of urban fringes may slow the rate of growth. In addition, decreases in the rural non-farm population will occur near some urban centres through the expansion of city boundaries to include what are now considered as rural areas.

On the prairie landscape, the few remaining vestiges of cultural distinctiveness associated with ethnic groups will slowly disappear. Less visible differences, such as language and customs, will become more muted, but still add an interesting and welcome diversity to Prairie rural communities.

Notes

1. Rural population by township, with no breakdown into farm and non-farm was published in the quinquennial censuses of Canada from 1901 to 1971; the data for 1976 were compiled but not published. Statistics Canada ceased even to assemble population by township after 1976, except at a prohibitive cost to the user. For this reason, Figures 15.3 and 15.4, which are based on the census data, show change in population and density of population only to 1976.

   The censuses of Canada define only "urban" for population purposes, with "rural" being the remainder. Until and including the 1946 census, people were considered urban if they lived in an incorporated centre, so that anyone not living in such a centre was rural. From 1951 to the present, the urban population has been defined as "people living in incorporated or unincorporated urban centres of 1,000 people or more, and people living in concentrations of high density elsewhere, usually on the fringes of large cities." Thus, people living in incorporated urban centres of less than 1,000 people are now considered rural, not urban, while people in unincorporated urban centres of 1,000 or more and in concentrations near but outside incorporated urban centres, who were once considered rural, are now defined as urban. However, the pre-1951 usage of rural has been maintained by the census of Canada for, and only for, determining rural population by township. These census data for townships were altered to fit the current meaning of "rural" in preparing Figures 15.1, 15.3, and 15.4. The current definitions of "urban" and "rural" were also used for Figure 15.2.

2. This statement applies to census farms, the definition of which has been changed several times since 1936. However, even if the 1936 definition had remained unchanged throughout the period, similar increases in the average size of farms would be obtained.

3. See also *Rural Education in Alberta* (Edmonton: King's Printer, 1929), 8–9.

4. Personal communication from P.W. Dyck, Executive Director, Regional Services, Saskatchewan Education. See also *Thirty-first Annual Report of the Department of Education of the Prairie of Alberta, 1935* (Edmonton: King's Printer, 1937), 92; and

Census of the Prairie Provinces 1936, vol. 1: *Population and Agriculture* (Ottawa: King's Printer, 1938), 232, 670, 1126.

5 Personal communication from P.W. Dyck, Executive Director, Regional Services, Saskatchewan Education. See also *Report of the Legislative Committee on Rural Education* (Edmonton: King's Printer, Sessional Paper, 136, 1935), 15; and *Rural High Schools in Alberta* (Edmonton: King's Printer, 1930), 9–11.

6. *Canadian Plains Bulletin* (Regina: Canadian Plains Research Center), vol. 8, no. 1, 1980, p. 11; vol. 10, no. 4, 1982, p. 14; and vol. 13, no. 2, 1985, p. 13. Some of these districts may still be in existence legally, even though they ceased long ago to have a school or school board.

7. Lists of operating schools obtained from departments of education in Manitoba, Saskatchewan and Alberta.

8. I am indebted to Dr. Simon Evans, Memorial University of Newfoundland, for providing me with much of the data shown on Figure 15.8. Michael Radcliffe of Baker, Zivot, Radcliffe, Murray and Sinnock (Barristers), in Winnipeg, and many Hutterite colonies provided valuable information on colonies recently established or being established, and on renegade colonies.

9. M. Radcliffe, personal communication, 19 February 1985.

10. K. Hoeppner, Consultant on Communal Farms, Alberta Municipal Affairs, personal communications, 4 January 1985 and 23 May 1985.

References

Artibise, A.F.A., and J. Friesen, eds. 1990. "Heritage Conservation." *Prairie Forum* 15:193–390.

Boldt, E.D. 1983. "The Recent Development of a Unique Population: The Hutterites of North America." *Prairie Forum* 8:235–40.

Canadian Grain Commission (CGC). 1983. *Grain Elevators in Canada, Crop Year 1983/84.* Ottawa: GCC.

Canadian International Grains Institute (CIGI). 1982. *Grains and Oilseeds: Handling, Marketing, Processing.* 3d ed., rev. Winnipeg: CIGI.

Carlyle, W.J. 1983a. "The Changing Family Farm on the Prairies." *Prairie Forum* 8:1–23.

———. 1983b. "Farm Layouts in Manitoba." *Canadian Geographer* 27:17–34.

———. 1987. "The Changing Geography of Administrative Units for Schooling and Local Government on the Canadian Prairies." *Prairie Forum* 12:5–35.

———. 1989. "Farm Population in the Canadian Parkland." *Geographical Review* 79:13–35.

Dawson, C.A., and E.R. Younge. 1940. "Pioneering in the Prairie Provinces: The Social Side of the Settlement Process." Vol. 3 of W.A. Mackintosh and W.L.G. Joerg, eds., *Canadian Frontiers of Settlement.* Toronto: Macmillan Company of Canada Ltd.

Eaton, J.W., and A.J. Mayer. 1954. *Man's Capacity to Reproduce: The Demography of a Unique Population.* Glencoe: The Free Press.

Friesen, R.J. 1977. "Saskatchewan Mennonite Settlements: The Modification of an Old World Settlement Pattern." *Canadian Ethnic Studies* 9:72–89.

Funk, J. 1971. "The Origin and Development of Consolidated School Districts in Saskatchewan." M.Ed. thesis, University of Saskatchewan.

Hart, J.F. 1975. *The Look of the Land.* Englewood Cliffs: Prentice-Hall.

Hoestetler, J.A. 1974. *Hutterite Society.* Baltimore and London: Johns Hopkins University Press.

Johnson, B D. 1984. "Prairie Ghost Towns: Life at the End of the Line." *Equinox,* May-June, 111–23.

Kerr, D., and D.W. Holdsworth, eds. 1990. *Historical Atlas of Canada.* Vol. 3: *Addressing the Twentieth Century, 1896–1961*, plate 17, by J.W. Carlyle, J.C. Lehr, and G.E. Millis.

Kulshreshtha, S.N. 1982. "Short-run Effects of an Inland Terminal on the Grain Handling System and Rural Communities: A Case Study of Weyburn." *Prairie Forum* 7:69–85.

Lehr, J.C. 1980. "The Log Buildings of Ukrainian Settlers in Western Canada." *Prairie Forum* 5:183–96.

Lehr, J.C., and D.W. Moodie. 1980. "The Polemics of Pioneer Settlement: Ukrainian Immigration and the Winnipeg Free Press." *Canadian Ethnic Studies* 12:88–101.

MacLennan, H. 1945. *Two Solitudes.* Toronto: Collins.

Martin, C. 1973. *"Dominion Lands" Policy.* Toronto: McClelland and Stewart.

Masson, J. 1985. *Alberta's Local Governments and their Politics.* Edmonton: Pica Pica Press.

Mitchell, E.B. 1981. *Western Canada Before the War.* Saskatoon: Western Producer Prairie Books. Reprint. London: J. Murray, 1915.

Peter, K.A. 1980. "The Decline of Hutterite Population Growth." *Canadian Ethnic Studies* 12:97–110.

Peter, K.A., and I. Whitaker. 1982. "The Changing Role of Hutterite Women." *Prairie Forum* 7:267–77.

Rees, R. 1988. *New and Naked Land.* Saskatoon: Western Producer Prairie Books.

Ryan, J. 1977. *The Agricultural Economy of Manitoba Hutterite Colonies.* Toronto: McClelland and Stewart.

Sawatzky, H.L. 1970. "Viability of Ethnic Group Settlement with Reference to Mennonites in Manitoba." *Canadian Ethnic Studies* 2:147–60.

———. 1979. "Prairie Potholes." *Blue Jay* 37:3–8.

Schlichtmann, H. 1976. "The Ethnic Architecture in the Prairies Conference: A Report and a Geographer's Reflections." *Prairie Forum* 1:69–75.

Smillie, B.G., ed. 1983. *Visions of the New Jerusalem.* Edmonton: NeWest.

Smith, P.J. 1984. "Urban Development Trends in the Prairie Provinces." In A.W. Rasporich, ed., *The Making of the Modern West: Western Canada Since 1945,* 133–43. Calgary: University of Calgary Press.

Vanderhill, B.G. 1982. "The Passing of the Pioneer Fringe in Western Canada." *Geographical Review* 72:200–17.

Warkentin, J. 1959. "Mennonite Agricultural Settlements of Southern Manitoba." *Geographical Review* 49:342–68.

Wilson, B. 1967. "The Development of Education in Manitoba." Ph.D. thesis, Michigan State University.

———. 1981. *Beyond the Harvest: Canadian Grain at the Crossroads.* Saskatoon: Western Producer Prairie Books.

Zasada, D. 1969. "Some Marketing Habits of Prairie Grain Producers." *Canadian Farm Economics* 4:15–19.

16 Growth and Decay in the Rural Maritimes: The Example of Pictou Island[1]

Eric Ross

One of the most striking differences between the Maritime provinces and the rest of Canada is that they have received no large groups of immigrants since the coming of the Irish nearly a century and a half ago. In this they differ greatly from all of the other provinces (except Newfoundland), which have taken in hundreds of thousands of migrants in the decades since Confederation. With few newcomers, it might have been expected that, by now, time and propinquity would have blended the early settlers of the Maritimes into one. But this has not been the case. Descendents of the various ethnic groups still predominate in many communities, and the old ways of their ancestors live on – whether native Indian, French, English, German, Scottish, Loyalist, or Irish – and are expressed every day in a hundred different ways. In fields such as language, religion, music, and folklore, links with the past can be quite obvious. In other areas, such as in choices of food, patterns of land use, and architecture they are sometimes more subtle. If space permitted, such links could be explored among the descendents of the Indians at Big Cove, the French at Memramcook, the Germans at Lunenburg, the Loyalists at Gagetown, or the Irish in Saint John. However, it does not, and so only one, small community will be visited here: the tiny Scottish Highland settlement that made its home on Pictou Island, which lies out in the Northumberland Strait between Nova Scotia and Prince Edward Island. Pictou Island's story during the past 150 years is typical of that of most small communities in the Maritimes, and to know it, in many ways, is to know the Maritimes as a whole.[2]

Although Pictou Island had been visited often by the Micmac Indians, it was not settled until the arrival of four Irish families in 1814 or soon after. In 1819, they were followed by the first of the Highlanders. The newcomers apparently feuded with the Irish who subsequently moved on.[3] More Highland settlers followed during the 1820s and 1830s from Mull and from the mainland of Ross and Argyll, with the last of them arriving in the early 1840s. By 1838, there were 17 families in a vigorous, young community of 119 souls. No family was without children still at home, and 13 of them shared a total of 58 children under the age of 14. Among the 17 heads of family – all of whom were male – were two carpenters and a blacksmith; the rest were farmers. Because land on the tiny island was limited – it was only seven and a quarter kilometers long and two kilometers wide – and since such a small community could support few tradesmen, most of the children eventually were forced to leave. Thus, by 1858 the population had reached a more or less fixed level of only 158 in 25 households, and remained at that level, with minor variations, until the end of the century when it was still only 159 although the number of households had climbed to 36. During the first two decades of the twentieth century, fishing, particularly for lobsters, became an important means of support, allowing the population to grow rapidly, to reach a peak of 227 in 37 households in 1921. However, by then (as will be shown later) changes in the fisheries were already taking place that would lead to the population falling as rapidly as it had risen. By 1951, it had dropped below the previous level of 158, and since then has continued to plummet until today only a handful live on the island all year long.

The island's shape – much like an elongated oatmeal loaf – allowed for an easy settlement pattern: the land was simply cut into 32 slices – each encompassing from 20 to 61 hectares (see Figure 16.1).[4] All the plots were long and narrow except for those towards the two "heels," which were sliced somewhat thicker to compensate for the narrowing of the island. As the population increased, some lots were divided into still thinner slices. All the houses were constructed in a line a short distance from the south shore. This, along with the narrowness of the lots, meant that neighbours were much closer to one another than was common in other pioneering communities.

Clearing the land was an heroic task, especially for men from the open straths and glens of Scotland, and it is still remembered today in tales passed down about the "old boys" who farmed all day and then pulled stumps at night and burned them so there would be enough light to pull more stumps. In time, the whole southern half of the island was swept clean of virtually every tree, until it resembled the land they had left. Hardly a twig was left to shelter the farms from the winter's blast. The northern half of the island was left in forest, thus providing each farm with an extensive woodlot from which to draw fuel, lumber, and materials for making boats, lobster-pots, and dyes. Each farm also had its "back fence," which marked the boundary between cleared and uncleared land. All of these fences were joined to form a continuous line from one end of the island to the other. In the spring, each farmer drove all his animals, except his milking cows, through the "back-fence gate" into the woods where they foraged together much as they might have done on common land at the head of some Scottish glen. With the animals out of the way the fields could be planted safely. After the harvest was gathered in the autumn, the gates were opened and soon most of the animals found their way back to their home farms. Any mix-ups were easily sorted out because the animals would have been marked before they were sent into the woods.

The absence of a harbour, or even a bay, along the smooth coastline of the island meant that there was no shelter for boats. Near the west end, there was a small wharf, but it was too exposed for boats to be left there safely. For these reasons, only small boats that could be hauled up easily were practical. Without larger craft, fishing was restricted mostly to the shallow waters near the island and, for many years, was regarded merely as a seasonal adjunct to farming. Most of the modest catch was for home consumption or was spread on the fields as fertilizer. Outside markets were impractical, given the technology of the time. Lobsters were plentiful – so plentiful in fact that they were held in low regard as food. It took an American firm, Shedd and Knox of Boston, to realize their worth and to provide a means for getting them to

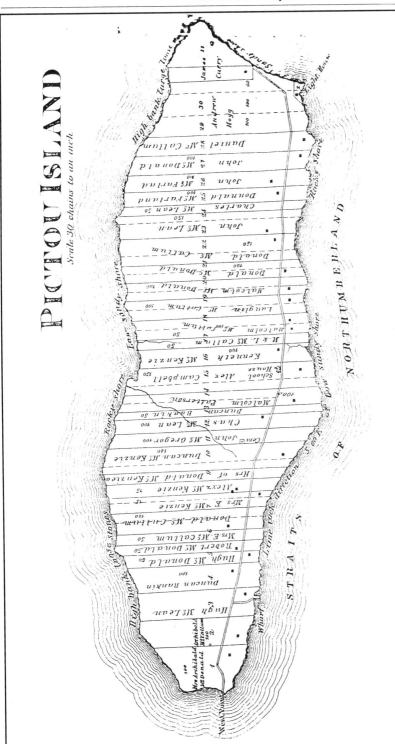

Figure 16.1 **Pictou Island, Nova Scotia, 1879**

Source: J.J. Meacham and Co., Pictou County Island

distant markets where they were appreciated. In the later 1870s Shedd and Knox established a factory at the east end of the island to can lobsters. In 1881, they moved to the mainland, but before long others followed their lead and built factories on the island. By the early 1900s, there were no fewer than five canneries in operation at the same time. For some islanders, fishing became more important than agriculture and, for the first time, there were those who began to regard themselves as fishermen rather than farmers.

The lobster fishery contributed much to the island's heyday between 1900 and 1950, but it did not do so alone. Potatoes, grains, beef, eggs, wool, and even milk also made their contributions. The community was then in its prime, and old-timers now living out their years in exile on the mainland remember it in a warm haze of nostalgia.

Snug in their homes on the southern side of their island, they felt safe and secure as they looked out across the strait to the blue hills of the Nova Scotia mainland. To their forebears these same hills had served as a modest reminder of the more rugged and dramatic land they had left behind in Scotland. Along the foot of the hills and dotting the shore-line were the tiny houses of their fellow Scots of Pictou County. On the horizon from the other side of the island could be seen Prince Edward Island, where many another Highland heart beat strong. In summer, the shallow waters of the strait could be remarkably pleasant and warm, allowing for safe and easy communication with the neighbouring shores; in winter they were choked with ice for months at a time, isolating the islanders from virtually all contact with the outside world.

This was a time of retreat and seclusion when the island became a world unto its own; a time when the islanders were knit into one big family; a time of music, story telling, and dancing; a time of weaving, hooking rugs, and making lobster-pots; and a time for enjoyment and preservation of the old ways. Summer brought contact with a somewhat wider world, but it too was largely Scottish and did little to modify the ways of the islanders. Their world may have been limited in space, but it was rich in time; it was a world where the past, present, and the future lived side by side, a world of ghost ships and tales of people and happenings from long ago, of the events of the present day, and of forerunners telling of future occurrences, particularly of death.

In the island's heyday, during the first half of this century, one year was much like another, from its beginning with Scottish rituals of New Year's Day to its ending with the rites of Hogmanay. On the evening of the day before New Year's Day, or Hogmanay, people would gather at certain houses to sing Gaelic songs and to dance – preferably to the skirl of the bagpipes – until "the peeping of the dawn." The more gregarious would then set out with flasks of whisky to wish their neighbours a happy New Year. Those who still had the ancient tongue – or, by that time of the day, thought they had – would tap on the door and "say a whole bunch of Gaelic." On at least one doorstep, the family still got out a broom and in Gaelic would say, "sweep out the old year and sweep in the new."

New Year's Day usually marked the end of easy communication with the mainland. The "hard" winter generally set in at about that time and for several months the island remained icebound – sometimes well into May. During the first decades of this century, signal fires of blazing straw were still the only means of communication with the mainland. Like the telegram, by then long in use elsewere in Canada, their message was rarely other than one of serious illness or death. The fire set on the mainland in January 1920 provides a typical case in point. When the islanders saw it, a crew set off over the ice. It was 45 hours before they returned to their anxious relatives with the news of the death of a resident of the island in the nearby town of Pictou. As on many other occasions, the crossing provided islanders with opportunities for acts of heroism. It was said that there was not a man who would not risk his life to go for medical aid. In some years an ice bridge would form, over which it was possible to cross. Occasionally, as in March 1932, it was possible to go by horse and sleigh all the way to Pictou, but normally the way was blocked by open stretches of water and by ten-metre piles of pack ice. Dog teams were not used for fear that the animals would drown or be crushed in the ice. Instead, the islanders resorted to dory-like hulls with runners. These could be both manhandled across the ice or rowed through open stretches of water. Often the ice-boats would leave the island in the morning and not reach Pictou until five or six o'clock in the evening. Sometimes they would be carried by the tide far from their intended landing place. Occasionally, they would be trapped in the ice for hours at a time as they inched through the chilling darkness towards the blazing shoreline beacon that had been set to guide it.

It was not until 1921 that a telephone cable was laid between the island and the mainland. However, it was frequently out of commission for weeks, and even months, at a time. Part of the problem was ice. In 1932, it was replaced by a new cable. A radio link was also established in the same year. This was fortunate since the cable was again damaged by ice in 1948, but by this time planes were flying back and forth several times a day, fulfilling a dream for communication by air expressed in the *Pictou Advocate* as far back as 1928. In the early days, the small planes landed in a farmer's field; later, they dodged the telephone poles to land on the narrow, dusty surface of the island's only road. No airstrip was ever built.

In spite of the isolation – or perhaps because of it – winter was the favourite season. Days began at five-thirty or six o'clock with a brisk sortie to the barns to milk the cows and do other chores. Only afterwards came the warmth of the kitchen stove and the homey smells of burning hardwood, of fresh bread being toasted over hot coals, and of the faintly acrid smoke of the oil lamp's flame as it cast its mellow circle over the breakfast table. The breakfast spread consisted of shorts porridge, sliced pork, oat cakes, raisin loaf, jam, molasses, and tea. Pork was an inevitable part of every meal of the day whether breakfast, dinner, supper, or lunch. Lunch was taken at bedtime and could be quite heavy with biscuits, bannock, molasses, and tea. Biscuits and bannock were part of nearly every meal, and it was said that not to have had a bannock on the table would have been grounds for divorce.

After breakfast, children went off to school, and the women got down to making bread and doing other household tasks. In the early years of this century, these might have included spinning, dyeing, and weaving. Meanwhile, the men set out to attend to outside tasks. On one day they might have walked a mile or two back into the woods to get on with the pleasant chore of making fence posts and cutting the year's supply of firewood – both for their homes and, in earlier years, for the lobster factories. On other days there was ice to be cut for ice houses and lobster-pots to be readied for the fishing season. By the time they returned home, it was usually getting dark but there was still the night wood to be split and carried in before supper.

After supper, hockey and skating easily lured people out when the ice was good. On other evenings there were house parties with singing, dancing, and cards, and, of course, there were the Saturday night frolics or ceilidhs in the community hall with step-dancing, lancers, strip-the-willow, and four-hand and eight-hand reels. The music was supplied by islanders playing the piano, fiddles, accordions, banjos, and guitars. Most of them played by ear, picking up tunes passed down from parents and grandparents. Saturday night could be rowdy with a great deal of drinking, but it was also a time of preparation for the sabbath. An island sabbath differed little from the sabbath held back in the Highlands. No one did any work; not even a bucket of water could be brought in.

There was never a tavern on the island, but in the years when there was a store operating, it became a favourite gathering place. It was there that the older folks gathered to swap stories after dark. Unheard (and almost unseen) in the darkened corners, silent children listened and absorbed the tales and lore that stretched back to the time the island was settled, and even across the ocean into the mists of the Highlands of long ago. Many of the tales touched on death, and the gifted story-teller could fill the room with a cozy aura of delicious gloom, seasoned here and there with quick flashes of black humour. To the children, it seemed that the old-timers were never happier than when they were miserable. Most of the stories were set on Pictou Island yet, had the children been able to journey to the land of their ancestors, they would have been amazed at how similar were the stories told there: stories of rattling chains, of ghosts, of second sight, and of prophesies of death.

Many islanders had witnessed the phantom ship, which appeared from time to time sailing to the eastward between the island and the mainland. It was an old-fashioned sailing ship with its rigging and sails on fire, and would stay in view for an hour or so before seeming to drifting off with the tide.

Bordering on the supernatural were stories told of the "grannies" or healing women. They were the last in a line of women who had been more numerous in the days before the rise of the medical profession, and the accompanying shift from women to men of the responsibility for delivering the babies and caring for the sick. From generation to generation, the grannies had passed on the mysteries of their healing arts, an essential element of which was the "charm," the secret word or words, carried over from Scotland, which helped in the healing process.

Illness and isolation loomed large in people's minds, especially in winter. When the telephone rang in the night, it was always assumed that someone was ill. People would get up and listen in on the party line and then, as likely as not, get dressed and go to visit the sick person. Tending the sick was a familiar part of life, and perhaps it was not surprising that a number of girls went away to places like Montreal, Boston, and Concord, New Hampshire, to train as nurses. As in other small, isolated communities, there was one medical problem almost too delicate for discussion: close intermarriage. Perhaps one of the old-timers put it best when he said that he had "seen a few mistakes . . . they should have read their Bibles."

The most important source of new blood came to the island with the lobster industry. The island factories required more workers than the island could provide, and so outsiders were drawn in at "fishing time." A few were fishermen, but most were women employed in packing the lobster meat into cans. Some were from Prince Edward Island and, with their similar Highland backgrounds, had much in common with the Pictou Islanders. The remainder were mostly from the Cape Bald (Cap-Pelé) area of New Brunswick and were of Acadian French origin.

The arrival of as many as 50 or 60 young women each spring caused great excitement among the young men of Pictou Island. Evenings were spent in coltish pursuit, and it was usually midnight before the youths got home to bed. No sooner were they asleep – or so it seemed – than their fathers were calling them to get up to go fishing again. Some found wives among the Prince Edward Islanders and occasionally one of the Prince Edward Island fishermen took home a Pictou Island bride, but there were almost no marriages with the Acadians. They were fun to go out with, but one did not marry them. Part of the reason may have been the difference in religion: the islanders were Protestant, and the Acadians were Roman Catholic. Island weddings were held in the best Highland tradition, with piping and dancing and a supper that "would stagger fourteen billy-goats."

Lobster fishing took place on the heels of the winter in May and June, and so all the preparations, including most of the boat-building and repairs, had to be completed before spring. Because "fishing time" occurred during the brief period when crops also had to be planted if they were to mature by the end of the short summer, there were some very hectic days.

July and August were easier months, and there was usually time to welcome summer visitors from the nearby mainland, and from the New England states and far off Upper Canada. Some former island residents drove back from the States in a "cawr" even though they had left in a "car" only a year earlier.

Early in May, the summer minister or catechist arrived. He was usually a student studying for the ministry. In August he would be joined for a day by "the reverend" from the mainland, who came over to give communion. Very occasionally – it happened in 1927 – there was a service in Gaelic and "all the old people that could get there was there with their ears wide open." As in other Maritime communities, the church was the institution most responsible for preserving the language and the old ways. Nearly all the islanders were Presbyterians and, in the early 1920s, they found themselves caught between the draw of their Scottish past and the new world pull of the emerging United Church of Canada. For many years the congregation was to be split into two denominations before reuniting under the Presbyterian banner.

About the time the summer minister was leaving in the autumn, the teacher was arriving for the winter. Both were birds of passage who seldom returned more than once or twice – if at all. Most of the teachers were young, female, and just out of normal school. If the minister represented a link with the past, the teacher represented the future, and provided a glimpse of the outside world. True, her background may not have been all that different from that of the islanders, but she was from a different community and showed a somewhat wider view of the world. Often she created in her pupils an awareness of possibilities other than farming and fishing. If she had special talents or training in music, art, or games, these were made freely available to the community.

Movement to and from the island in the autumn was by no means confined to the teacher and the minister. As in other Maritime communities, there was a great deal of toing and froing as people came and went to take up seasonal occupations. In later years, there were fishermen returning from the lobster season at Cape Tormentine, potato pickers returning from back-breaking work on Prince Edward Island, and sometimes as many as a half-dozen islanders coming back from the annual harvest excursion to the wheat fields of the far-off Prairies. At the beginning of winter there was more movement because some men left for the lumber woods of the neighbouring mainland. Late autumn was thus one of the few times of the year when most of the men were home.

November and December were busy months on the island dock: there were daily landings and shippings of potatoes, grain, fish, lumber, flour, livestock, and cranberries. This was also the time when people got in their winter supplies. They had to take in everything for six months: groceries, clothing, and Christmas presents alike. If they ran out later, they were out of luck. Scottish frugality was necessary. For instance, when the molasses was through running, the head was knocked out of the barrel to get at the sugar in the bottom. Nothing was wasted.

Each year ended as it began with the Scottish rituals of Hogmanay and New Year's Day. Among them was the custom of shaking hands on the first encounter in the new year. This marked a fresh beginning, and let neighbours know that the past was past and the slate was clean. Once again, the annual cycle could commence.

Like many Maritimers, Pictou Islanders look back with nostalgic hearts on what now seems to have been a golden age. They yearn for the strong sense of community that had grown out of a long tradition of sharing the work, the pleasures, and the suffering of this world – a tradition that had been successfully transplanted from Scotland and nurtured in the isolation of the island. It was a community that was largely self-sufficient; the few necessities not supplied by the island were met through trade with the nearby mainland and with Prince Edward Island, or through seasonable labour in those places. With the coming of the twentieth century, economic and social ties with the outside world became stronger. At first, these changes seemed to benefit the island, but later, especially after the Second World War, every structural change in the Canadian economy, every advance in technology and every piece of social legislation seemed to have an adverse effect on the community as a whole, although individuals did benefit. Whether one is speaking of the impact of the changing scale of and centralization of manufacturing and marketing, the coming of radio and television, the automation of lighthouses, the consolidation of the school system, or the impact of unemployment insurance cheques, all these things had an adverse affect on the community of Pictou Island.

In a hundred little ways, the islanders found themselves forming links with the mainland, which distanced them from one another. For instance, the coming of the gasoline engine for boats put an end to the teamwork that had been necessary for running sailing craft. One man could operate the "putt-putt" engine, whose fuel had to be bought on the mainland. Similarly, with the introduction of propane for cooking later on, the need for chopping frolics was diminished and dependence upon the mainland was increased.

There was remarkably little resistance to change. Most innovations were willingly adopted in the spirit of New World optimism. However, other changes, like the consolidation of the schools, which robbed the islanders of their children, were accepted with a sense of fatalism born long ago in the Highlands of Scotland.

Fishing proved to have the greatest success in surviving, and even benefiting, from the many changes taking place. Today, this industry still attracts many former residents back to the island to work during "fishing time." Few traces remain of the old island factories – they have moved to the mainland to be near the railway and to take advantage of the availability of electricity. It has been many years since these factories provided both seasonable jobs and a market for fuel-wood, eggs, and other foodstuffs from the island, which were used to feed the workers. From the factories, in turn, had come the vast quantities of lobster bodies, which were spread as fertilizer on the fields – the lime from the shells had helped to sweeten the acidic soils.

Most of the farms have been let go and are now returning to the forest. The reasons for this are many and are echoed elsewhere in the Maritimes. The closing of the lobster factories meant an end of a market for food and wood on the island; the introduction of Prince Edward Island's Wood Island Caribou Ferry allowed producers from there to flood Pictou Island's traditional potato market on the nearby mainland; the closing of easily accessible grist mills discouraged the production of grains; the mechanization of forestry meant that oats – traditionally the largest crop – were no longer needed for horses in the woods; tighter governmental regulations and transport difficulties spelled the end of dairying; and raising chickens fed on island wheat became less practical after foxes invaded the island, apparently crossing on the ice in winter, and after beef entered the local market from western Canada provided stiff competition for local producers. No wonder islanders felt buffeted by forces over which they had little control.

The first radio came to Pictou Island in 1930. By 1935, there were nine sets as the popularity of radio continued to increase. Television transmission began in the Maritimes in the late 1950s and it was not long before several island households installed little gasoline electric generators so they could operate television sets. During quiet winter evenings in the 1960s, one could hear the hum of generators up and down the island as people gathered to watch "Hockey Night in Canada," instead of going to the traditional Saturday night party and dance. Probably no force has been more destructive of the old ways than television – except, perhaps, for the consolidation of the schools.

As elsewhere in the Maritimes, Nova Scotian schools were consolidated in order that students – especially at the senior level – could have access to better facilities and teaching than was possible in smaller schools. For these reasons it was decided that students from the island who were read to attend high school, would be sent to the West Pictou School at Lyon's Brook, the closest regional school on the mainland. Rather than sending their children to board, some parents preferred to keep the family together by moving to the mainland. If there were also younger children, they, of course, went along as well. Soon, there were too few children left to justify keeping the island school open and, in 1971, it was closed. This forced the remaining parents with young children to follow the others to the mainland.

As individuals, the students probably benefited from being sent to Lyon's Brook. They gained from the science laboratories and the sports facilities, and gained an opportunity to form a wider circle of friends, which helped them to overcome the shyness inherent in members of a tight, little community. They learned to adjust to the values of the outside world – a necessary step before taking up occupations that demanding regular habits and a placement of one's own interests, and those of the employers, above those of the community. Fishing and farming were looked down on in the school. New skills were acquired and goals were set that could not be achieved on the island. In the end, few students found that they could ever again go home to live. As individuals, they were better able to cope with the wider world, but the community that had nourished them had been destroyed.

Young Pictou Islanders have blended into life on the mainland, and work at a variety of occupations in many different locations. For their parents, settling into regular jobs has not been as easy, and there has been a strong tendency for them to quit work and go back to the island during fishing time; they are still tied to the older rhythm of the seasons and the freedom of the fishing boat and farm, rather than to the relentless ticking of the clock on the confining walls of the factory or office.

No social benefit has had a greater impact on the island than the unemployment insurance cheque. Set up under a federal act proclaimed in 1949, unemployment insurance had little effect on the island at first because most of its population consisted of self-employed farmers and fishermen who were not eligible to receive benefits. However, in the 1950s, benefits were extended to fishermen who worked a specified number of weeks in the year (the number has changed from time to time). This led islanders to concentrate on fishing and to give up farming rather than combine fishing, farming, and perhaps another activity such as working in the woods or picking potatoes on Prince Edward Island, as had been done formerly. Because the lobster season was in late spring and early summer, the most convenient arrangement was to spend the winter on the mainland – especially if there were children in school – and the summer on the island. Thus, the combined effects of unemployment insurance, poor markets for agricultural produce, and the consolidation of the schools, has depopulated the island for much of the year. The Unemployment Insurance Commission also required that the applicants for benefit be readily available for employment and not on a remote island. Ironically, the Unemployment Insurance Commission – born out of the modern industrial state – has helped perpetuate the old rhythm of seasonable activities by replacing part of the annual cycle of work with an insurance cheque sent through the mail.

Unemployment insurance helped some members of a recent group of settlers to establish themselves on Pictou Island. Misnamed "hippies" by the old community, they were part of the back-to-the-land movement that swept the industrial world in the 1960s and 1970s and resulted in the sprouting of "communes" in many remote and abandoned communities in the Maritimes. With them came skills very different from those brought by the original pioneers in the early nineteenth century. They often knew little about farming, but unemployment insurance, tax laws, and welfare systems held few mysteries for them, and they were quite at ease with the whole alphabet of government granting agencies.

The old settlers carried from Scotland a way of life that had evolved over generations of living in an environment not all that dissimilar from Pictou Island. True, the winters were colder and the summers were warmer on Pictou Island and, instead of cutting peat for fuel, wood had to be chopped. Yet, in most essential ways, the old life could be carried on in the new land: the same crops could be grown and the same animals raised; wool could still be spun and woven into cloth; kelp could be gathered for the fields; and even the same fish could be found in the sea. The basis was there for carrying on the same, largely self-sufficent life of the old world. All that was needed was to transfer the old beliefs, customs, and religion. It was accepted that the family was important, and that the foundation of the family was the land. And in Nova Scotia, unlike Scotland, the settlers could own their land. Because of Pictou Island's small size, there was no agricultural frontier to tame and only those inheriting land had the means for remaining on the island. This led to a very stable and conservative population.

The recent settlers were usually well educated and idealistic but, unlike the original pioneers, they did not arrive with the skills necessary for self-sufficiency on the island. They came as individuals and formed bonds looser than those of marriage and family. In the beginning, although land was registered in one name, there was an attempt to hold property and farm equipment in common and to share expenses: "the whole pie-in-the-sky idea of a commune" as one of its members put it. Soon it was discovered that there was "always some greedy bastard who was taking more than his share and not contributing enough." So they said "the hell with it," and from then onward life became more and more private, and more and more like that of the old islanders. Individual members now own and maintain the equipment and each person is responsible for his rows in the garden. Like the old islanders, with their traditional head of the house, the newcomers have discovered that "what you need is a boss": someone to plan and organize the work, but no one seemed to want to take on the task. They have also discovered the need for privacy and have paired off into separate houses. At least one couple has now married and had children. Lastly, they have rediscovered what one old resident had always known when he said: "I've been working for 50 years, and I'm still not even near caught up."

Like those who were there before them, the newcomers have increasingly found their world shrinking to the limits of the island. Now they, in turn, resent the intrusion of outsiders – especially if they are buying land – at least as much as their arrival had been resented by the older residents a few years ago. By the mid-1970s, island land

Figure   **The Population of Pictou Island, 1838–1985**
16.2

had passed into the hands of residents of several Canadian provinces and at least six of the United States. Many owners were speculators who had never seen the island, but who had, nevertheless, helped bid up the price of the land far beyond its agricultural value. The only future now open to the island would seem to be as a recreational area. A few summer cottages have already been built, and the island is becoming increasingly popular with tourists. Thus, Pictou Island, like so many once self-sufficient communities in the Maritimes, has become almost totally dependant on the outside world – a world over which it has little control.

Today, nearly two dozen people live on the island the year round – about half are newcomers and half descendents of the old settlers (Figure 16.2). In the summer, the number rises to about 40, when a number of cottagers and former islanders arrive for the season. Only two of the permanent settlers are still farming. One of these is a man who worked for many years in Boston, repairing traffic meters, before returning to the island. In coming back, he typifies many Maritimers who spend large portions of their working lives in other regions before finally returning home to their roots. But for each one of these, there are many who, once they have left, seldom return except for visits. It is the outflow of these people and the rise of major industrial cities in other parts of the country that have caused the Maritime share of the Canadian population to steadily fall behind. In 1851, its share was 22 percent, by 1971 it had dropped to only 7.1 percent.

Outflow has varied from decade to decade, usually as a reflection of economic conditions both real and perceived. For example, even though earnings were still below those in the rest of Canada, the first decade of the century was a time of optimism in the Maritimes, coming as it did after a period of relative retardation in the latter years of the nineteenth century. Cape Breton steel was being developed and the future was looking brighter. Except for Prince Edward Island, which was then suffering its greatest population loss in this century, out-migration was lower than might have been expected. Being more dependant upon agriculture than the other two provinces, Prince Edward Island was already feeling stiff competition from the newly opened west. With the onset of the First World War, economic activity quickened, especially in the ice-free ports of Halifax and Saint John. Thousands of young men answered the imperial call, including seven from Pictou Island. Many others found work in wartime industries.

In the post-war period, the Maritime provinces were unable to adjust to the changed economic conditions, and the result was a rapid increase in the number of people leaving the region. The boom of 1926–29 largely passed them by, and both Nova Scotia and New Brunswick suffered their greatest population losses of this century. The migrants' favourite destination, by far, was the United States, especially nearby New England, known familiarly in the Maritimes as the "Boston States." Once settled, they made the pilgrimage back to the Maritimes, year after year, with "smart" gifts for their relatives and news of a more glamorous world where the future had already arrived. Some came up by steamer to Yarmouth or Halifax; others travelled on "The Gull," the overnight train that ran from Boston. Best of all, though, was to drive home in the finest car one could afford and add yet another exotic licence plate from Massachusetts or Connecticut to the dusty summer roads of the 1930s and 1940s. Incidentally, it was a man returning from the Boston States who taught the first Pictou Island car-owner how to drive his shiny new automobile.

In the 1930s the Maritimes were among the areas worst hit by the Great Depression. Yet emigration almost ceased during this time. Across the border, New England was among the hardest hit regions in the United States and could no longer serve as the land of opportunity for their northern neighbours. Without their traditional outlet, Maritimers stayed home and "made do" as best they could.

After the Second World War, migration patterns changed. Maritimers no longer looked to the United States: personal links, disrupted during the depression, were not re-established; the American military draft, unlike that in Canada, continued after the war was over, making the United States less attractive to young Canadian males; the New England economy was slowing down and the American border was being tightened. Although farther away than New England and much less appealing as a place to live, prosperous Ontario was becoming the new magnet for migrants. The distant Canadian West was costly to reach and did not exert a strong pull until the Alberta oil boom of the 1960s and 1970s. With the downturn in the oil industry in the 1980s, many former Maritimers are now returning home to "make do" once again. Like the Pictou Islander going home for the summer, Maritimers are drawn back to the region by the older ways of a long-settled community where life seems slower and the people "more friendly." In returning to an area that has received relatively few immigrants for many decades, they are often exchanging the ethnic variety and excitement found in the newer areas of the country for the comfortable and familiar. Undoubtedly, the ebb and flow will continue. At the moment, the U-haul trailers are accumulating at the Maritime end of the migration route.

Acknowledgements

Grateful acknowledgement is accorded to the following interviewees: the late Howard MacLean, the late Andy MacCallum and Mrs. MacCallum, Alfred MacLean, Carl MacCallum, Mr. and Mrs. Earnie Rankin, Jack "Happy" MacDonald and the late Mrs. MacDonald, Barry Mack, Billy MacMillan, Ken Banks, the late Mr. and Mrs. Campbell MacCallum, Mr. and Mrs. Chris Stafford, David Harding, Beth Munroe, Charlie Munroe, Florence MacMaster, Calvin MacCullum, Mr. and Mrs. Roy McCallum, Ona Glover, Ruth Munro, the late John Malcolm MacCallum, and Mr. and Mrs. Parker Lewis.

Notes

1. Some of the material in this chapter was published previously in E. Ross. "The Rise and Fall of Pictou Island," in L.D. McCann, ed., *People and Place: Studies of Small Town Life in the Maritimes* (Sackville and Fredericton: Acadiensis Press, 1987), 161–90.

2. See A.H. Clark, "Old World Origins and Religious Adherance in Nova Scotia," *Geographical Review* 50 (1960): 3.

3. G. Patterson, A *History of the County of Pictou, Nova Scotia*, 1877; Reprint, *The Pictou Advocate,* 1916, 178–80.

   The remainder of this chapter is based largely on interviews with inhabitants of Pictou Island past and present, on field observations, on census data, and on items from *The Pictou Advocate* (1895–1975). Most of the inteviews were conducted in the summers of 1975, 1976, 1984, and 1985.

4. The map is from J.H. Meachan & Co., *Illustrated Historical Atlas of Pictou County, Nova Scotia,* 1879 (edited by Mika Silk Screening Ltd., Belleville, Ontario, 1972).

17 The People of Newfoundland: A *Longue Durée* in Historical Geography

Alan G. Macpherson

The people of Newfoundland can be thought of as the result of two *longues durées*, two overlapping periods of long duration in which social, cultural, and economic evolution and development have occurred. A *grande longue durée*, associated with aboriginal North American peoples, began about 9,000 years ago with the arrival of Palaeolithic Indians on the North Shore of the Gulf of St. Lawrence and in the vicinity of the Strait of Belle Isle in Southern Labrador. A *petite longue durée* – longer in duration than elsewhere in North America north of the Caribbean and the Gulf of Mexico – began with the advent of European peoples on north-west Atlantic shores between Southern Labrador and Cape Race, the south-easternmost tip of the island of Newfoundland, about 500 years ago. From about 1500 A.D. to the present, the two *longues durées* have co-existed, usually in an uneasy and increasingly unequal relationship, but tending to converge, to some degree, into a single process in the twentieth century. The social and cultural characteristics of the people of Newfoundland at the latter end of the twentieth century are, in effect, deep reflections of these collective experiences through time.

17.1 The *"Grande Longue Durée"*

Archaeological investigations have established Amerindian presence at sites on the Labrador shore of the Strait of Belle Isle as early as 9,000 years ago, as well as the development of the Maritime Archaic tradition based upon their seasonal utilization of fish, marine mammals, and inland caribou. Bearers of this tradition had extended their domain north of Hamilton Inlet and Lake Melville by 6000 B.P. (c. 4000 B.C.), eventually reaching at least as far north as Saglek in Northern Labrador (see Figure 17.1). There is no evidence, as yet, of their advance southwards across the strait into the island until after 5000 B.P. (c. 3000 B.C.), when they appear at sites in the northern half as far south as Bonne Bay on the west coast and Bonavista Bay on the east coast (Tuck 1976).

Shortly after 4000 B.P. (c. 2000 B.C.) Palaeo-Eskimo hunters appeared in Northern Labrador, co-existing with later Maritime Archaic Indians and heralding the sudden advance of Dorset Eskimo into Northern and Southern Labrador and the island around 3000 B.P. (c. 1000 B.C.). The Dorset people had apparently withdrawn from Southern Labrador by 2500 B.P. (c. 500 B.C.), where they were replaced by resurgent late Maritime Archaic Indians, the probable ancestors of the modern Naskapi. Dorset people, however, continued to frequent the shores of Northern Labrador and the entire littoral of island Newfoundland until about 1300 B.P. (650

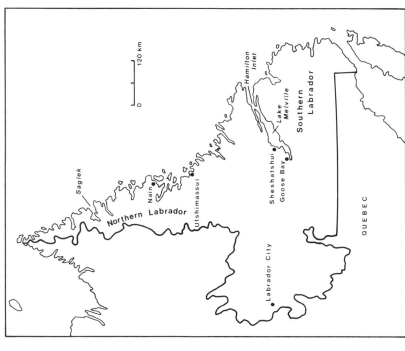

Figure 17.1b **Labrador**

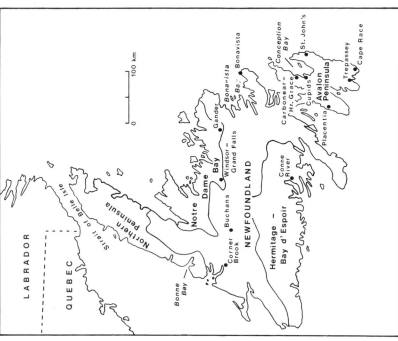

Figure 17.1a **Newfoundland**

A.D.), suggesting that they were present for over a millenium in two geographically isolated populations (McGhee 1978).

By 1200 B.P. (750 A.D.) Recent Indians, ancestors of the historic Beothuck, appear in the archaeological record for the island, and shortly thereafter they also replaced the ancient Dorset in Northern Labrador. In doing so they introduced a discontinuity between the Dorset Eskimo and the later Thule people, who succeeded them across the Canadian Arctic, similar to the hiatus filled by the Norse colonists when they arrived in Greenland in 986 A.D. The people of the vigorous Thule culture, ancestors of the modern Inuit of both Canada and Greenland, only advanced in Northern Labrador – as into Greenland – after 1200 A.D., suggesting that the natives who were observed and contacted by the Norse explorers and would-be colonists of Markland (Labrador) and Vinland (Newfoundland) in the first two decades of the eleventh century were Recent Indians. This seems to be confirmed by the fact that an enthusiastic trade in grey furs took place before the Norse withdrew to their base in medieval Greenland (Jones 1964).

With the advent of Europeans on the coasts of Newfoundland and Labrador around 1500 A.D., the cultural history of the aboriginal peoples entered a new phase, the tone of which was set by the forcible abduction of natives, both Beothuck and Inuit, by John Cabot in 1498 and by Gaspar Corte Real in 1501 (Howley 1915, 3–6). Coastal Inuit and nomadic Labrador Indians (Montagnais) moved into the southern end of Labrador during the sixteenth century, attracted by and in response to Basque whaling activities in the Strait of Belle Isle, part of the reshaping of aboriginal cultures around the Gulf of St. Lawrence that took place prior to European settlement. Perhaps the few bands of Naskapi Innu in the interior of Labrador were experiencing only the more distant shock of the early fur trade as it gained force among their relatives, the Montagnais, along the North Shore of the Gulf of St. Lawrence. In the case of the island Beothuck, the initial impact was one of steady encroachment upon summer fishing stations, particularly on the eastern shores of the Avalon Peninsula (Pastore n.d.). At the point of contact there were probably between one thousand and two thousand Beothuck on the island, while the Innu and Inuit in Labrador probably only numbered a few hundred each.

Pressure on the Beothuck took a more portentous turn in 1610 A.D. when the first party of English settlers arrived in Conception Bay to begin the process of colonization, and the first recorded party of Micmac Indians arrived on the island from Cape Breton Island to begin what appears to have been a pattern of seasonal or intermittent migration across the Cabot Strait, which lasted until the second half of the eighteenth century. These new departures meant further summer encroachment upon shore fishing stations, and winter competition for interior hunting and trapping grounds. More than two centuries of occasional atrocity, epidemic and endemic disease, and starvation ensued, causing the harassed Beothuck tribe to dwindle in numbers to the point of ultimate extinction at the end of the third decade of the nineteenth century. As they dwindled, their place was most effectively taken by the highly successful Micmac, who, like the Europeans, now came to settle permanently on the island. In fact the nineteenth century saw the Micmac spread their operating territory throughout the island, demonstrating that they could flourish in close proximity to a white society (Pastore 1978).

The inability of British authorities to protect and ensure the survival of the Beothuck was not repeated in the case of the Inuit. In 1769 the Unitas Fratrum or Moravian Church acquired from the British government a large tract of land in Northern Labrador for the express purpose of isolating the Inuit from the unruly whisky traders and summer fishermen in Southern Labrador (Lysacht 1766). From 1771, when the Nain mission was established, until the decade following Confederation with Canada in 1949, the Inuit remained under the ecclesiastical and commercial care of the Moravians. Inevitably subject to a considerable degree of acculturation, they had, by the 1840s, also achieved a high level of sustained literacy, albeit in their own language (Inuktitut), while nearby settler communities remained largely illiterate until after Confederation.

On the island, the first three decades of the twentieth century saw the rapid decline of the caribou herds and the concomitant end of traditional life for the Micmac, who then tended to concentrate at Conne River in Bay Despair. Loss of language and intermarriage during the last half century, as well as economic and social dependence upon government, have led provincial authorities to regard the 500-strong community at Conne River as just another rural community within the body politic and social fabric of Newfoundland. In spite of this, and indeed in response, the Micmacs have developed a new political consciousness that has reforged their links with Micmac in the Maritimes homeland, has brought them into touch with Indians across Canada, and has won them federal recognition as status Indians. Strenuous efforts have been made to redevelop a locally based economy, to assume some control over education, to re-invigorate their language (Paddock 1982), and to re-establish contact with people of mixed Micmac origin in other parts of the island. On the other hand, their controversial claim to aboriginal rights on the island is looked at askance by the provincial authorities and by the society at large.

The situation of the Indians in Labrador has been rather different. Traditional lifestyles prevailed, virtually untouched, until the arrival of the Hudson's Bay Company in the early nineteenth century. Subsequently, they have been socially marginalized by the advent of government intervention in 1942, when the company withdrew from responsibility; by the militarization of the local economy centred at Goose Bay in Central Labrador, which has continued apace since the Second World War; and by large-scale development of mineral, water, and forest resources. Nevertheless, the 700-strong Montagnais at Sheshatshui (formerly part of North West River) and the 200-strong Naskapi at Utshimassui (Davis Inlet), on the Northern Labrador coast south of Nain, have succeeded in retaining their language and have sustained their propensity to live a nomadic life for part of the year (Henriksen 1973). As the Innu of Labrador, they, and the Inuit, claim aboriginal rights to the land, and for some years have been engaged in negotiation with federal and provincial authorities to establish special rights to protect their culture and traditional way of life from further deterioration, and to compensate them for earlier environmental and cultural damage caused by large-scale developments in the Labrador economy.

The Inuit of Northern Labrador, now largely concentrated at Nain, have also moved into a socially dependent and marginalized position with respect to both the mainstream society and the regional economy since the 1950s, when the Moravian Church withdrew from its commercial monopoly, thereby abdicating its social control and opening the way for modernizing influences to enter. Resettlement, intermarriage, the imposition of education in English, and the consequent decline in the use of Inuktitut have all had their baleful and baneful effects upon the Inuit culture and way of life. Nevertheless, as in the case of the island Micmac and Innu of Labrador, the Inuit have become politically aware and, through the medium of radio in their case, have established communication with fellow Inuit from Alaska to Greenland.

Therefore, despite the pervasive and enervating effects of convergence with mainstream Canadian society, cultural resistance remains potent among the native peoples of Newfoundland and Labrador, and the last chapter in the *grande longue durée* has not yet been reached.

17.2 The *"Petite Longue Durée"*

The *petite longue durée* of those Newfoundlanders who trace their origins to European – predominantly British – homelands began with a series of exploratory voyages into the north-western Atlantic between 1480 and 1510. The single most significant outcome from John Cabot's expedition of 1497 was not his controversial landfall, but his observation that "the sea there is swarming with fish." It was the discovery of this attractive staple resource that set in train the whole course of events that have constituted the subsequent economic history and social evolution of Newfoundland; the fortunes of the fishery and their impact upon its personnel have dominated the *petite longue durée* throughout the past 500 years.

The *petite longue durée* can be best understood in terms of three distinct phases in which the population and mode of settlement evolved in conjunction with changes in the organization of the fishery. The first phase began with the exploratory expeditions and ended in 1610. The fishery was prosecuted as an open international activity, based in western France, northern Spain, Portugal, and south-western England, and was exclusively seasonal in character. St. John's harbour, for instance, enters the historical record for the first time in 1527, when it was occupied by one English, one Breton, two Portuguese, and eleven Norman fishing vessels (Hoffman 1961, 19). Although many thousands of fishermen frequented the bays, headlands, and drying beaches of the island in the course of the sixteenth century, no effective settlement occurred – indeed, no effective claim to exclusive sovereignty was made until 1583. Instead, the entire personnel of the summer fishery continued to return to their home bases in south-western Europe every fall. Basque whalers, who began to establish flensing and rendering stations along the Labrador shore of the Strait of Belle Isle from 1543 onwards, tended to stay a little longer in the season – sometimes inadvertently and disastrously staying over the winter – but had usually returned home by January, leaving no one other than native peoples to overwinter on the island or the strait (Barkham 1982, 53–95).

Although English colonization and the practice of overwintering were advocated as early as 1578, no change in the mode of prosecuting the fishery occurred until 1610. In that year, John Guy of Bristol's settlement at Cupids in Conception Bay, with a party of 40 men (who were joined by 16 women the following year), began the more complex and socially significant second phase. Twenty years of colonial experimentation ensued, involving a series of promotional land grants which resulted in the establishment of half a dozen plantations around the Avalon Peninsula (Cell 1969, 1982). Abortive in terms of commercial success, these formal plantations demonstrated, nevertheless, the feasibility of year-round habitation and, in conjunction with more enlightened fishing interests, spawned a score of thriving permanent settlements between Trepassey and Bonavista – the "Old English Shore" – by 1675. St. John's, where the first plantation houses appear to have been built in 1627 (Cell 1982, 274), a century after it was first used as a summer fishing station, soon came to dominate the new colony, challenged only by French Placentia (Plaisance) in the years between its establishment in 1662 and its demise as the French capital in 1713.

By the 1660s the second phase of the *petite longue durée* had become characterized by three concurrent and interrelated modes for prosecuting the fishery, all operating what was essentially a boat-fishery, whether offshore or inshore. The old migratory ship-fishery based in south-west England was still in operation, bringing hundreds of fishermen to their traditional fishing stations in Newfoundland every spring, and returning them home every fall. Associated with this was the byboat fishery, a Devon-based enterprise largely confined to the southern harbours of the colony and prominent in St. John's harbour, in which byboat masters and their fishing servants came and went as passengers on the fishing ships. By definition the byboat fishery was an inshore operation, and it was as seasonal and migratory as the ship-fishery on which it depended; neither included women among its operatives. The third mode was that of the overwintering planter and his indentured fishing servants, operating for the most part an inshore boat-fishery, but later in some instances acquiring banking vessels that could operate offshore. As they finished their three- or five-year indentures, the fishing servants, mostly young men and boys, were returned to England or Ireland in the fall, to be replaced the following spring by fresh recruits who also came as passengers on the seasonal fishing ships.

As the second phase unfolded, there was plenty of opportunity for both masters and men to move from one mode to another, and it might be argued that just as the byboat fishery grew out of the ship-fishery, so the overwintering and resident planter-fishery found its main recruitment of both masters and men in the ranks of the byboat-men. Acquisition of a shore fishing-room and the decision to overwinter with a working crew allowed the planter to bring his wife and family to join him in the enterprise. Thus, a population of resident Newfoundlanders grew alongside the migratory Newfoundland-men of Devon and Dorset, Wexford and Waterford (Head 1976).

Nevertheless, it must be emphasized that women were heavily outnumbered by men throughout the second phase, even in the winter, and that all categories of winter residents (including planters and their wives) were subject to marked and frequent

Persons

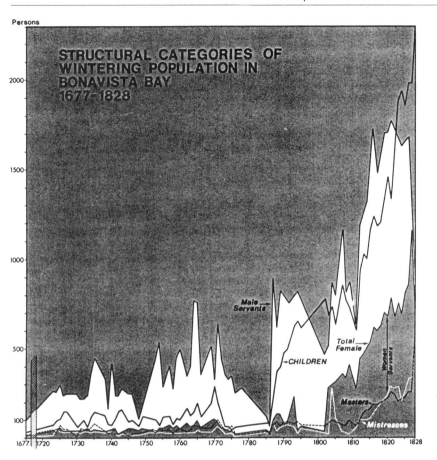

Figure 17.2   Structural Categories of Wintering Population in Bonavista Bay, 1677–1828

fluctuations in numbers, as exemplified in Bonavista Bay between 1677 and 1800 (Figure 17.2), indicating a fundamental turnover of personnel in sympathy with the fluctuating fortunes of the highly speculative fishery. Few agnatic surnames present in the 1670s survived this process into the mid-eighteenth century, and the number of women in the colony grew very slowly (Macpherson 1977, 102–9). Few of the planters and none of the men servants can have thought of themselves as permanent residents, destined to die and leave a progeny in Newfoundland.

The second phase ended, essentially, with the demise of the ancient ship-fishery and its ancillary byboat fishery at the end of the eighteenth century. The "winter" population, which began in 1610–11 with 40 persons who were 100 percent adult male and Protestant English, stood at 15,670 in the winter of 1796–97. Of these, 2,402 were women, representing 27 percent (a ratio of three men to every woman in the adult population), and some 6,700, or roughly 43 percent, were Catholic and Irish.

The third phase of the *petite longue durée* began as the second waned. It opened in the aftermath of the American Revolution and was further stimulated by the Napoleonic Wars, when a major wave of immigration, primarily from the traditional recruiting grounds of the older fisheries in south-western England and the south-east quarter of Ireland, passed into the island, swamping in volume the pre-revolutionary planter population (Handcock 1976, 1340; Handcock 1977, 15–48). It can be seen as it washed into Bonavista Bay after 1800, in Figure 17.2, and its shape, though not its volume, can be perceived in the graph of immigrant Irish marrying in St. John's and its vicinity between 1793 and 1856 (Figure 17.3). Immigrants were predominantly young, and many were single; marriage often followed closely upon arrival in the island. Marriage in Newfoundland (as recorded in the registers at the Basilica) can be used, therefore, as a surrogate for immigration to determine the temporal nature of the wave and the ratio of men to women involved. A graph of marriage among the immigrant English and few Scots would undoubtedly show a similar, if not identical, pattern.

Peaking in the period between 1811 and 1830, the wave of immigration was virtually expended by the 1860s, only isolated areas on the south and west coasts of the island and along the Southern Labrador coast receiving demographically significant numbers of immigrants thereafter. Between 1840 and 1880 southern parts of the old French fishing shore in the south-west corner of the island, such as the Codroy Valley and St. George's Bay, received a quite distinct immigration of British North American colonials: Acadians, Highland Scots, and Irish from Catholic Cape Breton (Ommer 1977, 212–33). In 1836, when the peak of the immigration wave had passed, the population of the colony was 64,701 persons, the sex ratio had reached parity, and the Irish component had risen to 52 percent. By 1869, when the wave had exhausted itself, the population was 146,536, a ten-fold increase in the population since the end of the eighteenth century.

These large-scale events effectively put their stamp upon the population as it has presented itself ever since. A century or more has elapsed since they occurred, and the community of Newfoundland in general has settled down to processes of indigenous growth, moderated by selective out-migration to the North American mainland and, since Confederation in 1949, by only partially compensating inflows of new blood. The population has undergone a four-fold increase since 1869. The question of quality remains.

17.3   The First Literacy Transition

The quality of a people of the industrial age is generally taken to be a fundamental element of its capacity for sustained social and economic growth. It is best measured by the level of the ability to read within the population, and it is taken as axiomatic – in terms of the usual order of events in what may well be a curtailed education – that the level of ability to read is higher than the level of ability to write. The ability to sign one's name is, therefore, an objective standard lying somewhere between the two, and represents an underestimate of the essential ability to read. Hard data in a marriage register, for instance, should be more reliable than subjective

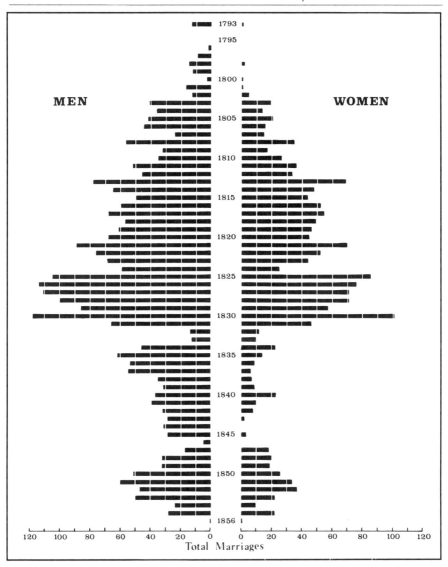

Figure   **Incidence of Irish Immigrant Marriages in Newfoundland,**
17.3   **1793–1856**

answers to census questions concerning the ability to read or write (Alexander 1978). Analysis of a marriage register has the further advantage that the ability to sign, on the part of the bride and groom, can be ascribed to a fairly representative cross-section of the population and to both sexes equally; above all, it relates overwhelmingly to young adults within 10 or 15 years of whatever formal education they may have received. As such, it represents a level of ability higher than that of the population at large.

The marriage register of the Anglican parish of Hermitage for the period 1844–1965 provides evidence of the literacy transition that has been achieved in a relatively remote rural area on the south coast of Newfoundland. To what extent it is representative of other places and other denominations is unproved, and one can expect more complex situations to have existed in larger, more central places such as St. John's. Its simple elegance, however, indicates that it can be approached with some confidence. In the analysis, the marrying couple, rather than the individual, has been used as the scoring unit, and each marriage has been assigned to one of four categories, in which neither, the man only, the woman only, or both, could sign the register (Table 17.1).

Table 17.1 **The First Literacy Transition: Hermitage Parish**

Period	Number of Marriages	Percentage Able to Sign				Population Literacy Rate
		Neither	Man	Woman	Both	
1844–55	58	93.1	3.4	0.0	1.7	3.4
1867–80	272	74.6	10.3	4.4	10.7	18.0
1881–90	215	60.0	13.0	14.0	13.0	26.5
1891–1900	243	51.0	13.2	17.3	18.5	33.7
1901–10	315	30.2	13.2	20.3	36.2	53.0
1911–20	158	29.1	17.1	22.2	31.6	51.3
1921–30	105	19.0	10.5	21.9	48.6	64.8
1931–40	157	3.8	1.3	15.9	79.0	86.6
1941–50	151	2.6	5.3	6.6	85.4	91.4
1951–60	154	2.6	2.6	8.4	86.4	91.9
1961–65	76	1.3	1.3	1.3	96.1	97.4

The experience of the young Anglicans of Hermitage suggests something of the historical or cultural mechanism by which literacy spread within the Newfoundland population. Prior to 1880 men tended to be more literate than women, a mark perhaps of the prevailing economy. But from the 1880s to the 1950s the young women of Hermitage, collectively, tended to be several percentage points ahead of the men they married. Similar differences have been observed between husband and wife on the land settlements established in various parts of the island during the 1930s. And as in the case of the land settlements, this tendency must have had an impact upon the education and educational aspirations of the next generation, raising literacy levels of both sexes. Nevertheless, if a 40 percent literacy level is a precondition for any kind of take-off into modern social and economic growth, then Newfoundland's population as a whole did not achieve it until the end of the nineteenth century (Alexander 1980). Nevertheless, rural Newfoundland, as represented by Hermitage, was steadily catching up with the more literate centres such as St. John's throughout the nineteenth century, although convergence probably did not occur until the 1930s.

17.4   Newfoundland's Population in 1981 and the Second Literacy Transition

In 1981 the population of Newfoundland stood at an all-time high of 567,681. Almost a quarter of this total (131,694 or 23.2 percent) resided in the urbanized metropolitan area of St. John's, while another 11 percent lived in places that held between 10,000 and 30,000 persons, most of them in the four larger urban centres of Corner Brook (24,204), Labrador City (14,688), Grand Falls–Windsor (14,107), and Carbonear–Harbour Grace (10,209). Smaller places, of between 1,000 and 10,000 persons, added a further 24 percent, to give a total "urban" component of 58.4 percent. Compared with the national figure of 75.7 percent, this seems low, while the 41.6 percent (234,783) classified as "rural" – the national figure being 24.3 percent – seems correspondingly high. The usual explanation is to hold responsible a time-lag in the province's transition to an urbanized modern society. However, Newfoundland differs from the other provinces in the virtual absence of a dispersed landward population; an overwhelming proportion of the "rural component" lives in agglomerated settlements below the arbitrary size of 1,000 persons. The distribution of the population and the settlement pattern are powerful reflections of the historical importance of the fisheries, which have always dominated the economy and social patterns of Newfoundland.[1]

The province is further distinguished within Confederation by having the highest level of patriation of its population: in 1981 over 98 percent were Canadian-born, 94 percent were Newfoundland-born, while the survivors of the immigration process constituted less than 10,000 persons, of whom 41 percent were United Kingdom–born and 23 percent American-born.[2]

Newfoundland stands culturally apart from the other provinces in other respects. With 94.7 percent of the people claiming ethnic origins in the British Isles (92.2 percent exclusively so), the province feels itself to be the most "British" part of Canada. At a distance of 2,900 kilometres it is, literally, the part of North America closest to the British homelands; it was the earliest part of the New World to be subject to English exploration, exploitation, and colonial expansion; and, in 1949, it was the last part of Canada to pass from British jurisdiction into Confederation. In 1981 ethnic origins in France were claimed by just 4.7 percent of Newfoundland residents (26,450 people), of whom 2.7 percent (15,355 people) claimed exclusive French background. In contrast with other parts of Canada, Newfoundland's population contained only tiny fractions of 1 percent claiming other ethnic origins: native (Amerindian and Inuit 0.6 percent, 0.78 percent if mixed origins are included), German (0.3 percent), Chinese, Dutch, Indo-Pakistani, and Scandinavian (0.1 percent each), Italian (0.07 percent), Pacific Islanders, mainly Filipino (0.06 percent), and Jewish (0.05 percent). Polish and Ukrainian origins, unlike elsewhere in Canada, are proportionally insignificant in Newfoundland.

In terms of location, the St. John's metropolitan area holds 27 percent of the total provincial population and 27.35 percent of the British component. Thus, there is little difference in ethnicity overall between the provincial capital and the rest of the province. However, the St. John's area has drawn high proportions of the ethnic streams of post-war immigrants. By 1981 it contained 64.8 percent of those claiming Indo-Pakistani origin, 57.5 percent of those of Chinese origin, and 39.8 percent of those of German origin, while less than 16 percent of the much older French component and less than 6 percent of the native component lived in the capital area. Significant proportions of the French and native elements, both Amerindian and Inuit, are associated with Labrador.[3]

Ethnic origin is a somewhat subjective measure, particularly for a population with roots as deep as those of the majority of people in the island of Newfoundland and mainland Labrador. Language affiliation is a more concrete measure, having the virtue of reflecting ethnicity to some degree but also providing a measure of cultural assimilation. Thus, over 99 percent of the people spoke English at home (97.3 percent monoglot), while only 0.32 percent (1,810 persons) spoke French at home, of which only 135 persons or 0.02 percent were monoglot.

Some 12,845 persons (2.3 percent of the total population) claimed to be bilingual, of whom 10,205 – virtually 80 percent – stated English to be their mother tongue. The last figure must have risen rapidly since the 1981 census, as French immersion programs have continued to spread throughout the education system. On the other hand, only 0.1 percent of those claiming English as their mother tongue (556,940 persons) used French as the language of the home, while 43 percent of those claiming French as their mother tongue (2,690 persons) used English as the language of the home. Table 17.2 indicates the preference for English as the general medium of communication as well as the degree of linguistic assimilation of natives and immigrants with mother tongues other than English and French.

The contrast in degree of linguistic assimilation between the Chinese and Indo-Pakistani groups undoubtedly reflects the legacy of the British Raj and greater familiarity with English prior to immigration on the part of the latter.The contrast between the two native mother tongue groups reflects the geographical and cultural isolation of the Inuit in Northern Labrador under the tutelage of largely German-speaking Moravian missionaries, and the protracted contact between English-speaking authorities and the Amerindians, particularly the Nova Scotia–based Micmacs now resident on the island.

The locational pattern of ethnic origins is reflected in the linguistic distribution. In 1981 the Census Metropolitan Area centred on St. John's contained 27 percent of the provincial population, but 61 percent of those whose mother tongue was Chinese, and only 18 percent of those claiming French as their mother tongue. Survivors of a century of Chinese immigration and presence in Newfoundland represent post-1945 arrivals (97 percent of them), whereas the French-speakers represent a mid-nineteenth-century influx of Acadians in south-west Newfoundland and a current generation of Quebecois largely associated with the opening of iron-ore resources in Western Labrador. Immigration from the Indian subcontinent and from the Philippines is essentially a post-1955 phenomenon.[4]

Religious affiliation introduces quite a different dimension of the social geography of Newfoundland as represented in the 1981 census (Table 17.3). Those of Protestant affiliation collectively equate with those of English and Lowland Scot

Table 17.2   **Distribution of Languages, 1981**

Mother Tongue	Total	% English	% French	% Mother Tongue	% Other
German	390	75.6	—	24.4	—
Amerindian	320	65.6	—	34.4	—
Indo-Pakistani	370	47.3	—	45.9	6.8
Other	1785	44.5	1.1	52.7	1.7
Inuktitut	800	36.3	—	63.7	—
Chinese	460	25.0	—	75.0	—

Source: *Census of Canada, 1981*

origins and, in the case of the Moravians, with the Inuit of Northern Labrador, while the adherents of the Roman Catholic Church are overwhelmingly of Irish origin, with enclaves of Scots Highland and Acadian origins in south-west Newfoundland.

Traditionally, religious affiliation in Newfoundland has been closely related to political attitudes and, constitutionally, to the provision of education. The dominance of the Roman Catholic, Anglican, and United Church (Methodist) communities reflects the historic primacy of those faiths, while the order in which the smaller denominations range themselves – again with the exception of the Moravians – is a measure of the order of their appearance in the province. Table 17.3 indicates that the Roman Catholics enjoy a greater intensity in the metropolitan population, almost 50 percent, than in the provincial population, while the smaller denominations have diminished presences. Thus, in terms of denominational social structure, St. John's

Table 17.3   **Religious Affiliation, 1981**

Denominations	Newfoundland Numbers	%	St. John's Numbers	%	Proportion in St. John's
Total	563,745	100	152,475	100	
Roman Catholic	204,430	36.3	74,025	48.5	36.2
Anglican	153,530	27.2	37,420	24.5	24.4
United Church	104,835	18.6	25,945	17.0	24.8
Salvation Army	45,115	8.0	4,325	2.8	9.6
Pentecostal	37,450	6.6	2,635	1.7	7.0
No preference	5,515	1.0	2,860	1.9	51.9
Presbyterian	2,700	0.5	2,000	1.3	74.1
Moravians	2,050	0.4	—	—	—
Jehovah's Witnesses	2,020	0.4	500	0.3	24.8

Source: *Census of Canada, 1981*

differs markedly from the rest of the province. The same contrast is obvious in the uneven distributions of the individual denominations, listed in the last column of Table 17.3. Not surprisingly, the metropolitan area has over half of those professing no affiliation.[5]

The levels of educational attainment that have emerged from the denominational system of education, and that characterize the human resource in the provincial economy, are also distinctive. In 1976 some 37 percent of the provincial population aged 15 and over indicated that they had less than a grade nine education; the national figure was 26 percent. By 1981 the provincial figure had dropped to 30.5 percent (the national to 20 percent). Although the gap with the rest of the country has been barely affected, a second literacy transition has evidently been progressing apace in Newfoundland for some time. The most favoured parts of the province in this respect have been the Avalon Peninsula, including the metropolitan area of St. John's, with 23.7 percent; the central part of the island (including the international airport town of Gander and the mining town of Buchans), with 24.1 percent; and Labrador (including the western iron-mining region and the militarized town of Goose Bay), with 24.6 percent. The least favoured have been the Hermitage–Bay Despair area on the south coast (48 percent), the Northern Peninsula (44 percent), Notre Dame Bay (42.9 percent), and Bonavista Bay (40.9 percent).

When these statistics are broken down by sex, a further distinction appears. In Canada as a whole there was less than one percentage point between men and women, slightly in favour of the men. In Newfoundland the gap was three-and-a-half points, and in favour of the women. Eight of the ten census divisions into which the province is divided showed the same tendency, the exceptions being Hermitage–Bay Despair and Labrador. The widest gap occurred in the Northern Peninsula where 40.24 percent of the women, and as much as 47.49 percent of the men, had failed to achieve that level of education.[6]

Populations with educational levels below grade nine are defined by UNESCO as living in a condition of functional illiteracy, characteristic of the Third World and disadvantageous for efficient living and work in a modernized economy. While numbers of individual Newfoundlanders can deny this definition as it might apply to their own lives, the fact that almost one-third of Newfoundland's adult population falls below that level is bound to have a deleterious and long-term effect on Newfoundland's economy and level of culture, and at the very least deter certain kinds of investment. Despite its crudity, such a measure is a good indicator of semi-periphery status within the national and global economies, even if the levels of attainment have been lowered by the out-migration of the more able.

At the other end of the educational scale, as measured by the census, 4.66 percent of the adult population of Newfoundland possess a bachelor's degree, against the national figure of 8 percent. When these figures are broken down by sex, the proportion for men in Newfoundland rises to 6.15 percent, and for women drops to 3.57 percent, against the national figures of 9.92 and 6.15 percent respectively. Although depleted by out-migration, the proportions for Newfoundland nevertheless emphasize the disparity under which the province labours within Confederation. This is further reflected in the rates of participation in the labour force, the unemployment rates, the average individual earnings, and the average family incomes for 1981 (Table 17.4). Dropping almost eight percentage points below the national figure in participation in the labour force, with more than double the national unemployment rate, and trailing the national averages in individual earnings and family income by 22.2 and 21.6 percent respectively, Newfoundland's people are stigmatized socially by their economic situation. It is not surprising, therefore, that the barometer birth cohort, which passed from the 15 to 19 age group to the 20 to 24 age group between 1976 and 1981, suffered a net loss in numbers amounting to 11,620 persons – an 18.63 percent loss.[7] Haemorrhages of this order, and occasionally as high as 25 percent, have been recorded for every cohort passing through this stage in their lives since Confederation. Whatever construction may be placed upon such statistics, they must be accepted as a potent measure of a persisting inability in the provincial economy to absorb a significant proportion of its young people into the labour force.

Level of educational attainment constitutes a problematic precondition in the provincial economy that is fundamental to the social and economic ills that afflict the provincial society as a whole. More vitally, it affects the futures of young Newfoundlanders – those who leave as well as those who stay. As such it is perhaps the most striking, and certainly the most crucial, of all the social indicators characterizing the people of Newfoundland at this point in their *longue durée*.

Table 17.4   **Economic Statistics: Newfoundland and Canada**

	Participation %	Unemployment %	Earnings $	Family Income $
Canada	64.8	7.4	16,918	26,748
Newfoundland	57.1	17.5	13,166	20,971

Source: Census of Canada, 1981

17.5   The People of Newfoundland in 1986

Between 1981 and 1986 the population of Newfoundland crept up a little further, to a total of 568,349. In the interval the fundamental patterns of the province's cultural geography remained essentially unchanged. The second literary transition, however, proceeded steadily, the proportion of the population over 15 with less than grade nine dropping a further four points to 26.6 percent and slightly closing the gap with the national figure of 17.7 percent. The transition,[8] which began at 68.7 percent in 1951, has entered the final, and perhaps most difficult, stage (Figure 17.4). The educational condition of the people nevertheless remains an inhibiting factor in the future prospects of the province; the fact that over a quarter of the adult population is functionally illiterate 40 years after Confederation calls into constitutional question the efficacy of the denominational education system.

Closer examination of the census data reveals that there are dimensions of age, gender, and regional location in the provincial situation. Functional illiteracy is

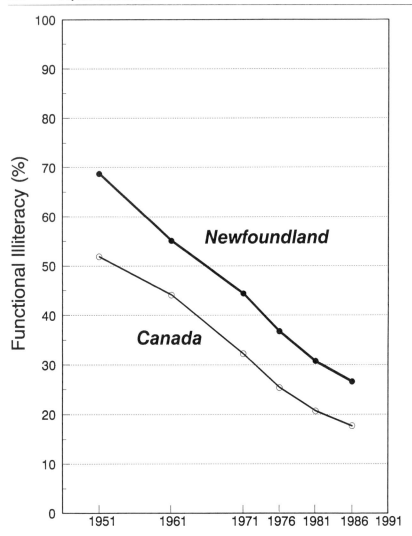

Figure 17.4 **Percentage of Functional Illiteracy, 1951–91**

largely a function of age, as is evident on both the provincial and national scales (Table 17.5); the anomalies in the 15 to 19 age groups reflect the fact that a significant number of individuals in these groups had not completed grade nine at the time of census. The disparity between total provincial and national levels at all ages is a measure of the historic difficulty in attaining national standards inherent in Newfoundland's economic structure, society, and peculiar settlement pattern. On the other hand, the marked widening of the gap in the 55 to 64 and 65 and over age groups – groups that received their education prior to 1949 – is an indication that Newfoundland benefited educationally by joining Canada. The disparity between men and women, which can be observed at all ages in the provincial population – a disparity barely visible in the national percentages – suggests that the cultural bias that appeared in elementary form in the 1880s is still powerful a century later. On the other hand, as the census data from which these percentages have been derived represent a residual population, the disparity between the sexes in the 1980s may also reflect a selective out-migration of better-educated males.[9]

The regional pattern of functional illiteracy remained the same as in 1981, with the Avalon Peninsula and metropolitan St. John's dropping four points to 19.8 percent but still two points behind the national figure, the central division dropping two points to 22.5 percent. The least favoured divisions made the most gains with the Hermitage–Bay Despair division dropping five points to 43.2 percent, the Northern Peninsula dropping five-and-a-half points to 38.6 percent, Notre Dame Bay dropping four points to 38.6 percent, and Bonavista Bay dropping five points to 35.8 percent. Despite their continued progress the latter divisions remain severely disadvantaged competitively within the province in terms of the basic quality of their work force.[10]

The traditional pattern of net out-migration continued between 1981 and 1986, the barometer cohort losing some 11,885 persons (6,525 men and 5,360 women) as it passed out of its late teens into its early twenties – a haemorrhage similar in size to that suffered by the preceding cohort at the same stage. All ten census divisions contributed to this 19 percent net loss – men 20.3 percent, women 17.3 percent – ranging from a minimal loss of 8.7 percent from the Avalon Peninsula to 33.5 percent from the south-west coast division.[11]

17.6   Newfoundland in 1991: A People in Crisis

Newfoundland waters, first described in the summer of 1497 as "swarming with fish," have always sustained an international fishery. The island shores have served as a base for prolific inshore and offshore bank fisheries for 400 years, during which time the people of Newfoundland and Labrador have gradually come to regard the marine resources of the adjacent waters as a major part of their cultural heritage. Following the extension of management jurisdiction out to the 200–nautical mile limit in 1977 in response to foreign over-fishing, they have called increasingly – rightly or wrongly – for exclusive rights in what have traditionally been considered to be common property resources as recognized under the law of the sea. The call, unfortunately, has come too late: under the terms of Confederation, Newfoundland surrendered jurisdiction over the marine area to Ottawa in 1949, to become the only province lacking control over its prime sustaining resource. Now, as Newfoundland prepares to celebrate the fifth centenary of its modern discovery, its historic relationship with its marine resources is in question – not to say, crisis.

The demise of the herring and inshore salmon fisheries, and the ban on the offshore "whitecoat" seal hunt on the spring sea-ice – a 200-year-old tradition along the north-east coast – have been followed by widespread failure of the cod and caplin fisheries, both offshore and inshore, accompanied by dire predictions of stock collapse on an unprecedented scale. Fish-plant closures and company bankruptcies; the more fundamental problem of licensed access affecting inshore fishermen, full-time as well as part-time; the political manipulation of the scientifically estimated

Table   **Functional Illiteracy by Age and Gender, 1986**
17.5

Age	NEWFOUNDLAND			CANADA		
Group	Total	Male	Female	Total	Male	Female
15–19	13.1	16.2	9.8	6.1	7.2	5.0
20–24	13.2	15.4	11.1	3.7	4.2	3.2
25–34	15.4	16.8	14.1	5.0	5.2	4.8
35–44	20.2	20.2	20.1	11.5	11.2	11.8
45–54	31.9	33.2	30.6	24.2	24.1	24.3
55–64	52.7	55.2	50.1	34.6	34.7	34.6
65<	63.2	68.8	58.5	45.6	46.4	45.0

(%)

Source: *Census of Canada, 1986*

"total allowable catch" and its allocation among inshore-men, near-shore longliners, and highly capitalized offshore dragger fleets from Newfoundland, the Maritime provinces, Quebec, and Europe; and the apparent inability or reluctance of the federal government to negotiate an end to serious over-fishing by European Community nations, all place the traditional society and settlement patterns of coastal Newfoundland and Labrador in immediate and future jeopardy. The threat is unlikely to be mitigated by onshore oil-related construction, begun in 1990 and highly localized in Trinity Bay, and may well be exacerbated by the imminent development of the Hibernia and other submarine oilfields, all subject to the environmental hazards of spring floe-ice and summer icebergs. Whatever may chance, the people of Newfoundland appear to be rapidly approaching a major turning point in their *longue durée*.

Notes

1. *Census of Canada, 1981*, Catalogue no. 93-901, Tables 3 and 5.
2. *Census of Canada, 1981*, Catalogue no. 93-925, Tables 7 and 8.
3. *Census of Canada, 1981*, Catalogue no. 93-925, Table 3.
4. *Census of Canada, 1981*, Catalogue no. 93-925, Tables 3 and 4.
5. *Census of Canada, 1981*, Catalogue no. 93-925, Table 5.
6. *Census of Canada, 1976*, Catalogue no. 92-826, Table 36; and *Census of Canada, 1981*, Catalogue no. 93-925, Table 11.
7. *Census of Canada, 1981*, Catalogue no. 93-949, Table 1, and no. 92–901, Table 1.
8. *Census of Canada, 1986*, Catalogue no. 93-110, Table 1.

9. *Census of Canada, 1986*, Catalogue no. 93-110, Table 2.
10. *Census of Canada, 1981*, Catalogue no. 93-925, Table 11; and *Census of Canada, 1986*, Catalogue no. 94-102, Newfoundland, part 2.
11. *Census of Canada, 1981*, Catalogue no. 98-901, Table 1; and *Census of Canada, 1986*, Catalogue no. 94-101, Newfoundland, part I.

References

Alexander, D. 1978. "Economic Growth in the Atlantic Region, 1880–1940." *Acadiensis* 8:47–76.

———. 1980. "Literacy and Economic Development in Nineteenth Century Newfoundland." *Acadiensis* 10:3–34.

Barkham, S. de L. 1982. In G.M. Story, ed., *Early European Settlement and Exploitation in Atlantic Canada,* 53–95. Selected papers from an International Symposium at Memorial University of Newfoundland, October 1979.

Cell, G.T. 1969. *English Enterprise in Newfoundland, 1577–1660.* Toronto: University of Toronto Press.

Cell, G.T., ed. 1982. *Newfoundland Discovered: English Attempts at Colonisation, 1610–1660.* London: The Hakluyt Society.

Handcock, W.G. 1976. "Spatial Patterns in a Trans-Atlantic Migration Field: The British Isles and Newfoundland during the Eighteenth and Nineteenth Centuries." In B.S. Osborne, ed., *The Settlement of Canada: Origins and Transfer,* 13–40. Proceedings of the 1975 British-Canadian Symposium on Historical Geography, Queen's University, Kingston.

———. 1977. "English Migration to Newfoundland." In J.J. Mannion, ed., *The Peopling of Newfoundland: Essays in Historical Geography*, 15–48. Social and Economic Papers, no. 8. St. John's: Institute of Social and Economic Research, Memorial University of Newfoundland.

Head, C.G. 1976. *Eighteenth Century Newfoundland: A Geographer's Perspective.* Ottawa: Carleton Library, no. 99.

Henriksen, G. 1973. *Hunters in the Barrens: The Naskapi on the Edge of the White Man's World.* Newfoundland Social and Economic Studies, no. 12. St. John's: Institute of Social and Economic Research, Memorial University of Newfoundland.

Hoffman, B.G. 1961. *Cabot to Cartier: Sources for a Historical Ethnography of North-eastern North America, 1497–1550.* Toronto: University of Toronto Press.

Howley, J.P. 1915. *The Beothucks or Red Indians, The Aboriginal Inhabitants of Newfoundland.* Toronto: Coles Canadiana Collection, Coles Publishing Co. Facsimile. Cambridge University Press, 1974.

Jones, G. 1964. *The Norse Atlantic Saga.* Oxford: Oxford University Press.

Lysacht, A.M. 1766. *Joseph Banks in Newfoundland and Labrador.* Facsimile. London, 1971.

McGhee, R. 1978. *Canadian Arctic Prehistory.* Canadian Prehistory Series, Archaeological Survey of Canada. Ottawa: National Museum of Man.

Macpherson, A.G. 1977. "A Modal Sequence in the Peopling of Central Bonavista Bay, 1676–1857." In J.J. Mannion, ed., *The Peopling of Newfoundland: Essays in Historical Geography*, 102–35. Social and Economic Papers, no. 8. St. John's: Institute of Social and Economic Research, Memorial University of Newfoundland.

Ommer, R.E. 1977. "Highland Scots Migration to Southwestern Newfoundland: A Study of Kinship." In J.J. Mannion, ed., *The Peopling of Newfoundland: Essays in Historical Geography,* 212–33. Social and Economic Papers, no. 8. St. John's: Institute of Social and Economic Research, Memorial University of Newfoundland.

Paddock, H.J. 1982. *Languages in Newfoundland and Labrador.* St. John's: Department of Linguistics, Memorial University of Newfoundland.

Pastore, R. n. d. "The Beothuks." *Museum Notes*, no. 1. St. John's: Newfoundland Museum.

———. 1978. "The Newfoundland Micmacs: A History of Their Traditional Life." *Newfoundland Historical Society Pamphlets*, no. 5. St. John's.

Tuck, J.A. 1976. *Newfoundland and Labrador Prehistory.* Canadian Prehistory Series, Archaeological Survey of Canada. Ottawa: Museum of Man.

18 Co-operatives as Instruments of Social Change for the Inuit of Canada

John K. Stager

18.1 Introduction

Change in the Canadian north, and especially for its Inuit people, began when a closed system was broken open.this system, which consisted of the co-existence of native people with the surrounding biological world, was entered by European contact and the subsequent intrusion of Euro-Canadian institutions and value systems. Recent among such interventions has been the establishment of co-operatives – collectively owned, directed, and managed business enterprises that provide a range of goods and services that are necessary in a modern, but still Inuit society. The co-operative movement will here be placed against a background of events and agents of change to establish its role both as a mechanism of change and also as a force for reconciling the current lifestyle of the Inuit with the abiding elements of their culture.

The present-day Inuit of Canada's Northwest Territories (NWT) and northern Quebec live in permanent settlements. The settlement sites, for the most part initially established as points of contact with the Inuit by whalers and fur traders, are at coastal or near coastal locations within the realm occupied by the Inuit in pre-contact days. Of a native population of nearly 25,000, 24 percent live in 25 settlements of between 60 and 400 people each. About 46 percent live in 16 settlements ranging in size from 500 to 800 people; 18 percent live in 5 settlements of approximately 1,000 population, and 11 percent live in 2 large settlements, one of which is over 2,000 people and the other over 3,000. With only one or two exceptions, the Inuit are dominant in numbers, usually making up in excess of 90 percent of the residents (Beaulieu 1980; *NWT Data Book, 1990–1991*). Nearly everyone lives in a house provided by the government, and modern schools, nursing stations, government offices, and other community facilities provide the social services commonly found in any small town or village. The principal commercial outlets for food, clothing, and hardware are owned either by the Northern Stores (formerly the Hudson's Bay Company) or the local co-operative, and both exist at many sites. There is an increasing number of other private stores and businesses associated with transportation, construction, and leisure-time activities. All communities have airstrips and most are served by scheduled commercial flights. Life for the Inuit in today's urban north contrasts quite starkly with the life of pre-settlement days. There are many people now living that can trace, in their own existence, the transition from traditional life on the land.

European contact with the aboriginal people first occurred in the sixteenth century when explorers were seeking the Northwest Passage. Beginning along the coast of Baffin Island, and then into Hudson Bay, this exploration was followed in the eighteenth century by the regular passage through Hudson Strait of supply ships for the Hudson's Bay Company forts in the southern part of Hudson Bay and James Bay. The whale fishery, which began in the 1820s and lasted until the early twentieth century, presented regular contact with certain Inuit groups along the north-east and, later, south Baffin coast. After 1860, whaling ships regularly returned each season to stations on Baffin Island and in northern Hudson Bay. There was short-lived but intense contact between natives and whalers in the Beaufort Sea region, which lasted into the first decade of the twentieth century (Bockstoce 1977). With the collapse of whaling in 1908, outside economic interest turned naturally to the fur trade, involving the Inuit essentially for the first time.

The establishment of present settlement sites is mainly a product of the fur trade. In general, between 1910 and 1920, posts were opened via the most accessible marine approaches on southern Baffin Island, Hudson Strait, Western Hudson Bay, and the Beaufort Sea. Deeper penetration to Foxe Basin and the Central Arctic coast occurred from 1920 to 1930, and more isolated posts were opened in the 1920s and even until the 1940s. High Arctic settlements such as Grise Fiord and Resolute Bay date from government-sponsored native migrations in the 1950s (Usher 1971). The fur trade, together with the spread of the Christian missions at post sites or nearby, brought about a gradual retreat from the distant reaches of tributary "tribal" lands and a movement towards the newly emerging centres of commerce, religion, and, to some extent, social activities. After the Second World War, the government of Canada began to pay more attention to the Canadian north and intervened with a series of social programs. When the new housing programs for native people accelerated in 1967, the people quite quickly moved off the land to take up permanent residence in the expanding settlements. In some parts of the Canadian Arctic it has been 400 years since the Inuit first saw the "Quallunaat" (white man), but the real effects of those first sightings on Inuit society were felt less than 100 years ago, and they gained real momentum only during the last four decades.

18.2   The Forces of Change

The impact of European exploration on Inuit life can almost be dismissed as an agent of change. Apart from a few unfortunate natives who were seized and carried off to Europe, and in those instances when exploration ships were trapped by ice for one, two, or even three winters, thereby allowing neighbouring natives to visit or trade souvenirs, few lasting effects are evident. Once whaling had moved to the "west side" of Baffin Bay after 1820, early intermittent and geographically dispersed landings by whaling ships were replaced by regular landings at preferred sites or whaling stations at Pond Inlet, Cumberland Sound, and Clyde Inlet, and a few other places on Baffin Island. From 1840 until whaling ended in this region in the first decade of this century, at least ten stations were repeatedly occupied at one time or another on Baffin Island. In addition, two of three sites along the west side of Roes

Welcome Sound and a station on Southampton Island in northern Hudson Bay were frequently occupied, as were four or more locations on the Beaufort Sea coast (Ross 1981). Repeated summer operations and overwintering of up to ten ships (and sometimes more) drew between 100 and 200 Inuit into the first semi-permanent "villages" at these sites. In some cases Inuit were transported temporarily from their home territories to new locations to work for the whalers. The contact and changes in lifestyle were most obvious in terms of material goods: tools, implements, and the like. The economic partnership emphasized for the Inuit that the value of furs and ivory had grown beyond their normal worth. The "sale" of labour was an entirely new concept. While the whaling captains fed their Inuit dependents, the native people did not abandon their preferred foods provided by traditional hunting. Social activities in the European mode – dances, music, games – were attractive to the native people. The negative side of the relationship included the introduction of alcoholic beverages, particularly in the western Arctic, cohabitation of native women with whalemen with the result of offspring, and, most devastating of all, the spread of fatal diseases previously unknown among the indigenous people. Indeed, a major decline of population, including the total demise of the Saglermuit of Southampton Island, was the result of foreign diseases (Ross 1977). For nearly 70 years this close and regular partnership persisted. It strengthened a dependency by the Inuit on a new economy that left the people totally unprepared to resume their aboriginal ways when the whaling industry collapsed in the early 1900s.

Even before the last whaling ships left the north for good, a period of decline in productivity caused fewer and fewer crews to return. The crews ceased over-wintering, came to depend more on supervised native whaling, and restricted the supplies and trade goods for the Inuit. The hardship and privation that followed increased the Inuit's receptiveness to the spread of fur-trading posts as free traders and the Hudson's Bay Company occupied the economic vacuum left by the departed whale ships. Instead of congregating at the "village" sites, the pursuit of furs moved people back onto their land, to their old territories, and, in some measure, reversed the centralizing influence of whaling and the effects of close social contact with large numbers of whites. The spread of new trading posts penetrated beyond the limited points of Inuit whaling contact. In a period of 25 years, posts were established among Inuit who previously knew of European goods and ways only through second-hand trading and hearsay. By 1940 no group of Inuit had not been introduced to the fur trade and a certain level of dependence upon it. The main product of the fur trade was white fox, but ermine, polar bear, wolverine, wolf pelts, and seal skins were also taken and exchanged in a barter system for goods. At first, the many free traders, along with the surviving Hudson's Bay Company, represented a marketing advantage to the trapper, but later, when government regulation and outside economic depression forced most independents from the scene, rationalization of posts reduced the several locations for trade down to the core sites of present-day settlement.

With only a few exceptions, trapping was not a new activity to the Inuit, but was added or grafted onto the round of hunting and fishing activities of the winter survival routine. The old ways of migration were modified to the extent that hunters had to visit their trap-lines repeatedly, and a pattern of movement evolved that more easily accommodated access to the trading posts. Trade items like guns, ammunition, metal tools and implements, steel traps, tobacco, cloth, and some food, brought a new technology to the native society. These products improved the efficiency of hunting and travelling, and were quickly adopted as either desirable or superior to the traditional things they replaced. The dependence upon the trade for its goods was enhanced by the sense of obligation or loyalty to traders that grew up with the credit/debt system associated with the barter exchange. However, the seemingly comfortable new life of the Inuit as hunter-trapper was vulnerable to the market place, and when fur prices declined in the 1940s, real hardship ensued, and the harsh realities of economic servitude came to the fore. Deprivation was reported, and actual starvation shocked both outside authorities and the public in Canada. There was no alternative but to engage the will and resources of the government to restore the situation, and to define what was to be normal if not necessarily desirable for the northern native citizens of the country (Jenness 1964, 99).

The federal government mission for the "New North" was conceived in a southern mode. Welfare concerns for the basics of good health, adequate housing, educational opportunity, and a reasonable standard of living were shipped north with the means to put them in place. All of this had to be set down at a site, and so the settlement pattern was re-entrenched into the landscape. Administrators accompanied these programs, and, in time, people collected in the settlements where the ultimate authority was imposed by a cadre of white professionals. The impact of all these events resulted in a profound intrusion into the familiar round of living that had been the Inuit way for a long time. It called upon that most characteristic resource of Inuit culture: adaptability. The difficult adjustments in their way of life that the people had to make during the first 30 years of change is nowhere more perceptively and sensitively told than in *The People's Land* by Hugh Brody (1975).

18.3   Settlements and Settlement Dwellers

Each settlement is provided with basic services: roads, water, waste removal, heat and fuel, electricity, communication links including airports, satellite television and telephone dishes, and radio installations. Government supplies their services and pays for the employment associated with the operation and maintenance. In addition, there are social services, including schools, nursing stations, and various other agencies related to social welfare and manpower improvement. With the build-up of community infrastructure, the government has encouraged the participation of local people who thereby gain influence and some authority over the policies and practices affecting life in the settlements. There are many committees with elected members that have both advisory and operating functions, such as committees on education, housing, recreation, social development, and wildlife management among others. The communities are self-governing with a range of autonomy and responsibility. When the adult members of the community are busy going from meeting to meeting, it is not necessary to understand all the subtleties of government-inspired involvement of local people to observe that there is a high degree of sociopolitical organization in what are essentially very small communities. In many ways, the north is overorganized, and the capable, politically astute leaders of the people are often overcommitted.

The demands upon native leadership are caused not only by the expanded committee work, but by a shortage of suitable people. It is always sobering to look at the demographics of native societies in Canada; they are extremely youthful. For example, 54 percent of Inuit are under 20 years of age, and most of them are still at school. The leadership of Inuit society is drawn mainly from people between 25 and 60 years of age. Thus, the leadership cohort is about 30 percent of the population; of this group, less than one-third are both between 25 and 30 years of age and possibly educated as far as grade 12. The second third of the leadership pool is between 30 and 40 years and could have had some schooling, but the remaining third, aged 40 to 60, basically lack formal education. Education, of course, does not equate with intelligence or wisdom, but through functional literacy it permits people to gain knowledge beyond that learned through direct experience. Thus, those who are capable of assuming executive leadership and who are aware of outside influences upon the north rarely make up more than 10 percent of the population in any one settlement; those who can be persuaded to enter local politics are even fewer.

Young people growing up in modern settlements are faced with different activities and priorities than were their parents. School is the major focus for a large part of the year, and the skills learned there, though valuable for entering the wage economy, bear little relation to life on the land. Moreover, "urban" living permits young people more freedom of individual behaviour away from parental supervision. Also, the invading material and entertainment world, with its radio and television advertising, has developed an attraction for instruments of amusement and self-gratification that are easily available if one only has the cash. The younger generation, therefore, has a value system and social behaviour increasingly like the youth of other Canadian towns or cities, and the social problems of the south are not absent from the north. What may be different in the north is the all-encompassing presence of government with an apparently unlimited supply of money at its disposal; this has contributed to an unreal perception of the value of money. It carries over into the domestic economy with personal spending priorities conditioned as much, or more, by desire as they are by need. There is, therefore, a great interest in having money, and the size of a salary or wage is frequently more attractive than the nature of a job, its challenge, or its interest. The completeness of government social support systems has further insulated people from the hard economic realities they would face if they had to rely on their own earnings to meet all their expenses. We are witnessing a change in the Inuit value system, one that threatens to replace self-reliance and personal industry with notions of entitlement, easy money, and unreal expectations (see also Vallee et al. 1984).

A walk down the street of a northern settlement today demonstrates all the complexity of any modern, small community. In the low light of winter you can see smoke from the rows of houses strung together by a net of power lines, frosted windows, snow drifts against the buildings, and its people moving about in warm, modern clothing. Snowmobiles are parked at almost every house or in groups outside the local store. Trucks bump along the roads while children play in the yard outside the school. In summer with the long days, those same prefabricated houses, painted various colours but looking much alike, have seal skins stretched on boards leaning up against them or drying on the clotheslines. Elsewhere, racks of drying fish attest to the continuing importance of traditional food. In the large settlements, like Iqaluit (formerly Frobisher Bay) (population 2,400) or Rankin Inlet (population 1,200) (Figure 18:1), the town centre is dominated by large government buildings or a hotel, testifying to their regional administrative roles and the frequent passage of travelling bureaucrats and businessmen. Modern stores, trucks, cars, and taxis signal a larger component of white population. The small communities are very much the same from place to place. The government houses are there, and in their midst is the school that is often the focus of the community because it doubles as a public gathering place for meetings and social events. Each community has its church, which still attracts a respectable congregation on Sundays. Everywhere, natives dominate the population, and occasionally you can catch a glimpse of an old man carving soapstone outside his house while children play baseball or run to the Northern Store or co-operative to buy candy and soft drinks.

18.4   The Co-operatives

The co-operative concept was introduced into the north to stimulate self-employment for a cash return at a time when fur prices were depressed and other opportunities to earn wages scarcely existed. A fishing/lumbering co-operative began at George River in 1959; within five years the idea had been taken up by 17 communities, and after ten years there were 30 such ventures (Figure 18.1). Co-operatives, based as they are on open membership, democratic governance, and dividends based upon patronage, are associations that allow people to help themselves by working together. Inuit society was traditionally based upon small group living, in which individual activity and behaviour was strongly conditioned by group welfare, so the formal co-operative structure was adopted easily and quickly. Early commercial successes were reported at the first co-operative conference in 1963 at Frobisher Bay where the first signs of collaboration among co-operatives emerged. It took the form of a defined need for central marketing of Inuit art and crafts. At the same time there was an early association of co-operatives with a common interest in the political power of native people (Myers 1980, xiv). A second conference at Povungnituk in 1966 raised the theme of federation. The growth within individual co-operatives increased the need for central services, information, and professional advice. The proposed joint effort to market crafts was pre-empted when Canadian Arctic Producers Limited (CAPL) was established in 1965 without accord from all the parties that claimed interest. Indeed, by 1966 the native co-operative movement had entered a political phase in charting the future, not because there were conflicting or particularly divergent views among the Inuit themselves, but because the "outside" advisors, supporters, and promoters found it difficult to agree. Therefore, in 1967, the five co-operatives in northern Quebec elected to form their

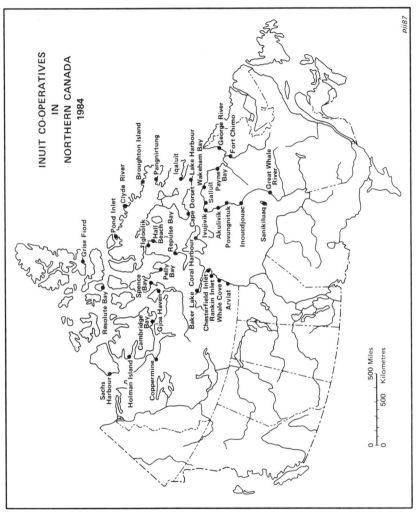

pji87

INUIT CO-OPERATIVES
IN
NORTHERN CANADA
1984

Grise Fiord

Pond Inlet

Clyde River

Broughton Island

Pangnirtung

Iqaluit

Lake Harbour

Wakeham Bay

George River

Fort Chimo

Payne
Bay

Great Whale
River

Saniluit

Cape Dorset

Ivujivik

Akulivik

Povungnituk

Inoucdjouac

Sanikiluaq

Resolute Bay

Igloolik

Hall
Beach

Repulse Bay

Spence
Bay

Pelly
Bay

Baker Lake

Coral Harbour

Chesterfield Inlet

Rankin Inlet

Whale Cove

Arviat

Cambridge
Bay

Gjoa Haven

Sachs
Harbour

Holman Island

Coppermine

500 Miles

500 Kilometres

0

0

Figure 18.1 Inuit Co-operatives in Northern Canada, 1984

own group, the Federation of Co-operatives of New Quebec (FCNQ) and, within a year, it added four newly incorporated co-operatives. It was the awakening interest of the government of Quebec in its north that encouraged the FCNQ to lead the way.

In the NWT, where the federal presence was unchallenged, the political preoccupation was with transferring federal functions to the government of the NWT. Enabling legislation, which was late in being passed, finally permitted the establishment of the Canadian Arctic Co-operative Federation Limited (CACFL) in 1972. By 1976 there were ten members-owners of FCNQ, and 41 members-owners of CACFL; in 1982, FCNQ had 12 members and CACFL had 33 members (these totals include nine Indian co-operatives). In 1983 CAFCL reorganized to become Arctic Co-operatives Limites (ACL). The growth of co-operative gross business and the payout remaining in communities is given in Table 18.1.

The growth in business mirrors the multiplication of functions that co-operatives initiated for commercial gain and service to the people. Now, nearly all co-operatives operate retail stores carrying food, clothing, hardware, and appliances, and will order almost anything; the stores also perform banking functions. Most co-operatives purchase carvings, crafts, and furs on occasion, and some buy traditional food (fish, muktuk) for resale to local people. Many co-operatives have contracts to distribute fuel, carry freight, operate taxis, deliver water, and act as airline agents. A few have tourist camps, restaurants, and recreation facilities. Listed in Table 18.2 are the main business activities of the 35 Inuit co-operatives in the north in 1984.

The retail store is regarded as the heart of the co-operative activity, and most people think of the store as the co-operative and not the association which runs it. In 29 settlements the co-operative competes with the Northern Stores. In most places, Northern Stores have the greater part of the business – about 60 percent except where recent modern co-operative stores have been built. In general, people shop at the co-operative for food and other expendables, but go to the Northern Stores for clothing and appliances because a better selection is offered. There is price competition, but prices at the co-operatives tend to be higher. Part of the reason for this lies in the cost of supporting the federations and paying for services like education and other human support features that are not strictly business costs. The variation in management efficiency is also reflected in prices, and the operating costs for heat, light, local transport, and warehouse storage are usually higher because many co-operatives' buildings have been converted from some previous use and are more difficult to maintain. However, in 11 communities, the co-operative is the only retail outlet. In summary, it could be said that there is considerable dependence upon the retail store for day-to-day living, including food. With advertising, and especially with television opening a window on materialism with its commercials, a strong consumerism has developed as part of the current northern scene.

Right from the beginning the co-operatives have had a leading role in the arts and crafts industry. The carving of soapstone and ivory was a new means for the Inuit to generate wealth just after the Second World War. The sale of carvings to the co-operatives added welcome cash to family budgets. Now, however, instead of carvings reaching the public exclusively through CAPL, the ACL agency, and

Table 18.1   **Financial Turnover of the Co-operatives**

	Gross Volume $	Community Payout $
1963	750,000	135,000
1966	2,000,000	—
1972	8,000,000	2,500,000
1980	27,000,000	9,100,000
1985	37,000,000	8,000,000

Sources: Department of Indian Affairs and Northern Development;
Arctic Co-operatives Ltd.

Table 18.2   **Business Activities of the Co-operatives**

Activity	Number of Co-operatives
Retail stores	34
Carving purchases	33
Service contracts	`26
Craft/sewing purchases	26
Hotel operation	11
Fur purchasing	9
Print/art production	7
Coffee shop/Pool room	6
Tourist camp/cabins	6
Community fishery	1
Bakery	1

Sources: Arctic Co-operative Ltd.; field survey

FCNQ, there is competition from the Northern Stores and other private dealers who go to the north to purchase stock; open purchasing has added new complications to pricing practices, a system that was already difficult to manage. Furthermore, ACL opened Northern Images stores in the NWT and, recently, outside the north in Edmonton, both retailing and wholesaling to other dealers. The carving industry is estimated to have produced an income for carvers of about $6.5 million in 1982, a drop from a peak of close to $9 million a year or so before (May, Pearson and Associates Ltd. 1983, vi; Stager 1982, 83). Growing market resistance at the retail end, associated with an economic downturn in southern Canada, and a fall-off in artistic quality of carvings themselves may be the cause. In the communities at the production end, the quantity made is influenced strongly by the ease with which there are other opportunities to earn cash. There is always pressure to pay good prices to carvers, and when co-operative purchasing agents are over-sympathetic to the local need for money, or remain unaware of the southern selling prices, they can pay out as much or more than can be recovered in retailing. With the addition of a profit margin to the northern purchase price, the system is pushing retail prices up and there is a growing inventory of unsold carvings. For example, in 1980 FCNQ bought a volume of carvings in one year that, on the basis of the sales record, would have required 18 months to sell. At the same time, CAPL held unsold inventory for which it paid $1.6 million; inventories are expensive to finance (Stager 1982, 39, 78). There are still difficulties in controlling the quality and quantity of the work, but new educational programs have helped the producers understand the need to accommodate market tastes and the importance of quality. In recent years, the opening of some new southern outlets and the introduction of more stringent purchasing controls have reduced inventory levels with considerable savings as a result. This was all the more necessary because the downturn in the general economy by 1984 had reversed a previously steady growth in sales of Indian and Inuit art.

Those involved in the production of Inuit prints are very much concerned with the quality that is properly designated as art. Resident art directors or advisors with training and experience assist most print shops in both technical and artistic matters. All prints require the approval of the Canadian Eskimo Art Council before they can go on the market and, over a period of years, Cape Dorset, Baker Lake, and Povungnituk have been joined by Holman, Clyde River, Pangnirtung, Salluit, and others renowned for their products. Prints, as well as wall hangings and other decorative sewing, have become an established art form of the Inuit that is both distinctive and valued. It adds a significant economic component to northern life, due mainly to the development work of the co-operatives.

Additional economic benefit to communities is provided by the employment generated in the co-operatives. In the NWT, about 300 full-time employees worked for co-operatives, and in 1984 they earned $4 million, an average of over $13,000 per capita (Arctic Co-operatives Limited, personal communication). Roughly 15 percent of all families in co-operative settlements benefit directly from wages, and there are a number of others employed casually or seasonally to help with fishing, sea-lift, or other part-time work (Stager 1982, 11). Besides the government service, the co-operatives are the largest employers in the north and, unlike government, in excess of 90 per cent of co-operative employees are native people. The major social benefit of working at a co-operative does not come from wages earned, although these are important, but from the experience of working within an imposed framework. The discipline such work teaches has touched many native people. It is estimated that in the last 20 years between 1,500 and 2,000 people have worked "at the co-op" in the NWT, and possibly 700 have done so in Quebec (Stager 1982, 11). Many young and not-so-young people who hold important salaried jobs as government employees or are in some other leadership role, have had their early working experience with the co-operatives. There can be little doubt that co-operatives have played, and continue to play, an important part in the development of human resources in Canada's north.

Despite 20 years of experience, growth, and expansion of functions, the co-operatives still have some imperfections. Management, for example, is the key to economic success or failure, and the uneven business success of co-operative history is mainly a reflection of management effectiveness. In Quebec, native management has always been the model; managers drawn from the community depend heavily upon the FCNQ to provide co-ordinated purchasing, book-keeping, auditing, and many other procedural mechanisms; the manager is like a branch manager of a larger network. Gradually, the managers have learned this role with the aid of constant supervision and training from Montreal. Nevertheless, with some notable exceptions, management skills and performances remain the weakest part of the system. Native managers do not have adequate formal education, and several are not completely aware of the implications of a federated business enterprise. Some have difficulty in making decisions, for example, on how much credit to extend, the appropriate prices to pay for carvings and craft, and how to recruit employees and deploy them. Such decisions have major local consequences, and managers are often subjected to heavy interpersonal pressures for favourable treatment coming from members of the community who are friends, neighbours, and relations. In the NWT, white managers were imported from the south when the business talent was not present. There have been some good, and long-term, white co-operative managers, but, more often, outside hiring produced high turnover, variable management skills and correspondingly uneven business success. Besides, this practice did not encourage local natives to aspire to management, and role models for successful natives in managerial careers did not emerge. During the last few years, a concerted effort to move to native management supported by a $2.5 million education program has been implemented. Using specially developed course manuals, seminars, teaching, and supervision by incumbent managers, native management trainees are given a comprehensive training program with success measured on the basis of acquired skills. The result has been that by 1985 there were 14 native general managers, and 8 more departmental managers in the 33 active co-operatives in the NWT (Arctic Co-operatives Limited, personal communication). The objective is to have all management positions occupied by northerners.

This same education program began a similar course for the directors of the co-operative boards. It emphasizes ownership and control of the co-operatives by its members, and the responsibilities of directors as representatives of membership. As important, however, is a concentration upon helping the directors understand business practices and statements, policy formation and meeting procedures. Unfortunately, the education program begun in 1982 was discontinued a year later for lack of funding. There is still a need for such training to strengthen the role of members-owners in directing their own co-operatives, and to increase the general community awareness of business and its ways.

A co-operative and its board really exist to serve the membership, but the success of the enterprise turns on the commitment of the members. At present in the NWT the 5,500 or so members represent 80 percent of the population over 25 years of age, which means that in the communities where co-operatives exist, practically all adults hold memberships. This is a significant measure of commitment. Co-operation has embedded in it the concept of dividends paid on the basis of patronage. Whenever this has occurred, membership booms, and the value of the co-operative becomes quite clear. When it comes to taking a direct interest in the affairs of a co-operative, commitment is not easy to measure, nor is it likely to be as strong as membership numbers suggest. For example, most Annual General Meetings rarely draw more than 50 people. The attendance is larger only when the subject for discussion is issue orientated – for example, a proposal to tighten credit. In northern communities there are more than enough meetings to attend, and people must get tired of them. Yet, field observations confirm a continued interest in the co-operative as an institution, even though there are criticisms of the local scene. In the early days, people joined forces to help the co-operative erect buildings and contributed other necessary free labour. Now, with cash so important, pay is almost a necessity to get help. On the other hand, when there is a crisis like threatened closure, the community becomes upset and new leadership emerges, tougher policies are accepted, debts are paid, and a general rescue takes place. At the same time, there is little being done to renew membership, and the younger people have not been attracted as they could be. There is a need for education of the membership to drive home the value of a community-owned enterprise and its need for care and tending.

The glue that holds the co-operatives together as organizations rather than as independent community associations, consists of the two federations. In both Quebec and NWT, the federations provide a range of services, important among which is the purchasing and transport division, which assists in bulk buying, warehouse assembly and sorting, and sea-lift or air-lift management. The federations also provide central accounting, audit services, and educational departments, and receive and market carvings and crafts. FCNQ, with ten Inuit co-operative member-owners, is very well integrated and the co-operatives are heavily dependent upon FCNQ services, with the federation budget very closely tied to the financial health of the co-operatives. The NWT federation, Arctic Co-operatives Limited, has faced an uphill battle to win the support of its member co-operatives. There are 33 members and many have strongly independent operating attitudes. This is reflected in a certain level of criticism of ACL's services, and some co-operatives act on their own to purchase goods and conduct their audits. In the past four years, however, ACL and the members are developing a sense of unity for common good. Thus, today there are co-operatives in Canadian Inuit communities that were the first all-native associations when they began, and have in time come together as integrated native organizations that remain important for both economic and human development.

18.5   The Future

To anticipate a continuing role for co-operatives in the north is to anticipate the changes in northern society. Population projections indicate a decreasing number of native people being added to the bottom of the age/sex pyramids as native fertility approaches the rates found in non-native society. At the same time, the children already born are moving into the working-age group, increasing the numbers of this cohort. Given the lack of substantial out-migration from the north, the need for gainful employment continues to increase, and in the age of a cash-orientated economy, there is real pressure for broader participation in existing work and for the generation of new economic activity.

Governments have responded by introducing various training and educational opportunities to increase native participation in the public sphere and in the private economy insofar as it exists. There are also programs to stimulate entrepreneurial initiatives that encourage Inuit to try their hand in various businesses, primarily in areas that service the needs of society. It is worth noting that despite the thrust of government policy towards private enterprise, the communities generally are not large enough to support duplication in businesses of either a service or commercial nature. For example, one coffee shop will survive where two cannot; most places need only one taxi company, one snowmobile repair shop, or one video rental service. Grise Ford (population 76) has only 3 businesses, including the co-operative, while Pond Inlet (population 880) has perhaps 10 to 12 businesses, including the co-operative, which runs the store, the hotel, and restaurant. Success in small business certainly requires knowledge of business methods, but it also emphasizes the role of the owner-manager whose loyalties are to the business and not necessarily to the community. It is a sharp break from the traditional Inuit culture in which fortune and misfortune were shared. Individuals as entrepreneurs also provide competition for the co-operatives in the search for new economic opportunity. Government choice in the letting of contracts or initiating services now seems to favour individuals, partly because the co-operatives are continuing entities that are sometimes overshadowed by their own reputations for variable success in the past. If an individual fails in business, he or she sinks out of sight, but if the co-operative fails in an enterprise, it remains with its faults exposed.

In the political sense, the Canadian north is very much at a crossroads. The issues of the future – the settlements of land claims, the role of native organizations, the future form of government, and the development of resources – are all intimately intertwined. Even in northern Quebec, where the James Bay Agreement has provided a blueprint for governance, the strengthening of native culture, economic self-determination, and resource development, events are not yet advancing smoothly. In Povingnituk, Ivujivik, and Salluit, dissident native groups, mainly of people who believe their co-operatives have a broader role to play as a community government, resisted parts of the agreement (D'Auglure 1984). A serious concern for the co-operatives, and FCNQ in particular, exists in the presence of the Makivik Corporation; Makivik is the development corporation set up by the agreement to be the steward of Inuit culture and the compensation funds of about $90 million for the Inuit of northern Quebec. The co-operatives worry that massed capital might provide direct and powerful economic competition in native communities where, because of the small size, business opportunities are few. The co-operatives, with a history of 30 years of people working hard together, could be eclipsed by the decisions made by development corporations in the name of the same people who built the co-operatives in the first place. There have been tentative moves for the co-operatives and Makivik to chart a future together, but nothing substantial has happened yet. The two organizations have co-existed for more than a decade and seem not to be in serious competition. In the Northwest Territories, events have proceeded more slowly than in

Quebec. Tungavik Federation of Nunavut (TFN), the Inuit organization, has negotiated an agreement-in-principle in their claims settlement with the federal government. It calls for $580 million in compensation over 20 years, ownership and resource rights to land, and the establishment of *Nunavut*, a new territory with Inuit majority governance. TFN formed the Nunasi Corporation to receive and manage compensation funds. ACL and its members were nervous about repeating the Quebec experience of corporate funds creating competitive businesses for the co-operatives at both the community and federation levels. Development corporations, although technically owned by all the people, are really directed by boards of directors, and to be successful, they must consider the profit motive to be a top priority. Recently, a series of regional development corporations have been created in the NWT that are likely to participate in compensation funds. The people at large do not understand Nunasi even though it is theirs. They are becoming familiar with the regional corporations and they do understand the co-operatives all of which they also own. Common sense suggests that no conflict need develop among the co-operatives, Nunasi, and the regional corporations, and that compensation funds from a settlement of claims could be available, at least in part, to support and strengthen the co-operatives. Despite the steady growth in business volume, equity, profits, and dividend payout between 1985 and 1990 (in 1989 ACL's 38 co-operatives had $37 million revenue and $1.7 million profit and returned $1.4 million in dividends), the co-operatives would benefit greatly by access to compensation funds to pay debts and improve or replace facilities. It would be equally important to co-ordinate the economic development programs of the corporations and the co-operatives. There are signs that this could happen; ACL now has a representative on the board of most of the regional corporations. If the co-operatives could be helped to take business initiatives at the community level, and the regional corporations encouraged to look for its sphere of activity in the regions, and Nunasi in the national or international business arena, then success in all organizations would combine to benefit the Inuit of the Northwest Territories.

The Inuit co-operatives of northern Canada have moved ahead over the past 30 years, partly through the vision and leadership of some dedicated people, but mainly as a result of the understanding, support, and hard work of the people who own them. The co-operatives and the federations have spent most of their energy in tending to their own business, and have been reluctant to recognize the importance of political activity that supports of their enterprises. To some extent, familiarity with the co-operatives has robbed them of their glamour, although new business success and dividend payments have sparked a re-awakening of members' interest. It is still important, however, for the federations to keep their programs of public education so that co-operatives as native-owned, -controlled, and -managed businesses can continue to fluorish in northern settlements.

References

Beaulieu, D. 1980. *The Co-operative Movement in Nouveau Québec*. Quebec: Ministère des consommateurs, Coopératives et institutions financières, Gouvernement du Québec.

Bockstoce, J.R. 1977. *Steam Whaling in the Western Arctic*. New Bedford, Mass.: Old Dartmouth Historical Society.

Brody, H. 1975. *The People's Land*. Harmondsworth: Penguin Books.

D'Anglure, B. 1984. "Contemporary Inuit of Quebec." In D. Damas, ed., *Handbook of North American Indians*. Vol. 5: *Arctic*, 683–88. Washington, D.C.: Smithsonian Institution.

Jenness, D. 1964. *Eskimo Administration: II, Canada*. Technical papers, no. 14. Montreal: Arctic Institute of North America.

May, Pearson and Associates Ltd. 1983. *The Production and International Marketing of Inuit Carvings: A Report and Recommendations for Arctic Co-operatives Ltd*. Toronto.

Northwest Territories Data Book, 1990–1991. Yellowknife: Outcrop.

Myers, B., ed. 1980. *Proceedings: Northern Co-operative Movement Conference III*. George River, 20–25 April 1980. Ottawa.

Ross, W.G. 1977. "Whaling and the Decline of Native Populations." *Arctic Anthropology* 14:1–8.

———. 1981. "Whaling, Inuit and the Arctic Islands." In M. Zaslow, ed., *A Century of Canada's Arctic Islands, 1880–1980*, 33–50. Ottawa: Royal Society of Canada.

Stager, J.K. 1982. *An Evaluation Study of the Federated Co-operatives in Nouveau Québec and the Northwest Territories after the Co-operative Development Program*. Ottawa: Evaluation Branch, Department of Indian Affairs and Northern Development.

Usher, P.J. 1971. *Fur Trade Posts of the Northwest Territories, 1870–1970*. Ottawa: Northern Science Research Group, Department of Indian Affairs and Northern Development.

Vallee, F.G., D.G. Smith, and J.D. Cooper. 1984. "Contemporary Canadian Inuit." In D. Damas, ed., *Handbook of North American Indians*. Vol. 5: *Arctic*, 662–75. Washington, D.C.: Smithsonian Institution.

Part Four

Planning, Society, and Environment

19 Introduction: Society and the Planned Management of Resources

Guy M. Robinson

19.1 Resource Development and Social Impacts

Studies of society by geographers cannot ignore the influence of government policies. These policies may address many issues and may mould social geography in an intricate fashion while generally attempting to foster notions of egalitarianism and reductions in inequalities between different groups of people. The complex inter-relationships between the social planning of federal and provincial governments, and the sectoral elements within particular plans give tremendous scope for study by a variety of disciplines. Work by sociologists such as Porter (1965) and Lucas (1971) has shown how various, ostensibly "economic," government policies impinge upon social organization and, in turn, spawn policies geared to correcting perceived "imbalances" in socio-economic development. For geographers, the study of planning in its broadest sense has been an important part of the growth of the discipline in the 1970s and 1980s, broadening the area of study with subject matter previously untouched. In some ways the most "obvious" area for the geographers to examine, with respect to policies and planning, has not been social planning, but resource management and evaluation. Some aspects of this topic are covered in the volume edited by T. O'Riordan and Wreford Watson (1977), and it forms the focus for the final part of this book, with special reference to the social impact of resource use and planning rather than to the environmental impact.

In Canada, government ownership of natural resources has provided the foundation for various management strategies and policies. Both federal and provincial governments have also acted as regulators of resource use, thereby attempting to play the roles of both developers of resources and mediators in conflicts arising over use of natural resources. Such conflicts have been common, occurring at a variety of scales and often involving the added dimension of the rights claimed by native peoples. In effect, government regulates natural resource use, but conflicts between provincial and federal governments, and between different ministries and agencies, make this regulation difficult to co-ordinate and operate for public benefit. For geographers there have been opportunities to influence the way in which policy has been formulated, and subsequently carried out, and there have also been roles in monitoring policy and examining its effects (see Mitchell 1989).

For social geographers the opportunities for more direct involvement in issues pertaining to resource development have evolved as part of the growth of government intervention in the way in which natural resources are utilized. For example, increasingly, policies have recognized the multiple demands made on resources and have taken greater note of environmental impact assessments and public hearings. Greater attention has been paid to questions of social costs and benefits. Indeed, in assessments of the impact of particular schemes or policies, the focus of expert input has tended to shift from the purely environmental impacts to the inclusion of social impacts. In 1973 this recognition of the need to consider the social dimension of development issues was made explicit in the establishment by the federal cabinet of an environmental and review process incorporating both biophysical and social aspects in the planning process. Guidelines have since been established for federal inquiries so that environmental and social impact statements are made on proposed developments, a public review is held, and recommendations are made to the federal minister by an appointed panel. The review is akin to a judicial process and enables public participation in the form of statements and presentation of information and opinions in a variety of forms (Bowles 1981; Finsterbusch 1980, 1981). This has meant that several different types of lobby group, and representatives of diverse public interests, have been represented at enquiries.

O'Riordan (chapter 20) examines the ways in which various public interests have affected public policies on resource management. He highlights the fact that only relatively recently have "destructive" resource developments been questioned by the public in a variety of forms: public inquiries, opinion polls, the assertion of native self-rights, and direct public action. From the range of environmental issues facing Canada, he concentrates upon environmental policies associated with resource development. He outlines recent phases in resource development activity, the growth of "environmental consciousness" in the 1970s, and the different challenges of the 1980s, including claims by native peoples. The sharing of responsibilities between federal and provincial governments, and the special problems this produces, is an integral part of his consideration (O'Riordan 1981).

The portrayal of economic development after 1945 emphasizes policies of rapid growth facilitated by cheap electricity. Initially, environmental and social issues were either little understood or were ignored, but certain problems associated with major energy projects helped increase public awareness of the consequences associated with rapid growth (e.g., Wilson 1966). Such awareness grew as native groups established themselves as a major political force, bringing about arrangements for compensation for the disruptions to their traditional way of life caused by large-scale developments, such as those on the Churchill River and the James Bay hydro project (Hamley 1987). From the early 1970s the management of environmental and social impacts was institutionalized with the creation of the Federal Department of Environment and provincial legislation introducing a statutory basis for environmental impact assessments (Lucas 1981; Mitchell and Turkheim 1977). Such assessments generally involved public hearings and avenues through which public groups could influence the development of projects. The example used by O'Riordan to illustrate this is the Berger Inquiry into the Mackenzie Valley pipeline proposal in the mid-1970s (Berger 1977; Sewell 1981).

O'Riordan refers to the growth of "environmental consciousness" in the 1970s during which not only did awareness of the social and environmental impacts of development grow, but also the nature of public participation in decision-making became more sophisticated (e.g., Howard 1980). One of the examples given is the changing nature of the reactions to the proposed Spadina expressway in central Toronto, also referred to by Collins in chapter 7. In cases such as this, greater consideration was being given to the likely effects of the development. In so doing, certain adjustments to project design could be made or, as in the case of the Spadina expressway, certain elements of development proposals could be scrapped completely. There were often problems, though, with the nature of evaluations and monitoring of projects. However, the establishment of the Canadian Environmental Assessment Research Council (CEARC) in 1984 has gone some way towards eliminating certain weaknesses. More recently, increased flexibility in the formulation of environmental assessments has brought further sophistication to the evaluation and monitoring of potentially environmentally harmful projects.

O'Riordan also considers the emerging environmental challenges of the 1980s. The changing economic circumstances have tended to reduce government willingness to extend environmental and social review processes in those parts of the country most affected by recession. However, new reviews have produced a re-evalu-ation of certain projects and kept environmental issues well to the fore. Examples of this include the concern over acid precipitation caused by industrial pollution, the destruction of fragile ecosystems, and chain-reaction damage to a variety of environ-ments stemming from the effects of national and international economic and trade policies.

The question of pollution has been raised frequently in the media and thereby has been kept well to the fore in terms of public interest and concern. Quality of environment has become of greater importance, stimulated by the debate over nuclear power and fears of "disasters" such as those at Bhopal and Chernobyl. Government reaction has been to introduce new standards for waste disposal, to develop better monitoring schemes, to restrict use of toxic chemicals, to introduce incentives encouraging recycling, to promote public education campaigns, and to extend penalties for those not meeting standards on pollution.

Particular attention has been paid to the need for both co-operation with the United States and the enforcement of pollution controls on both sides of the border, especially with a view to controlling emissions likely to produce acid rain (e.g., Carroll 1983). Monitoring of these and other types of pollution has increased greatly, but there is still public concern that insufficient action has been taken by government to limit pollution. In this respect it is pertinent to note that despite a post-Chernobyl with-drawal of government support for nuclear power in several countries, in Ontario there have been proposals to spend $17.2 billion on ten nuclear reactors over a 15-year period to 2015.

A central conflict could be seen as developing in the 1980s between governments' needs to stimulate growth at a time of recession and their requirement to protect the environment. This conflict was highlighted by the McDonald Report in 1985, which suggested that new schemes for resource exploitation should be accompanied by tighter controls upon the environmental impact. Thus the conflicting pressures posed by the issues of conservation versus development are likely to grow unless satisfactory regulatory mechanisms can be found. The federal-provincial jurisdictional problem adds difficulties concerning such issues, as does the fact that individual environmental problems, such as air pollution, loss of farmland, and disposal of toxic waste, continue to be dealt with by separate authorities and different arms of government.

To the types of environmental problem that Canada shares in common with many other developed countries must be added the dimension of the native peoples. The growth of environmental consciousness in the 1970s was also accompanied by a growing political awareness by native peoples and their supporters, of the natives' central role in the development of Canada's natural resources. Logging and mining operations, which could have dramatic environmental impacts, could threaten directly the lives and livelihood of native peoples. O'Riordan shows how conflicts between Indian groups in British Columbia and the provincial government have grown since the claims of the Nishga in 1970 to legal entitlement to their traditional land base. Yet, despite the establishment in the province of the Office of Native Claims, the provincial government does not recognize aboriginal title (see Tennant 1990). What has altered is federal policy, which has moved towards promotion of greater native self-government. Although offering native peoples more control over their own economic, social, and cultural affairs, this policy conflicts with the desire of others to utilize the lands and resources claimed by the Indian and Inuit groups.

This is one of the points also addressed by Sewell (chapter 21) who follows O'Riordan's more general treatment of the relationship between society and environment by focusing upon how an environmental policy was formulated in British Colombia, with special attention paid to the government's handling of conservation and development issues in wilderness areas. The example he uses of the problems linking conservation, resource exploitation, and native land claims is that of the Queen Charlotte Islands, the ancestral home of the Haida Nation. One of the mechanisms by which the provincial government attempted to deal with this conflict was through the formation of a Wilderness Advisory Committee. This committee studied 16 wilderness areas under review for possible boundary changes.

Sewell, himself a member of the committee, describes the way in which it reached its decisions, adopting some of the ideas on negotiating agreements as expounded by Fisher and Ury (1981). For the Queen Charlotte Islands, and especially their southernmost part, South Moresby, the prospect of agreement to any committee's findings rests upon a compromise between distinctive sets of interested parties: loggers and miners versus preservationists versus the Indians (in this case the Haida Nation). The latter group, failing to persuade either federal or provincial government to settle their land claims, made several peaceful protests in 1985 and also blocked some logging activity. Their actions virtually dictated that no solution could be formulated without at least giving the Haida some say in details of conservation management or the designation of land for resource development. Indeed, this was a recommendation of the committee, accompanied by a suggestion that a national or provincial park should be established on South Moresby. There was also a recommendation that the holder of logging rights in the area should be compensated and those rights be transferred elsewhere.

Given the entrenched positions of the various groups, it is not surprising that the committee's report met with a great deal of criticism. This was true for the Haida despite the suggestion that 94 percent of South Moresby should be set aside as a wilderness preserve. Thus, it seems that Indian claims and native peoples' general feelings of alienation are not going to be assuaged by setting aside more designated protected areas. It will take something more radical and far reaching for marginalized people, whose views of people-environment relationships are at variance with that of government and the majority of Canadian society, to lose their distrust of and objections to both "economic" and "environmental" solutions. Meanwhile, steps have been taken to implement some of the views presented in the committee's report. For example, both federal and provincial governments have considered extensions of protected areas as well as the designation of special recreational areas.

For South Moresby the recommendation that a national park be created was duly acted upon, and in July 1987 the federal and British Columbia governments reached an agreement to establish a national park and a national marine park (May 1990). Thus, South Moresby became the country's thirty-third national park, and the largest of the five national parks in British Columbia. It covers 145,000 hectares and includes the Ninstints Haida site already designated by UNESCO as a World Heritage Site of international cultural significance. Under the National Parks Act, the national park reserve has been established pending settlement of the Haida's land claim.

// Despite the establishment of the South Moresby National Park, the Haida do not regard this as satisfactory and have argued that continuation of logging beyond the park boundaries still violates their own land rights. Logging companies have also protested at the way the establishment of the park curtails their activities. To compensate the loggers for cessation of their work on South Moresby, the federal government paid over $22 million into a specially created South Moresby Forestry Compensation Account. A further $8 million was paid into the account by the government of British Columbia as compensation for forestry operations suspended as a result of the park's establishment. If these funds exceed the total amount of compensation ultimately awarded, the balance will go towards regional economic development initiatives in the rest of the Queen Charlotte Islands.[1] This illustrates an additional element of federal and provincial government policy towards the Queen Charlottes: combining enhanced environmental conservation in some areas with investment in development elsewhere. In all, the federal government allocated $106 million in 1987 to special programs for the Queen Charlottes, including $50 million for development initiatives.[2]

19.2   **Social Planning and Geographic Regions**

The question of government mediation in the relationship between society and the environment can be set in the general context of government regulation and control through social policy. The designation of specific areas for protection from development or for recreational purposes is just one aspect of government involvement in social welfare, which is actually at work at a variety of levels. This participation has helped shape several of the aspects of social geography considered in this book, but a more detailed guide is set out in chapter 22 by Weeks who considers one of the ways in which geographers can assist with social planning: the establishment of a better geographical framework for implementation and evaluation of policies.

Weeks outlines federal social policy under the categories of family allowances, old age pensions, unemployment insurance, assistance programs, health care, education, and regional policy. The key to the implementation of these policies has lain in the desire to provide minimum essential services throughout the country irrespective of provincial and local policy. Prompted especially by problems experienced during the depression of the 1930s, the federal government has tackled economic inequalities through universal welfare measures such as the Family Allowance Acts of 1944 and 1973, the Old Age Pension Act of 1927, the Old Age Security Act of 1951, and the Canada Pension Plan from 1965. Specific groups and areas are targeted through the Unemployment Insurance Program, and federal support for provincial policies on health and education is provided under legislation such as the 1958 Hospital and Diagnostic Services Act. These policies are often grouped together under the heading of social security and, as such, they are intended to maintain, protect, and raise the basic living standards of the citizenry. A fundamental aim is to replace income foregone by virtue of illness, accident, pregnancy, unemployment, old age, retirement, or the death or absence of the head of household. The expansion of social security referred to by Weeks includes the introduction of minimum wage legislation and some provision of income maintenance for costs of medical and hospital care and housing.

In terms of geographical investigation the significance of this wide range of measures lies in the way in which social security payments are unevenly spread spatially and sectorally. A Senate inquiry of 1969 revealed that one in four Canadians lived below the poverty line and subsequent studies have revealed the way in which this poverty is concentrated in particular districts (e.g., Economic Council of Canada 1977; Phillips 1983). Ontario, Alberta, and British Columbia have consistently maintained average personal incomes per inhabitant that are 70 percent higher than that found in Newfoundland and around 50 percent higher than that found in some parts of the Maritimes. Quebec's average personal income has also been consistently below the national average. The extent of the working poor, that is, people whose income from employment is insufficient to raise them above the "poverty line," was recognized in Saskatchewan, Manitoba, and Quebec by the introduction of supplementary incomes. At the federal level, inequalities in income have been tackled by means of regional development planning.

Regional variations in wealth and inequalities in socio-economic development have been addressed in several ways. In 1967 it was established that any province whose tax base was not able to provide per capita revenue equal to the national average would receive compensation from the federal government in the form of equalisation payments. Other measures, more related to development, were consolidated in the creation of the Department of Regional Economic Expansion (DREE) in 1969 and, later, with its successor, the Department of Regional Industrial Expansion (DRIE).

Reviews of policies during the 1980s have demonstrated the need for social policy to reach those sectors of the community most in need of assistance. Concern, too, has been voiced over the way in which those poorer sectors have continued to be unevenly distributed within Canada. Thus "targeting" of assistance is closely related to regional disparities in wealth and to the regional imbalances in economic development. Weeks argues that these regional imbalances need to be viewed at a sub-provincial level because disparities, with respect to critical "indicators" such as labour force participation rate and the rate of unemployment, are often greater within a province than between provinces. His contention is that an improved geographical framework for investigation is necessary for such regional variation to be described, and for its causes to be understood so that social policy can be adjusted accordingly.

This leads the geographer to utilize particular skills to contribute towards the planning of policy in the public domain, or what would generally be termed "applied geography." In this case those skills are ones related to the classification of space, or regionalization for the purposes of analyzing the data necessary for the process of social policy formulation. In the Canadian context Weeks suggests that the regionalization produced by Camu, Weeks, and Sametz (1964; Fremlin 1973, 241–50) provides a sound basis for this exercise because it enables assessment of the impact and usefulness of existing policies as well as the likely effects of future policies. The latter half of chapter 22 examines a modification of the Camu, Weeks, and Sametz regionalization, stimulated partly by renewed federal and provincial interest in the establishment of a suitable geographical framework for various policy formu-lations and evaluations. The regionalization so produced utilizes a methodology akin to that of the United States Bureau of Economic Analysis' economic areas. Its end-product (Figure 22.1) is a framework that can serve for federal, provincial, or local level socio-geographic studies, given the availibilty of data on particular social issues.

During his time as chief geographer of Canada, Wreford Watson dealt with many social problems on which he advised the government as to particular courses of action. This position, in which geographical skills were being allied to public policy concerns, placed him in the sort of position which, subsequently, more and more geographers have come to value and seek out. All three contributors to this final part of the book have been involved in shaping or monitoring public policy and in applying a geographical perspective to social and environmental problems and policies. The growth of this type of geography in which studies are problem oriented, and in which solutions are sought to questions of direct public concern, demonstrates an evolution of the discipline from the days when Watson was beginning his career and the regional paradigm held sway. It is pertinent to note that, although his former students, friends, and colleagues within the discipline of geography have often retained important elements of the "region," or a "sense of place," in their work, many have translated the skills of social geography in its broadest sense to practical problems. This tendency towards the practical has incorporated a desire to further the growth and evolution of society itself through the application of geographical skills. In this respect Watson's followers have been part of the blossoming of "applied geography" in the 1970s and 1980s. Three of these "applied" studies form the final part of this collection.

Notes

1. Environment Canada, *Environment Update* 9(1):4.
2. Environment Canada, *Annual Report, 1987–88*, 13.

References

Berger, T.R. 1977. *Northern Frontier, Northern Homeland.* Ottawa: Minister of Supply and Services Canada.

Bowles, R.T. 1981. *Social Impact Assessment in Small Communities.* Toronto: Butterworths.

Camu, P., E.P. Weeks, and Z. Sametz. 1964. *Economic Geography of Canada.* Toronto: Macmillan of Canada.

Carroll, J.E. 1983. *Environmental Diplomacy.* Ann Arbor: University of Michigan Press.

Economic Council of Canada. 1977. *Living Together: A Study of Regional Disparities.* Ottawa: Economic Council of Canada.

Finsterbusch, K. 1980. *Understanding Social Impacts: Assessing the Effects of Public Projects.* Beverly Hills: Sage Publications.

———. 1981. *Methodology of Social Impact Assessment.* 2d ed. Stroudsberg: Hutchison Ross Publishing Co.

Fisher, R., and W. Ury. 1981. *Getting to Yes: Negotiating Agreement Without Giving In.* New York: Penguin Books.

Fremlin, G., ed. 1973. *The National Atlas of Canada.* 4th ed. Ottawa: Surveys and Mapping Branch, Department of Energy, Mines and Resources.

Hamley, W. 1987. "Some Aspects and Consequences of the Development of the James Bay Hydro-Electric Complex." *British Journal of Canadian Studies* 2:250–62.

Howard, R. 1980. *Poisons in Public: Case Studies of Environmental Pollution in Canada.* Toronto: James Lorimer & Co.

Lucas, A.R. 1981. "The Canadian Experience." In S.D. Clark ed., *Environmental Assessment in Australia and Canada,* 141–89. Victoria, Austalia: Ministry of Conservation; and Vancouver: Westwater Research Centre, University of British Colombia.

Lucas, R.A. 1971. *Minetown, Milltown, Railtown: Life in Canadian Communities of Single Industry.* Toronto: University of Toronto Press.

May, E. 1990. *Paradise Won: The Struggle for South Moresby.* Toronto: McClelland and Stewart.

Mitchell, B. 1989. *Geography and Resource Analysis.* Harlow: Longman.

Mitchell, B., and R. Turkheim. 1977. "Environmental Impact Assessment. Principles, Practice and Canadian Experiences." In R.R. Krueger and B. Mitchell, eds., *Managing Canada's Renewable Resources,* 47–66. Toronto: Methuen.

O'Riordan, J. 1981. "The British Columbian Experience." In T. O'Riordan and W.R.D. Sewell, eds., *Project Appraisal and Policy Review,* 95–123. Chichester: John Wiley & Sons.

O'Riordan, T., and J.W. Watson, eds. 1977. *The American Environment, Perspectives and Policies.* London: John Wiley & Sons.

Phillips, P. 1983. *Regional Disparities.* Toronto: James Lorimer & Co.

Porter, J. 1965. *The Vertical Mosaic: An Analysis of Social Class and Power in Canada.* Toronto: University of Toronto Press.

Sewell, W. R. D. 1981. "How Canada Responded: The Berger Inquiry." In T. O'Riordan and W.R.D. Sewell, eds., *Project Appraisal and Policy Review,* 77–94. Chichester: John Wiley & Sons.

Tennant, P. 1990. *Aboriginal Peoples and Politics: The Indian Land Question in British Columbia, 1848–1989.* Vancouver: University of British Columbia Press.

Wilson, J.W. 1966. *People in the Way: The Human Aspects of the Columbian River Project.* Toronto: University of Toronto Press.

20 Society and Environment: How People Have Influenced Environmental Policies in Canada

Jonathan O'Riordan

20.1 Introduction

It is well known that Canada has a rich and varied natural resource base that has fuelled its growth over the past 200 years. Unfortunately, this impressive resource heritage has given succeeding governments, at both federal and provincial levels, a false sense of security: a feeling that the nation's vast quantities of water, minerals, fisheries, wildlife, and forests are virtually inextinguishable and will support Canada's relatively small population and export markets indefinitely. Only during the past 10 to 15 years has the public questioned the traditional policy of resource development at the expense of environmental quality, social-cultural stability, and protection of native groups' traditional values. As a result of this change, policies affecting resource exploitation have shifted dramatically in the past decade to accommodate social and environmental values. This essay discusses the influences that various public interests, both native and non-native, have had on changing government policies on resource management.

Canada, like most European countries and its neighbour, the United States, has witnessed several changes of pace in resource development over the past 20 years or so. The main dimensions of these development phases will be described to provide a background on resource and environmental issues facing Canada today. Imposed on this historical review will be consideration of the role that non-government interests have played in shaping policy towards resource management. This influence has been exerted not only through public hearings and inquiries, but also through more subtle ways such as public opinion polls, assertion of native rights, parliamentary lobbying, and more direct public action. The thesis of this essay is that policy changes in resource and environmental management have been led, not only by enlightened governments at both the federal and provincial levels, but also by visionary community leaders who have been able to articulate the frustrations, needs, and aspirations of the varied interest groups that together make up the complex society of Canada.

Full coverage of the range of environmental issues facing Canada or of the scope of the influence various public interests have brought to bear on the policy-working machinery cannot be encompassed in this essay. Although there are also many interesting facets to analysis of national resource policy in Canada, such as federal-provincial relations, revenue sharing, and legal rights, this survey will dwell almost exclusively on environmental policies associated with resource development.

Environmental policy-making is highly dynamic in Canada as in other western industrialized countries. This review can provide only a snapshot of the current situation. However, in the conclusion an attempt is made to forecast the dominant forces that will lead to future shifts in public policy and, thus, identify some of the changes in direction such policies might take.

20.2   Resource Development in Canada

Canada is a federal state. Under its Constitution, responsibilities for natural resource development are shared between the federal and provincial governments. However, the provinces exercise greater control over actual resource development activities because they own most resources and have statutory authority over development rights. The federal government has jurisdiction over inter-provincial and international trade, over taxation and revenue-sharing and, in the environmental field, over fisheries. By agreement, responsibility for managing inland fisheries has been delegated to the provinces, though the federal government retains an overall mandate to protect and conserve all fish under the British North America Act of 1867. Through this latter responsibility, the federal government has built up its environmental protection legislation to enforce its considerable powers under the Fisheries Act of 1970 to protect fish habitats and the quality of aquatic environments.

The provincial governments have jurisdictional responsibility over land use and resources such as forests, minerals, water resources, agriculture, and wildlife. Most of the responsibility for environmental management through pollution control, environmental protection laws, and the conduct of environmental assessments therefore lies with the provinces. In the past, the federal government's involvement in environmental assessments has generally been limited to reviewing development projects on federal lands, projects under federal jurisdiction such as national parks, ports, and airports, or projects on native Indian reserve lands. More recently, because of its mandate to protect fisheries, the courts have mandated the federal government to become directly involved in a wider range of project assessments.

Given these shared responsibilities, resource development in Canada has required cooperation between the two senior levels of government. This has not always been forthcoming. As Romanow (1985) puts it, "resource management has placed into stark relief the difficulties inherent in the Canadian federal system." Though much of this acrimony has arisen from revenue sharing, particularly for oil and gas, it also occurs over another central issue in resource management: that of native land claims. No survey of resource policy or the influence of public interests in shaping that policy in contemporary Canada can be complete without a review of the role played by native groups – Indian, Métis, and Inuit – in shaping public policy. This is now an issue that sets Canada uniquely apart from all other developed countries in the northern hemisphere.

Canada has experienced two distinct phases in resource development and environmental management. The first of these phases, from 1950 to 1971, covers the main era of resource exploitation accompanied by the awakening of environmental concerns. The second phase, from 1971 to the present, starts with the creation of a

Federal Department of Environment and, thus, encompasses the institutionalization of environmental management.

20.2.1 Economic Development Phase, 1950–1971

Throughout the 1950s and early 1960s, the primary emphasis of resource development was to stimulate economic development in the southern half of the nation. The period was dominated by large-scale hydro-electric projects for which environmental or social impact assessments were given short shrift. Examples of such projects are scattered across the nation and include the Alcan-Kemano hydro project on the Nechako River in north-central British Columbia, completed in 1952 to power the aluminum smelter in Kitimat; the gigantic power developments undertaken in the 1960s on the Columbia River, which were based on the Columbia River Treaty with the United States; the Churchill-Nelson diversion project in Northern Saskatchewan and Manitoba in 1970; the mammoth James Bay power development in northern Quebec in 1970; and the Churchill Falls scheme in Labrador (Figure 20.1).

During this period, the dominant public opinion favoured rapid economic growth facilitated by cheap electricity. Many environmental side-effects were either unknown or not considered to be critical in a country perceived to possess vast resources. Public agencies both in government and Crown corporations and in the private sector were largely managed by engineers and economists who placed high value on pragmatic goals of safe and cost-effective design, and who had little knowledge or understanding of environmental and social issues.

However, significant environmental and social impacts did occur as a result of such projects, and these began to force a change in policy in the early 1970s. Two important conferences were sponsored by the federal and provincial governments to review resource development policies, namely "The Resources for Tomorrow Conference" in 1961 and "Pollution and Our Environment Conference" in 1966. While these sessions had an important influence on public opinion, a more dramatic effect was public response to the actual environmental damage that resulted from the construction of some of these major energy projects. An example of these environmental effects is the severe de-watering of the Athabasca delta in Great Slave Lake, Alberta, as a result of the upstream impoundment on the Peace River in British Columbia caused by the construction of the W.A.C. Bennett Dam in the late 1960s (Peace-Athabasca Delta Project Group 1973). This project had profound effects on migrating waterfowl, on commercial fisheries, and on access to the lake. Similarly, the flooding of Southern Indian Lake as part of the Churchill-Nelson scheme resulted in a decline in the commercial whitefish populations and an increase in mercury content in both sport and commercial fish species caused by mobilization of mercury from the upper soil horizons due to flooding (Bodaly et al. 1985). There was also a considerable increase in shoreline erosion as the elevated water levels impinged on soft glacial tills instead of the bedrock that had been exposed at the lake's natural level. Similar effects on fisheries and fur-bearing mammals were observed at the giant Hydro-Quebec power project in James Bay (Paehlke 1980).

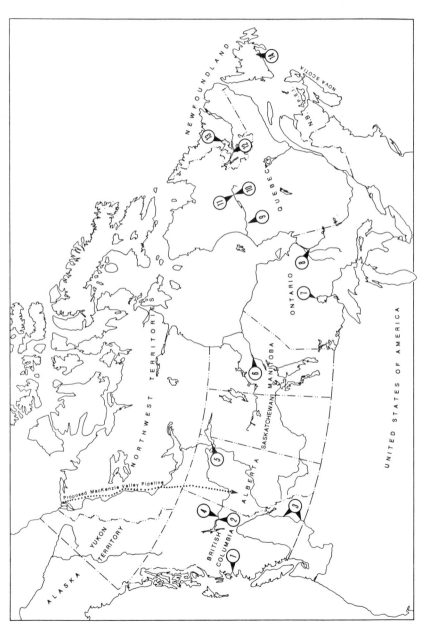

Figure 20.1 **Selected Major Hydro-electric Projects in Canada**

Projects cited in Figure 20.1

British Columbia
1. Nechako-Alcan
2. WAC Bennett Dam
3. Columbia Treaty Dams
4. Peace Site One and Site C

Alberta
5. Great Slave Lake Project

Manitoba
6. Churchill-Nelson Diversion

Ontario
7. Ogoki Diversion
8. Little Abitibi

Quebec
9. James Bay projects–Eastmain–Opinaca–La Grande
10. James Bay (Caniapisca–La Grande)
11. James Bay (Frigate–La Grande)

Newfoundland
12. Churchill Falls–Julian–Unknown
13. Churchill Falls–Naskaupi
14. Bay d'Espoir–Salmon Diversion

These environmental changes also produced severe social impacts through the loss of the resource base for native peoples and complete dislocation of communities. In the 1960s, there was little public sympathy with native groups in Canada, and a disruption to their traditional way of life was accepted as part of the costs of making economic progress. Little or no compensation was made to the native groups that were relocated around the giant Williston reservoir that formed behind the W.A.C. Bennett Dam on the Peace River in northern British Columbia (see Figure 20.1), or for the loss of community cohesion as a result of the reservoirs on the Columbia River (Wilson 1973).

But by the end of the 1960s, native groups had begun to establish themselves as a major political force in Canada. In northern Manitoba the three native communities affected by the Churchill River diversion joined with two non-native communities to form the Northern Flood Committee in 1974. As a legal entity, the committee threatened to obtain a court injunction to prevent Manitoba Hydro from proceeding with the project until compensation had been paid. After two years of negotiation between the committee and the federal and provincial governments, the Northern Flood Agreement was signed. This agreement provided provincial Crown land in exchange for flooded reserve lands, compensation for loss of hunting and fishing rights, and $3.2 million to be invested in an economic development corporation to assist the affected communities (Department of Indian and Northern Affairs 1984a).

A much more substantial settlement was made with the Cree Indians in Northern Quebec as a result of the James Bay Hydro project. This project, originally proposed in 1971, epitomized the changing attitudes of governments and industry to demands by native people. In 1972, after the initial protest by the Cree and Inuit groups affected by the project – there had been no consultation prior to the decision to undertake this project – these groups quickly banded together and sought a court injunction to stop construction in 1973. This injunction was granted by the Supreme Court of Quebec, though it was immediately suspended by the Quebec Court of Appeal. Nonetheless, the Quebec government could no longer ignore the Cree and Inuit case. Within five days of the decision, the Quebec government initiated negotiations on the native demands for aboriginal land claims and compensation for loss of livelihood.

An agreement was signed in 1975 by the James Bay Cree, the Inuit of Northern Quebec, the governments of Quebec and Canada, the James Bay Development Corporation, and Hydro Quebec. It recognized the aboriginal land claims, protected their remaining traditional fishing, hunting, and trapping rights, and paid cash compensation of $232.5 million over 21 years, divided proportionately between the Crees and the Inuit (Department of Indian and Northern Affairs 1979; Paehlke 1980).

20.2.2   The Rise of Environmental Consciousness in the 1970s and 1980s

As shown in Section 20.2.1, the management of environmental and social impact began to be implemented in the 1970s. The institutionalization of these policies occurred around 1971 with the creation of the federal Department of Environment and the application of environmental impact assessment (EIA) and, later, social impact assessment (SIA) by the federal and, eventually, all provincial governments. The combination of EIA and SIA is called environmental assessment (EA), the term used for the balance of this essay. Based on the American experience of costly and complicated law suits following its National Environment Protection Act in 1970, many Canadian jurisdictions initially kept their EA administration at the policy level rather than making it statutory. However, over time a number of provinces have introduced a statutory basis for EA, partly as a result of public pressure. Ontario led the way with its Environment Assessment Act in 1975, to be followed by Quebec in 1977, Newfoundland in 1980, and Saskatchewan in 1980. The federal government introduced draft legislation in June 1990, and this has been followed by major revisions or new assessment legislation by most provinces. This shift towards a legal basis for EA illustrates the powerful influence of public pressure, since many governments in Canada are philosophically inclined to encourage deregulation rather than more regulation. Departments and ministries of environment sprang up like mushrooms, generally as a result of renaming or reorganizing existing government agencies. Overall, a high political profile was given to environmental matters during the 1970s in Canada, as was the case in the United States (Gladwin 1980).

Public influence in the administration of these EA policies also increased during the 1970s. Many of the early attempts at EA resulted in large documentation of descriptive material, but little in the way of analysis and management of impacts. Governments, responding to public pressure, provided more and more avenues for consultation, generally through public hearings. Although these hearings often occurred too late in the decision-making process to have a real influence on whether a project was to be developed or not, the fact that EA documents were being publically scrutinized forced both the proponents and government agencies to become more disciplined in their analyses.

Perhaps the most persuasive example showing how public groups can influence project development as a result of expressing their environmental and social concerns is the Berger Inquiry into the Mackenzie Valley pipeline proposal (Berger 1977). Although the federal government had made a commitment to the United States to transport natural gas from the Canadian Arctic, it was persuaded by the growing political influence of native groups in the north to hold a public inquiry into the land-use, environmental, and social implications associated with two proposals by Arctic Gas and Foothills Pipelines Ltd. to build a pipeline for natural gas down the Mackenzie Valley to join existing pipelines in Northern Alberta (see Figure 20.1).

The government appointed Thomas Berger, a judge with the British Columbia (BC) Supreme Court, to head the inquiry in 1974. The process developed by Berger revolutionized the public inquiry system in Canada. The inquiry lasted for three years and cost over $5 million, with public meetings held in many small communities throughout the Northwest Territories and northern Yukon as well as some of the major cities in the south. Berger developed an obvious respect for the people of the north and encouraged them to articulate their concerns about the land, its resources, and their fears that economic development would irreversibly alter their traditional way of life. The inquiry also ensured that there was extensive coverage of all the hearings by the news media. The Canadian Broadcasting Corporation's Northern Service employed a team of six native reporters to broadcast a summary of each day's proceedings in all six native languages and in English, thus permitting the entire country access to the issues being discussed.

The inquiry also established two other precedents. First, it forced a much more scientific approach to predicting and managing the impact of development on the fragile northern environment. Until the early 1970s little attention had been paid to the ecology of the north, so scientists scurried not only to understand how these systems functioned in their undisturbed state, but also how resilient they would be to change. Second, Berger insisted that major public interest groups, which would not otherwise have the resources to participate at the hearings, receive financial support from the federal government. To ensure that there was a fair distribution of available funds, Berger developed the following criteria (Sewell 1981):

a) each group must represent a discernible public interest;
b) issues to be presented by each group must be relevant to the inquiry and not represented by other groups;
c) each group must have an established record for representing that interest; and
d) each group must present a clear proposal for the use of funds.

Subsequently, these criteria have been used to allocate funds in other major inquiries authorized by the federal government, such as the Beaufort Sea Oil and Gas Exploration EIA (FEARO 1984) and the Lysyk Inquiry into the Alaska Highway Gas Pipeline (Lysyk 1978).

Although the federal government had made a commitment to transport natural gas to the United States, Berger recommended in 1976 that there should be a ten-year moratorium on the development in the Mackenzie Valley to provide time for the federal government to settle native land claims and to increase development of renewable resources in the north so as to offset the boom-bust cycle that traditionally occurs with capital investment construction projects (Berger 1977). So the tide had turned. For the first time, a major energy project was deferred (now postponed indefinitely) as a result of public concern and a clear expression of social and environmental objectives for northern Canada (O'Malley 1976; Sewell 1986).

The Mackenzie Pipeline Inquiry became the prototype for a number of other influential inquiries into environmental and social implications of economic development proposals, some of which also reversed government thinking. Notable among these are the Thompson Inquiry into oil transportation off the west coast of British Columbia (the proposal was shelved by the federal government in 1979) (Sewell and Swainson 1981); the Bates Commission into uranium mining in 1980 (the B.C. government placed an indefinite moratorium on uranium mining in 1980); and the Porter Commission on electric power planning in Ontario (Porter 1980). This latter commission was established to counteract growing public criticism of Ontario Hydro's policy of supply side development, with the environmental consequences attendant upon transmission lines (loss of agricultural land), thermal generation (air pollution and acid precipitation), and uranium mining in northern Ontario and nuclear power plants (public risk and environmental health). The commission called for new emphasis on energy conservation, increased controls at nuclear generation plants and reductions in SO_2 emissions from thermal generation plants. Partly as a result of the economic recession that gripped Canada in 1982–83, but partly as a consequence of public concern, Ontario Hydro has adjusted its policies in the direction recommended by the Porter Commission.

Throughout this period of environmental consciousness-raising, public participation during the process of project review became increasingly more sophisticated (Sadler 1980; Elder 1980). Some individuals took it upon themselves to become "lay experts" in specific issues, such as the effects of pesticides on the environment, the siting of hazardous waste, and treatment and disposal facilities, and were able to challenge technical experts successfully in cross-examination (Howard 1980). The formation of Pollution Probe under the leadership of Donald Chant (1970) as an influential public environmental group in Toronto is a prime example of such a move. Other examples are cited by Howard (1980) in a series of case studies on how public groups affected policies of pesticide application. Often, groups banded together to form coalitions of interest groups, thereby raising sufficient funds to hire their own consultants and challenge government on more fundamental questions of policy. For example, a coalition of groups challenged B.C. Hydro in a hearing in 1983 about a proposed power project on the Peace River downstream from the Bennett dam. They argued that the project was not required at that period of time and that energy forecasts by B.C. Hydro and the government were substantially inflated. The independent panel agreed with the public case and recommended deferral of the project (B.C. Utilities Commission 1983).

As a result of public hearings, social issues such as changes to lifestyle and community cohesion were also given a much higher profile than the more traditional technical-fix associated with improvements to community infrastructure that dominated the early SIAs (Hanson 1986). Perhaps the most obvious example is the public opposition that developed against the Spadina expressway in central Toronto in the late-1960s and early-1970s. Although the route had been selected and construction started, public opinion and involvement through the inquiry process resulted in the termination of the project before it entered the downtown core (Nowlan 1970). The growing importance of social and community issues was largely responsible for the development of a new approach to EA known as adaptive environmental assessment and management (AEAM) (Holling 1978). Under this philosophy, accurate prediction of impacts on many behavioural systems was considered difficult, if not impossible, and a more effective management approach was proposed whereby effects were carefully monitored during and after project implementation, and adjustments made to design in order to mitigate undesirable impacts. In some cases, community leaders became part of the planning team and negotiated appropriate mitigatory measures with proponents, as with a major thermal coal and electrical generation project in central Alberta (Krawitz and Macdonald 1987).

More attention was also given to improving scientific understanding of cause and effect relationships associated with environmental change. A survey of contemporary practice in EA case studies across Canada in the early 1980s by Beanlands and Duinker (1983) revealed a lamentable disregard for proven scientific methods of analysis to predict and manage environmental impact. Despite almost a decade of experience and increased scrutiny of environmental reports by the public, many studies failed to predict with any degree of accuracy the consequences of environmental change. Furthermore, there was a lack of systematic evaluation and audit of projects following their construction to assess the adequacy of the predictions and mitigatory measures designed to offset environmental and social effects.

As a result of these weaknesses, the federal government sponsored the formation of an independent Canadian Environmental Assessment Research Council (CEARC) in 1984. The council is allocated a modest budget to commission applied research into a number of scientific, procedural, and institutional issues that currently limit the effectiveness of EA practice in Canada. Such an initiative is required because established research funding agencies in Canada look askance at research proposals that are interdisciplinary or applied. At present, the council is in the process of drafting research priorities in a number of areas including cumulative effects, post-project evaluation, social impacts, risk analysis, compensation/mitigation, and application of modelling techniques to improve impact prediction (CEARC 1985). The advent of a national body established to examine and improve EA applications is a rare, if not unique, institutional response in environmental policy-making.

20.3   Emerging Challenges

Although decision-makers have become more sensitized to public concern about social and environmental issues over the past decade, countervailing pressures have limited the adjustment of public policies to satisfy these public demands adequately. First, Canada, like other western industrial nations, suffered economic recession in the early 1980s, and, although the tempo of economic development has picked up in Ontario and Quebec, the resource-based economies in Western Canada and Atlantic Canada remain depressed. Thus provincial governments in these areas are tempted to approve almost any economic opportunity and are impatient with lengthy environmental and social review processes that might impede development. A continuing challenge to public agencies is the development of "fast-track" review procedures that permit timely decisions that are scientifically and socially responsible (O'Riordan 1986).

Second, a number of new environmental issues are now on the public agenda. One is the cumulative impact of multiple developments, each one of which may not create significant environmental problems, but that can, in combination with other activities, affect ecosystems profoundly. The classic example is acid precipitation due to transportation of air pollutants from the United States and eastern Canada. In the mid-1980s, several provinces and the federal government signed a multi-million dollar agreement to reduce the discharge of SO_2 and NO_2 by 50 percent between 1984 and 1990. Finally, in 1990, the U.S. passed its Clean Air Act and signed an agreement with Canada to control SO_2 (sulphur dioxide) emissions. Other examples of cumulative effects include the fragmentation of wildlife habitats in forest ecosystems as the result of a combination of logging practices, pesticide-spraying to control spruce budworm, and increased public access for hunting in New Brunswick (Baskerville 1986); loss of coastal wetlands on the south coast of British Columbia due to log storage, port and industrial development, and agricultural expansion (Dorcey 1979; 1986); and reduction in prairie wetlands due to improved drainage techniques and urban expansion. Because many of the activities that cause these incremental changes (prairie grain farming, coastal ports, and logging) are driven by national or international economic and trade policies, the cause and effect of such developments are so far removed that they have only recently been identified (CEARC 1986).

Other new challenges to sound environmental management include the safe development and use of toxic chemicals and the siting of environmentally secure disposal sites for such chemicals and for low level radio-active wastes (Levine 1982).

As in western Europe, following the Bhopal and Chernobyl disasters, public alarm has increased exponentially over environmentally risky technology such as nuclear power, chemical manufacturing plants, and transportation of hazardous goods. Public trust in both technology and its expert proponents has diminished considerably. The Ontario Waste Management Corporation, established in 1983 to develop a secure land disposal site for hazardous wastes, has already spent some $100 million in technical studies, examined many potential sites, and still faces strident and persistent public opposition. The public hearings required under the Ontario Environmental Assessment Act have yet to begin and will cost additional millions of dollars before construction of a selected site could begin.

Both federal and provincial governments are continually pressured by public opinion to react to these new challenges. In a series of public opinion polls taken by national firms over the past five years, there has been a consistently high public support for increasing the levels of environmental protection even at the expense of jobs (Decima Research 1986). Figure 20.2 indicates that the percentage of public support remained essentially unchanged even throughout the economic recession of 1982–83. Furthermore, over one-third of the public favours government action against companies that fail to meet environmental standards (Figure 20.3). Surprisingly, there has been a shift in public attitudes towards placing greater responsibility for pollution control onto federal and provincial governments rather than onto the private sector (Figure 20.4). This shows a certain amount of public inconsistency because there is a general concern over Canada's growing public debt. Yet, constant demands are made by various interest groups to increase public spending for their particular commitments.

In a province-wide survey undertaken in British Columbia in the depths of economic recession in 1982, the quality of environment was rated the third most important public issue after the state of the economy and quality of education (McIntyre and Mustel Research Associates 1982). Of the respondents, 63 percent felt that environmental quality in the province had deteriorated over the past five years, and half of all respondents felt that more legislation and government action was required to protect the environment.

Governments have begun to react to these demands. The Canadian Council of Ministers of the Environment (CCME), representing the federal and ten provincial environment ministries, has announced a co-ordinated strategy for handling and controlling the use of toxic materials "from the cradle to the grave." Strict national standards have been established for the disposal of such wastes, and environmental monitoring plans are being co-ordinated to check all transportation of wastes across provincial boundaries. Some jurisdictions, notably Ontario, have stepped up enforcement and prosecution capability to deal with offending polluters, and the federal government has enacted new legislation to control toxic chemical use in Canada. International co-operation has also increased with the signing of the new Great Lakes Water Quality Agreement in 1978 and the enforcement of waste management controls on industry and municipalities on both sides of the border (Munton 1980; Carroll 1983). As is the case with acid rain, Canada's strategy is to put its own house in order before negotiating with the United States. Also, Ontario announced a ten-year multi-billion dollar scheme to control municipal and industrial wastes and improve municipal infrastructure (Environment Ontario 1986).

20.3.1 Indian Land Claims

Although the governments are making some headway at tackling a few of the continuing environmental challenges, thus far they have substantially failed to deal with one other major issue that now has profound implications for resource development, especially in British Columbia, namely native land claims. By the end of 1986, native groups in British Columbia had successfully forced injunctions on logging operations on Meares Island and Deer Island off the west and east coasts of Vancouver Island respectively, and on the twin-tracking of the Canadian National railway through the Fraser and Thompson corridors. They also forced the preservation of the South Moresby national park on the Queen Charlotte Islands by both civil disobedience and court injunction, and took legal action in the British Columbia Supreme Court to claim aboriginal title over a vast tract of provincial Crown land in north-west British Columbia together with its substantial resources of timber, fish, wildlife, and minerals. Although the native groups lost this court case, they plan to appeal to the Supreme Court of Canada. Further details on native concerns over logging to protect wilderness values, and fish and wildlife resources on their claimed land base are provided by Derrick Sewell in the following chapter.

"Native land claims" and "aboriginal title" are related concepts pertaining to the traditional use of land and its resources enjoyed by native groups prior to settlement of the continent by Europeans. By royal proclamation in 1763, King George III dictated that the new settlers in Canada should acquire rights to lands by treaty, and over the ensuing one hundred years a number of treaties were signed in Ontario, Quebec, and the Prairie provinces. But British Columbia has steadfastly refused to negotiate treaties with native groups, apart from a few in southern Vancouver Island and in the north-eastern part of the province, which were signed prior to the province joining Confederation in 1871.

Under the British North America Act of 1867, the federal government is responsible for negotiating treaties. However, any such discussions must involve the province, which owns the land base and its resources. Over the past century, the government of British Columbia has made increasing commitments for resource development on its Crown lands without any regard for "aboriginal title." The major right it has given out has been for forest tenure, which provides private timber companies with long-term access to the forest base. Other rights include water licences, mineral leases, highway rights-of-way, grazing leases, and provincial parks. Out of a total of 86.5 million hectares of provincial Crown land (93 percent of the total land base), only 1.6 million hectares are unencumbered by these rights, and they are mostly unproductive, high-altitude areas (Council of Forest Industries 1986). Thus, as Berger (1981) has pointed out, the province had painted itself into a corner. Any negotiations for settlements of Indian land claims must now deal with these third party rights, either through compensation or through their removal.

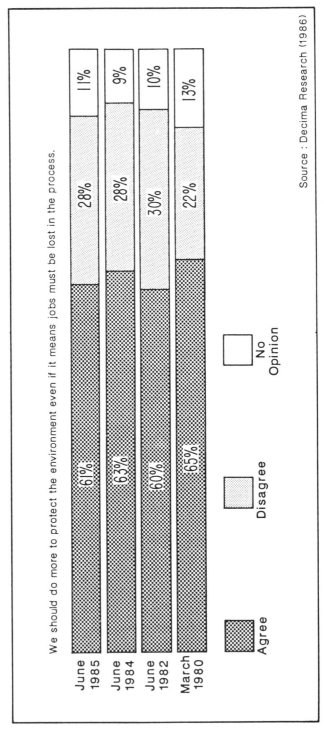

Figure 20.2 **Environmental Protection versus Jobs**

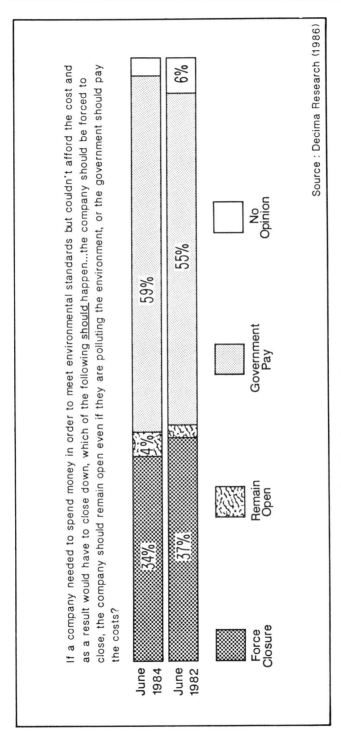

If a company needed to spend money in order to meet environmental standards but couldn't afford the cost and as a result would have to close down, which of the following should happen...the company should be forced to close, the company should remain open even if they are polluting the environment, or the government should pay the costs?

Force Closure

Remain Open

Government Pay

No Opinion

June 1984 — 34% / 4% / 59%

June 1982 — 37% / 55% / 6%

Source : Decima Research (1986)

Figure 20.3 **Preferred Action If a Company Cannot Meet Environmental Standards**

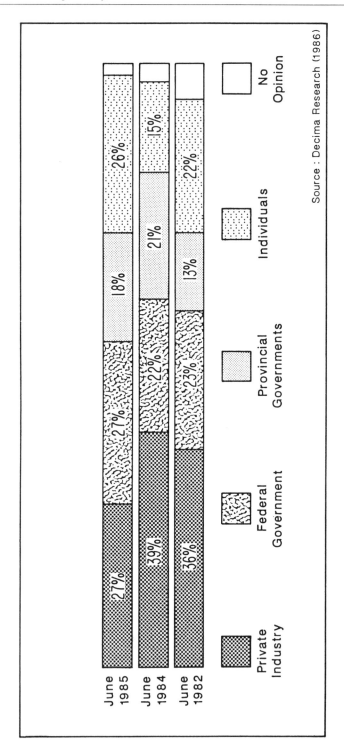

Figure 20.4 **Who Has the Primary Responsibility for Preventing Pollution?**

Until 1970, native groups watched helplessly as this pattern of rights was consolidated. But in 1970 the Nishga in north-west British Columbia took legal action in the B.C. Supreme Court to claim legal entitlement to its traditional land base. The court rejected the claim, declaring that while the ancient Nishga may have controlled the land in question, the current generation did not. The decision was appealed to the Supreme Court of Canada in 1973, which resulted in an historic split decision, three judges ruling in favour of the Indian band and three against; the seventh ruled against the Nishga but only on a legal technicality.

This moral victory for the Indians forced the federal government to take notice of land claims. In 1974 it set up an Office of Native Claims (ONC) to implement its new policy of negotiating comprehensive claims with native groups not already covered by a treaty. The federal government finally produced a formal policy for dealing with outstanding comprehensive claims after considerable political pressure by native groups (Department of Indian and Northern Affairs 1981). But progress has been painfully slow owing to the third party obligations mentioned earlier, overlapping claims (see Figure 20.5) and constant shifts in the position of native claimants (Berger 1981). Settlements were concluded with the Cree and Inuit in 1975, forced by the James Bay hydro project as discussed earlier, and with the Naskapi in Northern Quebec in 1978. Settlements with other native groups have occurred in the late 1980s.

In British Columbia, the ONC has accepted 14 claims for negotiation (Table 20.1 and Figure 20.5) and a further seven are currently under review. Figure 20.5 shows the areas of claims requested by various native Indian bands, and indicates their extent and overlaps. A number of these claims are associated with the resource developments noted earlier, namely the Nuu-Chah-Nulth Tribal Council claim to the west coast of Meares Island, which has tied up logging through a court injuction; the claim of the Council of Haida Nations on the Queen Charlotte Islands, which affects logging on Lyell Island; and the Alkali Lake Band claim, which has tied up the twin-tracking of Canadian National Railway's main line down the Thompson and Fraser Canyon. With these precedents, other potential proposals for resource development in northern British Columbia and the offshore islands are being affected before the claims issue is resolved either politically or through the courts.

The next steps in this process of dealing with native claims are still unclear. However, recently the province of British Columbia has indicated its willingness to negotiate native land claims and has become directly involved in the Nishga claim negotiations, together with the federal government. This more enlightened provincial policy has been implemented with the creation of the first "self-governing" Indian band in Canada, on the Sechelt Reserve on the coast, approximately 160 kilometres north of Vancouver.

The promotion of native self-government is an important new direction. Berger (1981) has argued that the collection of policies and legislation developed since Confederation are all institutional arrangements devised by non-natives to manage native affairs primarily for non-native convenience and interests. The native bands have matured significantly in political terms and are much more anxious and willing to fashion their own institutions, to see their economic base and culture flourish in a direction of their own choosing. As Berger puts it, "they are residents of the twentieth century [and] live in a world in which progress has an industrial and technological definition." However, implementation of this policy generally would depend on native access to lands and resources so they can pursue their more clearly articulated economic and social goals (O'Malley 1976; Richardson 1976). Eventually this question will have to be settled by the courts and/or through political will. The Gitskan-Wet'suwet'en Tribal Council, occupying lands adjacent to the Nishga claim (see Figure 20.5), launched a further court challenge on aboriginal title in the B.C. Supreme Court in the spring of 1987. In April 1991, this challenge was essentially struck down by the court, which argued that aboriginal title to resources was virtually extinguished as a result of provincial government enactments following Confederation. However, the B.C. Supreme Court did assert that the province had a fiduciary obligation to look after native interests with respect to resource use. This judgement is now being appealed to the Supreme Court of Canada.

Table 20.1   Status of Claim Negotiations between Federal Government and Native Groups in British Columbia

1. **ACCEPTED FOR NEGOTIATION** (date of acceptance)
   - Nishga Tribal Council (1974)
   - Kitwancool Band (1977)
   - Gitksan Wet'suwet'en Tribal Council (1977)
   - Kitimaat Village Council (1978)
   - Association of United Tahltans (1980)
   - Nuu-Chah-Nulth Tribal Council (1983)
   - Council of Haida Nation (1983)
   - Nuxaik Nation (Bella Coola) (1983)
   - Nazko-Kluskus Bands (1983)
   - Kaska Dena Council (1983)
   - Carrier-Sekani Tribal Council (1983)
   - Alkali Lake Band (1983)
   - Taku Tlingit (Atlin Band) (1984)

2. **CLAIMS UNDER REVIEW** (date of submission)
   - Kootenay Indian Area Council (1981)
   - Allied Tsimshian Tribes (1982)
   - Council of the Tsimshian Council (1983)
   - Kwakiutl First Nations (1984)
   - Nlaka' pamux Nation (1984)
   - Sechelt Band (1984)
   - Homalco Band (1985)

Sources: Council of Forest Industries (1986); Office of Native Land Claims

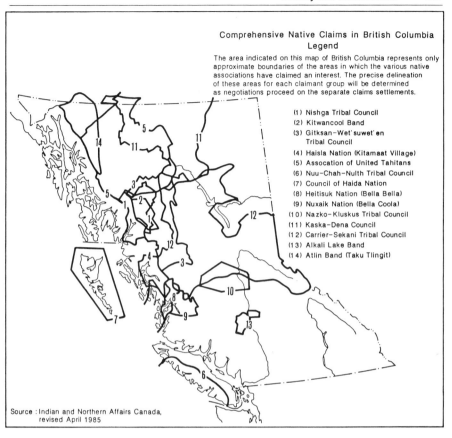

Figure 20.5 **Claims Accepted for Negotiation in British Columbia**

Native Indians have undoubtedly exerted greater political pressure on governments compared with non-native public interest groups regarding resource development and environmental management. Although a number of provinces have "green parties" that are registered political entities, generally their membership is small so they have little direct influence on the major parties' political agendas. Generally, the political influence of small, issue-specific interest groups is often quite limited. Greater political clout is developed when groups create coalitions of interests or act as a federation of individual provincial bodies. An example of such a group is the Fraser River Coalition, which represents around 20 public interest groups in the Greater Vancouver area of British Columbia, and which has applied pressure effectively on both the federal and provincial governments for improved environmental management of the Lower Fraser Estuary (Dorcey 1986). A public slide show presented by this group on problems of waste discharge into the Fraser River stimulated the provincial government to establish a special task force to check on all dischargers and lay charges wherever waste management permits were violated.

A second example of such a coalition is the B.C. Wildlife Federation and its parent group, the Canadian Wildlife Federation, both of which have influenced wild-life management policies through well-organized lobbying and direct participation in conservation projects. A number of members of the B.C. Wildlife Federation have been involved directly in salmonid enhancement projects to increase production of all Pacific salmon species under a ten-year federal-provincial agreement.

Over the past decade, the politics of confrontation have competed with the politics of co-operation. While many groups recognize that more influence can be gained through negotiation with public agencies and politicians, some, such as Greenpeace and the Western Canada Wilderness Committee, have continued confrontational activities, especially with respect to clear-cut logging. The effectiveness of the quiet diplomacy style is more difficult to evaluate than the direct confrontational style, because it is less overt. Certainly, the more combative approach has had success in protecting the South Moresby area in the Queen Charlotte Islands and in forcing a major review of forest practices in the Clayoquot Sound region on the west coast of Vancouver Island. However, as will be discussed in the next section, the future environmental issues are more complex, more strategic than many of the issues heretofore and thus generally more suited to the more patient negotiation styles of contemporary public groups.

20.4   Future Directions

As the end of the century approaches, Canada faces a somewhat mixed scorecard in terms of meeting society's needs for management of resources and the environment. On the positive side, there is a vastly improved process of EA in place in all provinces and at the federal level, with a reasonable degree of public access to decision-making through meetings, hearings, and inquiries. As shown in Environment Canada's recently published report, *State of the Environment – Report for Canada*, most indicators of environmental quality show improving trends, though there are some causes of concern. The diversity of floral and faunal species is declining, and there are reductions in wildlife populations that depend on climax, or undisturbed, habitats such as the grizzly bear, woodland caribou, and mountain goat. There has been some decline in air quality in major urban centres, but there are simply no data to determine the effect of this on human health. Statistical data are only now being measured on concentrations of toxic chemicals in humans and animals. Quantitative assessments of such trends will have to wait a few more years.

On the negative side, there is continuing perception in the mind of the average Canadian that the governments are not doing enough to protect the environment (Decima Research 1986; Law Reform Commission 1985). The issue of native land claims continues to smoulder, with frequent blockades at logging roads, and unless some substantive progress is made in negotiating such claims soon, the frustration of the natives may lead to more direct confrontations.

Perhaps the linkage between the environment and the economy epitomized by the native claim may yet lead to the full integration of government policies on management of resources and environment. In a recent public opinion survey, 82 percent of Canadians agreed that the economy is highly dependent on the state of the environment (Decima Research Ltd. 1986). The drive towards recognition of the links between the economy and the environment was also given a boost by the prestigious and voluminous *Royal Commission Inquiry on the Economic Union and Development Prospects for Canada* in 1985 (the Macdonald Report). The commission, which was established in 1983 to seek new ideas to stimulate Canada's economy and move it out of the recession, produced a far-reaching blueprint of social and economic change. But it also emphasized the need to protect the quality of the environment, argued for tougher EA legislation, and noted that sustained use of Canada's renewable resources was essential to economic growth. "Environmental goals should not be treated as incidental to other goals of resource and industrial policy. Commissioners seek a sustainable form of development that acknowledges that interdependence of society, the economy and the environment at both the national and international levels" (Macdonald 1985, Part 4).

This linkage between economic growth and environmental quality was also the central theme of a colloquium sponsored by the Economic Council of Canada in 1985. The discussions covered a range of issues from water and air quality, forest management, toxic waste disposal, climatic change, and the economic benefits of pollution controls. One speaker, Gustave Speth, graphically illustrated the linkage, however, by quoting a recent survey in the United States, which estimated that ozone damage to four crops – wheat, corn, soybeans, and peanuts – had reached US$3 billion annually (Speth 1985).

In response to the United Nations–appointed World Commission on the Environment and Development (Brundtland Commission 1987), Canada established the National Task Force on the Environment and the Economy (1988). This task force, made up of representatives from a wide spectrum of public interests, recommended that the federal and all provincial jurisdictions establish round tables on the environment and the economy to advise their respective governments on the preparation and implementation of sustainable development strategies for Canada. By 1990, all jurisdictions had established these round tables; they should collectively play an important role in shaping integrated environmental and economic policies for the balance of the decade.

All of these observations point to a number of dilemmas facing the policy-makers responsible for environmental management in Canada.

a) There is a decline in revenues to governments, yet strengthening demands from the public for additional government investments to ensure a clean and safe environment.

b) Industry is generally faced with diminishing profit margins and is, thus, unwilling or unable to pay for the full cost of pollution control.

c) There is a growing interest in local control and self-government, particularly from native groups, yet government at the federal and provincial levels are reluctant to relinquish their own power. This situation raises questions about efficiency and fairness in the decision-making process for resource management.

d) There is a gradual shift away from a resource-based economy to an economy based on information technology, service, and other less-polluting industries. This shift will have a ripple effect on changed lifestyles, greater recreational time, and higher expectations for enjoying a quality environment in both the cities and countryside.

Canada has long been a leader in preparing an inventory of its land and resources, and this database, the Canada Land Inventory, is now being substantially upgraded through remote sensing, sophisticated computer graphics, and field-work. Further improvements will still be required if Canada is to apply and evaluate conservation strategies to such sectors as agriculture, forestry, wildlife, and fisheries management. The State of the Environment Report for Canada clearly illustrated that neither the federal nor the provincial governments have been collecting the kinds of information required to assess whether conservation objectives are in fact being achieved. Now, at least the right questions are being asked, the information that is required has been identified, and the tools to collect and analyze this information are largely in place. It is more likely that conservation in the sense of balanced and sustainable growth will be adopted incrementally rather than through high-profile government endorsement.

Over the last few years, Canada and the provinces have undertaken major sectoral reviews of resource policies. Examples include the Pearse Inquiry into Pacific Fisheries Policy (1982), the same commissioner's inquiry into water resources (Pearse 1985), and a review of resource development policies in northern Canada's environments (Department of Indian and Northern Affairs 1984). In 1991, the B.C. Forest Resources Commission followed up the recommendations of the B.C. Wilderness Advisory Committee (1987) in outlining a land-use planning strategy for British Columbia to reduce conflict over resource-use decisions.

While these sectoral analyses of resource conservation represent an important step in safeguarding the sustainable utilization of resources, these policies, in total, do not constitute a national or provincial strategy. More effort is required to develop cross-sectoral strategies and supporting information systems. In Canada this means cross-jurisdictional co-operation. There are institutional arrangements in place to tackle this integration of policies, such as the CCME and various combinations of first ministers meetings, both regionally and nationally. Nonetheless, the will to co-operate nationally on environmental policies has developed only for perceived national crises such as acid precipitation, long-range transportation of air pollutants, and, recently, global warming. Other less critical issues at present, such as soil-loss in the Prairies and the gradual build-up of toxic chemicals in the food chain, have not yet reached the crisis stage that precipitates integrated national action.

Canada still faces important challenges on the national and international scale that, in turn, affect its resource development policies. There are strong regional imperatives for economic development that will continue to override national strategies for conservation. Politicians remain tied to electoral time-frames of four years or so. This provides a compelling reason for dealing with short-term, local needs that may be inconsistent with long-term sustainable development. The dictum of "anticipate and prevent" has yet to be embedded in the national psyche. However, progress is being made, and perhaps the creative tension that results from the conflict between meeting short-term objectives and longer term goals will provide the very energy that is required to achieve a truly integrated strategy for economic development and environmental conservation in Canada.

References

Baskerville, G. 1986. "Some Scientific Issues in Cumulative Impact Assessment." In *Proceedings of the Workshop on Cumulative Effects: A Binational Perspective,* 9–14. Ottawa: Canadian Environmental Assessment Research Council and United States National Research Council, Minister of Supply and Services.

Beanlands, G., and P.M. Duinker. 1983. *An Ecological Framework for Environmental Assessment in Canada.* Halifax: Institute of Resource and Environmental Studies, Dalhousie University.

Berger, T.R. 1977. *Northern Frontier, Northern Homeland. The Report of the Northern Mackenzie Valley Pipeline Inquiry.* 2 vols. Ottawa: Minister of Supply and Services.

———. 1981. *Fragile Freedoms: Human Rights and Dissent in Canada.* Toronto: Clark Irwin and Co. Ltd.

Berkes, F. 1977. "James Bay: The Cree Indian Coastal Fishery." *Canadian Geographic Journal* 93:60–65.

Bodaly, R.A., et al. 1985. "Ecological Effects of Hydroelectric Development in Northern Manitoba, Canada: The Churchill-Nelson River Diversion." In Scientific Committee on Problems of the Environment (SCOPE) of the International Council of Scientific Unions (ICSU), *Effects of Pollutants on Ecosystem Level.* Chichester and New York: John Wiley.

British Columbia Resources Commission. 1991. *The Future of our Forests.* Victoria.

British Columbia Utilities Commission. 1983. *Site C Report.* Vancouver: British Columbia Utilities Commission.

Canadian Council of Resource and Environment Ministers (CCREM). 1978. *Shore Management Symposium.* Proceedings of a Workshop Held in Victoria. Toronto.

———. 1988. *Report of the National Task Force on the Environment and the Economy.* Ottawa.

Canadian Environmental Assessment Research Council. 1985. *Philosophy and Themes for Research.* Ottawa: Minister of Supply and Services.

Canadian Environmental Assessment Research Council (CEARC) and United States National Research Council. 1986. *Cumulative Environmental Effects: A Binational Perspective.* Proceedings of a workshop. Ottawa: Minister of Supply and Services.

Carroll, J.E. 1983. *Environmental Diplomacy: An Examination and a Prospective of Canadian-United States Transboundary Environmental Relations.* Ann Arbor: University of Michigan Press.

Chant, D., ed. 1970. *Pollution Probe*. Toronto: New Press.

Conservation Council of Ontario. 1986. *Towards A Conservation Strategy for Ontario – An Assessment of Conservation and Development in Ontario*. Toronto: Conservation Council of Ontario.

Council of Forest Industries (COFI). 1986. *Native Land Claims in British Columbia. A Background Paper*. Vancouver: COFI.

Decima Research Ltd. 1986. *Special Report. Select Issues Bearing on Social Policy*. Toronto: Decima Research Ltd.

Department of Fisheries and Oceans. 1986. *Fish Habitat Management Policy*. Ottawa: DFO.

Department of Indian and Northern Affairs. 1979. *Negotiating a Way of Life: Initial Cree Experience with Administrative Structure Arising from the James Bay Agreement*. Ottawa: Minister of Supply and Services.

————. 1981. *In all Fairness: A Native Claims Policy*. Ottawa: Minister of Supply and Services.

————. 1984a. *Northern Flood Agreement: Backgrounder*. Winnipeg: DINA.

————. 1984b. *Report of the Task Force on Northern Conservation*. Ottawa: Minister of Supply and Services.

Dorcey, A.H.J., ed. 1979. *Coastal Resources in the Future of B.C.* Vancouver: Westwater Research Centre, University of British Columbia.

————. 1986. *Bargaining in the Covenance of Pacific Coastal Resources: Research and Reform*. Vancouver: Westwater Research Centre, University of British Columbia.

Economic Council of Canada. 1986. *Managing the Legacy*. Proceedings of a Colloquium on the Environment. Ottawa: Minister of Supply and Services.

Elder, P.S., ed. 1980. *Environmental Management and Public Participation*. Toronto: Canadian Environmental Law Association.

Emond, P. 1983. "Fairness, Efficiency and FEARO: An Analysis of EARP." In Canadian Institute of Resources Law, *Fairness in Environmental and Social Impact Assessment*. Calgary: Canadian Institute of Resources Law.

Environment Canada. 1981. *World Conservation Strategy: Federal Review*. Ottawa: Minister of Supply and Services.

————. 1986a. *State of the Environment: Report for Canada*. Ottawa: Minister of Supply and Services.

————. 1986b. *World Conservation Strategy – Canada. A Report on Achievements in Conservation*. Ottawa: Minister of Supply and Services.

Environment Ontario. 1986. *Municipal Industrial Strategy for Abatement (MISA)*. Toronto: Queen's Printer.

Federal Environmental Assessment and Review Office (FEARO). 1984. *Beaufort Sea Environmental Impact Assessment in Canada*. Halifax: Institute of Resource and Environmental Studies, Dalhousie University.

Gladwin, T. 1980. "Patterns of Environmental Conflict Over Industrial Facilities in the United States, 1970–78." *Natural Resources Journal* 20:243–74.

Government of Canada. 1985. *Report of the Royal Commission on the Economic Union and Development Prospects for Canada*. Ottawa: Minister of Supply and Services.

Hanson, P.P. 1986. *Environmental Ethics: Philosophical and Policy Perspectives.* Burnaby: Institute for the Humanities, Simon Fraser University.

Hecky, R.E., et al. 1984. "Environmental Impact Prediction and Assessment: The Southern Indian Lake Experience." *Canadian Journal of Fisheries and Aquatic Sciences* 41:720–32.

Holling, C.S., ed. 1978. *Adaptive Environmental Assessment and Management.* Toronto: John Wiley.

Howard, R. 1980. *Poisons in Public: Case Studies of Environmental Pollution in Canada.* Toronto: James Lorimer & Co.

IUCN, 1980. *World Conservation Strategy.* Gland: IUCN.

Krawitz, N., and W. McDonald. 1987. "Effective Monitoring in Canada. A Review of Effectiveness of Social Impact Monitoring and Management Approaches in Canada." *CEARC Background Paper.* Ottawa: Minister of Supply and Services.

Law Reform Commission of Canada. 1985. *Crimes Against the Environment.* Ottawa: Law Reform Commission of Canada.

Levine, A.G. 1982. *Love Canal: Science, Politics and People.* Lexington.

Lysyk, K.M., et al. 1978. *Alaska Highway Pipeline Inquiry.* Ottawa: Minister of Supply and Services.

McIntyre and Mustel Research Associates. 1982. *Public Opinion Issues Related to the Ministry of Environment.* Victoria: B.C. Ministry of Environment.

Munton, D. 1980. "Great Lakes Water Quality: A Study in Environmental Politics and Diplomacy." In O.P. Dwivedi, ed., *Resources and the Environment: Policy Perspectives for Canada,* 138–52. Toronto: McClelland and Stewart.

Nowlan, D., and N. Nowlan. 1970. *The Bad Trip: The Untold Story of the Spadina Expressway.* Toronto: House of Anasi.

O'Malley, M. 1976. *The Past and Future Land: An Account of the Berger Inquiry into the Mackenzie Valley Pipeline.* Toronto: Peter Martin Associates.

O'Riordan, J. 1986. "Environmental Assessment in British Columbia." *Northwest Environmental Journal* 2:63–84.

Paehlke, R. 1980. "James Bay Project: Environmental Assessment in the Planning of Resource Development." In O.P. Dwivedi, ed., *Resources and the Environment: Policy Perspectives for Canada,* 138–52. Toronto: McClelland and Stewart.

Peace-Athabasca Delta Project Group. 1973. *Peace-Athabasca Project Technical Report.* Ottawa: Information Canada.

Pearse, P.H. 1982. *Turning the Tide: A New Policy for Canada's Pacific Fisheries.* Report of the Royal Commission on Pacific Fisheries Policy. Ottawa: Minister of Supply and Services.

Pearse, P.H., et al. 1985. *Currents of Change.* Report of the Royal Commission on Federal Water Policy. Ottawa: Minister of Supply and Services.

Porter, A. 1980. *Report of the Royal Commission on Electric Power Planning.* Toronto: Queen's Printer of Toronto.

Richardson, B. 1976. *Strangers Devour the Land: A Chronicle of the Assault Upon the Last Coherent Hunting Culture in North America, the Cree Indians of Quebec and their Vast Primeval Homelands.* New York: Alfred Knopf.

Romanow, R. 1985. "Federalism and Resource Management." Paper presented to the Second Banff Conference on National Resources Law, Banff Centre, Banff.

Sadler, B., ed., 1980. *Public Participation in Environmental Decision-making: Strategies for Change.* Edmonton: Environmental Council of Alberta.

———. 1983. *Canada's Forests: Transition to Management.* Calgary: University of Calgary Press.

Science Council of Canada. 1986. *A Growing Concern: Soil Degradation in Canada.* Ottawa: Minister of Supply and Services.

Sewell, W.R.D. 1981. "How Canada Responded: The Berger Inquiry." In T. O'Riordan and W.R.D. Sewell, eds., *Project Appraisal and Policy Review,* 77–94. Chichester: J. Wiley and Sons.

Sewell, W.R.D. 1986. "Geography, Resources Policy and the Future." In P. Kivell, ed., *Geography, Planning and Policy-making,* 55–82. Norwich: Geobooks.

Sewell, W.R.D., and N.A. Swainson. 1981. "West Coast Oil Pollution Policies: Canadian Responses to Risk Assessment." In T. O'Riordan and W.R.D. Sewell, eds., *Project Appraisal and Policy Review,* 216–42. Chichester: J. Wiley and Sons.

Speth, G. 1985. "Environment, Economy, Security: A New Agenda for OECD Countries." Paper Presented at Colloquium on the Environment. Ottawa: Economic Council of Canada.

Standing Senate Committee on Agriculture, Fisheries and Forestry. 1984. *Soil at Risk: Canada's Eroding Future.* Ottawa: The Senate of Canada.

Wilson, J.W. 1973. *People in the Way: The Human Aspects of the Columbia River Project.* Toronto: University of Toronto Press.

21 "Getting to Yes" in the Wilderness: the British Columbia Experience in Environmental Policy Making

W.R. Derrick Sewell

A press conference held on 7 March 1986 in Victoria, British Columbia, furnished an important checkpoint in the evolution of environmental politics in the province because it marked the presentation of the B.C. Wilderness Committee's much anti-cipated report (B.C. Wilderness Advisory Committee 1986). At stake was the future of a number of areas that the provincial government had been considering as possible wilderness preserves. In some instances the deliberations had been going on for more than a decade, but so hardened had the positions of the "developers" and the "preservationists" become that no agreement had been reached. In at least one case the tensions had risen so high that physical confrontation between the two groups had been narrowly avoided.

The committee had had only four months in which to review this extremely complex and contentious situation, and to provide a report that represented a consensus of views of the committee, a group selected from a wide range of interests and backgrounds that were likely to come into serious conflict.

In the end the committee's hearings and its report served to highlight the fact that preservation of wilderness had become an important political issue in the province. No longer was it an isolated concern of a few parks enthusiasts, nature lovers, wildlife enthusiasts, or scientists pitted against a forest company or a mining enterprise in a particular area. Instead, it was a generic problem, involving a broad spectrum of the public, and embracing many different goals and value systems.

The purpose of this essay is to examine the ways in which this challenge has been met by governments, their agencies, interest groups, and the public at large. Basically it is a story of conflict resolution involving various types of bargaining. In particular, it is a commentary on how an independent body was able to reach a consensus on policy direction when the government itself was unable to do so.

21.1 Environmental Conflict and Models of Conflict Resolution
21.1.1 Confrontations

Confrontations over preservation of wilderness are part of a much broader area of conflict resolution: environmental management. Until relatively recently such management has been seen, for the most part, as an attempt to reconcile the goals and values of two fairly distinct sets of protagonists. Arrayed on the one side are those who wish to exploit various aspects of the environment to earn a living. On the other side are those who are in favour of preservation for a wide variety of reasons: ethical, aesthetic, or scientific.

In the past two decades, the two sets of interests have come increasingly into confrontation. Examining the record, it seems that it is becoming more and more difficult to reach agreement on issues involving the environment (Gladwin 1980). This is not necessarily because of a lack of good will, or absence of desire to find a solution, on the part of the contending parties. Often a consensus may be reached among government agencies as to a "reasonable course of action," but there may be hesitation on the part of government to act because there is uncertainty as to whether this reflects the will of the public at large.

21.1.2 Resolution of Environmental Conflicts

There are several possible ways in which a government might deal with environmental conflicts. Dorcey (1986) has described a spectrum of options, varying in the extent to which those involved are in contact with the decision-maker and with each other, and the manner in which trade-offs are made (Figure 21.1).

Although the most common option is authoritative decision-making, there is a growing interest in and explicit use of consultative modes of governance in environmental management. In British Columbia, for example, there are now established guidelines and referral processes for considering environmental and social impacts of resource development projects.

A common feature of all these modes of decision-making is bargaining. Even in the authoritative mode there is usually some interaction between interested parties prior to the issue of a directive. Typically, for example, the cabinet will obtain views of relevant ministries before making a decision about a major change in land use or the raising of user fees. Similarly, bargaining frequently takes place during the consultation process. This is, of course, the essence of negotiation.

21.1.3 Positional versus Principled Bargaining

Bargaining in most fields has tended towards confrontation, in which participants come to the table with a "position," representing what they believe is right and the minimum that their constituency would accept. They see each other as adversaries, make threats, insist on conditions for their participation, and regard

Authoritative Governance	Consultation in Governance	Negotiation in Governance
Decision imposed	Trade-off avoided or decision imposed by identification of consensus	Trade-off by agreement which is basis of decision

Figure 21.1 **Governance and Trade-offs**

"victory" as the goal. Such an approach is common to negotiations in the field of labour relations. It has also characterized many of the attempts to resolve major environmental conflicts in Canada in recent years (Dorcey and Riek 1987).

In contrast to such "positional" bargaining is what Fisher and Ury (1980) describe as "principled" bargaining in their book *Getting to Yes: Negotiating Agreement without Giving In*. They suggest that, at best, positional bargaining often results in failure to reach a satisfactory agreement. Principled bargaining, they claim, is more likely to lead to outcomes that are mutually acceptable and supportable. The latter approach requires the adoption of rules that are, in many respects, quite opposite to those followed in positional bargaining (Table 21.1).

Adoption of such principles is not easy. Typically, the institutions that exist in the fields of resources development and environmental management encourage the adoption of "positions." Legislation, policies, and administrative arrangements, for example, often focus either upon "development" *or* "environmental management," but never both. Vehicles used to review disputes between the two sides frequently result in the differences in viewpoint being emphasized rather than consensus or trade-offs being produced.

Table 21.1   Contrasts in the Characteristics of Positional and Principled Bargaining

POSITIONAL	PRINCIPLED
Participants are adversaries	Participants are problem solvers
The goal is victory	The goal is agreement
Concessions demanded as a condition of participation	No concessions demanded as a condition of participation
Participants adopt positions and stick to them	Participants focus upon interests, not on positions
Participants make threats	Participants explore what they have in common
Participants set a bottom line	Partipants avoid having a bottom line
Participants search for a single answer: the one they will accept	Participants explore multiple options from which they can select a mutually agreeable strategy
Participants insist on their own position	Participants agree upon criteria
Participants apply pressure	Participants reason: they yield to principle not pressure

Source: Based on Fisher and Ury, 1980

Over the past decade or so there have been a number of attempts in British Columbia to move from confrontational modes of bargaining in resources management to those involving principles of negotiation. One of these was introduced under the banner of "Integrated Resource Management," which recognized the interrelatedness of resources on the one hand and the need to bring together the various competing interests on the other (Apsey 1978). Several modifications were made to existing legislation, administrative structures, and procedures to accomplish this end. The establishment of an Environmental and Land Use Committee, together with a secretariat to provide technical advice and co-ordination, was one such modification. The creation of the Ministry of Environment was another. These helped materially in fostering interchange of information and ideas as well as in co-ordinating policy within the provincial government. There were also a number of efforts to improve communication between the latter and the public at large (O'Riordan 1986). More recently, there has been progress in bringing together fisheries and forestry interests to work out mutually acceptable policies (B.C. Ministry of Forests and Lands 1986). In the case of wilderness, however, there remain deficiencies in the process of bargaining, which have led to increasing levels of confrontation and frustration.

21.2   Wilderness Policy in British Columbia

The economy of British Columbia is based largely on the exploitation of natural resources. The forestry industry is its backbone. Over the past ten years it has provided about 10 per cent of the provincial GDP – almost 50 percent of the value of manufacturing shipments and more than half of the value of exports (Dorcey 1986). During this time it has furnished employment directly for 10 percent of the work force, plus another 15 percent indirectly. More than 100,000 workers depend in some way on the province's forest industry. Initially, the industry was concentrated on the coast, but today it is carried on throughout the province.

The second most important economic activity is mining. It accounts for about 7 percent of the provincial GDP, 20 percent of the value of provincial exports, about 1 percent of the direct employment, and an additional 2 percent in related activities (Dorcey 1986). Like the forest industry, mining is carried on in a wide diversity of locations.

Hydro-electric power has also been a cornerstone of economic development in British Columbia. The provision of large quantities of cheap electricity has fostered the growth of electro-processing industries as well as the forest industry in various parts of the province. Recently, tourism has become a major source of employment and income. In 1986 it furnished jobs for more than 105,000 people, and generated a total income in excess of $2.4 billion.

21.2.1   The "Developmental Ethic" versus Environmental Concerns

A "developmental ethic" has emerged in British Columbia in which the primary consideration of government policy has been to open up new opportunities for resource exploitation. There is no doubt that the province has benefited substantially from this commitment in attaining a very high standard of material well-being. Inevitably, however, it has had impact on the environment, and particularly upon specific aspects of the landscape that are treasured by various segments of the public as wilderness areas. Gradually, the "natural landscape" has been eroded away, and there is now serious concern that a number of unique ecosystems, rare species of wildlife or biota, and cultural heritage sites will disappear altogether.

21.2.2 Environmental Management Institutions

While the developmental ethic has tended to dominate in British Columbia, there has remained an underlying sensitivity about the management of the environment. Progressively, over the past three decades, the provincial government has introduced legislation and policies to protect wildlife, control pollution, and set aside certain areas as ecological reserves or parks (O'Riordan 1986). The Ministry of Environment was established in 1976 with a mandate for management of the environment. However, although the protection of wilderness has long been set as a desirable objective in the province, it has generally not been a major political issue.

No one agency has a clear mandate for protection of wilderness in British Columbia. For the most part, reliance has been placed upon the Ministry of Lands, Parks and Housing (and its predecessors) to set aside and manage wilderness areas, with related responsibilities being placed with the Ministry of Forests, and the Ministry of Environment. Various acts have been passed relating to wilderness, the most important being the Park Act. Today, British Columbia has about 370 parks and recreational areas, and one wilderness conservancy, all managed under the Park Act. There are also three national parks and two ecological reserves. Collectively these areas cover almost five million hectares or about 5 percent of the province's land area.

Proposals for wilderness designation have been generated either by various lobby groups (such as the Sierra Club, or the Canadian Parks and Wilderness Society) or by professionals in line agencies. A process has been in place for more than 15 years to review such suggestions within individual ministries and, where disputes have been involved, further consideration has been given in the Environment and Land Use Committee (O'Riordan 1986). Composed of ministers of seven line agencies, this is one of the most powerful committees in the cabinet. To help sharpen the focus of the issues, as well as to provide advice, the Environment and Land Use Technical Committee, composed of deputy ministers – who are civil servants – has been established. This decision-making process seemed to work reasonably well until the early part of the 1980s, at which point designation of wilderness became much more of a political issue.

21.2.3 The Emergence of Wilderness as a Political Issue

Four factors in particular have appeared to foster increasing confrontation in this matter. First, continued timber "liquidation" produced a decline of harvestable timber in the late 1970s, particularly in the coastal region. Little original forest remained. Some of the areas to which forest companies were now turning their attention contained within them, or were adjacent to, potential wilderness preserves.

Second, there was growing pressure from mining companies to extend the area in that they could undertake development. It was entirely possible, they argued, that valuable deposits were locked up in parks which had been set aside without any mineral surveys being undertaken, as occurred in Tweedsmsuir Provincial Park. Third, native peoples in the province had begun to voice their claims for lands in various parts of the province, based on aboriginal title. Emphasizing that some of the areas now being considered for forestry or mining development had profound historical, cultural, and spiritual value, leaders of native groups wanted them set aside. Fourth, there had emerged a highly committed, well-informed, and politically attuned environmental movement that recognized wilderness as a key issue.

The overall result of the interaction of these four forces was a series of confrontations between the "developers" and the "preservationists" in several parts of the province. In some places it was possible to resolve the conflict, but in several the outcome was either an impasse or indecision. The existing approach, apparently, did not enable the contending parties to "get to yes." While understanding had been reached between various ministries within the Environment and Land Use Committee, the cabinet did not always accept the resulting advice. Beyond this, there was often continuing disagreement between the developmental interests and the preservationist groups, and little opportunity for them to resolve their differences.

21.3   The Wilderness Advisory Committee

In October 1985 the government of British Columbia established the Special Advisory Committee on Wilderness (later to become known as the Wilderness Advisory Committee). Its task was to examine 16 areas that were under consideration for wilderness designation and eight parks containing wilderness lands that were under review for possible boundary changes (Figure 21.2). The proposed wilderness preserves varied considerably in size and characteristics (Table 21.2). One was an island of 15 hectares in the Nimpkish River of Northern Vancouver Island. It supports some of the oldest and tallest Douglas fir trees in the world. Many are more than 400 years old and still growing. Some approach 100 metres in height. Another was Robson Bight, a unique habitat for killer whales on the east coast of Vancouver Island. To ensure its preservation and non-disturbance of the whales, a proposal has been made to set aside a coastal strip of 515 hectares as an ecological reserve. Other proposals involved much larger areas, such as the 41,000-hectare reservation sought for the Cascade Wilderness, an area embracing magnificent scenery and several historic trails, or the 37,000-hectare Khutzeymateen watershed, north of Prince Rupert, which provides habitat for grizzly bears, now a species whose numbers in the province have been drastically reduced. These areas are all under the threat of the woodsman's axe. Others, including Akamina-Kishinina in south-eastern British Columbia, Kakwa in the Rocky Mountains, and a number of existing provincial parks, are all under pressure by mining interests for exploration and development.

The committee's task was formidable. It had but three months to prepare a report on issues that were highly complex and controversial. The majority of the members

Table   **Proposals under Review by the B.C. Wilderness Advisory**
21.2   **Committee: Characteristics and Issues**

PROPOSED AREA	CHARACTERISTICS	ISSUES
1. Akamina–Kishinena	An 11,000-hectare area in S.E. B.C. containing valued wildlife species, including Wyoming moose, Rocky Mountain wolf, grizzly, and elk.	Potential conflict with forestry and natural gas development.
2. Brooks Peninsula	A 20,000-hectare peninsula on Vancouver Island; not covered by glaciation in last Ice Age; habitat for unique species.	Potential conflict with forestry; mining claims widely staked.
3. Cascade Wilderness	A 41,000-hectare area northwest of Manning Prov. Park; location of former Indian and fur trading trails.	Potential conflict with forestry.
4. Duu Gwusd	In northern Queen Charlotte Islands; proclaimed as a "Tribal Park" in 1982 by Haida Indians.	Potential conflict with forestry and mining; subject of Indian land claims.
5. Gitnadoix	Undeveloped watershed in N.E. B.C. embracing a 58,000-hectare, highly scenic area.	Few conflicts.
6. Kakwa	Mountain range in the Rocky Mts. embracing 34,000 hectares; rugged terrain and magnificent scenery.	Possible conflict with mining and forestry.
7. Khutzeymateen	A 37,000-hectare watershed in N.E. B.C.; remote, narrow valley at the end of a fiord; provides habitat for endangered species of grizzly bear.	Possible conflict with forestry.
8. Mid-coast	Involves two study areas – the Hunter/Calvert Islands and the Mussel/Kynock Inlets area; includes magnificent vistas, beautiful beaches, and wildlife.	Few conflicts.
9. Nimpkish Island	A 15-hectare island in Nimpkish River on Vancouver Island; the site of some of the oldest and tallest Douglas firs in Canada	Negotiation between forest company and government for compensation.
10. Redfern Lake	A 40,000-hectare area in N.W. B.C. embracing glacial lakes.	Few conflicts.

PROPOSED AREA	CHARACTERISTICS	ISSUES
11. Robson Bight	Unique killer whale area on east coast of Vancouver Island, now a site for "whale watching"; proposal for 515-hectare Ecological Reserve to preserve coastal strip.	Marine Ecological Reserve is in place, but coastal strip is in the hands of a logging company
12. South Moresby	A 110-kilometre-long string of islands in the Queen Charlottes; the ancient home of the Haida Indians; contains unique biota; highly prized for its scenery and solitude.	Major conflicts between environmentalists and forest developers; the site of Indian land claims.
13. Stein Valley	The last major watershed within 150 kilometres of Vancouver that has not been logged or dammed; contains artifacts of native Indians; substantial recreational potential.	Major conflicts between environmentalists and forest developers; protests from native Indians.
14. Stikine	A 536-kilometre river widely regarded as a magnificent wild river with a spectacular canyon.	Potential conflicts with forestry and hydro-power development.
15. Tashish–Kwois	An 11,000-hectare wilderness watershed on N.W. Vancouver Island; largest stands of Sitka spruce in Canada.	Conflicts with forest development.
16. Tatshenshini–Alsek	Two rivers in N.W. corner of B.C., surrounded by glacier-topped mountains and wide valleys; river rafting a growing activity.	Some possibility of mineral development.
17. Park Boundary Reviews: Kokanee Glacier, Kwadacha, Purcell Wilderness, Strathcona, Stone Mountain, Tweedsmuir, Wells and Gray Provincial Parks, and Pacific Rim National Park	Parks created by provincial government under various designations, offering recreational potential and wilderness values, but also containing lands sought for forestry and/or mining development.	Potential conflicts between environmentalists and forest and mining interests.

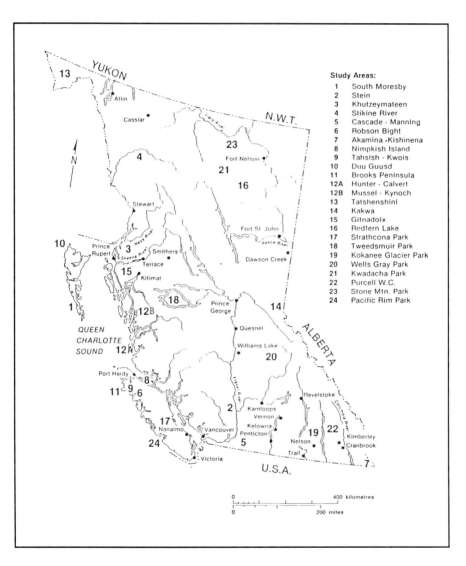

Figure **Location of Study Areas**
21.2

had other responsibilities besides those involved in the committee's work. Some observers claimed that the task was impossible and suggested that the committee should resign (Pynn 1986). A number of environmental groups said that the enterprise was a sham and decided to boycott the entire proceedings.[1]

21.3.1 Establishing a Process

In setting about its task, the committee wanted to ensure that the process of inquiry was seen to be open, fair, and efficient (B.C. Wilderness Advisory Committee 1986). To this end it took several steps.

1. It announced to the public what it understood to be its objectives. The committee thought that the terms of reference given by the government needed to be clarified.
2. The committee established a process of public involvement. It began by disseminating information about the committee's task through a special newsletter that was sent to interested parties and placed in local libraries. It called for briefs in an advertisement entitled "We Want to Hear from You." It also provided opportunities for the public to review all the submissions, and held a number of public meetings at various centres, at which individuals and groups were able to make presentations and pose questions.
3. The committee hired consultants to undertake studies of a number of issues on which particular expertise was required.
4. It also developed liaison with government agencies responsible for management of resources in the province through links with the Environment and Land Use Technical Committee.

Some of the features of the inquiry process adopted by the committee were similar to those employed by previous review bodies. Others, however, were new. One of the most innovative was the employment of a committee counsel to pose questions on behalf of participants in the hearings. In this way cross-examination was possible, focusing upon crucial issues without at the same time running the risk of lengthy speeches on the part of would-be questioners. Several important decisions were made with respect to the process, both by the government and by the committee. First, the government decided that there would be no funding of participants. Second, it opted to ban the appearance of its officials at the hearings.

A third issue was that of native land claims. Presently, as much as 70 percent of the territory of British Columbia is viewed by its native peoples as being part of their heritage. Several of the areas that were being considered by the committee were in regions where such claims have already been made or seem likely to be raised in the future. Because the issue is currently before the courts, the government felt it inappropriate for the committee to dwell upon it during its deliberations.

A fourth decision was made by the committee itself. This was to allow a certain degree of flexibility in the deadlines for the submission of briefs and replies thereto.

This was especially crucial for a number of interest groups that had limited financial resources, and where so little time was available to prepare a brief or reply.

Finally, the committee decided to allow native peoples to make presentations in their own, informal way. Instead of presenting briefs, they were able to convey their views through oral statements, sometimes in the form of a story or a poem.

21.3.2 The Conduct of the Inquiry

The committee began its task by familiarizing itself with background material relating to the 24 areas. Once briefed, the committee undertook a number of visits to the areas that had been designated for review. The next stage was the call for briefs. The response was overwhelming. More than 1,000 submissions were made, amounting to several thousands of pages of documentation.

Once the briefings had been received and there had been an opportunity for replies to be made by individuals who wished to do so, the committee staged a number of public meetings at which individuals and groups were able to make oral presentations and pose questions either to the committee or to other participants.

The site visits and both the volume and content of the submissions made it abundantly clear to the committee that the wilderness issue had become extremely important in the public mind. It was also evident that increasingly firm positions were being taken by the major interests involved.

21.3.3 The Quest for Consensus

Given their backgrounds, as well as the fact that some of them appeared to have had identifiable constituencies beyond the committee, it seemed unlikely that the members would reach a consensus on many of the areas involved, let alone the wilderness issue at large. A curious combination of leadership, a sense of responsibility, openness to mutual education, and camaraderie, however, produced agreement where previous processes had failed.

The chairman was a barrister with a well-established reputation in labour negotiations. A born organizer, he had a clear concept of the committee's task and of the route that would most likely lead to its successful accomplishment. His most important contribution, perhaps, was his insistence that the committee adopt an open process in its deliberations, canvassing as many viewpoints as possible. He also emphasized the importance of searching for alternative solutions, and not merely arguing about those that had been proposed already. In fact this proved to be the key to reaching agreement on several of the wilderness proposals, notably South Moresby.

While leadership was a crucial ingredient, it was only one of the factors that led to consensus. The individual members were highly committed to this task; they wanted the enterprise to succeed. They were ready to work long hours and, at times, endure considerable tension; they were willing to listen to each other, to reason, and to learn.

Increasingly, the committee's mettle was put to the test as it progressed through the list of areas under discussion. The committee decided to deal with the least

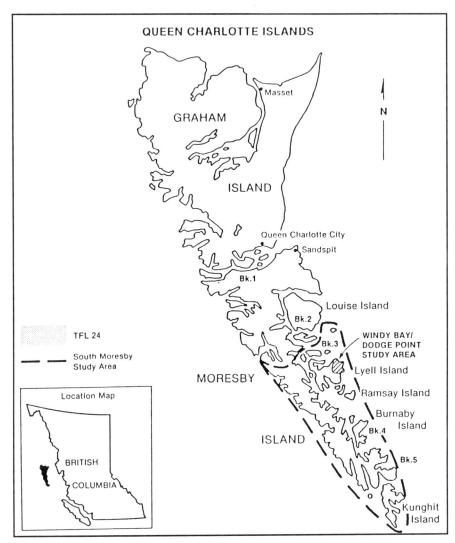

Figure   **The Queen Charlotte Islands**
21.3

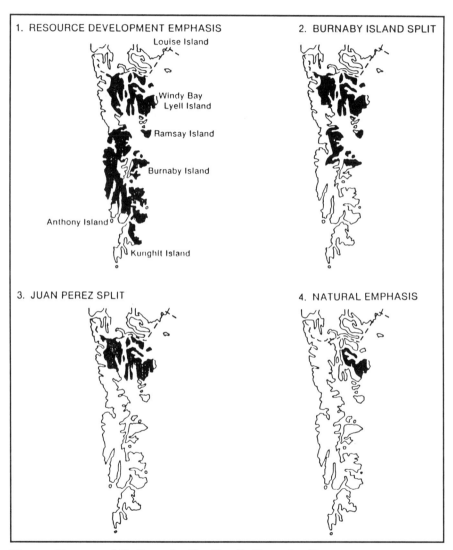

Figure   **Proposed Options by the South Moresby Resource**
21.4   **Planning Team**

Source: South Moresby Resource Planning Team
South Moresby Land Use Alternatives, Victoria B.C., 1981

complex issues first. This enabled it to gain experience in identifying issues, searching for alternatives, and agreeing upon trade-offs, before advancing to deal with the more difficult problems. Among the most controversial of all the areas was South Moresby in the Queen Charlotte Islands.

21.4   South Moresby: The Jewel in the Crown

South Moresby in many ways represents the wilderness issue in British Columbia in a microcosm (Young 1986). Located some 130 kilometres from the mainland, it forms the southernmost portion of the Queen Charlotte Islands (Figure 21.3). It is isolated and differs in important ways from the rest of the province. For example, some parts were left unglaciated during the last ice age. It presently provides a habitat for several rare species of animals and biota (Islands Protection Society 1984). It is also the home of the largest black bears in the world, the saw-whet owl, the golden pine marten, and numerous species of sticklebacks that are peculiar to the Queen Charlottes. It has the highest concentration of nesting sites of bald eagles in Canada, and supports more Peales peregrine falcons than anywhere in the world.

The Queen Charlottes are also the ancestral home of the Haida Nation, one of Canada's best-known native peoples. Said to have settled there as long ago as 10,000 years, the Haida have developed a lifestyle that is much in harmony with nature. They have become increasingly concerned about the changes that have been brought about by resource exploitation, particularly mining and forestry.

21.4.1 The Protagonists

The battle for South Moresby had begun. On the one side it involved developers who wanted to exploit the magnificent stands of red cedar, Douglas fir, hemlock, and spruce or to extract the mineral wealth. Much of the area is virgin forest, with certain stands reaching more than 100 metres in height. Volumes of timber are correspondingly huge. There are known reserves of various minerals, notably iron, copper, gold, and silver deposits, in which there is an ongoing interest among prospectors. There is also speculation that there may be considerable hydro-carbon resources in the offshore area south of South Moresby (Westcoast Offshore Exploration Assessment Panel 1986).

In opposition to development of such resources were the preservationists. They consisted of a wide diversity of groups, including environmentalists, scientists, recreationists, promoters of tourism, and artists, as well as various native peoples. They argued that it is possible to preserve South Moresby while at the same time sustaining a reasonable standard of living from activities that are environmentally benign (McConigle and Alden 1986). There is very little settlement in South Moresby. Apart from a temporary logging community at Powrivco Bay on Lyell Island, the area is largely deserted and is visited only by recreationists and tourists, mostly in the summer months. There are no road connections and access is limited to air and water transportation.

21.4.2 Escalation of the Conflict

The conflict between the developers and the preservationists is of relatively recent origin. It began just over a decade ago when a forest company submitted a five-year plan to harvest timber on Burnaby Island. This sparked a protest from the Skidegate Indian Band, which felt that its cultural heritage in that area would be destroyed. The provincial government responded in several ways. First, it denied permission for logging on the island. Second, it asked the Environment and Land Use Committee Secretariat in 1976 to provide an overview of the South Moresby situation. The third move was to create an ecological reserve at Windy Bay and Dodge Point on Lyell Island. Anthony Island was also established as a World Cultural Heritage preserve in 1979. The government, however, did allow logging in other parts of South Moresby and a major forest company, Western Forest Products, holds a licence permitting it to harvest timber on approximately one-third of the region. It is the proposals that the company has put forward to exercise this right that have sparked the conflict over South Moresby.

The provincial Ministry of Forests set up a South Moresby Resource Planning Team in 1979. Composed of representatives from provincial and federal agencies that had interests in the areas, together with appointees from industry and various interest groups, it carried out a detailed review of the South Moresby situation (South Moresby Resource Planning Team 1983). Its report, completed in 1983, outlined four options for government consideration. Option One called for a resource development emphasis, with recreational reservations set aside in three areas. Option Four focused on preservation of almost all of South Moresby, with forest development permitted only in areas already being logged on Lyell Island. Options Two and Three represented development situations that were compromises between the two ends of the spectrum (Figure 21.4).

The Environment and Land Use Committee visited the South Moresby area in June 1984 to familiarize itself with the four options. The cabinet also discussed the proposals. However, no specific actions followed. Meanwhile, the conflict escalated. The forest companies reiterated that they had the right to log. The preservationists mounted a wide range of demonstrations in Victoria and Vancouver. They took their case to Ottawa and alerted public concern across the country with a "whistle-stop campaign," carried out on a transcontinental train journey in late 1985.[2] The Haida, frustrated in their attempts to have their land claims settled, mounted a series of peaceful protests. Beginning in October 1985, they periodically blocked the passage of logging equipment on Lyell Island. The logging company, Frank Beban Logging, requested and was granted a court injunction to prevent such action. The Haida and a number of non-native supporters ignored the order. By mid-January 1986 some 72 people had been arrested for defiance and other offences related thereto.[3] Media coverage was intense and continuous. It became an international story.

The federal government has held a "watching brief" on the situation. Concerned on the one hand about environmental dimensions, and especially about the impact of logging on fisheries, but uneasy on the other about attempting to deal with the land claims issue (for which the provincial government believes the former has responsibility), it has tended to play a cautious role. Successive federal ministers of the environment in recent times suggested that they would be willing to support the creation of a national park. Since resource exploitation is not permitted in such areas, such a move was appealing to most of the preservationists, including the Haida. The forest companies endorsed it only if they were granted compensation.

21.4.3 Advisory Committee Review

The Wilderness Advisory Committee was keenly aware of the importance of the South Moresby issue, which had clearly played a major role in the government's decision to set up the committee. More mail or more briefs were received on South Moresby than on any other proposal reviewed. The committee made several visits to the area, gaining a sharp appreciation of what was at stake.

The public meetings that took place at Skidegate and Sandspit on the Queen Charlotte Islands were packed, and the tension was high. A logger summed up the views of one side of the issue in his closing statement, "You have our future in your hands. Think carefully about it." An environmentalist suggested, "The preservation of South Moresby is not just for a few of us who are here today but for those who will be here tomorrow." And a number of the Haida reminded everyone, "When you cut down a tree, you are not merely removing timber. You are removing part of us. The environment and the Haida are one. They are inseparable."

Faced with these opposing, well-established positions, the committee had to find a solution that would be acceptable to all sides – an enormous task. It agreed, first of all, that certain principles must apply:

1. Existing permits must be honoured, and where changes in these seemed in the general interest, compensation must be paid.
2. The widest range of options must be considered in trying to satisfy the needs of the contending parties.

In practical terms this meant that a search must be made for ways in which Western Forest Products might be persuaded to forego part of the logging area covered by its harvesting permit. Since monetary compensation is not of interest to a company that needs trees and forest land, this implied finding comparable sources of timber elsewhere on South Moresby or elsewhere in the province. It also meant that certain key elements that had been given priority by the protectionist groups would need to be set aside, such as particular ecosystems, scenic vistas, or places with special cultural or spiritual attributes.

To this end, the committee undertook studies to determine what possibilities there might be to provide compensation for loss of logging rights, and carried out reviews to try to identify crucial environmental and cultural attributes. It was aware that whatever proposal was made for compromise or trade-off, it would disappoint some. It hoped that it could find one that would appeal to the majority.

It is not possible to describe in detail how the committee arrived at its proposals on South Moresby. Suffice it to say it was a long, agonizing process with a conscious desire on the part of those involved to reach agreement rather than to declare that the latter was impossible. The results of the studies of alternative timber supplies showed that there was "no slack in the system." All the available sources had been allocated and there was no doubt that none of the current licence-holders would be willing to give up any of it. The only hope seemed to be in the possibility of persuading Western Forest Products to exchange part of its holdings for a portion of the area currently held by MacMillan Bloedel, who in turn would receive compensation by being granted permission to alter its tenure boundaries.

The committee made the following recommendations:

1. The provincial government should enter into negotiations with the federal government for the establishment of a national park on South Moresby.
2. If this were not acceptable to the former, or impossible to accomplish, then the provincial government should set up a provincial park, containing within it certain areas designated as wilderness conservancies.
3. Compensate the holder of logging rights on South Moresby by the transfer of rights on Louise Island, granting the present holder of the latter compensation through boundary changes.
4. Involve the Haida Nation in discussions relating to the management of the South Moresby area as a park.

The Wilderness Advisory Committee's recommendation for South Moresby is identified in Figure 21.5.

21.5   Recommendations and Reactions

The report of the Wilderness Advisory Committee is entitled *The Wilderness Mosaic* (B.C. Wilderness Advisory Committee 1986). This aptly describes the problems involved in determining what should be set aside for which purposes. At the same time, it reflects an attempt to bring a pattern of reasoning to a highly emotional and very complex situation. The recommendations were intended to convey principles as well as specific suggestions for action.

21.5.1 Proposals

Briefly, the committee put forward a new classification system for parks and protected areas, based upon intended uses (Table 21.3). This aimed to clarify the existing classification system and supplement it rather than totally replace it. Based on the new categorization, it made recommendations with respect to the 24 areas it had been asked to review (Table 21.4). The committee also made suggestions with respect to a number of generic issues, notably compensation to those who hold timber or other rights in areas designated for preservation, and the opening up of certain park areas for mineral exploration and development. Finally, it recommended a number of modifications to existing mechanisms for planning and policy-making, notably the introduction of the Natural Areas Protection Act and the establishment of the Wilderness Advisory Council.

The latter recommendations were especially important because they were intended to deal with the process by which decisions are made. The committee had been concerned that if it were to dwell solely upon the 24 areas referred to it, the basic problems that had led to its establishment would not have been solved.

21.5.2 Reactions

It was inevitable that the committee's report would not satisfy everyone. The positions of some of the groups had become so entrenched that anything short of what they had demanded would be seen by them as victory for the other side. Predictably, the forest industry was unhappy that proposals were made to limit their logging operations. Several spokesmen had said in briefs and at the public meetings that any reduction in the available timber base was unthinkable (Cruikshank 1986).

Some of the environmental groups were not pleased either. The Valhalla Wilderness Society, for example, which had urged environmentalists to boycott the committee's inquiry, was especially critical. It suggested that little had been solved, and that the major issues of wilderness disappearance and environmental degradation, as well as native land claims, still remained to be addressed (Valahalla Wilderness Society 1986).

The Haida were disappointed too. Although the committee had recommended that some 94 percent of South Moresby be set aside as a wilderness preserve, this was seen as insufficient. They were particularly chagrined at the recommendation that logging should continue on Lyell Island, the centre of the protest just four months earlier (Bohn 1986). Haida leader Miles Richardson commented, "Our position is that the forests of South Moresby and Duus Guusd are to remain in the state of nature in perpetuity."

Other observers, notably the media, were much more positive about the report. Recognizing the high level of confrontation and the considerable difficulties under which the committee had laboured, they praised the latter for its attempt to seek compromise. The general view, however, was that the committee had done its job, and it was now up to the government to respond.[4]

The immediate response of the government was congratulatory but cautious.[5] The minister of environment applauded the committee for its efforts and its ability to reach a consensus. Understandably, he needed time to review the report and obtain the opinions of his cabinet colleagues. Two months later, on 22 May 1986, he announced that the government had accepted the recommendations of the committee "in principle."[6]

Since then, the government has made a number of announcements relating to specific areas that were dealt with by the committee.[7] Briefly, there have been ongoing negotiations between the provincial government and the federal government to set South Moresby aside as a national park. Complicating such an agreement is the issue of Lyell Island, which the Haida want included but where the provincial government intends to permit logging, and the compensation that the federal government would give to British Columbia for the land being set aside as a national park. Meanwhile a major stumbling block in such negotiations has been removed, namely the payment by the federal government of compensation for lands set aside for Pacific Rim National Park. The federal government paid British Columbia $8 million as a first instalment on 28 February 1987. The balance of the $25 million due to the province was due by 31 March 1989 (Bohn 1987).

The government has also upgraded some areas from class B status (where activities in addition to recreation might be permitted) to class A status (where only conservation, protection, or recreation are allowed). These include parts of Tweedsmuir and Strathcona Parks. The major focus of the government's actions with respect to the committee's recommendation so far has been more upon the establishment of recreation areas than upon the permanent designation of wilderness reserves. The former are segments of land that cater for a variety of forms of recreation but also permit mining exploration and logging (and possibly development) for a limited period. To that end it has established the Brooks Peninsula, the Gitnadoix, Stone Mountain, and various parts of Strathcona, Tweedsmuir, Kokanee Glacier, and Akamina-Kishinena as recreation areas. Action still remains to be taken on other proposals reviewed by the advisory committee.

The overall reaction to the government's responses has been mixed. Given new opportunities for exploration and development, the mining lobby has been happy about the creation of recreation areas. The forest industry has said little. It awaits the outcome of deliberations about South Moresby and the Stein and a decision about whether and how much compensation will be paid. Environmentalists have become increasingly skeptical (George and Carr 1986).[8] While they were happy about the announcement that the governments were trying to reach an agreement on a national park for South Moresby, they have been displeased with the trend towards creation of recreation areas and the relatively small commitment to the establishment of wilderness areas (Husband 1986). Least satisfied of all are the Haida. They see no progress towards a settlement of their land claims, and fear that even the areas set aside as ecological reserves on Lyell Island may be damaged by logging adjacent to them. Frustrated by inaction, they have taken steps intended to increase confrontation, including the renouncing of Canadian citizenship by several Haida (McDonald 1986) and the passage of a constitution by an assembly of the Haida nation in late January 1987. Meanwhile, the prospect of further blockades to prevent logging on Lyell Island is growing.

21.6   Lessons Learned

The British Columbia experience with respect to formulation of wilderness policy suggests that bargaining takes place in three main areas of potential input. The first is that of inter-ministerial review, involving those agencies that have mandates that either involve the formulation and implementation of wilderness policy, or are affected in some major way by it. A second area where bargaining takes place is that of the public at large and the various interest groups. The third is in the cabinet, which, in an ideal situation, receives signals from the two other areas.

The Environment and Land Use Committee, and especially its technical arm (composed of deputy ministers), provides an extremely valuable forum in which

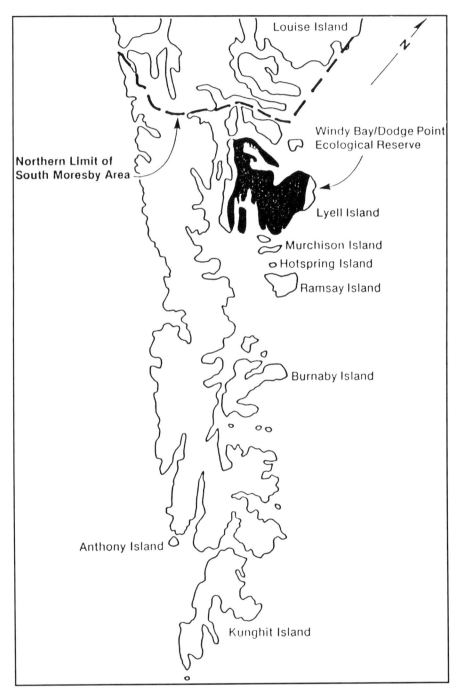

Figure   **Wilderness Advisory Committee Proposal for South Moresby**
21.5

Table **Proposed Categories of Natural Lands**
21.3

Intended Use	Designation	Definition	Prohibitions
1. Exclusively conservation, protection, or recreation	Ecological Reserve	Designated under Ecological Reserves Act for scientific purposes. Use by permit only. (See Appendix B)	Resource use and public use excluded.
	Nature Conservancy	Designated under Park Act as a roadless, natural area with recreation emphasis. (See Appendix B)	Resource use and hunting excluded.
	Park	Unit designated under Park Act, primarily for protection of natural, wild, and scenic areas for public enjoyment and recreation. (See Appendix B) It is recognized that the simple word "park" does not readily reveal the style or purpose of the park.	Resource use excluded; hunting in accordance with park management objectives.
	Wilderness Conservancy	Unit designated by Wilderness Act; roadless area with emphasis on wild, primitive conditions. To be managed by PORD, MoF, Wildlife Branch, as assigned.	Resource use excluded; hunting only in accordance with wildlife management objectives.
2. Mainly for conservation or recreation	Recreation Area	Unit designated under Park Act primarily for recreation; limited resource extraction permitted under direction of PORD, usually limited to pre-establishment tenures. (See Appendix B)	None, if not conflicting with recreation.
	Wildlife Management Area	Unit designated under Wildlife Act, primarily for conservation of wildlife; resource extraction permitted under direction of W.B.	None, if not conflicting with wildlife.
	Natural Area	Administrative unit designation by Ministry of Forests, in Provincial Forest, for retention of natural values; resource extraction permitted under direction of MoF.	None.
3. Preservation of Scenic Values	Scenic Corridor	Unit designated under ELUC Act primarily for management of scenic values and assigned to single agency.	None, if not conflicting with scenic values.
	Recreation Corridor	Planning designation for management of scenic and recreation values.	None.

NB: Adoption of this terminology requires that there be a review of the nomenclature for park categories and zones; for example, Kwadacha Wilderness Park, to achieve consistency.

Table **Recommendations of the Wilderness Advisory Committee and**
21.4 **Government Responses (as of 28 February 1987)**

Area or Topic	Recommendation	Action
1. South Moresby	National or provincial park, with logging on Lyell Island.	Ongoing negotiations on park logging commenced.
2. Stein Valley	Recreation area for Lower and Upper Stein. No road construction through canyon without consent of Lytton Indian band.	No decision.
3. Khutzey-mateen	Logging to be permitted but subject to logging plan to be approved by Ministries of Forests and Environment.	No decision.
4. Stikine/ Spatsizi	Set Upper Stikine aside as Class A park. Establish a recreation area in "Flood Reserve" region. Create a scenic corridor to embrace canyon region.	
5. Manning Park/ Cascade	Preservation of native and fur trading trails. Add Snass, and Skaist, Holding, and Tulameen drainages as a recreation area. Compensate forest land losses by deleting portions of Copper Creek drainage.	Major area to be added to the park as a recreation area. Copper Creek drainage to be deleted.
6. Robson Bight	Ecological Reserve.	No decision.
7. Akamina-Kishinena	Establish a Class A park, with a recreation area on Starvation Creek pending mineral exploration.	Established as a recreation area.
8. Nimpkish Island	Ecological Reserve with compensation to owner.	No decision.
9. Tahsish-Kwois	Manage on an integrated basis, but set aside two Ecological Reserves to protect the estuary and stands of tall Sitka spruce.	No decision.
10. Duu Guusd	No designation recommended.	No decision.
11. Brooks Peninsula	Recreation area until mineral claims extinguished, then Class A park status.	Recreation area established.
12. Mid-Coast	Recreation area, with Class A park status once land claims settled.	No decision.
13. Tatshen-shini-Alsek	Recreation corridor, no hydro power development. Further study.	Further studies under way.
14. Kakwa	Recreation area east of divide but strict control of ATV use. West of divide a combination of wilderness, ecological reserve, and recreation area.	No decision.

Area or Topic	Recommendation	Action
15. Gitnadoix	Class A park	Recreation area established.
16. Redfern Lake	Further study with possible designation as recreation area.	Further studies under way.
17. Strathcona Park	Develop master plan with public review. Add certain adjacent areas to the park and remove others to permit mineral development.	Preparations for a master plan under way. Some areas to be deleted and others to be added. Major section in the centre to be set aside as a recreation area. Remaining 200,000 hectares to be designated as Class A.
18. Tweedsmuir	Develop a master plan prior to any action. Consider upgrading portions to A status, adding some lands adjacent to the park, notably Rainbow Range, and deleting some areas on northern border.	Rainbow Range to be added as recreation area. Areas along northern border to be re-designated as recreation areas. Remaining 900,000 hectares to be designated as Class A park. Planning process now under way.
19. Kokanee Glacier	Consider rationalization of park boundaries, adding some lands and deleting others, leading ultimately to a Class A designation.	Various areas to be added and deleted, and some to be designated as recreation areas. Studies of mineral potential to be undertaken.
20. Wells Gray	Add various areas adjacent to the park, notably Trophy Mountain, Spanish Creek – Four Mill volcanoes, delete Mahood-Pendleton area.	Additions and deletions similar to recommendations of committee to be established.
21. Kwadacha	Reconfirm as a Class A park but delete south-western corner, which is a mineralized zone.	To be reconfirmed as a Class A park with the south-west corner designated as a recreation area. North-west corner of park to be deleted.
22. Purcell	Designate the area as a Class A park while also considering the merits of alternative uses of Carney Creek	Studies under way.
23. Stone Mountain–Wokkpash Valley	Add Wokkpash Valley to Stone Mountain Park with Class A status.	Recreation area established.
24. Pacific Rim National Park	Accept the boundaries proposed for Phase Three addition, and conclude compensation arrangements promptly.	Agreement concluded between federal and provincial governments for $34 million compensation.

conflicts between mandates and between objectives in the environmental field can be dealt with effectively. The technical committee had discussed many of the issues that were referred to the Wilderness Advisory Committee, and it is probable that agreement on some of them had been reached, at least in principle. Doubtless there were other issues, however, where there was uncertainty about the nature and strength of views about them.

In the case of the public at large, it seems clear that there was no consensus as to what action ought to be taken. While there had been concern within the forestry industry and the mining industry about "the wilderness issue," it was not yet a matter on which firm positions had been taken, either in terms of overall policy or with respect to particular park areas. The incidents on Lyell Island and the opposition to the construction of a road through the Stein River canyon served as stimuli for various parties favouring development to announce their positions. In contrast, those who were in opposition to this had begun to organize to make their views known through briefs to the government and statements to the press.

There was, however, no convenient opportunity for the developers and the preservationists to exchange views, except perhaps through the media. Certainly, the more conventional channels did not provide this facility. A possible exception, however, was the South Moresby Resource Planning Team, which included representatives from federal and provincial government agencies, the forest industry, and various interests within the public at large, including native peoples.

The planning team gathered a large amount of information about the South Moresby situation, including viewpoints expressed through correspondence, from places as far away as New York and Australia. To some degree, it acted as a bargaining forum. Its task, however, was not to reach a consensus on what to do, but to draw up a series of options from which the government might choose.

When the cabinet met in mid-1985 to determine a course of action on South Moresby and the Stein, it was somewhat uncertain as to the nature and strength of the positions likely to be taken by the various protagonists. The establishment of the Wilderness Advisory Committee as an independent body to review the situation and to make recommendations seemed an efficacious solution. It would buy time on the one hand and would furnish a more accurate assessment of viewpoints on the other. Besides examining the problems of South Moresby and the Stein, it would be asked to examine controversies surrounding a number of other wilderness management areas in the province.

Viewed in terms of the limited time-frame it was given, as well as the contentious nature of many of the issues it had to face, the Wilderness Advisory Committee must be regarded as a success. While none of the protagonists got all they wanted, they did agree that the process had been open and fair. The public at large, through letters to the committee following the publication of its report, expressed similar sentiments. An alternative, it seemed, had been found to the growing tendency toward confrontation in decision-making in environmental matters.

Care must be taken, however, not to regard this institutional innovation as a panacea. The Wilderness Advisory Committee was happy that it had been able to reach a consensus on the 24 areas it had been asked to review. It was equally concerned, however, that the process by which resources development and environmental decisions are made be improved. It spent a good deal of attention on such matters and made concrete recommendations about them. The government took an important first step towards improvement by consolidating the mandate for parks management under the roof of the Ministry of Environment, and by accepting the other recommendations in principle. Making the necessary alterations to existing institutions, however, may be even more of a challenge than implementing the recommendations on the 24 areas.

Acknowledgements

This chapter has benefited from the comments and suggestions of several people, notably P. Dearden, A.H.J. Dorcey, J. Dumbrell, G. Letcher, J.T. Morley, J. O'Riordan, T. O'Riordan, M. Rankin, and W.M. Ross. The opinions expressed, as well as any errors of omission or commission, are those of the author alone.

Notes

1. "Conservation Group Wants Panelist Out," *Vancouver Sun*, 13 November 1985.
2. "Hundreds Greet Save-Lyell Caravan," *Vancouver Province*, 16 March 1986.
3. "Mounties to Man Lyell When Logging Resumes," *Vancouver Sun*, 17 January 1986.
4. "Mosaic Offers Basis for Compromise," *Victoria Times–Colonist*, 9 March 1986.
5. "Minister Studies Wilderness Report," *Vancouver Sun*, 11 March 1986.
6. "A Seed Planted: A Park for Lyell," *Vancouver Sun*, 22 May 1986; and "Park Gem on Moresby is Nearing Reality," *Victoria Times–Colonist*, 22 May 1986.
7. "Park Boundaries Altered, Changing Terms on Mining," *Victoria Times–Colonist*, 30 January 1987.
8. "Reshaping a Park for Miners and Loggers," *Victoria Times–Colonist*, 13 February 1987.

References

Apsey, T.M. 1978. "Resource Management in British Columbia." In G. Drew, ed., *Integrated Management of Resources*.Vancouver: Centre for Continuing Education, University of British Columbia.

B.C. Ministry of Forests and Lands. 1986. *Coastal Fisheries-Forestry Guidelines*. Victoria: Queen's Printer.

B.C. Wilderness Advisory Committee. 1986. *The Wilderness Mosaic*. Vancouver: B.C. Wilderness Advisory Committee.

Bohn, G. 1986. "Wilderness Report Draws Fire." *Vancouver Sun*, 8 March 1986.

———. 1987. "South Moresby Park Threatened." *Vancouver Sun*, 20 February 1987.

Cruikshank, J. 1986. "Solution Sought to B.C. Struggle over Wilderness." *Globe and Mail,* 1 March 1986.

Dorcey, A.H.J. 1986. *Bargaining in the Governance of Pacific Coastal Resources: Research and Reform.* Vancouver: Westwater Research Centre, University of British Columbia.

Dorcey, A.H.J., and C.L. Riek. 1987. "Negotiation-Based Approaches to the Settlement of Environmental Disputes." Paper presented at a conference on the Place of Negotiation in EIA Processes, 19 and 20 February 1987, Toronto.

Fisher, R., and W. Ury. 1980. *Getting to Yes: Negotiating Agreement without Giving In.* New York: Penguin Books.

George, P., and A. Carr. 1986. "Advisory Committee Recommendations Increase Likelihood of Conflict." *The New Catalyst,* Summer, 19–20.

Gladwin, T.N. 1980. "Patterns of Environmental Conflict over Industrial Facilities in the United States, 1970–1980." *Natural Resources Journal* 20:243–74.

Husband, V. 1986. "Windy Bay's Treasures Could Soon Be Lost Forever." *Victoria Times–Colonist,* 28 November 1986.

Islands Protection Society. 1984. *Islands at the Edge: Preserving the Queen Charlotte Islands Wilderness.* Vancouver: Douglas and McIntyre.

McConigle, M., and T. Alden. 1986. "Wilderness Epitaph." *Equinox,* September/October, 46–58.

McDonald, S. 1986. "Nine Haida Seek to Renounce Citizenship in Lands Protest." *Vancouver Sun,* 14 July 1986.

O'Riordan, J. 1986. "Environmental Assessment in British Columbia." *Northwest Environment Journal* 2:63–64.

Pynn, L. 1985. "Public Preserve Pursuades Pelton." *Vancouver Sun,* 9 November 1985.

South Moresby Resource Planning Team. 1983. *South Moresby: Land Use Alternatives.* Victoria: Queen's Printer.

Valhalla Wilderness Society. 1986. *B.C. Environment in Big Trouble: Wilderness Advisory Committee Fails to Resolve Conflict.* New Denver, B.C.: Valhalla Wilderness Society.

Westcoast Offshore Exploration Environment Assessment Panel. 1986. *Offshore Hydrocarbon Exploration, Final Report.* Ottawa: Minister of Supply and Services.

Young, C. 1986. "The Last Stand: Confrontations Continue and Good Timber Is Running Low in B.C." *Canadian Geographic,* February/March 1986, 9–18.

22 Some Geographical Aspects of Social Policy and Evaluation

Ernest P. Weeks

This chapter seeks to review briefly social policy and practice, drawing attention to the broad geographic impact of social policies; to follow this with an explanation of the reasons why a better geographical framework for implementation and evaluation of policies is desirable; and, finally, to outline a proposed framework or system of areal units for such analysis of policy.

22.1 Federal Social Policies and Practices

Economic and social policies are so closely interrelated that it may often be preferable to consider them together or, at least, in parallel. For example, while employment and unemployment may result from economic policies and programs, the social implications are obvious. There is a greater or lesser call on Unemployment Insurance funds and on welfare payments as part of income maintenance. There are needs for training, not only to assist the individual in terms of future income, but also in terms of adjusting the individual to the rapidly changing nature of the economy and society. Related to this is the morale and quality of the labour force, which can deteriorate rapidly unless maintained through some activity with income support. The extent to which families and single persons fall below the poverty line can affect mental as well as physical health. The reverse relation is also significant, as changing social attitudes to education, leisure, or work can influence the economic situation.

A key factor in the historical development of federal policy has been the need and the desire to ensure that various regions of the country are able to provide minimum essential services, regardless of local conditions and without an unbearable burden of provincial and local taxation. The original British North America Act (BNA Act) of 1867 included no obligations on the part of federal or provincial authorities to provide welfare services. At that time social welfare was regarded as a matter that could best be handled by charitable individuals, religious institutions, or local government. Social assistance, such as it was, was assumed to be a provincial matter, with certain exceptions falling within the jurisdiction of the federal government, such as native peoples, militia, defence, and certain phases of public health including questions of jurisdiction over immigration. However, the relatively gradual changes in the economy before 1914 were greatly accelerated thereafter, resulting in the state assuming new social functions. As early as 1918 the federal government brought in the Children's Tax Exemption. This allowed parents to deduct a specified amount from taxable income for each child under 16 years of age. This was the first recognition of the fact that tax-paying parents carry a heavier financial burden than those taxpayers not supporting children. But for a poor family that paid no taxes at all, obviously there was no benefit.

The first major social policy change developed during the Great Depression of the 1930s when the central government had to assist badly stricken provinces, particularly in western Canada where a severe drought accentuated the economic misery of low prices. Various national social measures were proposed by the prime minister, R.B. Bennett, but he was defeated in 1935 and his legislation was declared ultra vires in 1937. The Rowell-Sirois Commission, set up in the same year, assessed many aspects of federal-provincial relations in its comprehensive report of 1940 and recommended policies, many of which were later adopted in various forms.

22.1.1 Family Allowances

A further significant report was prepared by Dr. Leonard Marsh in 1943.[1] Among other proposals, it advocated family allowances. The federal govern-ment adopted the general idea, not only as a welfare measure but also as an economic means to help prevent another post-war recession by redistributing income to sustain basic demand.

The Family Allowances Act was passed in 1944, and the first cheques went out in July the following year. In general, the allowance was paid for all children under 16 years of age for the "maintenance, care, training, education and advancement of the child." This allowance was intended particularly to supplement the incomes of poor families not assisted by the Children's Tax Exemption. At the same time, it would stimulate consumer spending and, thus, help to avoid a downturn in the post-war economy. The Family Allowances Act of 1973 extended the supplement to each dependent child under 18 years of age, and enabled allowances to be increased at the beginning of each year if the Consumer Price Index (CPI) for Canada increased. Special allowances were made payable for children under the age of 18 years and cared for or maintained in a government or approved private institution. The indexing was suspended for budgetary reasons for the year 1976, and it was limited to 6 percent in 1983 and 5 percent in 1984 for anti-inflationary reasons. Budgetary concerns were behind other new changes considered in the application of the indexing principle. In early 1986 amendments to the Family Allowances Act limited cost-of-living increases to rises in the CPI in excess of 3 percent per annum. A further move, this time in favour of the poorer sectors of society, was made with the Child Tax Credit in 1978. This was designed to give most benefit to families on low and modest incomes, and to exclude the better-off. For example, families earning more than $50,000 in 1985 did not qualify.

22.1.2 Old Age Pensions

Canada's Old Age Security (OAS) was introduced first under the Old Age Pension Act of 1927, which was replaced by the Old Age Security Act and the Old Age Assistance Acts of 1951. Under these acts and subsequent amendments, the OAS Pension is now paid to all persons aged 65 years and over, provided they have resided in Canada for ten years immediately preceding the approval of their application. Under an amendment in 1966, provision was also made for the payment of the Guaranteed Income Supplement: pensioners with no other income than their pension may receive the maximum monthly supplement; those with other sources up to a limit would receive less. Spouses allowances are given to the spouse (if aged 60 to 64 years) of an OAS pensioner, provided that the combined income of the couple is less than a certain amount. These pensions are indexed to the CPI, and an indication of their general social acceptance was the withdrawal of the budget proposal of May 1985 to partially de-index the OAS. In the case of both Family Allowances and Old Age Security, the federal government deals directly with the individuals concerned on a universal basis.

The Canada Pension Plan (CPP) is contributory and compulsory but is also earnings-related, and therefore covers most employed members of the labour force between the ages of 18 and 70 years. The CPP came into force in 1965, and covers all of Canada with the exception of Quebec, where there is a Quebec Pension Plan. Contributions amount to 1.8 percent of pensionable earnings falling within a certain range, and are made by employees and matched by the employer. Those who are self-employed pay 3.6 percent on the same range. The CPP is also indexed according to the CPI. Because of actuarial problems arising on the one hand from the increasing number of people aged over 65 years, and the relatively low contributions on the other, the federal government is considering the introduction of a significant increase in the annual contributions.

22.1.3 Unemployment Insurance

Unemployment Insurance was introduced as a direct result of experience during the Great Depression. The first legislation on unemployment and social insurance was the act of 1935, but in 1937 the judicial committee of the Privy Council declared it ultra vires of the federal government. The Privy Council considered that it came within the field of property and civil rights because it affected the contract of employment, and hence it was a provincial responsibility.

In 1940 all provinces agreed to an amendment of the BNA Act that gave the federal government exclusive jurisdiction under section 91 clause 2A. The 1940 act made unemployment insurance compulsory except for certain employments, but the list has been extended from time to time, for example to include fisheries in 1956. Contributions are paid by those employed in insurable employment on the basis of 2.25 percent of earnings. The employers' contributions are 1.4 times the employees' premiums. The government's share, prior to changes made in 1989, was one-fifth of the combined employee and employer payments. The government continues to cover the costs of management of the Unemployment Insurance Account, but otherwise only makes payments like any employer. Adjustments have been made to the period during which unemployment insurance may be collected to allow for regional differences in unemployment levels as compared with the national level. Workers living in regions suffering badly from unemployment are able to draw unemployment insurance after a shorter qualifying period and over a greater number of weeks than in more favoured parts of the country.

As compared with Family Allowances, Old Age Security, and the Canada Pension Plan, this system is a departure from uniform, nationwide application, and involves recognition of the social significance of regional economic differences. However, Unemployment Insurance, too, is being subjected to serious scrutiny by the federal authorities with respect to such aspects as time of entry, duration of payments, and varied applications in regions of heavy unemployment.

22.1.4 Assistance Programs

The Canada Assistance Plan of 1966 represents another step away from the universality of programs. This plan is designed to provide federal support for initiatives in the integration and improvement of provincial and municipal assistance programs, and thereby to encourage development and extension of social services intended to reduce or remove the causes and effects of poverty, child neglect, or dependence on public assistance. The federal government contributes 50 percent of the shareable costs. The only requirement for eligibility is that of locally determined need, regardless of its cause or nature. The services concerned may include counselling, case work, rehabilitation services, community development, day care, and home-maker and adoption services.

The report of the Royal Commission on the Economic Union and Development Prospects for Canada[2] made recommendations for sweeping changes in social policies. Some of these have obvious regional implications. For instance, on Unemployment Insurance the premium rates could be in proportion to the risk of unemployment and be treated on a firm-by-firm basis. The period of extended benefit based on regional unemployment rates could be eliminated, and the benefit rate limited to 50 percent of insurable earnings. To offset this the commission proposed a Transitional Adjustment Assistance (TAA) Fund to finance a program for individuals who had exhausted their Unemployment Insurance benefits or whose lay-offs appeared to be per-manent. Mobility, training, and early retirement would be the main thrusts; the system could include portable wage-subsidy programs, mobility grants, training programs, and the use of funds to encourage older workers to leave the labour force. Related to mobility was the provision that the fund could be used to pay compensation for loss of assets such as homes that had lost value because of the decline of communities.

On a broader scale, the commission recommended the introduction of a Universal Income Security Program (UISP). The commissioners believe that all Canadians have a duty and a right to share the costs of adjustment and to provide help for those who need it. Revisons to Unemployment Insurance and the TAA program would be an essential part of UISP and should be introduced at the same time. The essential aim of the UISP would be to replace various existing programs with a guaranteed payment (in 1985 dollars) of $2,750 per adult, and $750 per child, with benefits reduced at a 20 percent rate as other income became available. The existing programs replaced would include the Guaranteed Income Supplement, Family Allowances, Child Tax Credits, Married Exemptions, Child Exemptions, the federal share of the Canada Assistance Program, and federal social housing. Old Age Security and the Canada Pension Plan would not be affected.

22.1.5 Health Care

The Hospital Insurance and Diagnostic Services Act took effect in 1958. It is designed to provide eligible residents with a wide range of hospital and diagnostic services. Federal contributions are authorized for programs covering hospital costs and laboratory and other services in support of diagnosis. The provinces generally administer health services and may differ in organization and administrative practice. Their health insurance plans may differ as to source of funds (varying from premiums to coverage through a sales tax). Some of the responsibilities are delegated to local authorities.

Health has traditionally been acknowledged as primarily a provincial responsibility. However, the federal government, through the Department of Health and Welfare, is responsible for the overall promotion and protection of health to national standards. It also encourages fitness and amateur sport. Research, long-range health planning and standards, and consultation are other general federal undertakings. In addition, and more specifically, the federal responsibility extends to the health of Indians and Inuit, and to the Yukon and Northwest Territories in general. The Department of Veterans' Affairs is responsible for the health of veterans. Agriculture Canada deals with the health aspects of food production and food imports. Statistics Canada provides health and vital statistics. Other federal activities include the handling of food and drug protection, medical services in the fields of quarantine, immigration and civil aviation, disability assessment, and emergency health and welfare.

Medical insurance, which was introduced first as Medicare in Saskatchewan, was generally accepted by 1972, when all ten provinces and the two territories met the criteria required under the Medical Care Act as necessary conditions for the federal government to share in the costs. Comprehensive coverage to all eligible residents had to be provided for all medically required services rendered by a physician or surgeon. There was to be no dollar limit or exclusion, except on the ground that the services were not medically required (for example, cosmetic surgery). If these basic criteria as well as others in more detail are met, the federal government covers about 50 percent of the costs, but the provinces handle the administration. Considerable controversy has been raised by the desire of some doctors to make charges outside the plan, or beyond scheduled fees (so-called extra billing). The federal government has been opposed to extra billing and has so far succeeded in preventing its general use. The fundamental philosophy behind the Hospital and Medical Insurance flows has been to provide a general basic standard of assistance, regardless of income, and hence regardless of regional economic disparities.

22.1.6 Education

Education is basically a provincial responsibility. In the elementary and secondary school system, which may vary considerably from province to province, the local educational authorities or school boards receive support from the province in the form of universal grants per pupil to supplement income from the local tax base. The provincial contributions are often many times those of the local authorities, as the general aim is to secure minimum standards and thereby moderate the effect of disparities of wealth and income between different localities. The federal government makes a modest contribution to this level of education under a federal/provincial program for the development of bilingualism in education.

At the post-secondary level, traditionally the colleges and universities were private institutions that depended on tuition fees, alumni support, and some public grants. Pressures resulting from the post-war baby-boom supply of students and from higher educational expectations on the one hand, and from the demand for highly skilled people on the other, led to governments taking a much greater interest than hitherto in higher education. There was a considerable expansion, especially in technical colleges. By the end of the 1970s federal and provincial governments together were contributing over 80 percent of the total cost of higher education. Federal aid applies to all post-secondary institutions and these funds are transferred to the provincial governments, which then dispense the funds to the various institutions. The general policy supporting this federal involvement was based on the premise that increased inter-regional mobility of labour would mean that originating provinces or regions would be subsidizing their out-migrating workers. The receiving regions should therefore contribute through their federal taxes to the training of their in-migrating workers.

22.1.7 Regional Policy and Regional Impacts

After the Second World War, federal policies for socio-economic development became more regionally sensitive as they went through various stages. Following the end of hostilities, the federal government, through the Department of Reconstruction and Supply, was concerned about the economic and social effects of war industries closing down in "danger areas," and of the general deterioration or lack of infrastructure resulting from delayed public investment. This created a demand for more data and analysis at the level of the local area. During the Korean War this interest was greatly re-stimulated by the desire of the Department of Defence Production to know more about defence contracts and sub-contracts in various areas across the country.

At the inter-provincial level, a major innovation was the introduction of equalization payments under the Federal/Provincial Fiscal Arrangements Act of 1967, with related new acts in 1972 and 1977. The basic principle was that, in the interests of national equity, the federal government would compensate any province whose tax base was not adequate to provide per capita revenue equal to the national average. This compensation was intended to ensure that all citizens of the country would have comparable basic standards in public services.

Another method, which was more development oriented, was established through an interest in a more focused approach to specific regional socio-economic problems than that provided by equalization payments or universal measures of social security. Economic and social issues were closely interlinked in various regionally oriented agencies established for specific purposes or areas, such as the Agricultural and Rural Development Act of 1961, the Area Development Agency and the Atlantic Development Board established in 1962, and the Fund for Rural Economic Development in 1966.

A consolidation of these regional programs occurred with the establishment of the Department of Regional Economic Expansion (DREE) in 1969. This department was subsequently integrated in 1980 with components of the Department of Industry to become the current Department of Regional Industrial Expansion (DRIE).

This brief outline of social programs indicates that social policy may be viewed as fragmented – with diverse policies under the broad categories of taxation, income security, health, education, equalization payments, and regional economic development – or may be viewed as a unified system in their total effect. Many schemes are universal, applying uniformly to all of the specified recipient populations, while others are directed more specifically to particular persons, provinces, regions, or areas. Federal payments are made either directly to the individual or indirectly through the provinces or, in the case of regional stimuli, to specific firms or, in some cases, to municipalities. Federal and provincial responsibilities and policies vary according to categories, and the key question then concerns the balance of effects.

This key question comes into focus more acutely at the regional and zonal levels. The geographic aspects should be easily recognized because even universal schemes have different regional or zonal impacts. For example, with respect to federal income security, even universal Family Allowances and Old Age Security have varying area effects depending upon birth rates, death rates, family structure, proportion of senior citizens in the population, and the prevailing standards and costs of living. Thus, common levels of payment provide more real benefits in a Newfoundland outport than in metropolitan Toronto or Montreal. The same applies to Unemployment Insurance, which may become a significant income factor in certain areas, such as those where many seasonal fishermen or other seasonal workers reside. Yet the system of social welfare can represent a particularly heavy burden for the provinces and communities suffering from high levels of unemployment.

The Canada Pension Plan, being contributory and earnings-related, is clearly better for those who are regularly employed with a good income than for those who experience significant periods of unemployment or who have low incomes when they are working. Hence the impact of the plan in relatively prosperous areas is different from that in the less fortunate ones.

Support under the Canada Assistance Plan is based on locally determined need, and that need will obviously depend upon interrelated economic and social factors in the locality itself, and in its zonal and regional context.

With respect to health, federal contributions to provincial medicare schemes represent a cross-national approach, yet they particularly benefit those regions that would otherwise have lower medical services because of their poorer individual incomes and public tax base. The same principle applies to post-secondary education where the federal contribution helps to equalize the opportunities for education regardless of regional and local income levels. However, there is also the subsequent mobility of labour to the regions where the skills are required.

Federal policies of regional development covered by the General Development Agreements signed between the federal and provincial governments, and more recently by the Economic and Regional Development Agreements, provide for specific programs and projects. While these are usually of a direct economic nature, such as resource development, they may also include social infrastructure, such as training schools.

Many provincial policies are also designed to assist communities or areas to adjust to changes in markets and costs, or to the availability of resources. Assistance may also be provided to encourage communities to move into the new high-technology sectors of economic life and away from some of the declining, established industries.

The need for governments at all levels, and for non-governmental organizations and individuals, to devote more attention to local social and economic issues has been given new emphasis as the result of a study undertaken on behalf of the Institute for Research on Public Policy. This study, *The Social Policy Process in Canada*, published in 1986, was created to identify the agencies and other players in the field of social policy and how they perceived the major questions to be dealt with in the formation of social policy for the balance of the 1980s (Dobell and Mansbridge 1986). The findings suggested, among other things, the particular need for flexibility and adaptability to regional and local conditions.

A discussion paper for the study, based on the results of questionnaires, reflected many opinions that had a strong geographic theme. For example, local officials were concerned about tailoring social services to local conditions, and there was a general call to "humanize" and "personalize" social programs to meet the needs of local communities. Municipalities and regional and metropolitan types of government are often in a position to obtain the sort of sensitive and accurate information required to define and analyze such needs, and to evaluate programs that may be adopted. The database was a matter of great concern and was considered to be weak for purposes of assessing costs and benefits of social programs and, as a consequence, program evaluation was regarded as sporadic and often inefficient. It was felt that governments must supply comprehensive information and regular ongoing reporting of key social statistics.

The discussion paper referred to the growing interest in the better "targeting" of social resources as opposed to the continuing universality of many programs. In reactions to the paper it was emphasized that socio-economic policy needs to involve the integration of macro- and micro-planning.

22.2   Structural Adjustments and Poverty, as Basic Factors in Social Policy

The current rethinking or reassessment of federal social policy reflects the growing pressures on government finances, which are resulting in heavy and continuing budget deficits, and the political and social problems arising from the rapid, pervasive, and profound structural changes in the economy. The structural changes affect regions and sub-regions quite differently because of their relative dependence upon specific resources, industries, or services, and their relative, actual, or potential attractiveness for new or improved activities. The differences are not necessarily between broad regions such as the Atlantic region and central Canada, as the centre-periphery theorists emphasize, for indeed they are just as likely to be intraregional. For example, the north-east coast of Newfoundland is experiencing serious social and economic difficulties because of changes in the fishery and the shortage of alternative activities in that province, while the Halifax-Dartmouth area is relatively booming. Similarly, within British Columbia some forest areas are suffering the effects of severe adjustments, while the Victoria area is quite stable because of the high proportion of government services in the local economy and the presence of many retired persons on pensions.

There is a natural tendency to concentrate on socio-economic variations among the five main regions, or among the provinces. However, of equal or even greater importance is the wide range among regions or areas below the provincial level as shown in the Labour Force Survey for the Economic Regions defined therein. For purposes of illustration, data for June 1986 may be taken with respect to two factors: labour force participation rate and the rate of unemployment (Table 22.1). This shows that for labour force participation some of the economic regions of the "lowest" provinces were comparable with some regions in the "highest" provinces. Moreover, the differences within a province were greater in some cases than between provinces. Similarly, with unemployment, the range between the highest and lowest regions within provinces was quite large. The highest levels in Ontario, for example, were greater than the lowest in New Brunswick and Nova Scotia.

Similar variations within provinces could be indicated for other social data compiled on the current sub-provincial regions (SPRs) used by Statistics Canada, which are technical variants of the 1964 model devised by Camu, Weeks, and Sametz. A common system of sub-provincial regions, and a further breakdown into socio-economic zones, would not only allow the problems to be localized, but would also enable a more specific picture of the causes to be established.

The impact of poverty is obviously an essential element in the creation and continuance of social problems. The measurement of poverty is attempted in annual estimates made by the National Council of Welfare (1985a). The council points out that there is no single poverty line for all of Canada. Hence, the low-income cut-offs are varied according to two factors: the size of family and the place of residence. The latter factor is the one of particular interest for social geographers, and is broken down into five categories: metropolitan areas with 500,000 or more residents; large cities (100,000–499,999); medium-sized cities (30,000–99,999); smaller cities (15,000–29,999) and small urban areas (under 15,000); and rural areas, including farm and non-farm population. About 60 percent of the total population lives in cities of 30,000 or more.

This system does not provide for the analysis of economic and social relationships between different categories of urban centres, nor for relationships between rural and urban centres. However, on the basis of the established five categories, interesting geographical variations are well illustrated. A family of four may be taken as an example. The low-income lines for 1985 range from metropolitan areas down to rural areas as follows: $20,821, $19,787, $18,498, $17,206, and $15,316. Thus, the rural line is about 25 percent lower than that of the major urban areas. The same percentage variation applies for each size of family. On this basis a

Table   **Labour Force Participation and Unemployment:**
22.1   **Comparative Provincial and Sub-provincial Rates**

	Variation among Provinces %	Variation within Provinces (SPRs) %
LABOUR FORCE PARTICIPATION		
Highest		
Alberta	73.3	67.7–76.8
Ontario	70.2	63.0–73.5
Saskatchewan	68.3	62.2–70.5
Lowest		
Nova Scotia	61.1	52.5–71.6
New Brunswick	60.4	55.8–64.6
Newfoundland	58.4	52.3–61.5
UNEMPLOYMENT		
Highest		
Newfoundland	18.2	17.2–19.4
New Brunswick	14.4	10.4–20.0
Nova Scotia	12.3	8.8–22.7
Lowest		
Ontario	7.0	5.1–11.5
Saskatchewan	6.8	5.8–7.8
Manitoba	6.4	not available

Source: Statistics Canada, *The Labour Force*, June 1986

policy that provided the same level of assistance right across the country would have different effects on several categories. The Canadian Council on Social Development sets its poverty line at one-half of average family income, and makes no adjustments according to size of place of residence. It holds that living costs vary neither significantly nor systematically by size of community.

In their "Poverty Profile 1985" the National Council of Welfare (1985b) pointed out the large increases in family poverty between 1981 and 1984 in Alberta, British Columbia and Newfoundland. Over the same period, the unemployment rate went up considerably in these three provinces. The report does not provide details, but the variations by sub-provincial regions in both categories must also have been of some significance. In terms of the main regions, the highest rates of family poverty in 1984 were in the Atlantic region (18.4 percent) and Quebec (17.2 percent), with the Prairies (16.0 percent) next, followed by British Columbia (15.5 percent). Ontario (11.8 percent) had by far the lowest level. The difference between Ontario and all the other regions is noteworthy, especially the difference with the Atlantic region. There were large variations among the component provinces of the Atlantic and Prairie regions. Thus, nationally, Newfoundland had the highest figure at 23.0 percent, but

Prince Edward Island in the same region was the lowest with 12.4 percent. The range in the Prairies was from 17.0 percent in Saskatchewan to 14.6 percent in Manitoba.

All the main regions have had a significant increase in family poverty in the past few years, but western Canada has been particularly affected, with Alberta showing a 96.4 percent increase and British Columbia 64.9 percent for the 1981–84 period, as compared with a national average increase of 25.0 percent. The trends in family poverty do not show much difference on the basis of size of community, but this is scarcely surprising because the poverty lines were already established with variations according to size of place of residence. The poverty statistics do not reflect unemployment exactly, but move in the same direction, and the link is very clear for 1981–84 in Alberta, British Columbia, and Newfoundland.

In summary, if the actual causes of poverty and of the recent trends in different parts of the country are to be understood, and social policy adjusted accordingly, the determining factors must be assessed on a more specific regional basis below the provincial level.

22.3   Importance of an Improved Geographical Framework

In the implementation of social policy, an improved geographical framework, with the more detailed and meaningful production of data now feasible by use of computers, could make a valuable contribution to both the decisions on policies and programs, and to the evaluation of regional effects. Although the formulation of a framework of areal units to which policies may be developed is a fundamental geographical problem, social geographers do not seem to have been as interested in an overall national framework as in relatively small-scale areas. There may be several reasons for this, for example the small area is more tractable, and it may facilitate greater access to direct personal contact with people and issues. A national approach implies the use of large-scale statistical information within a meaningful framework. The familiar national frameworks of the ten provinces and two territories or the five regions of Canada[3] may be too general – given the wide range of differences in economic activity and social conditions within a province – and therefore the formulation of a better national framework may involve the use of sub-provincial regions and zones as units of analysis.

Various kinds of regional approach have been the subject of academic and applied presentations. Obviously, for economic and social analysis, the areas chosen should be more of the general-purpose type rather than the specific type such as for minerals, forests, or crops. The most systematic formulation of economic and social facts on a cross-country basis is Ray's (1971) *Dimensions of Canadian Regionalism.* However, the emphasis is structural rather than upon functional aspects. McCann (1982) provides no sub-provincial regional system or units aside from the separate treatment of the industrial heartland of southern Ontario and southern Quebec, and the separate analysis of the Canadian Shield as a region straddling five provinces and a corner of Alberta. Dhalla (1966) made a systematic compilation of socio-economic data on a sub-provincial basis, but he used Camu, Weeks, and Sametz's (1964) model as his framework.

In general, the major practical development of such frameworks is that spatial analyses are being carried out increasingly in terms of functional economic areas, such as the economic areas set up by the Bureau of Economic Analysis of the United States Department of Commerce. Similar regional characteristics have been utilized in Great Britain (Hall 1973) and Japan (Glickman 1976). From an economic- or social-geographic standpoint, the only consistent across-the-board systems are those of Camu, Weeks, and Sametz (1964), and the closely related 61-region system of Statistics Canada. These systems consist of the Labour Force Survey (LFS) economic regions based on a 1981 definition of boundaries, and the current SPRs.

These systems were proposed on the basis that for both social and economic policy, a database more detailed than that at the provincial level – at least down to SPRs and often down to smaller economic zones and sub-zones – would appear to be essential not only for federal and provincial departments and agencies, but also for private social agencies, business (for marketing), and academic research.

This more focused approach would apply most specifically in assessments of the impact and usefulness of existing policies and programs, in forecasting the need for action, and in the formulation of new policies and programs, or improvements of existing ones. New policies might be necessary because of changing regional and local conditions, the availability of financial resources, and shifts in the attitudes of the public and of governments as reflected in political, economic, and social priorities. For example, the problems of youth unemployment are different in a small town like Perth, Ontario, than in Toronto, and might call for different solutions. This may require an assessment even below SPRs, at the level of smaller zones and even sub-zones, whenever useful data are available. Such finer breakdowns would also be essential for the subsequent evaluation of the relative success of policies and programs and of the lessons to be learned.

The socio-economic policies and programs that could be particularly affected would be:

1. Federal measures below the provincial level, such as DRIE projects, and the Development Index, which is used to determine areas of application, and any specific steps taken to deal with different problems of unemployment and poverty;
2. Provincial measures that are at various levels between the province and the municipality, such as various types of job creation at a local level, resource areas, and tourist activity areas; and
3. Municipal measures that apply to a relatively wide area such as regional government units.

If areal units or zones are systematically defined to have economic and social meaning in both the functional and structural senses; to have hierarchical relationships with other zones, sub-zones, and sub-provincial regions; to become generally accepted federally and provincially; and to have relevant data available or generated for the areas concerned; then such zones provide an improved setting for forecasting the potential impact and hence the desirability and priority of programs and their assessment when undertaken. It is a case of providing action in the right places, or of minimizing the strains when downward adjustment must occur. Fine tuning becomes particularly important with the strains on the finances of governments at all levels resulting from continuing high unemployment and relatively slow growth in revenue, and hence the need for greater attention to costs and benefits, and to the priorities of programs and projects.

Fortunately, the use of the computer now makes it feasible to provide data quickly and cheaply on the level of zones, sub-zones, and even municipalities. But, for the detailed information to have most meaning and practical value, there must be a hierarchical grouping of census subdivisions into the sub-zones and zones, as well as sub-provincial regions. To obtain the best practical results for both levels of government and the private sector, the regions and zones should be general purpose; that is, they should serve social as well as economic analysis. Statistics Canada's SPRs need refinement, and new zonal levels should be introduced.

While limitations of space prevent presentation in detail, the purpose of the remainder of this essay is to outline a brief description of work on economic zoning in which Z.W. Sametz and I were engaged in 1984 for Statistics Canada. This has followed previous activities in the field at the Department of Reconstruction and Supply in the late-1940s and the Department of Defence Production in the 1950s, as well as our book in which we collaborated with Pierre Camu (Camu, Weeks, and Sametz 1964). The aim of the current work has been to contribute towards the provision of an improved multi-purpose regional and zonal system, which is now possible because of the availability of data on a more rapid and detailed basis through computerization.

The system proposed (Figure 22.1; Table 22.2) represents a modification of the 1964 model as reproduced in *The National Atlas of Canada* in 1973 (Fremlin 1973, 241–50), and enables analysis on the meso- or medio-level, that is, between the macro-level, which characterizes much of economic analysis, and the micro-level on which much social analysis has concentrated. Academic research has provided no systematic cross-country medio-analysis of various regional cultures (using the term in the broadest sense), sub-cultures or entities, or their comparative structures. However, Leonard Marsh (1970) used and recommended to others the 1964 model, modifications to which are considered below.

The revision of the 1964 model involved:

a) the establishment of a set of principles;
b) the application of these principles to a draft system of zones across the country, within a coded hierarchical framework that included provincial planning regions and SPRs above the zonal level, and sub-zones below it (the latter still only partially completed). Sub-zones are especially valuable for specific structural areas and they also permit adjustments of data to administrative boundaries and to various other existing regional divisions; and

c) the provision of a structure for basic discussion and decision-making by federal and provincial authorities.

The project was undertaken because of federal and provincial interest in developing a more meaningful geographical framework for policies and projects, especially those not applied on a universal basis.

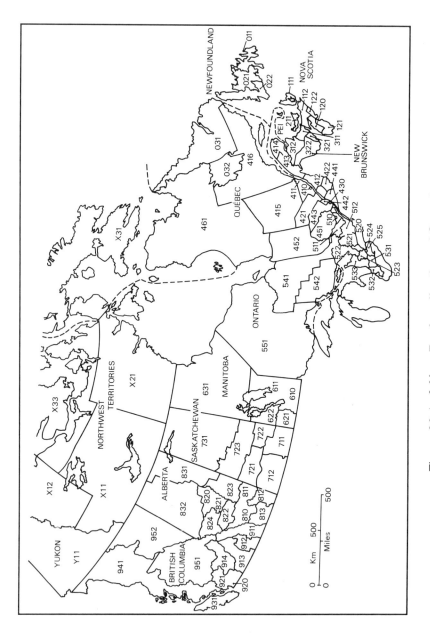

Figure 22.1 **A New Regionalization of Canada**

Table 22.2 A New Regionalization of Canada: Regional Codes

Province	Principal Region	Region
0 Newfoundland		
	01 Eastern Newfoundland	
	011	St. John's Metro–S.E. Newfoundland
	02 Western Newfoundland	
	021	Central Newfoundland
	022	Western Newfoundland Coastal
	07 Labrador 031	Eastern Labrador
	032	Western Labrador
1 Nova Scotia		
	11 Northern Nova Scotia	
	111	Sydney–Cape Breton
	112	Northumberland Strait
	12 Southern Nova Scotia	
	120	Halifax Metropole
	121	Yarmouth South Shore
	122	Annapolis Valley Region
2 Prince Edward Island		
	211	Prince Edward Island
3 New Brunswick		
	31 Eastern New Brunswick	
	311	Moncton/S.E. New Brunswick
	312	Northern New Brunswick
	32 Saint John's Valley	
	321	Saint John Metro–Fundy
	322	Upper Saint John's
4 Quebec		
	41 Eastern Quebec	
	410	Quebec Metropole
	411	Quebec Environs North
	412	Quebec Environs South
	413	Bas Saint-Laurent
	414	Gaspesie
	415	Chicoutimi–Jonquière Metro/Saguenay–Lac Saint Jean
	416	Côte-Nord
	42 Central Quebec	
	421	Trois Rivières Metro–Mauricie/Bois Francs
	422	Sherbrooke Metro–Est
	43 Montreal Metropole	
	430	Montreal Metropole
	44 Montreal Environs	
	441	Longeuil/Saint Jean–Monteregie
	442	Montreal Environs East/De Lanaudiere
	443	Montreal Environs North/Laurentides

Province	Principal Region	Region
	45 Western Quebec	
		451 Hull-Outaouais
		452 Abitibi-Temiscamingue
	46 Northern Quebec	
		461 Nord du Québec
5 Ontario		
	51 Eastern Ontario	
		510 Ottawa Metropole
		511 Ottawa Valley Environs
		512 Kingston Metro–St. Lawrence Valley
	52 Toronto–Central Ontario	
		520 Toronto Metropole
		521 Oshawa/Peterborough– Toronto East Environs
		522 Barrie–Toronto North Environs
		523 Kitchener/Guelph– Toronto West Environs
		524 Hamilton Metropole
		525 St. Catharines/Niagara/ Brantford–Hamilton South Environs
	53 South-western Ontario	
		531 London–Lake Erie
		532 Windsor/Sarnia–Lake St. Clair
		533 Stratford–Lake Huron
	54 North-eastern Ontario	
		541 North Bay–James Bay
		542 Sudbury/Sault Ste. Marie– Huron Industrial
	55 North-western Ontario	
		551 Thunder Bay–North Western
6 Manitoba		
	61 Winnipeg	
		610 Winnipeg Metropole
		611 Winnipeg Environs/S.E. Manitoba
	62 Western Manitoba	
		621 South-west Manitoba Prairie
		622 West Central Manitoba Parklands
	63 Northern Manitoba	
		631 Northern Manitoba
7 Saskatchewan		
	71 Southern Saskatchewan	
		711 Regina Metro–Southeastern Plains
		712 Saskatchewan Palliser
	72 Central Saskatchewan	
		721 Saskatoon Metro–Central Plains
		722 Saskatchewan S.E. Parklands
		723 Central Saskatchewan Parklands
	73 Northern Saskatchewan	
		731 Northern Saskatchewan Shield

Province	Principal Region		Region
8 Alberta			
	81 Southern Alberta		
		810	Calgary Metropole
		811	Calgary Environs–Drumheller
		812	Medicine Hat–S.E. Alberta/Palliser
		813	Lethbridge–S.W. Alberta
	82 Central Alberta		
		820	Edmonton Metropole
		821	Edmonton Central Environs
		822	Red Deer
		823	Edmonton East Environs
		824	Edmonton West Environs
	83 Northern Alberta		
		831	North-eastern Alberta
		832	North-western Alberta
9 British Columbia			
	91 Southern Interior B.C.		
		911	East Kootenay
		912	West Kootenay
		913	Kelowna–Okanagan
		914	Kamploops–South Central B.C.
	92 Vancouver Metropole		
		920	Vancouver Metropole
		921	Vancouver Environs
	93 Vancouver Island		
		931	Victoria Metro–Vancouver Island
	94 Pacific Coastal		
		941	North–western B.C.
	95 Northern B.C.		
		951	Prince George–North Central B.C.
		952	North-eastern B.C.
Y Yukon Territory			
	Y1 Yukon		
		Y11	Yukon Territory
X Northwest Territories			
	X1 Mackenzie		
		X11	Southern Mackenzie
		X12	Inuvik
	X2 Keewatin		
		X21	Keewatin
	X3 Franklin		
		X31	Eastern Franklin
		X32	Northern Franklin
		X33	Central Arctic

22.4   Outline of an Improved System of Socio-economic Areas

It is broadly accepted that any generally useful system of zones should cover all of Canada (including marine zones to which increasing attention is being devoted), with the same basic criteria applying in all parts of the country. Further, to be practical the approach must be generally acceptable to the provinces and hence respect provincial boundaries, although provision should be made to permit aggregations across boundaries for specific purposes, such as the Lloydminster area with its heavy oil development.

The actual delineation of boundaries has to be in accordance with well-defined concepts and should be both easy to describe and recognizable. The areas bounded should reflect the multiple requirements of users at large, both for purposes of private organizations and companies, as well as for public policy and its evaluation. The basic geographic unit in any particular study should be the minimum size for which data can be released and useful, and about which solid socio-economic generalizations can be made, depending upon the nature of the policy or problem.

To generate a manageable model, we aimed at a hierarchy of about 500 sub-zones for structural data; 250 zones, especially for functional data; 85 SPRs and 14 marine regions; and 35 principal provincial regions – or provincial planning regions (PPR) – and three marine planning regions (MPR).

So far, reference has been made to practical criteria and constraints. Above and beyond these criteria, there obviously must be a sound theoretical structure to give meaning to the regional and zonal data. The conceptual structure must make feasible the acceptance and digestion of significant disaggregated data in order that functional and structural characteristics of the regional and zonal areas may be identified, and changes seen in perspective. The 247 zones arrived at, and from which the 85 SPRs are built up, are the key elements of the system. The delineation was based on functional, structural, marketing, and production criteria. Allowance was also made for other factors, such as sociological factors, which include human spatial relationships and social and institutional structures. The four main factors were not isolated, but function and marketing were given more weight than structure and production because of their relation to central place theory.

This approach creates some practical problems. Regular published functional data on movements and relations of people, services, and goods are much more limited than those on, say, population, income, employment, unemployment, and industrial structure. Therefore it is harder to arrive at a functional model than a structural model. However, once arrived at, it provides a more useful framework for long-term socio-economic analysis, and becomes of greater interest to social geographers than the former structural models. Some recent adherents of the centre-hinterland approach have an ideological basis, but ours has been a purely technical-scientific development. The zones produced obviously differ widely in terms of area, population, and nature of economic and social activities. Hence, it is necessary for description and analysis to classify them into six different "orders," from zero to fifth inclusive. Each zone is a type of cell with a centre and a hinterland – unless it is a "metropole zone" with widespread relationships. This approach is different from that used in the poverty lines referred to earlier, where there are five different categories based primarily on population, and no types of relationships between hinterlands and centres. In short, the zones are intended to provide – with adequate data – a basis for analysis and evaluation of problems and preferable solutions.

In essence, this regionalization arrives independently at a methodology of delineation and a system of zones that is akin to that of the U.S. Bureau of Economic Analysis' (BEA) economic areas. The development of theory in the direction of systems of central places with functional relationships to their hinterlands was paralleled by their analytic move from the previous system of 501 State economic areas, which had been established on the basis of structural homogeneity, to the 173 BEA economic areas based formally on functional factors.

The 1984 draft model reflects the functional emphasis (but not exclusively) as distinct from the original 1953 (Defence Production) model (Economics and Statistics Branch 1953), which had used administrative operational-functional elements but still used major structural orientations from traditional geography, and the intermediate 1964 model where equal weighting was given to functional and structural perspectives. The sub-zones remain more structurally based, as were the 501 State economic areas.

Because of the wide variety of problems, principles, and practices involved, the question might well be posed as to why and how we arrived at these models of the zones and regions. It was, obviously, no short-term process. The "why" was easy. We were confronted with the huge problem of understanding the different areas of the country, of keeping track of area data, and of analyzing it meaningfully. In the period of post-war re-conversion, we had to analyze the danger areas of war production and the problems incumbent on re-conversion widening into general regional development. During the Korean War we had to analyze the problems of defence production and their area impact. Subsequently, it was problems of regional development in the Maritime provinces and Newfoundland. We were faced with a continuing intellectual challenge. The "how" was harder. We proceeded from areas to regions, and from one theoretical framework to another. The fundamentals of the system were sorted out prior to, and then in connection with, our original publication (Camu, Weeks, and Sametz 1964). At that time, statistical limitations forced the delineation of zonal boundaries along county or census division (CD) lines and this, naturally, resulted in certain anomalies because a given county or CD might have arbitrary boundaries and thus have within its confines two or more quite distinct economic structures, not to mention functional links. During the mid-1970s, we carried out a major review of the 1964 presentation, but were still hampered by the limited availability of data below the county level, although some CDs had been revised. The 1984 work for Statistics Canada represented a significant step forward, because some provinces were pressing to change the CDs or abandon the counties in favour of new municipalities or census subdivisions (CSDs), which could be combined into new "regions of concentration." The delineation could be based on data at the CSD level and boundaries could, thus, be drawn more realistically and meaningfully.

We have provided a carefully organized approximation, but no relatively permanent delineations can be established without the input and agreement of federal, provincial, and local officials, supplemented by the views of business and labour organizations, academic experts, and interested citizens. This general input becomes all the more important when one considers that the zones and regions should represent agreed social, as well as economic, units. Formal statistical data will have to be supplemented by quantitative data collected for special purposes at the local or private organizational level, including local academic research, and confirmed by qualitative information and judgement. Although it would appear that the social factors are given only a nominal weighting in the delineation of this multi-purpose socio-economic area system, most of the key social factors actually tend to work along with the economic factors, and they each reinforce the other. For example, the orientation to the commuting, or work-trip, factor is important to both perspectives. Thus, we feel that the model represents a socio-economic geographic system that could serve as the basis or framework for general as well as local social-geographic studies. If social geographers are to help us understand geographic differences in income and other social factors, they must develop or work within an analytical framework that is generally recognized, and that will facilitate the availability of the data necessary for analysis.

Notes

1. *Report on Social Security for Canada*, Committee on Post-War Reconstruction, 1943.
2. *Report of the Royal Commission on the Economic Union and Development Prospects for Canada* (Ottawa: Ministry of Supply and Services, 1985).
3. The five regions of Canada are Atlantic Canada, Quebec, Ontario, Prairies, and British Columbia.

References

Camu, P., E.P. Weeks, and Z.W. Sametz, 1964. *Economic Geography of Canada.* Toronto: Macmillan of Canada.

Dhalla, N.K. 1966. *These Canadians.* Toronto: McGraw-Hill.

Dobell, A.R., and S.II. Mansbridge. 1986. *The Social Policy Process in Canada.* Ottawa: Institute for Research on Public Policy.

Economics and Statistics Branch. 1953. *Economic Zoning of Canada and the D.P.P. Geographic Code.* Ottawa: Department of Defence Production.

Fremlin, G., ed. 1973. *The National Atlas of Canada.* 4th ed. Ottawa: Surveys and Mapping Branch, Department of Energy, Mines and Resources.

Glickman, N.J. 1976. "On the Japanese Urban System." *Journal of Regional Science* 16:317–36.

Hall, P., et al. 1973. *The Containment of Urban England*. London: George Allen and Unwin.

McCann, L.D., ed. 1982. *Heartland and Hinterland, a Geography of Canada*. Scarborough: Prentice-Hall.

Marsh, L. 1970. *Communities in Canada*. Toronto: McClelland and Stewart.

National Council of Welfare. 1985a. *1985 Poverty Lines*. Ottawa: Minister of Supply and Services.

———. 1985b. *Poverty Profile 1985*. Ottawa: Minister of Supply and Services.

Ray, D.M. 1971. *Dimensions of Canadian Regionalism*. Ottawa: Department of Energy, Mines and Resources.

Appendix:
An Appreciation of James Wreford Watson with a Bibliography of His Work

Guy M. Robinson

James Wreford Watson held honorary degrees from five Canadian universities.[1] This unique achievement is an indication of the recognition he achieved for his work in promoting the study of geography in Canada. At one time the holder of the title "Chief Geographer," he helped to establish departments of geography at both McMaster and Carleton universities, and while occupying the chair of geography at Edinburgh University for three decades, he forged close links with Canada through his role in establishing a Centre of Canadian Studies in Edinburgh. For many years his book *North America: Its Countries and Regions* (Watson 1963) was one of the standard texts through which geography students in the English-speaking world came to learn about both Canada and the United States. His other geographical writings on a wide range of urban, social, and economic issues, not to mention his poetry, which usually focused upon Canadian society and places, all combined to make him one of the major post-war figures within the geographical discipline. In his native Scotland and in his adopted home, Canada, his scholarship and the quality of his writing raised his academic standing to a level rarely obtained by someone owing allegiance to such an unfashionable subject as geography.

The scope of Wreford Watson's writing is large, and the topics he covered were many and varied, but I shall attempt here to chart its main themes and to identify its qualities while tracing the important influence of his allegiance to two countries, Canada and Scotland. For the sake of convenience, I have attempted to summarize his geographical writings under just four headings, but this distillation of over 50 major articles and books can provide only a bare outline of Watson's 50 years of scholarship, and can do little justice to the quality of his writing, which was its hallmark.

1   A Scot in Canada

James Wreford Watson was born in China in 1915, the son of Scottish Presbyterian missionaries. Although he spent little time in the land of his birth, one aspect of his origins showed up later in his lecturing style, which had more than a little of the preacher about it. He was educated in Edinburgh at George Watson's College before proceeding to Edinburgh University in 1931 where he read geography. The Department of Geography at the time comprised Alan Ogilvie, who became professor of geography in that year, and Arthur Geddes, son of Patrick, the biologist and sociologist. During the 1930s they were joined by David Linton, subsequently professor of geography at Birmingham University, T.W. Freeman, who attained the same position at Manchester University, and Catherine Snodgrass. Some of the influences of this quintet are apparent in Watson's early geographical work with its emphasis upon regions and regional differentiation. Ogilvie's concern with regional geography as the cornerstone of the study of geography played an important part. In his four-year undergraduate degree, Watson had at least one course of regional geography in every year, and every lecturer in the Department of Geography taught at least one regional course. Ogilvie's lectures on "The Mediterranean Lands" were regarded as masterpieces of description, and undoubtedly inspired Watson to emulate this particular art. However, Watson was not attracted by Ogilvie's emphasis upon vast numbers of facts, the use of which followed the tradition in economic geography set by Ogilvie's predecessor, George Chisholm. Instead, Watson was attracted to other branches of human geography, such as the social and regional topics covered by Arthur Geddes and containing "an overloading of ideas."

He graduated with a first class honours degree, won the Vans Dunlop Scholarship, and received the Royal Scottish Geographical Society's Universities' Medal, which denoted that he was considered the most outstanding geography graduate in Scotland that year. He embarked upon an academic career after graduating, being appointed as an assistant lecturer in geography at Sheffield University. Here he worked briefly under Professor Rudmose Brown and met Griffith Taylor who, at that time, was professor of geography at the University of Toronto. Within two years he had embarked on a lasting connection with Canada, becoming an instructor at McMaster University, Hamilton, in 1938 and registering as a Ph.D. student under Taylor at the University of Toronto to work on the growth of settlement and general economic development of the Niagara Peninsula. His thesis, completed in 1945, was entitled "The geography of the Niagara Peninsula, with special emphasis on changes in land use and settlement."

Although Taylor's cogently argued determinism was propounded strongly at Toronto, modifying elements in the form of Tathem's possibilism, Putnam's more pragmatic approaches, and Taylor's own revised "stop and go" determinism, together influenced Watson to take more account of differing philosophies within geography that had not featured largely in the curriculum at Edinburgh. His interest in the history of the philosophy of geography were broadened and this was reflected in the content of his teaching. This interest was extremely influential in the new departments of geography he established at McMaster, Carleton, and Queen's universities, and also in the fresh curricula he introduced to a new generation of geographers.

At McMaster he became lecturer in charge of the geography program, being appointed as the first professor of geography at the university in 1945 (see Johnson 1981). In all, he spent ten years at McMaster before leaving to help found a department of geography at Carleton University, Ottawa. He actually gave his first geography course at Carleton in 1945 where the first full-time lecturer in the subject was his wife Jessie, formerly Jessie Black, who had also graduated with a degree in geography from Edinburgh University. Indeed, as students at Edinburgh, Jessie Black and Wreford Watson had been instrumental in forming the first Edinburgh

University Geographical Society, in which Wreford Watson was its first president and Jessie Black its first secretary. At Carleton University, initially, he served on the part-time staff in the evening programs, Carleton catering especially to the demands of government employees requiring university courses and, at that time, not holding official university status. Later, he became professor of geography at Carleton while concurrently holding the appointment of chief geographer and director of the geographical branch of the Canadian federal civil service.

During his time at McMaster Watson's teaching had to cover the broad spectrum of the discipline, a fact that helps to explain his attempts to relate his own systematic interest in social geography to the main aspects of physical, human, and regional geography. The breadth of his teaching at this time is indicated by the titles of the four courses he taught each week throughout the academic year: "The Elements of Physical Geography," "The Human Geography of Settlement and Population," "The Regional Geography of Canada," and "The Regional Geography of Britain and Western Europe." This breadth was repeated in his book *General Geography* (Watson 1953), in which physical, human, and regional geography were covered in a text widely used in North America in both schools and universities. However, at a time when the systematic elements of geography were gradually starting to displace the overriding regional emphasis, his appointment as chief geographer began to strengthen a focus on what would today be termed "applied geography" and the development of new areas of interest. One of his main tasks was to prepare a national atlas covering both physical and human aspects of the country. Subsequently this led to his editing several atlases for Thomas Nelson and Sons, and also for Collins and Longmans (Watson 1958a, 1960, 1968c, 1968g). But other aspects of his job were much more practical: he had to give advice on public problems relating to land use, conservation, urban sprawl, rural depopulation, political boundaries, and industrial location. Undoubtedly this gave him a broader view of the discipline and helped him to focus attention on the major issues affecting society, as reflected, for example, in his later work on the United States (Watson 1971, 1982).

In 1954 Watson was appointed to the chair of geography at Edinburgh University and so returned to his alma mater. By no means did this sever his connections with Canada, and over the next three decades he and his wife became frequent trans-Atlantic travellers. For example, among the universities in which he held visiting professorships were Queen's (in 1959–60, 1963, and 1978), Manitoba (in 1969–70), British Columbia (in 1971), Simon Fraser (in 1976–77), and Calgary (in 1980–81 and 1983). Also, research continued to focus upon North America, necessitating frequent visits to both Canada and the United States. However, a more formal link with Canada was established after 1956 when he helped to found the School of North American Studies at Edinburgh University. Out of this was formed the Centre of Canadian Studies of which he was convener from 1972 to 1982.

The quality of Watson's work on the geography of North America has been recognized with a large and varied collection of awards from both Britain and North America. In North America he became a fellow of the Royal Society of Canada in 1954, two years after receiving the award of merit from the Association of American

Geographers at the International Geographical Congress in Washington D.C. The Canadian Association of Geographers made him a special award in 1978 for his services to Canadian geography, and his work in promoting Canadian Studies was recognized in the award of the Northern Telecom International Prize and Gold Medal of the International Council of Canadian Studies in 1984. In Britain he received two prestigious honours from the Royal Geographical Society: the Murchison Medal in 1960 and the Research Medal in 1964. In Scotland he became a fellow of the Royal Society of Edinburgh in 1958 and was awarded the Gold Medal of the Royal Scottish Geographical Society in 1984. Also, in addition to honorary degrees from five Canadian universities, a special scholarship entitled the Jessie and Wreford Watson Award in Geography was established at Carleton University by friends and colleagues, in recognition of the substantial role the Watsons played in the formative days of the discipline at Carleton.

2   Social Geography as a Systematic Study

It is significant that this book is entitled "A Social Geography" because one of the last articles written by Wreford Watson before he left Canada to take up the chair at Edinburgh was entitled "The Sociological Aspects of Geography" (Watson 1951), which was a contribution to Griffith Taylor's edited volume *Geography in the Twentieth Century.*

Watson's (1952) attempt to summarize the sociological aspects of geography was wide ranging. He assessed the contribution of social geography to physical geography, the cultural landscape, human regions, functional regions, and the sociological concept of natural area. In this he reflected the overriding concern of geography at that time for the region, a concern in which "regional geography . . . seeks to bring together in an areal setting various matters which are treated separately in topical geography" (James 1954, 9). The topic, or systematic aspect, was defined by Watson in the case of social geography by way of answering a four-part question: is social geography the distribution of social phenomena, the social adaptation of areas, the geographic basis of society, or regional differentiation in terms of social characteristics? His answer to this question produced the definition that social geography was "the identification of different regions of the earth's surface according to associations of social phenomena related to the total environment" (Watson 1951, 482). This indicates his view of the breadth of this systematic element within the geographic discipline. He placed general emphasis upon the regional differentiation of social characteristics and, as such, defined a smaller area of study than "human geography" despite the fact that some scholars have used the two terms interchangeably (e.g., Fitzgerald 1946). His list of systematic elements within human geography included racial, cultural, historical, economic, political, and social geography, though he recognized that the lines of division around the topics were not rigid and that social geography could not exist in isolation from the others.

In the Taylor volume, Watson's description of social geography drew heavily upon his studies of Hamilton. He not only distinguished the "social regions" of the city but also examined the stages in its growth and developed ideas of social distance and social space. His recognition of the importance of industry and city institutions in affecting the nature of the townscape was accompanied by a focus upon the way in which these factors had influenced the spatial patterns of urban society. He argued that social geography was concerned primarily with patterns, as these enabled the geographer to build up a picture of the world and to compare and contrast differences from place to place. These differences took the form of what he termed, "social regions" and, drawing upon the work of the Chicago school of social ecologists, he referred to transition zones, cultural shatter belts, and distinct zones associated with the different socio-economic groups within Hamilton. He recognized that though different groups might be separated merely by a railway line, in terms of social distance there could be a huge gulf between them. Such divisions within society were related to the operation of commercial and administrative institutions that helped to shape the fundamental character of the city.

Watson's clear statement on the nature of social geography was not taken up specifically and developed by other geographers working in this general area, though the work performed within this part of the discipline soon developed in a way which gave further emphasis to the notions of social regions as developed by Watson. This work, often termed "factorial ecology," sought to utilize statistical data and techniques to distinguish the different intra-urban regions that Watson distinguished by less formal means for Hamilton. In effect, factorial ecologies were refining the notion of classifying the city into distinctive spatial units, but often without Watson's concern with the forces producing the distinction (Berry 1971; Davies 1984; Murdie 1969). Meanwhile, Watson developed his ideas of social distance (Watson 1955) and retained an emphasis upon regionalization, using North America as a whole as his canvas rather than one particular city (Watson 1958b, 1962, 1963, 1965a, 1965c, 1968a, 1968b). The logical extension of his notions of social distance were taken up later in his work on both image geography and the importance of human perception and interpretation as factors in shaping geography (see Part 4).

The final developments of his 1951 statement on social geography were not made for nearly 30 years and, as it turned out, it was not Canada that provided the subject matter but the United States. First, his work on regionalization and regional distinctiveness led him to investigate the whole of North America, producing a major text on the regional geography of the continent (Watson 1963, 1968b). However, towards the end of his career he produced two books on the United States that combined aspects of traditional regional geography and the concern for the problems of society, which had become so much more evident within this branch of geography in the 1970s (Watson 1979a, 1982). Thus, though he never lost the strong emphasis on regional geography imparted in the 1930s by Ogilvie, and restated in his 1951 paper, Watson developed a concern for social problems and issues, which he first explored professionally as the chief geographer of Canada and subsequently expressed in the tenor of some of his regional writings.

Both *A Social Geography of the United States* (Watson 1979a) and *The United States: Habitation of Hope* (Watson 1982) combined a keen awareness of regional variation within the United States and a recognition of certain social problems.

Particularly in the former, these problems were foremost in a consideration of issues such as multi-racial development, the energy crisis, conservation of resources, and the environmental impact of development, urban decay, and suburban sprawl. This was Watson portraying the America that he had observed as a frequent visitor for four decades. The problems he examined were tied closely to the physical landscape, the nature of the emergence of economic specializations, and the processes that gave rise to distinctive regional characteristics. Throughout both texts one of Watson's trademarks was also evident: the frequent utilization of literature from beyond the academic realm of geography and the social sciences. Literature and poetry were cited regularly to convey a more complete "sense of place," so that the reader was given a more vivid portrayal of the "American reality." Thereby, Watson's writing frequently gained a luminescent quality that places it on a different level from the work of many other geographers: not only is it well written, but it has a certain style and finesse that is clearly that of the poet.

A simple indication of his style appears in his use of urban-centred novels such as Crane's (1896) *Maggie: A Girl of the Streets,* Farrell's (1934) *The Young Manhood of Studs Lonigan,* and Howells' (1884) *The Rise of Silas Lapham* as cogent underscorings of ethnic friction, class differences, and poverty in the city. These "secondary" sources were utilized masterfully to support particular themes based on a general historical-cultural approach. The United States was seen as a product of individualism promoting internal and external conflicts, a land of prospects but with problems that were only partially offset by certain "success stories" in the fields of women's liberation, environmental management, and opportunities for the young. This represented an approach and a perspective well removed from the deterministic views apparent in some of his earlier work, but throughout, he continues to display a fine use of language and a knowledge of many interesting philosophical points of view.

3   A Discipline in Distance

One of Watson's most concrete statements of his view of geography as a discipline was made in his inaugural lecture to the Edinburgh University Faculty of Arts upon his appointment to the university's chair of geography (Watson 1955). The content of this lecture foreshadowed one of the debates of the 1960s and 1970s that concerned the importance of space and distance in the recognition of a distinct and clearly defined geography. At a time when the region remained the uppermost concept in many geographers' formulations of their discipline, Watson produced powerful arguments to show that geographers could look beyond this concept to the factor of distance: "When distance is treated as the extent to which objects adapt themselves to, or dominate, their environment, then it offers valuable clues to their relationship with the environment, as relationship that leads geography on from description to explanation" (Watson 1955, 2).

But this was not simply an attempt to compartmentalize the earth's surface on the basis of division into manageable areal units defined by size. Instead, he was arguing that geographers should be interested in a variety of distances: "not only those made by nature, but those that form or perish within the mind of man." Here was the idea of mental distances and mental maps that he was to pursue later in his career. He illustrated the centrality of distance to the geographer by citing time distance, cost distance, and social distance as important elements that needed to be understood if geographers were going to explain particular spatial distributions. Both economic and ecological factors were included in this argument, and he reinforced his views on social geography and social distance by once more citing his work on Hamilton and the Niagara Peninsula.

In this inaugural lecture he also referred to the geographer's need to consider the way in which particular distributions have come about. This was not an endorsement of historical geography *per se*, but an indication of his belief in the dynamic nature of geography's subject matter and the need to be aware of the evolution of phenomena through time. Later, this was expressed specifically with reference to the nature of regions: "Most regions are dynamic entities – especially urbanised regions. They develop a considerable number of structures to support their functions. These structures are changing, or are resisting change, both in nature and form. Their geographical description should, therefore, be dynamic" (Watson 1959, 141). Thus, much of Watson's work on regions was set in a historical-cultural context, as, for example, were his vivid descriptions of how settlement and development in Canada responded to the natural environment (Watson 1949, 1950a, 1956a, 1962, 1965a). This recurrent theme of the human response to physical geography was also followed in later work on the United States (Watson 1972a, 1974, 1977a, 1977b). His view of the importance of historical development as a factor in shaping current geography is also set out in some of these works. In *Canada: Problems and Prospects* (Watson 1968a), the first chapter provides an excellent explanation of how Canada evolved into a nation separate from the United States. Other work in a similar vein focused upon specific features that act as "relicts" today, that is, representatives of earlier developments and processes: "The geographer is less concerned with individual remains than with fragments of whole landscapes that have persisted into, and become an integral part of the scene" (Watson 1959, 110).

While Watson maintained his work on regional geography (e.g., Watson 1963, 1968a), he followed his 1955 address on "a distance in discipline" by developing systematic work on social distance and the influence of people's images of places and their environment as translated into geographical reality (e.g., Watson 1965c, 1967b, 1972a). This marked a movement in step with the changing nature of the discipline and, initially, it appeared more as a change in the geography curriculum at Edinburgh than in Watson's own publications, which didn't focus upon mental images and perceived distances until the late 1960s and 1970s. The growth of systematic interests within geography in general were reflected at Edinburgh by the reduction in the number of regional courses offered and a burgeoning emphasis upon optional systematic courses. Watson taught both, offering the "Regional Geography of the United States and Canada" as well as "Social Geography." When the International Geographical Union met in Britain in 1964 he was asked to co-edit a volume on the systematic geography of Britain (Watson 1964a). In contrast, his predecessor,

Ogilvie (1928), had edited a volume of the regional geography of Britain. The systematic theme was also emphasized in Watson's convenorship at Edinburgh in the School of Scottish Studies. In this the concerns were with a combination of literature, folk art, music, material culture, and ethno-cultural identity. All were represented, too, during his ten-year tenure of office as editor of *Scottish Studies*. At the same time, he became deputy chairman of Edinburgh's School of the Built Environment where emphasis was placed not just on systematic study but also on interdisciplinary study, in which the overlap of geography, planning, architecture, and civil engineering were encouraged.

4   Geography as an Art

Wreford Watson has genuine claim to the title of "geographer-poet." He was one of few geographers who produced an output of published non-geographical literature of high quality: a quality recognized in 1954 with the award of the Governor General of Canada's Medal for Poetry. The award was specifically for his book of collected verses, *Of Time and the Lover*, published under the nom-de-plume of James Wreford (1953). Another of his books of verses, *Countryside Canada* (Wreford 1979), has Canada as its theme, as do many of his poems published in a variety of collections (see Birney 1953; Carman et al. 1954; Dudek and Layton 1952; Hambleton 1944; Smith 1943). He also published one set of poems under his own name (Watson 1985) and chose a Scottish topic for another literary work (Wreford 1973). However, it is perhaps in the Canadian poems that the greatest feeling of "sense of place" appeared within his writings. The importance to him of both this feeling and his poetry was suggested in his presidential address to the Institute of British Geographers in 1983 (Watson 1983a) in which he stressed the value of literature for geographers.

In the address he expressed some of the basic elements of his own philosophy in his chosen discipline. In charting the extent to which the content of geographical study had broadened since his student days, he showed that he felt this had given greater scope for the use of literature as a geographical source material – a movement away from literature as an embellishment to literature as a necessity (Watson 1983a, 385).

Thus, Watson recalled his student days, when "we often had Brunhes' words quoted at us, that geography 'must be first and above all the geography of the material,' of what was concrete in the landscape. Mere impressions by a writer were irrelevant. We were put off by the immaterial." But some of the more literary tradition, perhaps from his school days, prevailed, and he claimed, "I have never written an article or a book without an appeal to literature" (Watson 1983a, 387). These appeals were manifest in the use of relevant quotations from literature which, like geography, was concerned with people and places. This can be seen in his first published article (Watson 1939), in which he quoted Samuel Johnson to show how devoid of trees the Scottish Highlands had become by the eighteenth century, while also referring to scientific work on pollen analysis by Godwin. "Thus the eye of the writer was relied on as being as serviceable as the eye of the microscope" (Watson 1983a, 387).

It was this belief in the importance of qualitative views of place that underlay much of Watson's work on "image regions": "Not all geography derives from the earth; some of it springs from our ideas of the earth. This geography within the mind can at times be the effective geography to which men adjust" (Watson 1969, 10). Hence he became concerned less with the relief of the land and more with the topography of the mind. Canada, with its strong cultural contrasts and rich mosaic of cultures, proved particularly fertile ground for studying the way in which different groups built their own tastes and prejudices into systems of land development and settlement. These ideas were expressed in several of Watson's studies in the late 1960s and 1970s (e.g., Watson 1967b, 1969, 1970a, 1971, 1972c, 1974, 1977a, 1977b, 1977c) in which he demonstrated how personal tastes and individual decisions were translated into distinctive elements within particular cultural landscapes. For example, his presidential address to the Institute of British Geographers (Watson 1983a) contrasted the "irregular streets, incomplete squares, views shut off by bastions, narrow alleys and winding stairs" of French Quebec with the "great open views along broad straight boulevards" of English Montreal. These differences were part of the value landscape that geographers could perceive and record – a landscape adumbrated by writers and poets, such as Watson himself, so that literature and poetry became natural sources for the geographer to seek out.

Perhaps the clearest view of the importance of the topography of the mind was expressed in Watson's (1972c) address to the joint International Geographical Union/International Cartographers' Association meeting in Montreal, in which he claimed, "It is the mental image of a place, as much as the place itself, that counts." Behind a mental image lay social goals and prejudices, the dreams and illusions of individuals, which transformed geographical distance and physical space into mental distance. It was this transformation or falsification that "determined the real geography of social linkages" (Watson 1983a, 393).

In his concern for "Image Geography" Watson became one of the pioneers of a type of geographical study since popularized by the writings of Yi-fu Tuan, Meinig, Gould, Lowenthal, and Prince among others. In Watson's case the core of this aspect of his work was his attempt to show how images of America, held in the mind of Americans, were used to transform the American landscape to fit a particular image (e.g., Watson 1970a, 1974, 1977b). Here, too, was the opportunity for literature to play its part; the writings of Mark Twain, William Faulkner, Mike Fink, and John Steinbeck, for example, all have a role in expressing and creating the goals in the lives of their citizens, which then made an impression upon the land. Their writings were woven into Watson's theme that the freedom-loving Americans built up a market landscape in which the ethos of private enterprise and individual competition predominated.

He developed these ideas to suggest that image regions had a place within regional planning, a view echoed in Zelinsky's (1970, 2) comment that "a grass roots regionalism has been asserting itself throughout much of the world." Watson felt that planners should cater to this regional view and people's desire to retain particular images. He cited the case of the continued existence of Fife as a planning unit after the Scottish local government reforms of 1975, as an example of the retention of a particular historical image despite the fact that rational arguments were put forward for splitting the historical county between several other local authorities. "Instead of approaching a country or region as the combination of given natural forms with developed social functions, the geographer might begin by looking at the mental image of the area and then see how that image has worked itself out in the landscape" (Watson 1971, 33). Thus, he felt that image regions were an essential key to the rich variety of the earth, and that it was vital for geographers to recognize and study them.

5   Conclusion

This assessment of Watson's work under four headings has focused upon his published work. However, there are other important aspects of his career that should not be overlooked. He made a great personal commitment to furthering the aims of professional geographical organizations and institutions throughout the world. In so doing he held a series of high offices marking him as one of the most distinguished geographers of his generation. For instance, at the time of his appointment to the chair in Edinburgh, he was organizing chairman of the Canadian Association of Geographers and was instrumental in founding *The Canadian Geographer* (Watson 1950b). During his early years in Edinburgh he was a prominent organizer of International Geographical Congress meetings, chairing its cartographic section at the 1956 meeting in Brazil, and chairing its publications committee from 1960 to 1964. Within Britain he became president of the Institute of British Geographers in 1982–83, having been vice-president of the Royal Scottish Geographical Society from 1968 to 1976 and its president from 1976 to 1989. And in 1970 he was president of the geography section of the British Association for the Advancement of Science. In the broader sphere of education he was chairman of the Geography and Planning Committee of the Social Science Research Council from 1970 to 1975, the last four years of which he was a councillor on the research council. He occupied a similar role for a decade on the British Association of American Studies. He was a member of the British National Committee for Geography of the Royal Society, London, from 1960 onwards.

In Edinburgh Watson held positions on education committees of the city council in the 1960s and 1970s, and was a member of the Scottish Examinations Board. He was also dean of the Faculty of Social Science at Edinburgh and was a prime mover in establishing a university staff club. His evident affection for Edinburgh and his native Scotland led him to turn his academic writing away from North America from time to time to report on the changing scene in Scotland and especially Edinburgh itself (e.g., Watson 1965d, 1970b, 1976a, 1976b, 1979b).

Overall, Wreford Watson will be remembered by geographers for the quality of his writing and particularly for his ability to convey the real feel of a place. This was achieved because, as a poet as well as a geographer, he utilized poetry and literature to good effect in his geographical writing. He wrote two major articles on social geography and concepts of distance that deserved to be given a higher profile than they received within the discipline; they were ahead of their time. When the "new" geography of the 1960s and 1970s appeared, Watson's image regions and social distances found a more central role in the subject, though he never lost his attraction for the notion of the region as a central pillar of geographical thought. He will be remembered, too, for his writing on both Canada and the United States. But in Scotland and North America alike, the memories will be not of one Watson but of two, for Wreford and his wife, Jessie, had been a geographical team ever since their undergraduate days. Their collaboration in *The Canadians, How They Live and Work* (Watson 1978) gave them both, and many others, much pleasure.

Notes

1. Watson's honorary degrees were Hon. D.Litt. (York), Hon. LL.D. (Queen's), Hon. LL.D. (Carleton), Hon. LL.D. (Calgary), and Hon. LL.D. (McMaster).

References

Berry, B.J.L., ed. 1971. "Comparative Factorial Ecology." *Economic Geography* 47 (Supplement):209–367.

Birney, E., ed. 1953. *Twentieth Century Canadian Poetry.* Toronto: Ryerson.

Carman, B., L. Pierce, and V.B. Rhodemizer, eds. 1954. *Canadian Poetry in English.* Toronto: Ryerson.

Crane, S. 1896. *Maggie, A Girl of the Streets.* London: William Heinemann.

Davies, W.K.D. 1984. *Factorial Ecology.* Aldershot: Gower.

Dudek, L., and I. Layton, eds. 1952. *Canadian Poems.* Toronto: Contact Press.

Fitzgerald, W. 1946. "Correspondence: Geography and its Components." *Geographical Journal* 57:272–73.

Farrell, J.T. 1934. *The Young Manhood of Studs Lonigan.* New York: The Vanguard Press.

Hambleton, R. ed. 1944. *Unit of Five.* Toronto: Ryerson.

Howells, W.D. 1884. *The Rise of Silas Lapham.* Boston and New York: Houghton Mifflin & Co.

James, P.E. 1954. "Introduction: The Field of Geography." In P.E. James and C.F. Jones, eds., *American Geography: Inventory and Prospect,* 3–18. New York: Syracuse University Press.

Johnson, C.M. 1981. *McMaster University – The Early Years in Hamilton, 1930–1957.* Toronto: University of Toronto Press.

Murdie, R.A. 1969. "The Factorial Ecology of Metropolitan Toronto 1951–1961: An Essay on the Social Geography of the City." Research Papers, Department of Geography, University of Chicago, no. 116.

Ogilvie, A.G. ed. 1928. *Great Britain, Essays in Regional Geography.* Cambridge: Cambridge University Press.

Smith, A.J.M., ed., 1943. *The Book of Canadian Poetry*. Oxford: Oxford University Press.

Watson, J.W. 1985. *The Wounds of Love*. Watson, Kippford, Dumfries, and Galloway.

Wreford, J. 1953. *Of Time and the Lover*. Toronto: McClelland and Stewart.

————. 1973. *Scotland: The Great Upheaval*. Edinburgh: Bonaly Press.

————. 1979. *Countryside Canada*. Fredericton: Fiddlehead Press.

Zelinsky, W. 1970. "North America's Vernacular Regions." *Annals of the Association of American Geographers* 70:1–16.

J. Wreford Watson: A Bibliography

1939   "Forest or Man: Man the Deciding Factor." *Scottish Geographical Magazine* 55:148–62.

1943   "Urban Developments in the Niagara Peninsula." *Canadian Journal of Economic and Political Science* 9:463–86.

1944   "Canada in the American Balance." *Culture* 5:385–402.

1945a   "Hamilton and Its Environs." *Canadian Geographical Journal* 30:240–52.

1945b   "The Changing Industrial Pattern of the Niagara Peninsula." *Ontario Historical Society, Papers and Records* 37:49–58.

1946   "Mapping a Hundred Years of Change in the Niagara Peninsula." *Canadian Geographical Journal* 32:266–83.

1947   "Rural Depopulation in Southwestern Ontario." *Annals of the Association of American Geographers* 37:145–54.

1948   "The Influence of the Frontier on Niagara Settlements." *Geographical Review* 38:112–20.

1949   "Canada: Power Vacuum, or Pivot Area?" In H.W. Weigert, V. Stefanson, and R.E. Harrison, eds., *New Compass of the World*. New York: Macmillan.

1950a   "Canada: The Setting – Its Geography." In G.W. Brown, ed., *Canada*, 120–42. Toronto: University of Toronto Press.

1950b   The Canadian Association of Geographers: A Sketch of the Preliminaries." *Canadian Geographer* 1:1–3.

1951   "The Sociological Aspects of Geography." In G. Taylor, ed., *Geography in the Twentieth Century: A Study of Growth, Fields, Techniques, Aims and Trends*, 463–99. New York: Philosophical Library.

1952   "Geography in Relation to the Physical and Social Sciences." *Revue Canadienne de Geographie* 6:2–12.

1953a   *General Geography*. Toronto: Copp Clark.

1953b   "The Sociological Aspects of Geography." In G. Taylor, ed., *op. cit.* 2d ed.

1954a   "The Pattern of Canada's Post-war Growth." *Geography* 39:163–75.

1954b   "Basic Problems of Regional Planning in Canada." *Community Planning Review*, 488–92.

1955	"Geography – A Discipline in Distance." *Scottish Geographical Magazine* 71:1–13.
1956a	"The Land of Canada." *Canadian Geographical Journal* 52:136–66.
1956b	"Population Pressure and Marginal Lands." *Scottish Geographical Magazine* 72:107–21.
1957	"The Sociological Aspects of Geography." In G. Taylor, ed., *op. cit.*, 3d ed.
1958a	Editor.
	Nelson's Canadian Atlas. Toronto: Nelson's Canada.
1958b	"North America in the Changing World." *Journal of Geography* 47:381–89.
1959a	Edited with R. Miller.
	Geographical Essays in Honour of Alan G. Ogilvie. London: Thomas Nelson & Sons.
1959b	"Relict Geography in an Urban Community. Halifax: Nova Scotia." In W. Watson and R. Miller, eds., *Geographical Essays in Honour of Alan G. Ogilvie*, 110–43. London: Thomas Nelson & Sons.
1960	Editor.
	Nelson's World Atlas.London: Thomas Nelson & Sons.
1962	"Canada and Its Regions." *Scottish Geographical Magazine* 78:137–49.
1963	*"North America, Its Countries and Regions."* London: Longmans Green.
1964a	Edited with J.B. Sissons.
	The British Isles, a Systematic Geography. London: Thomas Nelson & Sons.
1964b	"The Individuality of Britain and the British Isles." In W. Watson and J.B. Sissons, eds., *The British Isles, a Systematic Geography*, 1–19. London: Thomas Nelson & Sons.
1964c	With J. Oliver and C.H. Foggo.
	Bermuda, a Geography. London: Collins.
1964d	"Geography and World Population." In "Developments in Geography." *Moray House Publications*, no. 3, 76–97.
1964e	Editor.
	Twentieth International Geographical Congress, United Kingdom, 1964: Congress Proceedings. London: IGC.
1965a	"Canada Divided: Problems of Region and State." *University of Edinburgh Journal*, Autumn, 146–58.
1965b	"Canadian Regionalism in Life and Letters." *Geographical Journal* 131:21–33.
1965c	"The City and the American Way of Life." *Philosophical Journal* 2:75–90.
1965d	"Geography and Growth in Scotland." *Journal of Geography* 64:398–414.
1967a	Section on "Urban Plans." In *Oxford Regional Economic Atlas of the United States and Canada*. Oxford: Oxford University Press.
1967b	"Mental Images and Geographical Reality in the Settlement of North America." *Cast Foundation Lectures*, no. 3, 3–24 (University of Nottingham).
1968a	*Canada: Its Problems and Prospects*. Don Mills: Longmans Canada.
1968b	*North America, Its Countries and Regions*. 2d ed. London: Longmans Green.
1968c	Editor.
	Advanced Atlas. London: Collins and Longmans.

1968d	"The United States: The Natural Scene." In A.N.J. den Hollander and S. Skard, eds., *American Civilization, an Introduction*. London: Longmans.
1968e	"Canada's Geography and Geographies of Canada." *Canadian Cartographer* 5:25–36.
1968f	*The Central Borders*. 2 vols. Prepared for the Scottish Development Department by the consultants in the University of Edinburgh, J.W. Watson, P. Johnson-Marshall, J.N. Wolfe, and the Faculty of Social Science. University of Edinburgh.
1968g	Edited with A.K. Wareham. *West African Secondary Schools Atlas*. London: Thomas Nelson & Sons.
1969	"The Role of Illusion in North American Geography."*Canadian Geographer* 13:10–27.
1970a	"Image Geography: The Myth of America in the American Scene." *British Association for the Advancement of Science* 27:1–9.
1970b	"Developments in Scotland." *Geographical Review* 60:570–82.
1971	"Geography and Image Regions." *Geographica Helvetica* 26:31–34.
1972a	"The United States – The Geographical Basis." In D. Welland, ed., *The United States*. London: Methuen.
1972b	"Canada and Its Environment." *Geographical Journal* 138:228–31.
1972c	"Mental Distance in Geography: Its Identification and Representation." In J.K. Fraser, ed., *Congress Proceedings, 22nd International Geographical Congress*. Montreal: IGC.
1972d	With R.W. Steel. "Geography in the United Kingdom, 1968–72." Report prepared on behalf of the British National Committee for Geography. *Geographical Journal* 138:139–53.
1974	"The Image of Nature." In W.R. Mead, ed., *The United States*. Aldine Press.
1975	Editor. *Advanced Atlas*. 2d. ed. London: Collins and Longmans.
1976a	"Land Use and Adam Smith: A Bicentennial Note." *Scottish Geographical Magazine* 92:128–34.
1976b	"Adam Smith, Wealth of Nations, and Edinburgh New Town." *Transactions of the Royal Society of Canada*, series 4, 14.
1977a	Edited with T. O'Riordan. *The American Environment, Perspectives and Policies*. London: John Wiley and Sons.
1977b	"Image Regions" and "The Image of Nature in America." In W. Watson and T. O'Riordan, eds., *The American Environment, Perspectives and Policies*, 15–28 and 63–78. London: John Wiley and Sons.
1977c	"Images of Canada." *Bulletin of Canadian Studies* 1:1–15.
1978	With Jessie W. Watson. *The Canadians, How They Live and Work*. Newton Abbot: David and Charles.
1979a	*Social Geography of the United States*. London: Longmans.
1979b	"Edinburgh – Concentration and Dispersal." *Ekistiks* 46:15–25.

1981   "Review Essay – The Development of Canadian Geography: The First Twenty-five Volumes of *The Canadian Geographer*." *Canadian Geographer* 25:391–98.

1982   *The United States: Habitation of Hope*. London: Longman.

1983a   "The Soul of Geography." *Transactions of the Institute of British Geographers* (new series) 8:385–99.

1983b   "Centre and Periphery: The Transfer of Urban Ideas from Britain to Canada." In J.H.C. Patten, ed., *The Expanding City: Essays in Honour of Professor Jean Gottmann*, 381–411. London: Academic Press.

Printed in Canada